T0238086

Lecture Notes in Computer Science

Commenced Publication in 1973
Founding and Former Series Editors:
Gerhard Goos, Juris Hartmanis, and Jan van Leeuwen

Dominique Borrione   Wolfgang Paul (Eds.)

Correct Hardware Design and Verification Methods

13th IFIP WG 10.5 Advanced Research
Working Conference, CHARME 2005
Saarbrücken, Germany, October 3-6, 2005
Proceedings

 Springer

Volume Editors

Dominique Borrione
TIMA Laboratory
46 Avenue Félix Viallet, 38031 Grenoble, France
E-mail: dominique.borrione@imag.fr

Wolfgang Paul
Saarland University, Department of Computer Science
P.O. Box 151150, 66041 Saarbrücken, Germany
E-mail: wjp@cs.uni-sb.de

Library of Congress Control Number: 2005932937

CR Subject Classification (1998): F.3.1, B, D.2.4, F.4.1, I.2.3, J.6

ISSN   0302-9743
ISBN-10   3-540-29105-9 Springer Berlin Heidelberg New York
ISBN-13   978-3-540-29105-3 Springer Berlin Heidelberg New York

Springer is a part of Springer Science+Business Media

springeronline.com

© IFIP International Federation for Information Processing 2005
Printed in Germany

Typesetting: Camera-ready by author, data conversion by Scientific Publishing Services, Chennai, India
Printed on acid-free paper   SPIN: 11560548   06/3142   5 4 3 2 1 0

Preface

This volume constitutes the proceedings of the 2005 *Advanced Research Working Conference on Correct Hardware-like Design and Verification Methods*. CHARME 2005 was held at the Victor's Residenz-Hotel, Saarbrücken, Germany, 3–6 October 2005.

CHARME 2005 was the thirteenth in a series of working conferences devoted to the development and the use of leading-edge formal techniques and tools for the specification, design and verification of hardware and hardware-like systems. Previous conferences under the CHARME name have been held in Turin (1991), Arles (1993), Frankfurt (1995), Montreal (1997), Bad Herrenalb (1999), Edinburgh (2001) and L'Aquila (2003). Prior events in the series were started in the early days of formal hardware verification, and were held under various names in Darmstadt (1984), Edinburgh (1985), Grenoble (1986), Glasgow (1988), and Leuven (1989). It is now well established that CHARME takes place on odd-numbered years, and rotates primarily in Europe. It is the biennial counterpart of its sister conference FMCAD, which has taken place every even year in the USA since 1996.

CHARME 2005 was sponsored by the IFIP TC10/WG10.5 Working Group on Design and Engineering of Electronic Systems and its Special Interest Group SIG-CHARME. It was organized by the Computer Science Department of Saarland University.

This year, two kinds of contributions were solicited: (i) full papers, describing original research work, intended for an oral plenary presentation, (ii) short papers, describing ongoing less mature research work intended for presentation as posters or research prototype demonstrations. Two very long sessions were allocated to poster and interactive presentations, with the aim of giving an emphasis on the "working" aspect of the working conference, where discussion of new or unfinished results and feedback are an essential aspect of the event. The community was extremely responsive to this viewpoint: we received a total number of 79 submitted papers, out of which 21 long contributions and 18 short contributions were accepted for presentation at the conference and inclusion in this volume. All papers received a minimum of three reviews.

For the conference program outside the refereed talks we put emphasis on the related topics of tool integration and pervasive system verification. The day preceding the working conference featured hands-on demonstrations for numerous verification tools; it also featured a tutorial on system verification by members of the Verisoft project. The overall program of CHARME 2005 included an invited keynote address by Wolfram Büttner on industrial processor verification and a round table discussion about mixed techniques for very large hardware-software systems initiated with an invited presentation by Masaharu Imai and Akira Kitajima.

A quality conference such as CHARME results from the work of many people. We wish to thank the members of the Program Committee and the external reviewers for their hard work in evaluating the submissions and in selecting high quality papers. The decision about many papers required long discussions among Program Committee members, who provided countless hours of their time to reach a consensus. On the organization side, we are grateful to the Web master Kristina Scherbaum, to Mark Hillebrand for his hard work in preparing the proceedings, and to Sabine Nermerich and Dirk Leinenbach. Our special thanks go to Tom In der Rieden who acted both as Finance Chair and Local Arrangements Chair, and could so efficiently find many ideas and solutions for the broadest range of questions. Finally, we would like to thank the TIMA Laboratory for mailing the CHARME 2005 call for papers, Saarland University for providing valuable support during the registration phase, and the companies who provided financial support for the organization of the event: IBM, Infineon, and Intel.

October 2005   Dominique Borrione and Wolfgang Paul

Organization

CHARME 2005 was organized by the Department of Computer Science of Saarland University, Germany.

Executive Committee

Conference Chair   Wolfgang Paul (Saarland University, Germany)
Program Chair   Dominique Borrione
    (Laboratoire TIMA, France)

Local Arrangements   Thomas In der Rieden
    and Finance Chair   (Saarland University, Germany)

Program Committee

Mark Aagaard (Univ. Waterloo, Canada)
Armin Biere (Johannes Kepler Univ. Linz, Austria)
Gianpiero Cabodi (Politecnico di Torino, Italy)
Rolf Drechsler (Univ. Bremen, Germany)
Emmanuelle Encrenaz (LIP6 – Université Paris 6, France)
Hans Eveking (Tech. Univ. Darmstadt, Germany)
Danny Geist (IBM Haifa Research Lab, Israel)
Ganesh Gopalakrishnan (Univ. Utah, USA)
Mike Gordon (Cambridge Univ., UK)
Alan Hu (Univ. British Columbia, Canada)
Warren Hunt (Univ. Texas at Austin, USA)
Steve D. Johnson (Indiana Univ., USA)
Thomas Kropf (Bosch & Univ. Tübingen, Germany)
Wolfgang Kunz (Univ. Kaiserslautern, Germany)
Panagiotis Manolios (Georgia Tech, USA)
Tiziana Margaria (Univ. Göttingen, Germany)
Andrew Martin (IBM, USA)
Ken McMillan (Cadence, USA)
Tom Melham (Oxford Univ., UK)
John O'Leary (Intel, USA)
Enric Pastor (UPC, Spain)
Laurence Pierre (Univ. Nice, France)
Carl Pixley (Synopsys, USA)
Mary Sheeran (Chalmers, Sweden)
Eli Singerman (Intel, USA)

Anna Slobodova (Intel, USA)
Enrico Tronci (Univ. Rome, Italy)
Miroslav Velev (Carnegie Mellon University, USA)

Additional Referees

In addition to the members of the Program Committee, the following persons acted as reviewers for contributions submitted to CHARME 2005.

Wolfgang Ahrendt
Charles André
Jason Baumgartner
Vincent Beaudenon
Robert Beers
Jesse Bingham
Per Bjesse
Bertrand Blanc
Cecile Braunstein
Ching-Tsun Chou
Jared Davis
Peter Dillinger
James R. Ezick
Xiushan Feng
Goerschwin Fey
Philippe Georgelin
Rami Gil
Sabine Glesner
Amit Goel
Daniel Große
Ziyad Hanna
Ravi Hosabettu

Christian Jacobi
Geert Janssen
Robert Jones
Gila Kamhe
Sava Krstic
Robert Krug
Jim Kukula
Hanbing Liu
Freddy Mang
John Matthews
Igor Melatti
Hari Mony
In-Ho Moon
Traian Muntean
Ingmar Neumann
Ziv Nevo
Minh Duc Nguyen
Sergio Nocco
Emmanuel Paviot-Adet
Lee Pike
Stefano Quer
David Rager

Sandip Ray
Erik Reeber
Ivano Salvo
Jun Sawada
Ohad Shacham
Sudarshan Srinivasan
Dominik Stoffel
Ofer Strichman
Sol Swords
Sami Taktak
Yann Thierry-Mieg
Alex Tsow
Rachel Tzoref
Noppanunt Utamaphethai
Moshe Vardi
Tatyana Veksler
Viswanath Vinod
Daron Vroon
Markus Wedler
Yu Yang
Karen Yorav
Qiang Zhang

Sponsoring Institutions

IBM Corporation
Infineon Technologies AG
Intel Corporation

Table of Contents

Invited Talks

Is Formal Verification Bound to Remain a Junior Partner of Simulation?
Wolfram Büttner 1

Verification Challenges in Configurable Processor Design with ASIP Meister
Masaharu Imai, Akira Kitajima 2

Tutorial

Towards the Pervasive Verification of Automotive Systems
Thomas In der Rieden, Dirk Leinenbach, Wolfgang Paul 3

Functional Approaches to Design Description

Wired: Wire-Aware Circuit Design
Emil Axelsson, Koen Claessen, Mary Sheeran 5

Formalization of the DE2 Language
Warren A. Hunt Jr., Erik Reeber 20

Game Solving Approaches

Finding and Fixing Faults
Stefan Staber, Barbara Jobstmann, Roderick Bloem 35

Verifying Quantitative Properties Using Bound Functions
Arindam Chakrabarti, Krishnendu Chatterjee, Thomas A. Henzinger,
Orna Kupferman, Rupak Majumdar 50

Abstraction

How Thorough Is Thorough Enough?
Arie Gurfinkel, Marsha Chechik 65

Interleaved Invariant Checking with Dynamic Abstraction
Liang Zhang, Mukul R. Prasad, Michael S. Hsiao 81

Automatic Formal Verification of Liveness for Pipelined Processors with
Multicycle Functional Units
Miroslav N. Velev 97

Algorithms and Techniques for Speeding (DD-Based) Verification 1

Efficient Symbolic Simulation via Dynamic Scheduling, Don't Caring, and
Case Splitting
Viresh Paruthi, Christian Jacobi, Kai Weber 114

Achieving Speedups in Distributed Symbolic Reachability Analysis Through
Asynchronous Computation
Orna Grumberg, Tamir Heyman, Nili Ifergan, Assaf Schuster 129

Saturation-Based Symbolic Reachability Analysis Using Conjunctive and
Disjunctive Partitioning
Gianfranco Ciardo, Andy Jinqing Yu 146

Real Time and LTL Model Checking

Real-Time Model Checking Is Really Simple
Leslie Lamport 162

Temporal Modalities for Concisely Capturing Timing Diagrams
Hana Chockler, Kathi Fisler 176

Regular Vacuity
Doron Bustan, Alon Flaisher, Orna Grumberg, Orna Kupferman,
Moshe Y. Vardi 191

Algorithms and Techniques for Speeding Verification 2

Automatic Generation of Hints for Symbolic Traversal
David Ward, Fabio Somenzi 207

Maximal Input Reduction of Sequential Netlists via Synergistic
Reparameterization and Localization Strategies
Jason Baumgartner, Hari Mony 222

A New SAT-Based Algorithm for Symbolic Trajectory Evaluation
Jan-Willem Roorda, Koen Claessen 238

Evaluation of SAT-Based Tools

An Analysis of SAT-Based Model Checking Techniques in an Industrial
Environment
*Nina Amla, Xiaoqun Du, Andreas Kuehlmann, Robert P. Kurshan,
Kenneth L. McMillan* 254

Model Reduction

Exploiting Constraints in Transformation-Based Verification
Hari Mony, Jason Baumgartner, Adnan Aziz 269

Identification and Counter Abstraction for Full Virtual Symmetry
Ou Wei, Arie Gurfinkel, Marsha Chechik 285

Verification of Memory Hierarchy Mechanisms

On the Verification of Memory Management Mechanisms
Iakov Dalinger, Mark Hillebrand, Wolfgang Paul 301

Counterexample Guided Invariant Discovery for Parameterized Cache
Coherence Verification
Sudhindra Pandav, Konrad Slind, Ganesh Gopalakrishnan 317

Short Papers

Symbolic Partial Order Reduction for Rule Based Transition Systems
Ritwik Bhattacharya, Steven German, Ganesh Gopalakrishnan 332

Verifying Timing Behavior by Abstract Interpretation of Executable Code
Christian Ferdinand, Reinhold Heckmann 336

Behavior-RTL Equivalence Checking Based on Data Transfer Analysis with
Virtual Controllers and Datapaths
Masahiro Fujita 340

Deadlock Prevention in the ÆTHEREAL Protocol
*Biniam Gebremichael, Frits Vaandrager, Miaomiao Zhang, Kees Goossens,
Edwin Rijpkema, Andrei Rădulescu* 345

Acceleration of SAT-Based Iterative Property Checking
Daniel Große, Rolf Drechsler 349

Error Detection Using BMC in a Parallel Environment
Subramanian K. Iyer, Jawahar Jain, Mukul R. Prasad, Debashis Sahoo,
Thomas Sidle   354

Formal Verification of Synchronizers
Tsachy Kapschitz, Ran Ginosar   359

A Parameterized Benchmark Suite of Hard Pipelined-Machine-Verification
Problems
Panagiotis Manolios, Sudarshan K. Srinivasan   363

Improvements to the Implementation of Interpolant-Based Model Checking
João Marques-Silva   367

High-Level Modelling, Analysis, and Verification on FPGA-Based Hardware
Design
Petr Matoušek, Aleš Smrčka, Tomáš Vojnar   371

Proving Parameterized Systems: The Use of Pseudo-Pipelines in Polyhedral
Logic
Katell Morin-Allory, David Cachera   376

Resolving Quartz Overloading
Oliver Pell, Wayne Luk   380

FPGA Based Accelerator for 3-SAT Conflict Analysis in SAT Solvers
Mona Safar, M. Watheq El-Kharashi, Ashraf Salem   384

Predictive Reachability Using a Sample-Based Approach
Debashis Sahoo, Jawahar Jain, Subramanian K. Iyer, David Dill,
E. Allen Emerson   388

Minimizing Counterexample of ACTL Property
ShengYu Shen, Ying Qin, SiKun Li   393

Data Refinement for Synchronous System Specification and Construction
Alex Tsow, Steven D. Johnson   398

Introducing Abstractions via Rewriting
William D. Young   402

A Case Study: Formal Verification of Processor Critical Properties
Emmanuel Zarpas   406

Author Index   411

Is Formal Verification Bound to Remain a Junior Partner of Simulation?

Wolfram Büttner

OneSpin Solutions GmbH,
Theresienhöhe 12, 80339 Munich, Germany
wolfram.buettner@onespin-solutions.com

Abstract. After decades of research the late eighties and the nineties have produced a number of "checkers" verifying complex aspects of industrial designs and thus raising the attention of early adopters. These achievements, however, have not led to wide adoption. The generally accepted explanation of this resistance is the required methodology change and the lacking ease of use. We see a more fundamental reason in the difficulty to set up a compelling value proposition based on isolated proven theorems.

With the advent of assertion-based verification the first two of the above obstacles are being successfully tackled. In this framework formal verification is piggybacking on advanced and established simulation platforms.

We foresee as a next step in the evolution of formal verification fully formal solutions for important functional verification tasks. Similar to formal equivalence checking these solutions will excel by extreme quality *and* improved productivity. This claim is exemplified by reporting about the formal verification of an industrial embedded processor within a large national initiative involving industry and academia.

D. Borrione and W. Paul (Eds.): CHARME 2005, LNCS 3725, p. 1, 2005.
© IFIP International Federation for Information Processing 2005

Verification Challenges in Configurable Processor Design with ASIP Meister

Masaharu Imai[1] and Akira Kitajima[2]

[1] Graduate School of Information Science and Technology, Osaka University, Japan
imai@ist.osaka-u.ac.jp
[2] Department of Computer Science, Osaka Electro-Communication University, Japan
kitajima@isc.osakac.ac.jp

Abstract. In this presentation, several verification problems in configurable processor design synthesis are illustrated. Our research group (PEAS Project) has been developing a novel design methodology of configurable processor, that includes higher level processor specification description, HDL description generation from the specification, Flexible Hardware Model (FHM) for resource management for HDL generation, compiler and ISS (Instruction Set level Simulator) generation. Based on this methodology, we develop a configurable processor design environment named *ASIP Meister*.

The processor design flow using ASIP Meister is as follows: Firstly, a designer describes an instruction set architecture as a specification of a target processor including pipeline specification, instruction formats, behavior description of each instruction and interrupts, data type specification, and so on. Secondly, the designer select resources for modules to implement some functions of instructions from FHM database, that can generate various resources, such as registers, selectors, adders, shifters, etc. Thirdly, the designer describes micro-operation level behavior description with selected resources in each pipeline stages for each instruction and interrupt. Finally, HDL description of the pipeline processor and machine-depend compiler information for a retargetable compiler are generated.

One of the most important issues in such a generation based design methodology is how to keep the consistency between a given instruction set architecture specification and implementations. In the most state-of-the-art processor core generation systems, including ASIP Meister, however, there are no efficient formal methods to guarantee the correctness of a generated HDL description and compiler that implement the given specification of instruction set architecture.

We will explain several problems that are expected to be solved by applying formal verification techniques as reasonable solutions.

D. Borrione and W. Paul (Eds.): CHARME 2005, LNCS 3725, p. 2, 2005.
© IFIP International Federation for Information Processing 2005

Towards the Pervasive Verification
of Automotive Systems

Thomas In der Rieden*, Dirk Leinenbach*, and Wolfgang Paul

Saarland University, Computer Science Dept., 66123 Saarbrücken, Germany
{idr, dirkl, wjp}@cs.uni-sb.de

Abstract. The tutorial reviews recent results from the Verisoft project [1]. We present a uniform mathematical theory, in which we can formulate pervasive correctness proofs for very large portions of automotive computer systems.

The basic ingredients of this theory are (i) correctness of processors with memory mamagement units and external interrupts [2], (ii) correctness of a compiler for (a subset of) C [3], (iii) correctness of the generic multitasking operating system kernel CVM [4], (iv) formal modeling of I/O devices and correctness of drivers [5], (v) correctness of serial interfaces [6], (vi) clock synchronization [7,8], (vii) worst case execution time analysis using abstract interpretation [9].

Using ingredients (i), (iv), (v), and (vi) one can construct electronic control units (ECU) consisting of processors and interfaces to a FlexRay like bus [10]; timers on the ECUs are kept synchronized. An OSEKTime like real time operating system is derived from CVM [11].

The programming model for applications under this operating system is very simple: several (compiled) C programs run on each ECU in so called *rounds* under a fixed schedule. With the help of system calls the applications can update and poll a set of shared variables. The times for updating each shared variable are fixed by the schedule, too. An update to a shared variable in round k is visible to all application programs that poll this variable in round $k + 2$. This programming model is very close to the model used in [12], where formal correctness proofs for a distributed emergency call application in cars are reported.

Worst case timing analysis permits to guarantee, that applications and drivers satisfy the requirements of the schedule. If the requirements of the schedule are satisfied and the interfaces are programmed as prescribed by the schedule, then one can show that the user model is implememented by compiler, operating system and hardware [6].

An effort for the formal verification of all parts of the theory presented here is under way [13]. We report also on the status of this effort.

References

1. The Verisoft Consortium: The Verisoft Project. http://www.verisoft.de/
2. Dalinger, I., Hillebrand, M., Paul, W.: On the verification of memory management mechanisms. In Borrione, D., Paul, W., eds.: Proceedings of the 13th Advanced Research Working Conference on Correct Hardware Design and Verification Methods (CHARME 2005). Springer (2005).

* Work funded by the German Federal Ministry of Education and Research (BMBF) in the Verisoft project under grant 01 IS C38.

3. Leinenbach, D., Paul, W., Petrova, E.: Towards the formal verification of a C0 compiler: Code generation and implementation correctness. In: Proceedings of the 3rd International Conference on Software Engineering and Formal Methods (SEFM 2005). IEEE Computer Society (2005).
4. Gargano, M., Hillebrand, M., Leinenbach, D., Paul, W.: On the correctness of operating system kernels. In Hurd, J., Melham, T.F., eds.: Proceedings of the 18th International Conference on Theorem Proving in Higher Order Logics (TPHOLs 2005), Springer (2005) 1–16
5. Hillebrand, M., In der Rieden, T., Paul, W.: Dealing with I/O devices in the context of pervasive system verification. In: Proceedings of the 23rd International Conference on Computer Design (ICCD 2005), IEEE Computer Society (2005)
6. Beyer, S., Böhm, P., Gerke, M., Hillebrand, In der Rieden, T., Knapp, S., Leinenbach, D., Paul, W.J.: Towards the formal verification of lower system layers in automotive systems. In: Proceedings of the 23rd International Conference on Computer Design (ICCD 2005). IEEE Computer Society (2005).
7. Schneider, F.B.: Understanding protocols for byzantine clock synchronization. Technical report, Ithaca, NY, USA (1987)
8. Rushby, J.: A formally verified algorithm for clock synchronization under a hybrid fault model. In: Proceedings of the 13th annual ACM Symposium on Principles of Distributed Computing (PODC 1994), New York, NY, USA, ACM Press (1994) 304–313
9. Ferdinand, C., Heckmann, R.: Verifying timing behavior by abstract interpretation of executable code. In Borrione, D., Paul, W., eds.: Proceedings of the 13th Advanced Research Working Conference on Correct Hardware Design and Verification Methods (CHARME 2005). Springer (2005).
10. FlexRay Consortium: FlexRay Communications System Specifications Version 2.1. (2005)
11. OSEK group: OSEK/VDX time-triggered operating system. (2001) http://www. osek-vdx.org/mirror/ttos10.pdf.
12. Botaschanjan, J., Kof, L., Kühnel, C., Spichkova, M.: Towards verified automotive software. In Press, A., ed.: Proceedings of the 2nd International ICSE Workshop on Software Engineering for Automotive Systems (SEAS 2005), ACM Press (2005).
13. In der Rieden, T., Knapp, S.: An approach to the pervasive formal specification and verification of an automotive system. In: Proceedings of the 10th International Workshop on Formal Methods for Industrial Critical Systems (FMICS 2005), IEEE Computer Society (2005).

Wired: Wire-Aware Circuit Design

Emil Axelsson, Koen Claessen, and Mary Sheeran

Chalmers University of Technology
{emax, koen, ms}@cs.chalmers.se

Abstract. Routing wires are dominant performance stoppers in deep sub-micron technologies, and there is an urgent need to take them into account already at higher levels of abstraction. However, the normal design flow gives the designer only limited control over the details of the lower levels, risking the quality of the final result. We propose a language, called Wired, which lets the designer express circuit function together with layout, in order to get more precise control over the result. The complexity of larger designs is managed by using parameterised connection patterns. The resulting circuit descriptions are compact, and yet capture detailed layout, including the size and positions of wires. We are able to analyse non-functional properties of these descriptions, by "running" them using non-standard versions of the wire and gate primitives. The language is relational, which means that we can build forwards, backwards and bi-directional analyses. Here, we show the description and analysis of various parallel prefix circuits, including a novel structure with small depth and low fanout.

1 Introduction

In deep sub-micron processes, the effects of wires dominate circuit behaviour and performance. We are investigating an approach to circuit generation in which wires are treated as first class citizens, just as components are. To successfully design high-performance circuits, we must reach convergence not only on functionality, but also *simultaneously* on other properties such as timing, area, power consumption and manufacturability. This demands that we mix what have earlier been separate concerns, and that we find ways to allow non-functional properties to influence design earlier in the flow. We must broaden our notion of correctness to include not only functionality but also performance in a broad sense. For example, we might like to do high-level floor-planning that takes account of the effects of the wires joining the top-level blocks, or to quickly explore the detailed timing behaviour of a number of proposed architectures for a given arithmetic block, without having to resort to full-custom layout. The Wired system is designed to solve both of these problems, though our initial work has concentrated on the latter: easing the design and analysis of data-paths.

Ever since the eighties, there has been much work on *module generation*. For example, Becker et al explored the specification and generation of circuits based on a calculus of nets [1]. As in μFP [8], the design notation took into account

D. Borrione and W. Paul (Eds.): CHARME 2005, LNCS 3725, pp. 5–19, 2005.

geometric and topological information. However, the designer viewed wires as "simple lines", and did not consider their exact position (although the associated synthesis tool produced real layout using sophisticated algorithms). The Wired user works at a lower level of abstraction and is in full control of the layout, including the exact positions of wires. Our own work with Singh at Xilinx on the use of Lava to give the designer fine control over the resources on the FPGA indicated that for regular circuits such as data-paths, mixing structure and behaviour in a single description gives good results [4]. Wired takes these ideas a step further. It is primarily aimed at giving the designer full control in standard-cell design. In both Lava and μFP, circuit behaviour is described as a *function* from input to output, and combinators capture common connection patterns. This use of functions can lead to a proliferation of connection patterns [8], whereas a relational approach, such as that in Ruby [6], abstracts from direction of data-flow and so avoids this problem. In Wired, the connection patterns provide a simple tiling, and the resulting behaviour is constructed by composing the relations corresponding to the tiles or sub-circuits. Thus, ideas from Ruby are reappearing. A major difference, though, is that Wired is embedded in Haskell, a powerful functional programming language, which eases the writing of circuit generators. As we shall see when we consider RC-delay estimation, the relational approach lends itself to circuit analysis by non-standard interpretation.

Typically, we start in Lava, and step down to the Wired level when it becomes necessary to consider effects that are captured only at that level. We have found that programming idioms used in Lava (that is the net-list generator level) translate surprisingly well into the lower Wired level. You might say that we aim to make circuit description and design exploration at the detailed wire-aware level as easy as it was at the higher net-list generator level – without losing the link to functional verification. In a standard flow, an application might be in the generation of modules that adapt to their context (for example to the delay profile of the inputs). The ideas are also compatible with recent work at Intel on the IDV system (Integrating Design and Verification [12]), which gives the designer full control in a setting based on refinement and a functional language. Our aim is to develop a practical approach to power-aware design in such a setting.

2   The Wired System

2.1   The Core Language

Wired is built around *combinators* with both functional and geometrical interpretations. Every description has a *surface* and a *surface relation*. A surface is a structure of contact segments, where each contact may or may not carry a signal. This structure specifies the interface of the description and keeps track of different signal properties. When flattened, it can represent the description's geometrical appearance. Figure 1(a) shows an example of a simple two-input and-gate. This is a 2-dimensional circuit, so the surface consists of four *ports*. The left- and right-hand ports are i-contacts (contacts without signals) of size 2. The inputs, on top, are two size 1 s-contacts (contacts with signals). The output,

(a)   **(b)**

Fig. 1. (a) Two-input and-gate (b) Beside composition, d1*||*d2

on the bottom, is a size 2 output signal. This gate has a clear signal flow from input to output, which is not always the case for Wired circuits.

The surface relation relates parts of the surface to each other. It can capture both structural and functional constraints. A structural relation can, for example, specify that the number of inputs is equal to the number of outputs, and a functional relation could specify that two signals are electrically connected.

Wired is embedded in the functional programming language Haskell. The data type that is used to represent descriptions internally is defined as:

```
data Description =   Primitive Surface Relation
                  |  Combined   Combinator Description Description
                  |  Generic    Surface (Surface -> Maybe Description)
```

A description is either a *primitive* defined by a surface and a relation, or a *combination* of two sub-descriptions. We will look more at *generic* descriptions in section 2.2. The combinator describes how the two sub-surfaces are combined into one, and indicates which surface parts are connected where the two blocks meet. This implicitly defines a new surface and relation for the combined description. Figure 2 illustrates a combination of two (not necessarily primitive) 2-dimensional circuits with relations R_1 and R_2.

Fig. 2. Combination of sub-descriptions

The combinator *||* (*"beside"*) places the first block to the left of the second, while *=* (*"below"*) places the first block below the second. Figure 1(b) illustrates d1*||*d2. Note how the resulting top and bottom ports are constructed. The top ports of the sub-circuits are named pB1 and pB2, and the resulting top port becomes the pair com [pB1,pB2]. The same holds for the side ports when using *=*. We will also use variations of these, which have the same geometrical meaning, but combine the surfaces differently. *||~ does the "cons" operation; if d1 has port pB1 and d2 has port com [pB21,pB22, ...], then the resulting port becomes com [pB1,pB21,pB22, ...]. ~||* does "cons" at the end of the list, and ~||~ and -||- are two variations of the "append" operation.

The surface structure may be partially unknown. For example, a wire (wires are normal descriptions, just like anything else) may not have a fixed length, but can be instantiated to whatever length it needs to have. Such instantiation is done – automatically by the system – by looking at the surrounding context of each sub-description. The surrounding surfaces form a so-called *context surface*, and we require, for all sub-descriptions, that the surface and the context surface are structurally equal. This means that if, for example, a stretchy wire is placed next to a block with known geometry, the wire will automatically be instantiated to the appropriate length. The wire also has a relation that states that its two sides have the same length. So, if we place yet another wire next to the first one, size information will be propagated from the block, through the first one and over to the new wire. In Wired, this circuit is written:

```
example1 = wireY *||* wireY *||* block3x3
```

`wireY` is a thin vertical wire with unknown length, and `block3x3` is a pre-defined block of size 3 × 3 units. Instantiating this description and asking for a picture (through an interactive menu system) gives the layout in Figure 3(a).

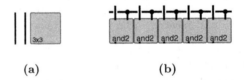

(a)   (b)

Fig. 3. (a) Layout after instantiation of `example1` (b) Layout of 5-bit bit-multiplier

In Lava, circuits are constructed by just running their Haskell descriptions, so most of the instantiation procedure comes for free, from Haskell. Since Wired is relational, we cannot use the same trick here. Instead we have a separate *instantiation engine*, which is implemented in Haskell. This engine works by fix-point iteration – it traverses the description iteratively, propagating surface information from contexts to sub-descriptions and instantiating unknown primitive surfaces, until no more information can be gained.

2.2 Generic Descriptions and Connection Patterns

In `example1` we saw wires that adapted to the size of their context. This is very useful since the designer doesn't have to give all wire sizes explicitly when writing the code. Sometimes we want to have sub-blocks whose entire content adapts to the context. For this we use the final constructor in the definition of descriptions (section 2.1) – `Generic`. A generic description is defined by a surface and an *instantiation function*. As the type (`Surface -> Maybe Description`) indicates, this function reads its current surface and may choose, depending on that information, to instantiate to a completely new description. Since this is a normal function on the Haskell level, it is possible to make clever choices here.

For example, in the context of non-functional analysis (section 3), we can choose between two different implementations depending on some estimated value.

The most common use for generic descriptions is in defining *connection patterns* which capture commonly used regular structures. The simplest connection pattern is the *row*, which places a number of copies of the same component next to each other. We can use it to define a bit multiplier circuit, for example:

```
bitMult = row and_bitM
    where and_bitM = and2 *=* (cro *||* crT0)
```

The primitives used are: and2, an and-gate with the surface from figure 1(a), cro, two wires crossing without connection and crT0, a T-shaped wire connection. Figure 3(b) shows the layout of this circuit instantiated for 5 bits.

We define row as follows:

```
row d = generic "row" xpSurf (row_inst d)

row_inst d surf = do len <- lengthX surf
                     case len of N 0 -> newInst thinEmptyY
                                 N _ -> newInst (d *||~ row d)
                                 _   -> noInst
```

The pattern is parameterised by a description d, and has unknown initial surface (xpSurf) and instantiation function row_inst (also parameterised by d). The instantiation function looks at the current surface and does a case analysis on its horizontal length. If the length is known to be 0 (the constructor N means known), the row becomes a thin empty block. This is the base-case in the recursive definition of row. For lengths greater than 0, we place one copy of d beside another row, using the *||~ combinator. If the length of the context has not yet been resolved (the last case), we do not instantiate.

A simpler alternative to the above definition of row is

```
rowN 0 _ = thinEmptyY
rowN n d = d *||~ rowN (n-1) d
```

This definition takes an extra length parameter n, and does the whole unrolling on the Haskell level instead, before instantiation. This is both simpler and runs faster, but has the down-side that the length has to be known in advance. In the normal row, instantiation automatically resolves this length.

Generic descriptions or partially unknown surfaces are only present during circuit instantiation. After instantiation, when we want to view the layout or extract a net-list, we require all surfaces to be complete, and that all generic parts have been instantiated away.

2.3   Signal Interpretation

Surfaces are structures of contact segments. A contact is a piece of area that may or may not carry a signal. However, it is possible to have more information here. The signal can, for example, be decorated with information about whether it is an input or an output, and about its estimated delay. This allows an analysis that checks that two outputs are never connected, and a way to compute the circuit's delay from input to output. We want to separate the description from the interpretation that we will later give to it, so that the same description can be used with different interpretations. This is done by abstracting the signal information on the Haskell type level. That is, we parameterise the `Description` type by the signal type `s`. This type variable can be kept abstract as long as we want, but before we instantiate the description, `s` must be given a particular type.

At the moment, possible signal types are:

`NoInfo`	No information, just a structural placeholder
`Direction`	Signal direction (in/out)
`UnitTime`	Delay estimation under unit delay model
`Resistance`	Output driving resistance
`Capacitance`	Input load capacitance
`Time`	Accurate RC-delay estimation

The operator `:+:` combines signal types. Such combinations are needed since it makes no sense to talk about delays if there is no notion of direction, for example. To increase readability, we define some useful type macros. For example,

```
type Desc_RCDelay = Description (Direction :+: Resistance :+: Capacitance :+: Time)
```

3   Non-functional Analysis

3.1   Direction and Unit-Delay

Wired is a relational language, and is thereby not bound to any specific direction of signal flow. Still, most circuits that we describe are functional, so we need to be able to check that a description has a consistent flow from input to output. Here we use the signal interpretation with direction. While it is usually known for gates which signals are inputs and outputs, wire junctions normally have undefined directions initially. However, we know that if one signal in a junction is an input (seen from inside the junction), all the others must be outputs, in order to avoid the risk of short-circuit. This constraint propagation can be baked into the circuit relation, and this is enough to help the instantiation engine resolve all directions (or report error). Figure 4 shows an example of a gate cell and a wire junction. Signal $s_{j,1}$ of the junction is indirectly connected to gate output $s_{g,5}$. If we assume that directions are propagated correctly through the intermediate wires, the context will eventually constrain $s_{j,1}$ to be an input, and by direction propagation, $s_{j,2}$ and $s_{j,3}$ will be constrained to outputs.

The simplest model for circuit delay estimation is the *unit-delay* model, in which each stage just adds a constant unit to the input delay – independent of electrical properties, such as signal drive strength and load. This gives a rather rough estimate of circuit delay.

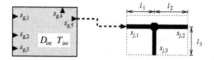

Fig. 4. Gate and wire junction

As with directions, unit-delay can be resolved by the instantiation engine, provided that delays are propagated correctly through gates and wires. The gate in the above example has intrinsic unit-delay D_{int} (and an accurate time delay T_{int}, which will be used in the next section). D_k refers to the unit-delay of signal s_k. As instantiation proceeds, delay estimates of the input signals will become available. Delay propagation can then set the constraints

$$D_{g,4} = D_{g,5} = max[D_{g,1}, D_{g,2}, D_{g,3}] + D_{int}$$

The model can easily be extended so that different input-output paths have different delays.

For the wire junction, we want to capture the fact that longer wires have more delay. This dependency is hidden in the function *conv*, which converts distance to unit-delay. By choosing different definitions for *conv*, we can adjust the importance of wire delays compared to gate delays. Once the delay of $s_{j,1}$ becomes available, the following propagation can be performed:

$$D_{j,k} = D_{j,1} + conv(l_1 + l_k) \quad \text{for } k \in [2, 3]$$

These two propagation methods work for all wires and gates, independent of number of signals and logical function, and they are part of the relations of all wire and gate primitives. Since information is only propagated from inputs to outputs, this is a *forwards analysis*. In the next section, we will use a combination of forwards and backwards analysis.

3.2   RC-Delay

For a more accurate timing analysis, we use the model in Figure 5. A gate output is a voltage source with intrinsic delay T_{int} and output resistance R_o. A wire is a distributed RC-stage with r and c as resistance and capacitance per length unit respectively. Gate input is a single capacitance C_g.

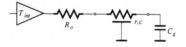

Fig. 5. Circuit stage from output to input

A signal change on an output gives rise to a signal *slope* on connected inputs. This slope is characterised by a *time constant*, τ. For output stages with equal rise and fall times (which is normally the case), it is standard to define wire delay as the time from an output change until the input slope reaches 50% of its final value. For a simple RC-stage, see Figure 6(a), the time constant is given by $\tau = RC$. The delay from the left terminal to the capacitor is then approximately equal to 0.69τ. For a distributed RC-stage (Figure 6(b)) with total resistance $R = rL$ and capacitance $C = cL$, it can be shown that $\tau_{dist} \approx RC/2$.

Figure 6(c) shows a fanout composition of n RC-stages. Based on Elmore's formula [7], the delay from the left terminal to capacitor C_i can be approximated by a simple RC-stage with the time constant

$$\tau_{1,i} = R_1 \cdot \left[\sum_{l \in [1..n]\backslash i} C_l \right] + (R_1 + R_i)C_i = \tau_1 + R_1 \cdot \left[\sum_{l \in [2..n]} C_l \right] + \tau_i \quad (1)$$

This formula also holds for distributed stages – R_i and C_i are then the total resistance and capacitance of stage i – or for combinations of simple and distributed stages. Note that the local time constants τ_1 and τ_i are computed separately and added, much as unit-delays of different stages were added. What is different here is the extra fanout term, where R_1 is multiplied by the whole load capacitance. It is generally the case that the stages on the right-hand side are themselves compound; the RC-stage is merely an approximation of their timing behaviour. Therefore, load capacitance needs to be propagated backwards from the load, through the stages and to the junction we are currently considering. So, for RC-delay analysis, we need a combination of forwards and backwards analysis. This is, however, a simple matter in a relational system like Wired.

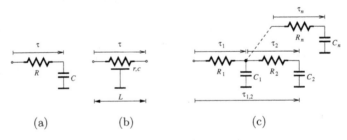

(a)   (b)   (c)

Fig. 6. (a) RC- and (b) distributed RC-stage (c) Composition of RC-stages

We describe gate and wire propagation from the example in Figure 4. Gates always have known output resistances and input capacitances, so no such propagation is needed. Therefore RC-delay propagation through gates behaves just like for unit-delay. Propagation through wire junctions is more tricky. We use R_k, C_k and τ_k to refer to the resistance, capacitance and RC-delay of the signal s_k. We also define R'_k, C'_k and τ'_k as the local resistance, capacitance and time constant of the piece of wire going from s_k to the junction. R'_k and C'_k can be computed directly from the corresponding length l_k, and $\tau'_k = R'_k C'_k/2$. The drive resistance and time constant of $s_{j,1}$, and the load capacitance of $s_{j,2}$ and $s_{j,3}$ will be resolved from the context.

The total load capacitance at the junction is given by $C_{junc} = C_{j,2} + C_{j,3} + C'_{j,2} + C'_{j,3}$. Backwards capacitance propagation can then be done directly by the constraint

$$C_{j,1} = C_{junc} + C'_1$$

From (1) we get the time constant at the junction as

$$\tau_{junc} = \tau_{j,1} + \frac{R_{j,1}C'_{j,1}}{2} + \tau'_{j,1} + (R_{j,1} + R'_{j,1}) \cdot C_{junc}$$

Finally, forwards resistance and RC-delay propagation is done as

$$R_{j,k} = R'_{j,k} \quad \text{and} \quad \tau_{j,k} = \tau_{junc} + \tau'_{j,k} \quad \text{for } k \in [2,3]$$

Now, to perform an RC-analysis of a circuit, say `bitMult` from section 2.2, we first select the appropriate signal interpretation:

```
bitMultRC = bitMult :: Desc_RCDelay
```

This description is then instantiated in a context surface that specifies resistance, capacitance and delay on the inputs or outputs of the circuit.

4   Parallel Prefix Circuits

A modern microprocessor contains many *parallel prefix circuits*. The best known use of parallel prefix circuits is in the computation of the carries in fast binary addition circuits; another common application is in priority encoders. There are a variety of well known parallel prefix networks, including Sklansky [11] and Brent-Kung [2]. There are also many papers in the field of circuit design that try to systematically figure out which topology is best for practical circuits. We have been inspired by previous work on investigating the effect of wire delay on the performance of parallel prefix circuits [5]. Our aim has been to perform a similar analysis, not by writing a specialised simulator, but by describing the circuits in Wired and using the instantiation engine to run RC-delay estimations.

4.1   The Parallel Prefix Problem

Given n inputs, $x_1, x_2, \ldots, x_n$, the problem is to design a circuit that takes these inputs and produces the n outputs $y_1 = x_1$, $y_2 = x_1 \circ x_2$, $y_3 = x_1 \circ x_2 \circ x_3$, $\ldots$ $y_n = x_1 \circ \ldots \circ x_n$, where $\circ$ is an arbitrary associative (but not necessarily commutative) binary operator. One possible solution is the *serial prefix circuit* shown schematically in Figure 7(a). Input nodes are on the top of the circuit, with the least significant input (x_1) being on the left. Data flows from top to bottom, and we also count the stages or levels of the circuit in this direction, starting with level zero on the top. An operation node, represented by a small circle, performs the $\circ$ operations on its two inputs. One of the inputs comes along the diagonal line above and to the left of the node, and the other along the vertical line from the top. A node always produces an output to the bottom

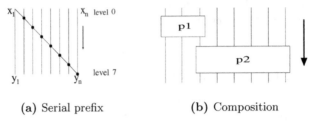

(a) Serial prefix   (b) Composition

Fig. 7.

along the vertical line. It may also produce an output along a diagonal line below and to the right of the node. Here, at level zero, there is a diagonal line leaving a vertical wire in the absence of a node. This is a fork. The *serial prefix* circuit shown contains 7 nodes, and so is said to be of *size* 7. Its lowest level in the picture is level 7, so the circuit has *depth* 7. The fanout of a node is its out-degree. In this example, all but the rightmost node have fanout 2, so the whole circuit is said to have fanout 2. Examining Figure 7(a), we see that at each non-zero level only one of the vertical lines contains a node. We aim to design *parallel* prefix circuits, in which there can be more than one node per level.

For two inputs, there is only one reasonable way to construct a prefix circuit, using one copy of the operator. Parallel prefix circuits can also be formed by composing two smaller such circuits, as shown in Figure 7(b). Repeated application of this pattern (and the base case) produces the serial prefix circuit.

For $2^n + 1$ inputs, one can use so-called forwards and backwards trees, as shown in Figure 8(a). We call a parallel prefix circuit of this form a *slice*. At the expense of a little extra fanout at a single level in the middle of the circuit, one can slide the (lower) backwards tree up one level, as shown in Figure 8(b). Composing increasing sized slices gives the well-known Brent-Kung construction [2] shown in Figure 9(a). A shallower n-input parallel prefix circuit can be ob-

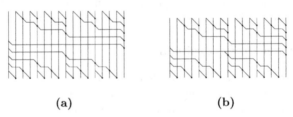

(a)   (b)

Fig. 8. (a) Parallel prefix construction using a forwards and a backwards tree (b) The same construction with the lower tree slid back by one level

tained by using the recursive Sklansky construction, which combines the results of two separate $n/2$-input parallel prefix circuits [11], as shown in Figure 9(b).

We have studied new ways to combine slices like those used to build Brent-Kung. By allowing the constrained use of fanout greater than 2, we have found a way to make slices in which the forward and backwards trees have different

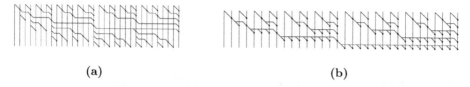

Fig. 9. (a) Brent Kung for 32 inputs (b) Sklansky for 32 inputs, with fanout 17

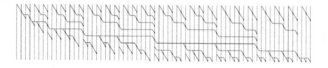

Fig. 10. A new arrangement of composed slices, with 67 inputs, depth 8 and fanout 4

depths, and this leads to parallel prefix structures that combine small depth with low fanout. An example of such a structure is shown in Figure 10.

4.2   Wired Descriptions

All of our parallel prefix circuits can be built from the primitives in Figure 11(a). d is the operator with inputs on the left and top ports, and output on the bottom. Its companion d2 additionally feeds the left input over to the output on the right-hand side. Although d2 is a primitive, it behaves as if there were a horizontal wire crossing on top of it. w1, w2 and w3 are unit-size wire cells, and w4 is a wire with adaptive length. Instead of hard-coding these into the descriptions, we will supply them as parameters, which allows us to use the same pattern with a different set of parameter blocks.

Just like for the row in section 2.2, we can choose between unrolling the structure during instantiation, or in advance on the Haskell level. Here we choose the latter, since it gives us more readable descriptions.

As shown in figure Figure 9(b), Sklansky consists of two smaller recursive calls, and something on the bottom to join their results. This leads to the following description in Wired:

```
sklansky 0   = thinEmptyX1
sklansky dep = join *=~ (sklansky (dep-1) ~||~ sklansky (dep-1))
  where
     join = (row w1 ~||* w3) -||- (row d2 ~||* d)
        where (d,d2,w1,_,w3,_) = params
```

The parameter blocks are taken from the global variable params. The local parameter dep determines the depth of the circuit. For each recursive call, this parameter is decreased by one. Figure 12 shows this structure instantiated for 16 inputs, both for bits and for pairs of bits. The distinction between the two cases is simply made by choosing parameter blocks from Figure 11(a) or (b).

Fig. 11. Parameters d, d2, w1, w2, w3 and w4 for (a) 1-bit, and (b) 2-bit computations

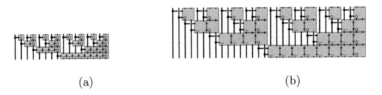

(a)   (b)

Fig. 12. 16-bit Sklansky: (a) For single bits (b) For pairs of bits

Brent-Kung consists of a sequence of the slices from Figure 8(b). Each slice contains a forwards and a backwards tree. The forwards tree is:

```
fwdTree 1   = thinEmptyX1
fwdTree dep = join *=~ (fwdTree (dep-1) ~||~ fwdTree (dep-1))
   where
     join = (row w1 ~||* w3) -||- (row w2 ~||* d)
       where (d,d2,w1,w2,w3,_) = params
```

Note the similarity to the definition of sklansky. Only a parameter to the second occurrence of row has changed.

backTree shares the same structure, but with extra control to take care of the slide-back (Figure 8(b)). Brent-Kung is then defined as

```
(d,_,w1,_,w3,w4) = params

bk True  1   = colN 1 $ w3 *||* d
bk _     1   = rowN 2 w4 ~=~ ((w1 *||* w3) *=* (w3 *||* d))
bk first dep = wFill ~=~ bk False (dep-1)
               ~||~ (backTree first True dep ~=~ fwdTree dep)
   where
     wFill = if depth==2 then thinEmptyX
                         else row w4 ~=~ (row w4 ~||* (w3 *=* w3))
```

The recursive case places a smaller Brent-Kung next to a slice consisting of a forwards and backwards tree. The rest of the code is a bit messy due to the fact that slide-back destroys the regularity around the base case.

The new structure in Figure 10 is also based on slices, and can be described in Wired without introducing any new ideas. Its Wired layout is shown in Figure 13.

Fig. 13. Wired layout of the new design

4.3   Results

The parameters used in our estimations are (see also Figure 5):

T_{int}	R_o	C_g	r	c
50.1ps	23.4kΩ	0.072fF	0.0229Ω/λ	1.43aF/λ

We analyse for a 100nm process ($\lambda = 50$nm, half the technology feature size), following a similar analysis by Huang and Ercegovac [5]. This is not a normal process node, but rather a speculative process derived from NTRS'97 [10]. The gate parameters refer to a min. size gate, but in the analyses, the output resistance is that of a 5× min. size device, while input capacitance is 1.5× min. size. Wiring parameters r and c are obtained by assuming a wire width of 4λ (see formula(4) in [5]). The operator cells are square, with a side length of 160λ.

The delays in nanoseconds resulting from the analsysis for Sklansky, Brent-Kung and the new structure for 64 bits are (starting from the least significant output):

Sklansky   0.010, 0.058, 0.10, 0.11, ... 0.42, 0.42, 0.42, 0.42
Brent-Kung   0.015, 0.066, 0.11, 0.12, ... 0.51, 0.51, 0.55, 0.36
New   0.012, 0.062, 0.11, 0.11, ... 0.40, 0.44, 0.44, 0.40

The result for Sklansky is very closely in line with those in [5], and the results for the new structure are promising.

5   Discussion

We have shown how the Wired system allows the user to describe and analyse circuits at a level of detail that captures not only the size and position of wires and components but also the overall behaviour. The descriptions are parameterised on the building blocks (such as gates, wires and junctions) used in the construction, and these blocks can also model non-functional aspects of circuit behaviour. This permits detailed circuit analyses such as the RC-delay estimation shown here. The instantiation engine that is used to propagate size information through the circuit based on information both from the circuit and its context is also used to perform these analyses. Circuit behaviour, whether functional or non-functional, is captured as a relation that is the composition of the relations for the sub-circuits. Thus, the analyses can be relational in nature (as the RC-delay estimation is), involving the flow of data in more than one direction, and multiple iterations before a fixed point is reached. Compared to a purely functional approach such as that used in Lava, this gives a strict increase in the range of analyses that can be performed by non-standard interpretation. Once the non-functional behaviour of the lowest level building blocks has been modelled, it becomes easy to explore the properties of a variety of different circuits to implement the same function. The fact that the descriptions are compact and quick to write is important here, and this has been demonstrated in our exploration of both standard and new parallel prefix circuits.

So far, we have only seen descriptions with 2-dimensional surfaces. We call these *hard* circuits, since they have a strict geometrical interpretation. Wired also supports hard *3-dimensional* and *soft* circuits. Hard 3D descriptions are used to make realistic circuits in processes with several metal layers, but if we only need to see and analyse a simplified layout, we prefer to use hard 2D descriptions, as they are much simpler. Soft descriptions do not have the geometrical constraints that hard descriptions have. They are used to fill in parts of the geometry that we don't want to describe exactly. It is possible to convert soft descriptions to hard, and vice versa. These operations only replace the outer surface of the description and keep the internal contents unchanged. Using these ideas about soft and hard circuits, we hope to return to the problem of high-level floor-planning that takes account of the effects of wires between blocks.

Currently, the only available output format is the kind of postscript picture shown here. The next step is to produce layout in a format such as GDSII. We will also, in the style of Lava, perform net-list extraction and produce input for verification tools. This will allow quick sanity checks during design exploration.

Work on Wired will continue to be driven by case studies. Building on our work on the generation of reduction trees [9] and on parallel prefix circuits, we plan to build, using Wired, a fast binary multiplier circuit. This will involve the study of buffer generation and of methods of folding circuits to improve layout.

The resulting circuit descriptions are *highly parameterised*, raising the question of how to provide *generic* verification methods. This is an important question, and we have no easy answers. We feel, however, that Hunt's work on the DUAL-EVAL language [3] and his current work that builds upon it is the best available starting point. We hope that others in the community will be inspired to tackle the problem of how to verify highly parameterised circuit generators.

Acknowledgements

This work receives Intel-custom funding from the SRC. We acknowledge an equipment grant from Intel Corporation. Thanks to Ingo Sander for comments on an earlier draft.

References

1. B. Becker, G. Hotz, R. Kolla, P. Molitor, and H.-G. Osthof. Hierarchical design based on a calculus of nets. In *DAC '87: Proceedings of the 24th ACM/IEEE conference on Design automation*, pages 649–653. ACM Press, 1987.
2. R.P. Brent and H.T. Kung. A regular layout for parallel adders. *IEEE Transactions on Computers*, C-31, 1982.
3. B. Brock and W.A. Hunt Jr. The DUAL-EVAL Hardware Description Language and Its Use in the Formal Specification and Verification of the FM9001 Microprocessor. *Formal Methods in System Design*, 11(1), 1997.
4. K. Claessen, M. Sheeran, and S. Singh. The Design and Verification of a Sorter Core. In *CHARME*, volume 2144 of *LNCS*. Springer, 2001.
5. Z. Huang and M. Ercegovac. Effect of Wire Delay on the Design of Prefix Adders in Deep-Submicron Technology. In *Proc. 34th Asilomar Conf.* IEEE, 2000.
6. G. Jones and M. Sheeran. Circuit design in Ruby. In J. Staunstrup, editor, *Formal Methods for VLSI Design*. North-Holland, 1990.
7. J.M. Rabaey et al. *Digital Integrated Circuits*. Prentice Hall, 2003.
8. M. Sheeran. *μFP, an algebraic VLSI design language, D.Phil. Thesis*. Oxford University, 1983.
9. M. Sheeran. Generating fast multipliers using clever circuits. In *Formal Methods in Computer-Aided Design (FMCAD)*, volume 3312 of *LNCS*. Springer, 2004.
10. SIA. *National Technology Roadmap for Semiconductors*. 1997.
11. J. Sklansky. Conditional-sum addition logic. *IRE Trans. Electron. Comput.*, EC-9, 1960.
12. G. Spirakis. Opportunities and challenges in building silicon products at 65nm and beyond. In *Design and Test in Europe (DATE)*. IEEE, 2004.

Formalization of the DE2 Language

Warren A. Hunt, Jr. and Erik Reeber

Department of Computer Sciences,
1 University Station, M/S C0500,
The University of Texas,
Austin, TX 78712-0233, USA
{hunt, reeber}@cs.utexas.edu

Abstract. We formalized the **DE2** hierarchical, occurrence-oriented finite state machine (FSM) language, and have developed a proof theory allowing the mechanical verification of FSM descriptions. Using the ACL2 functional logic, we have defined a predicate for detecting the well-formedness of **DE2** expressions. Furthermore, we have defined a symbolic simulator for **DE2** expressions which also serves as a formal cycle-based semantics for the **DE2** language. **DE2** is deeply embedded within ACL2, and the **DE2** language includes an annotation facility that can be used by programs that manipulate **DE2** descriptions. The **DE2** user may also specify and prove the correctness of programs that generate **DE2** descriptions. We have used **DE2** to mechanically verify components of the TRIPS microprocessor implementation.

1 Introduction

We present a formal description of and proof mechanism for the **DE2** hierarchical, occurrence-oriented finite state machine (FSM) description language, which we use to design and verify FSM-based designs or to optimize existing designs in a provably correct manner. This definition is primarily aimed at the representation and verification of hardware circuits, but **DE2** could also be used in other areas such as protocols and software processes. Defining a hardware description language (HDL) is difficult because of the many different ways in which it may be used; for example, a HDL may be used to specify a simulation semantics, define what circuits can be specified, restrict allowable names, enforce circuit interconnect types, estimate power consumption, and provide layout or other manufacturing information. We have formally described the **DE2** language using the ACL2 logic [16], and we have formally verified **DE2** descriptions using the ACL2 theorem prover.

 DE2 is designed to permit the rigorous hierarchical description and hierarchical verification of finite-state machines (FSMs). We call our language **DE2** (Dual-**E**val **2**) because of the two-pass approach that we employ for the language recognizers and evaluators. **DE2** is actually a general-purpose language for specifying FSMs; users may define their own language primitives. We recognize valid **DE2** descriptions with an ACL2 predicate that defines the permissible syntax,

D. Borrione and W. Paul (Eds.): CHARME 2005, LNCS 3725, pp. 20–34, 2005.

names, and hierarchy, of valid descriptions. The **DE2** language also provides a
rich annotation language that can be used to enforce syntactic and semantic
design restrictions.

We begin our presentation by listing **DE2** language characteristics, contrast-
ing the **DE2** language with other related efforts, and presenting some **DE2**
language examples. We next present the definition of **DE2**'s simulation-based
semantics. We conclude by describing how we use the **DE2** language to verify
circuits from the TRIPS microprocessor design [7].

2   DE2 Language Features

The development of **DE2** required balancing many demands. In particular, the
demand for hardware verification requires that it be as simple as possible to
evaluate, translate, and extend. In this section we list the resulting characteristics
of **DE2**.

- **Hierarchical:** A module is defined by connecting submodules.
- **Occurrence-Oriented:** Each reference to a previously defined module is
  called an occurrence. All named modules are defined as a sequence of occurrences (unnamed lambda modules are discussed in Section 4.2).
- **Deep Embedding in ACL2: DE2** modules are represented as ACL2 constants. Using the terminology defined by Boulton et al. [13], **DE2** is deeply
  embedded in the ACL2 language. This embedding allows us to write ACL2
  functions which simulate, analyze, generate, and manipulate **DE2** modules.
- **Annotation Mechanisms:** We use annotations to describe elements of a
  circuit which are not defined by evaluation (e.g. layout information). In **DE2**,
  annotations are first class objects.
- **Parameterized Finite Types:** In **DE2**, every module input and output
  is a bit vector of parameterized length. When the lengths of all the inputs
  and outputs are known, we may appeal to BDD- and SAT-based techniques
  for verification.
- **Two-pass Evaluation:** A **DE2** module is evaluated by twice interpreting
  its list of occurrences. This two-pass evaluation necessitates a level-order for
  the combination functions.
- **Representation of Internal State:** We represent the internal state of
  a module as an arbitrary block of memory that is implicitly part of the
  module's input and output and is updated during the second evaluation
  pass. This representation limits us to designing FSMs, but greatly simplifies
  the design and verification of these machines.
- **User-defined Primitive Modules:** We allow users to define primitive
  modules, rather than requiring that primitive modules be built into the language.
- **User-selectable Libraries:** Sets of primitives can become libraries. Libraries can be loaded into similar projects, which allows reuse of modules
  and verification efforts.

- **Verified DE2 Language Generators:** We can write ACL2 functions which generate **DE2** modules. Since the semantics of **DE2** have been formalized in ACL2, these functions can be shown to always generate correct **DE2** code.
- **Hierarchical Verification:** Our verification process involves verifying properties of submodules and then using these properties to verify larger modules built from these submodules. This hierarchical technique allows us to avoid reasoning about the internals of complex submodules.
- **Books for Verification Support:** We have defined a number of ACL2 "books" to assist the verification of **DE2** modules. When loaded into the theorem prover, these books use the ACL2 semantics of **DE2** to verify properties of **DE2** modules. We have used these books on a number of verification projects, some of which involve the verification of ACL2 functions that generate **DE2** circuits.

3   Related Work

The hardware verification community has taken two approaches [13] to defining the semantics of circuits: shallow and deep embedding. Shallow embedding defines a circuit description as a first-class object in a well-defined subset of a formal language. The syntax and formal semantics of the HDL are therefore a subset of the semantics of the formal language. Deep embedding defines a circuit description as a constant in a formal language. The syntax and semantics of the HDL are then written in the formal language.

The **DE2** language has been defined by deeply embedding it inside the ACL2 language, a primitive recursive functional subset of Lisp [17]. By embedding **DE2** within ACL2, we are given access to a theorem proving environment which has successfully verified large-scale hardware systems [8,9]. The formalization of the **DE2** language is similar in style to the embedding of the DUAL-EVAL HDL in NQTHM [11] and the DE language in ACL2 [10]. The DE language is different from DUAL-EVAL in that **DE** permits user-defined primitives, re-usable libraries, annotations, and contains a different structuring of data for state-holding elements. The **DE2** language contains the new features of DE, but also has a parameterized type system, a more sophisticated system for applying non user-defined primitives (implemented as ACL2 functions), and a more automated verification system.

In other hardware verification efforts with ACL2, hardware descriptions were translated directly to ACL2 models in the style of shallow-embedding [8,9]. These efforts do not permit the syntactic analysis of the circuits so represented; that is, it is not possible to treat the circuit descriptions as data so a program may be used to analyze its suitability.

Tom Melham used the HOL system [12] to deeply embed some elements of a hardware description language [12]. Boyer and Hunt attempted to deeply embed a subset of VHDL in the ACL2 logic, but this specification grew to more than 100 pages of formal mathematics, and its usefulness became suspect. Deeply embedding a HDL into another language brings great analytical power at the cost of having to manage all of the logical formalisms required—but these formalisms represent the real complexity that are inherit in such languages and in their associated analysis and simulation systems. To make such an embedding useful, a serious effort needs to be made to ensure an absolute economy of complexity, and there needs to be libraries that ease the use of such an embedding.

A significant amount of work has focused on the use of functional programming languages to simplify the writing of HDL-based descriptions. Mary Sheeran has developed the language Lava [1] and she has used it to design fast multipliers [2]. The strengths of Lava is its facilities to write programs that generate hardware—similar to the ACL2 programs we write to generate **DE2** descriptions —and its ability to embed layout information in the Lava language—similar to annotations in **DE2**. The Lava implementation does not include an associated reasoning system, but a user can appeal to SAT procedures to compare one Lava description with another.

Our recent verification methodology, which combines a SAT-based decision procedure with theorem proving, was partially inspired by the work at Intel combining symbolic trajectory evaluation with theorem proving. This work makes use of the functional languages Lifted-FL [4] and reFLect [3]. Some of the ways **DE2** differs from these languages include its simpler semantics (e.g. two pass evaluation), its simple syntax, its close correspondence to a subset of Verilog, and its embedding within a general-purpose theorem prover.

4   Example

The use of the **DE2** language is similar to the use of other hardware description languages. Circuits are specified in a hierarchical manner, and the syntactic form of the hierarchical circuit description also defines the hierarchical structure of a description's associated state. Here we give an example of a **DE2** circuit specification, and describe some of the restrictions imposed by the **DE2** language.

Our **DE2** language definition is a tremendous abstraction of the physical reality. The **DE2** language defines finite-state machines by permitting a user to define primitive elements. For this section, we assume the definition of Boolean connectives and state-holding elements have already been given. Issues such as clocking, wire delay, race conditions, power distribution, and heat, have been largely ignored.

Informally, the **DE2** language hierarchically defines Mealy machines—i.e. the outputs and next state of every module is a function of its inputs and internal state. By successively repeating the evaluation of an identified FSM, the **DE2** system can be used to emulate typical finite-state machine operation. **DE2** language definitions obey the syntax of Lisp constant expressions; that is, module definitions are represented as Lisp data rather than Lisp function definitions, macros, or other such constructs. We first give an example of several combinational circuits, where we exhibit some of the restrictions our evaluation approach imposes. Later we exhibit a sequential circuit.

4.1 Combinational Modules

Consider the circuit shown in Figure 1. In **DE2**, this circuit is represented as follows.

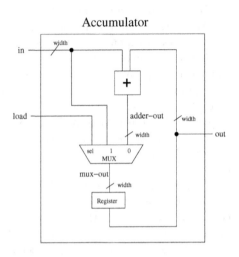

Fig. 1. Schematic of an Accumulator

```
(accumulator
 (params width)
 (outs (out width))
 (ins (in width) (load 1))
 (wires (adder-out width) (mux-out width))
 (sts reg)
 (labels (out 'data) (in 'data) (adder-out 'data)
         (mux-out 'data) (load 'control))
 (occs
  (reg (out) (register width 'data) (mux-out))
  (adder (adder-out) (bufn width 'data) ((bv-adder width in out)))
  (mux (mux-out) (bufn width 'data) ((bv-if load in adder-out)))))
```

A module is identified by its name, in this case `accumulator`. Each module is composed of a set of key-value pairs whose entries depend on the type of the module. All modules have lists of parameters, outputs, inputs, and states identified by `params`, `ins`, `sts`, and `outs`, respectively. Modules can also have a list of wires local to the module, identified by `wires`. This module also has a `labels` entry, which is an annotation. Annotations are not required, but can be used to enable optimizations, assist verification, or provide information to other tools. In this case, we use the `labels` annotation, along with a static checker, to ensure that we do not use a `data` wire when a `control` wire was expected or vice versa. Annotations can also be used to represent layout information or other physical attributes—a user may define their own annotations.

A module will also include occurrences which define the relationship between its inputs, outputs, and internal modules. Each occurrence consists of a unique occurrence name, a list of outputs, a module reference combined with its parameter list, and a list of inputs. For example, the first occurrence in the above example is named `reg`. The `reg` occurrence consists of an instance of a `register` module with the parameter `width`, input `mux-out`, and output `out`. The fact that `reg` occurs in the `accumulator` module's `sts` list denotes that it is a state-holding occurrence. Each input to an occurrence is specified by an ACL2 expression of the inputs and internal "wires" of the module. Our primitive simulation-based evaluator only defines a finite list of ACL2 functions (e.g. bv-adder and bv-if) for use in such an expression.

The **DE2** language evaluation semantics define the outputs of a module as a function of its inputs and internal state. The next state of a module is also a function of a module's inputs and internal state. Evaluation is discrete; that is, there is an implicit notion of time which is broken into discrete steps.

Module evaluation begins by binding input values to a module's inputs and binding state values to a module's states. Each occurrence is then evaluated in the order of its appearance. An occurrence is evaluated by binding its inputs and state to the specified arguments and then evaluating the reference itself. For the module defined above, the occurrence `reg` is evaluated first; the output of a register depends only on its internal state, not its inputs. After the value of `mux-out` is determined by evaluating the `mux` occurrence then internal state of the `reg` occurrence is updated.

In Section 6.1 we present some properties of this example which we have proven mechanically. Using the ACL2 theorem prover, we prove that for any data-path width a LOAD of A (i.e. `load` is high, `in` is A) followed by an ADD of B (i.e. `load` is low, `in` is B) produces the addition of A and B.

4.2 Primitives

A primitive module, corresponding to a hardware component built-in to a synthesis tool, has a similar definition to that of a non-primitive module. The difference between a primitive module is that rather than being defined in terms of occurrences of submodules, a primitive module is defined by lisp functions accessed through *lambda modules*. A lambda module has formals corresponding to the occurrence's list of parameters followed by the occurrence's list of inputs. The lambda module evaluates to a list with its first element being the state of the lambda module followed by its outputs. For example, the following is a definition of the primitive module `bufn`, which is a submodule of our accumulator.

```
(bufn
 (type primitive)
 (params n sig-type)
 (outs (q n))
 (ins (x n))
 (labels (q sig-type) (x sig-type))
 (occs (st (q)
           ((lambda (x) (list 'nil x)))
           (x))))
```

The `bufn` module instantiates a single lambda module. Since the `bufn` module has no state, this lambda expression evaluates to a list whose first element is `nil`. The output of the `bufn` module, which corresponds to the second element of the list, is equal to its input. The other primitive module found in our accumulator example, `register`, is defined as follows.

```
(register
 (type primitive)
 (params width sig-type)
 (outs (q width))
 (ins (d width))
 (sts st)
 (st-decls (st width))
 (labels (q sig-type) (d sig-type))
 (occs
  (st (q)
      ((lambda (width st d) (list d st)) width)
      (st d))))
```

The `register` example shows how a state-holding primitive is defined in **DE2**. The state of the `register` module is accessed through a lambda module named `st`, which turns the implicit input and output of state into an explicit input and output. The lambda module returns its input `d` as the next state and its state `st` as its output. Note that the `register` module also has a new field, `st-decls`, that declares the state element `st` to be a bit-vector of length `width`. This declaration is not a requirement of **DE2** modules, but enables the later use of decision procedures.

5   The DE2 Evaluator

The definition of the **DE2** evaluator is composed of two groups, each containing two mutually recursive functions. These four functions implement the entire hierarchical evaluation of the outputs and next-state values for any well-formed hierarchical FSM defined using the **DE2** language, except for the evaluation of the lambda and ACL2 (primitive) expressions. This set of functions was designed with a number of different goals in mind, so design decisions were made to attempt to implement the desired properties while keeping the size of the system as small as possible.

The **DE2** language can be thought of as having two parts: primitive operations and interconnect. We have defined different primitive evaluators, depending on our needs. The primitive evaluator we use for verification of gate-like primitives interprets such primitive modules by applying ordinary Boolean operations. If we are interested in the fan-out of a set of signals, we use a different primitive evaluator. If we want to generate a count of the number of and type of primitive modules required to implement a referenced module, we use a primitive evaluator that collects that information from every primitive encountered during an evaluation pass — note that this does not just count the number of defined modules, but it counts the number of every kind of modules required to realize the FSM being evaluated. If we want to compute a crude delay or power estimate, we use other primitive evaluators.

The semantic evaluation of a**DE2** design proceeds by binding actual (evaluated) parameters (both inputs and current states) to the formal parameters of the module to be evaluated; this in turn causes the evaluation of each submodule. This process is repeated recursively until a primitive module is encountered, and the specified primitive evaluator is called after binding the necessary arguments. This part of the evaluation can be thought of as performing all of the "wiring"; values are "routed" to appropriate modules and results are collected and passed along to other modules or become primary outputs. This set of definitions is composed of four (two groups of) functions (given below), and these functions contain an argument that permits different primitive evaluators to be used.

The following four functions completely define the evaluation of a netlist of modules, no matter which type of primitive evaluation is specified. The functions presented in this section constitute the entire definition of the simulator for the **DE2** language. This definition is small enough to allow us to reason with it mechanically, yet it is rich enough to permit the definition of a variety of evaluators. The se function evaluates a module and returns its primary outputs as a function of its inputs. The de function evaluates a module and returns its next state; this state will be structurally identical to the module's current state, but with updated values. Both se and de have sibling functions, se-occ and de-occ respectively, that iterate through each sub-module referenced in the body of a module definition. We present the se and de evaluator functions to make clear the importance we place on making the definition compact.

The se and de functions both have a `flg` argument that permits the selection of a specific primitive evaluator. The `fn` argument identifies the name of a module to evaluate; its definition should be found in the `netlist`. The `ins` and `st` arguments provide the primary inputs and the current state of the `fn` module. The `params` argument allows for parameterized modules; that is, it is possible to define modules with wire and state sizes that are determined by this parameter. The `env` argument permits configuration or test information to be passed deep into the evaluation process.

The se-occ function evaluates each occurrence and returns an environment that includes values for all internal signals. The se function returns a list of outputs by filtering the desired outputs from this environment. To compute the outputs as functions of the inputs, only a single pass is required.

```
(defun se (flg fn params ins st env netlist)
  (if (consp fn)
      ;; Primitive Evaluation.
      (cdr (flg-eval-lambda-expr flg fn params ins env))
    ;; Evaluate submodules.
    (let ((module (assoc-eq fn netlist)))
      (if (atom module)
          nil
        (let-names
```

```
     (m-params m-ins m-outs m-sts m-occs)
     (m-body module)
     (let*
       ((new-env      (add-pairlist m-params params nil))
        (new-env      (add-pairlist (strip-cars m-ins)
                                    (flg-eval-list flg ins env)
                                    new-env))
        (new-env      (add-pairlist m-sts
                                    (flg-eval-expr flg st env)
                                    new-env))
        (new-netlist (delete-assoc-eq-netlist fn netlist)))
       (assoc-eq-list-vals
        (strip-cars m-outs)
        (se-occ flg m-occs new-env new-netlist)))))))))

(defun se-occ (flg occs env netlist)
  (if (atom occs)   ;; Any more occurrences?
      env
    ;; Evaluate specific occurrence.
    (let-names
     (o-name o-outs o-call o-ins)
     (car occs)
     (se-occ flg (cdr occs)
             (add-pairlist
              (o-outs-names o-outs)
              (flg-eval-list
               flg (parse-output-list
                    o-outs
                    (se flg (o-call-fn o-call)
                        (flg-eval-list flg
                                       (o-call-params o-call)
                                       env)
                        o-ins o-name env netlist))
               env)
              env)
             netlist))))
```

Similarly, the functions de and de-occ perform the next-state computation for a module's evaluation; given values for the primary inputs and a structured state argument, these two functions compute the next state of a specified module. This result state is structured isomorphically to its input's state. Note that the definition of de contains a reference to the function se-occ; this reference computes the value of all internal signals for the module whose next state is being computed. This call to se-occ represents the first of two passes through a module description when DE is computing the next state.

```
(defun de (flg fn params ins st env netlist)
  (if (consp fn)
      (car (flg-eval-lambda-expr flg fn params ins env))
    (let ((module (assoc-eq fn netlist)))
      (if (atom module)
```

```
          nil
       (let-names
        (m-params m-ins m-sts m-occs) (m-body module)
        (let*
          ((new-env     (add-pairlist m-params params nil))
           (new-env     (add-pairlist (strip-cars m-ins)
                                      (flg-eval-list flg ins env)
                                      new-env))
           (new-env     (add-pairlist m-sts
                                      (flg-eval-expr flg st env)
                                      new-env))
           (new-netlist (delete-assoc-eq-netlist fn netlist))
           (new-env     (se-occ flg m-occs new-env new-netlist)))
          (assoc-eq-list-vals
           m-sts
           (de-occ flg m-occs new-env new-netlist))))))))

(defun de-occ (flg occs env netlist)
  (if (atom occs)
      env
    (let-names
     (o-name o-call o-ins) (car occs)
     (de-occ flg (cdr occs)
             (cons
              (cons
               o-name
               (de flg (o-call-fn o-call)
                   (flg-eval-list flg (o-call-params o-call) env)
                   o-ins o-name env netlist))
              env)
             netlist))))
```

This completes the entire definition of the **DE2** evaluation semantics. This clique of functions is used for all different evaluators; the specific kind of evaluation is determined by the `flg` input. We have proved a number of lemmas that help to automate the analysis of **DE2** modules. These lemmas allow us to hierarchically verify FSMs represented as **DE2** modules. We have also defined simple functions that use `de` and `se` to simulate a **DE2** design through any number of cycles.

An important aspect of this semantics is its brevity. Furthermore, since we specify our semantics in the formal language of the ACL2 theorem prover, we can mechanically and hierarchically verify properties about any system defined using the **DE2** language.

6 Our Use of the DE2 System

Having an evaluator for **DE2** written in ACL2 enables many forms of verification. In Figure 2 we illustrate our verification system, which is built around the **DE2** language.

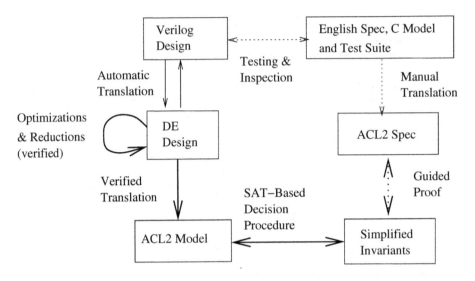

Fig. 2. An overview of the **DE2** verification system

We typically use the **DE2** verification system to verify Verilog designs. These designs are denoted in the upper left of Figure 2. Currently, the subset of Verilog includes arrays of wires (bit vectors), instantiations of modules, assignment statements, and some basic primitives (e.g. &, ?: and |). We also allow the instantiation of memory (array) modules and vendor-defined primitives.

We have built a translator that translates a Verilog description into an equivalent **DE2** description. Our translator parses the Verilog source text into a Lisp expression, and then an ACL2 program converts this Lisp expression into a **DE2** description.

We have also built a translator that converts a **DE2** netlist into a cycle-accurate ACL2 model. This translator also provides an ACL2 proof that the **DE2** description is equivalent to the mechanical produced ACL2 model. The process of translating a **DE2** description into its corresponding ACL2 model includes a partial cone-of-influence reduction; an ACL2 function is created for each module's output and parts of the initial design which are irrelevant to that output are removed. The **DE2** to ACL2 translator allows us to enjoy both the advantages of a shallow embedding (e.g. straightforward verification) and the advantages of a deep embedding (e.g. syntax resembling Verilog).

We start with an informal specification of the design in the form of English documents, charts, graphs, C-models, and test code which is represented in the upper right of Figure 2. This information is converted manually into a formal ACL2 specification. Using the ACL2 theorem prover, these specifications are simplified into a number of invariants and equivalence properties. If these properties are simple enough to be proven by our SAT-based decision procedure, we prove them automatically; otherwise, we simplify such conjectures using the ACL2 theorem prover until we can successfully appeal to some automated decision procedure.

We also use our system to verify sets of **DE2** descriptions. This is accomplished by writing ACL2 functions that generate **DE2** descriptions, and then proving that these functions always produce circuits that satisfy their ACL2 specifications.

Since **DE2** descriptions are represented as ACL2 constants, functions that transform **DE2** descriptions can be verified using the ACL2 theorem prover. By converting from Verilog to **DE2** and from **DE2** to back into Verilog, we can use **DE2** as an intermediate language to perform verified optimizations. Another use of this feature involves performing reductions or optimizations on **DE2** specifications prior to verification. For example, one can use a decision procedure to determine that two **DE2** circuits are equivalent and then use this fact to avoid verifying properties of a less cleanly structured description.

We can also build static analysis tools, such as extended type checkers, in **DE2** by using annotations. In **DE2**, annotations are first-class objects (i.e. annotations are not embedded in comments). Therefore an annotation, such as the labels annotation in Section 4, is parsed as easily as any core language feature. Such static checkers, since they are written in ACL2, can be analyzed and can also assist in the verification of **DE2** descriptions. Furthermore, annotations can be used to embed information into a **DE2** description to assist with synthesis.

6.1   Verification Example

To verify the **DE2** circuit in Section 4, we first generate an ACL2 model which is equivalent to the **DE2** circuit. The following theorems, which are proven automatically through a proof generated by our translator, prove that the ACL2 functions accumulator-next-st and accumulator-out produce the next state and the out output of the accumulator module from Section 4.

```
(defthm accumulator-de-rewrite
  (implies (accumulator-& netlist)
           (equal (de flg 'accumulator params ins st env netlist)
                  (let ((st (flg-eval-expr flg st env))
                        (in (get-nth-value 0 flg ins env))
                        (load (get-nth-value 1 flg ins env))
                        (width (nth 0 params)))
                    (accumulator-next-st st width in load)))))

(defthm accumulator-se-rewrite
  (implies (accumulator-& netlist)
           (equal (se flg 'accumulator params ins st env netlist)
                  (let ((st (flg-eval-expr flg st env)))
                    (list (accumulator-out st))))))
```

We now can prove properties about the ACL2 model using the ACL2 theorem prover. For example, consider the following theorem:

```
(thm
 (let* ((state1 (accumulator-next-st state0 width A (LOAD)))
```

```
        (state2 (accumulator-next-st state1 width B (ADD))))
     (equal (accumulator-out state2) (bv-adder width a b))))
```

In this theorem, state1 is the state of our accumulator after an arbitrary
LOAD instruction (i.e. the load input to the accumulator is high), and state2
is the state after following this LOAD with an ADD instruction (i.e. the load
input is low). The theorem then states that the output of the accumulator is
the addition of each cycles' inputs. We proved this theorem using the ACL2
theorem prover for any width accumulator. If we choose a specific width (e.g.
a 32-bit accumulator), then this theorem can be proven automatically with our
SAT-based decision procedure.

6.2   Verifying Components of the TRIPS Processor

We are using our verification system to verify components of the TRIPS processor. The TRIPS processor is a prototype next-generation processor being
designed by a joint effort between the University of Texas and IBM [7]. One
novel aspect of the TRIPS microprocessor is that its memory is broken up into
four pieces; each piece of memory has a separate cache and Load Store Queue
(LSQ). We plan to verify the LSQ design, based on the design described in
Sethumadhavan et al [6], using our verification system. We have already verified
properties of its Data Status Network (DSN) component.

The DSN hardware provides the communication and buffering between four
LSQ instances. Its design consists of 584 lines of Verilog code (including around
200 lines of comments), which we compile into a 427-line **DE2** description (with
no comments). We use our verifying compiler to translate this **DE2** description
into an ACL2 model and then prove the equivalence of the **DE2** description
and its ACL2 specification. Using a mixture of theorem proving and a SAT-
based decision procedure, we have proved properties that relate the output of
the four DSN instances, communicating with each other over multiple cycles, to
the output of a simplified machine; this simplified machine specifies the output
that would be immediately produced if all communication were instantaneous.

7   Conclusion

The definition of the **DE2** language provides a user with a hierarchical language for specifying FSMs. By deeply embedding the definition of **DE2** within
the ACL2 functional logic, we have provided a proof theory for verifying **DE2**
module descriptions with respect to a number of primitive interpretations. The
extensible structure of the **DE2** language and its general-purpose annotation
language allow a user to embed other types of information, such as a module's size, specification, layout, power requirements, and signal types. Instead of
just verifying large netlists, we often compare netlists or transform one netlist
into another netlist in a provably correct manner. We have extended the ACL2
theorem-proving system with a SAT procedure that can provide counter examples. We also have proved the correctness of functions that automatically

generate circuits; this can greatly reduce the amount of **DE2** module definitions written by a user.

We believe that the design of **DE2** more closely fulfills the needs of modern hardware design and specification than traditional HDLs. The increasing demands placed on hardware or FSM specification languages is presently being served by embedding all kinds of extra information in the form of comments into a traditional HDL. This process forces non-standard, non-portable use of HDLs, and prevents there from being a single design description that can be accessed by all pre- and post-silicon development tools. We believe that **DE2** is the first formal attempt to integrate disparate design data into a single formalism. We believe future design systems should include similar features.

The **DE2** language, annotation system, and semantics provide a user with a uniform means of specifying and verifying a wide variety of both functional and extrinsic properties. We continue to expand the size and type of designs that we have verified. In the future, we want to use **DE2** to capture existing design elements to ease the reuse problem. Typically, in an industrial design flow, when a previously designed and verified design element is used in a new design, the verification has to be completely redone. Our ability to specify and verify modules in a hierarchical manner permits the reuse of prior verifications, and perhaps this verification reuse is the real key. Being able to reuse the design and the effort required to validate it will greatly reduce the effort of reusing previously designed modules.

References

1. Per Bjesse, Koen Claessen, Mary Sheeran, and Satnam Singh. Lava: Hardware Design in Haskell. *The International Conference on Functional Programming (ICFP)*, pages 174–184, Volume 32, Number 1, ACM Press, 1998.
2. Mary Sheeran. Generating Fast Multipliers Using Clever Circuits. In Alan J. Hu and Andrew K. Martin, editors, *Formal Methods in Computer-Aided Design (FM-CAD)*, pages 6–20, LNCS, Volume 3312, Springer Verlag, 2004.
3. Sava Krstic and John Matthews. Semantics of the reFLect Language. *Principles and Practice of Declarative Programming (PPDP)*, pages 32–42, ACM Press, 2004.
4. Mark D. Aagaard, Robert B. Jones, and Carl-Johan H. Seger. Lifted-FL: A Pragmatic Implementation of Combined Model Checking and Theorem Proving. *Theorem Proving in Higher Order Logics (TPHOLs)*, LNCS, Volume 1690, Springer Verlag, 1999.
5. Mark D. Aagaard, Robert B. Jones, John W. O'Leary, Carl-Johan H. Seger, and Thomas F Melham. A methodology for large-scale hardware verification. In Warren A. Hunt, Jr. and Steve Johnson, editors, *Formal Methods in Computer-Aided Design (FMCAD)*, LNCS, Volume 1954, Springer Verlag, 2000.
6. S. Sethumadhavan, R.Desikan, D.Burger, C.R.Moore and S.W.Keckler. Scalable Hardware Memory Disambiguation for High ILP Processors (Load/Store Queue Design). *36th International Symposium on Microarchitecture (MICRO 36)*, pages 399–410, 2003.
7. The Tera-op Reliable Intelligently adaptive Processing System(TRIPS), http://www.cs.utexas.edu/users/cart/trips/

8. Bishop Brock, Matt Kaufmann, and J Moore. ACL2 Theorems about Commercial Microprocessors. In M. Srivas and A. Camilleri, editors, *Formal Methods in Computer-Aided Design (FMCAD'96)*, pages 275–293, LNCS, Volume 1166, Springer-Verlag, 1996.
9. Jun Sawada. Formal Verification of an Advanced Pipelined Machine. PhD Thesis, University of Texas at Austin, 1999.
10. Warren A. Hunt, Jr. The DE Language. *Computer-aided Reasoning: ACL2 case studies*, pages 151–166, Kluwer Academic Publishers, 2000.
11. Robert S. Boyer and J Strother Moore. *A Computational Logic Handbook*. Academic Press, Boston, 1988.
12. M. J. C. Gordon and T. F. Melham (editors). *Introduction to HOL: A Theorem Proving Environment for Higher-Order Logic*. Cambridge University Press, 1993.
13. Richard Boulton, Andrew Gordon, Mike Gordon, John Harrison, John Herbert, and John Van Tassel. Experience with Embedding Hardware Description Languages in HOL, *Theorem Provers in Circuit Design*, pages 129–156, IFIP Transactions A-10, Elsevier Science Publishers, 1992.
14. Mike Gordon. Why Higher-order Logic is a Good Formalism for Specifying and Verifying Hardware. Technical Report 77, University of Cambridge, Computer Laboratory, 1985.
15. Warren A. Hunt, Jr. and Bishop C. Brock. A Formal HDL and Its Use in the FM9001 Verification. In C.A.R. Hoare and M.J.C. Gordon, editors, Mechanized Reasoning and Hardware Design, pages 35–48, Prentice-Hall International Series in Computer Science, 1992.
16. Matt Kaufmann and J Strother Moore. ACL2: An Industrial Strength Version of NQTHM. *Eleventh Annual Conference on Computer Assurance (COMPASS-96)*, pages 23–34, IEEE Computer Society Press, 1996.
17. Guy Steele. Common Lisp: The Lanugage, Second Edition. Digital Press, 1990.
18. Phillip J. Windley and Michael L. Coe. A Correctness Model for Pipelined Microprocessors, *Theorem Provers in Circuit Design : Theory, Practice, and Experience*, LNCS, Volume 901, Springer Verlag, pages 33-51, 1995.

Finding and Fixing Faults*

Stefan Staber, Barbara Jobstmann, and Roderick Bloem

Graz University of Technology

Abstract. We present a method for combined fault localization and correction for sequential systems. We assume that the specification is given in linear-time temporal logic and state the localization and correction problem as a game that is won if there is a correction that is valid for all possible inputs. For invariants, our method guarantees that a correction is found if one exists. The set of fault models we consider is very general: components can be replaced by arbitrary new functions. We compare our approach to model based diagnosis and show that it is more precise. We present experimental data that supports the applicability of our approach, obtained from a symbolic implementation of the algorithm in the Vis model checker.

1   Introduction

Knowing that a program has a bug is good. Knowing its location is even better, but only a fix is truly satisfactory.

Even if a failure trace is available, it may be hard work to find the fault contained in the system. Researchers have taken different approaches to alleviate this problem. One approach is to make the traces themselves easier to understand. In the setting of model checking, [JRS02] introduces an approach that identifies points of choice in the failure trace that cause the error and [RS04] proposes a method to remove irrelevant variables from a counterexample derived using bounded model checking. Similarly, in the setting of software testing, Zeller and Hildebrandt [ZH02] consider the problem of simplifying the input that causes failure.

A second approach to help the user understand a failure (which is not necessarily the same as locating the fault) is to consider several similar program traces, some of which show failure and some success [Zel02, GV03, BNR03, RR03, Gro04]. The similarities between failure traces and their differences with the successful traces give an indication of the parts of the program that are likely involved in the failure.

A third approach, which aims to locate the fault, is based on a theory of diagnosis, originally developed for physical systems. We discuss this approach in Section 2 as it warrants a more detailed description.

In this paper, we take the view that a component may be responsible for a fault if it can be replaced by an alternative that makes the system correct. Thus fault localization and correction are closely connected, and we present an approach that combines the two. We assume a finite-state sequential system, which can be hardware or finite-state software. We furthermore assume that a (partial) specification is given in linear-time

---

* This work was supported in part by the European Union under contract 507219 (PROSYD).

D. Borrione and W. Paul (Eds.): CHARME 2005, LNCS 3725, pp. 35–49, 2005.

temporal logic (LTL), and we endeavor to find and fix a fault in such a way that the new system satisfies its specifications for all possible inputs. Our fault model is quite general: we assume that any component can be replaced by an arbitrary function in terms of the inputs and the state of the system.

Jobstmann et al. [JGB05] present a method for the repair of a set of suspect components. The most important weakness in that work is that a suspicion of the location of the fault has to be given by the user. We solve that weakness by integrating fault localization and correction.

We consider the fault localization and correction problem as an infinite game in which the system is the protagonist and the environment the antagonist. The winning condition for the protagonist is the satisfaction of the specification. The system first chooses which component is incorrect and then, at every clock cycle, which value to use as the output of the component. If for any input sequence, the system can choose outputs of the component such that the system satisfies the specification, the game is won. If the corresponding strategy is memoryless (the output of the component depends only on the state of the system and its inputs), it prescribes a replacement behavior for the component that makes the system correct. The method is complete for invariants, and in practice works well for general LTL properties, even though it is not complete.

Much work has been done in correcting combinational circuits. Typically, a correct version of the circuit is assumed to be available. (For instance, because optimization has introduced a bug.) These approaches are also applicable to sequential circuits, as long as the state space is not re-encoded. The work of [MCB89] and [LTH90] discusses formal methods of fault localization and correction based on Boolean equations. The fault model of [MCB89] is the same one we use for sequential circuits: any gate can be replaced by an arbitrary function. Chung, Wang, and Hajj [CWH94] improve these methods by pruning the set of possible faults. They consider only a set of *simple*, frequently occurring design faults. In [TYSH94] an approach is presented that may fix multiple faults of limited type by generating special patterns.

Work on sequential diagnosis and correction is more sparse. In the sequential setting, we assume that it is not known whether the state is correct at every clock tick, either because the reference model has a different encoding of the state space, or because the specification is given in a logic rather than as a circuit. Wahba and Borrione [WB95] discuss a method of finding single errors of limited type (forgotten or extraneous inverter, and/or gate switched, etc.) in a sequential circuit. The specification is assumed to be another sequential circuit, but their approach would presumably also work with a specification given in a temporal logic. Their algorithm finds the fault using a given set of test patterns. It iterates over the time frames, in each step removing from suspicion those gates that would, if changed, make a correct output incorrect or leave an incorrect output incorrect. Our work improves that of Wahba and Borrione in two respects: we use a more general fault model, and we correct the circuit for any possible input, not just for a given test sequence. Both improvements are important in a setting where a specification is available rather than a reference model. As far as we are aware, there are currently no complete approaches to correct a broken system with a fault model of comparable generality.

The paper is structured as follows. In Section 2, we discuss the relation of our approach to model based diagnosis and argue that the consistency-based approach is insufficiently precise. Section 3 gives the necessary definitions together with a motivating example. In Section 4, we show how the game can be solved and we prove the correctness and completeness of our approach. In Section 5, we show experimental evidence of the usability of our approach. We assume a basic understanding of LTL, see [CGP99] for an introduction.

2 Model Based Diagnosis for Fault Localization

Model based diagnosis provides a general, logic-based approach to fault localization. In this section, we describe the approach and discuss its shortcomings, which are addressed by our approach.

Model based diagnosis originates with the localization of faults in physical systems. Console et al. [CFTD93] show its applicability to fault localization in logic programs. In model based diagnosis, a model is derived from the source code of the program. It describes the actual, faulty behavior of the system. An oracle provides an example of correct behavior that is inconsistent with the actual behavior of the program. Using the model and the desired behavior, model based diagnosis yields a set of components that may have caused the fault.

Model based diagnosis comes in two flavors: abduction-based and consistency-based diagnosis [CT91]. Abduction-based diagnosis [PGA87] assumes that the set of fault models is enumerated, i.e., it is known in which ways a component can fail. Using these fault models, it tries to find a component of the model and a corresponding fault that explains the observation.

The set of fault models that we consider in this work is quite large (doubly exponential in the number of inputs and state variables to the system), and we do not consider it wise to enumerate all possible fault models. Thus, our approach should not be considered abductive.

Consistency-based diagnosis [KW87, Rei87] does not require the possible faults to be known, but rather tries to make the model consistent with the correct behavior by finding a component such that dropping any assumption on the behavior of the component causes the contradiction between the model and the correct behavior to disappear. In this setting, components are described as constraints, for example, an AND gate x with inputs i_1 and i_2 is described as

$$\neg\text{faulty}_x \Rightarrow (\text{out}_x \Leftrightarrow i_1 \wedge i_2),$$

where faulty_x means that x is considered responsible for the failure. Note that nothing is stated about the behavior of the gate when faulty is asserted. The task of consistency-based diagnosis is to find a minimal set Δ of components such that the assumption $\{\text{faulty}_c \mid c \in \Delta\} \cup \{\neg\text{faulty}_c \mid c \in \text{COMP} \setminus \Delta\}$ is consistent with the oracle (where COMP is the set of components).

Fahim Ali et al. [FAVS+04], for example, present a SAT-based method for consistency-based diagnosis of sequential circuits in which they unroll the circuits and use multiplexers with one free input instead of the faulty predicate.

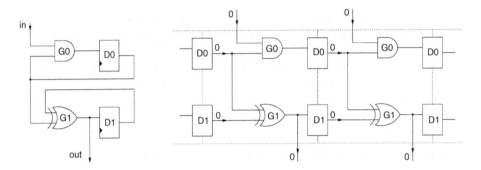

Fig. 1. Simple circuit   **Fig. 2.** Unrolling of circuit in Figure 1

Consistency-based reasoning has weaknesses when multiple instances of a component appear, for instance in the unrolling of a sequential circuit. (A similar observation is made in [SW99] for multiple test cases.) In diagnosis of sequential circuits, as in its combinational counterpart, the aim is to find a small set of components that explains the observations. A single incorrect trace is given and diagnosis is performed using the unrolling of the circuit as the model. A single faulty predicate is used for all occurrences of a given component. Hamscher and Davis [HD84] show that consistency-based diagnosis is indiscriminate in this setting: If dropping the constraints of a component removes any dependency between input and output, that component is a diagnosis. In sequential circuits, because of the replication of components, this is likely to hold for many components.

For instance, consider the sequential circuit shown in Figure 1. Suppose the initial state of the circuit is $(0, 0)$ and the specification is $(out = 0) \wedge G((out = 0) \leftrightarrow X(out = 1))$. Figure 2 shows the unrolling of the circuit corresponding to a counterexample of length 2. Consider the XOR gate. Any output is possible if the constraints on the outputs of this gate are removed, so it is a diagnosis. The AND gate is also a diagnosis.

The conclusion that either gate can be the cause of the failure, however, is incorrect. There is no replacement for the XOR gate that corrects the circuit: for the output of the circuit to be correct for the given inputs, the output of the XOR gate needs to be 0 in the first and 1 in the second time frame. This is impossible because the inputs to the gate are necessarily 0 in both time frames. The circuit can be corrected, but the only single consistent replacement to fix the circuit for the given input sequence is to replace the AND gate by a gate whose output is 1 when both inputs are 0.

In diagnosis of physical systems, faults may be intermittent, and a consistent explanation of the faulty behavior may not be required. In the setting of correction, however, the replacement must be consistent and functional. Thus, correctability is the proper notion for fault localization, and for maximum precision, the combination of fault localization and correction is essential.

Model based diagnosis gives a general, formal methodology of fault localization, but its two flavors each have significant shortcomings. The abduction-based approach can only handle a small set of possible faults, and the consistency-based method is unable to differentiate between correctable and non-correctable diagnoses. Furthermore, model based diagnosis does not deal with the problem of correcting a system for any possible input, but only finds a correction that is valid for a single input. Our approach is precise and finds corrections that are valid for all inputs.

3   Games for Localization and Correction

Using the simple example introduced in the previous section we explain the basic ideas of our approach. Additionally, we introduce some formalisms necessary for the proof of correctness in Section 4.2.

In order to identify faulty components, we need to decide what the components of the system are. In this paper, the components that we use for circuits are gates or sets of closely related gates such as full adders. For finite-state programs, our set of components consists of all expressions and the left-hand side of each assignment. Thus, for finite-state programs both diagnosis and correction are performed at the expression level, even though an expression may correspond to multiple gates on the implementation level.

Given a set of components our approach searches for faulty components and corresponding replacement functions. The range of the replacement function depends on the component model, the domain is determined by the states and inputs. Note that the formulation of our approach is independent of the chosen set of components.

We show how to search for faulty components and correct replacements by means of sequential circuits, where the specification F is the set of runs that satisfies some LTL formula φ. Our approach can handle multiple faults, but for simplicity we use a single fault to explain it. Thus, a correction is a replacement of one gate by an arbitrary Boolean function in terms of the primary inputs and the current state.

A circuit corresponds to a *finite state machine (FSM)* $M = (S, s_0, I, \delta)$, where S is a finite set of states, $s_0 \in S$ is the initial state, I is a finite set of inputs, and $\delta : S \times I \to S$ is the transition function. For example, if we are given the circuit in Figure 1 and we want it to fulfill the specification $(\text{out} = 0) \wedge G((\text{out} = 0) \leftrightarrow X(\text{out} = 1))$, we obtain the FSM shown in Figure 3.

We extend the FSM to a game between the system and the environment. A *game G* is a tuple $(S, s_0, I, C, \delta, F)$, where S is a finite set of states, $s_0 \in S$ is the initial state, I and C are finite sets of environment inputs and system choices, $\delta : S \times I \times C \to S$ is the complete transition function, and $F \subseteq S^\omega$ is the winning condition, a set of infinite sequences of states. To simplify matters, we translate the given specification in a corresponding set of sequences. In our example $(\text{out} = 0) \wedge G((\text{out} = 0) \leftrightarrow X(\text{out} = 1))$ corresponds to all sequences in which D_1 is 0 in the first two time frames and alternates between 1 and 0 afterwards.

Suppose we are given a circuit and the gates in the circuit are numbered by $0 \dots n$. We extend the corresponding FSM $M = (S, s_0, I, \delta)$ to a game by the following two steps

1. We extend the state space to $(S \times \{0 \dots n\}) \cup s_0'$. Intuitively, if the system is in state (s, d), we suspect gate d to be incorrect. s_0' is a new initial state. From this state, the system can choose which gate is suspect.
2. We extend the transition relation to reflect that the system can choose the output of the suspect gate.

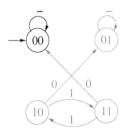

Fig. 3. Faulty system (grey parts are unreachable)

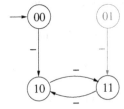

Fig. 4. Corrected system

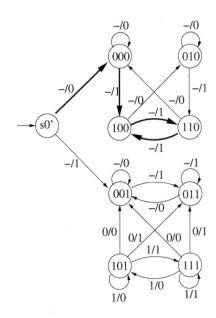

Fig. 5. Game to localize and correct the fault

If gate d is suspect, it is removed from the combinational logic of our circuit, and we obtain new combinational logic with one more input (and some new outputs, which we ignore). Let the function computed by this new circuit be given by $\delta_d : S \times I \times \{0,1\} \rightarrow S$, where the third argument represents the new input.

We construct the game $G = (S', s'_0, I, C', \delta', F')$, where

$$S' = (S \times \{0, \ldots, n\}) \cup s'_0,$$
$$C' = \{0 \ldots n\},$$
$$\delta'(s'_0, i, c) = (s_0, c),$$
$$\delta'((s, d), i, c) = (\delta_d(s, i, c \bmod 2), d),$$
$$F' = \{s'_0, (s_0, d_0), (s_1, d_1), \cdots \mid s_0, s_1, \cdots \in F\}.$$

Note that the full range of the system choice ($\{0 \ldots n\}$) is only used in the new initial state s'_0 to choose the suspect gate. Afterwards, we only need two values to decide the correct output of the gate (0 and 1), so we use the modulo operator. Also note that the decision which gate is suspect does not depend on the inputs: $\delta'(s'_0, i, c)$ does not depend on i.

For our simple example, we obtain the game shown in Figure 5. In the initial state the system chooses which of the gates (G_0 or G_1) is faulty. The upper part of the game in Figure 5 corresponds to an arbitrary function for gate G_0, the lower one represents a replacement of gate G_1. The edges are labeled with the values of environment input i and the system choice c separated by a slash, e.g., the transition from state 100 to 010 labeled with $-/0$ means that starting at $D_0 = 1$ and $D_1 = 0$ and assuming G_0 to be

Table 1. Function for the system choice

State $S \times \{0,1\}$ D_0 D_1 d			Input I i	Choice C' c
0	0	0	0	1
0	0	0	1	1
0	1	0	0	-
0	1	0	1	-
1	0	0	0	1
1	0	0	1	1
1	1	0	0	1
1	1	0	1	1

faulty, the system choice $C = 0$ forces the latches to be $D_0 = 0$ and $D_1 = 1$ in the next state regardless of the input.

Once we have constructed the game, we select system choices that restrict the game to those paths that fulfill the specification. In our example, first we choose a transition from s'_0 to either the upper or the lower part of the game. Choosing the transition from s'_0 to 000 means we try to fix the fault by replacing gate G_0. In state 000 we select transitions that lead to paths that adhere to the given specification. In Figure 5 the bold arrows only allow paths with the sequence 001010... for D_1 as required by the specification. Taking only these transitions into account we get the function shown in Table 1 for the system choice c. For the 3rd and 4th Line in Table 1 we can choose arbitrary values for the system choice. This choice gives us freedom in picking the desired correction. Since we aim for corrections that yield simple modified systems, we choose the simplest implementation, which sets $c = 1$ all the time. Using the corresponding transitions in the original model (Figure 3) yields the correct model shown in Figure 4.

Choosing the right transitions of the game corresponds to searching a memoryless winning strategy for the system that fulfills the winning condition F'. Formally, given a game $G = (S, s_0, I, C, \delta, F)$, a *memoryless strategy* is a function $\sigma : S \times I \to 2^C$, which fixes a set of possible responses to an environment input. A *play* on G according to σ is a finite or infinite sequence $\pi = s_0 \xrightarrow{i_0 c_0} s_1 \xrightarrow{i_1 c_1} \dots$, such that $c_i \in \sigma(s_i, i_i)$, $s_{i+1} = \delta(s_i, i_i, c_i)$, and either the play is infinite, or $\exists n : \sigma(s_n, i_n) = \emptyset$, which means that the play is finite. A play is *winning* (for the system) if it is infinite and $s_0 s_1 \dots \in F$. A strategy σ is *winning* on G if all plays according to σ on G are winning. Depending on the winning condition we distinguish different types of games. The winning condition of an *LTL game* is the set of sequences satisfying an LTL formula φ. A *safety game* has the condition $F = \{q_0 q_1 \dots \mid \forall i : q_i \in A\}$ for some A. The type of the game for localizing and correction depends on the specification. In Section 4, we explain how to obtain a winning strategy and we prove the correctness of our approach.

In order to handle multiple faults we extend the game to select a set of suspect components in the initial state. In every following state the system chooses an output for the suspect component. Thus, the range of the replacement function consists of tuples of outputs, one output for each suspect component.

4   Solving Games

In Section 4.1, we summarize the approach of [JGB05] to find a winning strategy for
a game, which we adopt. We describe the approach for safety games in some detail,
and briefly recapitulate how to find a strategy when the specification is given in LTL. In
Section 4.2, we prove that a winning strategy corresponds to a valid correction and that
for invariants a winning strategy exists iff a correction exists.

4.1   Strategies

For a set $A \subseteq S$ let

$$MX A = \{s \mid \forall i \in I \exists c \in C, s' \in A : (s, i, c, s') \in \delta\}$$

be the set of states from which, for any input, the system can force a visit to a state in
A in one step. We define $MG A = \nu Z.A \cap MX Z$ to be the set of states from which the
system can avoid leaving A. (The symbol ν denotes a greatest fixpoint, see [CGP99].)
Note that the MX operation is similar to the preimage computation in symbolic model
checking, apart from the quantification of the input variables. The MG operation mir-
rors EG.

   If the specification is an invariant A, the set $MG A$ is exactly the set of states from
which the system can guarantee that A is always satisfied. If the initial state is in $MG A$,
the game is won. The strategy for a safety game is then easily found. From any state,
and for any input, select any system choice such that the next state is in $MG A$:

$$\sigma(q, i) = \{c \in C \mid \delta(q, i, c) \in A\}.$$

Note that the strategy is immaterial for nodes that are unreachable. The same holds for
states that are not winning: they will never be visited.

   For LTL specifications, the situation is more intricate.

   A *finite-state strategy* determines the set of allowed system choices using a finite-
state machine that has a memory of the past input and system choices. A finite-state
strategy may, for example, alternately pick two different choices for one and the same
system state and input.

   We can compute a finite-state strategy for a game with winning condition φ by
finding a strategy on the product of the game and a deterministic automaton for φ. A
finite-state strategy corresponds to a correction in which the new FSM is the product
automaton. Thus, it would add state that corresponds to the automaton for φ.

   Finding a deterministic automaton for φ is hard in terms of implementation and
needs doubly exponential space. Furthermore, it is probably a bad idea to fix a simple fault by the addition of a large amount of state. Therefore, [JGB05] proposes a
heuristic approach. The approach constructs a nondeterministic Büchi automaton from
φ in the standard way [VW94], which causes only a singly exponential blowup. It then
constructs the product of the Büchi automaton and the game. The result is a Büchi
game, which in general has a finite-state strategy. To avoid adding state to the circuit,
[JGB05] presents a heuristic to turn a finite-state strategy into a memoryless strategy.
The heuristic works by finding choices that are common to all states of the finite-state

strategy. These two heuristics imply that the method is not complete: if the property is not an invariant, a correction may not be found even if it exists. We take the view that this tradeoff is necessary for efficiency and simplicity of the correction.

Jobstmann et al. [JGB05] show how a simple correction statement is extracted from a memoryless strategy.

The complexity of the approach is comparable to that of symbolic model checking of a property on the game that has $O(k \cdot \lg |COMP|)$ more Boolean state variables than the original system, where k is the number of faults assumed.

4.2 Localization and Correction

If a winning positional strategy for the system exists, it determines (at least) one incorrect gate plus a replacement function. To see this, we need some definitions. For a function $f : S \times I \to \{0, 1\}$, let $\delta[d/f]$ be the transition function obtained from δ by replacing gate d by combinational logic specified by f: $\delta[d/f](s, i) = \delta_d(s, i, f(s, i))$. Let $M[d/f]$ be the corresponding FSM. Let $\sigma : ((S \times \{0 \ldots n\}) \cup s_0') \times I \to 2^{\{0 \ldots n\}}$ be a winning finite-state strategy. Since the transition from the initial state s_0' does not depend on the input i, neither does the strategy for this state. Let $D = \sigma(s_0', i)$ for some i.

Let $\mathcal{F}_d$ be the set of all functions $f : S \times I \to \{0, 1\}$ such that $f(s, i) \in \{c \bmod 2 \mid c \in \sigma((s, d), i)\}$. We claim that D contains only correctable single-fault diagnoses and $\{\mathcal{F}_d\}_{d \in D}$ contains only valid corrections, and that for invariants there are no other single correctable diagnoses or corrections.

Theorem 1. *Let $d \in \{0 \ldots n\}$ and let $f : S \times I \to \{0, 1\}$. We have that $d \in D$ and $f \in \mathcal{F}_d$ implies that $M[d/f]$ satisfies F. If F is an invariant, then $M[d/f]$ satisfies F implies $d \in D$ and $f \in \mathcal{F}_d$.*

Proof. Suppose $d \in D$ and $f \in \mathcal{F}_d$. Let $\pi = (s_0', (s_0, d), (s_1, d), \ldots)$ be the play of G for input sequence $i_0', i_0, i_1, \ldots$ so that $(s_{j+1}, d) = \delta'((s_j, d), i_j, f(s_j, i_j))$. Since $f(s_j, i_j) \in \sigma((s_j, d), i_j) \pmod 2$, π is a winning run and $s_0, s_1, \cdots \in F$. Now note that $(s_{j+1}, d) = \delta'((s_j, d), i_j, f(s_j, i_j)) = (\delta_d(s, i_j, f(s_j, i_j)), d) = (\delta[d/f](s_j, i_j), d)$. Thus, $s_0, s_1, \ldots$ is the run of $M[d/f]$ for input sequence $i_0, i_1, \ldots$, and this run is in F.

For the second part, suppose F is an invariant, and say $M[d/f]$ satisfies F. Then for any input sequence, the run of $M[d/f]$ is in F, and from this run we can construct a winning play as above. The play stays within the winning region, and by construction of the strategy for a safety game, all system choices that do not cause the play to leave the winning region are allowed by the strategy. Thus, the play is according to the winning strategy, so $d \in D$ and $f \in \mathcal{F}_d$. $\qquad\square$

Note that for LTL properties, the theorem holds in only one direction. The primary reason for this is that a memoryless strategy may not exist for an LTL formula. Furthermore, even if a repair exists, our heuristics may fail to find it [JGB05].

5 Experiments

In this section we present initial experiments that demonstrate the applicability of our approach. We have implemented our algorithm in VIS-2.1 [B+96]. In the current version of the algorithm, the examples are manually instrumented in order to obtain and solve the corresponding games. The instrumentation can easily be automated.

The game constructed from a program proceeds in three steps:

1. decide which component is faulty,
2. read the inputs to the program, and
3. execute the extended version of the program, in which one component is left unimplemented.

Because the selection of the faulty component is performed before any inputs are passed to the program, the diagnosis does not depend on the inputs, and is valid regardless of the inputs.

Our implementation is still incomplete: it builds a monolithic transition relation for the corrected system, which is intractable for large designs. We are investigating the use of partitioned relations.

5.1 Locking Example

Figure 6 shows an abstract program which realizes simple lock operations [GV03]. Nondeterministic choices in the program are represented by $*$. The specification must hold regardless of the nondeterministic choices taken, and thus the program abstracts a set of concrete programs with different if and while conditions. The method lock() acquires the lock, represented by the variable L, if it is available. If the lock is already held, the assertion in Line 11 is violated. In the same way, unlock() releases the lock, if it is held. The fault is located in Line 6, which should be within the scope of the if command. This example is interesting because the error is caused by switching lines, which does not fit our fault model.

The components of the program that are considered for correction are the expressions in the if statement in Line 1, the while statement in Line 7, and the right-hand side (RHS) of the assignments to got_lock in Line 3 and 6.

In order to illustrate the instrumentation of the source code, Figure 8 shows an instrumented version of the program. In Line 0 we have introduced a variable diagnose. The game chooses one of four lines for diagnose. Function choose represents a system choice. The result of the function is one of its parameters: 11, 13, 16 or 17.

If a line is selected by diagnose, the game determines a new value for the right-hand side in that line (again represented by the function choose. Note that in the other suspect lines the original values are kept.

The algorithm finds three possible error locations: Line 1, 6, or 7. The correction for Line 1 suggests to set the if-condition to !L. Both lock() and unlock() are then called in every loop iteration. Note that the condition could also be set to true, but the algorithm cannot exclude the possibility of reaching Line 1 with L=1 before it fixes the strategy. The algorithm also suggests to set the loop condition to false in Line 7. Clearly that works, because the loop is now executed only once and the wrong value of got_lock does not matter. Finally, the algorithm suggests to set got_lock to 0 in Line 6. This is a valid correction, because now unlock() is only called if got_lock has been incremented before in Line 3. The last suggestion is satisfactory:

```
    int got_lock = 0;
    do {
1    if (*) {
2      lock();
3        got_lock = got_lock + 1; }
4    if (got_lock != 0) {
5      unlock(); }
6    got_lock = got_lock - 1;
7  } while (*)

   void lock() {
11   assert(L = 0);
12   L = 1; }

   void unlock() {
21   assert(L = 1);
22   L = 0; }
```

```
1   int least = input1;
2   int most = input1;

3   if (most < input2)
4     most = input2;
5   if (most < input3)
6     most = input3;
7   if (least > input2)
8     most = input2;
9   if (least > input3)
10    least = input3;

11 assert (least <= most);
```

Fig. 6. Locking Example   **Fig. 7.** MinMax Example

it is a correction for the program no matter which concrete conditions are used for the if and while conditions.

Note that our method does not recognize the intent of the designer to place the assignment to got_lock within the scope of the if, but it finds a correction regardless.

5.2 Minmax Example

Minmax is a simple program to evaluate the maximum and the minimum of three input values [Gro04]. The minimum is stored in least, the maximum is stored in most. The fault is located of Line 8 in Figure 7. Instead of assigning input2 to least the value is assigned to most.

We consider as possible faults the left-hand sides and right-hand sides of the assignments in Lines 4, 6, 8, and 10, and the expressions in Line 3, 5, 7, and 9. Note that a correction for a left-hand side should be independent of the state of the program. Therefore, the corrections for the left-hand side are decided together with the faulty components before the inputs are read. The assertion in Line 11 is replaced by if !(least <= most) error=1 and we check the property G(error = 0).

The algorithm provides two diagnoses and the corresponding corrections. The algorithm suggests to set the if-condition in Line 7 to false. In Line 8 more than one correction is possible. The algorithm suggests to change the LHS of the assignment to least, or to change the RHS either to input1 or to input3. It is obvious that all of the suggested corrections are valid for the assertion (least <= most), but that assertion does not guarantee the intended behavior of the program, namely that the minimum value is assigned to least and the maximum value to most. We make the specification more precise:

```
(least <= input1) && (least <= input2) && (least <= input3) &&
(most >= input1) && (most >= input2) && (most >= input3)
```

```
0      diagnose = choose{11, 13, 16, 17}
       int got_lock = 0;
       do{
1.0      if (diagnose = 11)
1.1         tmp = choose(true, false);
1.2      else
1.3         tmp = *;
1.4      if (tmp) {
2           lock();
3.0      if (diagnose = 13)
3.1         tmp = choose(0,..,n-1);
3.2      else
3.3         tmp = got_lock + 1;
3.4      got_lock = tmp;}
4        if (got_lock != 0) {
5           unlock();}
6.0      if (diagnose = 16)
6.1         tmp = choose(0,..,n-1);
6.2      else
6.3         tmp = got_lock - 1;
6.4      got_lock = tmp;
7.0      if (diagnose = 17)
7.1         tmp = choose(true, false);
7.2      else
7.3         tmp = *;
7.4      } while(tmp)
```

Fig. 8. Instrumented Lock Example

With this specification we find one diagnosis and correction: Change the LHS from most to least in Line 8.

As stated before, our approach is not restricted to invariants. In order to show the applicability of our approach, we change the program and the specification. In a modified program version we initialize error with 1 and set it to 0 if the assignment holds. We change the specification to the LTL formula $X\,X\,F(\text{error} = 0)$, meaning: "After two steps error must eventually be equal to 0". This is clearly not an invariant. Our algorithm is again able to find the correction.

5.3 Sequential Multiplier

The four-bit sequential multiplier shown in Figure 9 is introduced in [HD84]. The multiplier has two input shift-registers A and B, and a register Q which stores intermediate data. If input INIT is high, shift registers A and B are loaded with the inputs and Q is reset to zero. In every clock cycle register A is shifted right and register B is shifted left. The least significant bit (LSB) of A is the control input for the multiplexer. If it is high, the multiplexer forwards the value of B to the adder, which adds it to the intermediate result stored in register Q. After four clock cycles Q holds the product A ∗ B.

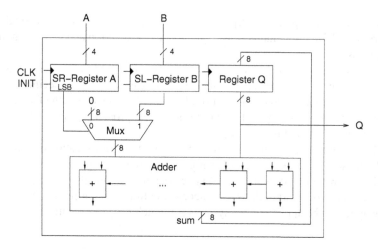

Fig. 9. Sequential Multiplier

The multiplier has a fault in the adder: The output of the single-bit full adder responsible for bit 0 always adds 1 to the correct output. The components we use for fault localization are the eight full adders in the adder, the eight AND gates in the multiplexer, and the registers A, B, and Q.

Our approach is able to find the faulty part in the adder and provides a correction for all possible inputs. It suggests to use a half adder for bit 0. This is simpler than the correction we expected and still correct: In the first time step, Q is 0 and in all subsequent steps, the LSB of B is 0 because B is shifted left. Thus, a carry never occurs.

Let us consider the candidates for correction that model-based diagnosis finds. If we load A and B with 6 and 9, respectively, the output is 58 instead of 54. Consistency-based diagnosis finds the registers B and Q, the AND gate for bit two in the multiplexer and the full adders for the three least significant bits as candidates. We can reduce the number of diagnoses by using multiple test cases and computing the intersection of the reported diagnoses. However, the full adder for bit one is a candidate in every test case. To see this, note that after four time slices the computed result is the correct value plus four. Regardless of the inputs, the carry bit of the full adder for bit 1 will have value 1 in at least one time step. If we change this value to 0, the calculated result of the multiplication is reduced by four and we obtain the correct result. Similarly Q is a diagnosis for every test case. This example shows once more that consistency-based diagnosis finds candidates that cannot have caused the fault.

The example can also be used to show that it is not possible to correct a fault using a single test case: for any single test case there is a valid correction for the full adder for bit one. There is not, however, one correction that is valid for all test cases. This conclusion can only be reached by considering multiple inputs, which is what our approach does.

6 Conclusions

We have presented an integrated approach to localizing and correcting faults in finite-state systems with a specification given in LTL. Our approach uses a very general fault model in which a component is replaced by an arbitrary new function. Though it has been formulated for single faults, it is applicable to localization and correction of multiple faults as well.

The approach, which is based on infinite games, is sound in the sense that a suggested correction is valid for all possible input sequences. If the specification is an invariant, our approach is complete: if a single point of failure exists, the fault is always found and corrected. For general LTL properties, the approach is sound and it performs well in practice, though it is not complete.

We have also shown that the most important competing localization method, model based diagnosis using consistency, does not provide the same precision in locating errors. Other known methods work with very restricted fault models, which are very useful when the fault is incurred during an incorrect optimization or re-encoding step, but does not appear to be applicable for systems for which no reference model is available.

References

[B⁺96]   R. K. Brayton et al. VIS: A system for verification and synthesis. In T. Henzinger and R. Alur, editors, *Eighth Conference on Computer Aided Verification (CAV'96)*, pages 428–432. Springer-Verlag, Rutgers University, 1996. LNCS 1102.

[BNR03]   T. Ball, M. Naik, and S. K. Rajamani. From symptom to cause: Localizing errors in counterexample traces. In *30th Symposium on Principles of Programming Languages (POPL 2003)*, pages 97–105, January 2003.

[CFTD93]   L. Console, G. Friedrich, and D. Theseider Dupré. Model-based diagnosis meets error diagnosis in logic programs. In *Proceedings of the International Joint Conference on Artificial Intelligence (IJCAI'93)*, pages 1494–1499. Morgan-Kaufmann, 1993.

[CGP99]   E. M. Clarke, O. Grumberg, and D. A. Peled. *Model Checking*. MIT Press, Cambridge, MA, 1999.

[CT91]   L. Console and P. Torasso. A spectrum of logical definitions of model-based diagnosis. *Computational Intelligence*, 7(3):133–141, 1991.

[CWH94]   P.-Y. Chung, Y.-M. Wang, and I. N. Hajj. Logic design error diagnosis and correction. *IEEE Transactions on Very Large Scale Integration (VLSI) Systems*, 2:320–332, 1994.

[FAVS⁺04] M. Fahim Ali, A. Veneris, S. Safarpur, R. Drechsler, A. Smith, and M. Abadir. Debugging sequential circuits using boolean satisfiability. In *International Conference on Computer Aided Design*, pages 204–209, 2004.

[Gro04]   A. Groce. Error explanation with distance metrics. In *International Conference on Tools and Algorithms for Construction and Analysis of Systems (TACAS'04)*, pages 108–122, Barcelona, Spain, March-April 2004. LNCS 2988.

[GV03]   A. Groce and W. Visser. What went wrong: Explaining counterexamples. In *Model Checking of Software: 10th International SPIN Workshop*, pages 121–135. Springer-Verlag, May 2003. LNCS 2648.

[HD84]   W. Hamscher and R. Davis. Diagnosing circuits with state: An inherently underconstrained problem. In *Proceedings of the Fourth National Conference on Artificial Intelligence (AAAI'84)*, pages 142–147, Austin, TX, 1984.

[JGB05]   B. Jobstmann, A. Griesmayer, and R. Bloem. Program repair as a game. To appear at Computer Aided Verification, 2005.

[JRS02]   H. Jin, K. Ravi, and F. Somenzi. Fate and free will in error traces. In *International Conference on Tools and Algorithms for Construction and Analysis of Systems (TACAS'02)*, pages 445–459, Grenoble, France, April 2002. LNCS 2280.

[KW87]   J. de Kleer and B. C. Williams. Diagnosing multiple faults. *Artificial Intelligence*, 32:97–130, 1987.

[LTH90]   H.-T. Liaw, J.-H. Tsiah, and I. N. Hajj. Efficient automatic diagnosis of digital circuits. In *Proceedings of the IEEE International Conference on Computer Aided Design*, pages 464–467, 1990.

[MCB89]   J. C. Madre, O. Coudert, and J. P. Billon. Automating the diagmosis and the rectification of design error with PRIAM. In *Proceedings of the IEEE International Conference on Computer Aided Design*, pages 30–33, 1989.

[PGA87]   D. L. Poole, R. Goebel, and R. Aleliunas. Theorist: a logical reasoning system for defaults and diagnosis. In N. Cercone and G. McCalla, editors, *The Knowledge Frontier: Essays in the Representation of Knowledge*, pages 331–352. Springer Verlag, 1987.

[Rei87]   R. Reiter. A theory of diagnosis from first principles. *Artificial Intelligence*, 32:57–95, 1987.

[RR03]   M. Renieris and S. P. Reiss. Fault localization with nearest neighbor queries. In *International Conference on Automated Software Engineering*, pages 30–39, Montreal, Canada, October 2003.

[RS04]   K. Ravi and F. Somenzi. Minimal assignments for bounded model checking. In *International Conference on Tools and Algorithms for Construction and Analysis of Systems (TACAS'04)*, pages 31–45, Barcelona, Spain, March-April 2004. LNCS 2988.

[SW99]   M. Stumptner and F. Wotawa. Debugging functional programs. In *Proceedings on the 16th International Joint Conference on Artificial Intelligence*, 1999.

[TYSH94]   M. Tomita, T. Yamamoto, F. Sumikawa, and K. Hirano. Rectification of multiple logic design errors in multiple output circuits. In *Proceedings of the Design Automation Conference*, pages 212–217, 1994.

[VW94]   M. Vardi and P. Wolper. Reasoning about infinite computations. *Information and Computation*, 115:1–37, 1994.

[WB95]   A. Wahba and D. Borrione. Design error diagnosis in sequential circuits. In *Correct Hardware Design and Verification Methods (CHARME'95)*, pages 171–188, 1995. LNCS 987.

[Zel02]   A. Zeller. Isolating cause-effect chains from computer programs. In *10th International Symposium on the Foundations of Software Engineering (FSE-10)*, pages 1–10, November 2002.

[ZH02]   A. Zeller and R. Hildebrandt. Simplifying and isolating failure-inducing input. *IEEE Transactions on Software Engineering*, 28(2):183–200, February 2002.

Verifying Quantitative Properties
Using Bound Functions

Arindam Chakrabarti[1], Krishnendu Chatterjee[1], Thomas A. Henzinger[1,4],
Orna Kupferman[2], and Rupak Majumdar[3]

[1] UC Berkeley, USA
[2] Hebrew University, Israel
[3] UC Los Angeles, USA
[4] EPFL, Switzerland

Abstract. We define and study a quantitative generalization of the traditional boolean framework of model-based specification and verification. In our setting, propositions have integer values at states, and properties have integer values on traces. For example, the value of a quantitative proposition at a state may represent power consumed at the state, and the value of a quantitative property on a trace may represent energy used along the trace. The value of a quantitative property at a state, then, is the maximum (or minimum) value achievable over all possible traces from the state. In this framework, model checking can be used to compute, for example, the minimum battery capacity necessary for achieving a given objective, or the maximal achievable lifetime of a system with a given initial battery capacity. In the case of open systems, these problems require the solution of games with integer values.

Quantitative model checking and game solving is undecidable, except if bounds on the computation can be found. Indeed, many interesting quantitative properties, like minimal necessary battery capacity and maximal achievable lifetime, can be naturally specified by *quantitative-bound automata*, which are finite automata with integer registers whose analysis is constrained by a bound function f that maps each system K to an integer $f(K)$. Along with the linear-time, automaton-based view of quantitative verification, we present a corresponding branching-time view based on a quantitative-bound μ-calculus, and we study the relationship, expressive power, and complexity of both views.

1 Introduction

Traditional algorithmic methods for the verification of finite-state systems, with a set P of *boolean* propositions, translate a system into a transition graph in which each vertex corresponds to a state of the system and is labeled by the propositions that hold in the state. A property of the system is specified by a temporal-logic formula over P or by an automaton over the alphabet 2^P. When the system is closed (i.e., its behavior does not depend on the environment), verification is reduced to *model checking* [7]; for open systems, verification requires

D. Borrione and W. Paul (Eds.): CHARME 2005, LNCS 3725, pp. 50–64, 2005.
© IFIP International Federation for Information Processing 2005

game solving [1]. While successful for verifying hardware designs [5] and communication protocols [12], this approach cannot adequately handle infinite-state systems that arise, for example, in general software verification. Much research has therefore focused on infinite-state extensions, such as models whose vertices carry a finite, but unbounded amount of information, e.g., a pushdown store, or integer-valued registers [14]. Much of the reasoning about such systems, however, has still focused on boolean specifications (such as "is the buffer size always bounded by 5?") rather than answering quantitative questions (e.g., "what is the maximal buffer size?"). Moreover, the main challenge in most infinite-state formalisms has been to obtain decidability for checking boolean properties, usually by limiting the expressive power of the models or properties.

In contrast, the solution of *quantitative* questions, such as system power requirements and system lifetime, has been considered on a property-by-property basis. Often the solution consists, however, of two basic steps: first, a suitable system of constraints is set up whose solution gives the intended quantitative answer (a "dynamic program"); and second, by considering the characteristics of the system (number of states or maximal initial battery power), a bound is provided on the number of iterations required to solve the dynamic program. We systematize this ad-hoc approach to answering quantitative questions about infinite-state systems in order to make it accessible to design engineers. For this purpose, we extend the traditional boolean verification framework to an *integer-based* framework, which due to its generality permits the modeling of a wide variety of quantitative aspects and properties of systems [6,4].[1] In particular, we generalize traditional boolean specification formalisms such as automata to the integer-based framework, so that an engineer can express the desired quantitative properties in a natural way. These quantitative automata are then automatically translated into dynamic programs for model checking and game solving. Finally, from parametric bounds given by the engineer, such as bounds on the value of a quantity or on the number of automaton steps necessary for computing a property, we automatically derive iteration bounds on solving the corresponding dynamic program. In all the examples we study, such as maximal lifetime of a system with given initial battery capacity, our generic, systematic approach matches the best known previous, property-specific algorithms.

Specifically, the models we consider, *quantitative structures*, are graphs with finitely many vertices, but every vertex is labeled by a set of *quantitative propositions*, each taking an integer value. For example, the label at each vertex may represent the amount of power consumed when the vertex is visited, or it may represent a buffer size, a time delay, a resource requirement, a reward, a cost, etc. The properties we check are quantitative properties of infinite paths, each representing a run of the system. For instance, we may ask for the peak power

---

[1] It should be noted that we use the term *quantitative*, as in quantitative verification, quantitative property, or quantitative μ-calculus, simply as referring to "integer-based" rather than "boolean." This is not to be confused with some literature, where the term *quantitative* is used to refer to "probabilistic" systems, and real values are obtained as results of evaluating boolean specifications [2,13,16,10].

consumption along a path, or for the lifetime of a battery along the path given a certain amount of initial battery power (i.e., the number of transitions along the path until the initial battery power is used up). Such properties can be specified by an extension of traditional automata. While a traditional automaton maps infinite paths of a graph with boolean propositions (i.e., infinite words over the alphabet 2^P) to "accept" or "reject", we define *quantitative* automata, which map each infinite path of a graph with quantitative propositions (i.e., infinite words over the alphabet $\mathbb{N}^P$) to an integer. For example, if the proposition $p \in P$ describes the amount of power consumed when the current input letter is read, then an automaton specifying battery lifetime, given initial power $a \in \mathbb{N}$, maps each word $o_1 o_2 o_3 \ldots$ to the maximal $k \geq 0$ for which $\sum_{i=1}^{k} o_i(p)$ is at most a. In model checking, boolean properties of infinite paths can be interpreted either in an existential or universal way, asking whether the property is true on some or all paths from a given state. In quantitative verification, we ask for the *maximal* or *minimal* value of a property over all paths from a state. For the battery life-time property, this amounts to computing the maximal or minimal achievable lifetime (note that this corresponds to the battery lifetime in the cases that a scheduler resolves all nondeterminism in a friendly vs. an adversarial manner). In a game, where two players (system components) decide which path is taken, boolean properties are interpreted in an ∃∀ fashion ("does player 1 have a strat-egy so that for all player 2 strategies the property is satisfied?"). Accordingly, we interpret quantitative properties in a *max min* fashion ("what is the maximal value of the property that player 1 can achieve no matter how player 2 plays?").

Since quantitative automata subsume counter machines, model checking and game solving are undecidable. However, unlike much previous work on infinite-state verification, we do not focus on defining decidable subclasses, but we note that in many examples that arise from verification applications, it is often easy and natural to give a *bound function*. This function specifies, for given system parameters (such as number of states, maximal constants, etc.), a threshold when it is safe to conclude that the value of a quantitative property tends to infinity. Accordingly, we specify a quantitative property as a *quantitative-bound automaton*, which is a pair consisting of a quantitative automaton and a bound function. Note that bounds are not constant but depend on the size of the struc-ture over which a specification is interpreted; they are *functions*. We consider *value-bound* functions, which constrain the maximal value of an automaton reg-ister, and *iteration-bound* functions, which constrain the maximal number of automaton transitions that need to be analyzed in order to compute the value of the property specified by the automaton. Iteration bounds directly give ter-mination bounds for dynamic programs, and thus better iteration bounds yield faster verification algorithms. In particular, for the battery lifetime property, the generic dynamic-programming algorithms based on iteration bounds are more efficient than the finite-state algorithms derived from value bounds, and they match the best known algorithms that have been devised specifically for the battery lifetime property [6]. Given a value-bound function f, we can always ob-tain a corresponding iteration-bound function g: for quantitative automata with

$|Q|$ control locations and k registers, and quantitative structures G, the iteration bound $g(G) = O(|Q| \cdot |G| \cdot f(G)^k)$ is sufficient and necessary. Moreover, for certain subclasses of quantitative automata it is possible to derive better iteration bounds. For instance, for *monotonic* quantitative-bound automata (without decreasing register values), we derive iteration-bound functions that are linear with respect to given value-bound functions.

The verification problems for properties specified by quantitative-bound automata are finite-state, and therefore decidable. However, instead of reducing these problems to boolean problems, we provide algorithms that are based on generic and natural, integer-based dynamic programming formulations, where the bound function gives a termination guarantee for the evaluation of the dynamic program. We expect these algorithms to perform well in practice, as they (1) avoid artificial boolean encodings of integers and (2) match, in all the examples we consider, the complexity of the best known property-specific algorithms. The use of bound functions can be viewed as a generalization of bounded model checking [3] from the boolean to the quantitative case. In bounded model checking, the engineer provides a bound on the number of execution steps of a system along with a property. However, the bound is usually a constant independent of the structure, whereas our bound functions capture when search can be terminated without losing information about the structure. Therefore, in bounded model checking, only the structure diameter constitutes a bound function in our sense, because smaller bounds may give counterexamples but not proofs. Of course, as in bounded model checking, our approach could be used to quickly find counterexamples for quantitative verification problems even if the bound function gives values that are smaller than necessary for proof.

Quantitative automata specify dynamic programs. There is a second natural way to specify iterative computation: through the μ-calculus [15]. In a quantitative extension of the μ-calculus, each formula induces a mapping from vertices to integers, and bound functions naturally specify a bound on the number of iterations for evaluating fixpoint expressions. More precisely, for a μ-formula φ, an iteration-bound function g specifies that if, during the iterative calculation of the value of a fixpoint expression in φ on a structure G, a stable value is not reached within $g(G)$ iterations, then the value is infinity. While quantitative extensions of the μ-calculus [13,16,10] have been defined before, they were interpreted over probabilistic structures and gave no iteration bounds. Finally, we give a translation from linear-time quantitative-bound automata to the branching-time quantitative-bound μ-calculus. For the purpose of game solving, as in the boolean case, the translation requires that the automaton is deterministic. This gives us symbolic algorithms for the quantitative verification of closed and open systems. Moreover, we show that the relationship [9] between boolean μ-formulas over *transition* graphs and boolean μ-formulas over *game* graphs carries over to the quantitative setting: a quantitative-bound μ-formula computes a particular quantitative property over two-player game graphs iff the formula computes the property over both existential and universal transition graphs (i.e., game graphs where one of the two players has no choices). This shows that the same integer-based symbolic iteration schemes can be used for verifying a quantitative property over both closed and open systems, provided the single-step operation is modified appropriately; this was previously known only for boolean structures, where the dynamic programs are degenerate [9].

2 The Integer-Based Quantitative Setting

Quantitative Properties. Let P be a nonempty, finite set of *quantitative propositions* (*propositions*, for short). A *quantitative observation* (*observation*, for short) is a function $o: P \to \mathbb{N}$ mapping each proposition to a natural number (possibly 0). Let $\mathcal{O}$ be the set of observations. A *quantitative trace* (*trace*, for short) is an infinite sequence $w \in \mathcal{O}^\omega$ of observations. A *quantitative property* (*property*, for short) is a function $\pi: \mathcal{O}^\omega \to \mathbb{N} \cup \{\infty\}$ mapping each trace to a natural number or to infinity. Let Π denote the set of properties. These definitions generalize the boolean interpretation [7], where observations are maps from propositions to $\{0,1\}$, and properties are maps from traces to $\{0,1\}$. The following examples describe some quantitative properties.

Example 1 (Response time). Let $P = \{p\}$. Given $a \in \mathbb{N}$, the property $rt_a: \mathcal{O}^\omega \to \mathbb{N}$ maps each trace w to $rt_a(w) = \sup\{k \mid \exists w' \in \mathcal{O}^*, w'' \in \mathcal{O}^\omega$ such that $w = w' \cdot (p \mapsto a)^k \cdot w''\}$. Thus, $rt_a(w)$ is the supremal number of consecutive observations mapping the proposition p to the value a in the trace w. This may model the maximal time between a request and a response. The supremum may be infinity. This happens if $w = w' \cdot (p \mapsto a)^\omega$, or if for all $k \geq 0$, the trace w contains a subsequence with at least k successive observations mapping p to a (for example, p may be mapped to $abaabaaabaaaab\ldots$). ∎

Example 2 (Fair maximum). Let $P = \{p,q\}$. The property $fm: \mathcal{O}^\omega \to \mathbb{N}$ maps each trace w to the supremal value of the proposition p on w if the proposition q is nonzero infinitely often on w, and to 0 otherwise. The proposition q may model a fairness condition on traces [6]. Formally, $fm(o_0 o_1 o_2 \ldots)$ is $\sup\{o_j(p) \mid j \geq 0\}$ if $\limsup\{o_j(q) \mid j \geq 0\} \neq 0$, and 0 otherwise. The supremum may be infinity. ∎

Example 3 (Lifetime). Let $P = \{p,c\}$. Given $a \in \mathbb{N}$, the property $lt_a: \mathcal{O}^\omega \to \mathbb{N}$ maps each trace $w = o_0 o_1 o_2 \ldots$ to $lt_a(w) = \sup\{k \mid \sum_{j=0}^{k}(-1)^{c_j} \cdot o_j(p) \leq a\}$, where $c_j = 0$ if $o_j(c) = 0$, and $c_j = 1$ otherwise. Intuitively, if a zero (resp., nonzero) value $o(c)$ denotes resource consumption (resp., resource gain) in a single step of $o(p)$ units, then $lt_a(w)$ is the supremal number of steps that can be executed without exhausting the resource, given a initial units of the resource. ∎

Example 4 (Peak running total). Let $P = \{p,c\}$ as in the previous example. The property $prt: \mathcal{O}^\omega \to \mathbb{N}$ maps each trace $w = o_0 o_1 o_2 \ldots$ to $prt(w) = \sup\{\sum_{j=0}^{k}(-1)^{c_j} \cdot o_j(p) \mid j \geq 0\}$, where again $c_j = 0$ if $o_j(c) = 0$, and $c_j = 1$ otherwise. Intuitively, if a resource is being consumed or gained over the trace w, then $prt(w)$ is the initial amount of the resource necessary so that the resource is never exhausted. ∎

Quantitative Structures. A *quantitative system* (*system*, for short) is a tuple $K = (S, \delta, s_0, \langle \cdot \rangle)$, where S is a finite set of states, $\delta \subseteq S \times S$ is a total transition relation, $s_0 \in S$ is an initial state, and $\langle \cdot \rangle : S \to \mathcal{O}$ is an observation function that maps each state s to an observation $\langle s \rangle$. A two-player *quantitative game structure* (*game*, for short) is a tuple $G = (S, S_1, S_2, \delta, s_0, \langle \cdot \rangle)$, where S, δ, s_0, and $\langle \cdot \rangle$ are as in systems, and $S_1 \cup S_2 = S$ is a partition of the state space into player-1 states S_1 and player-2 states S_2. At player-1 states, the first player chooses a successor state; at player-2 states, the second player. Note that systems are special cases of games: if $S_i = S$, for $i \in \{1, 2\}$, then the game is called a *player-i system*. We use the term *structure* to refer to both systems and games.

A *trajectory* of the structure G is an infinite sequence $t = r_0 r_1 r_2 \ldots$ of states $r_j \in S$ such that the first state r_0 is the initial state s_0 of G, and $(r_j, r_{j+1}) \in \delta$ for all $j \geq 0$. The trajectory t induces the infinite sequence $\langle t \rangle = \langle r_0 \rangle \langle r_1 \rangle \langle r_2 \rangle \ldots$ of observations. A trace $w \in \mathcal{O}^\omega$ is *generated* by G if there is a trajectory t of G such that $w = \langle t \rangle$. A *player-i strategy*, for $i \in \{1, 2\}$, is a function ξ_i: $S^* \times S_i \to S$ that maps every nonempty, finite sequence of states to a successor of the last state in the sequence; that is, $(s, \xi_i(t, s)) \in \delta$ for every state sequence $t \in S^*$ and state $s \in S_i$. Intuitively, $\xi_i(t, s)$ indicates the choice taken by player i according to strategy ξ_i if the current state of

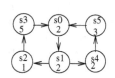

Fig. 1.

the game is s, and the history of the game is t. We write Ξ_i for the set of player-i strategies. For two strategies $\xi_1 \in \Xi_1$ and $\xi_2 \in \Xi_2$, the *outcome* t_{ξ_1, ξ_2} of ξ_1 and ξ_2 is a trajectory of G, namely, $t_{\xi_1, \xi_2} = r_0 r_1 r_2 \ldots$ such that $r_0 = s_0$ and for all $j \geq 0$ and $i \in \{1, 2\}$, if $r_j \in S_i$, then $r_{j+1} = \xi_i(r_0 r_1 \ldots r_{j-1}, r_j)$.

Consider the system K shown in Figure 1, with the initial state s_0. Each state s_i of K is labeled with the value $\langle s_i \rangle(p)$ for a proposition p. Consider the property rt_2 from Example 1. For all traces w that correspond to trajectories of K of the form $(s_0 s_1 s_2 s_3)^*$, we have $rt_2(w) = 2$. For all traces w that correspond to trajectories of the form $(s_0 s_1 s_4 s_5)^*$, we have $rt_2(w) = 3$. Moreover, $rt_2(w) \leq 3$ for all traces w generated by K. Now consider a game played on the same structure K, where the state s_1 is a player-2 state. Consider the property lt_{14} from Example 3, supposing that $\langle s \rangle(c) = 0$ for all states s of K. The goal of player 2 is to maximize lifetime given initially 14 units of the resource. Consider the strategy where player 2 chooses s_4 at the first visit to s_1, and chooses s_2 thereafter. This strategy generates a trace w along which p is mapped to $2223 (2215)^\omega$; hence $lt_{14}(w) = 7$. Note that all memoryless (i.e., history-independent) strategies lead to smaller lifetimes.

3   Quantitative-Bound Automata

3.1   Specifying Quantitative Properties

Syntax. We specify properties using automata. Let $\mathcal{O}$ be a given finite set of observations. Quantitative automata run over input traces in $\mathcal{O}^\omega$. The configuration of a quantitative automaton consists of a control location and an array of registers with values in $\mathbb{N}$. The transitions of quantitative automata are guarded by conditions on the values of the registers and the input observation, and involve, in addition to an update of the control location, also an update of the register values. A k-register *update function* is a recursive function $u: \mathbb{N}^k \times \mathcal{O} \rightharpoonup \mathbb{N}^k$ which may be partial. Let U denote the set of update functions. A *quantitative automaton* (*automaton*, for short) is a tuple $A = \langle Q, k, q_0, \gamma \rangle$, where Q is a finite set of control locations, $k \in \mathbb{N}$ is a number of registers, $q_0 \in Q$ is an initial location, and $\gamma: Q \to 2^{U \times Q}$ is a transition function that maps each location q to a finite set $\gamma(q)$ of pairs consisting of an update function and a successor location. We require that the transition function γ defines a total relation, namely, for each location $q \in Q$, each observation $o \in \mathcal{O}$, and all register values $\boldsymbol{x} \in \mathbb{N}^k$, there exists $(u, q') \in \gamma(q)$ such that $u(\boldsymbol{x}, o)$ is defined. For technical convenience, we furthermore assume that the automaton has a sink location $q_{halt} \in Q$: if the current location is q_{halt}, then for all observations, the next location is q_{halt} and the values of the registers remain unchanged; that is, $\gamma(q_{halt}) = \{(\lambda \boldsymbol{x}. \lambda o. \boldsymbol{x}, q_{halt})\}$. We write R for the array of registers, and $R[i] \in \mathbb{N}$ for the value of the i-th register, for $0 \leq i < k$.

Semantics. A *configuration* of the automaton A is a tuple $(q, v_0, v_1, \ldots, v_{k-1}) \in Q \times \mathbb{N}^k$ that specifies the current control location and the values of the registers. The initial configuration of the automaton is $c_{init} = (q_0, 0, 0, \ldots, 0)$, where all k registers are initialized to 0. For an input $o \in \mathcal{O}$, the configuration $c' = (q', v'_0, v'_1, \ldots, v'_{k-1})$ is an *o-successor* of the configuration $c = (q, v_0, v_1, \ldots, v_{k-1})$, denoted by $c \xrightarrow{o} c'$, if there is a transition $(u, q') \in \gamma(q)$ such that $u(v_0, v_1, \ldots, v_{k-1}, o) = (v'_0, v'_1, \ldots, v'_{k-1})$. A *run* of the automaton A over a trace $o_0 o_1 o_2 \ldots \in \mathcal{O}^\omega$ is an infinite sequence $c_0 c_1 c_2 \ldots$ of configurations such that $c_0 = c_{init}$, and $c_j \xrightarrow{o_j} c_{j+1}$ for all $j \geq 0$. The *value* of the run $r = c_0 c_1 c_2 \ldots$ is defined as $val_A(r) = \limsup\{R[0](c_j) \mid j \geq 0\}$, that is, the value of r is the maximal value of the register $R[0]$ which occurs infinitely often along r, if this maximum is bounded; and otherwise the value is infinity. In other words, $val_A(r) = \infty$ iff for all $k \geq 0$, the value of the register $R[0]$ is infinitely often greater than k.

An automaton is *monotonic* if along every run, the value of each register cannot decrease. An automaton is *deterministic* if for every configuration c and input $o \in \mathcal{O}$, there is exactly one o-successor of c. While a deterministic automaton has a single run over every input trace, in general an automaton may have several runs over a given trace, each with a possibly different value. According to the *nondeterministic* (or *existential*) interpretation of automata, the *value* of an automaton A over a trace w, denoted $val_A^{nondet}(w)$, is the supremal value of all runs of A over w. Formally, $val_A^{nondet}(w) = \sup\{val_A(r) \mid r \text{ is a run of } A \text{ with } \langle r \rangle = w\}$. An alternative is the *universal* interpretation of automata, where the *value* of A over a trace w, denoted $val_A^{univ}(w)$, is the infimal value of all runs of A over w; that is, $val_A^{univ}(w) = \inf\{val_A(w, r) \mid r \text{ is a run of } A \text{ with } \langle r \rangle = w\}$. Note that a deterministic automaton A can be viewed as both a nondeterministic and a universal automaton. The (nondeterministic) automaton A *specifies* (or *com-*

putes) the property $\pi \in \Pi$ if for all traces $w \in \mathcal{O}^\omega$, we have $val_A^{\text{nondet}}(w) = \pi(w)$. This definition captures traditional Büchi automata as a special case: keep one register $R[0]$, which is set to 1 whenever the automaton visits a Büchi accepting control location, and set to 0 otherwise.

Model Checking and Game Solving. Let K be a quantitative system. For a quantitative automaton A, the *max-value* of K with respect to A, denoted $val_A^{\text{max}}(K)$, is the supremal value of all traces generated by K, where we choose the nondeterministic (rather than the universal) interpretation of automata. Formally, $val_A^{\text{max}}(K) = \sup\{val_A^{\text{nondet}}(w) \mid w \text{ is a trace generated by } K\}$. The *min-value* of K with respect to A, denoted $val_A^{\text{min}}(K)$, is the infimal value of all traces generated by K; that is, $val_A^{\text{min}}(K) = \inf\{val_A^{\text{nondet}}(w) \mid w \text{ is a trace generated by } K\}$. Now consider a game G. The value of a strategy pair $\xi_1 \in \Xi_1$ and $\xi_2 \in \Xi_2$ with respect to a *deterministic* automaton A is the value $val_A(\xi_1, \xi_2) = val_A(t_{\xi_1, \xi_2})$ of A over the outcome of the strategies ξ_1 and ξ_2. The *game-value* of G with respect to a deterministic automaton A, denoted $val_A^{\text{maxmin}}(G)$, is defined as $\sup_{\xi_1 \in \Xi_1} \inf_{\xi_2 \in \Xi_2} val_A(\xi_1, \xi_2)$. This is the supremal value of A that player-1 can achieve against all player-2 strategies. The symmetric definition is omitted for brevity.

Given a system K and an automaton A, the *quantitative model-checking problem* (*model checking*, for short) is to determine $val_A^{\text{max}}(K)$ and $val_A^{\text{min}}(K)$. Given a game G and a deterministic automaton A, the *quantitative game-solving problem* (*game solving*, for short) is to determine $val_A^{\text{maxmin}}(G)$. Since registers can contain arbitrary natural numbers, we can encode 2-counter machines as monotonic automata, and hence the model-checking and game-solving problems are undecidable.

3.2   Bound Functions for Automata

Quantitative-Bound Automata. In order to solve model-checking problems and games, we equip quantitative automata with bound functions. A *quantitative-bound automaton* (QBA) (A, f) consists of a quantitative automaton A and a recursive function $f: \mathcal{G} \to \mathbb{N}$, where $\mathcal{G}$ is the set of quantitative structures (systems and games). To compute a property on a structure G, a QBA works with a bound $f(G)$ that depends on G. The motivation is that for many properties, the designer can provide a bound on the maximal value of the automaton registers, or on the number of automaton transitions that need to be executed in order to compute the value of the property if the value is finite. We thus have two interpretations of the bound function f: the *value-bound* interpretation, where $f(G)$ is a bound on the register values, and the *iteration-bound* interpretation, where $f(G)$ is a bound on the automaton transitions.

We define the value of a QBA over a trace generated by a structure for the two possible interpretations. Given a QBA (A, f), a structure G, and a trace w generated by G, let r be a run of the automaton A over w. The value of $r = c_0 c_1 c_2 \ldots$ over w for the value-bound interpretation, denoted $val_{\text{vbound}(A,f)}(r)$, is defined as follows: if there are an index $j \in \mathbb{N}$ and a register

$R[i]$, for $0 \leq i < k$, such that $R[i](c_j) > f(G)$, then $val_{\mathrm{vbound}(A,f)}(r) = \infty$; otherwise $val_{\mathrm{vbound}(A,f)}(r) = val_A(r)$. Intuitively, the value-bound interpretation maps every trace that causes some register to exceed the value bound at some point, to ∞. The value of the run r over w for the iteration-bound interpretation, denoted $val_{\mathrm{ibound}(A,f)}(r)$, is defined as follows: if for all $0 \leq i < k$, we have $\max\{R[i](c_j) \mid f(G) \leq j \leq 2 \cdot f(G)\} = \max\{R[i](c_j) \mid 2 \cdot f(G) \leq j \leq 3 \cdot f(G)\}$, then $val_{\mathrm{ibound}(A,f)}(r) = \max\{R[0](c_j) \mid f(G) \leq j \leq 2 \cdot f(G)\}$; otherwise $val_{\mathrm{ibound}(A,f)}(r) = \infty$. Intuitively, the iteration-bound interpretation checks if the maximal values of all registers stabilize within the iteration bound, and maps a trace to ∞ if some maximal register value does not stabilize.

Given a QBA (A, f), a system K, a game G, a trace generated by K or G, and two interpretations bound $\in \{\mathrm{vbound}, \mathrm{ibound}\}$, we define the values $val^{\mathrm{nondet}}_{\mathrm{bound}(A,f)}(w)$, $val^{\max}_{\mathrm{bound}(A,f)}(K)$, $val^{\min}_{\mathrm{bound}(A,f)}(K)$, and $val^{\mathrm{maxmin}}_{\mathrm{bound}(A,f)}(G)$ analogous to the corresponding definitions in Section 3.1 using $val_{\mathrm{bound}(A,f)}(r)$ instead of $val_A(r)$. The QBA (A, f) *specifies* (or *computes*) the property π on a structure G if for all traces w generated by G, we have $val^{\mathrm{nondet}}_{\mathrm{bound}(A,f)}(w) = \pi(w)$. The following examples illustrate the idea.[2]

Example 5 (Fair maximum). The following QBA (A, f) specifies the property *fm* from Example 2 on all structures G. There are two registers. The register $R[1]$ keeps track of the maximal value of proposition p seen so far. Whenever proposition q has a nonzero value, the value of $R[1]$ is copied to $R[0]$; otherwise $R[0]$ is set to zero. If q has a nonzero value infinitely often, then the maximal value of p occurs infinitely often in $R[0]$; otherwise from some point on, $R[0]$ contains the value 0. The bound function f is defined as follows: if G contains the maximal value Δ for p, then $f(G) = \Delta$ is a suitable value-bound function; if G has N states, then $f(G) = N$ is a suitable iteration-bound function. ∎

Example 6 (Lifetime). The property *lt$_a$* from Example 3 can be computed on all structures G by the following QBA (A, f). Let $A = \langle \{q_0, q_{halt}\}, 2, q_0, \gamma \rangle$, where for all inputs $o \in \mathcal{O}$, we have $\gamma(q_0) = \{(o(c) \neq 0 \wedge R'[0] = R[0] + 1 \wedge R'[1] = R[1] - o(p), q_0), (o(c) = 0 \wedge R[1] + o(p) \leq a \wedge R'[0] = R[0] + 1 \wedge R'[1] = R[1] + o(p), q_0), (o(c) = 0 \wedge R[1] + o(p) > a \wedge R'[0] = R[0] \wedge R'[1] = R[1], q_{halt})\}$. In register $R[0]$ the automaton stores the number of transitions already taken, and in $R[1]$ it tracks the amount of the resource used so far; it continues to make transitions as long as it has a sufficient amount of the resource. If G contains N states and the maximal value Δ for p, then $f(G) = a + (N + 1) \cdot \Delta$ is a suitable value-bound function, and $f(G) = N \cdot a + N \cdot (N + 1) \cdot \Delta$ is a suitable iteration-bound function. ∎

3.3 Quantitative-Bound Model Checking and Game Solving

Given a system K and a QBA (A, f), the *quantitative-bound model-checking* problem is to determine $val^m_{\mathrm{bound}(A,f)}(K)$, where bound $\in \{\mathrm{vbound}, \mathrm{ibound}\}$ and

---

[2] In the examples, we write update functions as relations $u(\boldsymbol{x}, o, \boldsymbol{x}')$, where unprimed variables denote the values of variables before the update, and primed variables denote the values after the update.

$m \in \{\text{max}, \text{min}\}$. Similarly, given a game G and a deterministic QBA (A, f), the problem of *solving quantitative-bound games* is to determine $val^{\text{maxmin}}_{\text{bound}(A,f)}(G)$, for bound $\in \{\text{vbound}, \text{ibound}\}$. Quantitative-bound model checking and game solving are decidable. In the case of value bounds, the state space is bounded by $O(|G| \cdot |Q| \cdot (f(G) + 2)^k)$, where $|Q|$ is the size of the automaton with k registers, $|G|$ is the size of the structure, and f is the value-bound function. Let G be a structure such that for all propositions $p \in P$ and states $s \in S$, we have $\langle s \rangle(p) \leq \Delta$. Let C_0 be the maximal constant that appears syntactically in the description of the automaton A, and let $C_1 = f(G)$. Call $B = \max\{\Delta, C_0, C_1\}$ the *oblivion bound* for the QBA (A, f) and structure G. Let $g(G) = |G| \cdot |Q| \cdot (B + 2)^k$, where A has k registers. Then $val^m_{\text{vbound}(A,f)}(G) = val^m_{\text{ibound}(A,g)}(G)$, for $m \in \{\text{max}, \text{min}, \text{maxmin}\}$. Thus, we can derive an iteration bound from a value bound.

Formally, the decision problem QBA-VMC (resp., QBA-VGS) takes as input a system K (resp., game G), a QBA (A, f), the oblivion bound B, and a value $a \in \mathbb{N} \cup \{\infty\}$, and returns "Yes" if $val^{\text{max}}_{\text{vbound}(A,f)}(K) \geq a$ (resp., $val^{\text{maxmin}}_{\text{vbound}(A,f)}(G) \geq a$). The decision problems QBA-IMC and QBA-IGS are defined analogously using $val^{\text{max}}_{\text{ibound}(A,f)}(K)$ and $val^{\text{maxmin}}_{\text{ibound}(A,f)}(G)$. We give the oblivion bound as an input to the problems, because the value of $f(G)$ can be unboundedly larger than the descriptions of f and G. We assume that updates take unit time.

Theorem 1. *(1) QBA-VMC is PSPACE-complete and QBA-IMC is EXPTIME-complete. (2) QBA-VGS and QBA-IGS are EXPTIME-complete. (3) Let $|G|$ be the size of the structure and $|Q|$ the automaton size for (A, f) and G. Let $S = |Q| \cdot |G| \cdot (f(G) + 2)^k)$. QBA-VMC and QBA-VGS can be solved in time $O(S)$ and $O(S^2)$ respectively. QBA-IMC and QBA-IGS can be solved in time $O(|Q| \cdot |G| \cdot f(G))$.*

Note that these complexity results reflect the sizes of the state space in which the solution lies. In practice, however, the reachable state space can be much smaller. Hence, on-the-fly state space exploration can be used instead of constructing the entire state space *a priori*. The following examples show that our approach, while being generic and capturing several interesting quantitative verification problems [6] as special cases, still remains amenable to efficient analysis.

Example 7 (Fair maximum). Consider the deterministic QBA (A, f) with value-bound function f from Example 5, which computes the property *fm* from Example 2. This property is exactly the winning condition for the "threshold Büchi games" described in [6]. For a game G, the state space with the value bound has size $O(|G| \cdot |Q| \cdot \Delta)$, where Δ is the maximal value of proposition p in G. This is exponential in $|G|$. However, the iteration bound for this problem is $|G|$, and this gives an $O(|G|^2)$ algorithm, which is the same complexity as the algorithm of [6].[3]   ∎

---

[3] However, computing an iteration-bound function automatically using the optimal value-bound function would lead to a suboptimal iteration-bound function $g(G) = |G| \cdot |Q| \cdot \Delta$.

Example 8 (Peak running total). The property *prt* from Example 4 is exactly the winning condition for the "energy games" of [6]. This property can be computed by a deterministic QBA with two registers and value-bound function $f(G) = |G| \cdot \Delta$, where Δ is the maximal value of p in G. A game-solving algorithm based on value bounds would require time $O(|G|^6 \cdot \Delta^4)$, whereas an algorithm designed specifically to solve this game [6] runs in time $O(|G|^3 \cdot \Delta)$. However, even for this problem, our generic approach, using the optimal iteration-bound function $h(G) = |G|^2 \cdot \Delta$ achieves the best known complexity of $O(|G|^3 \cdot \Delta)$. ∎

In the special case of monotonic automata, efficient iteration bounds can be automatically derived from value bounds. Consider a structure G with N states and a monotonic QBA (A, f) with value-bound function f, location set Q, and k registers. Since the value of each register only increases, within $|Q| \cdot k \cdot N \cdot f(G)$ steps of every run of A over a trace generated by G, either an automaton configuration repeats, or there is a register such that the value of the register has crossed the threshold $f(G)$. Thus $val^{\max}_{\text{vbound}(A,f)}(G)$ is achieved by a run within $|Q| \cdot k \cdot N \cdot f(G)$ steps. Since we only require the monotonicity of the registers in the limit, this observation can be generalized to *reversal-bounded automata* [18], where a bounded number of switches between increasing and decreasing modes of the registers are allowed.

Proposition 1. *Let A be a monotonic automaton with location set Q and k registers, let $f \colon \mathcal{G} \to \mathbb{N}$ be a recursive function, and let $g(G) = |Q| \cdot k \cdot N \cdot f(G)$ for all structures G with N states. Then $val^m_{\text{vbound}(A,f)}(G) = val^m_{\text{ibound}(A,g)}(G)$ for all structures G and $m \in \{\max, \min, \max\min\}$.*

As with the other components of a quantitative automaton, the designer has to provide the bound function f. Unfortunately, the task of providing a good value or iteration bound function f, that is, an f that satisfies $val^m_A(G) = val^m_{\text{bound}(A,f)}(G)$ for all structures G, cannot be automated.

Proposition 2. *There is a class of update functions involving only increment operations and equality testing on registers, such that the following two problems are undecidable: (1) given an automaton A, determine if there is a recursive function f such that $val^{\max}_A(K) = val^{\max}_{\text{vbound}(A,f)}(K)$ for all systems K; (2) given a QBA (A, f), determine if $val^{\max}_A(K) = val^{\max}_{\text{vbound}(A,f)}(K)$ for all systems K.*

4   The Quantitative-Bound μ-Calculus

We now provide an alternative formalism for defining quantitative properties: a fixpoint calculus. Our integer-based μ-calculus generalizes the classical μ-calculus [15], and provides an alternative set of iterative algorithms for model checking and game solving.

Unbounded Formulas. Let P be a set of propositions, let $\mathcal{X}$ be a set of variables, and let $\mathcal{F}$ be a set of recursive functions from $\mathbb{N} \times \mathbb{N}$ to $\mathbb{N}$. We require that $\max, \min \in \mathcal{F}$. The formulas of the *quantitative μ-calculus*[4] are defined as

---

[4] This is different from the μ-calculi over probabilistic systems defined by [13,10,16].

$$\varphi ::= k \mid p \mid X \mid upd(\varphi, \varphi) \mid pre(\varphi) \mid \mu[(X, \varphi), \ldots, (X, \varphi)] \mid \nu[(X, \varphi), \ldots, (X, \varphi)],$$

where k ranges over the constants in $\mathbb{N} \cup \{\infty\}$, p over the propositions in P, X over the variables in $\mathcal{X}$, and upd over the functions in $\mathcal{F}$. If pre ranges over the set $\{Epre, Apre\}$ of existential and universal next-time operators, we obtain the *system calculus*; if pre ranges over the set $\{Cpre_1, Cpre_2\}$ of player-1 and player-2 controllable next-time operators, we obtain the *game calculus*. Each least-fixpoint subformula $\mu[(X_1, \varphi_1), \ldots, (X_m, \varphi_m)]$ and each greatest-fixpoint subformula $\nu[(X_1, \varphi_1), \ldots, (X_m, \varphi_m)]$ binds a set $\{X_1, \ldots, X_m\}$ of variables. A formula φ is *closed* if all occurrences of variables in φ are bound.

The formulas of the quantitative μ-calculus are interpreted over quantitative structures (systems or games). Consider a game $G = (S, S_1, S_2, \delta, s_0, \langle \cdot \rangle)$. A *quantitative valuation (valuation, for short)* is a function $\theta \colon S \to \mathbb{N} \cup \{\infty\}$ that maps each state s to a natural number or infinity. We write Θ for the set of valuations. The semantics $[\![\varphi]\!]$ of a closed formula φ over the structure G is a valuation in Θ, which is defined as follows. An *environment* $\mathbb{E} \colon \mathcal{X} \to \Theta$ maps each variable to a valuation. Given an environment $\mathbb{E}$, we write $\mathbb{E}[X := \theta]$ for the environment that maps X to θ, and maps each $Y \in \mathcal{X} \setminus \{X\}$ to $\mathbb{E}(Y)$. Each update function $upd \in \mathcal{F}$ defines a transformer $[upd] \colon \Theta \times \Theta \to \Theta$ that maps a pair of valuations to the valuation obtained by the point-wise application of upd. Each next-time operator pre defines a transformer $[pre] \colon \Theta \to \Theta$ that maps valuations to valuations. Specifically, $[Epre](\theta)(s) = \max\{\theta(s') \mid (s, s') \in \delta\}$; $[Apre](\theta)(s) = \min\{\theta(s') \mid (s, s') \in \delta\}$; $[Cpre_1](\theta)(s) = [Epre](\theta)(s)$ if $s \in S_1$, and $[Cpre_1](\theta)(s) = [Apre](\theta)(s)$ if $s \in S_2$; $[Cpre_2](\theta)(s) = [Apre](\theta)(s)$ if $s \in S_1$, and $[Cpre_2](\theta)(s) = [Epre](\theta)(s)$ if $s \in S_2$. For an environment $\mathbb{E}$, the semantics $[\![\varphi]\!]_{\mathbb{E}}$ of a (not necessarily closed) formula φ over G is defined inductively:

$$[\![k]\!]_{\mathbb{E}}(s) = k; \quad [\![p]\!]_{\mathbb{E}}(s) = \langle s \rangle(p); \quad [\![X]\!]_{\mathbb{E}}(s) = \mathbb{E}(X)(s);$$
$$[\![upd(\varphi_1, \varphi_2)]\!]_{\mathbb{E}}(s) = [upd]([\![\varphi_1]\!]_{\mathbb{E}}, [\![\varphi_2]\!]_{\mathbb{E}})(s);$$
$$[\![pre(\varphi)]\!]_{\mathbb{E}}(s) = [pre]([\![\varphi]\!]_{\mathbb{E}})(s);$$
$$[\![\mu[(X_1, \varphi_1), \ldots, (X_m, \varphi_m)]]\!]_{\mathbb{E}}(s) = \limsup\{\mathbb{E}_j^{\mu}(X_1)(s) \mid j \geq 0\};$$
$$[\![\nu[(X_1, \varphi_1), \ldots, (X_m, \varphi_m)]]\!]_{\mathbb{E}}(s) = \limsup\{\mathbb{E}_j^{\nu}(X_1)(s) \mid j \geq 0\}.$$

The environment $\mathbb{E}_j^{\mu}$ is defined inductively by $\mathbb{E}_0^{\mu}(X_i) = (\lambda s. 0)$ and $\mathbb{E}_{j+1}^{\mu}(X_i) = [\![\varphi_i]\!]_{\mathbb{E}_j^{\mu}}$ for all $1 \leq i \leq m$; and $\mathbb{E}_j^{\mu}(Y) = \mathbb{E}(Y)$ for all $Y \in \mathcal{X} \setminus \{X_1, \ldots, X_m\}$ and $j \geq 0$. The environment $\mathbb{E}_j^{\nu}$ is defined like $\mathbb{E}_j^{\mu}$ except that $\mathbb{E}_0^{\nu}(X_i) = (\lambda s. \infty)$ for all $1 \leq i \leq m$. For monotone boolean formulas, the limsup semantics coincides with the usual fixpoint semantics of the μ-calculus [15]. For a closed formula φ, we define $[\![\varphi]\!]$ as $[\![\varphi]\!]_{\mathbb{E}}$, for an arbitrary environment $\mathbb{E}$. Given a structure G, the closed formula φ *specifies* the valuation $[\![\varphi]\!](G) = [\![\varphi]\!](s_0)$, where s_0 is the initial state of G.

Bound Functions. A *quantitative-bound μ-formula (QBF)* (φ, f) consists of a quantitative μ-formula φ and a recursive function $f \colon \mathcal{G} \to \mathbb{N}$ that provides a bound $f(G)$ on the number of iterations necessary for evaluating μ and ν subformulas on any given structure G. The semantics $[\![(\varphi, f)]\!]_{\mathbb{E}}$ of a QBF

(φ, f) over a structure G is defined like the semantics of the unbounded formula φ except that each fixpoint subformula is computed by unrolling the fixpoint only $O(f(G))$ times. Formally, a variable X is $f(G)$-*stable* at a state s with respect to a sequence $\{\mathbb{E}_j \mid j \geq 0\}$ of environments if $\max\{\mathbb{E}_j(X)(s) \mid f(G) \leq j \leq 2 \cdot f(G)\} = \max\{\mathbb{E}_j(X)(s) \mid 2 \cdot f(G) \leq j \leq 3 \cdot f(G)\}$. We define $[\![\mu[(X_1, \varphi_1), \ldots, (X_m, \varphi_m)], f]\!](s)$ to be $\max\{\mathbb{E}_j^\mu(X_1)(s) \mid f(G) \leq j \leq 2 \cdot f(G)\}$ if all variables X_i, for $1 \leq i \leq m$, are $f(G)$-stable with respect to $\{\mathbb{E}_j^\mu \mid j \geq 0\}$; otherwise $[\![\mu[(X_1, \varphi_1), \ldots, (X_m, \varphi_m)], f]\!](s) = \infty$. The semantics $[\![\nu[(X_1, \varphi_1), \ldots, (X_m, \varphi_m)], f]\!]$ of greatest-fixpoint subformulas is defined analogously, using the sequence $\{\mathbb{E}_j^\nu \mid j \geq 0\}$ of environments instead. A QBF formula (φ, f) defines an iterative algorithm for computing the valuation $[\![(\varphi, f)]\!](G)$ for any given structure G. Assuming updates take unit time, we can compute $[\![(\varphi, f)]\!](G)$ in $O(f(G)^\ell)$ time, where ℓ is the alternation depth of φ (i.e., the maximal number of alternations between occurrences of μ and ν operators; for a precise definition see [11]).

We now give examples for which a QBF (φ, f) can be found to specify the same property as the unbounded formula φ over all structures; that is, $[\![(\varphi, f)]\!](G) = [\![\varphi]\!](G)$ for all structures G. We use addition, subtraction, and comparison as update functions in $\mathcal{F}$, and we use the natural numbers 0 and 1 to encode booleans. For instance, we write $\varphi_1 = \varphi_2$ for $\min(\varphi_1 \leq \varphi_2, \varphi_2 \leq \varphi_1)$, and $\neg\varphi_1$ for $1 - \varphi$. The case formula $\mathrm{case}\{(\psi_1, \varphi_1), \ldots, (\psi_n, \varphi_n)\}$ stands for $\max(\min(\psi_1, \varphi_1), \ldots, \min(\psi_n, \varphi_n))$, where the n-ary max operator is obtained by repeated application of the binary max operator. In order to relate the branching-time framework of the quantitative μ-calculus to the linear-time framework of quantitative properties (and quantitative automata), we say that the closed QBF (φ, f) *computes* the property π if for all structures G, $[\![(\varphi, f)]\!](G) = \sup\{\pi(w) \mid w$ is a trace generated by $G\}$. In this way, linear and branching time are related *existentially* (through sup rather than inf); hence we use only the *Epre* operator to compute properties. Alternately, we could define a universal semantics where $[\![(\varphi', f)]\!](G) = \inf\{\pi(w) \mid w$ is a trace generated by $G\}$, and the *Apre* operator is used.

Example 9 (Fair maximum). Recall the property *fm* from Example 2. The property *fm* is computed over all structures G by the QBF (φ, f) with $\varphi = \mu[(X, \min\{\max\{p, X, \min\{Epre(X), Z\}\}, Z\})]$, where $Z = \nu[(X, \mu[(Y, Epre(\max\{\min\{q, X\}, Y\})])])]$, and $f(G) = N$, where N is the number of states of G. Since the longest simple path in G has length at most $N - 1$, every fixpoint is found in N iterations or less.   ∎

Example 10 (Lifetime). Over all structures G with N states, the property lt_a from Example 3 is computed by the QBF (φ, f) with $\varphi = \mu[(X, \mathrm{case}\{((c = 0) \wedge (p + Epre(Y) \leq a), X + 1), (c \neq 0, X + 1), (1, X)\}), (Y, \mathrm{case}\{(((c = 0) \wedge (p + Epre(Y) \leq a)), p + Epre(Y)), (c \neq 0, Epre(Y) - a), (1, Y)\})]$ and $f(G) = N \cdot a + N \cdot (N + 1) \cdot \Delta$, where Δ is the maximal value of the proposition p in G. If a fixpoint is not reached in $N \cdot a + N \cdot (N + 1) \cdot \Delta$ iterations, then there is a reachable cycle Γ in G with nonpositive resource consumption, and repeated traversal of Γ ensures an infinite lifetime.   ∎

Example 11 (Peak running total). Over all structures G with N states and maximal value Δ for the proposition p, the property prt from Example 4 is computed by the QBF (φ, f) with $\varphi = (\mu[(X, \text{case}\{(c = 0, p + \max\{0, Epre(X)\}), (c \neq 0, \max\{0, Epre(X)\} - p)\})], f)$ and $f(G) = N \cdot \Delta$. If a fixpoint is not reached in $N \cdot \Delta$ iterations, then there is no reachable cycle with nonpositive resource consumption, and it is not possible to traverse G forever starting with a finite amount of resources. ∎

From Automata Bounds to μ-Calculus Bounds. We establish the connection between properties specified by quantitative automata (a linear-time formalism) and those computed by the quantitative μ-calculus (a branching-time formalism). We show that every deterministic QBA can be converted to a QBF that computes the same property over all systems. This provides an alternative algorithm for quantitative model checking. We then show that the construction is robust [9], and hence, the resulting QBF can also be used for game solving. To formalize this, we define a quantitative μ-calculus over traces, extending the boolean linear-time μ-calculus [17]. The *quantitative-bound trace formulas* (QBTs) are identical to the quantitative-bound μ-formulas, except that they contain the single next-time operator Pre. A QBT is interpreted over the traces w generated by a given structure G. To define $[\![(\varphi, f)]\!](w)$ formally, we view the trace $w = o_0 o_1 o_2 \ldots$ as an infinite-state system without branching, analogous to the boolean definition in [9]. However, even though w is infinite-state, the evaluation of every fixpoint subformula in φ is bounded by $f(G)$, which is finite.

Consider a structure K, a game G, and a QBT (φ, f). The system value $val^{\max}_{(\varphi,f)}(K)$ (resp., $val^{\min}_{(\varphi,f)}(K)$) is the supremal (resp., infimal) value of the formula (φ, f) over all traces generated by K. Formally, $val^{\max}_{(\varphi,f)}(K) = \sup\{[\![(\varphi, f)]\!](w) \mid w \text{ is a trace generated by } K\}$, and $val^{\min}_{(\varphi,f)}(K)$ is the inf of the same set. For strategies $\xi_1 \in \Xi_1$ and $\xi_2 \in \Xi_2$, define $val_{(\varphi,f)}(\xi_1, \xi_2) = [\![(\varphi, f)]\!](\langle t_{\xi_1,\xi_2}\rangle)$. The game value $val^{\max\min}_{(\varphi,f)}(G) = \sup_{\xi_1 \in \Xi_1} \inf_{\xi_2 \in \Xi_2} val_{(\varphi,f)}(\xi_1, \xi_2)$ is the supremal value that player 1 can achieve against all player-2 strategies. The following two theorems generalize the results of [9] from boolean to quantitative verification: Theorem 2 establishes the connection between deterministic QBAs and QBTs; Theorem 3 presents a necessary and sufficient criterion, called *robustness*, when a QBT can be used for game solving. Moreover, the QBT constructed in Theorem 2 is robust. Given a QBT (φ, f), let $(\varphi[Epre], f)$ (resp., $(\varphi[Apre], f)$) be the QBF that results by replacing all occurrences of the next-time operator Pre with $Epre$ (resp., $Apre$).

Theorem 2. *Every deterministic QBA (A, f) can be translated into a QBT (φ, g) such that for all systems K, both $val^{\max}_{(A,f)}(K) = val^{\max}_{(\varphi,g)}(K) = [\![(\varphi[Epre], g)]\!](K)$ and $val^{\min}_{(A,f)}(K) = val^{\min}_{(\varphi,g)}(K) = [\![(\varphi[Apre], g)]\!](K).$*

Theorem 3. *Given a QBT (φ, f), the following two conditions, called robustness, are equivalent. (1) For all systems K, both $val^{\max}_{(\varphi,f)}(K) = [\![(\varphi[Epre], f)]\!](K)$ and $val^{\min}_{(\varphi,f)}(K) = [\![(\varphi[Apre], f)]\!](K)$. (2) For all games G, $val^{\max\min}_{(\varphi,f)}(G) = [\![(\varphi[Cpre_1], f)]\!](G).$*

Theorem 2 is proved using a standard (boolean) construction of a fixpoint formula from an automaton [8]. Theorem 3 follows from the existence of finite-memory optimal strategies for QBTs.

Acknowledgments. This research was supported in part by the ONR grant N00014-02-1-0671, the AFOSR MURI grant F49620-00-1-0327, and the NSF grants CCR-0225610, CCR-0234690, and CCR-0427202.

References

1. R. Alur, T.A. Henzinger, and O. Kupferman. Alternating-time temporal logic. *J. ACM*, 49:672–713, 2002.
2. A. Bianco and L. de Alfaro. Model checking of probabilistic and nondeterministic systems. In *FSTTCS*, LNCS 1026, pp. 499-513. Springer, 1995.
3. A. Biere, A. Cimatti, E.M. Clarke, and Y. Zhu. Symbolic model checking without BDDs. In *TACAS*, LNCS 1579, pp. 193–207. Springer, 1999.
4. P. Bouyer, A. Petit, and D. Thérien. An algebraic approach to data languages and timed languages. *Information & Computation*, 182:137–162, 2003.
5. J.R. Burch, E.M. Clarke, K.L. McMillan, D.L. Dill, L.J. Hwang. Symbolic model checking: 10^{20} states and beyond. *Information & Computation*, 98:142–170, 1992.
6. A. Chakrabarti, L. de Alfaro, T.A. Henzinger, and M. Stoelinga. Resource interfaces. In *EMSOFT*, LNCS 2855, pp. 117–133. Springer, 2003.
7. E.M. Clarke, O. Grumberg, and D. Peled. *Model Checking*. MIT Press, 1999.
8. M. Dam. CTL* and ECTL* as fragments of the modal μ-calculus. *Theoretical Computer Science*, 126:77–96, 1994.
9. L. de Alfaro, T.A. Henzinger, and R. Majumdar. From verification to control: Dynamic programs for ω-regular objectives. In *LICS*, pp. 279–290. IEEE, 2001.
10. L. de Alfaro, and R. Majumdar. Quantitative solution of concurrent games. *J. Computer & Systems Sciences*, 68: 374–397, 2004.
11. E.A. Emerson and C. Lei. Efficient model checking in fragments of the propositional μ-calculus. In *LICS*, pp. 267–278. IEEE, 1986.
12. G.J. Holzmann. *Design and Validation of Computer Protocols*. Prentice-Hall, 1991.
13. M. Huth and M. Kwiatkowska. Quantitative analysis and model checking. In *LICS*, pp. 111–122, IEEE, 1997.
14. O.H. Ibarra, J. Su, Z. Dang, T. Bultan, and R.A. Kemmerer. Counter machines: Decidable properties and applications to verification problems. In *MFCS*, LNCS 1893, pp. 426-435. Springer, 2000.
15. D. Kozen. Results on the propositional μ-calculus. *Theoretical Computer Science*, 27:333–354, 1983.
16. A. McIver and C. Morgan. Games, probability, and the quantitative μ-calculus. In *LPAR*, LNCS 2514, pp. 292-310. Springer, 2002.
17. M.Y. Vardi. A temporal fixpoint calculus. In *POPL*, pp. 250–259. ACM, 1988.
18. G. Xie, Z. Dang, O.H. Ibarra, and P.S. Pietro. Dense counter machines and verification problems. In *CAV*, LNCS 2725, pp. 93–105. Springer, 2003.

How Thorough Is Thorough Enough?

Arie Gurfinkel and Marsha Chechik

Department of Computer Science, University of Toronto
{arie, chechik}@cs.toronto.edu

Abstract. Abstraction is the key for effectively dealing with the state explosion problem in model-checking. Unfortunately, finding abstractions which are small and yet enable us to get conclusive answers about properties of interest is notoriously hard. Counterexample-guided abstraction refinement frameworks have been proposed to help build good abstractions iteratively. Although effective in many cases, such frameworks can include unnecessary refinement steps, leading to larger models, because the abstract verification step is not as conclusive as it can be in theory. Abstract verification can be supplemented by a more precise but much more expensive *thorough* check, but it is not clear how often this check really helps. In this paper, we study the relationship between model-checking and thorough checking and identify practical cases where the latter is not necessary, and those where it can be performed efficiently.

1 Introduction

Abstraction is arguably the most effective technique for dealing with the state explosion problem in model-checking. The goal of abstraction is to build a system which is small enough to analyze yet the one that allows to verify properties of interest. Such abstractions may be very hard to build; instead, we typically start with an abstraction which may be too crude for certain properties, and then refine it, attempting to reach a definite answer.

The best-known method for abstraction refinement, guided by counterexamples, has been suggested by Clarke et al. [5] and is outlined in Figure 1(a). This framework assumes that the abstraction K_α is an overapproximation of the system of interest K_c, i.e., every execution of K_c is an execution of K_α. When a universal property φ holds in K_α, this result can be trusted. Otherwise, either φ does not hold in K_c, or the abstraction is too crude. To tell between these cases, a counterexample obtained by verifying φ in K_α is checked for feasibility by playing it back in K_c. This either establishes the failure of φ, or enables the refinement of K_α that eliminates the spurious counterexample.

Several researchers [12,22,4,9,11] proposed an improvement of this framework that enables reasoning about arbitrary CTL formulas. In their framework, outlined in Figure 1(b), an abstract model K_α is 3-valued, which combines over- and under-approximation of K_c. Model-checking a CTL formula φ on K_α either yields true or false, which can be trusted without the need to resort to the counterexample, or it returns maybe, i.e., inconclusive. In this case, the counterexample can be used to refine the abstraction. Since building 3-valued models is no more expensive than classical [11], and neither is 3-valued model-checking [4] nor 3-valued counterexample generation [15,22], this

D. Borrione and W. Paul (Eds.): CHARME 2005, LNCS 3725, pp. 65–80, 2005.
© IFIP International Federation for Information Processing 2005

Goal: Check ACTL formula φ on a model K_c
  1. **repeat** until resources are exhausted
  2.   Build an abstract model K_α.
  3.   Model-check φ on K_α.
  4.   **if YES, return** "φ holds on K_c"
  5.   **else**
  6.   Check if the counterexample is feasible
  7.   **if YES, return** "φ fails on K_c"
  8.   **else** use the counterexample for refinement.
(a)

Goal: Check CTL formula φ on a model K_c
  1. **repeat** until resources are exhausted
  2.   Build a 3-val abstract model K_α.
  3.   Model-check φ on K_α.
  4.   **if YES, return** "φ holds on K_c"
  5.   **if NO, return** "φ fails on K_c"
  6.   **else** use the counterexample for refinement.
(b)

Fig. 1. Counterexample-guided abstraction refinement frameworks: (a) classical; (b) 3-valued

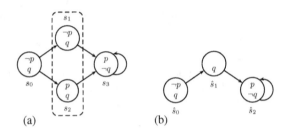

(a)   (b)

Fig. 2. (a) A concrete model K; (b) An abstraction K' of K

framework is not more expensive than classical, while allowing to reason about a larger class of temporal logic properties.

Both of these frameworks sometimes force a refinement step even though a conclusive result can be obtained from the existing model K_α. For example, consider checking a property $\varphi = A[(\neg p \wedge q) \ U \ p]$, where the original model K and its abstraction K' are shown in Figure 2. In K', states $\hat{s}_0$ and $\hat{s}_2$ correspond to s_0 and s_3 of K, respectively, whereas $\hat{s}_1$ is a merge of s_1 and s_2, indicated by dashed lines in Figure 2(a). In classical abstraction, we typically treat literals of the concrete models as atomic propositions of the abstract, thus both p and $\neg p$ are false in state $\hat{s}_1$ of K'. Our property φ fails in K', and a counterexample is produced. Clearly, this counterexample is not feasible, so refinement is necessary. On a closer inspection, we note that this counterexample is spurious not only in K but in *every* model that refines K'. There are two concretizations of this counterexample, and φ is true in both of them. Thus, it would be highly desirable to be able to conclude that the property holds, avoiding unnecessary refinement steps.

Godefroid and Jagadeesan [12] suggested that one can use an additional, *thorough*, check when the result of model-checking is inconclusive. This changes both algorithms in Figure 1 after step 5 as follows:

      5a.   Apply the thorough check of φ on K_α.
      5b.   **if** conclusive, tell user and stop.
      6.   **else** use the counterexample for refinement.

which we refer to as *classical thorough* and *3-valued thorough*, respectively. Even though the thorough check is exponentially more expensive than model-checking [12], this modification can potentially reduce the number of refinements. Since each refinement adds atomic propositions, and each additional atomic proposition doubles the size of the abstraction, the extra cost seems justified. Unfortunately, if the thorough check is still inconclusive, it does not help the refinement, but levies a heavy performance penalty. Without empirical evidence, it is not clear how useful this framework is in practice. We are thus interested to find out answers to the following questions:

1. Are there classes of problems where the thorough check is not necessary, i.e., it does not give a more precise result than model-checking?
2. In cases where the thorough check is required, can it be performed efficiently?

In this paper, we show that the thorough check of universal properties on models built using *predicate abstraction* [14] does not give an additional precision and thus can be skipped. For arbitrary abstraction, we give an algorithm for deciding ACTL formulas, where the thorough check can be performed efficiently. This approach combines the model-checking and the thorough step, resulting in an algorithm which is as precise as the thorough check, while being only marginally more expensive than model-checking. This algorithm also produces counterexamples which can be used for refinement.

The rest of this paper is organized as follows. We start by giving the necessary background in Section 2. In Section 3, we extend results of Godefroid and Jagadeesan [13] to show that 3-valued models in which each atomic proposition is either boolean (i.e., true or false), or maybe in each state, are as expressive as arbitrary 3-valued Kripke structures. This is used in Section 4 to show that 3-valued model-checking (referred to as *compositional*) and thorough checking correspond to different semantics of quantified temporal logic (QTL). We answer the questions posed above in Section 5, using previously established results for QTL. We compare our approach with related work in Section 6 and conclude the paper in Section 7.

2   Background

In this section, we provide the necessary background on model-checking, 3-valued reasoning, and quantified temporal logic.

3-Valued Kleene Logic. A 3-valued Kleene logic [18] is an extension of a classical two-valued logic of true and false, with an additional value maybe, representing uncertainty. Logical operators in the logic are defined via the *truth* ordering $\sqsubseteq$, where false $\sqsubseteq$ maybe $\sqsubseteq$ true. Intuitively, $a \sqsubseteq b$ indicates that a is *less true* than b. Conjunction and disjunction are given by meet (minimum) and join (maximum) operators of the truth ordering, respectively. Negation is defined as: $\neg$true $=$ false, $\neg$false $=$ true, and $\neg$maybe $=$ maybe. Kleene logic preserves most of the laws of classical logic, such as De Morgan laws ($\neg(a \wedge b) = \neg a \vee \neg b$), and an involution of negation ($\neg\neg a = a$), but not the laws of excluded middle ($a \vee \neg a =$ true) and non-contradiction ($\neg a \wedge a =$ false). The values of Kleene logic can also be ordered according to the *information* pre-order $\preceq$, where maybe $\preceq$ true and maybe $\preceq$ false. That is, maybe contains the least amount of information, whereas true and false are incomparable. We denote the set of boolean values true and false by **2**, and the set of values of Kleene logic by **3**.

$$||\ell||^K(s) \triangleq \ell$$
$$||\varphi \wedge \psi||^K(s) \triangleq ||\varphi||^K(s) \wedge ||\psi||^K(s)$$
$$||\neg\varphi||^K(s) \triangleq \neg||\varphi||^K(s)$$
$$||EG\varphi||^K(s) \triangleq ||\nu Z \cdot \varphi \wedge EXZ||^K(s)$$

$$||p||^K(s) \triangleq I(s,p)$$
$$||\varphi \vee \psi||^K(s) \triangleq ||\varphi||^K(s) \vee ||\psi||^K(s)$$
$$||EX\varphi||^K(s) \triangleq \bigvee_{t \in S}(R(s,t) \wedge ||\varphi||^K(t))$$
$$||E[\varphi U\psi]||^K(s) \triangleq ||\mu Z \cdot \psi \vee \varphi \wedge EXZ||^K(s)$$

Fig. 3. Semantics of CTL

Models. A model is a 3-valued Kripke structure $K = (S, R, S_0, AP, I)$, where S is a finite set of states, $R : S \times S \to \mathbf{3}$ is a total transition relation, $S_0 \subseteq S$ is a set of initial states, AP is a set of atomic propositions, and $I : S \times AP \to \mathbf{3}$ is an interpretation function, assigning a value to each atomic proposition $a \in AP$ in each state. A classical (two-valued) Kripke structure is a 3-valued Kripke structure that does not use the value maybe, i.e. the range of R and I is {true, false}.

Temporal Logic. *Computation Tree Logic* (CTL) [7] is a branching temporal logic, whose syntax is defined with respect to set AP of atomic propositions, as follows:

$$\varphi = \ell \mid p \mid \varphi \vee \varphi \mid \varphi \wedge \varphi \mid \neg\varphi \mid EX\varphi \mid AX\varphi \mid EF\varphi \mid AF\varphi$$
$$\mid EG\varphi \mid AG\varphi \mid E[\varphi U \varphi] \mid A[\varphi U \varphi],$$

where $p \in AP$ is an atomic proposition and $\ell \in \mathbf{2}$ is a constant. Informally, the meaning of the temporal operators is: given a state and all paths emanating from it, φ holds in one (EX) or all (AX) next states; φ holds in some future state along one (EF) or all (AF) paths; φ holds globally along one (EG) or all (AG) paths, and φ holds until a point where ψ holds along one (EU) or all (AU) paths.

The value of φ in state s of K is denoted by $||\varphi||^K(s)$; the value of φ in K is defined with respect to all initial states of K: $||\varphi||^K = \bigwedge_{s_0 \in S_0} ||\varphi||^K(s_0)$. Temporal operators EX, EG, and EU together with the propositional connectives form an adequate set [6]. The formal semantics of CTL is given in Figure 3. The only difference between the 2- and the 3-valued semantics is the change in the domain of ℓ. To disambiguate from an alternative semantics presented below, we refer to this semantics as *compositional*. Compositional semantics of CTL is interpreted over 3-valued Kripke structures with respect to Kleene logic.

We write $\varphi[x]$ to indicate that the formula φ may contain an atomic proposition x. An occurrence of x is *positive* (or of *positive polarity*) if it occurs under the scope of an even number of negations, and *negative* otherwise. An atomic proposition x is *pure* in φ if all of its occurrences have the same polarity, and is *mixed* otherwise. We write $\varphi[x \leftarrow y]$ for a formula obtained from φ by simultaneously substituting all occurrences of x by y. A formula φ is *universal* (or in ACTL) if all of its temporal operators are universal, and is *existential* (or in ECTL) if they are existential. In both cases, negation is only allowed at the level of atomic propositions.

Relationships Between Models. We revisit definitions of simulation and bisimulation for classical Kripke structures, and refinement for 3-valued Kripke structures.

Definition 1. *[20] Let K and K' be classical Kripke structures with identical sets of atomic propositions AP. A relation $\rho \subseteq S \times S'$ is a simulation iff $\rho(s, s')$ implies that*

1. $\forall p \in AP \cdot I'(s', p) \Leftrightarrow I(s, p)$, and
2. $\forall t' \in S' \cdot R'(s', t') \Rightarrow \exists t \in S \cdot R(s, t) \wedge \rho(t, t')$.

A state s *simulates* a state s' if $(s, s') \in \rho$. A Kripke structure K simulates K' iff every initial state of K' is simulated by an initial state of K. Simulation between K and K' preserves ACTL: for any $\varphi \in$ ACTL, $||\varphi||^K \Rightarrow ||\varphi||^{K'}$. K and K' are *bisimilar* iff exists a simulation ρ between K and K' such that ρ^{-1} is a simulation between K' and K. The set of all structures bisimilar to K is denoted by $\mathcal{B}(K)$. Bisimulation preserves CTL: $\forall \varphi \in$ CTL $\cdot \forall K' \in \mathcal{B}(K) \cdot ||\varphi||^K \Leftrightarrow ||\varphi||^{K'}$.

For a given a set of atomic propositions X, let K_{-X} denote the result of removing all atomic propositions in X from K, i.e., $AP_{-X} = AP \setminus X$. Let K and K' be Kripke structures such that $AP' = AP \cup X$. Then, K' is X-*bisimilar* to K iff K'_{-X} is bisimilar to K. The set of all X-bisimilar structures to K is denoted by $\mathcal{B}_X(K)$.

Definition 2. *[2] A relation $\rho \subseteq S \times S'$ is a* refinement *between 3-valued Kripke structures K and K' iff $\rho(s, s')$ implies*

1. $\forall p \in AP \cdot I(s, p) \preceq I'(s', p)$;
2. $\forall t \in S \cdot (R(s, t) \sqsupseteq \mathsf{true}) \Rightarrow \exists t' \in S' \cdot (R'(s', t') \sqsupseteq \mathsf{true}) \wedge \rho(t, t')$;
3. $\forall t' \in S' \cdot (R'(s', t') \sqsupseteq \mathsf{maybe}) \Rightarrow \exists t \in S \cdot (R(s, t) \sqsupseteq \mathsf{maybe}) \wedge \rho(t, t')$.

A state s is refined by s' ($s \preceq s'$) if there exists a refinement ρ containing (s, s'). A Kripke structure K is refined by K' ($K \preceq K'$) if there exists a refinement ρ relating their initial states: $\forall s \in S_0 \cdot \exists s' \in S'_0 \cdot \rho(s, s')$ and $\forall s' \in S'_0 \cdot \exists s \in S_0 \cdot \rho(s, s')$. Bisimulation and refinement coincide on classical structures, and refinement preserves 3-valued CTL:

Theorem 1. *[2] For 3-valued Kripke structures K and K' and a CTL formula φ, $K \preceq K'$ implies $||\varphi||^K \preceq ||\varphi||^{K'}$.*

Refinement can relate 3-valued and classical models as well. For a 3-valued Kripke structure K, let $\mathcal{C}(K)$ denote the set of *completions* [3] of K – the set of all classical Kripke structures that refine K. For any $K' \in \mathcal{C}(K)$, the structure K can be seen as less precise than K' in the sense that any CTL formula φ that evaluates to a definite value (either true or false) in K, evaluates to the same value in K', i.e., $(||\varphi||^K = \mathsf{true}) \Rightarrow (||\varphi||^{K'} = \mathsf{true})$ and $(||\varphi||^K = \mathsf{false}) \Rightarrow (||\varphi||^{K'} = \mathsf{false})$.

Thorough Semantics. Compositional semantics of CTL is inherently imprecise: if φ is maybe in K, it may or may not be true in every completion. To address this, Bruns and Godefroid [3] proposed an alternative semantics, calling it *thorough*. A formula φ is true in K under thorough semantics, written $||\varphi||^K_t = \mathsf{true}$, iff it is true in all completions of K; it is false in K if it is false in all completions; and maybe otherwise.

The additional precision comes at a cost of complexity. Model-checking φ under compositional semantics is linear in the size of the model and linear in the size of the formula, but model-checking φ under thorough semantics is EXPTIME-complete, with the best known algorithm quadratic in the size of the model and exponential in $|\varphi|$ [3].

Quantified CTL. Quantified CTL (QCTL) [19] is an extension of CTL with quantification over atomic propositions. Thus, QCTL formulas consist of all CTL formulas and formulas of the form $\forall x \cdot \varphi$ and $\exists x \cdot \varphi$. In this paper, we only use a fragment of QCTL in which all quantifiers precede all other operators. Thus, we consider formulas like $\forall x \cdot \exists y \cdot AG(x \Rightarrow AFy)$, but not like $AX(\exists x \cdot x \Rightarrow AFy)$, or $(\forall x \cdot EXx) \wedge (\exists y \cdot AXy)$

The syntax of QCTL does not restrict the domain of quantifiers. Thus, there are several different definitions of the semantics of QCTL with respect to a classical Kripke structure; we consider two of these in this paper: *structure* [19] and *amorphous* [10].

Structure Semantics. Under this semantics, each free variable x is interpreted as a boolean function over the statespace, i.e., $x \in [S \to \mathbf{2}]$. For example, $\forall x \cdot \varphi$ is true in K under structure semantics if replacing x by an arbitrary boolean function results in a formula that is true in K. Formally, the values of $\forall x \cdot \varphi$ and $\exists x \cdot \varphi$ over a Kripke structure K are defined as follows:

$$||\varphi||_s^K \triangleq ||\varphi||^K, \text{ if } \varphi \in \text{CTL} \qquad \text{(structure semantics)}$$
$$||\forall x \cdot \varphi||_s^K \triangleq \forall y \in [S \to \mathbf{2}] \cdot ||\varphi[x \leftarrow y]||_s^K$$
$$||\exists x \cdot \varphi||_s^K \triangleq \exists y \in [S \to \mathbf{2}] \cdot ||\varphi[x \leftarrow y]||_s^K$$

where $[S \to \mathbf{2}]$ denotes the set of all boolean functions over S.

Alternatively, structure semantics can be understood as follows. For Kripke structures K and K', we say that K' is an X-*variant* of K if there exists a set of atomic propositions X such that K and K'_{-X} are isomorphic. A formula $\forall x \cdot \varphi$ is satisfied by K under structure semantics iff φ holds in all $\{x\}$-variants of K. Note that if x is positive in φ, then $\forall x \cdot \varphi$ is equivalent to $\varphi[x \leftarrow \text{false}]$, and if x is negative – to $\varphi[x \leftarrow \text{true}]$.

Amorphous Semantics. Amorphous semantics of QCTL is defined as follows:

$$||\varphi||_a^K \triangleq ||\varphi||^K, \text{ if } \varphi \in \text{CTL} \qquad \text{(amorphous semantics)}$$
$$||\forall x \cdot \varphi[x]||_a^K \triangleq \forall K' \in \mathcal{B}_x(K) \cdot ||\varphi[x]||_a^{K'}$$
$$||\exists x \cdot \varphi[x]||_a^K \triangleq \exists K' \in \mathcal{B}_x(K) \cdot ||\varphi[x]||_a^{K'}$$

That is, a formula $\forall x \cdot \varphi$ is satisfied by K under amorphous semantics iff φ is satisfied by every $\{x\}$-bisimulation of K.

For formulas without existential ($\exists$) quantifiers, amorphous semantics implies structure semantics; further, the implication is strict [10].

3 Expressiveness of 3-Valued Models

In this section, we extend the results of Godefroid and Jagadeesan [13] on expressiveness of 3-valued models. In particular, we describe a transformation of 3-valued Kripke structures to Partial Kripke Structures (PKSs) – Kripke structures with boolean transition relation – and from there to Partial Classical Kripke Structures (PCKSs), where each atomic proposition is either always true or false, or is always maybe. This transformation enables us to use PCKSs as the theoretical model for developing our technical results. When compared to the original 3-valued Kripke structure, the transformation increases the number of atomic propositions. However, the transformation is used for theoretical purposes only – we never propose to apply this transformation during analysis. Furthermore, while increasing the number of atomic propositions, the transformation to PCKSs does not affect the number of bits required to encode the original Kripke structure.

$$T_1(p) = p \qquad\qquad T_1(\neg\varphi) = \neg T_1(\varphi)$$
$$T_1(\varphi \wedge \psi) = T_1(\varphi) \wedge T_1(\psi) \qquad T_1(\varphi \vee \psi) = T_1(\varphi) \vee T_1(\psi)$$
$$T_1(EX\varphi) = EX(tval \wedge T_1(\varphi)) \qquad T_1(EG\varphi) = \varphi \wedge EXEG(tval \wedge T_1(\varphi))$$
$$T_1(E[\varphi U \psi]) = T_1(\psi) \vee T_1(\varphi) \wedge EXE[tval \wedge T_1(\varphi) \ U \ tval \wedge T_1(\psi)]$$

Fig. 4. Transformation of a temporal logic formula

From 3-valued models to PKSs. A 3-valued Kripke structure that has a boolean transition relation ($R : S \times S \to \mathbf{2}$) is called a *Partial Kripke Structure* (PKS) [2]. An example of a PKS is shown in Figure 5(a).

PKSs are as expressive as 3-valued Kripke structures [13]. The transformation T_1 from 3-valued to Partial Kripke structures is very similar to a transformation from Labeled Transition Systems to Kripke structures (e.g., see [21]). Intuitively, we treat transition values as actions, and the transformation "pushes" them into states.

Given a 3-valued Kripke structure K, we construct a PKS $T_1(K) = (AP \cup \{tval\},$ $S \times \{0,1\}, S_0 \times \{0,1\}, T_1(R), T_1(I))$, where $T_1(R)$ and $T_1(I)$ are as follows:

1. $T_1(R)(\langle s, i\rangle, \langle t, 1\rangle) \Leftrightarrow (R(s,t) = \mathsf{true})$ and
   $T_1(R)(\langle s, i\rangle, \langle t, 0\rangle) \Leftrightarrow (R(s,t) = \mathsf{maybe})$,
2. for every $p \in AP$, $T_1(I)(\langle s, i\rangle, p) = I(s, p)$, and
3. the value of $tval$ is determined by the second component of the state:
   $T_1(I)(\langle s, i\rangle, tval)$ is true if $i = 1$, and maybe otherwise.

Intuitively, $tval$ represents the value of the transition relation. For example, since the value of $tval$ in a state $\langle t, 1\rangle$ is true, a transition between $\langle s, i\rangle$ and $\langle t, 1\rangle$ indicates that the transition between s and t in K is true.

The transformation T_1 is also extended to CTL formulas as shown in Figure 4. Intuitively, T_1 replaces every occurrence of EXp with $EX(tval \wedge p)$ in the fixpoint representation of the semantics of CTL (see Figure 3).

Theorem 2. *[13] Partial Kripke Structures are as expressive as 3-valued Kripke structures. For any 3-valued Kripke structure K and a formula φ, $||\varphi||^K = ||T_1(\varphi)||^{T_1(K)}$.*

From PKSs to PCKSs. A PKS in which every atomic proposition is either boolean (i.e., true or false in every state) or maybe (i.e. maybe in every state) is called a *Partial Classical Kripke Structure* (PCKS), an example of a PCKS is shown in Figure 5(b). Intuitively, a PCKS K is a classical Kripke structure extended with additional atomic propositions such that nothing except their name is known about them. We show that, for compositional semantics, PCKSs containing a *single* maybe atomic proposition are as expressive as PKSs.

A value of a propositional formula in a 3-valued Kripke structure is given by a 3-valued function $S \to \mathbf{3}$ over the statespace. Consider a PKS K shown in Figure 5(a). The value of p in K is given by a function that maps s_0 to true, s_1 to maybe, and s_3 to false. Next, consider the PCKS K' shown in Figure 5(b): it is the same structure, but with different atomic propositions. All atomic propositions of K' are boolean, except for m which is maybe in every state. Note that K' has two boolean atomic propositions p^t and p^m such that p^t is true in a state iff p is true in the same state of K, and p^m is true

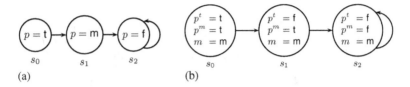

Fig. 5. (a) A PKS K. (b) A PCKS K'.

iff p is not false. The formula $p^t \vee (p^m \wedge m)$ in K' is semantically equivalent to p in K: for any state, both are true in s_1, maybe in s_2, and false in s_3. Thus, any propositional formula in K can be reduced to a semantically equivalent one in K'. Furthermore, temporal operators of CTL can be seen as predicate transformers operating on the semantic meaning of their arguments. Thus, the value of EXp in K is equivalent to the value of $EX(p^t \vee (p^m \wedge m))$ in K'.

Formally, we define a transformation T_2 from a PKS K to a PCKS $T_2(K) = (T_2(AP), S, S_0, R, T_2(I))$ as follows: (a) for each atomic proposition p of K, $T_2(AP)$ contains a pair of boolean atomic propositions p^t and p^m, (b) $T_2(I)(s, p^t)$ is true iff $I(s, p)$ is true, and $T_2(I)(s, p^m)$ is true iff $I(s, p)$ is *not* false, and (c) $T_2(AP)$ contains an atomic proposition m whose value is maybe in every state of $T_2(K)$.

For an atomic proposition p, $T_2(p)$ is defined as $p^t \vee (p^m \wedge m)$, and for a CTL formula φ, $T_2(\varphi)$ is obtained by replacing each atomic proposition p of φ with $T_2(p)$. For example, $T_2(AG(p \Rightarrow EFq)) = AG(T_2(p) \Rightarrow EFT_2(q))$.

Theorem 3. *Let K be a PKS, and φ be a CTL formula. Then, $||\varphi||^K = ||T_2(\varphi)||^{T_2(K)}$.*

Combining this result with Theorem 2, we obtain that PCKSs are as expressive (for compositional semantics) as 3-valued Kripke structures.

The transformation T_2 does not work in the case of thorough semantics: the value of φ in K is not necessarily equivalent to the value of $T_2(\varphi)$ in $T_2(K)$. For example, under thorough semantics, the value of $p \vee \neg q$ is maybe in a state where both p and q are maybe. However, since $p = $ maybe implies $p^t = $ false and $p^m = $ true, the transformed formula $T_2(p \vee \neg q) = (p^t \vee (p^m \wedge m)) \vee \neg(q^t \vee (q^m \wedge m))$ is logically equivalent to $m \vee \neg m$, which, in turn, is equivalent to true under thorough semantics. The problem is that in each state of $T_2(K)$, the atomic proposition m controls how *all* of the atomic propositions in this state are refined (i.e., either they are all set to true, or they are all set to false). This is easily avoided by introducing a different atomic proposition for each atomic proposition of K.

We define another transformation T_3 from a PKS K to a PCKS $T_3(K)$ as follows: (a) we first apply the transformation T_2, i.e., $T_3(K) = T_2(K)$, and (b) for each $p \in AP$ we add a new atomic proposition m_p to $T_3(AP)$, setting it to maybe in every state. For an atomic proposition p, $T_3(p)$ is defined as $p^t \vee (p^m \wedge m_p)$, and for a CTL formula φ, $T_3(\varphi)$ is obtained by replacing each atomic proposition p of φ with $T_3(p)$.

Theorem 4. *Let K be a PKS, and φ be a CTL formula. Then, $||\varphi||_t^K = ||T_3(\varphi)||_t^{T_3(K)}$.*

Combining this result with Theorems 2 and 3, we obtain that PCKSs are as expressive as 3-valued Kripke structures, for compositional and thorough semantics.

The distinction between transformations T_2 and T_3 highlights the key difference between compositional and thorough semantics. The former can be seen as a conservative approximation of laws of excluded middle and non-contradiction, i.e., if p is unknown, then so is $\neg p$, and thus $||p \vee \neg p|| = $ maybe $\vee$ maybe $= $ maybe. On the other hand, thorough semantics can be seen as applying these laws symbolically. Thus, even if the value of p is unknown, $||p \vee \neg p||_t$ is still true.

4   Quantified Temporal Logic and 3-Valued Model-Checking

In this section, we use the equivalence between 3-valued Kripke structures and PCKSs established in Section 3 to relate 3-valued model-checking and model-checking for QCTL.

The definition of 3-valued refinement, when restricted to PCKSs, is virtually identical to the definition of X-bisimulation. If K is a PCKS and X is the set of *all* of its maybe atomic propositions, then K' is a completion of K iff K'_{-X} is bisimilar to K_{-X}, i.e., K' is X-bisimilar to K_{-X}. Thus, deciding whether a formula φ is either true or false in a PCKS reduces to amorphous model-checking of a universally quantified formula, as stated in the theorem below.

Theorem 5. *Let K be a PCKS, $X \subseteq AP$ be the set of all of its* maybe *atomic propositions, and φ be an arbitrary CTL formula. Then, the value of φ in K under thorough semantics is:* $(||\varphi||_t^K = $ true$) \Leftrightarrow ||\forall X \cdot \varphi||_a^{K-X}$ *and* $(||\varphi||_t^K = $ false$) \Leftrightarrow ||\forall X \cdot \neg\varphi||_a^{K-X}$.

Similarly, compositional semantics is related to structure semantics for QCTL; however, the connection is somewhat more subtle. Let K be a PCKS, m be the *only* maybe atomic proposition of K, and φ be a CTL formula containing m. Furthermore, assume that all occurrences of m are positive. Then, $||\varphi||^K$ is true iff $||\varphi[m \leftarrow $ false$]||^{K-m}$ is true [16]. Next, consider the formula $\forall m \cdot \varphi$: since m is positive in φ, $||\forall m \cdot \varphi||_s^{K-m}$ is true iff $||\varphi[m \leftarrow $ false$]||^{K-m}$ is true [17]. Thus, in this case, deciding whether φ is true under compositional semantics reduces to checking $\forall m \cdot \varphi$ under structure semantics. Moreover, the result easily extends to the case where m occurs negatively.

The above does not hold when m is not of pure polarity in φ. For example, the value of $||m \vee \neg m||^K$ is maybe, but $||\forall m \cdot (m \vee \neg m)||_s^K$ is true. The problem is that compositional semantics treats positive and negative occurrences of the same atomic proposition independently. Thus, we can obtain the desired result by quantifying positive and negative occurrences of m separately. That is, we let m^+ and m^- denote positive and negative occurrences of m in $\varphi[m]$, respectively; then, $||\varphi[m]||^K$ is true iff $||\forall x, y \cdot \varphi[m^+ \leftarrow x, m^- \leftarrow y]||_s^K$ is true, and similarly $||\varphi[m]||^K$ is false iff $||\forall x, y \cdot \neg\varphi[m^+ \leftarrow x, m^- \leftarrow y]||_s^K$ is true. The following theorem formalizes this result for an arbitrary number of maybe atomic propositions.

Theorem 6. *Let K be a PCKS, and let $M = \{m_1, \ldots, m_n\}$ be the set of all* maybe *atomic propositions of K. For a CTL formula φ, let m_i^+ and m_i^- denote the positive and negative occurrences of m_i, respectively. Then,*

$$(||\varphi||^K = \text{true}) \Leftrightarrow ||\forall x_1, \ldots, x_n \cdot \forall y_1, \ldots, y_n \cdot \varphi'||_s^K \text{ and}$$
$$(||\varphi||^K = \text{false}) \Leftrightarrow ||\forall x_1, \ldots, x_n \cdot \forall y_1, \ldots, y_n \cdot \neg\varphi'||_s^K$$

where $\varphi' = \varphi[m_1^+ \leftarrow x_1, \ldots, m_n^+ \leftarrow x_n, m_1^- \leftarrow y_1, \ldots, m_n^- \leftarrow y_n]$.

A corollary of Theorem 6 is that if every maybe atomic proposition of K occurs with pure polarity in φ, then both thorough and compositional semantics reduce to deciding the same universally quantified formula, under amorphous and structure semantics, respectively. Furthermore, for universally quantified formulas, amorphous semantics imply structure ($||\forall X \cdot \varphi||_a \Rightarrow ||\forall X \cdot \varphi||_s$). Note that in general, for 3-valued semantics the implication is reversed, i.e., compositional semantics implies thorough $((||\varphi||^K = \text{true}) \Rightarrow (||\varphi||^K_t = \text{true})$. So, when every maybe atomic proposition is pure in φ, thorough and compositional semantics for φ coincide:

Theorem 7. *Let K be a PCKS and φ be a CTL formula such that all occurrences of* maybe *atomic propositions of K are of pure polarity in φ. Then, $||\varphi||^K_t = ||\varphi||^K$.*

Since every atomic proposition is either boolean or maybe in PCKSs, deciding whether all occurrences of maybe propositions in a formula φ are of pure polarity is trivial for these models. However, to determine this for arbitrary 3-valued Kripke structures, we first have to reduce them to PCKSs, which is not an option in practice since model-checking typically occurs on-the-fly during the construction of the model. In the next section, we use properties of particular abstractions to determine polarity of maybe propositions of φ and thus to decide when a thorough check is necessary.

5   Thorough Semantics and Abstraction

In this section, we exhibit practical cases where a thorough check does not give additional precision and thus can be eliminated, and cases where a thorough check can be performed efficiently.

5.1   Abstraction and 3-Valued Model Checking

Abstraction is a mapping between a concrete system and a smaller, abstracted, system. Here, we consider abstractions that map sets of concrete states into a single abstract state. Let K be a Kripke structure with statespace S and transition relation R. An *abstract domain* is a pair (S_α, γ), where S_α is a set of abstract states, and $\gamma : S_\alpha \to 2^S$ is a total *concretization function* that associates each abstract state with its interpretation as a set of concrete states.

Like Godefroid et al. [11], we use 3-valued Kripke structures to represent abstract models over an abstract domain (S_α, γ). A 3-valued Kripke structure K_α with a statespace S_α is an abstraction of a Kripke structure K if its transition relation R_α satisfies the following conditions:

$$(\mathbb{R}_\alpha(\hat{s}, \hat{t}) \sqsupseteq \text{true}) \quad \Rightarrow \forall s \in \gamma(\hat{s}) \cdot \exists t \in \gamma(\hat{t}) \cdot R(s, t)$$
$$(\mathbb{R}_\alpha(\hat{s}, \hat{t}) \sqsupseteq \text{maybe}) \quad \Leftarrow \exists s \in \gamma(\hat{s}) \cdot \exists t \in \gamma(\hat{t}) \cdot R(s, t)$$

Note that these conditions do not guarantee the precision of the abstract model. In particular, a 3-valued Kripke structure over S_α with a maybe transition between every pair of states satisfies the above conditions, and is a trivial abstraction of every classical Kripke structure over S.

Each atomic proposition of K_α corresponds to a predicate over the statespace of K. In an abstract state $\hat{s}$, an atomic proposition $\hat{p}$ is true iff the corresponding predicate p is true in every state of $\gamma(\hat{s})$, false if p is false in $\gamma(\hat{s})$, and maybe otherwise. Note that any predicate over the concrete statespace can be replaced by an atomic proposition. Thus, without loss of generality, we assume that every atomic proposition of the abstract system corresponds to an atomic proposition of the concrete.

As a 3-valued Kripke structure, an abstraction K_α of K is refined by K, i.e., $K_\alpha \preceq K$, which guarantees that K_α preserves arbitrary CTL formulas. Moreover, an arbitrary 3-valued Kripke structure is an abstraction of any model that refines it, where the concretization γ is induced by the refinement [11].

Predicate (or boolean) abstraction [14,1,11] is a popular technique for building abstractions, and has been successfully applied in practice [14,5]. Given a concrete system K and a set of n predicates $P = \{p_1, \ldots, p_n\}$, the abstract statespace of predicate abstraction consists of (at most) 2^n states, where each state assigns a boolean value to each of the predicates. The concretization γ is defined as follows:

$$\gamma(\hat{s}) = \{s \mid \forall p \in P \cdot ||p||(\hat{s}) = ||p||(s)\}$$

That is, an abstract state $\hat{s}$ corresponds to the set of all concrete states that agree with $\hat{s}$ on the values of all of the predicates in P. Thus, if K_α is a result of predicate abstraction, then its transition relation is 3-valued, but atomic propositions are boolean.

Cartesian abstraction [1,11] is an extension of predicate abstraction, where the statespace consists of 3^n states, and each state assigns one of true, false, or maybe to each of the predicates. The concretization γ is defined as follows:

$$\gamma(\hat{s}) = \{s \mid \forall p \in P \cdot ||p||(\hat{s}) \preceq ||p||(s)\}$$

That is, an abstract state $\hat{s}$ corresponds to the set of all concrete states that agree with $\hat{s}$ on the values of all of the predicates in P that have a definite value (i.e. true or false) in $\hat{s}$. Thus, if K_α is a result of a Cartesian abstraction, then both its atomic propositions and the transition relation are 3-valued.

Model-checking a property φ in the abstract system K_α is done with respect to compositional semantics. Thus, a maybe result from the model-checker does not necessarily indicate that the abstraction is at fault and must be refined. In these cases, it seems natural [12] that an additional check of φ under thorough semantics will yield more precise results. In what follows, we show that in many practical applications, thorough semantics does not offer an advantage over compositional.

5.2   Thorough Semantics and Predicate Abstraction

Let K_α be an abstract system constructed by predicate abstraction, and $K'_\alpha = T_1(K_\alpha)$ be a PKS corresponding to it. Note that all of the atomic propositions of K'_α are boolean, except for $tval$, which was added as part of T_1.

Assume that we want to check a CTL formula φ in K_α. By Theorem 2, there exists a CTL formula $\varphi' = T_1(\varphi)$ such that $||\varphi||^{K_\alpha} = ||\varphi'||^{K'_\alpha}$. Although φ does not mention $tval$ explicitly, each temporal operator of φ results in at least one occurrence of $tval$ in φ'. The polarity of these occurrences is positive for existential operators and negative for the universal ones. For example, EXp is transformed by T_1 into $EX(tval \wedge p)$, while AXp is transformed into $T_1(AXp) = T_1(\neg EX \neg p) = AX(tval \Rightarrow p)$.

Thus, if all temporal operators of φ are universal or all are existential, i.e., $\varphi \in$ ECTL or $\varphi \in$ ACTL, then φ' contains at most one non-boolean atomic proposition $tval$, and $tval$ is pure in φ'. Combining this with Theorem 7, we establish that in this case thorough and compositional semantics for φ in K_α coincide:

Theorem 8. Let K_α be a 3-valued Kripke structure constructed by predicate abstraction. Then, $\forall \varphi \in ECTL \cup ACTL \cdot ||\varphi||^{K_\alpha} = ||\varphi||_t^{K_\alpha}$.

In particular, this theorem implies that for predicate abstraction and for universal properties, the original abstraction-refinement framework of Clarke et al. [5] is as precise as the extension proposed by Godefroid and Jagadeesan [12].

In the case of Cartesian abstraction, K_α may contain 3-valued atomic propositions, and Theorem 8 is no longer applicable. One way to ensure that thorough and compositional semantics coincide in this case, is to require that all atomic propositions, not just $tval$, be of pure polarity. This gives rise to the following theorem:

Theorem 9. Let K_α be a 3-valued Kripke structure. Then, for any ACTL or ECTL formula φ in which every atomic proposition occurs with pure polarity, compositional and thorough semantics are equivalent.

For example, according to the above theorem, compositional and thorough semantics of $AG(\neg p \wedge q)$ are equivalent, since each atomic proposition occurs once, and polarity of p is negative, and polarity of q is positive. Of course, many interesting properties do contain atomic propositions of mixed polarity. For example, a property "in every state, only one of p and q holds" is expressed in CTL as $AG((\neg p \wedge q) \vee (p \wedge \neg q))$, and both of its atomic propositions are of mixed polarity. In this case, thorough semantics can offer additional precision. On the other hand, consider checking the property $AG(\neg q \wedge AF(p \wedge q))$ on the model in Figure 2(b). In this property, q occurs with mixed polarity, but it does not have value maybe in any reachable state of the model. For this and other properties where the proposition of mixed polarity does not have value maybe in the model, compositional semantics coincides with thorough, and the additional check is not required.

5.3   Thorough Model Checking for ACTL

In this section, we show that in the case of ACTL formulas, which are sufficient for expressing arbitrary safety properties, deciding whether a formula is true under thorough semantics can be done efficiently. Furthermore, in this case, the compositional check used in the abstraction-refinement framework of Clarke et al. [5] can be completely replaced by an efficient algorithm for implementing the thorough one.

We start by showing that for a classical Kripke structure and an ACTL formula φ, model-checking $\forall x \cdot \varphi[x]$ under amorphous semantics is reducible to model-checking $\varphi[x]$ (I). Using Theorem 5, we extend this result to an efficient algorithm for deciding whether an ACTL formula is true under thorough semantics on a PKS (II), and, finally, doing the same on an arbitrary 3-valued Kripke structure (III).

(I). Let K be a classical Kripke structure, x be an atomic proposition that does not appear in K, and φ be an ACTL formula containing x. Recall that $||\forall x \cdot \varphi||_a^K$ is true iff φ is true in every K' that is $\{x\}$-bisimilar to K. Let $T_4(K) = (T_4(AP), T_4(S), T_4(S_0), T_4(R), T_4(I))$ be a Kripke structure obtained from K by adding a new atomic proposition x that changes non-deterministically. The transformation T_4 is defined as follows:

$$T_4(AP) = AP \cup \{x\}$$
$$T_4(S) = S \times \{0, 1\}$$
$$T_4(S_0) = S_0 \times \{0, 1\}$$
$$T_4(R)(\langle s, i \rangle, \langle t, j \rangle) \Leftrightarrow R(s, t)$$
$$T_4(I)(\langle s, i \rangle, p) = I(s, p)$$
$$T_4(I)(\langle s, i \rangle, x) = \text{true if } i = 1 \text{ and}$$
$$\text{false otherwise}$$

Note that the value of each atomic proposition $p \in AP$ is determined by the first component of the state, and the value of x depends on the second component.

Clearly, $T_4(K)$ is $\{x\}$-bisimilar to K. Moreover, any Kripke structure that is $\{x\}$-bisimilar to K is *simulated* by $T_4(K)$ [17]. Since simulation preserves ACTL, $||\forall x \cdot \varphi||_a^K$ is equivalent to $||\varphi||^{T_4(K)}$. The result easily extends to an arbitrary number of universally-quantified atomic propositions of φ. Note that if x is of pure polarity in φ, the transformation T_4 is unnecessary, since $||\forall x \cdot \varphi[x]||_a^K$ is equivalent to either $||\varphi[x \leftarrow \text{true}]||^K$ or $||\varphi[x \leftarrow \text{false}]||^K$, depending on the polarity of x.

(II). Combining (I) with Theorem 5, we conclude that deciding whether an ACTL formula φ is true in a PKS K under thorough semantics is reducible to classical model-checking. In particular, for an ACTL formula φ, $||\varphi||_t^K = \text{true}$ iff $||\varphi||^{K'} = \text{true}$, where K' is a classical Kripke structure obtained from K via a process very similar to T_4, treating maybe atomic propositions non-deterministically. However, rather than splitting all states, we only split those where an atomic proposition has a value maybe. That is, if p is an atomic proposition and s is a state such that the value of p in s is maybe, then s is replaced by two states s' and s'' such that

(a) s' and s'' have the same successors as s,
(b) for every atomic proposition q different from p, s' and s'' assign the same interpretation as s ($I(s, q) = I(s', q) = I(s'', q)$),
(c) the value of p is true in s' and false in s'', and
(d) every transition from a state t to s is replaced by a pair of transitions from t to s' and s''.

This process is repeated until there are no more reachable states that assign maybe to an atomic proposition. Since each atomic proposition that is treated non-deterministically doubles the statespace, the statespace of K' is in the worst case exponential in the number of atomic propositions of K.

(III). From amorphous semantics, we know that $\forall x \cdot \varphi$ is equivalent to $\varphi[x \leftarrow \text{false}]$ if x is positive in φ, and to $\varphi[x \leftarrow \text{true}]$ if x is negative. Therefore, our translation can treat atomic propositions that are of pure polarity in φ as either true or false, depending on the polarity, whereas others must be treated non-deterministically. Thus, for a 3-valued Kripke structure K and an ACTL formula φ, deciding whether $||\varphi||_t^K = \text{true}$ is reducible to model-checking φ in K', obtained from K as follows:

(a) for every positive atomic proposition of φ, change its maybe occurrences in K to false,
(b) change maybe occurrences of negative ones to true,
(c) treat mixed ones as non-deterministic, and
(d) change all maybe transitions to true.

Note that transitions can be embedded into states using an atomic proposition $tval$ (see Section 3), which has negative polarity for ACTL. In the worst case, the size of K' is exponential only in the number of mixed atomic propositions of φ, which gives our algorithm the following complexity:

Theorem 10. *Let K be a 3-valued Kripke structure, and φ be an ACTL formula. Then, the complexity of deciding whether φ is* true *in K under thorough semantics is $O(2^n \times |K| \times |\varphi|)$, where n is the number of atomic propositions of mixed polarity in φ.*

Since we reduced the thorough check to classical model-checking, our algorithm either produces a definite result or generates a counterexample. Thus, it can completely replace step 3 in the abstraction refinement framework of Clarke et al. [5], shown in Figure 1(a). The resulting framework is as precise as the *classical thorough* framework (see Section 1 for definition), and requires the same number of iterations. Yet it is only marginally more expensive than the original framework. Moreover, in the case where all atomic propositions of φ are pure, the modified framework is the same as the original: same results, same running time. Finally, the algorithm can be applied on-the-fly, i.e., during the construction of the abstract model.

6   Discussion and Related Work

Dams et at. [9] developed a general framework for constructing abstractions based on the Abstract Interpretation [8] methodology. These abstractions are sound for full CTL (and richer logics such as CTL* and μ-calculus). Instead of 3-valued Kripke structures, their modeling formalism is Mixed Transition Systems (MTSs) – transition systems containing two kinds of transitions, where existential path quantifiers are interpreted over one kind and universal over the other. 3-valued Kripke structure can be seen as MTSs where truth of existential path quantifiers depends only on true transitions, while the truth of universal quantifiers depends on both true and maybe transitions [16].

The work of Dams et al. [9], as well as most other research on combining abstraction and model-checking (e.g., see [5,22,14]), handles explicit occurrences of negation in a formula by restricting negation to the level of atomic propositions and treating each literal of the concrete model as an atomic proposition of the abstract. For example, literals p and $\neg p$ are represented by two *distinct* atomic propositions, say, a and b. This looses information but ensures that all of the atomic propositions of a formula checked on an abstract model are pure, and thus a thorough check does not provide an additional advantage.

Thorough semantics was introduced by Bruns and Godefroid [3] via *generalized model-checking*, which is the problem of deciding whether there exists a completion of a 3-valued Kripke structure in which a given formula holds. This can be seen as a generalization of both satisfiability and model-checking: φ is true in the coarsest abstraction iff φ is satisfiable, and true in a classical Kripke structure K iff K is a model for φ. In this paper, we show that generalized model-checking can be also seen as an extension of amorphous semantics for existentially quantified temporal formulas from PCKSs to arbitrary 3-valued Kripke structures. In a sense, it combines amorphous quantification with the reduction to PCKSs.

The expressive power of various 3-valued models have been studied by Godefroid and Jagadeesan [13]. Our work completes the picture by showing that allowing for maybe atomic propositions is as expressive as allowing unrestricted occurrences of the value maybe in a model. The question whether or not 3-valued Kripke structures with boolean atomic propositions and a 3-valued transition relation are as expressive remains open. However, our results suggest that even if such a reduction exists, it is not trivial. In particular, this reduction would allow us to transform model-checking of ACTL under thorough semantics, which is EXPTIME-complete, into model-checking under compositional semantics, which is linear in the size of the model and the formula.

7 Conclusion

In this paper, we study the difference between compositional and thorough semantics for 3-valued model-checking. We show that the relationship between the two becomes more clear by casting 3-valued model-checking as model-checking for quantified temporal logic.

Our main motivation is a seemingly apparent advantage of thorough semantics over compositional in the abstraction refinement framework. However, we show that in many practically interesting cases, i.e., when properties are universal, thorough semantics is either no more precise than compositional, or can be efficiently combined with classical model-checking approaches. Although we used CTL as our temporal logic, our results depend only on its invariance to bisimulation, and thus naturally extend to other universal logics, such as LTL.

References

1. T. Ball, A. Podelski, and S. Rajamani. "Boolean and Cartesian Abstraction for Model Checking C Programs". In *TACAS'01*, volume 2031 of *LNCS*, pages 268–283, 2001.
2. G. Bruns and P. Godefroid. "Model Checking Partial State Spaces with 3-Valued Temporal Logics". In *CAV'99*, volume 1633 of *LNCS*, pages 274–287, 1999.
3. G. Bruns and P. Godefroid. "Generalized Model Checking: Reasoning About Partial State Spaces". In *CONCUR'00*, volume 1877 of *LNCS*, pages 168–182, 2000.
4. M. Chechik, B. Devereux, S. Easterbrook, and A. Gurfinkel. "Multi-Valued Symbolic Model-Checking". *ACM Trans. on Soft. Eng. and Methodology*, 12(4):1–38, 2003.
5. E. Clarke, O. Grumberg, S. Jha, Y. Lu, and H. Veith. "Counterexample-Guided Abstraction Refinement for Symbolic Model Checking". *Journal of the ACM*, 50(5):752–794, 2003.
6. E. Clarke, O. Grumberg, and D. Peled. *Model Checking*. MIT Press, 1999.
7. E.M. Clarke, E.A. Emerson, and A.P. Sistla. "Automatic Verification of Finite-State Concurrent Systems Using Temporal Logic Specifications". *ACM Trans. on Prog. Lang. and Systems*, 8(2):244–263, 1986.

8. P. Cousot and R. Cousot. "Abstract Interpretation: A Unified Lattice Model For Static Analysis of Programs by Construction or Approximation of Fixpoints". In *Proceedings of the 4th POPL*, pages 238–252, Los Angeles, California, 1977.

9. D. Dams, R. Gerth, and O. Grumberg. "Abstract Interpretation of Reactive Systems". *ACM Trans. on Prog. Lang. and Systems*, 2(19):253–291, 1997.

10. T. French. "Decidability of Quantifed Propositional Branching Time Logics". In *AI'01*, volume 2256 of *LNCS*, pages 165–176, 2001.

11. P. Godefroid, M. Huth, and R. Jagadeesan. "Abstraction-Based Model Checking Using Modal Transition Systems". In *Proceedings of CONCUR'01*, volume 2154 of *LNCS*, pages 426–440, 2001.

12. P. Godefroid and R. Jagadeesan. "Automatic Abstraction Using Generalized Model-Checking". In *CAV'02*, volume 2404 of *LNCS*, pages 137–150, 2002.

13. P. Godefroid and R. Jagadeesan. "On the Expressiveness of 3-Valued Models". In *VM-CAI'03*, volume 2575 of *LNCS*, pages 206–222, 2003.

14. S. Graf and H. Saïdi. "Construction of Abstract State Graphs with PVS". In *CAV'97*, volume 1254 of *LNCS*, 1997.

15. A. Gurfinkel and M. Chechik. "Generating Counterexamples for Multi-Valued Model-Checking". In *FME'03*, volume 2805 of *LNCS*, 2003.

16. A. Gurfinkel and M. Chechik. "Multi-Valued Model-Checking via Classical Model-Checking". In *CONCUR'03*, volume 2761 of *LNCS*, 2003.

17. A. Gurfinkel and M. Chechik. "Extending Extended Vacuity". In *FMCAD'04*, volume 3312 of *LNCS*, pages 306–321, 2004.

18. S. C. Kleene. *Introduction to Metamathematics*. New York: Van Nostrand, 1952.

19. O. Kupferman. "Augmenting Branching Temporal Logics with Existential Quantification over Atomic Propositions". *J. of Logic and Computation*, 7:1–14, 1997.

20. R. Milner. "An Algebraic Definition of Simulation between Programs". In *AI'71*, pages 481–489, 1971.

21. M. Müller-Olm, D. Schmidt, and B. Steffen. "Model-Checking: A Tutorial Introduction". In *SAS'99*, volume 1694 of *LNCS*, pages 330–354, 1999.

22. S. Shoham and O. Grumberg. "A Game-Based Framework for CTL Counter-Examples and 3-Valued Abstraction-Refinement". In *CAV'03*, volume 2725 of *LNCS*, pages 275–287, 2003.

Interleaved Invariant Checking
with Dynamic Abstraction

Liang Zhang[1], Mukul R. Prasad[2], and Michael S. Hsiao[3]

[1] Cadence Design Systems, San Jose, CA
[2] Fujitsu Laboratories of America, Sunnyvale, CA
[3] Dept. of Electrical & Computer Engineering,
Virginia Tech., Blacksburg, VA

Abstract. The notion of dynamic abstraction was recently introduced as a means of abstracting a model during the process of model checking. In this paper we show, theoretically and practically, how dynamic abstraction can be used with different algorithms for invariant checking, namely forward, backward and interleaved state-space traversal. Further, we formalize the correctness guarantees that can be made under different invariant checking algorithms operating on a dynamically abstracted model. We report experimental results on industrial strength benchmarks to further demonstrate the power and versatility of this abstraction mechanism in conjuction with interleaved state-space traversal.

1 Introduction

The application of formal verification techniques, such as model checking, to real-life industrial designs, has traditionally been hampered by what is commonly known as the *state explosion* problem. Dramatic increases in the size of digital systems and the corresponding exponential increases in the size of their state space have kept industrial designs well beyond the capacity of current model checkers. Abstraction refinement has recently emerged as a promising technology that has the potential to bridge this verification gap.

The basic idea behind *abstraction refinement* [13] is to verify the property at hand on a simplified version of the given design. This simplified version, or *abstraction*, is generated by removing elements from the original design that are not relevant to the proof of the given property. If the property passes on the abstract model, it is guaranteed to be true on the original design as well. However, if the property fails, counter-examples produced on the abstract model must be checked to see that they are true counter-examples on the original design. If however they are false counter-examples, the model checking process is iterated with another abstract model which approximates the original model more closely. The new abstract model can be obtained either by refinement, which embellishes the current abstraction with more details from the original design [5,22,23] or by re-generating a more detailed abstract model from the original design [11,17]. Usually the challenge in abstraction refinement is to construct as small an abstract model as possible so that the model checker can handle it easily. At the

D. Borrione and W. Paul (Eds.): CHARME 2005, LNCS 3725, pp. 81–96, 2005.
© IFIP International Federation for Information Processing 2005

same time, the abstract model should retain sufficient details so that the model checker can prove the property. Thus, the ideal technique for abstraction refinement is one which achieves a good balance between the *size* of the abstract model and its *accuracy*, with respect to being able to prove the given property.

Most previous work on abstraction refinement-based model checking has used *statically abstracted* models in that the abstract model produced by the abstraction step is never modified by the downstream model checker. The notion of *dynamic abstraction* was introduced in [26] whereby the initial abstract model of the design-under-verification is *further* abstracted during successive image computation steps of the model checking phase. Thus, dynamic abstraction provides for a more aggressive yet potentially more accurate abstraction methodology, effectively allowing the core model checking algorithm to work on smaller abstract models. The idea of dynamic abstraction is premised on the key observation that there may be state elements in the concrete model that are *partially abstractable*, *i.e.*, while a state element is necessary in the proof of the property, it may actually be required only in certain time-frames in the proof. For example, some latches in the design are solely present for initialization purposes and may effectively become *redundant* after a few initial time-frames, with respect to the given property.

The treatment in [26] implemented dynamic abstraction within an invariant checking algorithm using BDD-based forward state space traversal. However, as observed in several previous works such as [3,18], for many problem instances a backward state space traversal or a combination of forward and backward traversals (called *interleaved traversal*) may be significantly faster than a simple forward traversal. Such interleaved traversals can provide a more stable and balanced method of state space exploration and can be especially beneficial for failing instances where the failing trace may be constructed in part through forward and backward traversals respectively [18]. These facts are especially significant in the case of an iterative abstraction refinement framework, since a) abstraction can dramatically alter the state space of the model under verification, and b) *all* but the last iterations in iterative abstraction refinement produce failing models.

In the light of these arguments the main contributions of this paper are:

- We develop algorithms to implement dynamic abstraction within different state traversal techniques namely forward, backward and interleaved traversal, for invariant checking, in an abstraction refinement framework.
- We formalize the correctness guarantees that can be made under different invariant checking algorithms operating on a dynamically abstracted model.
- We present several optimizations to improve the performance of the basic techniques.

This paper is organized as follows. Section 2 surveys related work on abstraction refinement and state space traversal algorithms, followed by some background material in Section 3. In Section 4 we review the notion of dynamic abstraction as proposed in [26] and extend it to integrate different algorithms for state space traversal. We also present several simple but powerful optimizations to improve the performance of the basic algorithms. In Section 5 we present experimental results for the proposed algorithms and conclude the paper with directions for future work in Section 6.

2   Related Work

Abstraction Refinement: Abstraction refinement was first introduced by Kurshan [13] for verifying linear time properties. The last few years have seen a lot of research activities on this topic. Abstraction refinement methods can be broadly classified into two categories: 1) counter-example driven and 2) counter-example independent. Counter-example driven methods for abstraction refinement [2,5,7,15,23] typically work by iteratively refining the current abstraction so as to block *a particular* (false) counter-example encountered in model checking the previous abstract model. The refinement algorithm could use a combination of structural heuristics or functional analysis based on SAT or BDDs or some combination of these. A recent paper [8] enlarges the scope of the refinement by using multiple counter-examples from the previous abstract model. This notion is further generalized by Wang *et al.* in [22]. The GRAB tool described there uses a BDD representation for the entire set of shortest counter-examples in the previous abstract model, called *synchronous onion rings (SORs)*. Each iteration (referred to as a *generation*) performs a series of micro-refinements to eliminate all counter-examples represented in the SORs.

Counter-example independent abstraction refinement was introduced in [17] by Amla and McMillan and was also independently discovered by Gupta *et al.* [11]. The basic idea is to perform a SAT-based BMC [6] for the property, upto some depth k, on the original design and then generate the abstract model based on an analysis of the *proof of unsatisfiability* [9,25] of the BMC problem. Essentially, the abstraction excludes latches and/or gates that are not included in the proof of unsatisfiability of the BMC problem and thereby guarantees that the abstract model also does not have any counter-examples upto depth k. Successive abstract models are similarly generated by solving BMC problems of increasing depth. The main contribution of [11], compared to [17], lies in the use of BMC on successively smaller abstract models within an iterative framework so that the unbounded verification methods can have better chance to complete. As comparison, our proposed dynamic abstraction can be applied on top of [11,17] to further reduce the size of the abstract model. Recently, a hybrid scheme [1] has also been proposed to combine the strength of counter-example independent and counter-example driven abstraction refinement. Our current implementation uses counter-example independent abstraction refinement, although our ideas could help in counter-example driven frameworks as well.

Recent papers have also proposed improvements to other aspects of abstraction refinement-based model checking, most notably the concretization test and the granularity of abstraction. The use of BMC to concretize abstract counter-examples was first proposed in [23] and most of the current abstraction refinement frameworks use some variant of SAT or ATPG-based BMC for this task. Bjesse and Kukula [2] proposed an enhancement in that the concrete error trace need not have the same length as the abstract counter-example. Information from the abstract counter-example is used as a guide for the concretization algorithm. Other works [8,21] have generalized the granularity of the abstraction. Cut-points are inserted at selected points in the fanin cones of latches, and are used as abstraction points in addition to latch outputs. Li *et al.* [14] proposed a new search strategy for the SAT solver so that the proof of unsatisfiability will generate smaller abstract models.

State Space Traversal Algorithms: The second body of work that this paper draws upon, is the combination of forward and backward state space traversals to perform symbolic invariant checking. Several works such as [3,4,10,12] use a combination of forward and backward traversal whereby one sweep of traversal is used to approximate or prune the search space and subsequently the other sweep is used to perform the actual verification. This process may potentially be iterated. However, the work closest to the approach of this paper is that of [18] where forward and backward traversal are used simultaneously in one single pass. The motivation here is that the state space of some problems maybe best suited to backward traversal while others may have a propensity towards forward traversal. The algorithm tries to dynamically make this decision, with minimum overhead, and in the case of a buggy design it may construct the error trace partly through a forward traversal and partly through backward traversal.

Recently, the idea of *dynamic abstraction* was introduced in [26]. Previous work on abstraction refinement differs from dynamic abstraction in two key aspects. In previous work, 1) the abstraction step is algorithmically distinct from the model checking phase, *i.e.*, the abstraction is performed outside the model checker, and 2) the abstraction is purely structural in nature and has no temporal component. For example, the same static abstraction is used for each image computation step in BDD-based model checking. In contrast, dynamic abstraction first analyzes the temporal behavior of various latches. Then, based on the analysis it dynamically and progressively abstracts away a set of latches *during* different steps of model checking. For example, in the case of a BDD-based model checker, progressively more abstracted versions of the transition relation are used for successive image computation steps.

This paper further develops the theory and implementation of dynamic abstraction based invariant checking. In [26] dynamic abstraction was introduced in the context of a basic forward state traversal algorithm. In this work we develop algorithms to implement dynamic abstraction within different state traversal techniques namely forward, backward and interleaved traversal and formalize the correctness guarantees that can be made under different traversal techniques, operating on a dynamically abstracted model. Further, we present several optimizations to improve the performance of the basic techniques. As demonstrated by the experimental results in Section 5, on several industrial benchmarks the integration of dynamic abstraction and interleaved traversal is necessary to complete the verification. In other instances the combination and the proposed optimizations provide a significant performance improvement.

3   Background

For the purpose of this paper we will only consider model checking of invariants *i.e.*, CTL properties of the form **AG**p where p is a Boolean expression on the variables of the given circuit model. The circuit under verification can be modeled as a sequential circuit M with primary inputs $W = \{w_1, w_2, \ldots, w_n\}$, present state variables $X = \{x_1, x_2, \ldots, x_m\}$ and the corresponding next state variables $Y = \{y_1, y_2, \ldots, y_m\}$. Thus, M can be represented as $M = \langle T(X, Y, W), I(X) \rangle$, where $T(X, Y, W)$ is the *transition relation (TR)* and $I(X)$ is the set of initial states (more precisely the characteristic function of the set of initial states). M has a set of latches (state elements) $L = \{l_1, l_2, \ldots, l_m\}$. Thus, x_i and y_i would be the present state and next state variables corresponding to latch l_i. The transition relation T is a conjunction of the transition-relations of the individual latches. Thus,

$$T(X, Y, W) = \bigwedge_{i \in \{1 \ldots m\}} T_i(X, y_i, W)$$

Here, $T_i(X, y_i, W) = y_i \leftrightarrow \Delta_i(X, W)$ is the transition relation of latch l_i and $\Delta_i(X, W)$ is its transition function in terms of primary inputs and present state variables.

Given a subset of latches $L_{abs} = \{l_1, l_2, \ldots, l_q\}$, $L_{abs} \subseteq L$, that we would like to abstract away from the design, the abstract model can be constructed by cutting open the feedback loop of latches L_{abs} at their present-state variables X_{abs}, *i.e.* making the variables X_{abs} primary inputs and removing the logic cones of the transition functions of latches L_{abs} from the circuit model. Functionally, the abstracted transition relation $\widehat{T}$ can be defined as

$$\widehat{T}(\widehat{X}, \widehat{Y}, \widehat{W}) = \bigwedge_{i:l_i \in \widehat{L}} \widehat{T}_i(\widehat{X}, y_i, \widehat{W}) \tag{1}$$

where $\widehat{W} = W \cup X_{abs}$, $\widehat{X} = X - X_{abs}$, $\widehat{Y} = \{y_i : x_i \in \widehat{X}\}$, and for all i such that $y_i \in \widehat{Y}$, $\widehat{T}_i(\widehat{X}, y_i, \widehat{W}) = T(X, y_i, W)$.

A concept that will be frequently used in the sequel is that of the *proof of unsatisfiability (POU)* of a CNF SAT formula. As reported in [9,14,25], modern SAT solvers such as zchaff [24] can be modified to produce a proof of unsatisfiability when the CNF formula being solved is found to be unsatisfiable. The proof of unsatisfiability (denoted by $\mathcal{P}$ in the sequel) of an unsatisfiable SAT CNF formula is a sequence of resolution steps which derives the empty clause from the original clauses of the formula. It can be represented as a directed acyclic graph, the nodes of which are clauses and each node (other than the leaves) has precisely two children. The root of this graph is the empty clause and the leaves are clauses from the original CNF. All other nodes (including the root) such that they can be derived through a resolution operation on their two child clauses.

The basic framework for abstraction refinement in our current implementation is similar to the one developed in [17] and [11]. A simplified version of the algorithm used in [17] is shown in Algorithm 3.1. The basic algorithm used in [11] is similar to this except that the abstraction (line 5 and 6) is performed multiple times in an inner loop.

1: $k = $ InitValue
2: **if** SAT-BMC(M, p, k) is **SAT then**
3:     **return** "found error trace"
4: **else**
5:     Extract proof of unsatisfiability, $\mathcal{P}$ of SAT-BMC
6:     $M' = $ ABSTRACT$(M, \mathcal{P})$
7: **end if**
8: **if** MODEL_CHECK(M', p) returns **PASS then**
9:     **return** "passing property"
10: **else**
11:     Increase bound k
12:     **goto** Step 2
13: **end if**

Algorithm 3.1. Abstraction Refinement Using SAT-BMC [17]

Let v be a variable in the representation of the transition relation T. A k-step BMC problem is generated by unrolling and replicating T, k times. Let $v^1, v^2, \ldots, v^k$ denote the k instantiations of v in the unrolled BMC problem. The idea of the abstraction is to solve a k-step SAT-BMC [6] problem formulated on the original design and to analyze the POU returned by the SAT solver to generate the abstraction. The POU is analyzed to identify a set of latches L_{abs} such that for each $l \in L_{abs}$ the variables $l^1, l^2, \ldots, l^k$ do not appear in any of the clauses of the POU. These latches can then be abstracted away using Equation 1 (in the ABSTRACT operation in Step 6 of Algorithm 3.1). The rationale is that since these latches provably do not contribute to the property check in the first k time-frames, they might be irrelevant from the point of view of deciding this property for unbounded behaviors as well.

The model checking algorithm employed in Algorithm 3.1 (Step 8) may use a variety of methods. For the purpose of this paper we will assume a symbolic model checker using BDDs [16]. However, the ideas can easily be applied to other model checking methods such as SAT-based state-space traversal or even SAT-BMC. Algorithm 3.2 shows the pseudo-code for a generalized symbolic invariant checking algorithm that could use BDDs. The algorithm implements a combination of forward and backward state space traversal, henceforth referred to as *interleaved traversal* (after [18]). The traversal can be made a purely forward traversal, a purely backward one, or any interleaved combination of the two by an appropriate implementation of the *Choose_Direction* function (line 7 of Algorithm 3.2). Here B denotes the "bad states" *i.e.*, states that violate p and S_N^f and S_N^b denote the set of states currently reached through the forward and backward traversals respectively. Basically, the algorithm iteratively furthers the traversal in a direction governed by *Choose_Direction* till either the two traversals intersect (line 4) or either of the sets S_N^f or S_N^b reaches a fixpoint (line 3). A possible greedy heuristic for *Choose_Direction* would be to select the easier direction for image computation, which may be gauged by the final and/or peak BDD size of current image step, and other factors. The core steps implementing the traversal are the image (*Img*) and pre-image (*PreImg*) operations, defined in Equations 2 and 3 respectively. The *Img* operation on a set of states S, computes the states reachable from the states in S, in one step of computation, via the transition relation T. The *PreImg* operation simply performs the inverse computation.

$$Img(S) \equiv \exists X, W.\ S(X) \land T(X, Y, W) \tag{2}$$

$$PreImg(S) \equiv \exists Y, W.\ S(Y) \land T(X, Y, W) \tag{3}$$

$\underline{\text{Invariant Check}}(M\langle T, I\rangle,\ B)$

1: $S_N^f = I;\ S_N^b = B;\ S_C^f = \emptyset;\ S_C^b = \emptyset;$
2: $k_{fwd} = k_{bwd} = 0;\ j = 0;$
3: **while** $S_C^f \neq S_N^f$ **and** $S_C^b \neq S_N^b$ **do**
4:    **if** $S_N^f \cap S_N^b \neq \emptyset$ **then**
5:       **return** "found error trace";
6:    **end if**
7:    **if** *Choose_Direction*$() = $ "*forward*" **then**
8:       $S_C^f = S_N^f;$
9:       $S_N^f = S_C^f \cup Img(S_C^f);$
10:      $k_{fwd}++;$
11:   **else** {*Backward direction chosen*}
12:      $S_C^b = S_N^b;$
13:      $S_N^b = S_C^b \cup PreImg(S_C^b);$
14:      $k_{bwd}++;$
15:   **end if**
16:   $j++;$
17: **end while**
18: **return** "no bad state reachable";

Algorithm 3.2. Interleaved Symbolic Invariant Checking

4   Dynamic Abstraction

In order to make the paper self-contained, we begin by reviewing the notion of dynamic abstraction as developed in [26]. Given the original circuit M and the property $P = \mathbf{AG}p$ let us assume that a SAT-BMC problem on M of depth k has been solved and there is no counter-example. Further, suppose that the SAT solver generates a proof of unsatisfiability $\mathcal{P}$ for this problem as described in [9,25]. Figure 1, taken from [26], is a graphical representation of the POU from a 40-step SAT-BMC problem on a real circuit example. For each latch

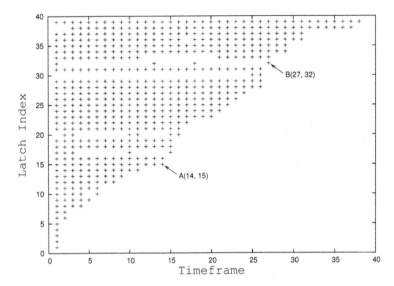

Fig. 1. Latch-based Unsatisfiability Analysis

(plotted for 40 representative latches on the y-axis) the plot shows the time-frames for which the corresponding instantiation of the latch variable appears in the POU of the SAT-BMC problem. The latches have been sorted on the y-axis for better readability of the data. Given a latch variable $l \in L$, we can define the *redundancy index*, $\rho(l)$ of l, with respect to the proof $\mathcal{P}$, as follows:

Definition 1 (Redundancy Index (RI)). *The redundancy index $\rho(l)$ of latch l with respect to the proof of unsatisfiability $\mathcal{P}$ is the smallest time-frame index such that for all time-frames j, $\rho(l) \leq j \leq k$, there does not exist a clause with variable l^j in $\mathcal{P}$.*

For example, in Figure 1 the points marked **A** and **B** show that latch number 15 has a redundancy index of 15 and latch 32 has a redundancy index of 28. Simply put, the redundancy index is the earliest time-frame at which the given latch stops participating in the POU of the *current* BMC problem. The situation depicted in Figure 1 is quite typical of a large variety of benchmarks we have experimented with. Most latches are not used in all time-frames of the POU. Moreover, there are several latches that are *only* used in the first few time-frames.

Note that the redundancy index analysis is typically done with respect to a particular SAT-BMC problem with a certain depth of unrolling. However, we conjecture that, by and large, the redundancy index calculated from a single SAT-BMC run can be a fairly good predictor of the unbounded behavior of a latch with respect to the given property. This intuition is supported by the data shown in Figure 2. The graph plots the redundancy indices for 4 randomly chosen latches from one of our benchmarks, generated from different BMC problems with varying depth k. Apart from minor fluctuations, the RI values of each latch

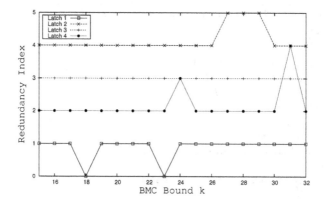

Fig. 2. Redundancy Index as a function of BMC-depth

are remarkably consistent, despite having been derived from *independent* BMC runs of *different* depth.

In the next section we develop an algorithm which uses the information about the redundancy indices of various latches to implement dynamic abstraction within state space traversal.

4.1   Interleaved Traversal with Dynamic Abstraction

At each step of image computation (measured by the iteration count variable j in Algorithm 3.2) we can define a *candidate set* of latches available to be abstracted through dynamic abstraction.

Definition 2 (Candidate set). *The candidate set of latches for iteration j of image computation in Algorithm 3.2 is denoted C_j and is defined as $C_j = \{l_i : l_i \in L, \rho(l_i) \leq k_{fwd}\}$.*

For example, consider the instance in Figure 1 , and suppose $k_{fwd} = 15$, *i.e.*, the *Choose_Direction* heuristic chooses forward traversal for the first 15 steps, then for time-frame $j = 15$, the candidate set consists of the first 16 latches, *i.e.*, $C_{15} = \{l_1, l_2, \ldots, l_{16}\}$, since the RIs of these latches are no greater than 15. A modified version of Algorithm 3.2, incorporating dynamic abstraction, is shown in Algorithm 4.1.

As in Algorithm 3.2, the state space traversal in Algorithm 4.1 can be implemented as purely forward, purely backward or any interleaved combination of these by an appropriate definition of the *Choose_Direction* function (line 11 of Algorithm 4.1). For example, if *Choose_Direction()* always returns "backward" the result will be a purely backward state space traversal. We maintain that an abstraction refinement algorithm employing dynamic abstraction in combination with an interleaved state-space traversal can yield a very powerful framework for invariant checking and this is the focal point of this paper. There are several reasons for this belief. First, as demonstrated in [26] the notion of dynamic abstraction provides a convenient mechanism to abstract away latches that become

Interleaved_Invariant_Check_DynamicAbstract $(M\langle T, I\rangle, B)$

1: $S_N^f = I$; $S_N^b = B$; $S_C^f = \emptyset$; $S_C^b = \emptyset$;
2: $k_{fwd} = k_{bwd} = 0$; $j = 0$;
3: **while** $S_C^f \neq S_N^f$ and $S_C^b \neq S_N^b$ **do**
4:    $L_{abs} = $ CHOOSE_ABSTRACTION_LATCHES(L);
5:    $T = $ ABSTRACT_TR(L_{abs}, T);
6:    $S_N^f = \exists X_{abs} \cdot S_N^f$;
7:    $S_N^b = \exists X_{abs} \cdot S_N^b$;
8:    **if** $S_N^f \cap S_N^b \neq \emptyset$ **then**
9:       **return** "found error trace";
10:    **end if**
11:    **if** $Choose_Direction() = $ "forward" **then**
12:       $S_C^f = S_N^f$;
13:       $S_N^f = S_C^f \cup Img(S_C^f)$;
14:       k_{fwd}++;
15:    **else** {*Backward direction chosen*}
16:       $S_C^b = S_N^b$;
17:       $S_N^b = S_C^b \cup PreImg(S_C^b)$;
18:       k_{bwd}++;
19:    **end if**
20:    j++;
21: **end while**
22: **return** "no bad state reachable";

Algorithm 4.1. Interleaved Symb. Invar. Checking with Dynamic Abstraction

"redundant" after a few steps of forward state space traversal, thereby focusing the invariant check on a smaller, but not necessarily less accurate, abstract model. On the other hand, [18] and several other works have noted that for certain state spaces, backward state traversal may be far more efficient than forward traversal. Further, in some failing instances, the optimum means of constructing an error trace may partly though a forward traversal and partly through a backward one. These two optimization mechanisms appear to be fairly complementary, especially since dynamic abstraction can simplify the transition relations for both forward and backward traversals. Thus, a combination of dynamic abstraction and interleaved traversal appears to be a reasonable means of harnessing the power of both. Second, as noted in [18] and also confirmed by our own experiments, interleaved traversal can work especially well in the case of failing properties since the forward and backward traversals can co-operate in the task of discovering the error trace. Given the fact that *all* but the last model produced during iterative abstraction refinement are failing instances, it seems to be an ideal candidate to benefit from the use of interleaved traversal. Our specific implementation of the interleaved traversal is discussed below, after a discussion of the CHOOSE_ABSTRACTION_LATCHES() function (line 11 in Algorithm 4.1).

As discussed in [26] a key determinant of the performance of dynamic abstraction is the latch selection heuristic CHOOSE_ABSTRACTION_LATCHES, that decides which latches, out of the current candidate set, should be abstracted at a given image computation step. The following definition of the latch selection heuristic allows us to place some correctness guarantees (Theorem 1 below) on the dynamically abstracted model.

Definition 3 (Choose_Abstraction_Latches()). *This heuristic chooses a subset of latches in C_j that have not already been abstracted away in previous iterations, for abstraction in the current iteration j of image computation in Algorithm 4.1.*

Our interleaving heuristic *i.e.*, the *Choose_Direction* function in Algorithm 4.1 maintains a cost for each direction of traversal (*i.e.*, forward and backward) based on peak BDD size and the increment of BDD size in the last image computation in that direction. In each iteration, the direction with the lower previous cost is chosen for traversal, with the exception that the the first few steps of traversal are always in the forward direction. This is because as per Definition 2 the candidate set open for abstraction, for both forward *and* backward traversal grows monotonically with the number of *forward* image computations performed. Thus, after a few initial forward images, the transition relation is usually reduced through dynamic abstraction and this same reduced transition relation (*i.e.*, its inverse) is used for potential backward traversal, thereby enhancing its efficiency.

Theorem 1. *Algorithm 4.1 will not find any counter-example to the given property in the first k steps of image computation, where $k = k_{fwd} + k_{bwd}$.*

Proof outline: [1] The proof of this result is along the lines of the main result in [17]. It is based on the observation that the above dynamic abstraction scheme can be equivalently formulated as a SAT-BMC by unrolling T for k time-frames and then cutting open the the unrolled latches in the corresponding time-frames at which these latches were abstracted away by the dynamic abstraction algorithm. It can be shown that the original POU $\mathcal{P}$ is still fully contained in this abstracted SAT-BMC problem, provided the latches dynamically abstracted during invariant checking conform to Definition 3. Thus, the dynamic abstracted model will not have any counter-example to the given property in the first k steps. Note that the above holds for *any* sequence of *forward* or *backward* choices made by the *Choose_Direction* heuristic in Algorithm 4.1. In that sense Theorem 1 is a strict generalization of the main result of [26].

4.2   Optimizations

In the following we describe some inexpensive optimizations that can be used to further improve the performance of a model checking algorithm that performs dynamic abstraction as described above.

Bypassing the Error Check: A simple corollary of Theorem 1 is the following.

---

[1] The complete proof is omitted for lack of space.

Corollary 1. *The error state check $S_N^f \cap S_N^b \neq \emptyset$ (line 8) in Algorithm 4.1 will always yield* `false` *in the first k iterations of the algorithm, $k = k_{fwd} + k_{bwd}$.*

This simple result obviates the need to perform the error state intersection check (line 8 of Algorithm 4.1) in the first k iterations of image computation. This check can be fairly expensive at deeper image computation steps and/or when the target states are not simply the negation of the property but an enlarged target computed through a few pre-image computation steps. For example, in case of benchmark $D7$ in Table 1 the error-state check at depth 11 costs more than 1600 secs. Note that this result is equally applicable to frameworks that only use static abstraction.

Early Quantification Re-scheduling: Typically the transition relation (TR) is maintained in an implicitly conjoined and partitioned form, along with an early quantification scheduling. During dynamic abstraction some state variables may be quantified out from the TR. As a result, the original early quantification scheduling may become sub-optimal to the modified TR. Our implementation solves this problem by modifying the early quantification scheduling when the TR changes.

Cone of Influence Reduction: As proposed in [17], an abstraction of some latches may create opportunities for further abstraction by applying the standard *cone of influence (COI)* reduction on the abstracted model. While the optimization was proposed in the context of the static abstraction procedure, the same can be done after each abstraction step in our dynamic abstraction algorithm. The key point is that any subsequent abstraction due to the COI reduction *does not* increase the space of allowable behaviors of the design. Thus, the quality of the abstraction is not diminished in any way, but the design becomes smaller and more tractable for the model checking.

5   Experimental Results

Experimental Set-Up: We have implemented the proposed algorithms for dynamic abstraction and state traversal within the VIS framework [19]. The static abstraction algorithms of [11,17] have also been implemented in the same framework, for comparison. We use the CUDD package for BDD computations, and zChaff [24] as the SAT solver for BMC. The POU extraction in zChaff has been modified to perform the analysis necessary for dynamic abstraction.

The following specific heuristic for CHOOSE_ABSTRACTION_LATCHES() (line 4 of Algorithm 4.1), proposed in [26] has been used for the purpose of these experiments. More involved and potentially better options are of course possible and could further enhance the proposed algorithms.

***Heuristic:** Dynamically abstract just once at $\lceil \delta \cdot k \rceil$ time-steps, $(0 < \delta < 1)$, and abstract all latches in the candidate set at this point.*

The philosophy behind this heuristic is to minimize the overhead of abstraction by doing it only once and being aggressive by choosing all candidates for

Table 1. Results: Static Abstraction and Proposed Dynamic Abstraction

Problem	Pass/ cex leng.	Concrete Model			Static Abstraction	Time (secs.)	Dynamic Abstraction		
		# PIs	# FFs	# Gates	# FFs		# FFs (diff.)	Fwd (secs.)	Intrlvd (secs.)
D1	Pass	85	161	1385	101	472	73(-28)	128	**13**
D2	Pass	118	375	1562	161	>24h(30)	129(-32)	952	**288**
D3	36	289	654	4826	170	>24h(28)	160(-10)	**1069**	1400
D4	29	289	654	4823	201	52333	168(-33)	10098	**617**
D5	60	308	746	3837	123	272	81(-42)	261	**216**
D6	Pass	330	1158	5155	264	67	204(-60)	**41**	58
D7	27	356	1644	7408	257	>24h(11)	244(-13)	>24h(13)	**456**
D8	Pass	1015	2971	10044	286	236	216(-70)	**100**	144
D9	Pass	1950	5564	19161	224	811	187(-37)	**114**	323
blackjack_5	Pass	7	109	1061	95	**460**	94(-1)	18104	7143
vsa16a_7	Pass	34	205	1939	108	24	105(-3)	32	**8**
s38584_2	73	13	615	2575	93	>24h(20)	66(-27)	>24h(39)	**10506**

abstraction. δ is kept fairly low to increase the likelihood of the latches being redundant for future image computations. We used $\delta = 0.2$ in our experiments.

Since the tools of [11,17] are not publicly available, a direct comparison against those approaches is neither fair nor intended. However, we have attempted to incorporate the essence of these works and used them to derive the initial static model on which dynamic abstraction based invariant checking is applied.

We have tested our tool for safety properties on different modules from four real-life industrial designs. In addition we have also experimented with circuits from the VIS Verilog suite [20] and some of the larger ISCAS89 sequential circuits. In the case of the ISCAS'89 circuits the property is the justification of a randomly generated state.

All experiments were run on a 3.0 GHz Pentium 4 Linux machine with 1G RAM, and a 24 hour time-out limit for each problem. Table 1 shows results for a subset of our benchmarks, representative of most of the interesting scenarios we encountered. *D1 - D9* are problem instances from in-house industrial designs, *blackjack_5* and *vsa16a_7* are benchmarks from the VIS Verilog suite while *s38584_2* is an instance from the ISCAS'89 circuits. The second column shows if the property is a passing property or the length of the shortest counterexample if it is a failing property. Column 6 shows the number of latches in the statically abstracted model, while column 8 reports the number of latches in the final dynamically abstracted model. Column 7 is the cumulative CPU time for iterative static abstraction refinement and invariant checking. Columns 9 and 10 report similar times but for dynamic abstraction with forward and interleaved model checking respectively. Both these times include the time for static abstraction as well, since the static abstraction is the starting point for dynamic abstraction based invariant checking. Note that Column 9 represents the results of [26], albeit enhanced with the optimizations of Section 4.2. In cases where the model checking timed out after 24 hours, the number of image computation steps successfully completed, in the last iteration of abstraction refinement, is noted in parenthesis.

Analysis of Results: As shown in Table 1, the proposed method of combining dynamic abstraction with interleaved state space traversal, during invariant checking, shows significant improvements over plain static abstraction refinement (column 7) as well as over dynamic abstraction with plain forward invariant checking (column 9), for both passing and failing properties. In some cases, such as *D7*, the improvement can be quite dramatic. In a few cases such as *D3*, *D6*, *D8* and *D9*, the interleaved method is moderately slower than dynamic forward invariant checking. These are passing properties, where the forward direction turns out to be the optimum direction of traversal and any mis-predicted backward traversal performed by the interleaved method merely serves as an overhead. In the very rare case, such as *blackjack_5*, where the both dynamic abstraction methods are slower than plain static abstraction, the dynamic interleaved method actually improves upon the dynamic forward method, thereby offsetting some of the losses incurred in using dynamic abstraction. In that sense the combination of interleaved traversal and dynamic abstraction is a more stable algorithmic configuration. Overall, our conclusions are that the combination of interleaved state space traversal with dynamic abstraction, in a framework for abstraction refinement, can provide significant performance gains over either plain static abstraction or even dynamic abstraction with pure forward traversal. In several cases, this combination can successfully complete the verification where the other methods time-out. The slow-down due to the overhead of mis-predicted interleaved traversals is usually moderate and, in our opinion, an acceptable trade-off considering the stability and significant performance improvements offered by the method.

6   Conclusions and Future Work

The notion of dynamic abstraction was recently introduced [26] as a means of abstracting a model during the process of model checking. In this paper we have extended the theory and implementation of this idea in several ways. We have presented algorithms to implement dynamic abstraction within different state traversal techniques namely forward, backward and interleaved traversal and formalized the correctness guarantees that can be made under different traversal algorithms operating on a dynamically abstracted model. We have also presented several optimizations to enhance the performance of the proposed algorithms. Our experiments on several large benchmarks from industrial designs as well as the public domain demonstrate that in several instances the integration of dynamic abstraction and interleaved traversal is necessary to complete the invariant check. In other cases the use of interleaved traversal either provide a significant performance improvement or a modest overhead.

There are several avenues for enhancing the proposed algorithms. One of the possibilities would be to reduce the overhead that the interleaved traversal incurs. This could be done by refining the heuristic for choosing the direction of traversal or by use of the "2-DD manager" idea proposed in [18]. Another direction would be to integrate the proposed algorithms into a hybrid framework combining counter-example guided and proof based abstraction such as the one proposed in [1].

References

1. N. Amla and K. L. McMillan. A hybrid of counterexample-based and proof-based abstraction. In A. J. Hu and A. K. Martin, editors, *Proc. of Formal Methods in CAD*, volume 3312 of *LNCS*, pages 260–274. Springer, Nov 2004.
2. P. Bjesse and J. Kukula. Using Counter Example Guided Abstraction Refinement to Find Complex Bugs. In *Proc. of the Design Automation and Test in Europe*, pages 156–161, February 2004.
3. G. Cabodi, P. Camurati, and S. Quer. Efficient State Space Pruning in Symbolic Backward Traversal. In *Proc. of the Intl. Conf. on Computer Design*, pages 230–235, October 1994.
4. G. Cabodi, S. Nocco, and S. Quer. Mixing Forward and Backward Traversals in Guided-Prioritized BDD-Based Verification. In E. Brinksma and K. Larsen, editors, *Proc. of the Intl. Conf. on Computer Aided Verification*, volume 2404 of *LNCS*. Springer, July 2002.
5. P. Chauhan, E. M. Clarke, J. Kukula, S. Sapra, H. Veith, and D. Wang. Automated Abstraction Refinement for Model Checking Large State Spaces using SAT based Conflict Analysis. In M. Aagaard and J. W. O'Leary, editors, *Proc. of the Intl. Conf. on Formal Methods in CAD*, volume 2517 of *LNCS*, pages 33–51, Nov. 2002.
6. E. Clarke, A. Biere, R. Raimi, and Y. Zhu. Bounded Model Checking Using Satisfiability Solving. *Formal Methods in System Design*, 19(1):7–34, July 2001. Kluwer Academic Publishers.
7. E. M. Clarke, A. Gupta, J. Kukula, and O. Strichman. SAT-based Abstraction Refinement Using ILP and Machine Learning Techniques. In E. Brinksma and K. Larsen, editors, *Proc. of the Intl. Conf. on Computer Aided Verification*, volume 2404 of *LNCS*, pages 265–279. Springer, July 2002.
8. M. Glusman, G. Kamhi, S. M.-H., R. Fraer, and M. Y. Vardi. Multiple-Counterexample Guided Iterative Abstraction Refinement: An Industrial Evaluation. In H. Garavel and J. Hatcliff, editors, *Proc. of the Intl. Conf. on Tools and Algorithms for the Construction and Analysis of Systems*, volume 2619 of *LNCS*, pages 176–191. Springer, April 2003.
9. E. Goldberg and Y. Novikov. Verification of proofs of unsatisfiability for CNF formulas. In *Proc. of the Design Automation and Test in Europe*, pages 886–891, March 2003.
10. S. G. Govindaraju and D. L. Dill. Verification by approximate forward and backward reachability. In *Proc. of Intl. Conf. on CAD*, pages 366–370, Nov. 1998.
11. A. Gupta, M. Ganai, Z. Yang, and P. Ashar. Iterative Abstraction Using SAT-based BMC with Proof Analysis. In *Proc. of the Intl. Conf. on CAD*, pages 416–423, Nov. 2003.
12. H. Iwashita and T. Nakata. Forward model checking techniques oriented to buggy designs. In *Proc. of Intl. Conf. on CAD*, pages 400–404, Nov. 1997.
13. R. P. Kurshan. *Computer-Aided Verification of Coordinating Processes: The Automata-Theoretic Approach*. Princeton University Press, 1995.

14. B. Li and F. Somenzi. Efficient Computation of Small Abstraction Refinements. In *Proc. of the Intl. Conf. on CAD*, Nov. 2004.
15. F. Y.-C. Mang and P.-H. Ho. Abstraction Refinement by Controllability and Co-operativeness Analysis. In *Proc. of the Design Automation Conf.*, pages 224–229, June 2004.
16. K. L. McMillan. *Symbolic Model Checking: An approach to the State Explosion Problem.* Kluwer Academic Publishers, 1993.
17. K. L. McMillan and N. Amla. Automatic abstraction without counterexamples. In Hubert Garavel and John Hatcliff, editors, *Proc. of the Intl. Conf. on Tools and Algorithms for the Construction and Analysis of Systems (TACAS'03)*, volume 2619 of *LNCS*, pages 2–17. Springer, April 2003.
18. C. Stangier and T. Sidle. Invariant Checking Combining Forward and Backward Traversal. In A. J. Hu and A. K. Martin, editors, *Proc. of 5th Intl. Conf. on Formal Methods in CAD*, volume 3312 of *LNCS*, pages 414–429. Springer, Nov. 2004.
19. The VIS Group. VIS: A system for Verification and Synthesis. In R. Alur and T. Henzinger, editors, *Proc. of the Intl. Conf. on Computer Aided Verification*, volume 1102 of *LNCS*, pages 428–432. Springer, July 1996.
20. VIS Verilog Benchmarks. http://vlsi.colorado.edu/~vis.
21. C. Wang, G. D. Hachtel, and F. Somenzi. Fine-Grain Abstraction and Sequential Don't Cares for Large Scale Model Checking. In *Proc. of the Intl. Conf. on Computer Design*, October 2004.
22. C. Wang, B. Li, H. Jin, G. D. Hachtel, and F. Somenzi. Improving Ariadne's Bundle by Following Multiple Threads in Abstraction Refinement. In *Proc. of the Intl. Conf. on CAD*, pages 408–415, Nov. 2003.
23. D. Wang, P.-H. Ho, J. Long, J. Kukula, Y. Zhu, T. Ma, and R. Damiano. Formal Property Verification by Abstraction Refinement with Formal, Simulation and Hybrid Engines. In *Proc. of the Design Automation Conf.*, pages 35–40, June 2001.
24. http://ee.princeton.edu/~chaff/zchaff.php, Dec. 2003.
25. L. Zhang and S. Malik. Validating SAT Solvers using an Independent Resolution-based Checker: Practical Implementations and Other Applications. In *Proc. of the Design Automation and Test in Europe*, pages 880–885, March 2003.
26. L. Zhang, M. R. Prasad, M. Hsiao, and T. Sidle. Dynamic Abstraction Using SAT-based BMC. In *Proc. of the Design Automation Conf.*, pages 754–757, June 2005.

Automatic Formal Verification of Liveness for Pipelined Processors with Multicycle Functional Units

Miroslav N. Velev

http://www.ece.cmu.edu/~mvelev
mvelev@ece.cmu.edu

Abstract. Presented is a highly automatic approach for proving bounded liveness of pipelined processors with multicycle functional units, without the need for the user to set up an inductive argument. Multicycle functional units are abstracted with a placeholder that is suitable for proving both safety and liveness. Abstracting the branch targets and directions with arbitrary terms and formulas, respectively, that are associated with each instruction, made the branch targets and directions independent of the data operands. The observation that the term variables abstracting branch targets of newly fetched instructions can be considered to be in the same equivalence class, allowed the use of a dedicated fresh term variable for all such branch targets and the abstraction of the Instruction Memory with a generator of arbitrary values. To further improve the scaling, the multicycle ALU was abstracted with a placeholder without feedback loops. Also, the equality comparison between the terms written to the PC and the dedicated fresh term variable for branch targets of new instructions was implemented as part of the circuit, thus avoiding the need to apply the abstraction function along the specification side of the commutative diagram for liveness. This approach resulted in 4 orders of magnitude speedup for a 5-stage pipelined DLX processor with a 32-cycle ALU, compared to a previous method for indirect proof of bounded liveness, and scaled for a 5-stage pipelined DLX with a 2048-cycle ALU.

1 Introduction

Previous work on microprocessor formal verification has almost exclusively addressed the proof of *safety*—that if a processor does something during a step, it will do it correctly—as also observed in [2], while ignoring the proof of *liveness*—*that a processor will complete a new instruction after a finite number of steps*. Several authors used theorem proving to check liveness [15][16][17][19][23][28][32][34], but invested extensive manual work. This paper is the first to prove liveness for pipelined processors with multicycle functional units in an automatic way.

Functional units in recent state-of-the-art processors usually have latencies of up to $20-30$ cycles, and rarely up to 200 cycles, but it is expected that the memory latencies in next generation high-performance designs will reach 1,000 cycles [13]. Thus, the need to develop automatic techniques to prove the liveness of pipelined processors where the functional units can have latencies of up to thousands of cycles.

In the current paper, the implementation and specification are described in the high-level hardware description language HDL [46], based on the logic of Equality with Uninterpreted Functions and Memories (EUFM) [7]. In EUFM, word-level values are abstracted with terms (see Sect. 4) whose only relevant property is that of equality with other terms. Restrictions on the style for describing high-level processors [35][36] reduced the number of terms that appear in both positive and negated equality comparisons—and are so called *g-terms* (for general terms)—and increased the number of

D. Borrione and W. Paul (Eds.): CHARME 2005, LNCS 3725, pp. 97–113, 2005.

terms that appear only in positive polarity—and are so called *p-terms* (for positive terms). The property of Positive Equality [35][36] allowed us to treat syntactically different p-terms as not equal when evaluating the validity of an EUFM formula, thus achieving significant simplifications and orders of magnitude speedup. (See [5] for a correctness proof.)

The formal verification is done with an automatic tool flow, consisting of: 1) the term-level symbolic simulator TLSim [46], used to symbolically simulate the implementation and specification, and produce an EUFM correctness formula; 2) the decision procedure EVC [46] that exploits Positive Equality and other optimizations to translate the EUFM correctness formula to an equivalent Boolean formula, which has to be a tautology in order for the implementation to be correct; and 3) an efficient SAT-solver. This tool flow was used at Motorola [18] to formally verify a model of the M•CORE processor, and detected bugs.

The rest of the paper is organized as follows. Sect. 2 defines safety and liveness. Sect. 3 discusses related work. Sect. 4 summarizes the logic of EUFM, the property of Positive Equality, and efficient translations from EUFM to CNF. Sect. 5 presents a previous indirect method for proving liveness of pipelined processors by exploiting Positive Equality. Sect. 6 explains the application of that indirect method to proving the liveness of pipelined DLX processors having ALUs with latencies of up to 2048 cycles. Sect. 7 describes an abstraction for multicycle ALUs that is applicable to proving both safety and liveness of pipelined processors. The next three sections present optimizations that speed up the automatic formal proof of liveness for pipelined processors with multicycle functional units: Sect. 8 describes techniques for abstracting the branch targets and directions of instructions; Sect. 9 makes the observation that the branch targets of newly fetched instructions can be considered to be in the same equivalence class, and so can be replaced with the same fresh term variable; and Sect. 10 shows an approach to avoid the abstraction function along the specification side of the commutative correctness diagram for liveness. Sect. 11 presents experimental results, and Sect. 12 concludes the paper.

2   Definition of Safety and Liveness

The formal verification is done by correspondence checking—comparison of a pipelined implementation against a non-pipelined specification. The abstraction function, *Abs*, maps an implementation state to an equivalent specification state, and is computed by *flushing* [7]—feeding the implementation pipeline with bubbles (combinations of control signals that do not modify architectural state) until all partially executed instructions are completed. The safety property (see Fig. 1) is expressed as a formula in the logic of EUFM, and checks that one step of the implementation corresponds to between 0 and k steps of the specification, where k is the issue width of the implementation. F_{Impl} is the transition function of the implementation, and F_{Spec} is the transition function of the specification. We will refer to the sequence of first applying *Abs* and then F_{Spec} as the *specification side* of the diagram in Fig. 1, and to the sequence of first applying F_{Impl} and then *Abs* as the *implementation side*.

The safety property is the inductive step of a proof by induction, since the initial implementation state, Q_{Impl}, is arbitrary. If the implementation is correct for all transitions that can be made for one step from an arbitrary initial state, then the implementation will be correct for one step from the next implementation state, Q'_{Impl}, since that state will be a special case of an arbitrary state as used for the initial state, and so on for any number of steps. For some processors, e.g., where the control logic is optimized by using unreachable states as don't-care conditions, we may have to impose *invariant constraints* for the initial state in order to exclude unreachable states. Then, we need to prove that those constraints are satisfied in the implementation state after one step, Q'_{Impl}, so that the correctness will hold by induction for that state, and so on for all subsequent states. (See [1][2] for a discussion of correctness criteria.)

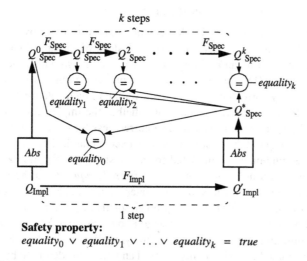

Safety property:
$$equality_0 \lor equality_1 \lor \ldots \lor equality_k = true$$

Fig. 1. The safety correctness property for an implementation processor with issue width k: one step of the implementation should correspond to between 0 and k steps of the specification, when the implementation starts from an arbitrary initial state Q_{Impl} that is possibly restricted by a set of invariant constraints.

To illustrate the safety property in Fig. 1, let the implementation and specification have three architectural state elements—Program Counter (PC), Register File, and Data Memory. Let PC^i_{Spec}, $RegFile^i_{Spec}$, and $DMem^i_{Spec}$ be the state of the PC, Register File, and Data Memory, respectively, in specification state Q^i_{Spec} ($i = 0, \ldots, k$) along the specification side of the diagram. Let PC^*_{Spec}, $RegFile^*_{Spec}$, and $DMem^*_{Spec}$ be the state of the PC, Register File, and Data Memory in specification state Q^*_{Spec}, reached after the implementation side of the diagram. Then, each disjunct $equality_i$ ($i = 0, \ldots, k$) is defined as:

$$equality_i \leftarrow pc_i \land rf_i \land dm_i,$$

where

$$pc_i \leftarrow (PC^i_{Spec} = PC^*_{Spec}),$$
$$rf_i \leftarrow (RegFile^i_{Spec} = RegFile^*_{Spec}),$$
$$dm_i \leftarrow (DMem^i_{Spec} = DMem^*_{Spec}).$$

That is, $equality_i$ is the conjunction of pair-wise equality comparisons for all architectural state elements, thus ensuring that they are updated in synchrony by the same number of instructions. In processors with more architectural state elements, an equality comparison is conjuncted for each additional state element. Hence, for this implementation processor, the safety property is:

$$pc_0 \wedge rf_0 \wedge dm_0 \vee pc_1 \wedge rf_1 \wedge dm_1 \vee ... \vee pc_k \wedge rf_k \wedge dm_k = true.$$

We can prove liveness by a modified version of the safety correctness criterion—by symbolically simulating the implementation for a finite number of steps, n, and proving that:

$$equality_1 \vee equality_2 \vee ... \vee equality_{n \times k} = true \qquad (1)$$

where k is the issue width of the implementation. The formula proves that n steps of the implementation match between 1 and $n \times k$ steps of the specification, when the implementation starts from an arbitrary initial state that may be restricted by invariant constraints. Note that (1) *guarantees that the implementation has made at least one step*, while the safety correctness criterion allows the implementation to stay in its initial state when formula $equality_0$ (checking whether the implementation matches the initial state of the specification) is *true*. The correctness formula is generated automatically in the same way as the formula for safety, except that the implementation and the specification are symbolically simulated for many steps, and formula $equality_0$ is not included. As in the formula for safety, every formula $equality_i$ is the conjunction of equations, each comparing corresponding states of the same architectural state element. That is, formula (1) consists of top-level positive equations that are conjuncted and disjuncted but not negated, allowing us to exploit Positive Equality when proving liveness. The minimum number of steps, n, to symbolically simulate the implementation, can be determined experimentally, by trial and error, or identified by the user after analyzing the processor (see Sect. 6).

The contribution of this paper is a highly automatic method to prove bounded liveness of pipelined processors with multicycle functional units. The proposed method enables the liveness check for a 5-stage pipelined DLX processor [13] with a 2048-cycle ALU, while producing 4 orders of magnitude speedup for a pipelined DLX with a 32-cycle ALU compared to a previous method for indirect proof of bounded liveness [42] (see Sect. 5).

3   Related Work

Safety and liveness were first defined by Lamport [20]. Most of the previous research on formal verification of processors has addressed only safety, as also observed in [2]. The most popular theorem-proving approach for proving microprocessor liveness is to prove that for each pipeline stage that can get stalled, if the stalling condition is *true* then the instruction initially in that stage will stay there, and if the stalling condition is *false* then the instruction will advance to the next stage. It is additionally proved that if the stalling condition is *true*, then it will eventually become *false*, given the implementation of the control logic and fairness assumptions about arbiters. Liveness was proved in this way by Srivas and Miller [34], Hosabettu et al. [15], Jacobi and Kröning

[16], Müller and Paul [28], Kröning and Paul [17], and Lahiri et al. [19]. Sawada [32] similarly proved that if an implementation is fed with bubbles, it will eventually get flushed. However, note that a buggy processor, where the architectural state elements are always disabled, may pass the check that stall signals will eventually become *false*, and that the pipeline will eventually get flushed, as well as satisfy the safety correctness criterion (where formula $equality_0$ will be *true*), but will fail the liveness check done here. Using a different theorem-proving approach, Manolios [23] also accounted for liveness by proving that a given state can be reached from a flushed state after an appropriate number of steps. McMillan [27] used circular compositional reasoning to check the liveness of a reduced model of an out-of-order processor with ALU and move instructions. His method requires the manual definition of lemmas and case-splitting expressions; the manual reduction of the proof to one that involves two reservation stations and one register; and the manual introduction of fairness assumptions for the abstracted arbiter. The approaches in the above nine papers will require significant manual work to apply to the models that are automatically checked for both safety and liveness in the current paper. Aagaard et al. [1] formulated a liveness condition, but did not present results.

Henzinger et al. [14] also enriched the specification, using a different method than ours, but had to do that even to prove safety of a 3-stage pipeline with ALU and move instructions. Biere et al. [3][4] enriched a model with a witnessing mechanism that records whether a property has been satisfied, thus allowing them to model check liveness of a communication protocol as safety. Pnueli et al. [29] proved the liveness of mutual-exclusion algorithms by deriving an abstraction, and enriching it with conditions that allowed the efficient liveness check in a way that implies the liveness of the original model. A method for indirect proof of liveness for pipelined processors was presented in [42]—see Sect. 5. Another approach suitable for proving both safety and liveness of pipelined processors was proposed in [24], but was not applied to designs with multicycle functional units.

4   EUFM, Positive Equality, and Efficient Translation to CNF

The syntax of EUFM [7] includes *terms* and *formulas*. Terms are used to abstract word-level values of data, register identifiers, memory addresses, as well as the entire states of memory arrays. A term can be an Uninterpreted Function (UF) applied to a list of argument terms, a term variable, or an *ITE* operator selecting between two argument terms based on a controlling formula, such that *ITE(formula, term1, term2)* will evaluate to *term1* if *formula = true*, and to *term2* if *formula = false*. The syntax for terms can be extended to model memories by means of the functions *read* and *write* [7][39]. Formulas are used to model the control path of a microprocessor, and to express the correctness condition. A formula can be an Uninterpreted Predicate (UP) applied to a list of argument terms, a Boolean variable, an *ITE* operator selecting between two argument formulas based on a controlling formula, or an equation (equality comparison) of two terms. Formulas can be negated and combined by Boolean connectives. We will refer to both terms and formulas as *expressions*. UFs and UPs are used to abstract the implementation details of functional units by replacing them with "black boxes" that satisfy no particular properties other than that of *functional consistency*—that equal values of the inputs to the UF (UP) produce equal output values.

The efficiency from exploiting Positive Equality is due to the observation that the truth of an EUFM formula under a maximally diverse interpretation of the p-terms implies the truth of the formula under any interpretation. A maximally diverse interpretation is one where the equality comparison of a term variable with itself evaluates to *true*; that of a p-term variable with a syntactically distinct term variable (a p-equation) evaluates to *false*; and that of a g-term variable with a syntactically distinct g-term variable (a g-equation) could evaluate to either *true* or *false*, and can be encoded with Boolean variables [10][30][41].

In the formal verification tool flow, we can apply an optimization [44] that produces Boolean formulas with many ITE-trees. An ITE-tree can be translated to CNF with a unified set of clauses [44], without intermediate variables for outputs of ITEs inside the tree. ITE-trees can be further merged with one or more levels of their AND/OR leaves that have fanout count of 1. We can also merge other gate groups [43][44]. Merging of ITE-trees and other gate groups results in fewer variables and clauses, i.e., reduced solution space, and so less Boolean Constraint Propagation (BCP) and fewer cache misses.

5   Indirect Proof of Liveness

This section summarizes one of the results from [42]. To avoid the validity checking of the monolithic liveness correctness formula (1), which becomes complex for designs with long pipelines and many features, we can prove liveness indirectly:

THEOREM 1. *If after n implementation steps, $equality_0$ = false under a maximally diverse interpretation of the p-terms, and the safety property is valid, then the liveness property is valid under any interpretation.*

Note that under an interpretation that is not a maximally diverse interpretation of the p-terms, the condition $equality_0$ may become *true*, e.g., in the presence of software loops, or if multiple instructions raise the same exception and so update the PC with the same exception-handler address. However, the liveness condition (1) will be still valid, since it can only get disjuncted with other formulas that result from equations between syntactically distinct p-terms that become equal under an interpretation that is not a maximally diverse interpretation of the p-terms.

Since $equality_0$ is the conjunction of the pair-wise equality comparisons for all architectural state elements, it suffices to prove that one of those equality comparisons is *false* under a maximally diverse interpretation of the p-terms. In particular, we can prove that $pc_0 = false$, where pc_0 is the equality comparison between the PC state after the implementation side of the diagram (see Fig. 1), and the PC that is part of the initial specification state. Note that choosing the Register File or the Data Memory instead would not work, since they are not updated by each instruction, and so there can be infinitely long instruction sequences that do not modify these state elements. Note that proving *forward progress*—*that the PC is updated at least once after n implementation steps*, i.e., proving $pc_0 = false$ under a maximally diverse interpretation of the p-terms—is done without the specification. However, the specification is used to prove safety, thus inductively the correctness for any number of steps.

6   Processor Benchmarks and Their Liveness

Experiments will be conducted with variants of a 5-stage pipelined DLX processor [13] that can execute ALU, branch, load, and store instructions. The 5 pipeline stages are: Fetch, Decode, Execute, Memory, and Write-Back. The Execute stage contains an ALU that can take either a single cycle or up to m cycles to compute the result of an ALU instruction. The actual latency may depend on the instruction opcode, the values of the data operands, etc., and so the choice between 1 and m cycles is made non-deterministically [37] in order to account for any actual implementation of the ALU. The processor benchmarks are named DLX-ALU4, DLX-ALU8, ..., and DLX-ALU2048, for values of m equal to 4, 8, ..., and 2048, respectively. The branch instructions have both their target address and their direction (indicating whether the branch is taken or not taken) computed in the Execute stage in a single cycle. ALU results, data memory addresses, branch targets, and branch directions depend on the instruction opcode, and two data operands read from the Register File (in the Decode stage) at locations specified by source register identifiers. ALU and load instructions also have a destination register identifier, indicating the Register File location where the result will be stored. Data hazards are avoided by forwarding logic in the Execute stage. While the ALU is computing the result of a multicycle operation, the instructions in previous stages are stalled, and bubbles are inserted in the Memory stage.

   To illustrate the choice of number of steps, n, for the liveness proof of one of the above benchmarks where the ALU has a maximum latency of m cycles, note that the longest delay before such a processor fetches a new instruction that is guaranteed to be completed is $m + 3$ cycles. This will happen if the Decode stage contains a branch that will be taken, but the Execute stage contains an ALU instruction that will take m cycles. Then, the branch will be stalled for $m - 1$ cycles, followed by one cycle to go through Decode, another cycle to go through Execute (where the branch target and direction will be computed), a third cycle to go through Memory (where the PC will be updated with the branch target, and all subsequent instructions that are in previous pipeline stages will be cancelled), and a fourth cycle to fetch a new instruction that is guaranteed to be completed since the pipeline will be empty by then. Thus, a correct version of these processors has to be simulated symbolically for $m + 3$ steps in order to fetch a new instruction that is guaranteed to be completed.

7   Placeholder for Abstracting Multicycle Functional Units for Proving Safety and Liveness

Multicycle functional units are abstracted with a placeholder that is suitable for proving both safety and liveness (see Fig. 2), a modified version of a placeholder suitable for proving only safety [37]. Uninterpreted function ALU abstracts the functionality of the replaced multicycle functional unit.

In Fig. 2, when signal Flush is *false* (during regular symbolic simulation) and a multicycle instruction is in the pipeline stage of the abstracted functional unit, as indicated by signal Take_m being *true* in that stage, then the chain of $m - 1$ latches will be used to delay the multicycle computation for m cycles before the result of that computation is allowed to continue to the next stage. When signal Flush becomes *true* during the computation of the abstraction function by flushing, then the chain of $m - 1$ latches will be cleared on the next clock cycle; signal Complete will become *true* for 1 clock cycle as long as the placeholder contains a valid instruction in flight, thus completing that instruction; and signal Stall will be *false*, thus allowing the instructions in the previous pipeline stages to advance. Hence, this placeholder of a multicycle functional unit can be used for proving both safety (by setting Flush to *false* for one cycle of regular symbolic simulation, and then setting Flush to *true* in order to quickly complete partially executed instructions during flushing) and liveness (by setting Flush to *false* for as many cycles as required, and then setting Flush to *true* in order to quickly complete partially executed instructions during flushing). Multicycle memories are abstracted similarly, by using a memory model instead of the uninterpreted function ALU.

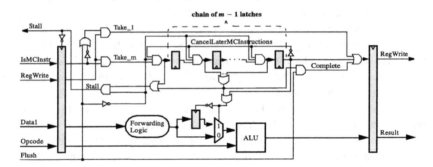

Fig. 2. Abstracting a multicycle ALU with a placeholder suitable for proving both safety and liveness of the pipelined processor. The latency is 1 cycle when signal Take_1 is *true* (i.e., RegWrite is *true* and IsMCInstr is *false*) or m cycles when signal Take_m is *true* (i.e., RegWrite is *true* and IsMCInstr is *true*). The chain of $m - 1$ latches delays signal IsMCInstr for m cycles in the stage of the functional unit. The previous pipeline stages are stalled by signal Stall when the functional unit takes more than 1 cycle for an operation. Signal CancelLaterMCInstructions avoids the need to impose and check an invariant that at most one latch in the chain has value *true*.

An alternative implementation of the placeholder is without the feedback loop of signal CancelLaterMCInstructions that clears the $m - 1$ latches when a multicycle operation completes. Instead, constraints are imposed that at most one of the $m - 1$ latches contains a valid instruction. These constraints have to be checked for invariance after 1 cycle of regular symbolic simulation.

8   Abstracting the Branch Targets and Directions

The indirect proof of liveness (see Sect. 5) checks that the PC is modified by at least one new instruction after n implementation steps. However, for this proof it does not matter what the actual values of the branch targets and branch directions are when the

PC is updated. The safety proof already guarantees that those values will be correct. Thus, we can abstract each instruction's branch target and direction with an oracle term and an oracle formula, respectively, such that there is a 1-to-1 relation between the instruction and its oracles. This can be done by either extending the Instruction Memory to produce the oracles, or introducing a new uninterpreted function and a new uninterpreted predicate, respectively, that depend on the PC of the instruction.

The oracles for the branch target and direction are propagated along the processor pipeline in the same way as the instruction's opcode. These oracles are used in the Execute stage only when proving liveness, by being connected (e.g., by means of a multiplexor controlled by a signal indicating whether the proof is for liveness) to the signals for the branch target and branch direction, respectively, which are otherwise computed by an uninterpreted function and an uninterpreted predicate, respectively, when proving safety. The introduction of auxiliary state in a processor can be viewed as *design for formal verification*. Note that the oracle branch target and branch direction can be used as abstractions for the final actually chosen branch target and branch direction, respectively, in a design where several branch targets and branch directions are prioritized for each instruction. This abstraction technique, using oracles to abstract result terms and formulas, is general and applicable to other functional units, once it is proven that their operands are provided correctly for each instruction.

Since the above abstractions make the branch targets and directions independent of the data operands, we can perform *automatically* a cone-of-influence reduction to simplify the processor for its liveness proof by removing any circuitry that does not affect the PC—the only architectural state element in the EUFM formula for the indirect proof of liveness. That allows us to remove the uninterpreted function and uninterpreted predicate abstracting the functionality of, respectively, the functional unit computing the branch target and that computing the branch direction in the Execute stage; the forwarding logic for those functional units; the uninterpreted function abstracting the functionality of the multicycle ALU in the Execute stage, since the produced result no longer affects the updating of the PC; the forwarding logic for the multicycle ALU; the Register File and the Data Memory, since the data operands that they produce no longer affect the updating of the PC; and all connections for transferring of data operands. What is left after an automatic cone-of-influence reduction is a *timing abstraction* of the pipelined processor with multicycle functional units. The timing abstraction does not depend on the data operands in the original implementation, but only on signals that affect the stalling and squashing of the oracle branch targets and oracle branch directions in the reduced pipelined design.

LEMMA 1. If the timing abstraction of a pipelined processor model satisfies the condition $pc_0 = false$ under a maximally diverse interpretation of the p-terms after n steps, then that condition is also satisfied by the pipelined processor model itself.

Sketch of the proof: Because of the way that the oracles are generated and then propagated along the processor pipeline together with the instruction opcode, there is a 1-to-1 correspondence between each instruction and its oracles. Also, since the oracles are not constrained in any way—i.e., the oracles for the branch targets and branch directions are arbitrary terms and formulas, respectively—then each such oracle can be viewed as a "placeholder" for the actual value of a branch target or a branch direction, respectively. The safety proof already guarantees that any actual branch target and branch direction will be computed correctly. Furthermore, since no control decisions are made based on the values of the oracles for the branch targets, then those oracle terms will be classified as p-terms, allowing us to exploit Theorem 1. (In the case of pipelined processors with branch prediction, where the actual branch targets are compared for equality with predicted branch targets in order to correct a branch misprediction, we can use special abstractions that turn the actual and predicted branch targets into p-terms [42].) Hence, a liveness proof based on arbitrary terms for the branch targets and arbitrary formulas for the branch directions will account for any outcome of the branches, and will ensure that the PC will be updated by at least one new instruction after any sequence of instructions executed during n implementation steps. Then, there will be no execution scenario of stalling or cancelling of instructions over n implementation steps, resulting in violation of the indirect liveness condition, $pc_0 = false$, under a maximally diverse interpretation of the p-terms. $\qquad\square$

9   Abstracting the Branch Targets of New Instructions with a Dedicated Term Variable

Recall that we want to prove that formula pc_0 is *false* under a maximally diverse interpretation of the p-terms, which implies that $equality_0 = false$, and thus from Theorem 1 that the liveness condition holds (see Sect. 5). That is, we want to prove that the representation of pc_0 as $(PC^0{}_{Spec} = PC^*{}_{Spec})$ is *false* under a maximally diverse interpretation of the p-terms, where $PC^0{}_{Spec}$ is the PC term after flushing the implementation along the specification side of the diagram in Fig. 1, and $PC^*{}_{Spec}$ is the PC term after n regular implementation steps followed by flushing along the implementation side of the diagram.

After abstracting the branch targets with arbitrary terms, the term for $PC^0{}_{Spec}$ will be a nested-*ITE* expression that has as leaves the term variables for branch targets of instructions that are initially in the pipeline. The term for $PC^*{}_{Spec}$ will too be a nested-*ITE* expression that also has as leaves all of those term variables, as well as the terms for the branch targets of new instructions fetched during the n regular implementation steps. Because of modeling restrictions [35][36], all branch targets will appear as p-terms. Thus, in formula pc_0 the branch target p-terms of new instructions will be compared for equality with only branch target p-terms of instructions that are initially in the pipeline. Since the branch target p-terms of new instructions are syntactically distinct from the branch target p-terms that are initially in the pipeline, then such low-level equations will simplify to *false* when evaluating pc_0 under a maximally diverse interpretation of the p-terms. The only low-level equations in pc_0 that will evaluate to *true* are those where both arguments are the same p-term variable that is initially in the pipeline. Hence, the value of pc_0 under a maximally diverse interpretation of the p-terms will be preserved if all branch target p-terms of new instructions are considered to be in the same equivalence class, representing branch target p-terms that are syntactically distinct from those that are initially in the pipeline. *This observation allows us to abstract the branch targets of newly fetched instructions with the same dedicated* *fresh term variable.* By reducing the number of distinct p-term variables that are leaves of the nested-*ITE* arguments of equation pc_0, we will improve the efficiency of evaluating pc_0 under a maximally diverse interpretation of the p-terms.

Note that along the implementation side of the diagram, the PC is also updated with SequentialPC terms produced by an uninterpreted function that maps the current PC term to a term for the sequential instruction address. Hence, applications of that uninterpreted function will also appear as leaves of term PC^*_{Spec}. Applying the above reasoning, we can replace all applications of that uninterpreted function with the dedicated fresh term variable used to abstract the branch targets of newly fetched instructions, since the PC is not updated with its sequential values during flushing along the specification side of the diagram. However, this will result in updating the PC with the dedicated fresh term variable on many clock cycles, and then in fetching the same symbolic instruction from the Instruction Memory on the next cycles. In order to prove liveness for an arbitrary instruction sequence executed over n implementation steps, we can abstract the Instruction Memory with a generator of arbitrary values [37], thus producing a completely arbitrary symbolic instruction and associated oracles on every clock cycle. As before, we will prove that there is no execution scenario that will prevent the fetching and completion of at least one new instruction.

10   Avoiding the Abstraction Function Along the Specification Side of the Diagram

Instead of checking that $(PC^0_{Spec} = PC^*_{Spec})$ is *false* under a maximally diverse interpretation of the p-terms, we can check that $(new\_PC\_var = PC^*_{Spec})$ is *true* under a maximally diverse interpretation of the p-terms, thus proving that the PC is overwritten with the dedicated fresh term variable new_PC_var after all execution sequences of length n. If that holds, then PC^*_{Spec} evaluates to new_PC_var under a maximally diverse interpretation of the p-terms, so that $(PC^0_{Spec} = PC^*_{Spec})$ is equivalent to $(PC^0_{Spec} = new\_PC\_var)$, which will be *false* under a maximally diverse interpretation of the p-terms, since new_PC_var is not a leaf of PC^0_{Spec} because by the definition of flushing new_PC_var is not written to the PC along the specification side of the diagram for liveness. Thus, we avoid the specification side of the diagram, since PC^0_{Spec} is no longer needed.

Additionally, we can automatically introduce an auxiliary circuit that when simulated symbolically will construct a formula that is equivalent to the formula $(new\_PC\_var = PC^*_{Spec})$ but is much simpler to evaluate. Intuitively, we can push the equation $(new\_PC\_var = PC^*_{Spec})$ to the leaves of PC^*_{Spec}, where PC^*_{Spec} is a nested-*ITE* expression with leaves that are term variables representing branch targets, and *ITE*-controlling formulas that are the enabling conditions for the updates of the PC along the implementation side of the diagram for liveness. Then, we can introduce an auxiliary circuit where a new latch is used to track whether each new update of the PC has value that is equal to new_PC_var, such that the latch is initialized with *false*, since the initial PC value is syntactically different from new_PC_var. This latch is updated under the same conditions that control the PC updates, but with the formula $(new\_PC\_var = new\_PC\_term)$, where new_PC_term is the new term that is written to the PC in that clock cycle. Furthermore, we can apply automatically a retiming trans-formation [25][26], and move the equation (*new_PC_var* = *new_PC_term*) across pipeline latches that provide versions of *new_PC_term* in different clock cycles. The effect is to replace the term-level signal for a version of *new_PC_term* in each pipeline latch with a bit-level signal, indicating whether the initial version of *new_PC_term* in that pipeline latch is syntactically equal to *new_PC_var*. This transformation replaces the term-level signal for branch targets with a bit-level signal, having initial values *false* in all pipeline latches (since the term variables representing the initial state of branch targets in pipeline latches are syntactically distinct from *new_PC_var*), while the value of this signal in the first pipeline stage is *true* (since the original term-level signal there is exactly *new_PC_var* that is fed both to the PC instead of the Sequen-tialPC and to the first pipeline latch). This transformation is applied entirely automati-cally. Thus, we obtain a modified circuit, where a new latch records whether the PC has been updated with *new_PC_var*, such that the new latch is controlled by the enable signal for the original PC (that is no longer needed), but is updated with formulas. The formula built in the new latch represents directly the result from evaluating (*new_PC_var* = PC^*_{Spec}) under a maximally diverse interpretation of the p-terms, and thus avoids the increase in memory and CPU time necessary for an EUFM decision procedure to evaluate (*new_PC_var* = PC^*_{Spec}). Damm et al. [9] also reduced the domain to {0, 1} when formally verifying pipelines with a certain structure.

11 Results

The processor benchmarks from Sect. 6 were first checked for safety—each bench-mark required less than 0.2 seconds—and then for liveness—see Tables 1 – 5. The term-level symbolic simulator TLSim [46] was used to symbolically simulate all mod-els. The resulting EUFM correctness formulas were translated to equivalent proposi-tional formulas by the decision procedure EVC [46] that then applied efficient translations to CNF [43][44][45]. Equations between g-term variables were encoded with the e_{ij} encoding [10]. The SAT-solvers siege_v4 [31] and BerkMin621 [11][12] —two of the top performers in the SAT'03 competition [21]—were used for all exper-iments; siege_v4 was faster on all of the resulting CNF formulas, but could not process a formula with more than 2^{19} CNF variables (see Table 2)—that formula was solved with BerkMin621. The computer was a Dell OptiPlex GX260 with a 3.06-GHz Intel Pentium 4, having a 512-KB on-chip L2-cache, 2 GB of memory, and running Red Hat Linux 9.0.

From Table 1, the previous method for indirect proof of liveness [42] (see Sect. 5) scaled up to the model with a 32-cycle ALU, DLX-ALU32, for which the proof took 2,483 seconds.

Table 2 shows the results after abstracting the branch targets and branch directions with oracles, thus making the branch targets and directions independent from the data operands, and then performing automatically a cone-of-influence reduction to elimi-nate all logic associated with the computation, transfer, and storage of operands (see Sect. 8). The time for the automatic cone-of-influence reduction was less than 0.1 sec-ond for each benchmark and is included in the time for symbolic simulation with

TLSim. This approach produced *3 orders of magnitude speedup* for DLX-ALU32, reducing the total time for the liveness check from 2,483 seconds to 1.6 second (1,552× speedup). For this benchmark, the CNF variables were reduced almost 3×, the clauses more than 10×, and the literals almost 50×. The approach enabled scaling up to the model with a 128-cycle ALU, for which the proof took 258 seconds.

Table 1. Results from the previous method for indirect proof of liveness by proving $pc_0 = false$ under a maximally diverse interpretation of the p-terms [42]

Processor	CNF			Formal Verification Time [sec]			
	Variables	Clauses	Literals	TLSim	EVC	SAT	Total
DLX-ALU4	3,249	32,239	142,749	0.02	0.49	0.05	0.56
DLX-ALU8	7,905	102,699	555,272	0.03	5.72	0.22	5.97
DLX-ALU16	18,597	381,414	2,937,085	0.03	42.53	1.36	44
DLX-ALU32	63,285	2,137,614	26,113,861	0.06	2,462.94	20.20	2,483

Table 2. Results from indirect proof of liveness after also abstracting the branch targets and branch directions with oracles, and performing a cone-of-influence reduction

Processor	CNF			Formal Verification Time [sec]			
	Variables	Clauses	Literals	TLSim	EVC	SAT	Total
DLX-ALU32	23,735	171,974	551,002	0.04	1.24	0.32	1.60
DLX-ALU64	165,159	1,195,077	3,841,960	0.08	12.31	37.59	50
DLX-ALU128	784,587	6,198,558	20,833,828	0.19	100.68	157.13[a]	258
DLX-ALU256	—	—	—	0.39	> mem.	—	—

a. BerkMin621 was used, since siege_v4 cannot process CNFs with more than 2^{19} variables.

Table 3. Results from indirect proof of liveness after also using a dedicated fresh term variable for all branch targets of newly fetched instructions, and abstracting the Instruction Memory with a generator of arbitrary values

Processor	CNF			Formal Verification Time [sec]			
	Variables	Clauses	Literals	TLSim	EVC	SAT	Total
DLX-ALU32	1,827	34,979	105,580	0.04	0.29	0.09	0.42
DLX-ALU64	5,635	220,243	663,052	0.08	1.79	0.88	2.75
DLX-ALU128	19,395	1,566,643	4,708,684	0.18	18.26	11.11	30
DLX-ALU256	71,491	11,832,947	35,532,748	0.46	234.36	158.13	393

Table 4. Results from indirect proof of liveness after also abstracting the multicycle ALU with a placeholder without feedback loops

Processor	CNF			Formal Verification Time [sec]			
	Variables	Clauses	Literals	TLSim	EVC	SAT	Total
DLX-ALU32	1,991	23,857	72,519	0.05	0.26	0.11	0.42
DLX-ALU64	5,959	130,369	392,887	0.11	1.08	0.61	1.80
DLX-ALU128	20,039	854,369	2,566,551	0.33	8.60	2.60	12
DLX-ALU256	72,775	6,181,281	18,550,615	1.78	92.30	36.24	130

Table 5. Results from indirect proof of liveness after also implementing the equation with the dedicated fresh term variable for the new PC values as an auxiliary circuit and avoiding the specification side of the diagram

Processor	CNF			Formal Verification Time [sec]			
	Variables	Clauses	Literals	TLSim	EVC	SAT	Total
DLX-ALU32	837	6,562	20,768	0.05	0.09	0.08	0.22
DLX-ALU64	1,783	21,278	63,129	0.11	0.22	0.35	0.68
DLX-ALU128	3,422	71,234	226,927	0.32	0.78	0.89	1.99
DLX-ALU256	6,995	259,793	914,040	1.77	3.46	13.95	19
DLX-ALU512	13,907	978,001	3,465,464	8.24	19.79	43.22	71
DLX-ALU1024	27,731	3,790,673	13,483,512	71	252	210	533
DLX-ALU2048	51,276	16,992,534	55,198,573	899	4,117	1,042	6,058

Table 3 presents the results after using a dedicated fresh term variable for all branch targets of newly fetched instructions, and abstracting the Instruction Memory with a generator of arbitrary values. This approach produced an order of magnitude speedup of the liveness check for the model with a 64-cycle ALU, DLX-ALU64, reducing the total time from 50 seconds to 2.75 seconds. The speedup was more than 8× for the model with a 128-cycle ALU, DLX-ALU128, for which the total time was reduced from 258 seconds to 30 seconds. Most importantly, this approach enabled scaling up to the model with a 256-cycle ALU, for which the proof took 393 seconds.

Table 4 presents the results after abstracting the multicycle ALU with a placeholder without feedback loops, and using a constraint to restrict the initial state of that place-holder so that it contains at most one valid instruction in the chain of $m - 1$ latches. Checking the invariance of this constraint took less than 1 second for each of the benchmarks. This approach resulted in 3× speedup of the liveness check for the model with a 256-cycle ALU, DLX-ALU256, reducing the total time from 393 seconds to 130 seconds. Furthermore, while the CNF variables increased only slightly, the CNF clauses and literals were almost halved for DLX-ALU128 and DLX-ALU256.

Table 5 presents the results after implementing the equation with the dedicated fresh term variable for the new PC values as an auxiliary circuit and avoiding the specifica-tion side of the diagram (see Sect. 10). The auxiliary circuit was introduced automati-cally—that required less than 0.2 seconds for each benchmark and the exact time is included in the time for symbolic simulation with TLSim. This approach resulted in a 6.5× speedup for the model with a 256-cycle ALU, DLX-ALU256, reducing the total time from 130 seconds to 19 seconds, while the CNF variables, clauses and literals were reduced by an order of magnitude. Most importantly, this approach enabled the scaling for the model with a 2048-cycle ALU, DLX-ALU2048, for which the liveness check took 6,058 seconds. *Note that the speedup for DLX-ALU32 is 4 orders of magni-tude relative to the previous method for indirect proof of liveness* (see Table 1).

12   Conclusions

Presented was an approach for proving liveness of pipelined processors with multicy-cle functional units, without the need for the user to set up an inductive argument. The method scaled for a 5-stage pipelined DLX with a 2048-cycle ALU, and resulted in 4 orders of magnitude speedup for a design with a 32-cycle ALU, compared to a previous method for indirect proof of liveness [42]. Given that functional units in recent state-of-the-art processors usually have latencies of up to $20-30$ cycles, and rarely up to 200 cycles, the presented approach will enable the automatic formal verification of liveness for realistic pipelined processors targeted to embedded and DSP applications. Future work will improve the scaling of the new approach.

References

[1] M.D. Aagaard, N.A. Day, and M. Lou, "Relating multi-step and single-step microprocessor correctness statements," *Forma l Methods in Computer-Aided Design (FMCAD '02)*, LNCS 2517, Springer-Verlag, November 2002.

[2] M.D. Aagaard, B. Cook, N.A. Day, and R.B. Jones, "A framework for superscalar microprocessor correctness statements," Software Tools for Technology Transfer (STTT), Vol. 4, No. 3 (May 2003).

[3] A. Biere, C. Artho, and V. Schuppan, "Liveness checking as safety checking," Electronic Notes in Theoretical Computer Science 66, 2002.

[4] V. Schuppan, and A. Biere, "Efficient reduction of finite state model checking to reachability analysis," International Journal on Software Tools for Technology Transfer (STTT), Vol. 5, No. 2–3, Springer-Verlag, March 2004.

[5] R.E. Bryant, S. German, and M.N. Velev, "Processor verification using efficient reductions of the logic of uninterpreted functions to propositional logic," ACM Transactions on Computational Logic (TOCL), Vol. 2, No. 1 (2001).

[6] R.E. Bryant, and M.N. Velev, "Boolean satisfiability with transitivity constraints," ACM Transactions on Computational Logic (TOCL), Vol. 3, No. 4 (October 2002), pp. 604–627.

[7] J.R. Burch, and D.L. Dill, "Automated verification of pipelined microprocessor control," *CAV '94*, June 1994.

[8] J.R. Burch, "Techniques for verifying superscalar microprocessors," *33rd Design Automation Conference (DAC '96)*, June 1996.

[9] W. Damm, A. Pnueli, and S. Ruah, "Herbrand Automata for Hardware Verification," *9th International Conference on Concurrency Theorey (CONCUR '88)*, D. Sangiorgi and R. de Simone, *eds.*, Springer-Verlag, LNCS 1466, 1988.

[10] A. Goel, K. Sajid, H. Zhou, A. Aziz, and V. Singhal, "BDD based procedures for a theory of equality with uninterpreted functions," *Computer-Aided Verification (CAV '98)*, LNCS 1427, Springer-Verlag, June 1998, pp. 244–255.

[11] E. Goldberg, and Y. Novikov, "BerkMin: A fast and robust sat-solver," *DATE '02*, March 2002, pp. 142–149.

[12] E. Goldberg, and Y. Novikov, SAT-solver BerkMin621, June 2003.

[13] J.L. Hennessy, and D.A. Patterson, *Computer Architecture: A Quantitative Approach*, 3rd ed., Morgan Kaufmann, San Francisco, 2002.

[14] T.A. Henzinger, S. Qadeer, and S.K. Rajamani, "Decomposing refinement proofs using assume-guarantee reasoning," *International Conference on Computer-Aided Design (ICCAD '00)*, 2000.

[15] R. Hosabettu, M. Srivas, and G. Gopalakrishnan, "Proof of correctness of a processor with reorder buffer using the completion functions approach," *Computer-Aided Verification (CAV '99)*, LNCS 1633, Springer-Verlag, 1999.

[16] C. Jacobi, and D. Kröning, "Proving the correctness of a complete microprocessor," *30. Jahrestagung der Gesellshaft für Informatik*, Springer-Verlag, 2000.

[17] D. Kröning, and W.J. Paul, "Automated pipeline design," *Design Automation Conference (DAC '01)*, June 2001.

[18] S. Lahiri, C. Pixley, and K. Albin, "Experience with term level modeling and verification of the M•CORE™ microprocessor core," *International Workshop on High Level Design, Validation and Test (HLDVT '01)*, November 2001.

[19] S.K. Lahiri, S.A. Seshia, and R.E. Bryant, "Modeling and verification of out-of-order microprocessors in UCLID," *Formal Methods in Computer-Aided Design (FMCAD '02)*, LNCS 2517, Springer-Verlag, November 2002.

[20] L. Lamport, "Proving the correctness of multiprocess programs," IEEE Trans. on Software Engineering," Vol. 3, No. 2 (1977).

[21] D. Le Berre, and L. Simon, "Results from the SAT'03 solver competition," *6th International Conference on Theory and Applications of Satisfiability Testing (SAT '03)*, 2003. http://www.lri.fr/~simon/contest03/results/

[22] S. Malik, A.R. Wang, R.K. Brayton, and A. Sangiovani-Vincentelli, "Logic Verification Using Binary Decision Diagrams in a Logic Synthesis Environment," *International Conference on Computer-Aided Design*, November 1988.

[23] P. Manolios, "Mechanical verification of reactive systems," Ph.D. Thesis, Computer Sciences, Univ. of Texas at Austin, 2001.

[24] P. Manolios, and S.K. Srinivasan, "Automatic verification of safety and liveness for XScale-like processor models using WEB refinements," *Design, Automation and Test in Europe (DATE '04)*, Vol. 1, February 2004.

[25] J. Matthews, and J. Launchbury, "Elementary microarchitecture algebra," *Computer-Aided Verification (CAV '99)*, N. Halbwachs, and D. Peled, *eds.*, LNCS 1633, Springer-Verlag, July 1999, pp. 288–300.

[26] J.R. Matthews, "Algebraic specification and verification of processor microarchitectures," Ph.D. Thesis, Department of Computer Science and Engineering, Oregon Graduate Institute of Science and Technology, October 2000.

[27] K.L. McMillan, "Circular compositional reasoning about liveness," Technical Report, Cadence Berkeley Labs, 1999.

[28] S.M. Müller, and W.J. Paul, *Computer Architecture: Complexity and Correctness*, Springer-Verlag, 2000.

[29] A. Pnueli, J. Xu, and L. Zuck, "Liveness with (0, 1, infinity)-counter abstraction," *CAV '02*, LNCS 2404, Springer-Verlag, July 2002.

[30] A. Pnueli, Y. Rodeh, O. Strichman, and M. Siegel, "The small model property: how small can it be?", Journal of Information and Computation, Vol. 178, No. 1 (October 2002), pp. 279–293.

[31] L. Ryan, Siege SAT Solver v.4. http://www.cs.sfu.ca/~loryan/personal/

[32] J. Sawada, "Verification of a simple pipelined machine model," in *Computer-Aided Reasoning: ACL2 Case Studies*, Kluwer Academic Publishers, Boston/Dordrecht/London, 2000.

[33] H. Sharangpani, and K. Arora, "Itanium processor microarchitecture," IEEE Micro, Vol. 20, No. 5 (2000).

[34] M.K. Srivas, and S.P. Miller, "Formal verification of an avionics microprocessor," Tech. Report CSL-95-4, SRI International, 1995.

[35] M.N. Velev, and R.E. Bryant, "Exploiting positive equality and partial non-consistency in the formal verification of pipelined microprocessors," *36th Design Automation Conference (DAC '99)*, June 1999.

[36] M.N. Velev, and R.E. Bryant, "Superscalar processor verification using efficient reductions of the logic of equality with uninterpreted functions to propositional logic," *CHARME '99*, LNCS 1703, September 1999, pp. 37–53.

[37] M.N. Velev, and R.E. Bryant, "Formal verification of superscalar microprocessors with multicycle functional units, exceptions, and branch prediction," *37th Design Automation Conference (DAC '00)*, June 2000.

[38] M.N. Velev, "Formal verification of VLIW microprocessors with speculative execution," *Computer-Aided Verification (CAV '00)*, E.A. Emerson, and A.P. Sistla, *eds.*, LNCS 1855, Springer-Verlag, July 2000.

[39] M.N. Velev, "Automatic abstraction of memories in the formal verification of superscalar microprocessors," *Tools and Algorithms for the Construction and Analysis of Systems (TACAS '01)*, LNCS 2031, April 2001, pp. 252–267.

[40] M.N. Velev, and R.E. Bryant, "Effective use of boolean satisfiability procedures in the formal verification of superscalar and VLIW microprocessors," Journal of Symbolic Computation (JSC), Vol. 35, No. 2 (February 2003).

[41] M.N. Velev, "Automatic abstraction of equations in a logic of equality," *Automated Reasoning with Analytic Tableaux and Related Methods (TABLEAUX '03)*, LNAI 2796, Springer-Verlag, September 2003.

[42] M.N. Velev, "Using positive equality to prove liveness for pipelined microprocessors," *Asia and South Pacific Design Automation Conference (ASP-DAC '04)*, January 2004.

[43] M.N. Velev, "Efficient translation of Boolean formulas to CNF in formal verification of microprocessors," *Asia and South Pacific Design Automation Conference (ASP-DAC '04)*, January 2004.

[44] M.N. Velev, "Exploiting signal unobservability for efficient translation to CNF in formal verification of microprocessors," *Design, Automation and Test in Europe (DATE '04)*, February 2004.

[45] M.N. Velev, Comparative Study of Strategies for Formal Verification of High-Level Processors, 22nd International Conference on Computer Design (ICCD '04), October 2004, pp. 119–124.

[46] M.N. Velev, and R.E. Bryant, "TLSim and EVC: A term-level symbolic simulator and an efficient decision procedure for the logic of equality with uninterpreted functions and memories," International Journal of Embedded Systems (IJES), Special Issue on Hardware-Software Codesign for Systems-on-Chip, 2004.

Efficient Symbolic Simulation via Dynamic Scheduling, Don't Caring, and Case Splitting

Viresh Paruthi[1], Christian Jacobi[2], and Kai Weber[2]

[1] IBM Systems Group, Austin, TX
[2] IBM Deutschland Entwicklung GmbH, Boeblingen, Germany

Abstract. Most computer-aided design frameworks rely upon building BDD representations from netlist descriptions. In this paper, we present efficient algorithms for building BDDs from netlists. First, we introduce a dynamic scheduling algorithm for building BDDs for gates of the netlist, using an efficient hybrid of depth- and breadth-first traversal, and constant propagation. Second, we introduce a dynamic algorithm for optimally leveraging constraints and invariants as *don't-cares* during the building of BDDs for intermediate gates. Third, we present an automated and complete *case splitting* approach which is triggered by resource bounds. Unlike prior work in case splitting which focused upon variable cofactoring, our approach leverages the full power of our don't-caring solution and intelligently selects arbitrary functions to apply as constraints to maximally reduce peak BDD size while minimizing the number of cases to be explored. While these techniques may be applied to enhance the building of BDDs for arbitrary applications, we focus on their application within cycle-based symbolic simulation. Experiments confirm the effectiveness of these synergistic approaches in enabling optimal BDD building with minimal resources.

1 Introduction

Many applications in computer-aided design rely to some degree upon building BDD representations from netlist descriptions, such as combinational and sequential equivalence checking, bounded, unbounded, and inductive property checking, and design optimization and abstraction algorithms. Even modern satisfiability solvers, increasingly finding applications in domains for which BDD-based techniques were long considered the only alternative (such as unbounded verification), are likely to use a hybrid-algorithm scheme integrating BDDs for optimality [16,15].

In this paper, we present an efficient set of synergistic algorithms for building BDDs from a netlist. First, we present a new scheduling algorithm for optimal BDD building. Our proposed resource-constrained interleaved depth-first and (modified) breadth-first schedule heuristically converges upon an optimal schedule for building BDDs. The scheme dynamically alternates between a depth-first and breadth-first schedule with progressively increasing resources until all BDDs for the netlist nodes have been built. Such a scheme combines the advantages of building BDDs with either of the two schedules, and augments it further by doing so in a resource-constrained manner resulting in a robust summation of their strengths. Furthermore the resource-constrained scheme handles constant propagation very efficiently which is particularly effective in property checking and equivalence checking frameworks.

D. Borrione and W. Paul (Eds.): CHARME 2005, LNCS 3725, pp. 114–128, 2005.

Second, we present a novel method to take advantage of constraints and invariants to optimize intermediate BDDs. Constraints arise as user-specified restrictions of the environment, and also as a means to perform manual case splitting for computational efficiency. Essentially, constraints and invariants are applied as don't-cares when building BDDs in an attempt to optimize their size by heuristically factoring in the constraints early. This is closely intertwined with the scheduling algorithm described above such as to realize its benefits at each step of the BDD building process. Additionally, this is controlled by BDD size thresholds resulting in a tight and robust algorithm that dynamically trades-off resources invested with the desired reduction in BDD sizes.

Third, we describe an automatic and complete case splitting strategy that decomposes the problem into smaller problems, thus enabling building BDDs of the netlist without exceeding resources. In addition to case splitting on inputs, we present techniques for case splitting on internal signals by *constraining* them to constant values, and propagating these constraints to other BDDs. This is equivalent to restricting the inputs in the support of the chosen internal signal to values that cause it to assume the selected constant value. Note that this nicely interacts with the resource-constrained BDD building and its efficient constant propagation, and with the don't-care optimization of intermediate node BDDs. We additionally present new heuristics to choose signals to case split upon. Completeness is ensured by applying all possible values to the case split inputs and signals. The method gracefully degrades into underapproximate analysis once global resources are exceeded by not exploring all case split branches.

In this paper we present the described algorithms in the context of a cycle-based symbolic simulation (CBSS) [5] engine. A CBSS performs a cycle-by-cycle symbolic simulation of the design under test, and thus extends the cycle simulation methodology to symbolic values. The simulator essentially performs forward bounded symbolic simulation starting from the initial states. Symbolic values (represented as BDD variables) are assigned to the inputs in every cycle and propagated through the circuit to the outputs and state variables. This technique enables simulating large input spaces in parallel due to the inputs assuming symbolic values at each time-step. The bottleneck of the approach lies in the possible explosion of the BDD representations of the netlist nodes and state variables; this is alleviated by our proposed BDD-building scheme, don't-care optimization, and case splitting strategy.

We briefly describe synergies of this engine with other transformation and verification algorithms in a *Transformation-Based Verification* (TBV) [18] framework. By utilizing a sequence of transformation engines we may achieve significant reductions in the size of the design in a manner that benefits simulating it symbolically using the described algorithm. Additionally, the simulator may be leveraged as a falsification and proof algorithm in a number of settings.

Related Work. Other researchers [20,21,23] have studied various scheduling techniques (e.g., DFS, BFS, hybrid) for BDD operations inside a BDD package, eg. in which order to traverse the BDD sub-graphs when ANDing two BDDs. The order of processing in BDD operations themselves is a different (and independent) question from the order in which BDDs for gates in a netlist are built. The latter question pertains to our work, and has also been studied by Aloul et al. [2]. They propose the use of partitioning and placement information to obtain a min-cut based scheduling for the gates, i.e. gates which are close together in the circuit are scheduled close together as well. A drawback of their method is that they spend a considerable amount of time obtaining a schedule. Our method is more robust and dynamically adapts itself to different circuit topologies.

Rather then looking at a schedule for the whole netlist, Murgai et al. [19] delve into finding an optimal schedule for combining BDDs at the inputs of a multi-input AND gate when attempting to build the BDD for the gate output. They select which two BDDs to combine next based on a size- and support-based analysis of the candidate BDDs. Their approach is complementary to our approach and may easily be integrated into our overall netlist schedule. DFS and BFS are commonly used schedules for building BDDs for netlists. We extend these by proposing a hybrid DFS-BFS schedule for this task and further optimize by building BDDs in a resource-constrained manner and propagating constants efficiently.

Algorithms for optimizing BDDs with respect to don't-care sets has been studied in [10,11]. We utilize and extend these algorithms by dynamically choosing the BDD-minimization algorithm based on size thresholds. We additionally propose the novel application of constraints as don't-cares during intermediate BDD building which often substantially reduces peak BDD size.

Wilson et al. [22] use ternary symbolic simulation (X-values) to abstract internal nodes to deal with the computational complexity. They also briefly mention case splitting on input variables, but do not detail their algorithms for selecting case split nodes, or the management of case splits. Our method extends their work by also being able to split upon internal nodes and using different heuristics to select nodes to case split upon. Completeness in our approach is ensured by symbolically simulating all possible values of the case split inputs and signals, and is handled automatically unlike the manual case splitting technique presented in [1]. In contrast to the approximating approach presented by Bertacco et al. [5,6] our approach is complete in that it checks the design exhaustively.

A recent body of work addresses the generally exponential relation between the number of variables in the support of a BDD and its size by *reparameterizing* the representation onto a smaller set of variables, e.g. [4]. This technique has been extended to cycle-based symbolic simulation by reparameterizing unfolded input variables [5,6,8]. Such approaches are complementary to the techniques presented in this paper. Our techniques may be used to more efficiently compute the desired BDDs for the functions to be reparameterized. After reparameterization, our approach may again be used to continue the computations, seeded by the results of the reparameterization.

Organization. The rest of the paper is organized as follows. The next section (Section 2) introduces some notation used throughout the paper to aid in describing our approach. Section 3 gives a high-level overview of the CBSS algorithm. In Section 4 we present an optimal scheduling technique for building BDDs for gates in a netlist representation of a design. Next we describe a method to optimally utilize constraints and invariants in Section 5. Section 6 describes efficient techniques to perform case splitting to deal with the complexity of symbolic analysis, and Section 7 delves into synergies of symbolic simulation with other algorithms in a Transformation-Based Verification framework. Lastly we present experimental results in Section 8, followed by concluding the paper.

2   Netlists: Syntax and Semantics

A *netlist* is a tuple $N = \langle\langle V, E\rangle, G, Z\rangle$ comprising a directed graph with nodes V and edges $E \subseteq V \times V$. Function $G : V \mapsto types$ represents a semantic mapping from nodes to gate *types*, including constants, primary inputs (i.e., nondeterministic bits), registers (denoted as the set $R \subset V$), and combinational gates with various functions. Function $Z : R \mapsto V$ is the initial value mapping $Z(v)$ of each register v, where $Z(v)$ may not contain registers in its transitive fanin cone. The *semantics of a netlist N* are defined in terms of traces: $\{0, 1\}$ valuations to netlist nodes over time which are consistent with G. We denote the value of gate v at time i in trace p by $p(v, i)$.

Our verification problem is represented entirely as a netlist, and consists of a set of *targets* $T \subseteq V$ correlating to a set of properties $AG(\neg t), \forall t \in T$. We thus assume that the netlist is a composition of the *design under test*, its *environment* (encoding *input assumptions*), and its *property automata*. The goal of the verification process is to find a way to drive a '1' to a target node, or to prove that no such assertion of the target is possible. If the former, a counterexample trace showing the sequence of assignments to the inputs in every cycle leading up to the fail is generated.

A set of *constraints* $C \subseteq V$ may be used to filter the stimulus that can be applied to the design. In the presence of constraints, a target $t \in T$ is defined to be hit in trace $p \in P$ at cycle i if $p(t, i) = 1$ and $p(c, i') = 1$ for all $c \in C, i' \leq i$. A target is *unreachable* if it cannot be hit along any path. Algorithmically, when searching for a way to drive a '1' to a target, the verification process must prune its search along paths which violate constraints.

A set of *invariants* $I \subseteq V$ specify properties inherent in the design itself. I.e. invariants will always evaluate to '1' in every time-step along every trace, at least until a constraint is violated. Invariants encode "truths" about a design that may be utilized as constraints to tighten overapproximate techniques (such as induction) to enhance proof capability. Invariants may be generated using a variety of mechanisms, e.g. the negation of targets previously proven unreachable.

We map all designs into a netlist representation containing only primary inputs, one "constant zero" node, 2-input AND gates, inverters, and registers, using straightforward logic synthesis techniques to eliminate more complex gate types [16]. Inverters are represented implicitly as edge attributes in the representation.

3   Background

A Cycle-based Symbolic Simulator (CBSS) [5] performs a cycle-by-cycle symbolic simulation of the design under test, typically using BDDs. It applies symbolic values at the inputs in every cycle, and propagates those to the state-variables and targets. Hence, state-variables and targets are always expressed in terms of symbolic input values, i.e., as Boolean functions of the symbolic inputs applied in the current and all prior cycles. If a target is hit, counterexample traces are generated by simply assigning concrete values to the symbolic input values in the cycles leading up to the fail.

Figure 1 gives an outline of the algorithm. The algorithm applies symbolic inputs in the form of new BDD variables at the inputs in every cycle, in func-

```
Algorithm cycle_sym(num_cycles) {
  for (cycle_num = 0; cycle_num ≤ num_cycles; cycle_num++) {
    create_variables(inputs); // Create new BDD variables for inputs in the current cycle
    if (cycle_num == 0) {
      build_node_bdds(initial_state_fns); // Build BDDs for the initial states
      update_state_variables(initial_state_fns); // Initialize the design
    }
    build_node_bdds(constraints); // Build BDDs for the constraints
    build_node_bdds(targets); // Build BDDs for the targets
    constrain_node_bdds(targets, constraints); // Constrain target BDDs
    check_targets(targets); // Check targets for being hit
    if (all_targets_solved(targets)) return;
    build_node_bdds(next_state_fns); // Build BDDs for the next-functions
    update_state_variables(next_state_fns); // Update state-vars
  }
}
```

Fig. 1. Generic cycle-based symbolic simulation algorithm

tion **create_variables**. At the outset, BDDs for the initial-states of the state-variables are computed and stored at the respective state-variables via function **update_state_variables**. Next, BDDs for the constraints and targets are obtained by evaluating the combinational logic of the netlist starting with the new BDD variables at the inputs and the current BDDs at the state-variables. The computation of the constraints ANDs the constraint valuations (BDDs) from the previous cycles to the BDDs obtained for the constraint nodes in the current cycle. These "accumulated" constraint BDDs are then ANDed with the target BDDs (function **constrain_node_bdds**) before the targets are checked for being hit in function **check_targets** to ensure that the target valuations are consistent with the *care set* defined by the constraints. Thereafter, the combinational next-state logic of the state-variables is evaluated (again starting at the current BDD variables of the primary inputs and current state-variable BDDs), followed by updating the state-variables with the valuations obtained at the respective next-state functions. The process is iterated until all targets are *solved* (i.e. hit) or the design has been simulated symbolically for the specified maximum number of cycles.

4   Dynamic BDD Scheduling Algorithm

The bulk of the time during symbolic simulation is spent building BDDs for nodes in a netlist graph (function **build_node_bdds** in Fig. 1). A set of nodes whose BDDs are required to be built at each step, called "sinks," are identified. Sinks correspond to targets, constraints, invariants, initial-state and next-state functions of state variables. BDDs of some netlist nodes are available at the beginning of each cycle, namely those of the current content of state-variables, and new BDD variables created for the primary inputs (function **create_variables** in Fig. 1). The BDD building task is to compute BDDs for the sink nodes, starting at nodes for which BDDs exist, according to the semantics of the gates in the underlying combinational network.

It is known that different schedules for building BDDs for nodes of a netlist lead to significantly different peak numbers of BDD nodes [19,2]. It is of utmost importance that this peak number be kept as low as possible. A large number of BDD nodes results in bad memory and cache performance, and severely degrades performance of expensive optimization algorithms such as Dynamic Variable Reordering (DVO) and Garbage Collection. Optimal DVO has an impractically high computational complexity in the worst case (the problem is known to be NP-Hard [7]). Practical DVO approaches look for local minima based on time or memory limitations. They are likely to find better variable orderings when they are called on smaller number of active BDD nodes.

The BDDs for the sink nodes are built topologically starting at the inputs and state-variables, nodes for which BDDs exist at the beginning of a cycle. Two standard and commonly used schedules for building BDDs are depth-first (DFS) traversal of the netlist starting at the sink nodes, and breadth-first (BFS) traversal starting at the inputs and state-variables. Each of the two schedules have certain advantages and drawbacks depending on the structure of the netlist. Intuitively, when a netlist has many "independent components" which do not fan out to other parts of the netlist, DFS is often more efficient. This is because it builds BDDs for the components successively, hence only has the intermediate BDDs of a single component "alive" at any time. The algorithm is able to free BDDs for nodes in the component as soon as BDDs of their fanouts have been built. In contrast, the levelized nature of BFS builds BDDs of all components simultaneously causing many intermediate BDDs to be "alive" at the same time. But if a netlist node n has many fanouts, each processed by DFS along separate branches, the levelized BFS schedule is likely to perform better. The BDD for n can be freed as soon as all fanout gates of n are built, which often happens sooner with BFS particularly when the fanouts of n are level-wise close to n. This reduces the average "lifetime" of BDDs thus reducing the peak number of alive nodes. The experimental results in Section 8 demonstrate that each method outperforms the other method on some examples.

We extend the standard DFS- and BFS-based BDD building algorithms by applying them in a resource-constrained manner, using the algorithm of Figure 2. The algorithm builds BDDs for netlist nodes per the chosen schedule, but builds BDDs for gates in the netlist only up to a certain BDD size limit, i.e. it gives up building the BDD for a node if it exceeds an imposed size limit. After all node BDDs within this limit have been built, the limit is increased and the algorithm is applied again. We extend this further by alternating between DFS- and BFS-based schedules. Once all node BDDs within the current size limit have been built, the algorithm increases the size limit and switches to the other BDD building schedule. Such an interleaved hybrid DFS-BFS scheme brings together both a DFS and a BFS scheme in a tight and robust integration combining the advantages of both, and alleviating some of their drawbacks. The new scheme works in a "push-pull" manner by going back and forth between the two schedules. The DFS or the "pull" scheme uncovers any paths building BDDs along which may suffice to build the BDD for a sink node. The "push" or the levelized BFS traversal causes BDDs to be propagated quickly from the inputs toward the outputs with a tight control on the consumed resources.The resource limits further ensure that the overall algorithm does not get stuck in any one computation that does not contribute to the final result.

Building BDDs iteratively in a resource-constrained manner has several advantages over conventional approaches. First, since we restrict the BDD sizes at each iteration, DVO algorithms are able to converge on a good variable order when BDDs are small, causing larger BDDs that are computed later to be more compact and smaller. Second, the resource-constrained scheme ensures that nodes that have small BDDs can be computed and gotten out of the way early (and subsequently freed), to "make way" for larger BDDs later. Third, the resource-constrained algorithm can uncover and propagate constants very effectively. Note that if an input to an AND gate evaluates to a constant '0' there is no need to evaluate its other input function. Traditional BDD building approaches may spend a large amount of time and memory computing the BDD of that other fanin node function. Our resource-bounded scheme will effectively iterate between evaluating the function of both the fanin nodes under increasing size limits. If BDD size limits along either branch are exceeded, the scheme gives up building the BDD for this branch and moves on to the next node in the schedule, heuristically discovering the constant without the need to evaluate the more complex branch. This situation arises frequently in real designs, e.g. at multiplexers where some multiplexer data input functions may have significantly higher BDD complexity than the others and the selector signal is a constant, thus enabling the multiplexer to be evaluated by sampling the simpler data input. Once we discover a constant at a node we recursively propagate it along all the fanouts of this node.

We generalize this further to efficiently derive constants at partially evaluated multi-input AND (and OR) gates. It is frequently the case that the BDD for such a gate cannot be computed due to exceeding BDD size limits on some of the inputs, but the available BDDs together already imply a constant for the gate output, for example due to complimentary inputs along two branches. We recognize and exploit this situation by building a "partial" BDD for the multi-input AND structure by successively combining BDDs of the available fanin nodes within the current BDD size limit. If this evaluates to a constant at any point, we don't need to build the BDDs for the remaining fanin nodes, and instead we trigger constant propagation as described above.

5   Dynamic Don't Caring Under Constraints and Invariants

Constraints are often used in verification to prune the possible input stimulus of the design. Semantically, the verification tool must discard any states for which a constraint evaluates to a '0'. In that sense, constraints impose "hard restrictions" on the evaluations performed by the verification tool, splitting the input space into two parts - the "valid" or the "care" set, and the "invalid" or the "don't-care" set. In the CBSS algorithm this is achieved by ANDing the accumulated constraints of the current and past cycles to the targets before they are checked for being hit. Recall that, during overapproximate search, our framework treats invariants as constraints.

We have found that constraints may be efficiently exploited as don't-cares to optimize intermediate BDDs during the course of the overall computation. This is achieved by modifying the intermediate BDDs in a manner such that they evaluate to the same Boolean values within the care set, but they are free to assume values in the don't-care set towards the goal of minimizing the size of the BDD [10,11]. In some applications of constraints, like manual case splitting [13], or automatic case splitting (cf. Sect. 6), this minimization is key to the successful completion of the symbolic simulation without memory explosion.

We present a technique to exploit constraints and invariants optimally in a symbolic simulation setting. At each time-step of the symbolic simulation process BDDs for the

Algorithm build_node_bdds(*sink_nodes*) {
   // Compute DFS and BFS schedules for nodes in the cone-of-influence
   dfs_schedule = **compute_dfs_schedule**(*sink_nodes*);
   bfs_schedule = **compute_bfs_schedule**(*sink_nodes*);
   bdd_size_limit = INITIAL_BDD_SIZE_LIMIT;
   while (1) {
      // Attempt building BDDs within the current bdd-size-limit using a DFS schedule
      build_node_bdds_aux(*dfs_schedule, bdd_size_limit*);
      if (**all_sink_node_bdds_built**(*sink_nodes*))
         return SUCCESS;
      if (*bdd_size_limit* ≥ MAX_BDD_SIZE_LIMIT))
         return INCOMPLETE;
      bdd_size_limit = *bdd_size_limit* + DELTA_BDD_SIZE_LIMIT;
      // Attempt building BDDs within the current bdd-size-limit using a BFS schedule
      build_node_bdds_aux(*bfs_schedule, bdd_size_limit*);
      if (**all_sink_node_bdds_built**(*sink_nodes*)
         return SUCCESS;
      if (*bdd_size_limit* ≥ MAX_BDD_SIZE_LIMIT)
         return INCOMPLETE;
      bdd_size_limit = *bdd_size_limit* + DELTA_BDD_SIZE_LIMIT;
   }
}

Fig. 2. Interleaved DFS-BFS resource-constrained BDD building algorithm

constraints and invariants are computed and subsequently applied as don't-cares when building BDDs for the netlist nodes. This is done in a manner that ensures BDD sizes do not increase as a result of the don't-caring. The don't-caring is done by using one of the BDD *constrain* [10], *restrict* [10] and *compact* [11] operations. These algorithms ensure that the BDD valuations within the care set are unchanged, but for all values outside the care set they freely choose a '0' or a '1' value to minimize the BDD size.

Intuitively, don't-caring heuristically factors in the constraints early, and doing so helps to reduce the BDD representation of the intermediate nodes. The behaviors added by the intermediate application of the don't-cares will ultimately be eliminated before targets are checked for being hit (function **constrain_node_bdds** in Fig. 1). In a sense, our scheme rules out and/or adds behaviors precluded by the constraints early on by application of the constraints when building intermediate BDDs, as opposed to doing this only at the end once all the exact BDDs have been built.

Exact minimization is known to be NP-hard [11]; the *constrain, restrict*, and *compact* operators are therefore heuristic minimization algorithms. In the listed order, they are increasingly powerful in minimizing BDD sizes, at the cost of (often dramatically) increased runtime. Therefore, in our symbolic simulation algorithm we apply the cheapest, or the least computationally expensive, operation *constrain* first, and depending on size thresholds automatically switch to more expensive algorithms. This ensures a dynamic compromise between time and memory requirements. Also, this threshold-based scheme applies the cheap and fast minimization operation to the many small BDDs, and applies the more expensive operations to the only (hopefully) few large BDDs.

```
Algorithm dont_care_node_bdd(node_bdd, constraint_bdds) {
    if (bdd_size(node_bdd) < BDD_SIZE_THRESHOLD_CONSTRAIN)
        return node_bdd; // return if too small
    foreach (constraint_bdd in constraint_bdds) {
        if (supports_intersect(node_bdd, constraint_bdd)) {
            res_bdd = bdd_constrain_threshold(node_bdd, constraint_bdd); // constrain
            if (bdd_size(res_bdd) ≥ BDD_SIZE_THRESHOLD_RESTRICT)
                res_bdd = bdd_restrict_threshold(node_bdd, constraint_bdd); // restrict
            if (bdd_size(res_bdd) ≥ BDD_SIZE_THRESHOLD_COMPACT)
                res_bdd = bdd_compact(node_bdd, constraint_bdd); // compact
            node_bdd = res_bdd;
        }
    }
    return node_bdd;
}
```

Fig. 3. Algorithm for optimizing node BDDs using don't-cares

Note that some verification problems use constraints only for restricting the input stimulus, and have only minimal BDD reduction potential. Applying the expensive minimization algorithms to such designs will only marginally decrease the BDD size, but may have a severe impact on runtime. For such problems it is best to set the thresholds of the expensive operations very high. The *constrain* operator is so fast that it usually is worthwhile even on such examples.

Figure 3 gives an outline of the algorithm. Whenever a BDD for a netlist node has been built, the BDD is optimized by applying all the constraint BDDs as don't-cares, in function **dont_care_node_bdd**.[1] If the BDD size is below the threshold for the application of the *constrain* operator, the function immediately returns. Otherwise, any don't-caring first checks for the intersection of the cone-of-influence of the BDDs of the constraints with that of the node (function **supports_intersect**), and applies only those constraints that have some overlap. Functions **bdd_constrain_threshold** and **bdd_restrict_threshold** apply the *constrain* and *restrict* operators respectively, but additionally ensure that the size of the resultant BDD is no greater than the argument BDD by returning the argument BDD if the application of these operators causes the BDD size to increase (which is possible [10]).

It may be noted that the BDD for a constraint in any time-step is a conjunction of the BDD obtained for it in the current and all previous time-steps. If at any point the BDD for the constraint becomes a zero BDD, it implies that the design does not have a legal state-space beyond this time-step and any unsolved targets are trivially unreachable.

6   Automated Case Splitting

In this section we describe automated case splitting strategies to ameliorate the BDD explosion which may occur during symbolic simulation. The described method ensures that the total number of BDD nodes does not exceed a specified limit, ultimately enabling symbolic simulation to complete computations which otherwise would be prone

---

[1] Note that we cannot use don't-care minimization when building BDDs for the constraint nodes themselves; if we did, we could alter their care set.

to memory-out conditions. In our proposed method we address the memory blow-up when computing intermediate BDDs as follows:

- If the total number of BDD nodes exceed a certain threshold, we select a netlist node to case split on, and a constant value to be applied to the selected node.
- Upon case splitting the BDD sizes drop significantly and we continue with the symbolic analysis. Note that we may case split on any number of netlist nodes at different steps and stages of the symbolic simulation.
- Once the symbolic analysis completes, i.e. the design has been symbolically simulated for the required number of time-steps, we "backtrack" to the last case split (and the time-step in which it was applied) and set the selected netlist node to the other constant, and complete the symbolic analysis on this branch. This is continued until all case splits are covered, ensuring completeness.

All case splits are entered onto a stack that snapshots BDDs for the non-chosen value of the case split node (and discards the current BDDs at the node) to enable back-tracking to this case split. The case splitting decomposes the problem into significantly smaller subproblems each of which is then individually discharged. Expensive BDD operations such as DVO benefit greatly from such a decomposition due to the subproblems being much smaller, and the fact that they can be solved independently of the others; in particular, DVO can apply different variable orderings along different branches of the case splits. A parallel may be drawn between case splitting and satisfiability (SAT) approaches with the case split nodes representing decision variables - the BDDs encode all possible solutions of the netlist nodes for the particular value of the case split node as opposed to SAT systematically exploring the solutions one-by-one.

We propose two techniques to select the netlist node or nodes to case split upon. We have found these to be very effective in managing space complexity of BDD operations. We describe these in the context of selecting a single node to case split upon, but they can be easily extended to case split on multiple nodes in one step:

- *Case split on the "fattest" variable(s)*. The fattest variable, at a given point in time, is defined as a variable that has the largest number of BDD nodes in all the live BDDs. Hence, setting this variable to a constant causes the largest reduction in the number of BDD nodes.
- *Case split on an internal node via constraining*. Here we select a netlist node other than inputs to case split upon based on algorithmic analysis. The analysis may include the reduction potential by examining the netlist graph and BDDs available for internal nodes. Next, the BDD for the selected case split node or its inverse is treated as a constraint, which is then added to the list of constraints as a *derived* constraint. The new constraint is subsequently used for minimizing all other BDDs by means of don't-caring as described in the previous section. The derived constraint is later removed from the list of constraints when the algorithm backtracks. For the other branch of the split, the inverse of the case split BDD is applied as a constraint. As an example, we may try don't-caring all live BDDs with the BDD for each node, and select the one that gives maximal reduction. Note that a constraint is effectively a restriction on the variables in its support and divides the input space according to the constraint BDD. Essentially, case splitting on an internal netlist node

in a certain cycle of the symbolic simulation is equivalent to removing the logic in the cone-of-influence of this node up to the current time-step in an unfolded version of the netlist - and then using the Boolean consequences of this reduction for minimizing other BDDs.

If the global resources are exhausted this case splitting gracefully degrades into underapproximate analysis by not exploring all branches. In underapproximate analysis, at every case split the algorithm heuristically chooses the branch to explore next, which enables semi-formal analysis. For example, the case split algorithm can be configured to always select the simpler branch first (i.e. the smaller one after case splitting) in order to reach very deep into the state space. Using underapproximate symbolic simulation thus balances the benefits of standard binary simulation (reaching very deep) with the power of symbolic simulation, effectively simulating a large number of input combinations in parallel, hence visiting a large number of states.

7   Transformation Synergies

Here we briefly sketch scenarios and interactions of this engine with other algorithms that we have found to be useful. We have deployed the symbolic simulator as an engine in the IBM internal TBV [18] system *SixthSense*. Such a system is capable of maximally exploiting the synergy of the transformation and verification algorithms encapsulated in the system as engines against the verification problem under consideration.

Approaches that build BDDs from netlist representations tend to benefit dramatically from prior simplifying transformations applied to the netlist. For example, redundancy removal and logic rewriting algorithms [16] that reduce the number of gates in the netlist reduce the number of distinct BDDs that need to be built, and may even reduce the cutwidth of the netlist implying a need for fewer live BDD nodes. In a CBSS approach, reductions to the sequential netlist are particularly useful, as they reduce the complexity of every subsequent time-frame of the symbolic evaluation. In particular, we have found the input reductions enabled by structurally abstracting the netlist through reparameterization [4] to be very beneficial to symbolic simulation, often times improving performance by orders of magnitude. Note that this is complementary to traditional approaches that reparameterize state sets during symbolic simulation [1,5,6,8]. In fact, both these can be combined into a powerful two-step process that reparameterizes the structural sequential netlist, followed by reparameterizing the next-state BDDs at every time-step of the symbolic simulation.

In a semi-formal setting when performing a directed search of the state-space of the design, symbolic simulation performs a broad simulation of the design within specified resources. The engine thus uncovers large portions of the state space, and allows for probabilistically uncommon scenarios to be exposed that cause the fail events to be hit. When performing an exhaustive k-step bounded model check of the design, the symbolic simulator often outperforms SAT-based bounded model checking [16], particularly when the number of inputs is not too large or for small values of k. Additionally, we have found this engine to be very useful when attempting proofs via k-step BDD-based induction. Furthermore, the engine may be used to obtain proofs in conjunction with an engine that computes a *diameter* estimate of the design [3].

Table 1. Details of examples used in the experiments

| S.No. | Design | Design Size | | | | | |
		#Inputs	#Registers	#Gates	#Targets	#Constraints	#Cycles
1	FPU_ADD	440	5025	79105	84	5	26
2	FPU_FMA	452	5785	72272	82	4	18
3	IBM_03	25	119	2460	1	2	33
4	IBM_06	37	140	3157	1	2	32
5	SLB	57	692	3754	1	0	8
6	CHI	112	92	732	1	0	9
7	SCU	71	187	810	1	0	23

Table 2. BDD node count and runtimes for the different schedules without DVO

| S.No. | DFS | | Res. DFS | | BFS | | Res. BFS | | DFS-BFS | |
	T(s)	$N(10^6)$	T(s)	$N(10^6)$	T(s)	$N(10^6)$	T(s)	$N(10^6)$	T(s)	$N(10^6)$
1	inf	inf	40.06	0.17	inf	inf	45.46	0.24	40.22	0.17
2	inf	inf	14580	101.14	inf	inf	inf	inf	10399	96.78
3	57.2	3.12	54.7	3.14	59.1	3.75	58.1	3.68	52.1	3.14
4	7392	96.56	7916	111.39	8991	129.79	8150	118.23	7897	106.60
5	1901	329.44	2094	291.84	1982	304.73	1976	291.84	1832	291.83
6	1000	91.26	907	83.85	1019	89.27	1021	88.57	910	85.94
7	112	6.58	91	6.18	120	74.31	113	74.08	84	6.28

Localization [17] augmented with counterexample-guided abstraction refinement [9] has been shown to be an effective technique for obtaining proofs. Such paradigms rely upon exhaustive bounded search to provide counterexamples from which to refine the abstracted design. A symbolic simulation engine is apt for performing such bounded analysis of the localized design. Additionally, the exhaustive representation using BDDs may be inherently exploited to derive minimally sized refinements.

8   Experimental Results and Conclusions

In order to gauge the effectiveness of various aspects of our symbolic simulation algorithm we chose a diverse set of industrial designs to conduct our experiments on (see Table 1). All experiments were run on an IBM pSeries computer with POWER4 processors running at 1.4GHz using the IBM internal verification tool *SixthSense*. All designs were put through reductions using a BDD-based combinational redundancy removal engine [16] before the symbolic simulator was applied. FPU_ADD and FPU_FMA are the verification problems of the dataflow for a floating-point "add" and "fused-multiply-add" instruction respectively [13]. IBM_03 and IBM_06 are examples from the IBM Formal Verification Benchmarks [12]. These were randomly chosen from among those with constraints. SLB is a Segment Lookaside Buffer, CHI is a Channel Interface and SCU is a Storage Control Unit. SLB, CHI, and SCU are optimized control intensive circuits that have been put through a number of design transformations.

We ran experiments to measure the resources (time/memory) required to symbolically simulate the above designs with all three scheduling schemes, namely BFS, DFS and DFS-BFS, in different settings. In order to show the benefits of resource constrain-

Table 3. BDD node count and runtimes for the different schedules with DVO

S.No.	DFS		Res. DFS		BFS		Res. BFS		DFS-BFS	
	T(s)	N(10^6)	T(s)	N(10^6)	T(s)	N(10^6)	T(s)	N(10^6)	T(s)	N(10^6)
3	236	2.54	239	2.65	168	2.98	172	2.97	215	2.64
4	24507	94.13	25135	100.19	26979	100.91	26103	101.47	24369	100.01
5	648	7.7	577	6.80	1122	14.78	1127	7.68	631	6.81
6	2643	61.39	1346	53.43	3042	16.86	2270	25.66	2000	30.69
7	382	59.66	398	55.57	582	69.35	524	67.48	311	56.40

Table 4. BDD node count and runtimes with and without don't-caring using constraints

S.No.	Without don't-caring		With don't-caring	
	Time(s)	Nodes(10^6)	Time(s)	Nodes(10^6)
1	inf	inf	40.22	0.17
2	inf	inf	10399	96.78
3	48.44	3.50	52.11	3.14
4	7990	109.40	7897	106.60

ing, we ran the DFS and BFS schemes with and without resource constraints. The results are given in Table 2. A value of "inf" indicates that the particular run exploded (> 500 million) in the number of BDD nodes. The "#Nodes" in the tables is the peak number of BDD nodes reported by the BDD package [14]. In the first set of experiments we turned Dynamic Variable Reordering (DVO) off to get a true comparison since DVO can skew results due to its heuristic nature. The table also compares and contrasts the three scheduling techniques. The benefits of resource constraining are amply clear from the results. It is indispensable for the FPU designs where we see the runs explode without any resource constraining, and go through easily with resource constraining. This is likely due to the propagation of a large number of constants which resource constraining specializes in taking advantage of, in particular when many such constants are created due to constraints [13]. The effects are somewhat less pronounced in some other examples due to the fact that they have symbolic initial values or are highly optimized, causing less constants to propagate. Note that resource constraining is inherent in the hybrid DFS-BFS interleaved scheme as it enables switching between the two underlying schemes. It is clear that each of DFS and BFS outperforms the other on different examples. The hybrid DFS-BFS scheme clearly stands out as the most robust, and nicely combines the individual benefits of DFS and BFS schedules. By and large it has a peak number of BDD nodes that is close to or less than the lower of the peaks of the two underlying schemes, and runtime that is close to or better than the faster one.

We repeated the above experiment this time with DVO enabled (Table 3). We observed a somewhat similar pattern, though things varied a bit more. We attribute this to the heuristic nature of DVO, and the fact that we used low effort DVO. The heuristic nature of DVO is clearly demonstrated by the FPU examples that explode now in both non-resource-constrained as well as in the resource-constrained case. The hybrid DFS-BFS scheme again comes across as the best overall and shows consistent performance in different scenarios re-enforcing our claim. It provides the benefits of both resource constraining as well as a summation of the strengths of DFS and BFS schedules resulting in a powerful and robust approach that works for all cases.

Table 5. BDD node count and runtimes with and without case splitting using constraints

Design	Target Status	No case splitting		Case split on fattest variables			Evaluation
		T(s)	N(10⁶)	T(s)	N(10⁶)	#Cases	
2	Reachable	57.11	3.48	40.07	1.06	4(0)	Underapprox
4	Reachable	7897	106.6	16097	11.70	5(4)	Underapprox
5	Unreachable	631	6.81	570	6.24	3	Complete
6	Unreachable	910	85.94	806	36.44	4	Complete

Next we measured the impact of handling constraints as don't-cares during inter-mediate BDD building. The hybrid DFS-BFS scheme was used for the purposes of this experiment. The results are summarized in Table 4. Only designs containing con-straints were used for this experiment. The intermediate don't-caring using constraints (cf. Section 5) is absolutely essential to get the FPU examples through - the runs simply explode otherwise. The impact of factoring in constraints early can have a significant impact on reducing intermediate BDD sizes, or it may not depending on the nature of the constraints and the design. If a constraint prunes a fair amount of the input stimulus it may be very effective in reducing BDD sizes, but on the other hand if the BDDs of the internal nodes are already optimized then it may not do much. Hence, in our scheme we use threshold based don't-caring that is cheap for the most part, and apply more aggressive but computationally complex don't-caring only for very large BDDs. Such an approach was essential to automatic verification of FPUs as described in [13].

Lastly, we ran those designs with a large number of nodes with case splitting enabled (Table 5). The results are a mix of underapproximate evaluation (with some backtracks) for designs in which the targets were hittable, and others for which complete case split-ting was done to prove that the targets are not hittable boundedly. The benefits of case splitting in both cases is clear. It helps to hit the reachable targets much sooner while visiting a large number of states of the design and within resources bounds, and enables completing exhaustive bounded checks on designs with unreachable targets without ex-ploding in memory. Essentially, it trades-off complexity in memory with time, but is a compromise that is worth it to complete analysis on a design which otherwise may not - though for example #6 the overall performance is much better possibly due to a re-duced number of BDD nodes to deal with. The numbers in parenthesis in the "#Cases" column indicates the number of case splits for which the other branch was evaluated as well. Hence, in the case of example #4, 4 of the 5 case splits were fully evaluated. Case splitting on internal nodes was necessary to verify FPU designs using formal methods in a fully-automated manner, as detailed in [13].

Conclusion. We presented a robust set of algorithms for building BDDs efficiently for netlists. We presented a scheduling scheme that dynamically converges upon a heuris-tically optimal schedule for computing BDDs using an efficient hybrid of depth- and breadth-first search called out in an interleaved manner under resource constraints. We introduced a dynamic algorithm, tightly integrated with the scheduling scheme, to opti-mally leverage constraints and invariants as don't-cares when building BDDs for inter-mediate gates in the netlist. Additionally, we described an automatic and complete case splitting approach that is triggered and controlled by resource bounds to decompose the overall problem into simpler parts which are then solved individually. The presented approach takes advantage of the full power of our don't-caring solution and smartly selects arbitrary functions to apply as constraints to maximally reduce peak BDD size while minimizing the number of cases to be explored.

References

1. M. D. Aagaard, R. B. Jones, and C.-J. H. Seger. Formal verification using parametric representations of Boolean constraints. In *DAC*, 1999.
2. F. A. Aloul, I. L. Markov, and K. A. Sakallah. Improving the efficiency of Circuit-to-BDD conversion by gate and input ordering. In *ICCD*, 2002.
3. J. Baumgartner, A. Kuehlmann, and J. Abraham. Property checking via structural analysis. In *Computer-Aided Verification*, July 2002.
4. J. Baumgartner and H. Mony. Maximal input reduction of sequential netlists via synergistic reparameterization and localization strategies. In *CHARME*, 2005.
5. V. Bertacco, M. Damiano, and S. Quer. Cycle-based symbolic simulation of gate-level synchronous circuits. In *Design Automation Conference*, June 1999.
6. V. Bertacco and K. Olukotun. Efficient state representation for symbolic simulation. In *Design Automation Conference*, June 2002.
7. R. E. Bryant. Symbolic Boolean manipulation with ordered binary-decision diagrams. *ACM Computing Surveys*, 24(3), Sept. 1992.
8. P. Chauhan, E. Clarke, and D. Kroening. A SAT-based algorithm for reparameterization in symbolic simulation. In *Design Automation Conference*, June 2004.
9. E. M. Clarke, O. Grumberg, S. Jha, Y. Lu, and H. Veith. Counterexample-guided abstraction refinement. In *Computer-Aided Verification*, July 2000.
10. O. Coudert, C. Berthet, and J. Madre. Verification of synchronous sequential machines based on symbolic execution. In *Automatic Verification Methods for Finite State Systems*, 1989.
11. Y. Hong, P. A. Beerel, J. R. Burch, and K. L. McMillan. Safe BDD minimization using don't cares. In *Design Automation Conference*, June 1997.
12. IBM Formal Verification Benchmark Library. http://www.haifa.il.ibm.com/projects/verification/RB_Homepage/fvbenchmarks.html.
13. C. Jacobi, K. Weber, V. Paruthi, and J. Baumgartner. Automatic formal verification of fused-multiply-add floating point units. In *DATE*, 2005.
14. G. Janssen. Design of a pointerless bdd package. In *IWLS*, 2001.
15. H.-S. Jin, M. Awedh, and F. Somenzi. CirCUs: A satisfiability solver geared towards bounded model checking. In *CAV*, 2004.
16. A. Kuehlmann, V. Paruthi, F. Krohm, and M. Ganai. Robust Boolean reasoning for equivalence checking and functional property verification. *IEEE Trans. CAD*, 21(12), 2002.
17. R. P. Kurshan. *Computer-Aided Verification of Coordinating Processes*. Princeton University Press, 1994.
18. H. Mony, J. Baumgartner, V. Paruthi, R. Kanzelman, and A. Kuehlmann. Scalable automated verification via expert-system guided transformations. In *FMCAD*, 2004.
19. R. Murgai, J. Jain, and M. Fujita. Efficient scheduling techniques for ROBDD construction. In *VLSI Design*, pages 394–401, 1999.
20. H. Ochi, K. Yasuoka, and S. Yajima. Breadth-first manipulation of very large binary-decision diagrams. In *International Conference on Computer-Aided Design*, 1993.
21. J. V. Sanghavi, R. K. Ranjan, R. K. Brayton, and A. L. Sangiovanni-Vincentelli. High performance BDD package by exploiting memory hiercharchy. In *DAC*, pages 635–640, 1996.
22. C. Wilson, D. L. Dill, and R. E. Bryant. Symbolic simulation with approximate values. In *Formal Methods in Computer-Aided Design*, pages 335–353, Nov. 2000.
23. B. Yang, Y.-A. Chen, R. E. Bryant, and D. R. O'Hallaron. Space- and time-efficient BDD construction via working set control. In *ASP-DAC*, pages 423–432, 1998.

Achieving Speedups in Distributed Symbolic Reachability Analysis Through Asynchronous Computation

Orna Grumberg, Tamir Heyman, Nili Ifergan *, and Assaf Schuster

Computer Science Department, Technion, Haifa, Israel
Computer Science Department, Technion, Haifa 32000, Israel
Phone: 972-4-8294929
inili@cs.technion.ac.il

Abstract. This paper presents a novel BDD-based distributed algorithm for reachability analysis which is completely asynchronous. Previous BDD-based distributed schemes are synchronous: they consist of interleaved rounds of computation and communication, in which the fastest machine (or one which is lightly loaded) must wait for the slowest one at the end of each round.

We make two major contributions. First, the algorithm performs image computation and message transfer concurrently, employing non-blocking protocols in several layers of the communication and the computation infrastructures. As a result, regardless of the scale and type of the underlying platform, the maximal amount of resources can be utilized efficiently. Second, the algorithm incorporates an adaptive mechanism which splits the workload, taking into account the availability of free computational power. In this way, the computation can progress more quickly because, when more CPUs are available to join the computation, less work is assigned to each of them. Less load implies additional important benefits, such as better locality of reference, less overhead in compaction activities (such as reorder), and faster and better workload splitting.

We implemented the new approach by extending a symbolic model checker from Intel. The effectiveness of the resulting scheme is demonstrated on a number of large industrial designs as well as public benchmark circuits, all known to be hard for reachability analysis. Our results show that the asynchronous algorithm enables efficient utilization of higher levels of parallelism. High speedups are reported, up to an order of magnitude, for computing reachability for models with higher memory requirements than was previously possible.

1 Introduction

This work presents a novel BDD-based asynchronous distributed algorithm for reachability analysis. Our research focuses on obtaining high speedups while computing reachability for models with high memory requirements. We achieve this goal by designing an asynchronous algorithm which incorporates mechanisms to increase process utilization. The effectiveness of the algorithm is demonstrated on a number of large circuits, which show significant performance improvement.

---

* corresponding auhtor.

D. Borrione and W. Paul (Eds.): CHARME 2005, LNCS 3725, pp. 129–145, 2005.

Reachability analysis is a main component of model checking [10]. Most temporal safety properties can easily be checked by reachability analysis [2]. Furthermore, liveness property checking can be efficiently translated into safety property checking [3].

Despite recent improvements in model checking techniques, the so-called state explosion problem remains their main obstacle. In the case of industrial-scale models, time becomes a crucial issue as well. Existing BDD-based algorithms are typically limited by memory resources, while SAT-based algorithms are limited by time resources. Despite recent attempts to use SAT-based algorithms for full verification (pure SAT in [23,8,21,16] and SAT with BDDs in [19,17,18]), it is still widely acknowledged that the strength of SAT-based algorithms lies primarily in falsification, while BDD-based model checking continues to be the de facto standard for verifying properties (see surveys in [28] and [4]). The goal of this work is verification of large systems. Therefore, we based our techniques on BDDs.

The use of distributed processing to increase the speedup and capacity of model checking has recently begun to generate interest [5,29,22,1,27,20,15,30,24]. Distributed techniques that achieve these goals do so by exploiting the cumulative computational power and memory of a cluster of computers. In general, distributed model checking algorithms can be classified into two categories: explicit state representation based [29,22,1,27] and symbolic (BDD-based) state representation based [20,15]. Explicit algorithms use the fact that each state is manipulated separately in an attempt to divide the work evenly among processes; given a state, a hash-function identifies the process to which the state was assigned. The use of hash-functions is not applicable in symbolic algorithms which manipulate *sets* of states, represented as BDDs. In contrast to sets of explicit states, there is no direct correlation between the size of a BDD and the number of states it represents. Instead, the workload can be balanced by partitioning a BDD into two smaller BDDs (each representing a subset of the states) which are subsequently given to two different processes.

The symbolic work-efficient distributed synchronous algorithm presented in [15] is the algorithm that is closest to ours. In [15], as well as in our algorithm, processes (called workers) join and leave the computation dynamically. Each worker *owns* a part of the state space and is responsible for finding the reachable states in it. A worker splits its workload when its memory overflows, in which case it passes some of its owned states to a free worker.

Unlike the algorithm proposed in this work, the one in [15] works in synchronized iterations. At any iteration, each of the workers applies image computation and then waits for the others to complete the current iteration. Only then do all workers send the non-owned states discovered by them to their corresponding owners.

The method in [15] has several drawbacks. First, the synchronized iterations result in unnecessary and sometimes lengthy idle time for "fast" processes. Second, the synchronization phase is time-consuming, especially when the number of processes is high. Consequently, processes split as infrequently as possible in an attempt to reduce the overhead caused by synchronization. This leads to the third drawback: processes underutilize the given computational power, since available free processes are not used until there is absolutely no other choice but to join them in. These drawbacks make the algorithm insufficiently adaptive to the checked system and the underlying parallel environment. Furthermore, the combined effect of these drawbacks worsens with two factors: the size of the parallel environment and the presence of heterogeneous resources in it (as are commonly found today in non-dedicated grid and large-scale systems). These drawbacks limit the scalability of the algorithm and make it slow down substantially.

In order to exploit the full power of the parallel machinery and achieve scalability, it was necessary to design a new algorithm which is asynchronous in nature. We had to change the overall scheme to allow concurrency of computation and communication, to provide non-blocking protocols in several layers of the communication and the computation infrastructures, and to develop an asynchronous distributed termination detection scheme for a dynamic system in which processes join and leave the computation. In contrast to the approach presented in [15], the new algorithm does not synchronize the iterations among processes. Each process carries on the image computations at its own pace. The sending and receiving of states is carried out "in the background," with no coordination whatsoever. In this way, image computation and non-owned state exchange become *concurrent* operations.

Our algorithm is aimed at obtaining high speedup while fully utilizing the available computational power. To this end, when the number of free processes is relatively high the splitting rate is increased. This mechanism imposes *adaptive early splitting* to split a process even if its memory does not overflow. This approach ensures that free computational power will be utilized in full. In addition to using more processes, splitting the workload before memory overflows means that processes will handle smaller BDDs. This turned out to be a critical contribution to the speedup achieved by the new approach because a smaller BDD is easier to manipulate (improved locality of reference, faster image computation, faster and less frequent reorders, faster slicing, etc.).

In the asynchronous approach, when a process completes an iteration it carries on to the next one without waiting for the others. Consequently, splitting the workload with new processes is an efficient method for speeding up the computation since the overhead in adding more workers is negligible. However, this approach poses a huge challenge from the viewpoint of parallel software engineering. Given that the state space partition varies dynamically and that the communication is asynchronous, messages containing states may reach the wrong processes. By the time a message containing states is sent and received, the designated process may cease to own some or all of these states due to change of ownerships. Our algorithm overcomes this problem by incorporating a *distributed forwarding mechanism* that avoids synchronization but still assures that these states will eventually reach their owners. In addition, we developed a new method for opening messages containing packed BDDs which saves local buffer space and avoids redundant work: the mechanism ensures that only the relevant part of the BDD in the message is opened at every process visited by the message.

Distributed termination detection presents another challenge: although a certain process may reach a fixpoint, there may be states owned by this process that were discovered (or, are yet to be discovered) by others and are on their way to this process (in the form of BDDs packed in messages). The two-phase Dijkstra [11,12] termination detection algorithm is an efficient solution in such cases. However, we had to face yet another algorithmic complication that was not addressed by Dijkstra: the number of processes in the computation can vary dynamically and cannot be estimated or bounded in advance.

We found no solution to this problem in the distributed computing literature. Thus, we had to develop the solution ourselves as an extension of the Dijkstra algorithm.

Related Work. Other papers suggest reducing the space requirements for sequential symbolic reachability analysis by partitioning the work into several tasks [25,7,13]. However, these schemes use a single machine to sequentially handle one task at a time, while the other tasks are kept in external memory. These algorithms, as well as the distributed symbolic algorithms [20,15], are based on strict phases of computation and synchronization, which are carried out until a global fixpoint is reached. As a result, these schemes cannot scale well, and cannot take advantage of contemporary large-scale distributed platforms, such as huge clusters, grid batch systems and peer-to-peer networks, which are commonly non dedicated and highly heterogeneous.

The rest of the paper is organized as follows. In Section 2 we discuss the distributed approach. Section 3 describes sending and forwarding of BDD messages. In Section 4 we detail the algorithm performed by processes. Section 5 describes the asynchronous termination detection algorithm. Section 6 describes the operation of the coordinators. Experimental results are given in Section 7. Finally, we conclude in Section 8 with a summary and directions for future research.

2   The Distributed Asynchronous Approach

We begin by describing the sequential symbolic (BDD-based) reachability algorithm. The pseudo-code is given in Figure 1. The set of reachable states is computed sequentially by applying Breadth-First Search(BFS) starting from the set of initial states S_0. The search is preformed by means of *image computation* which, given a set of states, computes a set containing their successors. In general, two sets of states have to be maintained during reachability analysis:

1) The set of reachable states discovered so far, called R. This set becomes the set of reachable states when the exploration ends.
2) The set of reached but not yet developed states, called N. These states are developed in each iteration by applying image computation on N.

The distributed reachability algorithm relies on the notion of Boolean function slicing [26]. The state space is partitioned into *slices*, where each slice is *owned* by one process. A set, $w_1 \ldots w_k$, of Boolean functions called *window functions* defines for each process the slice it owns. The set of window functions is complete and disjoint, that is, $\bigvee_{i=1}^k w_i = 1$ and $\forall i \neq j : w_i \wedge w_j = 0$, respectively. States that do not belong to the slice owned by a process are called *non-owned* states for this process.

```
Reachability(S_0)
1)  R = N = S_0
2)  while  (N ≠ φ)
3)     N = Image(N)
4)     N = N \ R
5)     R = R ∪ N
6)  return R
```

Fig. 1. Sequential Reachability Analysis

As noted earlier, reachability analysis is usually carried out by means of a BFS exploration of the state space. Both the sequential algorithm (Figure 1) and the distributed synchronous algorithm (see [20,15]) use this technique: in iteration i, image computation is applied to the set of states, N, which are reachable in i steps (and no fewer than i steps) from the set of initial states. Thus, when iteration i is finished, all the states which are reachable in at most $i + 1$ steps have already been discovered. While in a sequential search the states in N are developed by a single process, in a distributed search the states in N are developed by a number of processes, according to the state space partition. In the latter, the processes synchronize on a barrier at the end of each iteration, i.e., wait until all processes complete the current iteration. Only then do the processes exchange their recently discovered non-owned states and continue to the next iteration.

However, reachability analysis need not be performed in such a manner. Note that reachability analysis would be correct even if, in iteration i, not all the states which are reachable in i steps are developed, as long as they will be developed in a future iteration. Thus, when a process completes iteration i, it does not have to wait until the other processes complete it. It can continue in the image computation on the newly discovered states and receive owned states discovered by other processes at a later time. This is one of the key ideas behind the asynchronous approach employed in the computational level.

Like [20,15], our algorithm uses two types of processes: workers and coordinators. The distributed platform consists of a non-dedicated pool of workers. Workers can join and leave the computation dynamically. Workers participating in the computation are called *active*. Otherwise, they are called *free*. Each active worker *owns* a slice of the state space and is responsible for discovering the reachable states within its slice. The algorithm is initialized with one active worker that runs a symbolic reachability algorithm, starting from the set of initial states. During its run, workers are allocated and freed. Each worker works iteratively. At each iteration, the worker computes an image and exchanges non-owned states, until a global fixpoint is reached and termination is detected. During image computation, the worker computes the new set of states that can be reached in one step from its owned part of N. The new computed set contains owned as well as non-owned states. During the exchange operation, the worker asynchronously sends the non-owned states to their corresponding owners. The novelty of our algorithm is that the iterations are not synchronized among workers. In addition, image computation and state exchange become concurrent.

Image computation and the receiving of owned states from other workers are critical points in which memory overflow may occur. In both cases, the computation stops and the worker splits its ownership into two slices. One slice is left with the overflowed worker and one given to a free worker. While distributed synchronous algorithms use splitting only when memory overflows, our approach also uses splitting to attain speedups. The *adaptive early splitting* mechanism splits a worker according to progress of its computation and availability of free workers in the pool. Besides utilizing free workers, this mechanism aims at increasing the asynchrony of the computation by splitting workers whose progress in the computation is not fast enough. An additional mechanism merges ownerships of several workers with low memory requirements to one worker, where the others return to the pool of free workers.

The concurrency between image computation and state exchange is made possible by the asynchronous sending and receiving of states. Non-owned states are transformed into BDD messages. BDD messages are sent "in the background," by the operating system. Note that asynchronous communication is usually implemented in a manner which allows minimum CPU intervention. As a result, a worker that sends a BDD message to a colleague is not blocked until the BDD message is actually sent or received. Similarly, a worker need not immediately process a BDD message that it receives. Received BDD messages are accumulated in a buffer called *InBuff*. The worker can retrieve them whenever it chooses. The worker retrieves BDD messages from *InBuff* during image computation, transforms them to BDDs, and stores them in a set called *OpenBuff* until the current image operation is completed. To summarize, a worker has to maintain three sets of states, N, R, and *OpenBuff*, as well as one buffer, *InBuff*, during the distributed asynchronous reachability analysis.

In addition, our algorithm uses three coordinators: the `exch_coord`, which holds the current set of owned windows and is notified on every split or merge. The `exch_coord` is also responsible for termination detection; the `pool_mgr`, which keeps track of free workers; and the `small_coord`, which merges the work of underutilized workers. Following is an explanation of how we handle BDD messages. The algorithm itself will be explained in detail in Sections 4, 5 and 6.

3   Forwarding and Sending of BDD Messages

Workers often exchange non-owned states during reachability analysis. BDDs are translated into and from messages as described in [15]. A BDD message represents the content and pointers of each BDD node as an element in an array. This method reduces the original BDD by 50%. Thus, BDD messages are transferred across the net efficiently. Moreover, recall that there is no exchange phase in which the processes send BDD messages all at once; messages are sent and received asynchronously during the computation. In addition, received BDD messages are opened during image computation and pending messages do not accumulate. As a result, the communication overhead is negligible and the memory required to store BDD messages that are waiting to be sent or opened is relatively small. These observations held in all the experiments we conducted.

As noted earlier, messages of non-owned states may reach the wrong worker (some or all of the states in the BDD message do not belong to the worker). Our algorithm thus incorporates a *distributed forwarding mechanism* that avoids synchronization but still ensures that these states will eventually reach their owners. In addition, the mechanism enables forwarding BDD messages without transforming them to a BDD form (which may be a time consuming operation). To this end, we attach a window to each BDD message. We refer to a BDD message as a pair $\langle T, w \rangle$, where T is the BDD in an array form and w is the attached window. Before worker P_i sends worker P_j a BDD message, it receives from the `exch_coord` the window w'_j which P_j owned when it last updated the `exch_coord`. This is the window P_i *assumes* P_j owns. As illustrated in Figure

Fig. 2. (a)P_i sends P_j a BDD message with an assumed window w'_j (b) P_j forwards a BDD message to P_k with an assumed window w'_k

2(a), when P_i sends a message to P_j it attaches the window w'_j it assumes P_j owns. If P_j is required to forward this message to worker P_k with an assumed window w'_k, it will change the window to $w'_j \wedge w'_k$ before doing so (see Figure 2(b)).

The Open_Buffer procedure, described in Figure 3, retrieves BDD messages from *InBuff*. Recall that those messages are received asynchronously into *InBuff* by the operating system. When a worker retrieves BDD messages from *InBuff*, it requests and receives from the exch_coord the list of window functions owned by the workers. Next, it asynchronously forwards each BDD message to each worker whose window's intersection with the message window is non-empty. Then it opens the BDD message.

In this work we developed a new method for opening BDD messages which saves local buffer space and avoids redundant work: only the relevant part of the BDD in the message is opened at every process visited by the message. The new method, called *selective opening*, extracts from a BDD message only those states that are under a given window (the window of the message intersected with the window of the worker), without transforming the entire message to BDD form. The worker holds the owned states extracted from the BDD message in *OpenBuff*.

Though the selective opening method only extracts the required states, the operation may fail due to memory overflow. In this case, the worker splits its ownership and thereby reduces its workload. Note that, despite the split, the BDD messages pending in *InBuff* do not require special handling; the next time the worker calls the Open_Buffer procedure and retrieves a pending BDD message, it forwards it according to the updated state partition given by the exch_coord and extracts the owned states according to its new window.

4   The Worker Algorithm

A high level description of the algorithm performed by a worker with ID my_id is shown in Figure 3. We will first describe each procedure in general and then in detail.

During the Bounded_Image procedure, a worker computes the set of states that can be reached in one step from N, and stores the result in N. During the computation, the worker also calls the Open_Buffer procedure and extracts owned states into *OpenBuff*. N and R will be updated with those states only in the Exchange procedure. If memory overflows during image computation or during the opening of a buffer, the worker splits its window w and updates N, R and *OpenBuff* according to the new window. The same holds true if early splitting occurs.

During the Exchange procedure the worker sends out the non-owned states $(N \setminus w)$ to their assumed owners and updates N, R with new states accumulated in *OpenBuff* (new states are states that do not appear in R).

If only a small amount of work remains, i.e., N and R are very small, the worker applies the Collect_Small procedure. The Collect_Small procedure merges the work of several workers into one task by merging their windows. As a result, one worker is assigned the unified ownership (merges as owner) and the rest become "free" ($w = \varnothing$, merge as non-owners) and return to the pool of free workers.

procedure **Open_Buffer**($w, OpenBuff$)
  $\{\langle T, w' \rangle\} \leftarrow$ BDD messages from $InBuff$
  $\{\langle P_j, w_j \rangle\} \leftarrow$ receive windows from exch_coor
  foreach ($\langle T, w' \rangle$)
    foreach (($j \neq my\_id$) $\wedge$ ($w' \cap w_j \neq \varnothing$))
      send $\langle T, w' \cap w_j \rangle$ to P_j
    Res=Selective_Opening($T, w' \cap w, Failed$)
    if $Failed = TRUE$
      return BDD message to $InBuff$
      Split($R, w, N, OpenBuff$)
    else $OpenBuff = OpenBuff \cup Res$

procedure **Reach_Task** ($R, w, N, OpenBuff$)
  loop forever
    Bounded_Image($R, w, N, OpenBuff$)
    Exchange($OpenBuff$)
    if (Terminate() = $TRUE$)
      return R
    Collect_Small(R, w, N)
    if ($w = \varnothing$)
      send $\langle$'to_pool', $my\_id \rangle$ to pool_mgr
      return to pool (keep forwarding BDD messages)

procedure **Exchange**($OpenBuff$)
  $\{\langle P_j, w_j \rangle\} \leftarrow$ receive windows from exch_coor
  foreach ($j \neq my\_id$)
    send $\langle N \cap w_j, w_j \rangle$ to P_j
  $N = N \setminus w_j$
  $N = N \cup OpenBuff$
  $N = N \setminus R$; $R = R \cup N$
  $OpenBuff = \varnothing$

procedure **Bounded_Image**($R, w, N, OpenBuff$)
  $Completed = FALSE$
  while $Completed = FALSE$
    Bounded_Image_Step($R, w, N, Max, Failed, Completed$)
    if (($Failed = TRUE$)$\vee$(Early_Split() = $TRUE$))
      Split($R, w, N, OpenBuff$)
    Open_Buffer($w, OpenBuff$)

function **Terminate**()
  if ($N = \varnothing \wedge InBuff = \varnothing \wedge$ 'all async' sends are complete)
    if ($TerminationStatus = $ 'no_term')
      $TerminationStatus = $ 'want_term'
      send exch_coord $\langle TerminationStatus, my\_id \rangle$
      return $FALSE$
    else if ($TerminationStatus = $ 'want_term')
      $TerminationStatus = $ 'regret_term'
      $\langle action \rangle \leftarrow$ receive from exch_coord *if any*
      if ($action = $ 'regret_termination_query')
        send $\langle$'regret_status', $TerminationStatus, my\_id \rangle$
      if ($action = $ 'reset_term')
        $TerminationStatus = $ 'no_term'
      if ($action = $ 'terminate')
        $TerminationStatus = $ 'terminate'
        return $TRUE$
    return $FALSE$

Fig. 3. Pseudo-code for a worker in the asynchronous distributed reachability computation

After performing Collect_Small, the worker checks whether its window is empty and it needs to join the pool of free workers. The window of a worker can be empty if it merged as non-owner in the Collect_Small procedure, or if it joined the computation with an empty window (this will be discussed later).

A worker is called *freed* if it participated in the computation once and then joined the pool of free workers. Freed workers may still receive misrouted BDD messages and thus need to forward them. For example, before worker P_i is freed, another worker may send it a message containing states that were owned by P_i. Should this message reach P_i after it was freed, P_i must then forward the message to the current owner(s) of these states. Methods for avoiding this situation will be discussed later. Note that if freed workers are required to forward BDD messages, they must participate in the termination algorithm. Following is a detailed description of each procedure.

The **Bounded_Image Procedure** is described in Figure 3. The image is computed by means of Bounded_Image_Step operations, which are repeated until the computation is complete. This algorithm uses a *partitioned transition relation*. Each partition defines the transition for one variable. The conjunction of all partitions gives the transition of all variables. Each Bounded_Image_Step applies one more partition and adds it to the intermediate result. The Bounded_Image_Step procedure receives as an argument the maximal amount of memory that it may use. If it exceeds this limit, the procedure stops and *Failed* becomes true.

The technique for computing an image using a partitioned transition relation was suggested by Burch et al.[6] and used for the synchronous distributed algorithm in [15]. Using bounded steps to compute the image allows memory consumption to be monitored and the computation stopped if there is memory overflow. Also explained in [15] is how the partitioned transition relation helps to avoid repeating an overflowed computation from the beginning: each worker resumes the computation of its part of the image from the point at which it stopped and does not repeat the bounded steps that were completed in the overflowed worker.

Our asynchronous algorithm exploits the partitioned computation even further. During image computation, between each bounded step, we retrieve pending BDD messages from *InBuff*, forward them if necessary, and extract owned states into *OpenBuff*. By doing so, we free the system buffer which contained the messages and produce asynchronous send operations, if forwarding is needed. Note that R and N are updated with *OpenBuff* only after the current image computation is completed. In addition, during image computation, the worker can perform early split according to the progress of its computation and availability of free workers in the pool. We chose to implement the Early_Split function by checking whether the amount of free workers in the pool is above a certain threshold and whether the worker has not split for a while.

The **Exchange Procedure** is described in Figure 3. First, the worker requests and receives from the exch_coord the list of window functions owned by the other workers. Then it uses this list to asynchronously send recently discovered non-owned states to the other workers. Afterwards, it updates N, R with states accumulated in *OpenBuff* and recalculates N, R.

Collect_Small Procedure.[1] An underutilized worker, i.e., one with small N and R, informs the small_coord of their size. The small_coord gives the worker one of the following commands: exit the procedure (in case it has no other worker to merge with or it is not small enough), merge as owner, or merge as non-owner. In case the worker's ownership changed, it informs the exch_coord of its new window. Note that workers with large R sets can not be merged since the memory required to store the united R set may not fit in the memory of a single machine.

A worker which merges as non-owner is freed. As mentioned before, freed workers keep forwarding BDD messages. However, this can be avoided. A freed worker can stop forwarding BDD messages if all the other workers have already requested and received a set of windows that does not include this freed worker. This ensures that no new messages will be sent to it. In addition, to ensure that all the already sent BDD messages have arrived, we can either bound the arrival time of a BDD message or run a termination-like algorithm. The termination algorithm will be discussed later.

---

[1] The pseudo-code for the Collect_Small procedure is not given in this paper due to space limitations.

Split Procedure.[2] This procedure starts by asking the pool_mgr for a free worker. We use a *Slice* procedure, which when given a BDD, computes a set of two windows that partition the BDD into two parts. This slicing algorithm was suggested in [20].

Two pairs of window functions are computed using the Slice procedure, one for N and one for R and *OpenBuff*. The two pairs are computed in an attempt to balance both the current image computation (by slicing N) and the memory requirements (by slicing R and *OpenBuff*). Note that the new windows the workers will own are the ones obtained by slicing R and *OpenBuff*. If R and *OpenBuff* are relatively small, only N is sliced. Thus, the overflowing worker's ownership remains unchanged and the new worker will have an empty window. Such a worker is called a *helper*. A helper simply assists the overflowed worker with a single image computation. Once the computation is complete, the helper sends the states it produced to their owners and joins the pool of free workers in the Reach_Task procedure. In our experiments, we observed that the creation of helpers is a common occurrence. After computing the partitions, the splitting worker sends the other worker its new window and its part of R, *OpenBuff* and N. It also updates the exch_coord with the new windows.

5 Asynchronous Termination Detection

Our termination detection algorithm is an extension of the two-phase Dijkstra [11,12] termination detection algorithm. Dijkstra's algorithm assumes a fixed number of processes and synchronous communication. In our extension, the communication is asynchronous and processes may join and leave the computation.

The presented termination detection algorithm has two phases: the first phase during which the exch_coord receives *want_term* requests from all the active and freed workers, and the second phase, during which the exch_coord queries all the workers that participated in the previous phase as to whether they regret the termination. After receiving all responses, it decides whether to terminate or reset termination and notifies the workers of its decision. The part of the exch_coord in the termination detection is discussed in Section 6.

Each worker detects termination locally and notifies the exch_coord when it wants to terminate. Upon receiving a regret query, the worker answers as to whether it regrets its request. The next message the worker will receive from the exch_coord will command it to terminate or reset termination. Note that the communication described above is asynchronous and thus does not block the workers.

The pseudo-code for the Terminate function performed by a worker is given in Figure 3. The termination status of a worker can be one of the following: *no_term*, if it does not want to terminate; *want_term*, if it wants to terminate; *regret_term*, if its status was *want_term* when it discovered that it still has work to do; *terminate*, if it should terminate. The initial termination status is *no_term*.

Upon entering the Terminate function the worker checks whether all of the following three conditions hold: It does not have any new states to develop ($N = \oslash$); it does not have any pending BDD messages in *InBuff*; all its asynchronous send operations have been completed. We will clarify the last condition. If a worker receives a BDD

---

[2] The pseudo-code for the Split procedure is not given in this paper due to space limitations.

function **Exch_Coord**()
$Ws[0] = one$
$ActiveWL = \{0\}; FreedWL = \oslash$
Loop-forever
$\langle cmd \rangle$ = receive from *any* worker
if $cmd = \langle 'collect\_small', P_{id}, w_{id}, P_i \rangle$
$Ws[P_{id}] = w_{id}$
$ActiveWL = ActiveWL \setminus P_i$
$FreedWL = FreedWL \cup P_i$
send $\langle 'release' \rangle$ to P_i and to P_{id}
if $cmd = \langle 'split', P_{id}, NewW_s = \{(p_i, w_i)\}\rangle$
foreach $(p_i, w_i) \in NewW_s$
$Ws[p_i] = w_i$
$ActiveWL = ActiveWL \cup P_i$
$FreedWL = FreedWL \setminus P_i$
send $\langle 'release' \rangle$ to P_{id}
TerminationDetection(cmd)

procedure **MoveToRegretPhaseIfNeeded**(P_i)
$WantTermL = WantTermL \setminus \{P_i\}$
if $(WantTermL = \oslash \wedge TPhase = 'want\_term')$
$TPhase = 'regret\_phase'$
$\forall P_j \in RegretQueryL :$
send $\langle 'regret\_termination\_query' \rangle$ to P_j

procedure **ResetOrTerminateIfNeeded**(P_i)
$RegretTermL = RegretTermL \setminus \{P_i\}$
if $(RegretTermL = \oslash \wedge CancelTerm = FALSE)$
$\forall P_j \in ResetOrTermL :$ send $\langle 'terminate' \rangle$ to P_j
if $(RegretTermL = \oslash \wedge CancelTerm = TRUE)$
$\forall P_j \in ResetOrTermL :$ send $\langle 'reset\_term' \rangle$ to P_j
$ResetOrTermL = \oslash; CancelTerm = FALSE$
$TPhase = 'no\_term'$

function **TerminationDetection**(cmd)
Initialization:
$CancelTerm = FALSE$
$RegretQueryL = \oslash$
$TPhase = 'no\_term'$
if $cmd = \langle 'want\_term', P_i \rangle$
if $TPhase = 'no\_term'$
$WantTermL = ActiveWL \cup FreedWL$
$TPhase = 'want\_term'$
if $TPhase = 'regret\_term'$ (P_i is a split colleague)
send $\langle 'regret\_termination\_query' \rangle$ to P_i
$RegretQueryL = RegretQueryL \cup \{P_i\}$
MoveToRegretPhaseIfNeeded(P_i)
if $cmd = \langle 'regret\_status', stat, P_i \rangle$
$CancelTerm = CancelTerm \vee (stat = regret)$
$ResetOrTermL = ResetOrTermL \cup \{P_i\}$
ResetOrTerminateIfNeeded(P_i)
if $(cmd = \langle 'split', P_{id}, \{(P_i, w_i)\}\rangle \wedge$
$\qquad TPhase \neq 'no\_term')$
$CancelTerm = TRUE$
if $TPhase = 'want\_term'$
$WantTermL = WantTermL \cup \{P_i | P_i \in \{(P_i, w_i)\}$
if $(cmd = \langle 'collect\_small', P_{id}, w_{id}, P_i \rangle \wedge$
$\qquad TPhase \neq 'no\_term')$
$CancelTerm = TRUE$

Fig. 4. The pseudo-code for the exch_coord

message, the sender will not consider the send operation complete until it receives an acknowledgement from this worker. Without acknowledgement, there could be a BDD message that was sent but not yet received, and no worker would know of its existence. Note that the acknowledgement is sent and received asynchronously.

If the termination status is *no_term* and all conditions hold, the termination status is changed to *want_term*. The worker will notify the exch_coord that it wants to terminate and exit the function (with return value false). If the termination status is *want_term* and one of the conditions does not hold, it may have more work to do. Thus, the termination status is changed to *regret_term*. If the worker has a pending command from the exch_coord, it acts accordingly. It can be prompted to send its termination status, or else to set it to either *no_term* or *terminate*.

6   The Coordinators

The exch_coord. Figure 4 describes the pseudo-code for the algorithm performed by the exch_coord. The exch_coord maintains a set of window functions Ws, where $Ws[P_i]$ holds the window owned by P_i. The exch_coord also maintains two lists: a list of active workers, *ActiveWL*, and a list of freed workers, *FreedWL*. The exch_coord receives notifications from workers and acts accordingly; when workers split or perform Collect_Small, it updates Ws, as well as the *ActiveWL* and *FreedWL* lists.

The exch_coord detects termination according to the TerminationDetection procedure. The *TPhase* variable indicates the termination phase and can have one of the following values: *no_term*, which means that no termination request has yet been received; *want_term*, where the exch_coord collects termination requests; *regret_term*, where the exch_coord collects regret termination responses. The initial value of *TPhase* is *no_term*. In addition, the exch_coord holds the following three lists: the *WantTermL* list, which is used in the *want_term* phase and contains all the active and freed workers that have **not** sent a termination request; the *RegretQueryL* list, which is used in the *regret_term* phase and contains all the workers that have **not** sent a regret response; and the *ResetOrTermL* list, which contains all the workers that will be notified of the termination decision when the *regret_term* ends.

The phase changes are triggered by commands received from the workers. The exch_coord can receive one of four commands and proceed accordingly. The *want_term* phase begins upon receiving a *want_term* request. Then the *WantTermL* is assigned the value of all active and freed workers. During this phase, the exch_coord receives *want_term* requests from all the workers in this list. Each worker that sends a request is removed from the *WantTermL* list and added to the *RegretQueryL*. When the *WantTermL* list becomes empty, the *regret_term* phase begins. All the workers in the *RegretQueryL* are sent a regret query. During this phase, those workers send a response to the query (their regret status). Each worker that sends a response is removed from the list and added to the *ResetOrTermL*. Only when the *RegretQueryL* becomes empty are the workers in the *ResetOrTermL* sent the decision as to whether or not to terminate. The exch_coord decides not to terminate if one of the workers regretted the termination or if split or merge occurred. In the latter case, the exch_coord also updates the appropriate lists.

The small_coord. The small_coord collects as many underutilized workers as possible. It receives merge requests from small (underutilized) workers. The small_coord stops a small worker for a predefined time; if timeout occurs and no other small worker has arrived in the meantime, it releases the worker. If a small worker arrives while another is waiting, it matches the two for merging.

The pool_mgr. The pool_mgr keeps track of free workers. During initialization it marks all workers as free, except for one. When a worker becomes free, it returns to the pool. When a worker splits, it sends the pool_mgr a request for a free worker. The pool_mgr sends in reply the *ID* of a free worker, which is then removed from the pool. If the pool_mgr is asked for a worker and there is no free worker in the pool, it stops the execution globally and announces "workers overflow."

7   Experimental Results

We implemented our algorithm on top of Division [14], a generic platform for the study of distributed symbolic model checking which requires an external model checker. We used FORECAST [13] for this purpose. FORECAST is an industrial strength high-performance implementation of a BDD-based model checker developed at Intel, Haifa.

Circuit Name	# Vars	# Steps	Forecast		Forecast-D		Forecast-AD		
			Max. Step	Time(m)	Time(m)	# Workers	Time(m)	# Workers	Speedup (AD Vs. D)
s1269	55	9	9	45	50	12	15	6	3.3
s330	172	8	8	141	85	6	52	14	1.64
D_1	178	36	36	91	100	8	70	10	1.43
D_5	310	68	68	1112	897	5	150	18	5.98
D_6	328	94	94	81	101	5	76	3	1.3
Head_1_1	300	98	ovf(44)	-	9180	10	900	15	10.2
Head_2_0	276	85	ovf(44)	-	2784	4	390	55	7.14
Head_2_1	274	85	ovf(55)	-	1500	8	460	50	3.26
I1	138	139	ovf(102)	-	7178	18	2760	36	2.6

Fig. 5. A comparison between FORECAST, FORECAST-D and FORECAST-AD. If FORE-CAST was unable to complete an image step, we reported the overflowing step in parentheses. FORECAST-D and FORECAST-AD reached a fixpoint on all circuits. Column 10 shows the speedup when comparing FORECAST-AD and FORECAST-D run times.

This section describes our experimental results on certain large benchmarks that are known to be hard for reachability analysis. Most publicly available circuits are small or medium sized and can be computed sequentially. Therefore, we focused mostly on industrial-scale examples. We conducted experiments on two of the largest ISCAS89 benchmarks (s1269, s3330). Additional large-size examples are industrial designs taken from Intel. Our parallel testbed included a maximum of 56 PC machines, 2.4GHz Xeon processor with 4GB memory. The communication between the nodes was via LAM MPI over fast Ethernet. We used daemon-based communication, which allows true asynchronous message passing (i.e., the sending of messages progresses while the user's program is executing).

Our results are compared to FORECAST and to the work-efficient distributed synchronous implementation in [15]. The work-efficient implementation originally used NuSMV [9] as an external BDD-based model checker. For comparability, we replaced it with FORECAST. The work-efficient implementation which uses FORECAST will be referred to as FORECAST-D (Distributed FORECAST), and our prototype as FORECAST-AD (Asynchronous FORECAST-D).

Figure 5 clearly shows a significant speedup on all examples, up to an order of magnitude. When comparing FORECAST-D to FORECAST-AD, we were able to obtain a speedup even when the number of workers decreased. For instance, in the s1269 circuit, we obtained a speedup of 3.3 even though the number of workers decreased by a factor of 2. It can also be seen that the early splitting mechanism in FORECAST-AD enables using more workers than in FORECAST-D. Using more workers clearly increases efficiency: for example in the Head_1_1 circuit, FORECAST-AD uses 1.5 times more workers, but the speedup is of an order of magnitude.

We analyzed worker utilization when using the early splitting mechanism. Figure 6 provides utilization graphs for the Head_2_0 circuit, with this mechanism enabled and disabled. The Head_2_0 is a large circuit, difficult for reachability analysis. As can be seen in Figure 5, FORECAST is unable to reach a fixpoint on this circuit and overflows at step 44, while FORECAST-D requires over 46 hours to reach a fixpoint. Figure 6(a)

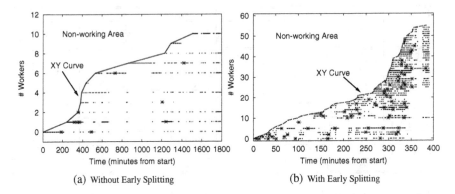

(a) Without Early Splitting   (b) With Early Splitting

Fig. 6. FORECAST_AD worker utilization with and without the early splitting mechanism in the Head_2_0 circuit. In each graph, the Y axis represents the worker's ID. The X axis represents the time(in minutes) from the beginning of the distributed computation. For each worker, each point indicates that it computed an image at that time; a sequence of points represents a time segment in which a worker computed an image; a sequence in which points do not appear represents a time segment in which a worker is idle (it does not have any new states to develop). An asterisk on the time line of a worker represents the point when it split. The XY curve connects times at which workers join the computation. This curve separates the **working** from the **non-working** area. Note that the scales of the two graphs (both X axis and Y axis) are different.

clearly shows that when the early splitting mechanism is disabled, the workers are idle for much of the time. For instance, between 850 and 1100 minutes, only P_7 is working. This situation occurs when workers do not have any new states to develop and wait to receive new owned states. In this case, only when P_7 finds non-owned states and sends them to their corresponding owners are those workers utilized again. It is evident in Figure 6(b) that early splitting can significantly reduce such a phenomenon. As can be seen, the phenomenon still exists, but on a much smaller scale, for instance between 360 and 380 minutes. In addition, when using early splitting, we are able to use more machines more quickly. In Figure 6(a) it takes 1600 minutes for 10 machines to come into use, whereas in Figure 6(b) this takes 70 minutes.

Circuit Name	# Vars	Forecast-AD				Speedup (A Vs. B)
		No Early Splitting (A)		Early Splitting (B)		
		Time(m)	# Workers	Time(m)	# Workers	
s330	172	120	8	52	14	2.3
D_5	310	617	14	150	18	4.1
Head_1_1	300	1140	4	900	15	1.3
Head_2_0	276	1793	11	390	55	4.6
Head_2_1	274	1200	5	460	50	2.6

Fig. 7. The early splitting effect in FORECAST-AD. The "Speedup" column reports the speedup obtained when using the early splitting mechanism.

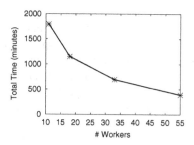

Fig. 8. The speedup obtained when increasing the number of workers on the Head_2_0 circuit (in FORECAST-AD). The X axis represents the time required to reach a fixpoint. The Y axis represents the maximal number of workers that participated in the computation. An asterisk on the (x, y) coordinate indicates that when the threshold of free workers is set to x, the reachability analysis ended after y minutes.

Figure 6 also illustrates that when the number of workers increases, the relative size of the non-working area (the area above the XY curve) increases significantly. In the working area (the area below the XY curve), workers are dedicated to the distributed computation, whereas in the non-working area, workers are in the pool and can be used for other computations. Thus the *effectiveness* of the mechanism, i.e, the relation between the speedup and the increase in the number of workers, should actually be measured with respect to the relative size of the working area. Figure 7 presents the speedup obtained on several circuits, when using the early splitting mechanism.

As can be seen in Figure 8, there is an almost linear correlation between the increase in computational power and the reduction in runtime on the Head_2_0 circuit. As the number of workers increases, the effectiveness decreases slightly. This can be explained by the fact that the relative size of the non-working area becomes larger as the number of workers increases (since we are not able to utilize free workers fast enough).

8 Conclusions and Future Work

This paper presents a novel algorithm for distributed symbolic reachability analysis which is asynchronous in nature. We employed non-blocking protocols in several layers of the communication and the computation infrastructures: asynchronous sending and receiving of BDD messages (concurrency between image computation and state exchange), opening of messages between bounded image steps, a non-blocking distributed forwarding mechanism, non-synchronized iterations, and an asynchronous termination detection algorithm for a dynamic number of processes. Our dynamic approach tries to utilize contemporary non-dedicated large-scale computing platforms, such as Intel's Netbatch high-performance grid system, which controls all (tens of thousands) Intel servers around the world.

The experimental results show that our algorithm is able to compute reachability for models with high memory requirements while obtaining high speedups and utilizing the available computational power to its full extent.

Additional research should be conducted on better adaption of the reorder mechanism to a distributed environment. One of the benefits of the distributed approach which we exploit is that each worker can perform reorder independently of other workers and thus find the best order for the BDD it holds. We did not elaborate on this matter since it is not the focus of the paper. Our adaptive early splitting approach not only better utilizes free workers but also results in processes handling smaller-sized BDDs, which are easier to manipulate. In particular, the reorders in small BDDs are faster and less frequent. Nevertheless, the BDD package still spent a considerable time on reordering. We intend to explore the use of splitting as an alternative method for reordering.

References

1. J. Barnat, L. Brim, and J. Stribrna. Distributed LTL model-checking in SPIN. In *Proceedings of the 8th international SPIN workshop on Model checking of software*, pages 200–216. Springer-Verlag, 2001.
2. I. Beer, S. Ben-David, and A. Landver. On-The-Fly Model Checking of RCTL Formulas. In *CAV*, pages 184–194, 1998.
3. A. Biere, C. Artho, and V. Schuppan. Liveness Checking as Safety Checking. In *Proceedings of the 7th International ERCIM Workshop, FMICS'02*. Electronic Notes in Theoretical Computer Science, 66(2). Elsevier, July 2002.
4. A. Biere, A. Cimatti, E.M. Clarke, O. Strichman, and Y. Zue. *Bounded Model Checking*. Advances in Computers. Volume 58, Academic Press, 2003.
5. V. A. Braberman, A. Olivero, and F. Schapachnik. Issues in distributed timed model checking: Building Zeus. *STTT*, 7(1):4–18, 2005.
6. J. R. Burch, E. M. Clarke, and D. E. Long. Symbolic Model Checking with Partitioned Transition Relations. In *Proceedings of Internation Conference on Very Large Integration*, pages 45–58, 1991.
7. G. Cabodi, P. Camurati, and S. Quer. Improved Reachability Analysis of Large FSM. In *Proceedings of the IEEE International Conference on CAD*, pages 354–360, 1996.
8. Pankaj Chauhan, Edmund M. Clarke, and Daniel Kroening. Using SAT based Image Computation for Reachability Analysis. Technical report, Carnegie Mellon University, School of Computer Science, 2003.
9. A. Cimatti, E.M. Clarke, F. Giunchiglia, and M. Roveri. NuSMV: a new Symbolic Model Verifier. In *CAV'99*, pages 495–499.
10. E. M. Clarke, O. Grumberg, and D. Peled. *Model checking*. MIT Press, 1999.
11. E. W. Dijkstra, W. H. J. Feijen, and A. J. M. van Gasteren. Derivation of a Termination Detection Algorithm for Distributed Computations. *Information Processing Letters*, pages 217–219, 1983.
12. E. W. Dijkstra and C.S. Scholten. Termination Detection for Diffusing Computations. *Information Processing Letters*, pages 1–4, 1980.
13. R. Fraer, G. Kamhi, Z. Barukh, M.Y. Vardi, and L. Fix. Prioritized Traversal: Efficient Reachability Analysis for Verification and Falsification. In *CAV'00*, volume 1855 of *LNCS*.
14. O. Grumberg, A. Heyman, T. Heyman, and A. Schuster. Division System: A General Platform for Distributed Symbolic Model Checking Research, 2003.
15. O. Grumberg, T. Heyman, and A. Schuster. A Work-Efficient Distributed Algorithm for Reachability Analysis. In *CAV*, LNCS, 2003.
16. O. Grumberg, A. Schuster, and A. Yadgar. Memory Efficient All-Solutions SAT Solver and its Application for Reachability Analysis. In *FMCAD'04*.
17. A. Gupta, A. Gupta, Z. Yang, and P. Ashar. Dynamic Detection and Removal of Inactive Clauses in SAT with Application in Image Computation. In *DAC*, pages 536–541. ACM Press, 2001.

18. A. Gupta, Z. Yang, P. Ashar, L. Zhang, and S. Malik. Partition-Based Decision Heuristics for Image Computation using SAT and BDDs. In *ICCAD*, pages 286–292. IEEE Press, 2001.
19. Aarti Gupta, Zijiang Yang, Pranav Ashar, and Anubhav Gupta. SAT-Based Image Computation with Application in Reachability Analysis. In *FMCAD*, volume 1954 of *LNCS*, 2000.
20. T. Heyman, D. Geist, O. Grumberg, and A. Schuster. A Scalable Parallel Algorithm for Reachability Analysis of Very Large Circuits. *Formal Methods in System Design*, pages 317 – 338, 2002.
21. H. Kang and I. Park. SAT-based Unbounded Symbolic Model Checking. In *DAC*, 2003.
22. F. Lerda and R. Sisto. Distributed-Memory Model Checking with SPIN. In *Proceedings of the 5th and 6th International SPIN Workshops on Theoretical and Practical Aspects of SPIN Model Checking*, pages 22–39. Springer-Verlag, 1999.
23. K. L. McMillan. Applying SAT Methods in Unbounded Symbolic Model Checking. In *CAV'00*.
24. K. Milvang-Jensen and A. J. Hu. BDDNOW: A Parallel BDD Package. In *FMCAD '98, LNCS*, Palo Alto, California, USA, November 1998.
25. A. Narayan, A. Isles, J. Jain, R. Brayton, and A. L. Sangiovanni-Vincentelli. Reachability Analysis Using Partitioned-ROBDDs. In *Proceedings of the IEEE International Conference on Computer Aided Design*, pages 388–393, 1997.
26. A. A. Narayan, J. Jawahar, M. Fujita, and A. Sangiovanni-Vincenteli. Partitioned-ROBDDs. In *CAV*, pages 547–554, 1996.
27. D. M. Nicol and G. Ciardo. Automated Parallelization of Discrete State-Space Generation. *J. Parallel Distrib. Comput.*, 47(2):153–167, 1997.
28. M. R. Prasad, A. Biere, and A. Gupta. A Survey of Recent Advances in SAT-Based Verification. To appear in STTT, 2005.
29. U. Stern and D. L. Dill. Parallelizing the Murφ Verifier. In *CAV*, pages 256–278, 1997.
30. T. Stornetta and F. Brewer. Implementation of an Efficient Parallel BDD Package. In *33rd Design Automation Conference*, 1996.

Saturation-Based Symbolic Reachability Analysis Using Conjunctive and Disjunctive Partitioning[*]

Gianfranco Ciardo and Andy Jinqing Yu

Dept. of Computer Science and Engineering,
Univ. of California, Riverside
{ciardo, jqyu}@cs.ucr.edu

Abstract. We propose a new *saturation*-based symbolic state-space generation algorithm for finite discrete-state systems. Based on the structure of the high-level model specification, we first disjunctively partition the transition relation of the system, then conjunctively partition each disjunct. Our new encoding recognizes *identity transformations* of state variables and exploits *event locality*, enabling us to apply a recursive fixed-point image computation strategy completely different from the standard breadth-first approach employing a global fix-point image computation. Compared to breadth-first symbolic methods, saturation has already been empirically shown to be several orders more efficient in terms of runtime and peak memory requirements for asynchronous concurrent systems. With the new partitioning, the saturation algorithm can now be applied to completely general asynchronous systems, while requiring similar or better run-times and peak memory than previous saturation algorithms.

1 Introduction

Formal verification techniques have received much attention in the past decade. In particular, BDD-based [4] symbolic model checking [10,17] has been successfully applied in industrial settings. However, even if BDDs can result in great efficiency, symbolic techniques remain a memory and time-intensive task.

We focus on symbolic state-space generation, a fundamental capability in symbolic model checking, and target asynchronous concurrent systems, including asynchronous circuits, distributed software systems, and globally-asynchronous locally-synchronous systems (GALSs), which are increasingly being used in complex hardware and embedded systems, such as System-on-Chip designs.

The standard approach to state-space generation uses a breadth-first strategy, where each iteration is an image computation. This corresponds to finding a "global" fixed-point of the transition relation. The *saturation* algorithm we introduced in [6] uses instead a completely different iteration strategy, which has been shown to excel when applied to asynchronous concurrent systems.

---

[*] Work supported in part by the NSF under grants CNS-0501747 and CNS-0501748.

D. Borrione and W. Paul (Eds.): CHARME 2005, LNCS 3725, pp. 146–161, 2005.

Saturation recognizes and exploits the presence of *event locality* and recursively applies multiple "local" fixed-point iterations, resulting in peak memory requirements, and consequently runtimes, often several orders of magnitude smaller than for traditional approaches. As introduced, however, saturation requires a *Kronecker-consistent* decomposition of the high-level model into *component models*. While this is not a restriction for some formalisms (e.g., ordinary Petri nets, even if extended with inhibitor and reset arcs), it does impose constraints on the decomposition granularity in others (e.g., Petri nets with arbitrary marking-dependent arc cardinalities or transition guards). For some models, these constraints may prevent us from generating the state space because each component model is too large. A particularly important example is the analysis of software.

In [20], Miner proposed a saturation algorithm applicable to models not satisfying Kronecker consistency, but its cost approaches that of an explicit generation in models where an event affects many state variables. In this paper, after giving an overview of state-space and transition relation encodings, we formalize previous saturation algorithms in a unifying framework (Sect. 2). Then, we present a new transition relation encoding based on a *disjunctive-conjunctive partition* and *identity-reduced* decision diagrams (Sect. 3). This allows us to define a new saturation algorithm that does not require Kronecker consistency, like [20], nor a priori knowledge of the state variable bounds, like [7], and is exponentially more efficient in certain models (Sect. 4). We present preliminary memory and runtime results for our approach and compare it to NuSMV [9] and SPIN [14] (Sect. 5). Finally, we report related work and our conclusions (Sect. 6).

2   Preliminaries

We consider a discrete-state model represented by a Kripke structure $M = (\widehat{S}, S_{init}, \mathcal{R}, L)$, where $\widehat{S}$ is a finite set of states, $S_{init} \subseteq \widehat{S}$ is a set of initial states, and $\mathcal{R} \subseteq \widehat{S} \times \widehat{S}$ is a transition relation. We assume the *(global)* model state to be a sequence of K *local state* variables, $(x_K, ..., x_1)$, where, for $K \geq l \geq 1$, $x_l \in \{0, 1, ..., n_l - 1\} = S_l$, for some $n_l \in \mathbb{N}$. Thus, $\widehat{S} = S_K \times \cdots \times S_1$ and we write $\mathcal{R}(i_K, ..., i_1, i'_K, ..., i'_1)$, or $\mathcal{R}(\mathbf{i}, \mathbf{i'})$, if the model can transition from the *current state* $\mathbf{i}$ to a *next state* $\mathbf{i'}$ in one step (unprimed symbols denote current states, primed symbols denote next states). We let $\mathbf{x}_{(l,k)}$ denote the (sub)state $(x_l, ..., x_k)$, for $K \geq l \geq k \geq 1$. Given a function f on the domain $\widehat{S}$, $Supp(f)$ denotes the set of variables in its support. Formally, $x_l \in Supp(f)$ if there are states $\mathbf{i}, \mathbf{j} \in \widehat{S}$, differing only in component l, such that $f(\mathbf{i}) \neq f(\mathbf{j})$.

2.1   Symbolic Encoding of State Space and Transition Relation

State space generation consists of building the smallest set of states $S \subseteq \widehat{S}$ satisfying (1) $S \supseteq S_{init}$ and (2) $S \supseteq Img(S)$, where the *image computation* function gives the set of successor states: $Img(\mathcal{X}) = \{\mathbf{x'} : \exists \mathbf{x} \in \mathcal{X}, (\mathbf{x}, \mathbf{x'}) \in \mathcal{R}\}$. The most common symbolic approach to store the state space uses $\lceil n_l \rceil$ boolean variables to encode each state variable x_l, thus it encodes a set of states $\mathcal{Z}$ through its *characteristic function* $f_\mathcal{Z}$, using a BDD with $\sum_{K \geq l \geq 1} \lceil n_l \rceil$ levels.

Instead of BDDs, we prefer *ordered multi-way decision diagrams* (MDDs) [18] to encode sets of states, where each variable x_l is directly encoded in a single level, using a node with n_l outgoing edges. Not only this results in a simpler discussion of our technique, but it also allows us to more clearly pinpoint an important property we exploit, *event locality*.

Definition 1. An MDD over $\widehat{S}$ is an acyclic edge-labeled multi-graph where:

- Each node p belongs to a *level* in $\{K, ..., 1, 0\}$, denoted $p.lvl$.
- There is a single *root* node.
- Level 0 contains the only two *terminal* nodes, *Zero* and *One*.
- A node p at level $l > 0$ has n_l outgoing edges, labeled from 0 to $n_l - 1$. The edge labeled by i_l points to node q, with $p.lvl > q.lvl$; we write $p[i_l] = q$.

Finally, one of two reductions ensures canonicity. Both forbid *duplicate* nodes:

- Given nodes p and q at level l, if $p[i_l] = q[i_l]$ for all $i_l \in \mathcal{S}_l$, then $p = q$.

Then, the *fully-reduced* version [4] forbids *redundant* nodes:

- No node p at level l can exist such that, $p[i_l] = q$ for all $i_l \in \mathcal{S}_l$.

While the *quasi-reduced* version [19] forbids arcs from spanning multiple levels:

- The root is at level K.
- Given a node p at level l, $p[i_l].lvl = l - 1$ for all $i_l \in \mathcal{S}_l$.   □

Definition 2. The set encoded by MDD node p at level k w.r.t. level $l \geq k$ is

$$\mathcal{B}(l, p) = \begin{cases} \mathcal{S}_l \times \mathcal{B}(l-1, p) & \text{if } l > 0 \wedge l > k \\ \bigcup_{i_l \in \mathcal{S}_l} \{i_l\} \times \mathcal{B}(l-1, p[i_l]) & \text{if } l > 0 \wedge l = k \end{cases},$$

with the convention that $\mathcal{X} \times \mathcal{B}(0, Zero) = \emptyset$ and $\mathcal{X} \times \mathcal{B}(0, One) = \mathcal{X}$.   □

Most symbolic model checkers, e.g., NuSMV [9], generate the state space with breadth-first iterations, each consisting of an image computation. At the dth iteration, $\mathcal{Z}$ contains all the states at distance exactly d, or at distance up to d (either approach can be the most efficient, depending on the model). When using MDDs, we encode $\mathcal{Z}(\mathbf{x})$ as a K-level MDD and $\mathcal{R}(\mathbf{x}, \mathbf{x}')$ as a $2K$-level MDD whose unprimed and primed variables are normally interleaved for efficiency. Furthermore, the transition relation can be conjunctively partitioned into a set of *conjuncts*, $\mathcal{R}(\mathbf{x}, \mathbf{x}') = \bigwedge_\alpha \mathcal{C}_\alpha(\mathbf{x}, \mathbf{x}')$, or disjunctively partitioned into a set of *disjuncts*, $\mathcal{R}(\mathbf{x}, \mathbf{x}') = \bigvee_\alpha \mathcal{D}_\alpha(\mathbf{x}, \mathbf{x}')$ [16], stored as a set of MDDs, instead of a single monolithic MDD. Heuristically, such partitioned relations have been shown effective for synchronous and asynchronous systems, respectively.

2.2   A General Partitioning Methodology for the Transition Relation

In general discrete-state systems, both asynchronous and synchronous behavior can be present. Thus, given a model expressed in a high-level formalism, we first exploit the asynchronous aspects, by first disjunctively partitioning the transition relation $\mathcal{R}$ into a set of disjuncts, where each disjunct $\mathcal{D}_\alpha$ corresponds to a different *event* α in the set $\mathcal{E}$ of system events, i.e., $\mathcal{R}(\mathbf{x}, \mathbf{x}') \equiv \bigvee_{\alpha \in \mathcal{E}} \mathcal{D}_\alpha(\mathbf{x}, \mathbf{x}')$.

Then, each event can synchronously update several state variables. We assume that, for each disjunct $\mathcal{D}_\alpha$, the high-level model description specifies both:

- A set of *enabling conjuncts* specifying when event α can occur, or *fire*. The support of conjunct $Enable_{\alpha,m}$ is a subset of $\{x_K, ..., x_1\}$.
- A set of *updating conjuncts* describing how the state variables are updated when α fires. The support of conjunct $Upd_{\alpha,n}$ is a subset of $\{x_K, x'_K, ..., x_1, x'_1\}$.

Thus, the partitioned transition relation can be represented as:

$$\mathcal{R}(\mathbf{x}, \mathbf{x}') \equiv \bigvee_{\alpha \in \mathcal{E}} \mathcal{D}_\alpha(\mathbf{x}, \mathbf{x}') \equiv \bigvee_{\alpha \in \mathcal{E}} \left(\bigwedge_m Enable_{\alpha,m}(\mathbf{x}) \wedge \bigwedge_n Upd_{\alpha,n}(\mathbf{x}, \mathbf{x}') \right).$$

We assume a particularly important class of models, where each updating conjunct only updates one primed variables, so that we can write:

$$\mathcal{R}(\mathbf{x}, \mathbf{x}') \equiv \bigvee_{\alpha \in \mathcal{E}} \mathcal{D}_\alpha(\mathbf{x}, \mathbf{x}') \equiv \bigvee_{\alpha \in \mathcal{E}} \left(\bigwedge_m Enable_{\alpha,m}(\mathbf{x}) \wedge \bigwedge_{K \geq l \geq 1} Upd_{\alpha,l}(\mathbf{x}, x'_l) \right). \quad (1)$$

As a running example, we consider an event α corresponding to the following pseudocode statement in a larger program:

> if $x_5 > 2$ and $x_6 \leq 1$ then $\langle x_3, x_6 \rangle \leftarrow \langle x_4, (x_7 + x_6) \bmod 6 \rangle$;

where the state variables are $x_7, ..., x_1 \in [0..5]$ and the "$\langle$ $\rangle$" pairs enclose v (two, in our case) distinct variables to be simultaneously assigned, and the corresponding v expressions, which are evaluated before performing any assignment. The disjunct $\mathcal{D}_\alpha$ has then two enabling conjuncts, $Enable_{\alpha,1} \equiv [x_5 > 2]$ and $Enable_{\alpha,2} \equiv [x_6 \leq 1]$, and seven updating conjuncts, one for each variable x_k, $k \in [7, ..., 1]$, $Upd_{\alpha,3} \equiv [x'_3 = x_4]$, $Upd_{\alpha,6} \equiv [x'_6 = (x_7 + x_6) \bmod 6]$, and $Upd_{\alpha,k} \equiv [x'_k = x_k]$, for $k \in \{7, 5, 4, 2, 1\}$.

2.3   Event Locality

We now examine the ways an event α can be "independent" of a state variable and show how the standard concept of support for a function is inadequate when applied to the disjuncts of the transition relation. Recalling that $\mathcal{D}_\alpha$ is just a function of the form $\widehat{S} \times \widehat{S} \to \mathbb{B}$, we can consider the following cases:

- If $x_l \notin Supp(\mathcal{D}_\alpha)$, the value of x_l affects neither the enabling of event α nor the value of any x'_k, for $K \geq k \geq 1$, including $k = l$, when α fires. In our running example, this is the case for x_3.
- If $x'_l \notin Supp(\mathcal{D}_\alpha)$, the value of x'_l is independent of that of x_k, for $K \geq k \geq 1$, including $k = l$, when α fires. This corresponds to nondeterministically setting x'_l to any value in $\mathcal{S}_l$. Of course, given the expression of Eq. 1, we already know that x'_l affects neither the enabling of α nor the values of x'_k, for $k \neq l$.

When encoding $\mathcal{D}_\alpha$ with a fully-reduced $2K$-level MDD, the above two cases are reflected in the absence of node at level l, or l', respectively. Indeed, it is even possible that both $x_l \notin Supp(\mathcal{D}_\alpha)$ and $x'_l \notin Supp(\mathcal{D}_\alpha)$ hold, thus neither l nor l' would contain any node. However, these two cases are neither as important nor as common as the following type of "independence":

- If $x_l \notin Supp(\bigwedge_m Enable_{\alpha,m} \wedge \bigwedge_{k \neq l} Upd_{\alpha,k})$ and $Upd_{\alpha,l} \equiv [x'_l = x_l]$, the value of x_l affects neither the enabling of event α nor the value of any x'_k, for $k \neq l$, while the firing of α does not change the value of x_l.

This common situation is not exploited by ordinary MDD reductions; rather, it results in the presence of (possibly many) *identity patterns*: a node p at level l such that, foreach $i_l \in \mathcal{S}_l$, $p[i_l] = q_{i_l}$, and $q_{i_l}[j_l] = Zero$ for all $j_l \in \mathcal{S}_l$, except for $q_{i_l}[i_l] = r$, where node $r \neq Zero$ does not depend on i_l (the gray pattern in Fig. 1). It is instead exploited by Kronecker encodings of transition matrices [6,8].

We define $\mathcal{V}_\alpha^{indep}$ to be the set containing any such (unprimed) variable, and $\mathcal{V}_\alpha^{dep} = \{x_K, ..., x_1\} \setminus \mathcal{V}_\alpha^{indep}$, and say that *event locality* is present in a system when $\mathcal{V}_\alpha^{dep}$ is a strict subset of $\{x_K, ..., x_1\}$. We further split $\mathcal{V}_\alpha^{dep}$ into $\mathcal{V}_\alpha^{upd} = \{x_l : Upd_{\alpha,l} \neq [x'_l = x_l]\}$, the set of unprimed variables whose corresponding primed variable can be *updated* by the firing of α, and $\mathcal{V}_\alpha^{unchanged} = \mathcal{V}_\alpha^{dep} \setminus \mathcal{V}_\alpha^{upd}$, the set of unprimed variables that affect the enabling of α or the value of some primed variable, but whose corresponding primed variable is *not updated* by the firing of α. For our running example, $\mathcal{V}_\alpha^{upd} = \{x_6, x_3\}$, $\mathcal{V}_\alpha^{unchanged} = \{x_7, x_5, x_4\}$ and $\mathcal{V}_\alpha^{indep} = \{x_2, x_1\}$. By definition, $\mathcal{V}_\alpha^{upd} \cup \mathcal{V}_\alpha^{unchanged} \cup \mathcal{V}_\alpha^{indep} = \{x_K, ..., x_1\}$ and, based on these sets, we can partition the transition relation as:

$$\mathcal{R}(\mathbf{x}, \mathbf{x}') \equiv \bigvee_{\alpha \in \mathcal{E}} \left(\bigwedge_m Enable_{\alpha,m}(\mathbf{x}) \wedge \bigwedge_{x_k \in \mathcal{V}_\alpha^{upd}} Upd_{\alpha,k}(\mathbf{x}, x'_k) \wedge \bigwedge_{x_k \notin \mathcal{V}_\alpha^{upd}} [x'_k = x_k] \right).$$

Definition 3. Let $Top(\alpha)$ and $Bot(\alpha)$ be the highest and lowest variable indices in $\mathcal{V}_\alpha^{dep}$: $Top(\alpha) = \max\{k : x_k \in \mathcal{V}_\alpha^{dep}\}$, $Bot(\alpha) = \min\{k : x_k \in \mathcal{V}_\alpha^{dep}\}$. ☐

We can then group the disjuncts $\mathcal{D}_\alpha$ according to the value of $Top(\alpha)$:

$$\mathcal{R}(\mathbf{x}, \mathbf{x}') \equiv \bigvee_{K \geq k \geq 1} \mathcal{R}_k(\mathbf{x}, \mathbf{x}') \equiv \bigvee_{K \geq k \geq 1} \left(\bigvee_{\alpha: Top(\alpha)=k} \mathcal{D}_\alpha(\mathbf{x}, \mathbf{x}') \right). \qquad (2)$$

2.4 Kronecker Encoding of the Transition Relation to Exploit Locality

The performance evaluation community working on Markov chains has long recognized that Kronecker techniques can be used to encode large (real) transition matrices while naturally exploiting the presence of identity transformations for state variables [25]. However, such an encoding requires a *Kronecker consistent* model. In our setting, this means that the following two properties must hold:

- The support of each enabling conjunct contains only one unprimed variable. Thus, $Enable_{\alpha,l}(x_l)$ simply lists the set of values $\mathcal{S}_{\alpha,l} \subseteq \mathcal{S}_l$ for x_l in which the event may be enabled: $Enable_{\alpha,l}(x_l) \equiv [x_l \in \mathcal{S}_{\alpha,l}]$. Of course, when $\mathcal{S}_{\alpha,l} = \mathcal{S}_l$, the conjunct does not enforce any restriction on the enabling of event α.
- The support of the updating conjunct for x_l' contains only x_l, in addition to x_l': $Upd_{\alpha,l}(x_l, x_l') \equiv [x_l' \in \mathcal{N}_{\alpha,l}(x_l)]$, where $\mathcal{N}_{\alpha,l}(x_l) \subseteq \mathcal{S}_l$.

Such a model is called Kronecker consistent because, letting $\mathcal{R}_{\alpha,l}(x_l, x_l') \equiv [x_l \in \mathcal{S}_{\alpha,l} \wedge x_l' \in \mathcal{N}_{\alpha,l}(x_l)]$, and storing it as an $n_l \times n_l$ boolean matrix $\mathbf{R}_{\alpha,l}$, we can write $\mathcal{R}(\mathbf{x}, \mathbf{x}') \equiv \bigvee_{\alpha \in \mathcal{E}} \bigwedge_{K \geq l \geq 1} \mathcal{R}_{\alpha,l}(x_l, x_l')$ and the matrix $\mathbf{R}$ corresponding to the overall transition relation $\mathcal{R}$ can be expressed as $\mathbf{R} = \sum_{\alpha \in \mathcal{E}} \bigotimes_{K \geq l \geq 1} \mathbf{R}_{\alpha,l}$, where "$\sum$" indicates boolean sum and "$\otimes$" Kronecker product of matrices. Our notion of locality becomes apparent: for $x_l \in V_\alpha^{indep}$, $\mathcal{R}_{\alpha,l}(x_l, x_l') \equiv [x_l' = x_l]$, thus $\mathbf{R}_{\alpha,l}$ is an identity matrix, which of course is not explicitly stored.

A model can be made Kronecker consistency in two ways. We can *merge* state variables into new "larger" variables, so that each new variable can depend only on the original state variables that were merged into it; in our running example, we could merge variables x_4 and x_3 into a new variable, and variables x_7 and x_6 into another new variable. Or we can *split* a disjunct $\mathcal{D}_\alpha$ based on a Shannon expansion, so that each new "smaller" disjunct satisfies Kronecker consistency; in our example, we can split along variables x_7 and x_4 and write $\mathcal{D}_\alpha = \bigvee_{i_7 \in \{0,\dots,5\}, i_4 \in \{0,\dots,5\}} \mathcal{D}_{\alpha,x_7=i_7,x_4=i_4}$, where each $\mathcal{D}_{\alpha,x_7=i_7,x_4=i_4}$ satisfies Kronecker consistency. However, neither approach is satisfactory for models with intricate dependencies; excessive merging results in few or even just a single state variable, i.e., an explicit approach, while excessive splitting causes an exponential growth in the number of events, i.e., the storage for the $\mathbf{R}_{\alpha,l}$ matrices.

2.5 Previously Proposed Variants of the Saturation Algorithm

The saturation algorithm exploits event locality through lightweight recursive fixed point image computations where the disjunctive partitioning of the transition relation is organized according to the value of $Top(\alpha)$, for each $\alpha \in \mathcal{E}$:

$$\mathcal{R}(\mathbf{x}, \mathbf{x}') \equiv \bigvee_{K \geq l \geq 1} \bigvee_{\alpha : Top(\alpha)=l} \mathcal{D}_\alpha(\mathbf{x}, \mathbf{x}') \equiv \bigvee_{K \geq l \geq 1} \mathcal{R}_l(\mathbf{x}_{(l,1)}, \mathbf{x}'_{(l,1)}) \wedge [\mathbf{x}'_{(K,l+1)} = \mathbf{x}_{(K,l+1)}].$$

A node p at level l is saturated if the set of states it encodes cannot be enlarged by applying events α such that $Top(\alpha) \leq l$, i.e., $\mathcal{B}(l, p) \supseteq Img_{\leq l}(\mathcal{B}(l, p))$, where $Img_{\leq l}$ is the image computation restricted to $\mathcal{R}_k$, for $l \geq k \geq 1$:

$Img_{\leq l}(\mathcal{X}) = \{\mathbf{x}'_{(l,1)} : \exists \mathbf{x}_{(l,1)} \in \mathcal{X}, \exists k \leq l, \mathcal{R}_k(\mathbf{x}_{(k,1)}, \mathbf{x}'_{(k,1)}) \wedge \mathbf{x}_{(l,k+1)} = \mathbf{x}'_{(l,k+1)}\}.$

Thus, if, before saturating it, p encoded the set $\mathcal{B}(l,p) = \mathcal{X}_0$, at the end of its saturation, p encodes the least fixed point $\mathcal{B}(l,p) = \mu\mathcal{X}.(\mathcal{X}_0 \cup Img_{\leq l}(\mathcal{X}))$. To encode this fixed point, p is modified *in place*, i.e., the pointers $p[i_l]$ are changed, so that they point to nodes that encode increasingly larger sets, while the pointers to p from nodes above it are unchanged.

Starting from the MDD encoding the initial state(s), the nodes of this MDD are *saturated* in bottom-up order. In other words, whenever the application of $\mathcal{R}_l$ causes the creation of a node at a level $k < l$, this new node must be immediately saturated, by applying $\mathcal{R}_k$ to it. Thus, during the bottom-up process of saturating all nodes, only $\mathcal{R}_l$ must be applied to a node p at level l, since all $\mathcal{R}_k$, for $k < l$, have been already applied to saturate its children.

In the original saturation algorithm for Kronecker-consistent models [6], we store each $\mathcal{D}_\alpha$ as the set of matrices $\mathbf{R}_{\alpha,l}$, for $Top(\alpha) \geq l \geq Bot(\alpha)$; of course, for $Top(\alpha) > l > Bot(\alpha)$, we might have $x_l \in \mathcal{V}_\alpha^{indep}$, in which case $\mathbf{R}_{\alpha,l}$ is the identity and is not stored. For state-space generation of GALS, we showed how the peak memory and runtime requirements of saturation can be several orders of magnitude better than a traditional breadth-first iteration.

In [7], we extended the algorithm to models where the state variables have unknown bounds, which must then be discovered "on-the-fly". During the generation process, each matrix $\mathbf{R}_{\alpha,l}$ contains rows and columns corresponding to the *confirmed* values for $\mathbf{x}_l$, i.e., values i_l that appear as the lth component in at least one global state $\mathbf{i}$ known to be reachable, but also columns corresponding to *unconfirmed* values for $\mathbf{x}_l$, i.e., values j_l such that $\mathcal{R}_{\alpha,l}(i_l, j_l)$ is a possible transition in isolation from a confirmed state i_l, but we don't yet know whether α is enabled in a global state $\mathbf{i}$ whose l^{th} component is i_l. Thus, the algorithm interleaves the building of rows of $\mathbf{R}_{\alpha,l}$, obtained through an explicit (local) state-space exploration of the model restricted to variable x_l, with the (global) symbolic exploration of the state space.

In [20], Miner showed how to deal with models that do not satisfy the Kronecker-consistency requirement. The transition relation is encoded using K-level *matrix diagrams (MxDs)*, which we introduced in [8]. Essentially, these are $2K$-level MDDs where the nodes of levels x_l and x'_l are merged into "matrix" nodes having $n_l \times n_l$ edges, but, unlike ordinary decision diagrams, the reduction rule requires to remove a node p if it describes an identity, i.e., if $p[i_l, j_l] = Zero$ for $i_l \neq j_l$ and $p[i_l, i_l] = q$ for all $i_l \in \mathcal{S}_l$. Thus, MxDs combine the generality of decision diagrams (they can represent any relation over $\widehat{\mathcal{S}}$) with the advantages of a Kronecker representation (they can reveal and exploit event locality).

A single MxD can encode $\mathcal{R}_l$, but [20] requires $\mathcal{R}_l(\mathbf{x}, \mathbf{x}')$ to be expressed as

$$\mathcal{R}_l(\mathbf{x}_{(l,1)}, \mathbf{x}'_{(l,1)}) \equiv \bigvee_{\alpha:\, Top(\alpha)=l} \left(\bigwedge_g Group_{\alpha,g}(\mathbf{x}_{(l,1)}, \mathbf{x}'_{(l,1)}) \wedge \bigwedge_{x_k \in \mathcal{V}_\alpha^{indep},\, k<l} [x'_k = x_k] \right),$$

where $Supp(Group_{\alpha,g})$ is a set of "unprimed-primed" variable pairs, and groups have disjoint supports: $g \neq h$ implies $Supp(Group_{\alpha,g}) \wedge Supp(Group_{\alpha,h}) = \emptyset$.

Thus, each "coarse-grain" $Group_{\alpha,g}$ corresponds to the intersection of all the enabling and updating conjuncts that depend on its support, including the updating conjuncts of the form $[x'_k = x_k]$, for $x_k \in \mathcal{V}_\alpha^{unchanged} \cap Supp(Group_{\alpha,g})$.

Then, [20] maintains an MxD for each $Group_{\alpha,g}$, and updates it every time a new local state $i_k \in \mathcal{S}_k$ is confirmed, if $x_k \in Supp(Group_{\alpha,g})$. In turn, this triggers the rebuilding of the MxD for $\mathcal{R}_l$, by performing the appropriate MxD intersection and union operations. Just like in [7], these updates following the confirmation of a local state require one step of explicit state space exploration in a portion of the model. However, instead of considering a single variable x_k, we must now consider **all** the unprimed variables in $Supp(Group_{\alpha,g})$ whenever the set of possible values for **any** of these variables is extended. For example, if $Supp(Group_{\alpha,g}) = \{x_7, x'_7, x_5, x'_5, x_2, x'_2\}$ and $i_5 \in \mathcal{S}_5$ is confirmed, [20] explicitly explores the possible transitions from each state in $\mathcal{S}_7 \times \{i_5\} \times \mathcal{S}_2$.

3   Fine-Grain Partitioning with MDD-Based Encodings

The cost of building the coarse-grain disjoint partitioned groups $Group_{\alpha,g}$ of [20] can be large, since each group $Group_{\alpha,g}$ is built explicitly, at an exploration cost $O(\prod_{x_k \in Supp(Group_{\alpha,g})} |\mathcal{S}_k|)$. The disjoint partitioning requirement may result in too coarse a conjunctive-partitioning for event α or even, in the worst case, in a single group, as in the shift register example of Sect. 5.

We propose a fine-grain partitioned approach, using the more familiar $2K$-level MDDs to encode the transition relation. We express $\mathcal{R}_l(\mathbf{x}_{(l,1)}, \mathbf{x}'_{(l,1)})$ as:

$$\mathcal{R}_l(\mathbf{x}_{(l,1)}, \mathbf{x}'_{(l,1)}) = \bigvee_{\alpha:\, Top(\alpha)=l} \left(\mathcal{D}_\alpha^{Part}\left(\mathbf{x}_{(l,1)}, \mathbf{x}'_{(l,1)}\right) \wedge \bigwedge_{x_k \notin \mathcal{V}_\alpha^{upd},\, k \leq l} [x'_k = x_k] \right), \quad (3)$$

where the "partial" relation $\mathcal{D}_\alpha^{Part}\left(\mathbf{x}_{(l,1)}, \mathbf{x}'_{(l,1)}\right)$ is defined as:

$$\mathcal{D}_\alpha^{Part}\left(\mathbf{x}_{(l,1)}, \mathbf{x}'_{(l,1)}\right) = \bigwedge_m Enable_{\alpha,m}\left(\mathbf{x}_{(l,1)}\right) \wedge \bigwedge_{x_k \in \mathcal{V}_\alpha^{upd}} Upd_{\alpha,k}\left(\mathbf{x}_{(l,1)}, x'_k\right).$$

We use a fully-reduced MDD for each enabling conjunct $Enable_{\alpha,m}$ and each updating conjunct $Upd_{\alpha,k}$ of each event α with $Top(\alpha) = l$, where $x_k \in \mathcal{V}_\alpha^{upd}$. The variables of each such MDD are only those in the support of the encoded conjunct; because of our new encoding technique, we do not store the updating conjuncts of the form $[x'_k = x_k]$, for $x_k \notin \mathcal{V}_\alpha^{upd}$, $k \leq l$, even if $x_k \notin \mathcal{V}_\alpha^{indep}$.

The fully-reduced MDD encoding $\mathcal{D}_\alpha^{Part}$ is then obtained as the intersection (boolean conjunction) of the MDDs of all its $Enable_{\alpha,m}$ and $Upd_{\alpha,k}$ conjuncts, thus $Supp(\mathcal{D}_\alpha^{Part})$ is the union of the supports of these conjuncts.

3.1   Fully-Identity Reduced $2K$-Level MDD Encoding of the Disjuncts

To efficiently build $\mathcal{R}_l$ from Eq. 3 and exploit event locality in the MDD, we introduce a new canonicity-preserving *identity* reduction rule. In our particular application, we use a *fully-identity* reduced $2K$-level MDD to encode each $\mathcal{R}_l$:

- Each unprimed level, l (for variable x_l) $K \geq l \geq 1$, is fully-reduced, i.e., no node at level l can be redundant, and is immediately followed by the corresponding primed level l' (for variable x'_l).
- Each level l' is *identity-reduced* w.r.t. to level l: (1) if node p is at level l and $p[i_l]$ reaches q at level l', then q is not a *singular-i_l* node, i.e., it is not a node with $q[i_l] \neq Zero$ and $q[j_l] = Zero$ for all $j_l \in S_l \setminus \{i_l\}$; (2) a singular-$i_l$ node at level l', for any $i_l \in S_l$, must be pointed by a node at level l.

Fig. 1 shows three examples of MDDs that are either fully-fully (left) or fully-identity (right) reduced for the unprimed and primed levels, respectively. In the first example, the entire identity pattern clearly visible in the fully-fully case is absent in the fully-identity case, because nodes q_0 and q_1 are eliminated first (due to the identity-reduced rule for level l') and the remaining node p is now redundant and eliminated (due to the fully-reduced rule for level l). In the second example, singular-0 node q_0 is eliminated, but redundant node q is added while, in the third example, singular-1 node q_1 requires the introduction of node p, which is not redundant in the fully-identity reduction case.

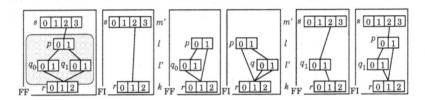

Fig. 1. Comparing fully-fully (FF) and fully-identity (FI) reductions for MDDs

---

$Build(\mathcal{R}_l)$

1 **foreach** α s.t. $Top(\alpha) = l$ **do**
2     $\mathcal{D}_\alpha^{Part} \leftarrow \bigwedge_m Enable_{\alpha,m} \wedge \bigwedge_{x_k \in \mathcal{V}_\alpha^{upd}} Upd_{\alpha,k}$;   •*intersection of fully-fully MDDs*
3     $\mathcal{D}_\alpha \leftarrow FullyIdentity(\mathcal{D}_\alpha^{Part})$;   •*change fully-fully MDD into fully-identity MDD*
4 $\mathcal{R}_l \leftarrow \bigvee_{\alpha: Top(\alpha) = l} \mathcal{D}_\alpha$;   •*union of fully-identity MDDs*

Fig. 2. Algorithm to build $\mathcal{R}_l$ from the disjuncts and conjuncts

From the fully-fully reduced MDD for $\mathcal{D}_\alpha^{Part}$, the fully-identity reduced $2K$-level MDD for $\mathcal{D}_\alpha$ is built using a recursive procedure. Then, the $2K$-level fully-identity reduced MDD encoding of $\mathcal{R}_l$ is built using a recursive *union* for fully-identity reduced MDD on the disjuncts $\mathcal{D}_\alpha$ for which $Top(\alpha) = l$ (Fig. 2).

Our fully-identity reduced $2K$-level MDDs, while strongly related to MxDs used in [20] to encode disjuncts, can be even more compact. Only matrix nodes corresponding to levels $l \in \mathcal{V}_\alpha^{indep}$ can be eliminated in MxDs, while, in addition to eliminating these entire identity patterns, our fully-identity reduced MDDs also eliminate nodes at primed levels $k \in \mathcal{V}_\alpha^{unchanged}$.

4   A New Saturation Algorithm for State-Space Generation

Based on the new encoding technique for partitioned transition relations, we propose new saturation algorithms for models with known or unknown variable bounds, respectively (Fig. 3 and 4). As in previous saturation algorithms, the state space is encoded in a *quasi-reduced* K-level MDD, since $\mathbf{R}_l$ must be applied also to redundant nodes at level l; if fully-reduced MDDs were used, these nodes would have to be re-inserted to saturate them during bottom-up saturation. For simplicity, the pseudocode of Fig. 3 4 assumes that either both or neither levels k and k' are skipped in the MDD of the disjuncts $\mathcal{R}_l$, for $K \geq l \geq 1$; our actual implementation also manages the case when only one of them is skipped.

$Saturate(\text{MDD } p)$

  1 $l \leftarrow p.lvl$;
  2 **repeat**
  3     $\mathcal{B}(l,p) \leftarrow \mathcal{B}(l,p) \cup \bigcup_{i_l \in \mathcal{S}_l, i'_l \in \mathcal{S}_l} \{i'_l\} \times ImgSat\left(p[i_l], \mathcal{R}_l[i_l][i'_l]\right)$
  4 **until** $\mathcal{B}(l,p)$ is not changed

$ImgSat(\text{MDD } q, \text{MDD2 } f)$

  1 **if** $q = Zero$ or $f = Zero$ **then** return $\emptyset$;
  2 $k \leftarrow q.lvl$; $m \leftarrow f.lvl$; $s \leftarrow$ a new MDD node s at level k;
  3 **if** $k > m$ **then**
  4     $\mathcal{B}(k,s) = \bigcup_{i_k \in \mathcal{S}_k} \{i_k\} \times ImgSat\left(q[i_k], f\right)$;
  5 **else**   •k is equal to m
  6     $\mathcal{B}(k,s) = \bigcup_{i_k \in \mathcal{S}_k, i'_k \in \mathcal{S}_k} \{i'_k\} \times ImgSat\left(q[i'_k], f[i_k][i'_k]\right)$;
  7 $Saturate(s)$;
  8 **return** $\mathcal{B}(k,s)$.

Fig. 3. A saturation algorithm for models with known variable bounds

4.1   Saturation When State Variables Have Known Bounds

For models where state variables have known bounds, e.g., circuits and other hardware models, each conjunct can be built separately a priori, considering all the possible transitions when the conjunct is considered in isolation. Then, the MDD encodings of the disjunctive partition $\mathcal{R}_K, ..., \mathcal{R}_1$, can be built by the $Build(\mathcal{R}_l)$ procedure of Fig. 2, prior to state-space generation. The saturation algorithm for the case when $\mathcal{R}_K, ..., \mathcal{R}_1$ are built this way is shown in Fig. 3.

    $Saturate(p)$ recursively compute a fixed-point on node p at level l. It iteratively selects a child $p[i_l]$; for each $i'_l \in \mathcal{S}_l$, it calls $ImgSat(p[i_l], \mathcal{R}_l[i_l][i'_l])$ to compute the (possibly new) reachable states in $\mathcal{S}_{l-1} \times ... \times \mathcal{S}_1$; finally, it adds the states $\{i'_l\} \times ImgSat(p[i_l], \mathcal{R}_l[i_l, i'_l])$, a subset of $\mathcal{S}_l \times ... \times \mathcal{S}_1$, to $\mathcal{B}(l,p)$.

    The $ImgSat(q, f)$ procedure takes a K-level MDD node q at level k and a $2K$-level MDD node f at level m as inputs, where $m \leq k$, since the K-level MDD for the state space is quasi-reduced. If either node q or node f is $Zero$, the empty set is returned, since no transitions are possible in this case. If node f is at a level m below k, our fully-identity reduction implies the identity-transformation of variable x_k. If node f is instead at level k, for each possible transition of variable x_k from i_k to i'_k, a recursive call on the children nodes is made. These (possibly) new states are encoded in a MDD node s at level k, which is *Saturated* prior to returning it to the calling procedure.

The state-space generation starts with an MDD encoding for the initial state(s), then follows with a bottom-up saturation of these initial MDD nodes, until all of them are saturated. The final result is the encoding of the state space.

4.2 Saturation When State Variables Have Unknown Bounds

For systems with unknown variable bounds, the partitioned transition relations cannot be built prior to state-space generation. We must instead interleave building partitioned transition relation i.e., calls to the *Confirm* procedure, with symbolic state-space generation (Fig. 4).

We define the *confirmed* set $\mathcal{S}^c_l \subseteq \mathcal{S}_l$ for variable x_l as the values of variable x_l that appear in a global state currently encoded by the MDD. $\mathcal{S}_l \backslash \mathcal{S}^c_l$ contains instead the *unconfirmed* states that appear only in the l' level of the transition relation; these are "locally" but not necessarily "globally" reachable. For any node p at level l, $p[i_l] = Zero$ for any such unconfirmed local state i_l.

Saturate is then modified so that, at each iteration, any new values for x_l that are now known to be reachable (appears in a path leading to *One* in the MDD encoding the state-space) are confirmed by calling $Confirm(x_l, i'_l)$, and $\mathcal{R}_l$ is rebuilt if needed, i.e., if any of its conjuncts has changed. The selection of (i_l, i'_l) in statement 5 of course avoids repeating a pair unless $p[i_l]$ or $\mathcal{R}_l[i_l][i'_l]$ have changed; this check is omitted for clarity.

Saturate(MDD p)

1 $l \leftarrow p.lvl$;
2 **repeat**
3    $Confirm(x_l, i_l)$ for any state $i_l \in \mathcal{S}_l \setminus \mathcal{S}^c_l$ s.t. $p[i_l] \neq Zero$;
4    $Build(\mathcal{R}_l)$;
5   pick $i_l \in \mathcal{S}^c_l, i'_l \in \mathcal{S}_l$ s.t. $\mathcal{R}_l[i_l][i'_l] \neq Zero$;
6    $\mathcal{B}(l, p) \leftarrow \mathcal{B}(l, p) \cup \{i'_l\} \times ImgSat\,(p[i_l], \mathcal{R}_l[i_l][i'_l])$
7 **until** $\mathcal{B}(l, p)$ is not changed

Confirm(x_l, i_l)

1 $\mathcal{S}^c_l \leftarrow \mathcal{S}^c_l \cup \{i_l\}$;
2 **foreach** enabling conjunct $Enable_{\alpha,m}$, s.t. $x_l \in Supp(Enable_{\alpha,m})$ **do**
3   **foreach** $\mathbf{i}_{sub} \in \{i_l\} \times \times_{x_k \in Supp(Enable_{\alpha,m}) \backslash \{x_l\}} \mathcal{S}^c_k$ **do**
4   **if** $ModelEnable_{\alpha,m}(\mathbf{i}_{sub})$ **then** $Enable_{\alpha,m} \leftarrow Enable_{\alpha,m} \cup \{\mathbf{i}_{sub}\}$;
5 **foreach** updating conjunct $Upd_{\alpha,n}$, s.t. $x_l \in Supp(Upd_{\alpha,n})$ **do**
6   **foreach** $\mathbf{i}_{sub} \in \{i_l\} \times \times_{x_k \in \{x_K, \ldots, x_1\} \cap Supp(Upd_{\alpha,n}) \backslash \{x_l\}} \mathcal{S}^c_k$ **do**
7      $\mathcal{I}'_n \leftarrow ModelUpd_{\alpha,n}(\mathbf{i}_{sub})$; $\bullet$*states reachable from* $\mathbf{i}_{sub}$ *in one step*
8      $Upd_{\alpha,n} \leftarrow Upd_{\alpha,n} \cup \{\mathbf{i}_{sub}\} \times \mathcal{I}'_n$;
9      $\mathcal{S}_n \leftarrow \mathcal{S}_n \cup \mathcal{I}'_n$;

Fig. 4. A saturation algorithm for models with unknown variable bounds

Procedure *Confirm* takes a new value i_l for variable x_l and updates each conjunct with x_l in its support. This requires to explicitly query the high-level model for each (sub)state $\mathbf{i}_{sub}$ that can be formed using the new value i_l and any of the values in the confirmed set $\mathcal{S}_k^c$ of any unprimed variable x_k in the support of such a conjunct. Functions *ModelEnable*$_{\alpha,m}$ and *ModelUpd*$_{\alpha,n}$ are analogous to *Enable*$_{\alpha,m}$ and *Upd*$_{\alpha,n}$, but they are assumed to be "black-boxes" that can be queried only explicitly; they return, respectively, whether α is enabled in $\mathbf{i}_{sub}$, and what is the set of possible values for x_n' when α fires in $\mathbf{i}_{sub}$ in isolation, i.e., considering only the restriction of the model to the particular conjunct. Thus, our cost is still of the form $O(\prod_{x_k \in Supp(f)} |\mathcal{S}_k|)$, as in [20], but f is now *Enable*$_{\alpha,m}$ or *Upd*$_{\alpha,n}$, which can have a much smaller support than *Group*$_{\alpha,g}$.

We stress that, while our presentation assumes that the support of each updating conjunct contains a single primed variable, this is is not required by our approach. Thus, a situation where an event α "nondeterministically either increments both x_5 and x_4 or decrements both x_5 and x_4" is captured with an updating conjunct of the form *Upd*$_{\alpha,\{4,5\}}$ having both x_5' and x_4' in its support. Indeed, our implementation heuristically merges enabling or updating conjuncts for efficiency reasons: if $Supp(Enable_{\alpha,m}) \subset Supp(Upd_{\alpha,l})$, we can merge the effect of *Enable*$_{\alpha,m}$ in the definition of *Upd*$_{\alpha,l}$; if $Supp(Upd_{\alpha,l}) \setminus \{x_l'\} \subseteq Supp(Upd_{\alpha,k}) \setminus \{x_k'\}$, we can merge the two updating conjuncts, into a conjunct *Upd*$_{\alpha,\{l,k\}}$ having the union of the supports. As long as no new unprimed variable is added to the support of a conjunct, the enumeration cost of explicitly building the conjunct is not affected, but the number of conjuncts is reduced.

5   Experimental Results

We now show some experimental results for our new technique, run on a 3 Ghz Pentium IV workstation with 1GB memory, on a set of models whose state-space size can be controlled by a parameter N. We compare the new proposed saturation algorithm for the unknown bound case (for ease of model specification) with the saturation algorithm in [20], the symbolic model checker NuSMV [9], and the explicit model checker SPIN [14], which targets asynchronous software verification and applies partial-order reduction and other optimizations such as minimized automaton storage for reachable states and hash compaction.

Table 1 reports the parameter N, the size $|\mathcal{S}|$ of the original and the reduced (by partial-order reduction) state space, and the runtimes and peak memory requirements for the four approaches, SPIN, SMV (NuSMV), QEST (the approach in [20]), and NEW (our new encoding technique). Both QEST and NEW are implemented in our tool SMART [5]. We studied the following models:

- A *Slotted-ring* network protocol [24] where N processors can access the medium only during the slot allocated to them.
- The classical *Queen* problem where the N queens must be placed on an $N \times N$ chessboard, in sequential order from row 1 to N without attacking each other.

- A *Fault-tolerant* multiprocessor system described in [11]. While [11] requires 1200 seconds for $N = 5$, we require 0.07 seconds for $N = 5$ and we can generate the state space for $N = 100$ in 485 seconds. [20] reports similar improvements, but uses over twice as much memory.
- A *Leader* election protocol among N processes, a simplified version of [12], where the broadcasting of the winner identity is omitted. Messages are sent asynchronously via FIFO message queues.
- A *Bubble-sort* algorithm where an array of N numbers initialized to $N, ..., 1$ need to be sorted into the result $1, ..., N$.
- A *Swapper* program [1] where a boolean array of size $2N$ is initialized with 0's in the first half and 1's in the second half, and the two halves are swapped through neighbor-only exchanges. While the best tool considered in [1] requires 90 seconds for $N = 40$, we require 0.03 seconds for $N = 40$ and can generate the state space for $N = 2,000$ in 50 seconds.
- A *Round-robin* mutex protocol [13] where N processes require exclusive access to a resource.
- A *Bit-shifter* where, at each step, a new random bit b_0 is generated, and bit b_k is set to bit b_{k-1}, for $N \geq k \geq 1$.
- An analogous *Int-shifter*, which shifts values in the range $\{1, ..., N\}$.

Defining equivalent models (with the same number of states) was a challenge. For *Leader*, from the SPIN distribution, we were able to define equivalent models for NuSMV and SMART. For all other models, initially defined in SMART, we defined equivalent NuSMV and SPIN models, except that, for SPIN, our *Queen* model has approximately $1/3$ more states, and we have no *Fault-tolerant* model.

From Table 1, we can observe that, compared with QEST, NEW has better runtime and memory consumptions for essentially all models and parameter combinations. In the only two cases where QEST is (negligibly) faster than NEW, *Bubble-sort* and *Fault-tolerant*, NEW's memory consumption is much better. Especially for *Bit-shifter* and *Int-shifter*, NEW has enormously better performance. This is because QEST requires conjuncts (groups) with non-intersecting supports; for these two models, the resulting groups are very large and prevent QEST from analyzing a 256-bit shifter or an 8-int shifter.

Compared with SMV, both QEST and NEW achieve much better runtime and memory consumptions for all models except *Bit-shifter* and *Int-shifter*, where QEST reports much worse results than SMV, while NEW still greatly outperforms SMV in both time and memory.

Considering now SPIN, clearly, all symbolic approaches greatly outperform SPIN unless its partial-order reduction techniques are applicable. One case where this happen is *Leader*, for which only $10N$ states are explored in the reduced state space, while the actual state space S grows exponentially. Nevertheless, for *Leader*, NEW can generate the state space for $N = 30$, greatly outperforming SMV and QEST in time and memory; indeed NEW's peak number of MDD nodes for S is $22N - 23$, just one more than the final number. For all other models, instead, SPIN fails to reduce any states, thus its explicit exploration is limited to small parameter values.

Table 1. Experimental results

N	Original $\lvert \mathcal{S} \rvert$	Reduced $\lvert \mathcal{S} \rvert$	CPU time (sec)				Peak memory (KB)			
			SPIN	SMV	QEST	NEW	SPIN	SMV	QEST	NEW
Slotted-ring: $K = N$, $\lvert \mathcal{S}_k \rvert = 15$ for all k										
6	575,296	575,296	8.2	0.13	0.03	0.03	401,130.5	5,660.6	33.3	36.8
15	1.5×10^{15}	—	—	1285.1	0.17	0.15	—	21,564.2	262.7	155.8
200	8.4×10^{211}	—	—	—	—	204.8	153.6	—	—	362,175.8	176,934.1
Queen: $K = N$, $\lvert \mathcal{S}_k \rvert = N + 1$ for all k										
11	166,926	228,004	0.7	14.0	3.9	1.8	21,308.4	17,018.4	14,078.6	5,302.2
12	856,189	1.2×10^{6}	3.8	105.9	19.5	8.9	103,307.3	53,218.3	63,828.6	23,276.7
Fault-tolerant: $K = 10N + 1$, $\lvert \mathcal{S}_k \rvert \le 4$ for all k except $\lvert \mathcal{S}_1 \rvert = N + 1$										
5	2.4×10^{13}	n/a	n/a	n/a	152.0	0.14	0.07	n/a	18,576.8	171.4	120.2
100	1.0×10^{262}	n/a	n/a	n/a	—	480.2	485.0	n/a	—	52,438.7	23,406.1
Leader: $K = 2N$, $\lvert \mathcal{S}_k \rvert \le 19$ for all k										
7	1.5×10^{6}	70	0.013	491.7	1.6	0.7	7,521.3	91,270.2	607.2	42.1
20	3.3×10^{17}	200	0.024	—	93.4	28.2	7,521.3	—	7,281.3	86.6
30	1.8×10^{26}	300	0.047	—	568.9	145.6	9,618.4	—	20,271.7	114.3
Bubble-sort: $\lvert \mathcal{S} \rvert = N!$, $K = N$, $\lvert \mathcal{S}_k \rvert = N$ for all k										
11	4.0×10^{7}	4.0×10^{7}	1,042.8	125.3	1.7	1.7	848,498.7	19,704.4	7,217.6	2,505.7
12	4.8×10^{8}	—	—	859.9	5.3	5.5	—	43,948.3	21,680.7	7,438.5
Swapper: $\lvert \mathcal{S} \rvert = N!/((N/2)!)^2$, $K = N$, $\lvert \mathcal{S}_k \rvert = 2$ for all k										
20	184,756	184,756	0.9	0.2	0.01	0.01	37,006.3	6,831.6	30.8	23.5
40	1.4×10^{11}	—	—	241.6	0.06	0.03	—	14,795.2	100.4	34.3
2,000	2.0×10^{600}	—	—	—	742.3	49.8	—	—	187,266.0	58,970.9
Round-robin: $K = N + 1$, $\lvert \mathcal{S}_k \rvert = 10$ for all k except $\lvert \mathcal{S}_K \rvert = N + 1$										
16	2.3×10^{6}	2.3×10^{6}	43.0	0.34	0.11	0.07	1,046,004.7	7,060.3	290.0	125.5
50	1.3×10^{17}	—	—	11.7	2.1	1.2	—	61,239.0	6,041.3	1,299.2
200	7.2×10^{62}	—	—	—	336.3	77.0	—	—	351,625.7	47,833.1
Bit-shifter: $\lvert \mathcal{S} \rvert = 2^{N+2}$, $K = N + 3$, $\lvert \mathcal{S}_k \rvert = 2$ for all k except $\lvert \mathcal{S}_{N+3} \rvert = \lvert \mathcal{S}_{N+2} \rvert = 3$										
16	262,144	262,144	1.2	0.03	12.7	0.01	306,798.6	4,449.4	8,326.6	44.2
256	4.6×10^{77}	—	—	447.7	—	2.63	—	16,723.4	—	4,988.2
1,000	4.3×10^{301}	—	—	—	—	64.52	—	—	—	97,060.2
Int-shifter: $\lvert \mathcal{S} \rvert = 2N^{N+1}$, $K = N + 3$, $\lvert \mathcal{S}_k \rvert = N$ for all k except $\lvert \mathcal{S}_{N+3} \rvert = \lvert \mathcal{S}_{N+2} \rvert = 3$										
7	1.2×10^{7}	1.2×10^{7}	137.6	0.05	281.4	0.04	680,857.6	4,767.9	157,344.0	120.1
24	6.4×10^{34}	—	—	29.2	—	2.87	—	14,827.8	—	8,096.1
32	9.4×10^{49}	—	—	—	—	11.3	—	—	—	24,221.1

6   Related Work and Conclusions

For traditional breadth-first state space generation, the efficiency of image computation has been extensively studied. A *conjunctive partition* of the transition relation is the dominant approach for synchronous systems; the *conjunctive scheduling problem* [21] consider efficient clustering of the conjuncts and ordering of the clusters to minimize the size of the intermediate results during image computation. Traditionally, coarse-grain conjunctive partitioning is used to build the transition relation, and conjuncts are split only as necessary. A fine-grain conjunctive partition is instead used in [15], where bit-level conjuncts are conjoined into clusters. A *disjunctive partition* of the transition relation is instead naturally applied to asynchronous systems, but also to synchronous systems based on a Shannon's expansion [23]. [22] proposes an approach combining conjunctive partition with disjunctive recursive splitting; this differs from our approach which performs a conjunction on the results of the disjunction by events.

The presence of identities in disjunctive partitions of asynchronous circuits is suggested in [10], by limiting the image computation using disjuncts to the *dependent* variables. For software models, [2] shows how to translate conjuncts into disjuncts and vice versa. Their disjuncts modify only one state variable and the program counter, while we allow disjuncts to concurrently modify any number of state variables. Thus, [2] uses conjuncts not to "decompose" the disjuncts but to perform a pre-model-checking reduction. Furthermore, the image computation uses partial disjuncts, as in [10], but there is no merging of the partial-disjuncts while still exploiting the identity transformations, as allowed by our fully-identity reduced $2K$-MDDs.

Finally, regarding iteration orders other than breadth-first, only [20] uses a saturation-based approach; [3] uses a guided search in symbolic CTL model checking, in the hope to obtain a witness or counterexample without exploring the entire state space; and [26] uses a mixed breadth-first/depth-first approach in state-space generation based on the idea of *chaining*, a precursor to saturation.

To summarize our contribution, we introduced a new encoding for the transition relation of a discrete-state model, based on a new disjunctive-conjunctive partition and a new fully-identity reduction rule for MDDs. With this encoding, we perform symbolic state-space generation using the efficient *saturation* algorithm without having to satisfy the *Kronecker consistency* requirement. This new algorithm retains the efficiency of the original version, but has general applicability. In particular, it can be used to study models of software, for which the consistency requirement hindered the use of previous versions of saturation.

Remarkably, for saturation, encoding the transition relation with (at most) one MDD for each state variable turns out to be more efficient than the finer encoding with one MDD for each event. This suggests that **a disjunctive partition improves efficiency as long as it enables the recognition of event locality, but exploiting identity transformations is what truly matters**.

References

1. P. A. Abdulla, P. Bjesse, and N. Eén. Symbolic reachability analysis based on SAT-solvers. *TACAS*, LNCS 1785, pp.411–425, 2000.
2. S.Barner and I.Rabinovitz. Efficient symbolic model checking of software using partial disjunctive partitioning. *CHARME*, LNCS 2860, pp.35–50, 2003.
3. R.Bloem, K.Ravi, and F.Somenzi. Symbolic guided search for CTL model checking. *DAC*, pp.29–34, 2000.
4. R.E. Bryant. Graph-based algorithms for boolean function manipulation. *IEEE Trans. Comp.*, 35(8):677–691, 1986.
5. G.Ciardo, R.L. Jones, A.S. Miner, and R.Siminiceanu. Logical and stochastic modeling with SMART. *Tools*, LNCS 2794, pp.78–97, 2003.
6. G.Ciardo, G.Luettgen, and R.Siminiceanu. Saturation: An efficient iteration strategy for symbolic state space generation. *TACAS*, LNCS 2031, pp.328–342, 2001.
7. G.Ciardo, R.Marmorstein, and R.Siminiceanu. Saturation unbound. *TACAS*, LNCS 2619, pp.379–393, 2003.
8. G.Ciardo and A.S. Miner. A data structure for the efficient Kronecker solution of GSPNs. *PNPM*, pp.22–31, 1999.
9. A.Cimatti, E.Clarke, F.Giunchiglia, and M.Roveri. NuSMV: A new symbolic model verifier. *CAV*, LNCS 1633, pp.495–499, 1999.

10. E.M. Clarke, O.Grumberg, and D.A. Peled. *Model Checking*. MIT Press, 1999.
11. S.Derisavi, P.Kemper, and W.H. Sanders. Symbolic state-space exploration and numerical analysis of state-sharing composed models. *NSMC*, 167–189, 2003.
12. D.Dolev, M.Klawe, and M.Rodeh. An $O(n \log n)$ unidirectional distributed algorithm for extrema finding in a circle. *J. of Algorithms*, 3(3):245–260, 1982.
13. S.Graf, B.Steffen, and G.Lüttgen. Compositional minimisation of finite state systems using interface specifications. *Formal Asp. of Comp.*, 8(5):607–616, 1996.
14. G.J. Holzmann. *The SPIN Model Checker*. Addison-Wesley, 2003.
15. H.Jin, A.Kuehlmann, and F.Somenzi. Fine-grain conjunction scheduling for symbolic reachability analysis. *TACAS*, LNCS 2280, pp.312–326, 2002.
16. J.R. Burch, E.M. Clarke, and D.E. Long. Symbolic model checking with partitioned transition relations. *VLSI*, 49–58, 1991. IFIP.
17. K. L. McMillan. *Symbolic Model Checking*. Kluwer, 1993.
18. T.Kam, T.Villa, R.Brayton, and A.Sangiovanni-Vincentelli. Multi-valued decision diagrams: theory and applications. *Multiple-Valued Logic*, 4(1–2):9–62, 1998.
19. S.Kimura and E.M. Clarke. A parallel algorithm for constructing binary decision diagrams. *ICCD*, pp.220–223, 1990.
20. A.S. Miner. Saturation for a general class of models. *QEST*, pp.282–291, 2004.
21. I.-H. Moon, G.D. Hachtel, and F.Somenzi. Border-block triangular form and conjunction schedule in image computation. *FMCAD*, LNCS 1954, pp.73–90, 2000.
22. I.-H. Moon, J.H. Kukula, K.Ravi, and F.Somenzi. To split or to conjoin: the question in image computation. *DAC*, pp.23–28, 2000.
23. A.Narayan, A.J. Isles, J.Jain, R.K. Brayton, and A.Sangiovanni-Vincentelli. Reachability analysis using partitioned-ROBDDs. *ICCAD*, pp.388–393, 1997.
24. E.Pastor, O.Roig, J.Cortadella, and R.Badia. Petri net analysis using boolean manipulation. *ATPN*, LNCS 815, pp.416–435, 1994.
25. B.Plateau. On the stochastic structure of parallelism and synchronisation models for distributed algorithms. *SIGMETRICS*, pp.147–153, 1985.
26. M.Solé and E.Pastor. Traversal techniques for concurrent systems. *FMCAD*, LNCS 2517, pp.220–237, 2002.

Real-Time Model Checking Is Really Simple

Leslie Lamport

Microsoft Research

Abstract. It is easy to write and verify real-time specifications with existing languages and methods; one just represents time as an ordinary variable and expresses timing requirements with special timer variables. The resulting specifications can be verified with an ordinary model checker. This basic idea and some less obvious details are explained, and results are presented for two examples.

1 Introduction

Numerous special languages and logics have been proposed for specifying and verifying real-time algorithms. There is an alternative that I call the *explicit-time* approach, in which the current time is represented as the value of a variable *now* and the passage of time is modeled by a *Tick* action that increments *now*. Timing constraints are expressed with timer variables.

Hardly anything has been written about the explicit-time approach, perhaps because it is so simple and obvious. As a result, most people seem to believe that they must use special real-time languages and logics. It has already been shown that an explicit-time approach works fine for specifying and proving properties of real-time algorithms [1]. Here, I consider model checking explicit-time specifications.

The major advantage of the explicit-time approach is that it can be used with any language and logic for describing concurrent algorithms. This is especially important for complex algorithms that can be quite difficult to represent in the lower-level, inexpressive languages typical of real-time model checkers. For example, distributed message-passing algorithms have queues or sets of messages in transit, each with a bound on its delivery time. Such algorithms are difficult or impossible to handle with most real-time model checkers. Section 2 briefly explains the explicit-time approach with a simple distributed algorithm. A complete specification of the algorithm in TLA$^+$ [8], a high-level mathematics-based language, appears in [9].

Explicit-time descriptions can use either continuous or discrete time. Section 3 shows that when discrete time is used, these descriptions can be checked with ordinary model checkers. This simple fact has been known for quite a while and is implicit in several published results [5]. However, a direct statement of it does not seem to have appeared before in print. Moreover, there are some aspects

D. Borrione and W. Paul (Eds.): CHARME 2005, LNCS 3725, pp. 162–175, 2005.

of model checking explicit-time specifications that may not be obvious, including the use of view symmetry and a method for checking that a specification is nonZeno [1].

Section 4 describes the result of checking the algorithm described in Section 2 with TLC, a model checker for TLA$^+$ specifications, and with Uppaal [10], the only real-time model checker I know of that can handle this example. It also compares TLC, Spin [6], and SMV [11] with Uppaal on the Fischer mutual exclusion algorithm [13]. More details appear in [9].

2   Writing Explicit-Time Specifications

In an explicit-time specification, time is represented with a variable *now* that is incremented by a *Tick* action. For a continuous-time specification, *Tick* might increment *now* by any real number; for a discrete-time specification, it increments *now* by 1. Timing bounds on actions are specified with one of three kinds of timer variables: a *countdown* timer is decremented by the *Tick* action, a *count-up* timer is incremented by *Tick*, and an *expiration* timer is left unchanged by *Tick*.[1] A countdown or count-up timer expires when its value reaches some value; an expiration timer expires when its value minus *now* reaches some value. An upper-bound timing constraint on when an action A must occur is expressed by an enabling condition on the *Tick* action that prevents an increase in time from violating the constraint; a lower-bound constraint on when A may occur is expressed by an enabling condition on A that prevents it from being executed earlier than it should be.

I illustrate how one writes explicit-time specifications using the example of a simple version of a classic distributed algorithm of Radia Perlman [12]. The original algorithm constructs a spanning tree rooted at the lowest-numbered node, called the *leader*. The tree is maintained by having the leader periodically propagate an *I'm Leader* message down it that informs each node of its distance to the leader. A new tree is constructed if a failure causes some node to time out before receiving the *I'm Leader* message. I have simplified it by eliminating failures, so correctness means simply that every node learns the leader within some fixed length of time. A complete TLA$^+$ specification of the algorithm appears in [9]. Here, I describe only the TLA$^+$ specification of the *Tick* action.

The algorithm has three timing parameters, *Period*, *MsgDelay*, and *TODelay*. Each node n has a countdown timer $timer[n]$. Setting $timer[n]$ to τ causes a timeout to occur between τ and $\tau + TODelay$ seconds later. By letting τ be the minimum timeout interval, this models both delay in reacting to a timeout and variation in the running rate of physical timers. When its timeout occurs, node n sends an *I'm Leader* message and sets $timer[n]$ to *Period*. If n receives an *I'm Leader* message from a lower-numbered node, it resets $timer[n]$ to a suitable value. A message is assumed to be received at most *MsgDelay* seconds after it is sent, a constraint enforced with a *rcvTimer*

---

[1] Dutertre and Sorea [3] use a different kind of timer variable that predicts the time at which an action will occur.

$Tick \triangleq \exists d \in \{r \in Real : r > 0\} :$
$\qquad \land \forall n \in Node : timer[n] + TODelay \geq d$
$\qquad \land \forall ms \in BagToSet(msgs) : ms.rcvTimer \geq d$
$\qquad \land now' = now + d$
$\qquad \land timer' = [n \in Node \mapsto timer[n] - d]$
$\qquad \land msgs' = \text{LET } Updated(ms) \triangleq$
$\qquad\qquad\qquad\qquad [ms \text{ EXCEPT } !.rcvTimer = ms.rcvTimer - d]$
$\qquad\qquad\quad \text{IN} \quad BagOfAll(Updated, msgs)$
$\qquad \land \text{UNCHANGED } \langle ldr, dist \rangle$

Fig. 1. The *Tick* action's definition for the leader algorithm

countdown timer field in the message. The algorithm achieves stability if, upon receiving a message from its leader, a node n sets $timer[n]$ to a value no smaller than $Period + TODelay + dist[n] * MsgDelay$, where $dist[n]$ is the distance from n to the leader.

Figure 1 contains the definition of the *Tick* action from the TLA$^+$ specification. It can't be completely understood without seeing the rest of the specification and having some knowledge of TLA$^+$ (including the definitions of the operators *BagToSet* and *BagOfAll* from the standard *Bags* module). However, it will indicate how timing constraints are specified and also give an idea of the high-level nature of TLA$^+$. This version is for a continuous-time specification, in which *now* is incremented by some real value d. We obtain a discrete-time specification by replacing "$\exists d \in \{r \in Real : r > 0\} :$" with "LET $d \triangleq 1$ IN".

The action's first two conjuncts enforce the upper-bound constraints. The first prevents $timer[n]$ from becoming less than $-TODelay$, for each node n. The second prevents the timer $ms.rcvTimer$ from becoming negative, for all messages ms in the bag (multiset) msg of messages in transit.

The action's remaining conjuncts assert how the variables are changed. The third conjunct asserts that *now* is incremented by d. The fourth and fifth conjuncts assert that all the timers are decremented by d, the fourth for each $timer[n]$ and the fifth for the timer component $ms.rcvTimer$ of each message ms. The final conjunct asserts that the specification's other variables are unchanged.

The complete specification asserts the additional timing constraint that a timeout action of node n cannot occur before $timer[n]$ has counted down past 0. This constraint is expressed by the conjunct $timer[n] < 0$ in that action's definition.

3   Model Checking Explicit-Time Specifications

Most real-time system specifications are symmetric under time translation, meaning that system actions depend only on the passage of time, not on absolute time values. This section explains what symmetry and model checking under symmetry mean and describes a simple method of model checking explicit-time specifications that are symmetric under time translation.

3.1   Specifications and Temporal Properties

Let a *state* of a specification be an assignment of values to all the specification's variables, and let its *state space* be the set of all such states. A *state predicate* is a predicate (Boolean function) on states, and an *action* is a predicate on pairs of states. The formula $s \xrightarrow{A} t$ asserts that action A is true on the pair s, t of states. A *behavior* is a sequence of states. A *temporal property* is a predicate on behaviors. Temporal properties are represented syntactically as temporal formulas.

Assume a specification $\mathcal{S}$ that consists of an initial predicate *Init*, a next-state action *Next*, and a liveness assumption L that is a temporal property, possibly equal to TRUE. The initial predicate and next-state action form the *safety part* $\overline{\mathcal{S}}$ of specification $\mathcal{S}$. A behavior $s_1, s_2, \ldots$ satisfies $\overline{\mathcal{S}}$ iff s_1 satisfies *Init* and $s_i \xrightarrow{Next} s_{i+1}$ for all i; it satisfies $\mathcal{S}$ iff it satisfies both $\overline{\mathcal{S}}$ and L.

3.2   Symmetry

A *symmetry* is an equivalence relation on states. A state predicate P is *symmetric with respect to* a symmetry $\sim$ iff, for any states s and t with $s \sim t$, predicate P is true in state s iff it is true in state t. An action A is *symmetric with respect to* $\sim$ iff, for any states s_1, s_2, and t_1,

$$
\begin{array}{ccc}
s_1 \xrightarrow{A} t_1 & & s_1 \xrightarrow{A} t_1 \\
\wr & \text{implies there exists } t_2 \text{ such that } \wr & \wr \\
s_2 & & s_2 \xrightarrow{A} t_2
\end{array}
$$

In other words, for any states s_1 and s_2 with $s_1 \sim s_2$ and any state t_1, if $s_1 \xrightarrow{A} t_1$ then there exists a state t_2 with $t_1 \sim t_2$ such that $s_2 \xrightarrow{A} t_2$.

A symmetry $\sim$ is extended to an equivalence relation on behaviors in the obvious way by letting two behaviors be equivalent iff they have the same length and their corresponding states are equivalent. A temporal property is *symmetric* (with respect to $\sim$) iff, for every pair of behaviors σ and τ with $\sigma \sim \tau$, the property is true of σ iff it is true of τ.

A temporal formula is constructed from state predicates and actions by applying temporal operators, logical connectives, and ordinary (non-temporal) quantification. The formula is symmetric if each of its component state predicates and actions is symmetric.

3.3   Model Checking

An explicit-state model checker works by computing the directed graph $\mathcal{G}$ of a specification $\mathcal{S}$'s reachable states. The nodes of $\mathcal{G}$ are states, and $\mathcal{G}$ is the smallest graph satisfying the following two conditions: (i) $\mathcal{G}$ contains all states satisfying *Init*, and (ii) if state s is a node of $\mathcal{G}$ and $s \xrightarrow{Next} t$, then $\mathcal{G}$ contains the node t and an edge from s to t. Paths through $\mathcal{G}$ (which may traverse the same node many times) starting from an initial state correspond to behaviors satisfying $\overline{S}$. Those behaviors that also satisfy its liveness assumption are the ones that satisfy S.

The model checker constructs $\mathcal{G}$ by the following algorithm, using a set $\mathcal{U}$ of unexamined reachable states. Initially, $\mathcal{G}$ and $\mathcal{U}$ are both empty. The checker first sequentially enumerates the states satisfying $Init$, adding each state not already in $\mathcal{G}$ to both $\mathcal{G}$ and $\mathcal{U}$. It does the following, while $\mathcal{U}$ is nonempty. It chooses some state s in $\mathcal{U}$ and enumerates all states t satisfying $s \xrightarrow{Next} t$. For each such t: (i) if t is not in $\mathcal{G}$ then it adds t to $\mathcal{G}$ and to $\mathcal{U}$; (ii) if there is no edge from s to t in $\mathcal{G}$, then it adds one.

Model checking under a constraint P is performed by constructing a subgraph of $\mathcal{G}$ containing only states that satisfy the state predicate P. To compute the subgraph, this procedure is modified to add a state to $\mathcal{G}$ and $\mathcal{U}$ only if the state satisfies P.

Model checking under a symmetry $\sim$ consists of constructing a smaller graph $\mathcal{E}$ by adding a state to $\mathcal{E}$ and $\mathcal{U}$ only if $\mathcal{E}$ does not already contain an equivalent state. The graph $\mathcal{E}$ constructed in this way satisfies the following properties: (i) $s \nsim t$ for every distinct pair of nodes s, t of $\mathcal{E}$; (ii) for every state s satisfying $Init$, there is a node t in $\mathcal{E}$ such that t satisfies $Init$ and $s \sim t$; (iii) for every node s of $\mathcal{E}$ and every state t such that $s \xrightarrow{Next} t$, the graph $\mathcal{E}$ contains a node t' with $t \sim t'$ and an edge from s to t'. The specification is then checked as if $\mathcal{E}$ were the reachable-state graph.

Here, I ignore practical concerns and assume a theoretical model checker that can perform this algorithm even if the state graph is infinite. All the results apply *a fortiori* if the state graph is finite.

For model checking with symmetry to be equivalent to ordinary model checking, the following condition must hold:

SS. A behavior satisfies $\overline{S}$ iff it is equivalent (under $\sim$) to a behavior described by a path through $\mathcal{E}$ starting from an initial state.

This condition does not imply that the behaviors described by paths through $\mathcal{E}$ satisfy $\overline{S}$, just that they are equivalent to ones that satisfy $\overline{S}$. Condition SS is true if the specification satisfies the following two properties:

S1. (a) *Init* is symmetric, or
    (b) No two states satisfying *Init* are equivalent.
S2. *Next* is symmetric.

The specification is defined to be *safety symmetric* iff it satisfies S1 and S2.

An explicit-state model checker checks that a correctness property F holds by checking that $L \Rightarrow F$ holds for every behavior described by a path through the reachable-state graph starting from an initial state, where L is the specification's liveness assumption. A symmetric property is true of a behavior iff it is true of any equivalent behavior. Condition SS therefore implies that model checking with symmetry is equivalent to ordinary model checking for verifying that a safety symmetric specification with a symmetric liveness assumption satisfies a symmetric property.

The simplest kind of temporal property is a state predicate P, which as a temporal formula asserts that P is true initially. If the specification satisfies S1(b), then model checking with symmetry is equivalent to ordinary model checking for verifying that P is satisfied, even if P is not symmetric.

3.4   View Symmetry

A view symmetry is defined by an arbitrary function on states called a *view*. Two states are equivalent under a view V iff the value of V is the same in the two states. Many explicit-state model checkers test if a state s is in the state graph $\mathcal{G}$ constructed so far by keeping the set of fingerprints of nodes in $\mathcal{G}$ and testing if $\mathcal{G}$ contains a node with the same fingerprint as s. Such a checker is easily modified to implement checking under view symmetry by keeping fingerprints of the views of states rather than of the states themselves. TLC supports view symmetry as well as symmetry under permutations of a constant set.

View symmetry is equivalent to abstraction [2,4] for a symmetric specification $\mathcal{S}$. Abstraction consists of checking $\mathcal{S}$ by model checking a different specification $\mathcal{A}$ called an abstraction of $\mathcal{S}$. The view corresponds to the abstraction mapping from states of $\mathcal{S}$ to states of $\mathcal{A}$.

3.5   Symmetry Under Time Translation

Time-translation symmetry is a special kind of symmetry in which two states are equivalent iff they are the same except for absolute time. I now define what this means, using the notation that $s.v$ is the value of variable v in state s.

A *time translation* is a family of mappings T_d on the state space of the specification $\mathcal{S}$ that satisfies the following properties, for all states s and all real numbers d and e: (i) $T_d(s).now = s.now + d$, (ii) $T_0(s) = s$, and (iii) $T_{d+e}(s) = T_d(T_e(s))$. Specification $\mathcal{S}$ is defined to be *invariant under* this time translation iff it satisfies the following two conditions, for all real numbers d.

T1. (a) A state s satisfies *Init* iff $T_d(s)$ does, or
    (b) $s.now = t.now$ for any states s and t satisfying *Init*.
T2. $s \xrightarrow{Next} t$ iff $T_d(s) \xrightarrow{Next} T_d(t)$, for any states s and t.

Given a time translation, we define the *time-translation symmetry* $\sim$ by $s \sim t$ iff $s = T_d(t)$ for some d. T1 and T2 imply S1 and S2 for this symmetry. Hence, a specification that is invariant under a time translation is symmetric under the corresponding time-translation symmetry. Invariance under time translation is stronger than time-translation symmetry because, in addition to implying SS, it implies the following property.

TT. Let $s_1, \ldots, s_k$ and $t_1, t_2, \ldots$ be two behaviors satisfying $\overline{\mathcal{S}}$ (the second behavior may be finite or infinite). If $s_k = T_d(t_j)$, then the behavior $s_1, \ldots, s_k, T_d(t_{j+1}), T_d(t_{j+2}), \ldots$ also satisfies $\overline{\mathcal{S}}$.

To define a time translation, we must define $T_d(s).v$ for every real number d, state s, and variable v. Explicit-time specifications have three kinds of variables:

now, timer variables, and "ordinary" variables that are left unchanged by the *Tick* action. We know that $T_d(s).now$ equals $s.now + d$. Time translation should not change the value of an ordinary variable v, so we should have $T_d(s).v = s.v$ for such a variable. For a timer variable t, we should define $T_d(s).t$ so that the number of seconds in which t will time out is the same in s and $T_d(s)$. The value of a countdown or count-up timer directly indicates the number of seconds until it times out, so $T_d(s).ct$ should equal $s.ct$ for such a timer ct. Whether or not an expiration timer et has timed out depends on the value of $et - now$. The time translation T_d preserves the number of seconds until et times out iff $T_d(s).et - T_d(s).now$ equals $s.et - s.now$, which is true iff $T_d(s).et = s.et + d$.

With this definition of the T_d, any explicit-time specification is invariant under time translation, and hence safety symmetric under time-translation symmetry, if it expresses real-time requirements only through timer variables. Let $v_1, \ldots, v_m$ be the specification's ordinary variables and countdown and count-up timer variables, and let $et_1, \ldots, et_n$ be its expiration timer variables. Then symmetry under time translation is the same as view symmetry with the view $\langle v_1, \ldots, v_m, et_1 - now, \ldots, et_n - now \rangle$.

3.6   Periodicity and Zeno Behaviors

Let *NZ* be the temporal property asserting that time increases without bound. A specification $\mathcal{S}$ is *nonZeno* iff every finite behavior satisfying $\mathcal{S}$ can be extended to an infinite one satisfying $\mathcal{S}$ and *NZ* [1]. Property *NZ* is not symmetric under time translation; by replacing states of a behavior with ones translated back to the behavior's starting time, we can construct an equivalent behavior in which *now* never changes. Thus, model checking with time-translation symmetry cannot be used to check that a specification is nonZeno. However, we can take advantage of time-translation invariance as follows to use ordinary model checking to show that a specification is nonZeno.

Let $\mathcal{S}$ be a specification that is invariant under time translation. For simplicity, we assume that the initial condition of $\mathcal{S}$ asserts that *now* equals 0, so $s.now \geq 0$ for all reachable states s. For any reachable state s, let *LeastTime*(s) be the greatest lower bound of the values $t.now$ for all states t equivalent to s (under time-translation symmetry). The *period* of $\mathcal{S}$ is defined to be the least upper bound of the values *LeastTime*(s) for all reachable states s of $\mathcal{S}$. Intuitively, if a system's specification has a finite period λ, then all its possible behaviors are revealed within λ seconds. More precisely, any λ-second segment of a system behavior is the time translation of a segment from the first λ seconds of some (possibly different) behavior.

Define the condition NZ_λ as follows, where λ is a positive real number.

NZ_λ. Every finite behavior satisfying $\overline{\mathcal{S}}$ that ends in a state s with $s.now \leq \lambda$ can be extended to a behavior satisfying $\overline{\mathcal{S}}$ that ends in a state t with $t.now \geq \lambda + 1$.

It can be shown that if a specification $\mathcal{S}$ is time-translation invariant, has a period less than or equal to the real number λ, and satisfies NZ_λ, then it is nonZeno. Therefore, we can check that S is nonZeno by verifying that S has a period of at most λ and that it satisfies NZ_λ.

Here is how we can use model checking under time-translation symmetry to find an upper bound on the period of S. Let $\mathcal{E}$ be the state graph constructed by model checking under this symmetry. Because every reachable state is equivalent to a node in $\mathcal{E}$, the period of S is less than or equal to the least upper bound of the values $s.now$ for all nodes s of $\mathcal{E}$. (Since all initial states have $now = 0$, the period of most specifications will equal this least upper bound for a model checker that, like TLC, uses a breadth-first construction of the state graph.) Debugging features allow the TLC user to insert in the specification expressions that always equal TRUE, but whose evaluation causes TLC to perform certain operations. Using these features, it is easy to have TLC examine each state s that it finds and print the value of $s.now$ iff $s.now > t.now$ for every state t it has already found.[2] This makes computing an upper bound on the period of S easy. An explicit-state model checker that lacks the ability to compute the upper bound can verify that λ is an upper bound on the period by verifying the invariance of $now \leq \lambda$, using time-translation symmetry.

To check that S satisfies NZ_λ, we must show that from every reachable state with $now \leq \lambda$, it is possible to reach a state with $now \geq \lambda + 1$. We can do this by model checking with the constraint $now \leq \lambda + 1$, in which the model checker ignores any state it finds with $now > \lambda + 1$. It is easy to verify NZ_λ under this constraint with a model checker that can check possibility properties. With one like TLC that checks only linear-time temporal properties, we must show that S together with fairness assumptions on subactions of its next-state action imply that the value of now must eventually reach $\lambda + 1$ [1,7]. That is, we add fairness assumptions on certain actions and check that eventually $now \geq \lambda + 1$ holds, using the constraint $now \leq \lambda + 1$.

All of this, including the definition of $period$, has been under the assumption that $now = 0$ for all initial states. Extending the definition of $period$ to the general case is not hard, but there is no need to do it. Invariance under time translation requires that either (a) the set of initial states is invariant under time translation, or (b) the value of now is the same in all initial states. In case (b), that value will probably either be 0 or else a parameter of the specification that we can set equal to 0. In case (a), we conjoin the requirement $now = 0$ to the initial predicate. Invariance under time translation implies that, in either case, modifying the specification in this way does not affect whether or not it is nonZeno.

4   Comparison with Uppaal

4.1   The Leader Algorithm

I have checked the TLA$^+$ specification of the leader algorithm with the TLC model checker. Although the specification is time-translation invariant, the correctness property is not. It asserts $(now > c(n)) \Rightarrow P(n)$ for each node n,

---

[2] One of the features needed was added to TLC after publication of [8].

where $c(n)$ is a constant expression and $P(n)$ does not contain *now*. We could add a timer variable and restate the property in terms of it. (This is what is done in the Uppaal model.) However, I instead had TLC check the property under a symmetry $\sim$ defined as follows. Let Σ be the maximum of $c(n)$ for all nodes n. Then $s \sim t$ iff $s.now$ and $t.now$ are both equal or both greater than Σ. Both the specification and the correctness property are symmetric under $\sim$. This symmetry is view symmetry under the view consisting of the tuple $\langle v_1, \ldots, v_k, \text{IF } now > \Sigma \text{ THEN } \Sigma + 1 \text{ ELSE } now \rangle$, where the v_i are all the variables except *now*.

Real-time model checkers use much lower-level modeling languages than TLA$^+$. Uppaal [10] is the only one I know of whose language is expressive enough to model this algorithm. Arne Skou, with the assistance of Gerd Behrmann and Kim Larsen, translated the TLA$^+$ specification to an Uppaal model. Since Uppaal's modeling language is not as expressive as TLA$^+$, this required some encoding. In particular, Uppaal cannot represent the potentially unbounded multiset of messages in the TLA$^+$ specification, so the Uppaal model uses a fixed-length array instead. To ensure that the model faithfully represents the algorithm, Uppaal checks that this array does not overflow.

TLC and Uppaal were run on different but roughly comparable machines. As indicated, some Uppaal executions were run on a 30-machine network. More detailed results are presented in [9].

The parameters of the specification are the number N of nodes, a constant operator that describes the graph, and the timing constants *Period*, *TODelay*, and *MsgDelay*. The latter two are upper-bound constraints, which implies that the number of reachable states is an increasing function of their values. Figure 2 shows the results of checking the correctness property on two different graphs, with 3 and 4 nodes, for some haphazardly chosen values of the timing bounds. Uppaal timings are given for a single machine and for the 30-machine network; *fail* means that Uppaal ran out of memory.

We expect that increasing a timing bound will increase the number of reachable states, and hence TLC's execution time, since it increases the number of possible values of the timer variables. The time required by Uppaal's algorithm depends only on the ratios of the timing bounds, not on their absolute value. The results show that Uppaal's execution time is strongly dependent on the ratio *MsgDelay/Period*. For ratios significantly less than .6, Uppaal's execution time depends almost entirely on the graph and not on the other parameters. TLC's execution time depends on the magnitude of the parameters as well as on this ratio. Hence, if Uppaal succeeds, it is usually faster than TLC for small values of the parameters and much faster for larger values. Using 30 processors extends the range of parameters for which Uppaal succeeds. TLC can be run on multiple computers using Java's RMI mechanism. Tests have shown that execution speed typically increases by a factor of about .7 times the number of computers. This suggests that, run on a network of processors, TLC's execution speed is comparable to Uppaal's for the range of instances tested. However, since increasing the timing-constraint parameters increases the number of reachable states, TLC will be slower than Uppaal for large enough values of these parameters.

$N = 3$ $N = 4$

$1 <^{\displaystyle 2}_{\displaystyle 3}$ with 2—3 $1 - 2 - 3 - 4$

N	Period	MsgDelay	TODelay	MsgDelay/Period	TLC	Uppaal	30-proc Uppaal
3	10	3	5	.3	255	9.4	2.9
	3	1	1	.33	4	9.4	13.4
	5	2	5	.5	70	11.2	2.9
	5	3	1	.6	13	30.8	3.0
	5	3	5	.6	265	fail	20.9
	3	2	1	.67	7	10.2	3.0
	3	2	2	.67	20	fail	16.6
	5	4	1	.8	27	32.5	9.2
	5	4	5	.8	980	fail	fail
	2	2	1	1	11	fail	fail
	1	2	1	2	270	fail	fail
	1	2	2	2	1280	fail	fail
4	10	3	5	.3	1385	42.2	2.5
	3	1	1	.33	6	43.9	2.7
	5	2	2	.4	42	48.3	4.2
	5	2	5	.4	390	93.0	4.3
	2	1	1	.5	6	48.2	3.7
	5	3	1	.6	28	72.8	3.8
	5	3	5	.6	1770	fail	84.6
	3	2	1	.67	12	73.1	9.8
	3	2	2	.67	44	fail	73.1
	5	4	5	.8	6760	fail	fail
	2	2	1	1	13	fail	fail
	1	2	1	2	390	fail	fail
	1	2	2	2	1650	fail	fail

Fig. 2. Comparison of Uppaal and TLC execution times in seconds for the indicated graphs with 3 and 4 nodes

The overall result is that Uppaal can check models with larger timing-constraint parameters, and hence with a finer-grained choice of ratios between the parameters. However, TLC can check a wider range of ratios among the parameters. For finding bugs, the ability to check parameter ratios of both 1:2 and 2:1 is likely to be more useful than the ability to check ratios of both 1:2 and 11:20.[3]

---

[3] The Uppaal model was subsequently rewritten to improve its performance. Because the TLA^{+} specification was written to be as simple as possible, with no consideration of model-checking efficiency, the fairest comparison seems to be with the first Uppaal model. Uppaal can check the new model on a single computer an average of 4.5 times faster for the $N = 3$ instances of Figure 2 and 50 times faster for the $N = 4$ instances, but it still fails when MsgDelay/Period is greater than about 1. The new model therefore does not alter the basic result that Uppaal is faster than TLC for the range of parameter ratios it can handle, but it cannot handle as wide a range.

Period	MsgDelay	TODelay	$\dfrac{MsgDelay}{Period}$	reachable states	msgs in transit max	mean
2	2	1	1	6579	6	3.46
1	2	1	2	240931	12	6.57
3	2	2	.67	20572	6	3.69
10	3	5	.33	247580	6	3.85

Fig. 3. The number of messages in transit

The dependence on the *MsgDelay/Period* ratio can be explained as follows. Since *Period* is a lower bound on the time between the sending of messages and *MsgDelay* is an upper bound on how long it takes to deliver the message, the maximum number of messages that can be in transit at any time should be roughly proportional to this ratio. The table of Figure 3 gives some idea of what's going on, where the results are for the 3-node graph. The first two rows show the dramatic effect of changing *Period* and leaving the other parameters the same. The second two rows show that the *MsgDelay/Period* ratio is just one of the factors determining the number of messages in transit and the number of reachable states.

It is possible that these results reflect some special property of this example. However, the sensitivity to the *MsgDelay/Period* ratio suggests that it is the messages in transit that pose a problem for Uppaal. Each message carries a timer, and the performance of real-time model checkers tends to depend on the number of concurrently running timers. Perhaps the most common use of real time in systems is for constraints on message transit time—constraints that are modeled by attaching timers to messages. This suggests that Uppaal might have difficulty checking such systems if there can be many messages in transit. However, more examples must be tried before we can draw any such conclusion.

TLC was also used to check that some of the instances in Figure 2 were nonZeno. For $N = 3$, this took about twice as long as checking the correctness property; for $N = 4$ the two times were about the same.

4.2   Fischer's Algorithm

I also compared the explicit-state approach to the use of Uppaal on a version of Fischer's mutual exclusion algorithm [13] that is distributed with Uppaal. Because TLA$^+$ is a very high-level language, TLC must "execute" a specification interpretively. It is therefore significantly slower than conventional model checkers for verifying simple systems. I also obtained data for two other popular model checkers whose models are written in lower-level languages: the explicit-state model checker Spin [6] and the symbolic checker SMV [11] that uses binary decision diagrams. The Spin model was written and checked by Gerard Holzmann, and the SMV model was written and checked by Ken McMillan. Checked were the safety properties of mutual exclusion and deadlock freedom (except for SMV) and a simple liveness property.

K	states	Safety				Liveness		
		TLC^s	TLC	Spin	SMV	TLC	Spin	SMV
2	155976	9	29	.7	1.3	128	3.7	2.5
3	450407	10	78	2.4	3.8	385	13	6.3
4	1101072	16	194	6.9	6.5	1040	49	10
5	2388291	26	399	19	10	3456	171	16
6	4731824	47	784	51	14	5566	468	22
7	8730831	78	1468	142	25	13654	1317	40
8	15208872	132	2546	378	35		3593	54
9	25263947	244	4404	977	46		5237	73
10	40323576	446	7258	2145	62			95
Uppaal						135		

Fig. 4. Execution times in seconds for a simple version of Fischer's algorithm with 6 threads, where TLC^s is TLC with symmetry under thread permutations

This version of Fischer's algorithm uses a parameter K that is both an upper- and lower-bound timing constraint. All the models were tested for 6 threads, which is the smallest number for which Uppaal takes a significant amount of time. The results for different values of K are shown in Figure 4. Uppaal's execution time is independent of K. For checking safety, TLC was run both with and without symmetry under permutations of threads. (The liveness property is not symmetric.) The speedups obtained by the 6-fold symmetry should not be taken very seriously; in real examples one at best obtains only 2- or 3-fold symmetry.

Since Uppaal's execution time is independent of K, we know that for large enough values of K it will be faster than a model checker whose running time depends on K. All of the model checkers could check the specification for large enough values of K to provide reasonable confidence of its correctness, though the numbers do not bode well for the ability of TLC and Spin to check liveness for more complicated examples. We do not expect TLC's performance on liveness checking to be good enough for large applications. But because Fischer's algorithm is so simple, it is dangerous to infer from these numbers that the performance of Uppaal and SMV would be good enough.

5   Conclusion

Experts in the field will not be surprised that one can write and check explicit-time specifications using ordinary model checkers. But this is apparently not widely appreciated because it has not been stated clearly in the literature. Moreover, the use of view symmetry and the method described here for checking that a specification is nonZeno may be new even to experts.

I know of no previous comparisons of the explicit-state approach with the use of a real-time model checker. The results reported here do not tell us how the two methods will compare on other examples. But they do indicate that verifying explicit-time specifications with an ordinary model checker is not very much worse than using a real-time model checker. Indeed, the results for the leader algorithm suggest that the explicit-time approach is competitive with Uppaal for distributed algorithms. The results of using TLC to check two more complicated versions of Fischer's algorithm are reported in [9]. They too suggest that TLC can be used in practice to check explicit-time specifications.

The main advantage of an explicit-time approach is the ability to use languages and tools not specially designed for real-time model checking. There are practical reasons for using a higher-level language like TLA$^+$ instead of one designed expressly for model checking. As one industrial user remarked, "The prototyping and debug phase through TLA$^+$/TLC is so much more efficient than in a lower-level language."

References

1. Martín Abadi and Leslie Lamport. An old-fashioned recipe for real time. *ACM Transactions on Programming Languages and Systems*, 16(5):1543–1571, September 1994.
2. Edmund M. Clarke, Orna Grumberg, and David E. Long. Model checking and abstraction. *ACM Transactions on Programming Languages and Systems*, 16(5):1512–1542, September 1994.
3. Bruno Dutertre and Maria Sorea. Modeling and verification of a fault-tolerant real-time startup protocol using calendar automata. In *Formal Techniques, Modelling and Analysis of Timed and Fault-Tolerant Systems, Joint International Conferences on Formal Modelling and Analysis of Timed Systems, FORMATS 2004 and Formal Techniques in Real-Time and Fault-Tolerant Systems, FTRTFT 2004, Grenoble, France, September 22-24, 2004, Proceedings*, volume 3253 of *Lecture Notes in Computer Science*, pages 199–214. Springer, 2004.
4. Susanne Graf and Claire Loiseaux. Property preserving abstractions under parallel composition. In Marie-Claude Gaudel and Jean-Pierre Jouannaud, editors, *TAPSOFT'93: Theory and Practice of Software Development*, volume 668 of *Lecture Notes in Computer Science*, pages 644–657. Springer, 1993.
5. Thomas A. Henzinger and Orna Kupferman. From quantity to quality. In Oded Maler, editor, *Proceedings of the International Workshop on Hybrid and Real-Time Systems (HART '97)*, volume 1997 of *Lecture Notes in Computer Science*, pages 48–62. Springer-Verlag, 1997.
6. Gerard J. Holzmann. *The Spin Model Checker*. Addison-Wesley, Boston, 2004.
7. Leslie Lamport. Proving possibility properties. *Theoretical Computer Science*, 206(1–2):341–352, October 1998.
8. Leslie Lamport. *Specifying Systems*. Addison-Wesley, Boston, 2003. A link to an electronic copy can be found at http://lamport.org.
9. Leslie Lamport. Real time is really simple. Technical Report MSR-TR-2005-30, Microsoft Research, March 2005.
10. Kim Guldstrand Larsen, Paul Pettersson, and Wang Yi. UPPAAL in a nutshell. *International Journal of Software Tools for Technology Transfer*, 1(1/2):134–152, December 1997.
11. K. L. McMillan. *Symbolic Model Checking*. Kluwer, 1993.

12. Radia Perlman. An algorithm for distributed computation of a spanningtree in an extended LAN. In *Proceedings of the Ninth Symposium on Data Communications*, pages 44–53. SIGCOMM, ACM Press, 1985.
13. Fred B. Schneider, Bard Bloom, and Keith Marzullo. Putting time into proof outlines. In J. W. de Bakker, C. Huizing, W.-P. de Roever, and G. Rozenberg, editors, *Real-Time: Theory in Practice*, volume 600 of *Lecture Notes in Computer Science*, pages 618–639, Berlin, Heidelberg, New York, 1992. Springer-Verlag.

Temporal Modalities for Concisely Capturing Timing Diagrams

Hana Chockler[1,2] and Kathi Fisler[1]

[1] Department of Computer Science, WPI,
100 Institute Road, Worcester, MA 01609, USA
[2] MIT CSAIL, 32 Vassar street,
Cambridge, MA 02139, USA
{hanac, kfisler}@cs.wpi.edu

Abstract. Timing diagrams are useful for capturing temporal specifications in which all mentioned events are required to occur. We first show that translating timing diagrams with both partial orders on events and don't-care regions to LTL potentially yields exponentially larger formulas containing several non-localized terms corresponding to the same event. This raises a more fundamental question: which modalities allow a textual temporal logic to capture such diagrams using a single term for each event? We define the shapes of partial orders that are captured concisely by a hierarchy of textual linear temporal logics containing future and past time operators, as well Laroussinie *et al*'s forgettable past operator and our own unforeseen future operator. Our results give insight into the temporal abstractions that underlie timing diagrams and suggest that the abstractions in LTL are significantly weaker than those captured by timing diagrams.

1 Introduction

Timing diagrams are a commonly used visual notation for temporal specifications. Although designers instinctively know when information can conveniently be expressed as a timing diagram, few researchers have explored the formal connections between timing diagrams and textual temporal logics. Understanding these formal connections would be useful for understanding what makes specifications designer-friendly, as well as for developing tools to visualize temporal logic specifications. Ideally, we would like to have constructive decision procedures for determining when a specification, given in a temporal logic or a specification language (such as LTL or PSL), can be rendered as a timing diagram. These could aid in both understanding and debugging specifications.

Identifying diagrammable LTL specifications appears to be very hard. Its complexity stems partly from the fact that a timing diagram contains several different visual elements (events, orderings and timings between events, event synchronization) which must be located within the more uniform syntax of a temporal logic formula. In addition, LTL formulas that capture timing diagrams appear to be at least one order of magnitude (and sometimes two) larger than the diagrams and use multiple logical terms for the same event. Before we can write an algorithm to recognize timing diagrams in temporal logic formulas, we need to understand how the patterns over visual elements that underlie timing diagrams would appear textually.

This paper explores this question by trying to identify textual temporal logic operators that capture timing diagrams concisely; the rendering problem would then reduce

D. Borrione and W. Paul (Eds.): CHARME 2005, LNCS 3725, pp. 176–190, 2005.

to recognizing uses of these operators in LTL. The core of a timing diagram is the partial order it imposes on events. We view a formula as capturing a partial order *concisely* if the formula characterizes instances of the partial order using *exactly one term* for each event in the partial order. We study a progression of linear temporal logics including LTL, PLTL, PLTL with forgettable past [10] and PLTL with forgettable past and unforeseeable future (which we have defined for this work). We identify the set of partial orders that each logic can capture concisely and show that some partial orders defy concise representation in even the richest of these logics. We do not address the rendering question in this paper, as our results indicate that additional theoretical work is required before pursuing that question.

Our results cover timing diagrams with both partial orders and don't-care regions (Section 2). To illustrate the subtleties in representing timing diagrams in LTL, Section 3 presents a translation from diagrams to LTL and argues that a small translation seems impossible. We provide a counterexample that shows that introducing don't-care regions explodes the size of the formula by forcing it to separately handle all possible total-order instances of the partial order. Section 4 presents our algorithm for efficient translation of a particular class of diagrams to formulas in LTL with the past-time and forgettable-past-and-future modalities; this section also identifies a class of diagrams that this logic cannot capture. Related work is mentioned throughout the paper.

2   Timing Diagrams

Timing diagrams depict changes in values on signals (*events*) over time. Figure 1 shows an example. Waveforms capture each signal (lower horizontal lines represent false and higher ones true), arrows order events, arrow annotations constrain the time within which the tail event must follow the head event, vertical lines synchronize behavior across signals, and bold lines indicate *care regions* in which the signal must hold the depicted value. Non-care regions between events are called *don't-care regions*; they allow the signal value to vary before the event at the end of the region occurs. The diagram in Figure 1 has signals a, b, and c. The rising transition on b must occur 2 to 4 cycles after the rising transition on a. The falling transition on a and the rising transitions on b and c may occur in any order (since no arrows order them). Once c rises, it must remain true until the second rising transition on a (due to the care region on c and the vertical lines that synchronize the transition on a and the value on c into a single event). The value of b may vary after its rise, since a don't-care region follows the rise.

The timing diagrams literature contains many variations on this core notation: diagrams may support events that contain no transitions, busses, bi-directional arrows, assumption events (to represent input from the environment) [3], or combinations of timing diagrams using regular expression operators [2]. This paper considers timing diagrams with don't-care regions and partial orders between events.

Definition 1. The syntax of timing diagrams is captured as follows:

- A *signal* is a proposition; p and $\neg p$ denote true and false values on signal p.
- A *transition* is a proposition annotated with a directional change: $p{\downarrow}$ and $p{\uparrow}$ denote falling and rising transitions, respectively.

$$\begin{array}{c|cccccccccc}
a & 0 & 1 & 0 & 0 & 0 & 0 & 1 & 1 & 1 & 1 \\
b & 0 & 0 & 0 & 0 & 1 & 1 & 0 & 0 & 1 & 0 \\
c & 0 & 0 & 1 & 1 & 1 & 1 & 0 & 0 & 0 & 1 \\
\hline
  & 0 & 1 & 2 & 3 & 4 & 5 & 6 & 7 & 8 & 9
\end{array}$$

Fig. 1. A timing diagram with a word that satisfies its semantics

- An *event* is a conjunction of values and at least one transition on signals.
- A *timing diagram* is a tuple $\langle E, C, M \rangle$ where E is a set of events, C (the care regions) is a set of tuples $\langle e_1, e_2, p, v \rangle$ where e_1 and e_2 are (uniquely identified[1]) events in E, p is a signal name and v is a boolean value, and M (the timing constraints) is a set of tuples $\langle e_1, e_2, l, u \rangle$ where e_1 and e_2 are events in E, l is a positive integer, and u is either an integer at least as large as l or the symbol ∞. For each signal, any region that is not within a care region is called a *don't-care region*.

The semantics of timing diagrams is defined in terms of languages over finite or infinite words in which characters are assignments of boolean values to signals. A word models a timing diagram if the earliest occurrence of each event that respects the partial order in the timing constraints respects the care regions and durations of timing constraints. The earliest occurrence requirement keeps the language unambiguous. Formally, we define what it means for an index into a word to satisfy an event, map events to indices in the word, and check that those mappings respect the diagram.

Definition 2. Let E be an event $v_1 \wedge \ldots \wedge v_k$ where each v_i is a proposition, its negation, or a rising or falling transition on a proposition. Let W be a word and i an index into W. Let $W_i(q)$ denote the value of proposition q at index i of W. Index i *satisfies* E if for every v_i, $W_i(p) = 0$ if $v_i = \neg p$, $W_i(p) = 1$ if $v_i = p$, $W_i(p) = 0$ and $W_{i+1}(p) = 1$ if $v_i = p \uparrow$, and $W_i(p) = 1$ and $W_{i+1}(p) = 0$ if $v_i = p \downarrow$.

Definition 3. Let $\langle E, C, M \rangle$ be a timing diagram, W be a word, and I a function from E to indices into W (I is called an *index assignment*). I is *valid* iff

- For every event $e \in E$, $I(e)$ satisfies e,
- For every care region $\langle e_1, e_2, p, v \rangle$, $W_i(p) = v$ for all $I(e_1) < i \leq I(e_2)$, and
- For every timing constraint $\langle e_1, e_2, l, u \rangle \in M$, $l \leq I(e_2) - I(e_1) \leq u$.

I is *minimal* iff for each event $e \in E$, $I(e)$ is the smallest index into W that satisfies e and occurs after all indices assigned to events that must precede E (by the partial order induced by M).

Definition 4. Let D be a timing diagram and let W be a word. $W \models D$ if there exists a minimal and valid index assignment I for D and W. The set of all such words forms the *language* of D (denoted $\mathcal{L}(D)$).

---

[1] A numbering scheme could distinguish syntactically similar events.

The semantics captures one occurrence of a timing diagram, rather than the multiple occurrences needed to treat a timing diagram as an invariant. The one-occurrence semantics provides a foundation for defining different multiple-occurrence semantics [5] and enables efficient complementation of timing diagrams [6].

3   Translating Timing Diagrams to LTL

Formulas of linear temporal logics describe computations on infinite paths where each state is labeled with a subset of atomic propositions AP that are true in that state. For a computation $\pi = w_0, w_1, \ldots$ and $i \geq 0$, let π^i be the computation π starting at the state w_i. In particular, $\pi^0 = \pi$. We use $\pi, i \models \varphi$ to indicate that a formula φ holds in a computation π with w_i taken as a start position. The relation $\models$ is inductively defined for each of the logics we define in this paper.

LTL. Given a set AP of atomic propositions, the LTL formulas over AP are:

- **true, false**, p, or $\neg p$, for $p \in AP$,
- $\neg \psi$ or $\psi \vee \varphi$, where ψ and φ are LTL formulas, or
- $G\psi$, $X\psi$, or $\psi U\varphi$, where ψ and φ are LTL formulas.

The temporal operators G ("always"), X ("next") and U ("until") describe time-dependent events. F ("eventually") abbreviates $\mathbf{true}U$.

For LTL, $\pi, i \models \varphi$ is equivalent to $\pi^i, 0 \models \varphi$, since formulas in LTL are not concerned with past events. We use $\pi \models \varphi$ as a shorthand for $\pi, 0 \models \varphi$.

- For all paths π, $\pi \models \mathbf{true}$ and $\pi \not\models \mathbf{false}$.
- For an atomic proposition $p \in AP$, $\pi \models p$ iff $p \in L(w_0)$.
- $\pi \models \neg\psi$ iff $\pi \not\models \psi$.
- $\pi \models \psi \vee \varphi$ iff $\pi \models \psi$ or $\pi \models \varphi$.
- $\pi \models \psi \wedge \varphi$ iff $\pi \models \psi$ and $\pi \models \varphi$.
- $\pi \models G\psi$ iff for all $i \geq 0$, $\pi^i \models \psi$.
- $\pi \models X\psi$ iff $\pi^1 \models \varphi$.
- $\pi \models \psi U\varphi$ iff there exists $i \geq 0$ such that $\pi^i \models \varphi$ and for all $j < i$, $\pi^j \models \psi$.

The rest of this section presents a translation from timing diagrams with partial orders on events and don't-care regions into LTL. Previous work [6] translated timing diagrams with don't-care regions and total orders on events to LTL. We could reuse the prior algorithm by enumerating all the total orders corresponding to the partial order and logically disjoining the result of converting each totally-ordered diagram to LTL. This approach has the obvious drawback of potentially requiring exponentially many disjuncts in the translated formula. We therefore wish to consider alternate approaches.

Amla *et al.* translate timing diagrams with partial orders but no don't-care regions to *universal finite automata (∀FA)* [1]. ∀FA differ from standard NFAs in accepting those words on which *all* possible runs (rather than some run) through the automaton end in a final state. Amla *et al*'s automata spawn one run for each event in the diagram, as well as one run for each waveform in the diagram.

Fig. 2. Timing diagram motivating the need for an *end* marker

Since proper handling of partial orders is new for translations to LTL, we first focus on this issue, returning afterwards to include don't cares. For partial orders, we use a similar idea to Amla *et al*'s: we construct a formula for each event and timing constraint in the diagram, and then conjoin these formulas into one LTL formula. The translation to LTL, however, is more difficult because LTL is inherently defined on infinite words. To see why this is a problem, consider the diagram in Figure 2 (the arrow from the rising to falling transition on a is dashed to indicate that it is implicit from the waveform). Clearly, the formula must locate the rise and fall of a and the rise of b and capture the ordering constraint (that the fall of a follows the rise of b).

We want a formula that is polynomial in the size of the diagram. Writing formulas to capture the individual waveform shapes is easy but capturing the ordering constraint is not. We cannot capture the waveforms together with the ordering constraint in one pass through the diagram due to the unspecified order between the fall of a and the rise of b. Writing one formula to capture that the fall of a follows the rise of a and another formula to capture that the rise of b follows the rise of a also doesn't work because both formulas must locate *the same fall of a*. Separate constraints would accept the word $w = (\bar{a}\bar{b}) \cdot (a\bar{b}) \cdot (\bar{a}\bar{b}) \cdot (a\bar{b}) \cdot (ab) \cdot (\bar{a}b)^{\omega}$ which does not satisfy the diagram (where $\bar{p}$ stands for $\neg p$). To align the searches for events, we will use LTL augmented with existential quantification over atomic propositions to introduce a special symbol called *end* into the word to mark the end of the diagram.[2] This problem does not exist in ∀FA, since all copies of the automaton must finish in an accepting state at the same time. Thus, in some sense, the *end* marker is implicitly present in ∀FA.

Returning to capturing timing constraints, assume we want to define an LTL formula $\varphi(a, i)$ that is true at the ith transition on a, which happens to be a rise. Assume that n_a is the number of transitions on a, $finish(a)$ is the literal for the final value of a in the diagram, and that we have a proposition *end* identifying the end of the diagram. Then

$$\varphi(a, i) = \neg a \land X(aU(\neg aU(\ldots U(finish(a)Uend)\ldots))),$$

where the number of U operators is $n - i - 1$. Intuitively, the formula first describes whether the transition is a rise or a fall (a fall would begin with $a \land X\neg a U\ldots$), then captures the rest of the waveform as the second argument to the first U.

Using such formulas, the formula for a whole timing constraint $\langle a_i, b_j, l, u \rangle$, where a is the ith transition on a and b_j is the jth transition on b, and the transition on b happens within the $[l, u]$-interval after the one on a, is captured by $\xi(a_i, b_j, l, u)$, where

---

[2] In general, adding quantification over atomic propositions increases the expressive power of temporal logics [12,13,14]. The restricted version that we use here does not add expressiveness, however, as all formulas that are created from timing diagrams can be translated to equivalent formulas in LTL with both past and future modalities using Gabbay *et al*'s work [7,8].

$$\xi(a_i, b_j, l, u) = F(\varphi(a, i) \wedge (aU\varphi(b, j)))$$

if a rises at i, and

$$\xi(a_i, b_j, l, u) = F(\varphi(a, i) \wedge (\neg aU\varphi(b, j)))$$

if a falls at i. If the timing constraint has time bounds (say $[l, u]$), then we replace $aU\varphi(b, j)$ with $\bigvee_{k=l}^{u} \psi \wedge X\psi \wedge \ldots \wedge X^{k-2}\psi \wedge X^{k-1}\varphi$, where X^m stands for m nested X operators, and l and u are natural numbers. Let $\Xi(D)$ be the set of all formulas $\xi(a_i, b_j, l, u)$, for all timing constraints in D.

For synchronization lines, the formulas that capture the fact that the ith transition on a happens simultaneously with the jth transition on b are

$$\gamma(a_i, b_j) = F(\varphi(a, i) \wedge \varphi(b, j)).$$

Let $\Gamma(D)$ be the set of all formulas $\gamma(a_i, b_j)$ for all synchronization events.

Timing diagrams contain implicit ordering arrows between each pair of consecutive events on a single waveform. Rather than encode these through ξ, we create a single formula that precisely captures the shape of its waveform. For a signal a, let $start(a)$ be the literal for the initial value of a in the diagram (either a or $\neg a$), and let $finish(a)$ be the literal that corresponds to the final value of a in the diagram. The formula ψ_a that describes the waveform of a is

$$\psi(a) = start(a)U(\neg start(a)U(start(a)U \ldots U(finish(a)Uend)\ldots)) \quad (1)$$

where the number of U operators equals the number of transitions on a in the diagram.

Finally, we combine all these formulas into a formula $\theta(D)$ that describes the language of the timing diagram D. The formula states that a word w belongs to the language of D iff there exists a position r in w such that when $w[r]$ is labeled with end, the word can be mapped to D. The formula $\theta(D)$ is as follows.

$$\theta(D) = \exists! end : \bigwedge_{a \in AP} \psi_a \wedge \bigwedge \Xi(D) \wedge \bigwedge \Gamma(D)), \quad (2)$$

where $\exists! end$ means that exactly one position is labeled with end.

Example 1. As an illustration, consider a diagram D and its waveform formulas:

$$\psi(a) = \neg aU(aU(\neg aU end))$$
$$\psi(b) = \neg bU(bU(\neg bU end))$$
$$\psi(c) = \neg cU(cU end)$$

The arrows connect the rise of a with the rise of c, the rise of c with the fall of a, and the fall of a with the fall of b. The rise of a is characterized by the formula $\varphi(a, 1) = \neg a \wedge X(aU(\neg aU end))$, and similarly for other transitions. The timing constraints are

$$\xi(a_1, c_1, 2, 5) = \varphi(a, 1)U_{[2,5]}\varphi(c, 1)$$
$$\xi(c_1, a_2, 1, \infty) = \varphi(c, 1)U\varphi(a, 2)$$
$$\xi(a_2, b_2, 3, 9) = \varphi(a, 2)U_{[3,9]}\varphi(b, 2)$$

Finally, the formula $\theta(D)$ is

$$\exists! end : \psi(a) \wedge \psi(b) \wedge \psi(c) \wedge \xi(a_1, c_1, 2, 5) \wedge \xi(c_1, a_2, 1, \infty) \wedge \xi(a_2, b_2, 3, 9)).$$

Observation 1 (Complexity of $\theta(D)$). The formula $\theta(D)$ is polynomial in the size of the diagram D. Let D be a timing diagram of size n. The number of waveform formulas $\psi(a)$ is equal to the number of signals in D. The size of a waveform formula $\psi(a)$ is linear in the number of transitions, thus is $O(n)$. Since $\varphi(a)$ is a subformula of $\psi(a)$, we have that $|\varphi(a)| = O(n)$. The number of events in D is bounded by n. Therefore, the total size of $\theta(D)$ is bounded by $O(n^2)$.

Observation 2 (Adding Don't Cares). The ξ and γ formulas capture the diagram's constraints *under the assumption that the ith transition as identified from the end of the diagram is the ith transition from the beginning of the diagram.* This assumption may be false in the presence of don't-care regions; the *end* marker does not help because it isn't clear which occurrences of events should count. Handling both partial orders and don't cares seems to require enumerating the total orders for the partial order, which yields a formula of a (possibly) exponential complexity in the size of the diagram.

4 Cleanly Capturing Diagrams Through Textual Logics

The previous section shows the complex structure of an LTL formula that captures a timing diagram with partial orders and don't cares. Some of this complexity arises from using separate subformulas for waveforms and timing constraints, which is needed to capture partial orders on events. The diagram in Figure 2 illustrates a core incompatibility between timing diagrams and LTL: LTL cannot cleanly capture separate paths converging on a future event while timing diagrams express this naturally.

This problem suggests that timing diagrams rely on a different set of temporal abstractions than those provided by the LTL operators. This raises an interesting question: how fundamental are these differences? Visually, timing diagrams define (potentially overlapping) windows that are bounded by events and contain other events and windows. In LTL, $[\phi U \psi]$ defines a window bounded on the left by the current position in a word and bounded on the right by positions satisfying ψ. Since the occurrence of ϕ can extend beyond that of ψ (if ψ were Fp, for example), LTL also supports some degree of overlapping windows. The future-time nature of LTL biases window locations towards future positions in a word, however, and leads to blowup when windows align on the right boundaries. Past-time temporal operators, however, could capture windows that align on right boundaries. Our question is *whether operators that fix window boundaries on one end of the word are rich enough to capture the window structure in timing diagrams while using only one term for each event in the diagram.*

The restriction to one term per event is important because it is a distinguishing feature of timing diagrams. We are trying to understand the differences between textual temporal logics and timing diagrams from a logical perspective. In this work, we hold formulas to the one-term requirement and study the restrictions that this in turn places on the semantics of the operators. For the rest of this paper, we consider timing diagrams with ordering between events but no timing constraints on those orders. Such diagrams

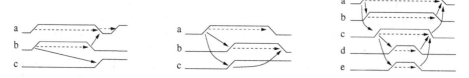

Fig. 3. Timing diagrams with various shapes of partial order

still blow up when translated to LTL but allow us to focus on the fundamental question of how well LTL-like logics capture the partial orders allowed in timing diagrams. We begin with several examples of timing diagrams with different shapes of partial orders and discuss which textual temporal logic operators capture them cleanly.

Tree-Shaped Partial Orders. Two observations arise from the diagram in Figure 2. First, we could cleanly capture the diagram in LTL if the common event lay at the beginning of the partial order (i.e., if the orderings on events were reversed): we would locate the first event, then independently locate the remaining two events. Second (though related), this diagram appears easier to capture if we use past-time operators: we could locate the falling transition on a that is common to both chains of events, then look *backwards* to find the (now independent) rising transitions on a and b. These observations give rise to our first two claims about partial orders and clean temporal logic formulas: partial orders that form trees (or forests) can be cleanly translated into LTL, while those that form trees with their edges reversed can be cleanly translated into Past-LTL. Note that Past-LTL here means LTL with *only* past-time temporal operators. We will use PLTL to mean the temporal logic with both future time and past-time operators.

Partial Orders with Multiple Minimal Events. The leftmost diagram in Figure 3 has multiple minimal events. A formula capturing this diagram cannot start simultaneous (i.e. conjoined) searches from the rising transitions on a and b because those searches converge on the falling transition on a. Using both past and future-time operators, however, a formula could search for the first rising transition on a followed by the falling transition on a; at that point, the search could split into two independent searches: one forward for the second rise on a, and another backward for the transitions on b followed by a forward search for the transition on c. All of the edges in the partial order are edges in the tree specifying this search, but some of those edges are reversed in the tree. Intuitively, this criterion characterizes when a search can be captured in PLTL.

Diamond-Shaped DAGs. The events in the middle diagram in Figure 3 form a diamond (between the rising transition on a and the falling transition on b). If a formula searches for the rising transition on a first, it cannot then spawn independent searches for the rising transitions on b and c (the "bulge" of the diamond) because they must meet up again at the falling transition on b. Searching first for the falling transition in b causes similar problems. We could conduct this search cleanly if we had a way to "remember" the location of the rising transition on a, then search forwards for the falling transition on b, then backwards for the rising transitions on b and c, but with these last two searches bounded by the remembered position of the search on a.

Laroussinie, Mackey, and Schoebelen's linear temporal logic with forgettable past (NLTL) does exactly this. It adds an operator N to PLTL that restricts the path to the suffix starting from the position at which the N is encountered. Using N, we could capture the diamond pattern roughly as $FN(a\uparrow \wedge F(b\uparrow \wedge F(b\downarrow \wedge P(c\uparrow))))$. The N prevents the backwards search for $c\uparrow$ from going beyond the location of $a\uparrow$.

The rightmost diagram in Figure 3 contains one diamond pattern nested inside another. This diagram is hard to capture cleanly using just NLTL because both prefixes and suffixes must be truncated during the search. We therefore introduce an analogous operator to N, called $\tilde{N}$, that limits the scope of a search to a prefix of the path.

The following subsections formalize our observations about the temporal operators needed to cleanly capture various shapes of partial orders. We define the logics PLTL and NÑLTL and present an algorithm for translating a subset of partial orders into formulas in NÑLTL. We prove that the translation is correct and show a richer partial order that NÑLTL cannot capture. Characterizations of the partial orders captured by LTL, PLTL, and Past-LTL follow from the correctness of the translation algorithm.

4.1   The Logics

PLTL. The logic PLTL (LTL+Past) is the logic LTL extended with past time modalities: Y ("yesterday") is the opposite of X, that is, it denotes an event that happened in the previous step; P ("past") is the opposite of F, that is, it denotes an event that happened somewhere in the past; and S ("since") is the opposite of U. We refer to Y, P, and S as *past modalities*, and to X, U, F, and G as *future modalities*. The semantics for the past modalities is as follows.

- $\pi, i \models Y\psi$ iff $i > 0$ and $\pi, i-1 \models \psi$.
- $\pi, i \models \psi S\varphi$ iff $\pi, j \models \varphi$ for some $0 \leq j \leq i$ such that $\pi, k \models \psi$ for all $j < k \leq i$.

We use P as a shortcut for $\mathbf{true}S$.

The N and $\tilde{N}$ Modalities. The logic NLTL (*LTL with forgettable past*) is defined by extending the logic PLTL with the unary modality N [10]. The semantics of N is defined as follows: $N\varphi$ is satisfied in the ith position of a path π iff φ is satisfied in the path $\rho = \pi^i$. In other words, N ignores everything that happened in π prior to the position i. Formally, $\pi, i \models N\varphi$ iff $\pi^i, o \models \varphi$.

NÑLTL includes N and a similar modality for the *unforeseeable future*. The unforeseeable future modality ("up to now") is denoted by $\tilde{N}$. Semantically, $\tilde{N}\varphi$ is satisfied in the ith position of a path π iff φ is satisfied in the last position of the finite path ρ obtained from π by cutting off its suffix π^{i+1}. That is, $\rho = \pi[0..i]$.

Gabbay [7,8] proved that any linear-time temporal property expressed using past-time modalities can be translated into an equivalent (when evaluated at the beginning of the path) pure future formula. In other words, PLTL is not more expressive than LTL. Gabbay's proof can be extended to NLTL as well [10]. Since the modality $\tilde{N}$ is symmetrical to N; the same proof applies to NÑLTL. Gabbay's translation yields a

Gen-Formula(P)

    if P contains multiple connected components $P_1, \ldots P_k$ **return** $\bigwedge_{i=1}^{i=k}$ Gen-Formula(P_i)

    elseif P has a valid schedule tree T and no dividing events **return** Gen-Tree(P, T, root(T))

    else let $e_1, \ldots, e_n$ be a sequence of dividing events for P

      return $\varphi_{e_1} \wedge \tilde{N}(\text{Gen-Formula}(R_0))$

                $\wedge XNF(\varphi_{e_2} \wedge \tilde{N}(\text{Gen-Formula}(R_1))$

                          $\wedge XNF(\varphi_{e_3} \wedge \ldots \wedge XNF(\varphi_{e_n} \wedge \tilde{N}(\text{Gen-Formula}(R_{n-1}))$

                                    $\wedge XNF(\text{Gen-Formula}(R_n)) \ldots)$

Gen-Tree(P,T,e)

    if e has no successors **return** φ_e

    else let $en_1, \ldots, en_k$ be successors of e in T in same direction as in P

      let $ep_1, \ldots, ep_j$ be successors of e in T in opposite direction as in P

      return $\varphi_e \wedge \bigwedge_{i=1}^{k}(XF\text{Gen-Tree}(P, T, en)) \wedge \bigwedge_{i=1}^{j}(P\text{Gen-Tree}(P, T, ep))$

Fig. 4. The formula generation algorithm. φ_e denotes the formula that captures an event e: $\neg a \wedge X(a)$ captures $a \uparrow$ and $a \wedge X(\neg a)$ captures $a \downarrow$.

---

formula whose size is assumed to be non-elementary in the size of the initial formula. It was recently proved that PLTL is at least exponentially more succinct than LTL, and that NLTL is at least exponentially more succinct than PLTL [9]. It is easy to see that the proof of exponential gap in succinctness can be used almost without change for $\tilde{N}$. That is, introducing either N or $\tilde{N}$ is enough for the exponential gap. Observe that in general, chopping off the prefix is not equivalent to chopping off the suffix, since the former leaves us with an infinite path, while the latter preserves only a finite portion of the path. However, Laroussinie *et al.*'s proof uses only propositional formulas. The same proof therefore works if we reverse the direction of the input, switch past and future modalities in formulas and use $\tilde{N}$ instead of N. While using both N and $\tilde{N}$ modalities proves to be helpful in translating timing diagrams, it seems that having both of them does not introduce an additional gap in succinctness as opposed to having only one. That is, the logic NÑLTL seems to be no more succinct than NLTL.

4.2 Compiling Partial Orders to NÑLTL

The diagrams in Figure 3 illustrate how the events in timing diagrams bound windows in which other events must occur. Our discussion illustrates how the N and $\tilde{N}$ operators are useful for enforcing these boundaries in temporal logic. Our translation strategy is to use N and $\tilde{N}$ to (recursively) scope the window boundaries at the outermost levels and to use PLTL to capture the events that fall within these windows. This approach works when the contents of windows form forests (or can be further decomposed into subwindows). We limit the algorithm to these cases, then show a richer structure that NÑLTL is not capable of capturing.

    The algorithm appears in Figure 4. It finds window boundaries by locating *dividing events* in the partial order.

Definition 5. An event e of a diagram D is a *dividing event* iff there exists a partition of the events of D minus e into sets E_1 and E_2 such that $e \succ e_1$ for all $e_1 \in E_1$ and

$e \prec e_2$ for all $e_2 \in E_2$. Given a sequence of dividing events, $e_1 \prec e_2 \prec \ldots \prec e_n$, the *region* R_i is the set of events e such that $e_i \prec e \prec e_{i+1}$ (with R_0 containing those events that precede e_1 and R_n containing those events that follow e_n).

By definition, the dividing events are totally ordered and thus can be captured by a sequence of nested LTL F operators. All remaining events fall into regions encapsulated by the dividing events. Our translation algorithm bounds these regions in the formula by inserting N and $\tilde{N}$ at the beginning and the end of regions.

If a partial order contains no dividing events, then each connected component within the partial order is compiled to a formula in PLTL. This translation relies on a *schedule tree* that specifies the order in which to search for each event in the component.

Definition 6. Given a partial order P, a *schedule tree* T of P is a tree with directed edges such that the set of nodes in T is the set of nodes in P. We call a schedule tree *valid* if for each edge $e_1 \to e_2$ in T, P contains either an edge from e_1 to e_2, or an edge from e_2 to e_1. In other words, all edges in T must be justified by edges in P, but the edges in T may occur in the reversed direction from those in P.

Note that a single partial order could have several schedule trees. As a simple example, the partial order $a \prec b$, $b \prec c$, and $a \prec c$ could schedule b or c in either order.

Definition 7. Given a partial order P, a *schedule forest* F of P is a set of trees with directed edges such that the set of nodes in F is the set of nodes in P and each tree in F is a schedule tree for its subset of nodes.

The following theorem establishes that the result of Gen-Formula(P) is a formula that recognizes all valid instances of P.

Theorem 3. *Let D be a diagram with partial order P. Let $\mathcal{R}$ be the set of regions (sub-orders) between each pair of subsequent dividing events of P. Then, if the partial order for each region $R \in \mathcal{R}$ can be translated to a schedule forest, Gen-Formula(P) is of size $O(|P|)$ and defines the same language as D.*

Proof. We argue the size and correctness claims from the theorem separately, starting with size. Formulas describing individual events are constant in size. Each dividing event is included in the formula one time (in the final **return** of Gen-Formula). The formula returned from Gen-Tree has linear size in the number of events in the tree by construction. Each non-dividing event appears in at most one schedule tree, so the formula resulting from Gen-Formula(P) has linear size in the number of events in P.

For the correctness claim, we will prove that Gen-Formula(P) requires exactly those event orderings contained in P. Let φ be the result of Gen-Formula(P). We first show that the formula enforces every ordering edge in P. Let $e \to e'$ be an edge in P. One of the following cases must hold:

- e is a dividing event in some portion of P. Then φ contains the subformula $\varphi_e \wedge \phi \wedge X N \psi$ where the term for e' occurs in ψ. The use of N ensures that e occurs no later than e' and the use of X ensures that e occurs strictly later than e'.

- e' is a dividing event in some portion of P. Then e must lie in the region preceding e' (unless e was a dividing event, which the previous case covered). φ contains the subformula $\varphi_{e'} \wedge \tilde{N}(R)$, where R is the region containing e. The $\tilde{N}$ ensures that e occurs before e' (no X is needed here because $\tilde{N}$ cuts off the future between the two halves of e' while two positions are needed to capture both halves of e).
- Neither e nor e' is a dividing event, which means the subformula containing their terms was generated by a call to Gen-Tree on some schedule tree T over a portion of P. By the definition of valid schedule trees, T must contain an edge between e and e' (in one direction or the other). If $e \rightarrow e'$ was an edge in T, then the XF in the output of Gen-Tree ensures that e occurs before e'. If $e' \rightarrow e$ was an edge in T, then the P in the output of Gen-Tree ensures that e occurs before e'.

We now argue that φ does not require any event orders beyond those in P. Let e_1 and e_2 be unordered events (directly or transitively) in P. Since e_1 and e_2 are unordered, no dividing event can occur between them, so they must lie in the same region R of the diagram. There are two possible cases:

- e_1 and e_2 are in different connected components of R. Gen-Formula connects separate components only through $\wedge$, which induces no temporal ordering, so φ respects the lack of order between e_1 and e_2.
- e_1 and e_2 are in the same connected component of R. In this case, both events will be in the schedule tree T for their enclosing component. If e_1 and e_2 are in different branches within T, φ relates them only by $\wedge$ and thus respects their lack of ordering. Assume that e_1 and e_2 are on a common branch, and assume without loss of generality that e_1 is closer to the root of T than is e_2. The path from e_1 to e_2 must contain at least one edge that occurs in the same direction as in P and one that occurs in the opposite direction as in P (otherwise, P would order e_1 and e_2). This means that both an F and a P operator will separate e_1 and e_2 in φ. This allows e_2 to occur on either side of e_1 (no N or $\tilde{N}$ operator can intervene because those are dropped only at dividing events), so the theorem holds. $\square$

Lemma 1. *If the directed graph induced by partial order P forms a tree, then there exists a formula in LTL that recognizes P.*

Proof. In this case, P is a valid schedule tree of itself. Gen-Tree uses only future time operators when the edges in the schedule tree match the edge direction in P.

Lemma 2. *If the directed graph constructed by reversing every edge in a partial order P forms a tree, then there exists a formula in Past-LTL that recognizes P.*

Proof. Follows by similar argument as for Lemma 1. The expressions for events that use the X operator can be rewritten to use Y.

Lemma 3. *If the graph induced by partial order P is a tree with multiple minimal events, then there exists a formula in PLTL that captures P.*

Proof. True by the definition of Gen-Tree since such a P has a valid schedule tree.

Note that don't cares are handled implicitly by not being present as events in P. The care regions are present in P as separate events for each care position, and the complexity in this case would also depend on the unary representation of the length of the care region.

4.3   Limitations of NÑLTL

The Gen-Formula algorithm uses the F and P operators only to search for events. These uses all take the form $F/P(e \wedge \psi)$, where e is an event and ψ is an NÑLTL formula. We call these forms of F and P *search operators*. NÑLTL restricted to search operators cannot capture all timing diagrams using only one term per event. Consider the following diagram D_{bad}, which has no dividing events and as many arrows as it does events (which precludes a schedule tree). The partial order over events in this diagram appears on the right. The rise and subsequent fall of a correspond to the events e_1 and e_2, and the rise and subsequent fall of b correspond to the events e_4 and e_3, respectively.

D_{bad} is expressible in NÑLTL as $F(F(e_2) \wedge F(e_3) \wedge P(e_1) \wedge P(e_4))$. The outermost F locates an index lying within the windows on a and b from which to start the search; it effectively performs existential quantification on the starting position. This is a rather different use of F from the search operators. The following lemma argues that D_{bad}'s partial order cannot be expressed concisely in NÑLTL using only search operators.

Lemma 4. *No NÑLTL formula restricted to search operators captures D_{bad} with exactly one term per event.*

Proof (sketch). Any NÑLTL formula that captures D_{bad} using only search operators must search for the events in some tree-shaped order (corresponding to the order in the formula's parse tree). The restriction that each event appear once in the formula allows the proof to exhaustively consider each order of the four events. Intuitively, N and $\tilde{N}$ cannot be used since there is no common minimal or maximal event: dropping an N marker at e_1 or e_4 before the other has been located would induce an unwanted ordering between these events; a similar problem with $\tilde{N}$ governs e_2 and e_3. Therefore, no event can serve as a valid starting point for the search embodied in the parse tree. None of the remaining operators help encode constraints in which one node is incident on two others. Any attempt to construct a formula that captures all orderings therefore either omits an arrow or imposes an order that does not exist in the diagram.   □

D_{bad} has the simplest partial order with n events and n non-transitive edges forming an undirected cycle. Larger orders of this form cannot be expressed in NÑLTL even by using F to search for a starting position. The analogous formula for the order on the right, for example, would induce unwanted constraints on unrelated events (such as e_2 and e_4).[3] We defer the proof to a full paper.

---

[3] Thanks to Shriram Krishnamurthi for suggesting this example.

Note that while the partial order in D_{bad} is diamond shaped, the direction of the arrows is different from the expressible diamond shape in the middle diagram from Figure 3. The diamond in the Figure 3 diagram has one minimal and one maximal event, while D_{bad} has two minimal and two maximal events. Multiple extremal events (and their common incident events) are at the heart of the argument for Lemma 4 because they preclude dividing events that decompose the search.

5   Conclusions and Future Work

LTL is often viewed as the canonical linear temporal logic for formal specification. Although newer logics such as PSL and OVA challenge this view in practical settings, LTL is still a benchmark logic for theoretical verification research. Timing diagrams are often viewed as just a pretty interface for LTL. This paper questions that view by illustrating the distance between the LTL operators and the temporal abstractions that timing diagrams express so naturally. Our translation from timing diagrams to LTL—the first to handle both partial event orders and don't-care regions—illustrates the gap, while our results on concisely capturing various shapes of partial orders in temporal logics put the mismatch in a formal context.

Perspective.   Our results relating partial orders to temporal logics serve two purposes. First, they suggest temporal abstractions that we would need to be able to recognize in textual formulas (in any logic) in order to render specifications as timing diagrams. Translating textual specifications to diagrams is attractive as an aid for understanding and debugging complex specifications. One interpretation of our work is that we have partly reduced the problem of recognizing that a formula can be drawn as a diagram to one of recognizing when an LTL formula captures a (more compact) NÑLTL formula. Our work suggests that recognizing diagrams in formulas might not make sense for LTL, as we do not expect designers would ever write LTL formulas as complicated as our translations of timing diagrams. Rendering diagrams that *approximate* temporal specifications may be a more realistic approach that would still benefit from our observations.

Second, our results suggest than a good textual analog to timing diagrams needs a different semantic philosophy than LTL. LTL and its extensions break paths into windows in which subformulas are satisfied, but these windows are strictly bounded at one end. This characteristic captures nested windows and windows that are ordered on one side, but not windows that overlap one another with constraints on both ends. Timing diagrams capture these richer spatial operators between windows. The inexpressible diagram in Section 4.3 provides an example of complex constraints between windows that do not fit within the styles of operators traditional in LTL extensions.

Future Work.   Characterizing the class of diagrams for which there are no equivalent NÑLTL formulas of the same size remains an open problem. Section 4.3 presents initial steps in this direction. Given such a characterization, we must confirm that our algorithm handles all expressible partial orders other than D_{bad}. We have not yet considered the impact of timing constraints on our conciseness results. Logics such as

PSL in which windows in words are an explicit part of the semantics may provide a better textual analog for timing diagrams. We intend to perform a similar analysis to the one in this paper for PSL. This exercise should give a different perspective on the temporal operators that are fundamental to timing diagrams yet natural to capture textually. If existing windows-based logics also prove insufficient for cleanly capturing timing-diagram-like specifications, developing native verification techniques for timing diagrams may well prove beneficial. Similar comparisons to interval-based temporal logics would also be instructive [4,11]. Finally, it would be useful to understand the shapes of partial orders that designers frequently express in timing diagrams in practice. While we have seen examples that require rich partial orders, we lack more detailed data about the frequency of each of these shapes in practice.

Acknowledgments. Research funded by NSF grants CCR-0132659 and CCR-0305834.

References

1. N. Amla, E. A. Emerson, and K. S. Namjoshi. Efficient decompositional model checking for regular timing diagrams. In *IFIP Conference on Correct Hardware Design and Verification Methods*, 1999.
2. N. Amla, E. A. Emerson, K. S. Namjoshi, and R. J. Trefler. Visual specifications for modular reasoning about asynchronous systems. In *International Conference on Formal Techniques for Networked and Distributed Systems*, pages 226–242, 2002.
3. E. Cerny, B. Berkane, P. Girodias, and K. Khordoc. *Hierarchical Annotated Action Diagrams*. Kluwer Academic Publishers, 1998.
4. L. Dillon, G. Kutty, L. Moser, P. M. Melliar-Smith, and Y. S. Ramakrishna. A graphical interval logic for specifying concurrent systems. *ACM Transactions on Software Engineering and Methodology*, 3(2):131–165, Apr. 1994.
5. K. Fisler. Timing diagrams: Formalization and algorithmic verification. *Journal of Logic, Language, and Information*, 8:323–361, 1999.
6. K. Fisler. On tableau constructions for timing diagrams. In *NASA Langley Formal Methods Workshop*, 2000.
7. D. Gabbay. The declarative past and imperative future. In B. Banieqbal, H. Barringer, and A. Pnueli, editors, *Temporal Logic in Specification*, volume 398 of *Lecture Notes in Computer Science*, pages 407–448. Springer-Verlag, 1987.
8. D. Gabbay, A. Pnueli, S. Shelah, and J. Stavi. On the temporal analysis of fairness. In *Proc. 7th ACM Symp. on Principles of Programming Languages*, pages 163–173, January 1980.
9. F. Laroussinie, N. Markey, and P. Schnoebelen. Temporal logic with forgettable past. In *Proc. 17th IEEE Symp. Logic in Computer Science (LICS'2002)*, pages 383–392, 2002.
10. F. Laroussinie and P. Schnoebelen. A hierarchy of temporal logics with past. In *Proc. 11th Symp. on Theoretical Aspects of Computer Science*, Caen, February 1994.
11. B. Moszkowski. A temporal logic for multi-level reasoning about hardware. *IEEE Computer*, pages 10–19, February 1985.
12. A. Pnueli and R. Rosner. On the synthesis of a reactive module. In *Proc. 16th ACM Symp. on Principles of Programming Languages*, pages 179–190, Austin, January 1989.
13. A. Sistla. *Theoretical issues in the design of distributed and concurrent systems*. PhD thesis, Harvard University, Cambridge, MA, 1983.
14. A. Sistla, M. Vardi, and P. Wolper. The complementation problem for Büchi automata with applications to temporal logic. *Theoretical Computer Science*, 49:217–237, 1987.

Regular Vacuity

Doron Bustan[2], Alon Flaisher[1], Orna Grumberg[1], Orna Kupferman[3,*],
and Moshe Y. Vardi[2,**]

[1] Technion Haifa
[2] Rice University
[3] Hebrew University

Abstract. The application of model-checking tools to complex systems involves a nontrivial step of modelling the system by a finite-state model and a translation of the desired properties into a formal specification. While a positive answer of the model checker guarantees that the model satisfies the specification, correctness of the modelling is not checked. Vacuity detection is a successful approach for finding modelling errors that cause the satisfaction of the specification to be trivial. For example, the specification "every request is eventually followed by a grant" is satisfied vacuously in models in which requests are never sent. In general, a specification φ is satisfied vacuously in a model M if φ has a subformula ψ that does not affect the satisfaction of φ in M, where "does not affect" means we can replace ψ by a universally quantified proposition. Previous works focus on temporal logics such as LTL, CTL, and CTL*, and reduce vacuity detection to standard model checking.

A major feature of recent industrial property-specification languages is their regular layer, which includes regular expressions and formulas constructed from regular expressions. Our goal in this work is to extend vacuity detection to such a regular layer of linear-temporal logics. We focus here on RELTL, which is the extension of LTL with a regular layer. We define when a regular expression does not affect the satisfaction of an RELTL formula by means of universally quantified intervals. Thus, the transition to regular vacuity takes us from monadic quantification to dyadic quantification. We argue for the generality of our definition and show that regular-vacuity detection is decidable, but involves an exponential blow-up (in addition to the standard exponential blow-up for LTL model checking). This suggests that, in practice, one may need to work with weaker definitions of vacuity or restrict attention to specifications in which the usage of regular events is constrained. We discuss such weaker definitions, and show that their detection is not harder than standard model checking. We also show that, under certain polarity constraints, even general regular-vacuity detection can be reduced to standard model checking.

1 Introduction

Model-checking tools are successfully used for checking whether systems have desired properties [9]. The application of model-checking tools to complex systems involves

* Supported in part by BSF grant 9800096, and by a Minerva Program grant.
** Supported in part by NSF grants CCR-9988322, CCR-0124077, CCR-0311326, IIS-9908435, IIS-9978135, EIA-0086264, and ANI-0216467, by BSF grant 9800096, by Texas ATP grant 003604-0058-2003, and by a grant from the Intel Corporation.

D. Borrione and W. Paul (Eds.): CHARME 2005, LNCS 3725, pp. 191–206, 2005.
© IFIP International Federation for Information Processing 2005

a nontrivial step of modelling the system by a finite-state mathematical model, and translation of the desired properties into a formal specification. When the model does not satisfy the specification, model-checking tools accompany a negative answer with a counterexample, which may point to a real error in the system [8]. It is often the case, however, that there is an error in the modelling of the system and/or in the formal specification. Such errors may not be detected when the answer of the model-checking tool is positive: while a positive answer does guarantee that the model satisfies the specification, the answer to the real question, namely, whether the system has the desired properties, may be different.

The realization of this unfortunate situation has led to the development of several *sanity checks* for formal verification. The goal of these checks is to detect errors in the modelling of the system and the properties. Sanity checks in industrial tools are typically simple, often ad hoc, tests, such as checking for enabling conditions that are never enabled [20]. A more systematic approach is based on *vacuity detection*. Intuitively, a specification is satisfied vacuously in a model if it is satisfied in some non-interesting way. For example, the LTL specification $\theta = $ globally $(req \rightarrow $ eventually $grant)$ ("every request is eventually followed by a grant") is satisfied vacuously in a model with no requests. While vacuity checking cannot ensure that whenever a model satisfies a formula, the model is correct, it does capture inconsistencies between the model and the verified property. Being automatic, vacuity checking avoids hidden false assumptions made by the verifier, and thus it is more likely to capture modelling and specification errors.

Several years of experience in practical formal verification have convinced the verification group in IBM Haifa Research Laboratory that vacuity is a serious problem [5]. To quote from [5]: "Our experience has shown that typically 20% of specifications pass vacuously during the first formal-verification runs of a new hardware design, and that vacuous passes always point to a real problem in either the design or its specification or environment." The first formal treatment of vacuity is described in [5]. Consider a model M satisfying a specification φ. A subformula ψ of φ *does not affect* (the satisfaction of) φ in M if M also satisfies all formulas obtained by modifying ψ. In the example above, the subformula $grant$ does not affect θ in a model with no requests. Now, M satisfies φ vacuously if φ has a subformula that does not affect φ in M. A general method for vacuity detection was presented in [19], who showed that when all the occurrences of ψ in φ are of a *pure polarity* (that is, they are either all under an even number of negations (positive polarity), or all under an odd number of negations (negative polarity)), then ψ does not affect φ iff M satisfies the formula obtained from φ by the single extreme modification of ψ (to **true** in case ψ has a negative polarity, and to **false** otherwise). This observation reduces vacuity detection to model checking. The usefulness of vacuity analysis is also demonstrated via several case studies in [22]. For more recent work on vacuity checking, see [16,15].

As shown in [19], the method described there can be used when subformulas of φ are of a *mixed polarity*. In practice, however, one often needs to cope with mixed polarity. For example, the subformula ψ has a mixed polarity in formulas of the (commonly seen) form globally $(\psi \rightarrow \theta) \wedge$ eventually ψ. In fact, industrial-strength property-specification languages such as Sugar [4], ForSpec [3], and the recent standards PSL 1.01 and SVA 3.1a [1] contain operators in which even a single occurrence of ψ may not have a pure polarity (e.g., ψ XOR θ or $\psi \leftrightarrow \theta$).

Once we allow subformulas of a mixed polarity, there is a need to re-examine the definition of when ψ does not affect φ in M. Indeed, it is only in the pure-polarity case that the various modifications of ψ may be restricted to the single extreme modification. Such a re-examination was done in [2], who considered vacuity detection for LTL specifications. While the modifications to ψ in [5] are *syntactic*; i.e., M has to satisfy all formulas $\varphi[\psi \leftarrow \psi']$, namely formulas obtained from φ by substituting ψ by an LTL formula ψ', Armoni et al. argued that a right definition is one in which the modifications to ψ are *semantic*; i.e., M has to satisfy the formula $(\forall x)\varphi[\psi \leftarrow x]$, obtained by substituting ψ by a universally quantified proposition [1]. Gurfinkel et al further extend this definition to CTL* in [15] arguing that it is more robust than other definitions. . It is shown in [2] that, under such a semantic interpretation, vacuity detection of LTL formulas can still be reduced to LTL model checking. A tool used at Intel for vacuity detection is also described in [2].

As mentioned earlier, the work in [2] was motivated by the need to extend vacuity detection to recent industrial property-specification languages, which are significantly richer syntactically and semantically than LTL. A major feature of these languages, which does not exist in LTL, is a *regular layer*, which includes regular expressions and formulas constructed from regular expressions. The regular layer does not only add to the expressive power of the specification language s.t. it can express the whole ω-regular spectrum, but it also seemed to be more intuitive to hardware engineers. For some languages like SVA 3.1a, the only way to express temporal properties is using regular expressions.

As an example of the use of the regular layer, consider the ForSpec formula e seq θ, where e is a regular expression and θ is a formula, asserts that some e sequence is followed by θ, and the ForSpec formula e triggers θ, asserts that all e sequences are followed by θ. Our goal in this paper is to extend vacuity detection to such a regular layer of linear-temporal logics. Rather than treat the full complexity of industrial languages, we focus here on RELTL, which is the extension of LTL with a regular layer. Thus, we need to define, and then check, the notion of "does not affect," not only for subformulas but also for regular expressions. We refer to the latter as *regular vacuity*. As an example, consider the property $\varphi =$ globally $((req \cdot (\neg ack)^* \cdot ack)$ triggers $grant)$, which says that a grant is given exactly one cycle after the cycle in which a request is acknowledged. Note that if $(\neg ack)^* \cdot ack$ does not affect the satisfaction of φ in M (that is, replacing $(\neg ack)^* \cdot ack$ by any other sequence of events does not cause M to violate φ), we can learn that acknowledgments are actually ignored: grants are given, and stay on forever, immediately after a request. Such a behavior is not referred to in the specification, but can be detected by regular vacuity. Note that if the same regular expression appears in the left-hand side of both seq and triggers formulas or on both sides of a triggers formula, then this expression has mixed polarity.

In order to understand our definition for regular vacuity, consider a formula φ over a set AP of atomic propositions. Let Σ be the set of Boolean functions over AP, and

---

[1] A model M satisfies a formula $(\forall x)\varphi(x)$ if φ is satisfied in all computations π that differ from a computation of M only in the label of the proposition x. Note that different occurrences of a state in π may have different x labels.

let e be a regular expression over Σ appearing in φ. The regular expression e induces a language – a set of finite words over Σ. For a word $w \in \Sigma^\omega$, the regular expression e induces a set of intervals [3]: these intervals define subwords of w that are members in the language of e. By saying that e does not affect φ in M, we want to capture the fact that we could modify e, replace it with any other regular expression, and still M satisfies φ. As has been the case with propositional vacuity, there is no known algorithmic approach to handle such syntactic modifications in the presence of regular expressions of mixed polarity. Accordingly, as in [2], we follow a semantic approach to modifications of e, where "does not affect" is captured by means of universal quantification. Thus, in RELTL vacuity there are two types of elements we need to universally quantify to check vacuity. First, as in LTL, in order to check whether an RELTL subformula ψ, which is not a regular expression, affects the satisfaction of φ, we quantify universally over a proposition that replaces ψ. In addition, checking whether a regular expression e that appears in φ affects its satisfaction, we need to quantify universally over intervals. Thus, while LTL vacuity involved only *monadic* quantification (over the sets of points in which a subformula may hold), regular vacuity involves *dyadic* quantification (over intervals – sets of pairs of points, in which a regular expression may hold). In Section 3, we discuss two weaker alternative definitions: a restriction of the universally quantified intervals to intervals of the same duration as e, and an approximation of the dyadic quantification over intervals by monadic quantification over the Boolean events referred to in the regular expressions. As discussed there, the definition in terms of dyadic quantification is the most general one.

The transition from monadic to dyadic quantification is very challenging. Indeed, while monadic second-order logics are often decidable [7,23], this is not the case for dyadic second-order logics. For example, while monadic second-order theory of one successor is decidable [7], this is not the case for the dyadic theory [6]. The main result of this work is that regular vacuity is decidable. We show that the automata-theoretic approach to LTL [27] can be extended to handle dyadic universal quantification. Unlike monadic universal quantification, which can be handled with no increase in computational complexity [2], the extension to dyadic quantification involves an exponential blow-up (in addition to the standard exponential blow-up of handling LTL [25]), resulting in an EXPSPACE upper bound, which should be contrasted with a PSPACE upper bound for RELTL model checking. Our NEXPTIME-hardness lower bound, while leaving a small gap with respect to the upper bound, shows that an exponential overhead on top of the complexity of RELTL model checking seems inevitable. The above results suggest that, in practice, one may need to restrict attention to specifications in which regular expressions are of pure polarity. We show that under this assumption, the techniques of [19] can be extended to regular vacuity, which can then be reduced to standard model checking. In addition, for specifications of mixed polarity, the two weaker definitions we suggest for regular vacuity can also be checked in PSPACE – like standard RELTL model checking.

2   RELTL

The linear temporal logic RELTL extends LTL with a regular layer. We consider LTL in a positive normal form, where formulas are constructed from atomic propositions and their negations by means of Boolean ($\land$ and $\lor$) and temporal (next, until, and its dual release) connectives. For details, see [21]. Let AP be a finite set of atomic propositions, and let $\mathcal{B}$ denote the set of all Boolean functions $b : 2^{AP} \to \{\textbf{false}, \textbf{true}\}$ (in practice, members of $\mathcal{B}$ are expressed by Boolean expressions over AP). Consider an infinite word $\pi = \pi_0, \pi_1, \ldots \in (2^{AP})^\omega$. For integers $j \geq i \geq 0$, and a language $L \subseteq \mathcal{B}^*$, we say that $\pi_i, \ldots, \pi_{j-1}$ *tightly satisfies* L, denoted $\pi, i, j \models L$, if there is a word $b_0 \cdot b_1 \cdots b_{j-1-i} \in L$ such that for all $0 \leq k < j - i$, we have that $b_k(\pi_{i+k}) = \textbf{true}$. Note that when $i = j$, the interval $\pi_i, \ldots, \pi_{j-1}$ is empty, in which case $\pi, i, j \models L$ iff $\epsilon \in L$.

The logic RELTL contains two regular modalities: $(e \text{ seq } \varphi)$ and $(e \text{ triggers } \varphi)$, where e is a regular expression over the alphabet $\mathcal{B}$, and φ is an RELTL formula. Intuitively, $(e \text{ seq } \varphi)$ asserts that some interval satisfying e is followed by a suffix satisfying φ, whereas $(e \text{ triggers } \varphi)$ asserts that all intervals satisfying e are followed by a suffix satisfying φ. Note that the seq and triggers connectives are essentially the "diamond" and "box" modalities of PDL [11]. Formally, let π be an infinite word over 2^{AP} then,[2]

- $\pi, i \models (e \text{ seq } \varphi)$ if for some $j \geq i$, we have $\pi, i, j \models L(e)$ and $\pi, j \models \varphi$.
- $\pi, i \models (e \text{ triggers } \varphi)$ if for all $j \geq i$ such that $\pi, i, j \models L(e)$, we have $\pi, j \models \varphi$.

In the automata-theoretic approach to model checking, we translate temporal logic formulas to automata [27]. A *nondeterministic generalized Büchi word automaton* (NGBW, for short) is a tuple $A = \langle \Sigma, S, \delta, S_0, \mathcal{F} \rangle$, where Σ is a finite alphabet, S is a finite set of states, $\delta : S \times \Sigma \to 2^S$ is a transition function, $S_0 \subseteq S$ is a set of initial states, and $\mathcal{F} \subseteq 2^S$ is a set of sets of accepting states. A run ρ of A is an infinite sequence of states in S that starts in a state in S_0 and obeys δ. Let $inf(\rho) \subseteq S$ denote the set of states that are visited infinitely often in ρ. Since the run is infinite and S is finite, it must be that $inf(\rho)$ is not empty. An NGBW A accepts an infinite word π if it has an infinite run ρ over π such that for every $F \in \mathcal{F}$, we have $inf(\rho) \cap F \neq \emptyset$. The full definition of NGBW is given in the full version. We now describe a translation of RELTL formulas to NGBW. The translation can be viewed as a special case of the translation of ETL to NGBW [27] (see also [17]), but we need it as a preparation for our handling of regular vacuity.

Theorem 1. *Given an RELTL formula φ over AP, we can construct an NGBW A_φ over the alphabet 2^{AP} such that $L(A_\varphi) = \{\pi | \pi, 0 \models \varphi\}$ and the size of A_φ is exponential in φ.*

Proof: The translation of φ goes via an intermediate formula ψ in the temporal logic ALTL. The syntax of ALTL is identical to the one of RELTL, only that regular expressions over $\mathcal{B}$ are replaced by nondeterministic finite word automata (NFW, for short) over 2^{AP}. The adjustment of the semantics is as expected: let $\pi = \pi_0, \pi_1, \ldots$ be an infinite path over 2^{AP}. For integers i and j with $0 \leq i \leq j$, and an NFW Z with alphabet 2^{AP}, we say that $\pi_i, \ldots, \pi_{j-1}$ *tightly satisfies* $L(Z)$, denoted $\pi, i, j, \models L(Z)$, if

---

[2] In industrial specification languages such as ForSpec and PSL the semantics is slightly different. There, it is required that the last letter of the interval satisfying $L(e)$ overlaps the first letter of the suffix satisfying ψ. In the full version we describe a linear translation between these two semantics.

$\pi_i, \ldots, \pi_{j-1} \in L(Z)$. Then, the semantics of the **seq** and **triggers** modalities are as in RELTL, with $L(Z)$ replacing $L(e)$.

A regular expression e over the alphabet $\mathcal{B}$ can be linearly translated to an equivalent NFW Z_e with a single initial state [18]. To complete the translation to ALTL, we need to adjust the constructed NFW to the alphabet 2^{AP}. Given the NFW $Z_e = \langle \mathcal{B}, Q, \Delta, q_0, W \rangle$, let $Z'_e = \langle 2^{AP}, Q, \Delta', q_0, W \rangle$, where for every $q, q' \in Q$, and $a \in 2^{AP}$, we have that $q' \in \Delta'(q, a)$ iff there exists $b \in \mathcal{B}$ such that $q' \in \Delta(q, b)$ and $b(a) = \mathbf{true}$. It is easy to see that for all π, i, and j, we have that $\pi, i, j \models L(e)$ iff $\pi, i, j \models L(Z'_e)$. Let ψ be the ALTL formula obtained from φ by replacing every regular expression e in φ by the NFW Z'_e. It follows that for every infinite word π and $i \geq 0$, we have that $\pi, i \models \varphi$ iff $\pi, i \models \psi$.

It is left to show that ALTL formulas can be translated to NGBW. Let ψ be an ALTL formula. For a state $q \in Q$ of an NFW Z, we use Z^q to denote Z with initial state q. Using this notation, ALTL formulas of the form $(Z'_e \text{ seq } \varphi)$ and $(Z'_e \text{ triggers } \varphi)$ now become $(Z'^{q_0}_e \text{ seq } \varphi)$ and $(Z'^{q_0}_e \text{ triggers } \varphi)$. The closure of ψ, denoted $cl(\psi)$, is the set $\{\xi | \xi$ is a subformula of $\psi\} \cup \{(Z^q \text{ seq } \xi) | (Z^q \text{ seq } \xi)$ is a subformula of ψ and q' is a state of $Z^q\} \cup \{(Z^{q'} \text{ triggers } \xi) | (Z^q \text{ triggers } \xi)$ is a subformula of ψ and q' is a state of $Z^q\}$. Let $seq(\psi)$ denote the set of **seq** formulas in $cl(\psi)$. A subset $C \subseteq cl(\psi)$ is *consistent* if the following hold: (1) if $p \in C$, then $\neg p \notin C$, (2) if $\varphi_1 \wedge \varphi_2 \in C$, then $\varphi_1 \in C$ and $\varphi_2 \in C$, and (3) if $\varphi_1 \vee \varphi_2 \in C$, then $\varphi_1 \in C$ or $\varphi_2 \in C$.

Given ψ, we define the NGBW $A_\psi = \langle 2^{AP}, S, \delta, S_0, \mathcal{F} \rangle$, where $S \subseteq 2^{cl(\psi)} \times 2^{seq(\psi)}$ is the set of all pairs (L_s, P_s) such that L_s is consistent, and $P_s \subseteq L_s \cap seq(\psi)$. Intuitively, when A_ψ reads the point i of π and is in state (L_s, P_s), it guesses that the suffix $\pi_i, \pi_{i+1}, \ldots$ of π satisfies all the formulas in L_s. In addition, as explained below, the set P_s keeps track of the seq formulas in L_s whose eventuality needs to be fulfilled. Accordingly, $S_0 = \{(L_s, \emptyset) \in S : \psi \in L_s\}$.

Before we describe the transition function δ, let us explain how subformulas of the form $(Z^q \text{ seq } \psi)$ and $(Z^q \text{ triggers } \psi)$ are handled. In both subformulas, something should happen after an interval that tightly satisfies Z^q is read. In order to "know" when an interval $\pi_i, \pi_{i+1}, \ldots \pi_{j-1}$ tightly satisfies Z^q, the NGBW A_ψ simulates a run of Z^q on it. The **seq** operator requires a single interval that tightly satisfies Z^q and is followed by a suffix satisfying ψ. Accordingly, A_ψ simulates a single run, which it chooses nondeterministically. For the **triggers** operator, the requirement is for every interval that tightly satisfies Z^q. Accordingly, here A_ψ simulates all possible runs of Z^q. Formally, $\delta : (S \times 2^{AP}) \to 2^S$ is defined as follows: $(L_t, P_t) \in \delta((L_s, P_s), a)$ iff the following conditions are satisfied:

- For all $p \in AP$, if $p \in L_s$ then $p \in a$, and if $\neg p \in L_s$ then $p \notin a$.
- If $(\text{next } \varphi_1) \in L_s$, then $\varphi_1 \in L_t$.
- If $(\varphi_1 \text{ until } \varphi_2) \in L_s$, then either $\varphi_2 \in L_s$, or $\varphi_1 \in L_s$ and $(\varphi_1 \text{ until } \varphi_2) \in L_t$.
- If $(\varphi_1 \text{ release } \varphi_2) \in L_s$, then $\varphi_2 \in L_s$ and either $\varphi_1 \in L_s$, or $(\varphi_1 \text{ release } \varphi_2) \in L_t$.
  Let $Z = \langle 2^{AP}, Q, \Delta, q_0, W \rangle$ be an NFW.
- If $(Z^q \text{ seq } \psi) \in L_s$, then (a) $q \in W$ and $\psi \in L_s$, or (b) $(Z^{q'} \text{ seq } \psi) \in L_t$ for some $q' \in \Delta(q, a)$.
- If $(Z^q \text{ triggers } \psi) \in L_s$, then (a) if $q \in W$, then $\psi \in L_s$, and (b) $(Z^{q'} \text{ triggers } \psi) \in L_t$ for all $q' \in \Delta(q, a)$.

– If $P_s = \emptyset$, then $P_t = L_t \cap seq(\varphi)$. Otherwise, for every $(Z^q \text{ seq } \psi) \in P_s$, we have that (a) $q \in W$ and $\psi \in L_s$, or (b) $(Z^{(q')} \text{ seq } \psi) \in P_t \cap L_t$ for some $q' \in \Delta(q, a)$.

Finally, the generalized Büchi acceptance condition is used to impose the fulfillment of until and seq eventualities. Thus, $\mathcal{F} = \{\Phi_1, \ldots, \Phi_m, \Phi_{seq}\}$, where for every $(\varphi_i \text{ until } \psi_i) \in cl(\varphi)$, we have a set $\Phi_i = \{(L_s, P_s) \in S | \psi_i \in L_s \text{ or } (\varphi_i \text{ until } \psi_i) \notin L_s\}$, and in addition we have the set $\Phi_{seq} = \{(L_s, P_s) \in S | P_s = \emptyset\}$. As in [27], we count on the fact that as long as a seq formula has not reached its eventuality, then some of its derivations appear in the successor state. In addition, whenever P_s is empty, we fill it with new seq formulas that need to be fulfilled. Therefore, the membership of Φ_{seq} in $\mathcal{F}$ guarantees that the eventualities of all seq formulas are fulfilled. The correctness of the construction is proved in the full version.   □

The exponential translation of RELTL formulas to NGBW implies a PSPACE model-checking procedure for it [27]. A matching lower bound is immediate from LTL being a fragment of RELTL [25]. Hence the following theorem.

Theorem 2. *The model-checking problem for RELTL is PSPACE-complete.*

3   Regular Vacuity

As discussed in Section 1, we follow the semantic approach to vacuity [2]. According to this approach, a subformula ψ of an RELTL formula φ *does not affect* φ in a model M if M satisfies $(\forall x)\varphi[\psi \leftarrow x]$, where $\varphi[\psi \leftarrow x]$ is the result of replacing in φ all the occurrences of the subformula ψ with the variable x. Thus, ψ is replaced by a universally quantified *propositional variable*. Unlike a subformula ψ, which defines a set of points in a path π (those that satisfy ψ), a regular expression e defines a set of intervals (that is, pairs of points) in π (those that tightly satisfy e). Accordingly, we are going to define "does not affect" for regular expressions by means of universally quantified *interval variables*. For that, we first define QRELTL, which is a technical extension of RELTL; it extends RELTL by universal quantification over a single interval variable.

Recall that the regular expressions of RELTL formulas are defined with respect to the alphabet $\mathcal{B}$ of Boolean expressions over AP. Let y be the interval variable, and let φ be an RELTL formula whose regular expressions are defined with respect to the alphabet $\mathcal{B} \cup \{y\}$. Then $(\forall y)\varphi$ and $(\exists y)\varphi$ are QRELTL formulas. For example, $(\forall y)$ globally $[(y \text{ seq } \psi) \wedge (ab^* \text{ triggers } \neg\psi)]$ is a well-formed QRELTL formula, while $\psi \vee [(\exists y)(y \text{ seq } \psi)]$ is not.

We now define QRELTL semantics. Let $I = \{(i, j) | i, j \in \mathbb{N}, j \geq i\}$ be a set of all (natural) intervals. An *interval set* is a set $\beta \subseteq I$. The interval variable y ranges over interval sets and is associated with β. Thus, $(i, j) \in \beta$ means that y is satisfied over an interval of length $j - i$ that starts at i. For a universally (existentially) quantified formula, satisfaction is checked with respect to every (some) interval set β. We first define when a word $\hat{\pi} = \pi_i \ldots \pi_{j-1}$ over 2^{AP} tightly satisfies, with respect to β, a language L over $\mathcal{B} \cup \{y\}$. Intuitively, it means we can partition $\hat{\pi}$ to sub-intervals that together correspond to a word w in L. Note that since some of the letters in w may be

y, the sub-intervals may be of arbitrary (possibly 0) length, corresponding to intervals in β. Formally, we have the following.

Definition 1. *Consider a language $L \subseteq (\mathcal{B} \cup \{y\})^*$, an infinite path π over 2^{AP}, indices i and j with $i \leq j$, and an interval set $\beta \subseteq I$. We say that $\pi_i, \ldots, \pi_{j-1}$ and β tightly satisfy L, denoted $\pi, i, j, \beta \models L$ iff there is $w \in L$ such that either $w = \epsilon$ and $i = j$, or $w = w_0, w_1, \ldots, w_n$ and there is a sequence of integers $i = l_0 \leq l_1 \leq \cdots \leq l_{n+1} = j$ such that for every $0 \leq k \leq n$, the following conditions hold:*

- *If $w_k \in \mathcal{B}$, then $w_k(\pi_{l_k}) = \mathbf{true}$ and $l_{k+1} = l_k + 1$.*
- *If $w_k = y$, then $(l_k, l_{k+1}) \in \beta$.*

For example, if $AP = \{p\}$, $\beta = \{(3,3), (3,4)\}$, and $\pi = \{\{p\}, \emptyset\}^\omega$, then $\pi, 2, 4, \beta \models \{p \cdot y\}$ since $p(\{p\}) = \mathbf{true}$ and $(3,4) \in \beta$. Also, $\pi, 2, 4, \beta \models \{p \cdot y \cdot \neg p\}$, since $p(\{p\}) = \mathbf{true}$, $(3,3) \in \beta$, and $\neg p(\emptyset) = \mathbf{true}$. Note that when the required w does not contain y, the definition is independent of β and coincides with tight satisfaction for languages over $\mathcal{B}$.

The semantics of the RELTL subformulas of a QRELTL formula is defined inductively as in RELTL, only with respect to an interval set β. In particular, for the seq and triggers modalities, we have

- $\pi, i, \beta \models (e \text{ seq } \varphi)$ iff for some $j \geq i$, we have $\pi, i, j, \beta \models L(e)$ and $\pi, j, \beta \models \varphi$.
- $\pi, i, \beta \models (e \text{ triggers } \varphi)$ iff for all $j \geq i$ s.t. $\pi, i, j, \beta \models L(e)$ we have $\pi, j, \beta \models \varphi$.

In addition, for QRELTL formulas, we have

- $\pi, i \models (\forall y)\varphi$ iff for every interval set $\beta \subseteq I$, we have $\pi, i, \beta \models \varphi$.
- $\pi, i \models (\exists y)\varphi$ iff there exists an interval set $\beta \subseteq I$, such that $\pi, i, \beta \models \varphi$.

An infinite word π over 2^{AP} satisfies a QRELTL formula φ, denoted $\pi \models \varphi$, if $\pi, 0 \models \varphi$. A model M satisfies φ, denoted $M \models \varphi$, if all traces of M satisfy φ.

Definition 2. *Consider a model M. Let φ be an RELTL formula that is satisfied in M and let e be a regular expression appearing in φ. We say that e does not affect φ in M iff $M \models (\forall y)\varphi[e \leftarrow y]$. Otherwise, e affects φ in M. Finally, φ is regularly vacuous in M if there exists a regular expression e that does not affect φ.*

As an example for regular vacuity, consider the property

$$\varphi = \text{globally } ((req \cdot \mathbf{true} \cdot \mathbf{true}) \text{ triggers } ack)$$

which states that an ack is asserted exactly three cycles after a req. When φ is satisfied in a model M, one might conclude that all requests are acknowledged, and with accurate timing. However, the property is also satisfied in a model M that keeps ack high at all times. Regular vacuity of φ with respect to $(req \cdot \mathbf{true} \cdot \mathbf{true})$ will be detected by showing that the QRELTL formula $(\forall y)\varphi[(req \cdot \mathbf{true} \cdot \mathbf{true}) \leftarrow y]$ is also satisfied in M. This can direct us to the erroneous behavior.

In the previous example we considered regular vacuity with respect to the entire regular expression. Sometimes, a vacuous pass can only be detected by checking regular vacuity with respect to a subexpression. Consider the property

$$\varphi = \text{globally } ((req \cdot (\neg ack)^* \cdot ack) \text{ triggers } grant)$$

which states that when an ack is asserted sometime after req, then $grant$ is asserted one cycle later. Regular vacuity on the subexpression $((\neg ack)^* \cdot ack)$ can detect that ack is actually ignored, and that $grant$ is asserted immediately after req and remains high. On the other hand, regular vacuity would not be detected on the regular expression $e = (req \cdot (\neg ack)^* \cdot ack)$, as it does affect φ. This is because φ does not hold if e is replaced by an interval $(0, j)$, in which req does not hold in model M.

We now describe two alternative definitions for "does not affect" and hence also for regular vacuity. We argue that the definitions are weaker, in the sense that a formula that is satisfied vacuously with respect to Definition 2, is satisfied vacuously also with respect to the alternative definitions, but not vice versa (i.e., it may declare vacuity when the general definition does not.) On the other hand, as we discuss in Section 5, vacuous satisfaction with respect to the alternative definitions is computationally easier to detect.

Regular Vacuity Modulo Duration. Consider a regular expression e over $\mathcal{B}$. We say that e is of *duration* d, for $d \geq 0$, if all the words in $L(e)$ are of length d. For example, $a \cdot b \cdot c$ is of duration 3. We say that e is of a *fixed duration* if it is of duration d for some $d \geq 0$. Let $e = a \cdot b \cdot c$ and let $\varphi = e$ triggers ψ. The property φ states that if the computation starts with the Boolean events a, b, and c, then ψ should hold at time 3. Suppose now that in a model M, the formula ψ does not hold at times 0,1, and 2, and holds at later times. In this case, φ holds due to the duration of e, regardless of the Boolean events in e. According to Definition 2, e affects φ (e.g., if $\beta = \{(0, 1)\}$). On the other hand, e does not affect φ if we restrict the interval variable y to intervals of length 3. Thus, e does not affect the truth of φ in M modulo its duration iff φ is still true when e is replaced by an arbitrary interval of the *same* duration (provided e is of a fixed duration). Formally, for a duration d, let $I_d = \{(i, i + d) : i \in \mathbb{N}\}$ be the set of all natural intervals of duration d. The logic *duration-QRELTL* is a variant of QRELTL in which the quantification of y is parametrized by a duration d, and y ranges over intervals of duration d. Thus, $\pi, i \models (\forall_d y)\varphi$ iff for every interval set $\beta \subseteq I_d$, we have $\pi, i, \beta \models \varphi$, and dually for $(\exists_d y)\varphi$.

Definition 3. *Consider a model M. Let φ be an RELTL formula that is satisfied in M and let e be a regular expression of duration d appearing in φ. We say that e does not affect φ in M modulo duration iff $M \models (\forall_d y)\varphi[e \leftarrow y]$. Finally, φ is regularly vacuous in M modulo duration if there exists a regular expression e of a fixed duration that does not affect φ modulo duration.*

We note that instead of requiring e to have a fixed duration, one can restrict attention to regular expressions of a finite set of durations (in which case e is replaced by intervals of the possible durations); in particular, regular expressions of a bounded duration (in which case e is replaced by intervals shorter than the bound). As we show in Section 5, vacuity detection for all those alternative definitions is similar.

Regular Vacuity Modulo Expression Structure. Consider again the formula $\varphi = e$ triggers ψ, for $e = a \cdot b \cdot c$. The formula φ is equivalent to the LTL formula $\varphi' = a \rightarrow X(b \rightarrow X(c \rightarrow X\psi))$. If we check the vacuity of the satisfaction of φ' in a system M, we check, for each of the subformulas a, b, and c whether they affect the satisfaction of φ'. For that, [2] uses universal monadic quantification. In regular vacuity modulo expression structure we do something similar – instead of replacing the whole regular expression with a universally quantified dyadic variable, we replace each of the Boolean functions in $\mathcal{B}$ that appear in the expression by a universally quantified monadic variable (or, equivalently, by a dyadic variable ranging over intervals of duration 1). Thus, in our example, φ passes vacuously in the system M described above, as neither a, b, nor c affect its satisfaction. Formally, we have the following[3].

Definition 4. *Consider a model M. Let φ be an RELTL formula that is satisfied in M and let e be a regular expression appearing in φ. We say that e does not affect φ in M modulo expression structure iff for all $b \in \mathcal{B}$ that appear in e, we have that $M \models (\forall_1 y)\varphi[b \leftarrow y]$. Finally, φ is regularly vacuous in M modulo expression structure if there exists a regular expression e that does not affect φ modulo expression structure.*

4   Algorithmic Aspects of Vacuity Detection

In this section we study the complexity of the regular-vacuity problem. As discussed in Section 3, vacuity detection can be reduced to model checking of a QRELTL formula of the form $(\forall y)\varphi$. We describe an automata-based EXPSPACE solution to the latter problem, and conclude that regular vacuity is in EXPSPACE. Recall that we saw in Section 2 that RELTL model checking is in PSPACE. As shown in [2], vacuity detection for LTL is not harder than LTL model checking, and can be solved in PSPACE. In the full version we show that regular vacuity is NEXPTIME-hard. Thus, while the precise complexity of regular vacuity is open, the lower bound indicates that an exponential overhead on top of the complexity of RELTL model checking seems inevitable.

We describe a model-checking algorithm for QRELTL formulas of the form $(\forall y)\varphi$. Recall that in the automata-theoretic approach to LTL model checking, one constructs, given an LTL formula φ, an automaton $A_{\neg\varphi}$ that accepts exactly all paths that do not satisfy φ. Model checking is then reduced to the emptiness of the product of $A_{\neg\varphi}$ with the model M [27]. For a QRELTL formula $(\forall y)\varphi$, we need to construct an automaton $A_{(\exists y)\neg\varphi}$, which accepts all paths that do not satisfy $(\forall y)\varphi$. Since we considered RELTL formulas in a positive normal form, the construction of $\neg\varphi$ has to propagate the negation inward to φ's atomic propositions, using De-Morgan laws and dualities. In particular, $\neg(e\ \mathsf{seq}\ \varphi) = (e\ \mathsf{triggers}\ \neg\varphi)$ and $\neg(e\ \mathsf{triggers}\ \varphi) = (e\ \mathsf{seq}\ \neg\varphi)$. It is easy to see that the length of $\neg\varphi$ in positive normal form is linear in the length of φ.

Theorem 3. *Given an existential QRELTL formula $(\exists y)\varphi$ over AP, we can construct an NGBW A_φ over the alphabet 2^{AP} such that $L(A_\varphi) = \{\pi | \pi, 0 \models (\exists y)\varphi\}$, and the size of A_φ is doubly exponential in φ.*

Proof: The translation of $(\exists y)\varphi$ goes via an intermediate formula $(\exists y)\psi$ in the temporal logic QALTL. The syntax of QALTL is identical to the one of QRELTL, only that regular expressions over $\mathcal{B} \cup \{y\}$ are replaced by NFW over $2^{AP} \cup \{y\}$. The closure of QALTL formulas is defined similarly to the closure of ALTL formulas. The adjustment

---

[3] Note that Definition 4 follows the semantic approach of [2]. A syntactic approach, as the one taken in [5,19], would result in a different definition, where Boolean functions are replaced by different Boolean functions.

of the semantics is similar to the adjustment of RELTL to ALTL described in Section 2. In particular, the adjustment of Definition 1 to languages over the alphabet $2^{AP} \cup \{y\}$ replaces the condition "if $w_k \in B$ then $w_k(\pi_{l_k}) = \textbf{true}$ and $l_{k+1} = l_k + 1$" there by the condition "if $w_k \in 2^{AP}$, then $w_k = \pi_{l_k}$ and $l_{k+1} = l_k + 1$" here.

Given a QRELTL formula $(\exists y)\varphi$, its equivalent QALTL formula $(\exists y)\psi$ is obtained by replacing every regular expression e in $(\exists y)\varphi$ by Z'_e, where Z'_e is as defined in Section 2. Note that the alphabet of Z'_e is $2^{AP} \cup \{y\}$. It is easy to see that for all π, i, j, and β, we have that $\pi, i, j, \beta \models L(e)$ iff $\pi, i, j, \beta \models L(Z'_e)$. Thus, for every word π and $i \geq 0$, we have that $\pi, i \models (\exists y)\varphi$ iff $\pi, i \models (\exists y)\psi$.

The construction of the NGBW A_φ from $(\exists y)\psi$ is based on the construction presented in Section 2. As there, when A_φ reads π_i and is in state (L_s, P_s), it guesses that the suffix $\pi_i, \pi_{i+1} \ldots$ satisfies all the subformulas in L_s. Since, however, here A_φ needs to simulate NFWs with transitions labelled by the interval variable y, the construction here is more complicated. While a transition labelled by a letter in 2^{AP} corresponds to reading the current letter π_i, a transitions labelled by y corresponds to reading an interval $\pi_i, \ldots, \pi_{j-1}$ in β. Recall that the semantics of QALTL is such that $(\exists y)\psi$ is satisfied in π if there is an interval set $\beta \subseteq I$ for which π, β satisfies ψ. Note that triggers formulas are trivially satisfied for an empty β, whereas seq formulas require β to contain some intervals. Assume that A_φ is in point i of π, it simulates a transition labelled y in an NFW that corresponds to a seq formula in L_s, and it guesses that β contains some interval (i, j). Then, A_φ has to make sure that all the NFWs that correspond to triggers formulas in L_s and that have a transition labelled y, would complete this transition when point j is reached. For that, L_s has to be associated with a set of triggers formulas.

Formally, for a set $L_s \subseteq cl(\psi)$, we define $wait(L_s) = \{(Z^{q'} \textsf{ triggers } \xi) | (Z^q \textsf{ triggers } \xi) \in L_s \text{ and } q' \in \Delta(q, y)\}$. Intuitively, $wait(L_s)$ is the set of triggers formulas that are waiting for an interval in β to end. Once the interval ends, as would be enforced by a seq formula, the members of $wait(L_s)$ should hold. Let $seq(\psi)$ and $trig(\psi)$ be the sets of seq and triggers formulas in $cl(\psi)$, respectively. An *obligation* for ψ is a pair $o \in seq(\psi) \times 2^{trig(\psi)}$. Let $obl(\psi)$ be the set of all the obligations for ψ. Now, to formalize the intuition above, assume that A_φ is in point i and it simulates a transition labelled y in the NFW Z for some $(Z^q \textsf{ seq } \xi) \in L_s$. Then, A_φ creates the obligation $o = ((Z^q \textsf{ seq } \xi), wait(L_s))$ and propagates it until the end of the interval.

The NGBW $A_\varphi = \langle 2^{AP}, S, \delta, S_0, \mathcal{F} \rangle$, where the set of states S is the set of all pairs (L_s, P_s) such that L_s is a consistent set of formulas and obligations, and $P_s \subseteq L_s \cap (seq(\psi) \cup obl(\psi))$. Note that the size of A_φ is doubly exponential in φ. The set of initial states is $S_0 = \{(L_s, P_s) | \psi \in L_s, P_s = \emptyset\}$. The acceptance condition is used to impose the fulfillment of until and seq eventualities, and is similar to the construction in Section 2; thus $\mathcal{F} = \{\Phi_1, \ldots, \Phi_m, \Phi_{seq}\}$, where $\Phi_i = \{s \in S | (\varphi_i \text{ until } \xi_i), \xi_i \in L_s \text{ or } (\varphi_i \text{ until } \xi_i) \notin L_s\}$, and $\Phi_{seq} = \{s \in S | P_s = \emptyset\}$. We define the transition relation δ as the set of all triples $((L_s, P_s), a, (L_t, P_t))$ that satisfy the following conditions:

1. For all $p \in AP$, if $p \in L_s$ then $p \in a$.
2. For all $p \in AP$, if $\neg p \in L_s$ then $p \notin a$.
3. If (next φ_1) $\in L_s$, then $\varphi_1 \in L_t$.

4. If $(\varphi_1 \text{ until } \varphi_2) \in L_s$, then either $\varphi_2 \in L_s$, or $\varphi_1 \in L_s$ and $(\varphi_1 \text{ until } \varphi_2) \in L_t$.
5. If $(\varphi_1 \text{ release } \varphi_2) \in L_s$, then $\varphi_2 \in L_s$ and either $\varphi_1 \in L_s$, or $(\varphi_1 \text{ release } \varphi_2) \in L_t$.
6. If $(Z^q \text{ seq } \xi) \in L_s$, then at least one of the following holds:
   (a) $q \in W$ and $\xi \in L_s$.
   (b) $(Z^{q'} \text{ seq } \xi) \in L_t$ for some $q' \in \Delta(q, a)$.
   (c) $\Delta(q, y) \neq \emptyset$ and $o = ((Z^q \text{ seq } \xi), wait(L_s)) \in L_s$. In this case we say that there is a y-transition from $(Z^q \text{ seq } \xi)$ to o in L_s.
   If conditions a or b hold, we say that $(Z^q \text{ seq } \xi)$ is *strong* in L_s w.r.t. $((L_s, P_s), a, (L_t, P_t))$.
7. If $(Z^q \text{ triggers } \xi) \in L_s$, then the following holds:
   (a) If $q \in W$, then $\xi \in L_s$.
   (b) $(Z^{q'} \text{ triggers } \xi) \in L_t$ for all $q' \in \Delta(q, a)$.
8. For every $(Z^q \text{ seq } \xi) \in P_s$, at least one of the following holds:
   (a) $q \in W$ and $\xi \in L_s$.
   (b) $(Z^{q'} \text{ seq } \xi) \in P_t \cap L_t$ for some $q' \in \Delta(q, a)$.
   (c) $\Delta(q, y) \neq \emptyset$ and $o = ((Z^q \text{ seq } \xi), wait(L_s)) \in P_s$. In this case we say that there is a y-transition from $(Z^q \text{ seq } \xi)$ to o in P_s.
   If conditions a or b hold, we say that $(Z^q \text{ seq } \xi)$ is strong in P_s w.r.t. $((L_s, P_s), a, (L_t, P_t))$.
9. If $o = ((Z^q \text{ seq } \xi), \Upsilon) \in L_s$ then at least one of the following holds:
   (a) For some $q' \in \Delta(q, y)$, we have that $(Z^{q'} \text{ seq } \xi) \in L_s$ and $\Upsilon \subseteq L_s$. In this case we say that there is a y-transition from o to $(Z^{q'} \text{ seq } \xi)$ in L_s.
   (b) $o \in L_t$.
   If condition b holds, we say that o is strong in L_s w.r.t. $((L_s, P_s), a, (L_t, P_t))$.
10. If $o = ((Z^q \text{ seq } \xi), \Upsilon) \in P_s$ then at least one of the following holds:
   (a) For some $q' \in \Delta(q, y)$, we have that $(Z^{q'} \text{ seq } \xi) \in P_s$ and $\Upsilon \subseteq L_s$. In this case we say that there is a y-transition from o to $(Z^{q'} \text{ seq } \xi)$ in P_s.
   (b) $o \in P_t$.
   If condition b holds, we say that o is strong in P_s w.r.t. $((L_s, P_s), a, (L_t, P_t))$.
11. If $P_s = \emptyset$, then $P_t = L_t \cap (seq(\varphi) \cup obl(\varphi))$.
12. If $wait(L_s) \subseteq L_s$, then for every element in $L_s \cap (seq(\varphi) \cup obl(\varphi))$ there exists a path (possibly of length 0) of y transitions to a strong element w.r.t. $((L_s, P_s), a, (L_t, P_t))$. Note that the y-transitions are local in L_s and defined in rules 6, 8, 9, 10.
13. If $wait(L_s) \subseteq L_s$, then for every element in $P_s \cap (seq(\varphi) \cup obl(\varphi))$ there exists a path (possibly of length 0) of y transitions to a strong element w.r.t. $((L_s, P_s), a, (L_t, P_t))$.

We now explain the role of conditions 12 and 13 of δ. As explained above, for every formula $(Z^q \text{ seq } \xi)$ that should hold at point i, the NGBW A_φ simulates a run of Z^q that should eventually accept an interval of π. Since Z^q has transitions labelled by y, it is possible for Z^q to loop forever in (L_i, P_i) (when $(i, i) \in \beta$). Conditions 12 and 13 force the run of Z^q to eventually reach an accepting state, and prevent such an infinite loop. The correctness of the construction is proved in the full version. $\square$

In the automata-theoretic approach to linear model checking, we translate a formula ψ to an automaton that accepts exactly all the computations that satisfy ψ. While traditional translations use nondeterministic automata (cf., [13]), recent translations go through alternating automata (cf., [12,26]). Then, the state space of the automaton consists of subformulas of ψ, the construction is considerably simpler, and the intermediate automata are exponentially more succinct. In particular, the translation of RELTL formulas to NGBW described in Theorem 1 can be replaced by a simpler translation, to alternating automata. For vacuity detection, however, we have to use nondeterministic automata. To see why, note that reasoning about the QRELTL formula $(\exists y)\varphi$ involves a guess as to where intervals associated with y end. Therefore, a translation of the formula to an alternating automaton results in an automaton in which the different copies need to coordinate in order to synchronize at the position when y ends. Such a synchronization is impossible for alternating automata.

Given a model M and the NGBW A_φ for $(\exists y)\varphi$, the emptiness of their intersection can be tested in time polynomial or in space polylogarithmic in the sizes of M and A_φ (note that M and A_φ can be generated on the fly) [27]. A path in the intersection of M and A_φ is a witness that e affects φ. It follows that the problem of deciding whether a regular expression e affects φ in M can be solved in EXPSPACE. Since the number of regular expressions appearing in φ is linear in the length of φ, we can conclude with the following upper bound to the regular-vacuity problem. As detailed in the full version, the lower bound follows from a reduction of the exponential bounded-tiling problem to regular vacuity.

Theorem 4. *The regular-vacuity problem for RELTL can be solved in EXPSPACE and is NEXPTIME-hard.*

In Section 5, we analyze the complexity of regular vacuity more carefully and show that the computational bottle-neck is the length of regular expressions appearing in triggers formulas in φ. We also describe a fragment of RELTL for which regular vacuity can be solved in PSPACE.

5   Regular Vacuity in Practice

The results in Section 4 suggest that, in practice, because of the computational complexity of general vacuity checking, one may need to work with weaker definitions of vacuity or restrict attention to specifications in which the usage of regular expressions is constrained. In this section we show that under certain polarity constraints, regular vacuity can be reduced to standard model checking. In addition we show that even without polarity constraints, detection of the weaker definitions of vacuity, presented in Section 3, is also not harder than standard model checking.

Specifications of Pure Polarity. Examining industrial examples shows that in many cases the number of trigger formulas that share a regular expression with a seq formula is quite small. One of the few examples that use both describes a clock tick pattern and is expressed by the formula $tick\_pattern = (e\ \mathsf{seq\ true}) \wedge$ $\mathsf{globally}\ (e\ \mathsf{triggers}\ (e\ \mathsf{seq\ true}))$, where e defines the clock ratio, e.g. $e = clock\_low \cdot clock\_low \cdot clock\_high \cdot clock\_high$.

As shown in the previous section, the general case of regular vacuity adds an exponential blow-up on top of the complexity of RELTL model checking. A careful analysis of the state space of A_φ shows that with every set L_s of formulas, we associate obligations that are relevant to L_s. Thus, if L_s contains no seq formula with an NFW that reads a transition labelled y, then its obligation is empty. Otherwise, $wait(L_s)$ contains only trigger formulas that appear in L_s and whose NFWs read a transition labelled y. In particular, in the special case where seq and trigger subformulas do not share regular expressions, we have $|obl(\varphi)| = 0$. For this type of specifications, where all regular expressions have a *pure polarity*, regular vacuity is much easier. Rather than analyzing the structure of A_φ in this special case, we describe here a direct algorithm for its regular-vacuity problem.

We first define *pure polarity* for regular expression. As formulas in RELTL are in positive normal form, polarity of a regular expression e is not defined by number of negations, but rather by the operator applied to e. Formally, an occurrence of a regular expression e is of *positive polarity* in φ if it is on the left hand side of a seq modality, and of *negative polarity* if it is on the left hand side of a triggers modality. The polarity of a regular expression is defined by the polarity of its occurrences as follows. A regular expression e is of *positive polarity* if all occurrences of e in φ are of positive polarity, of *negative polarity* if all occurrences of e in φ are of negative polarity, of *pure polarity* if it is either of positive or negative polarity, and of *mixed polarity* if some occurrences of e in φ are of positive polarity and some are of negative polarity.

Definition 5. *Given a formula φ and a regular expression of pure polarity e, we denote by $\varphi[e \leftarrow \bot]$ the formula obtained from φ by replacing e by $\mathbf{true}^*$, if e is of negative polarity, and by $\mathbf{false}$ if e is of positive polarity.*

We now show that for e with pure polarity in φ, checking whether e effects φ, can be reduced to RELTL model checking:

Theorem 5. *Consider a model M, RELTL formula φ, and regular expression e of pure polarity. Then, $M \models (\forall y)\varphi[e \leftarrow y]$ iff $M \models \varphi[e \leftarrow \bot]$.*

Since the model-checking problem for RELTL can be solved in PSPACE, it follows that the regular-vacuity problem for the fragment of RELTL in which all regular expressions are of pure polarity is PSPACE-complete.

Weaker Definitions of Regular Vacuity. In Section 3, we suggested two alternative definitions for regular vacuity. We now show that vacuity detection according to these definitions is in PSPACE – not harder than RELTL model checking.

We first show that the dyadic quantification in duration-QRELTL can be reduced to a monadic one. Intuitively, since the quantification in duration-QRELTL ranges over intervals of a fixed and known duration, it can be replaced by a quantification over the points where intervals start. Formally, we have the following:

Lemma 1. *Consider a system M, an RELTL formula φ, a regular expression e appearing in φ, and $d > 0$. Then, $M \models (\forall_d y)\varphi[e \leftarrow y]$ iff $M \models (\forall x)\varphi[e \leftarrow (x \cdot \mathbf{true}^{d-1})]$, where x is a monadic variable.*

Universal quantification of monadic variables does not make model checking harder: checking whether $M \models (\forall x)\varphi$ can be reduced to checking whether there is a computation of M that satisfies $(\exists x)\neg\varphi$. Thus, as detailed in [2], when we construct the intersection of M with the NGBW for $\neg\varphi$, the values for x can be guessed, and the algorithm coincides with the one for RELTL model checking. Since detection of vacuity modulo duration and modulo expression structure are both reduced to duration-QRELTL model checking, Theorem 2 implies the following.

Theorem 6. *The problem of detecting regular vacuity modulo duration or modulo expression structure is PSPACE-complete.*

We note that when the formula is of a pure polarity, no quantification is needed, and e may be replaced, in the case of vacuity modulo duration, by **false** or **true**^{d} according its polarity. Likewise, in the case of vacuity modulo expression structure, the Boolean formulas in e may be replaced by **false** or **true**.

6 Concluding Remarks

We extended in this work vacuity detection to a regular layer of linear-temporal logics. We focused here on RELTL, which is the extension of LTL with a regular layer. We defined the notion of "does not affect," for regular expressions in terms of universal dyadic quantification. We showed that regular vacuity is decidable, but involves an exponential blow-up (in addition to the standard exponential blow-up for LTL model checking). We showed that under certain polarity constraints on regular expressions, regular vacuity can be reduced to standard model checking. Our decidability result for dyadic second-order quantification is of independent interest. It suggests that the boundary between decidability and undecidability can be charted at a finer detail than the current monadic/dyadic boundary. A related phenomenon was observed in the context of descriptive complexity theory, see [10,14].

We suggested two alternative definitions for regular vacuity and showed that with respect to these definitions, even for formulas that do not satisfy the polarity constraints, vacuity detection can be reduced to standard model checking, which makes them of practical interest. The two definitions are weaker than our general definition, in the sense that a vacuous pass according to them may not be considered vacuous according to the general definition. It may seem that working with a more sensitive definition would be an advantage, but experience with vacuity detection in industrial settings shows that flooding users with too many reports of vacuous passes may be counterproductive. Thus, it is difficult to make at this point definitive statements about the overall usability of the weaker definitions, as more industrial experience with them is needed.

References

1. Accellera - www.accellera.org.
2. R. Armon, L. Fix, A. Flaisher, O. Grumberg, N. Piterman, A. Tiemeyer, and M. Vardi. Enhanced vacuity detection for linear temporal logic. In *Proc 15th CAV*, LNCS 2725, 2003.

3. R. Armoni et al. The ForSpec temporal logic: A new temporal property-specification logic. In *8th TACAS*, LNCS 2280, pages 296–211, 2002

4. I. Beer, S. Ben-David, C. Eisner, D. Fisman, A. Gringauze, and Y. Rodeh. The temporal logic sugar. In *Proc. 13th CAV*, LNCS 2102, pages 363–367, 2001.

5. I. Beer, S. Ben-David, C. Eisner, and Y. Rodeh. Efficient detection of vacuity in ACTL formulas. *FMSD* 18(2):141–162, 2001.

6. E. Börger, E. Grädel, and Y. Gurevich. *The Classical Decision Problem.* 1996.

7. J. Büchi. On a decision method in restricted second order arithmetic. In *Proc. Internat. Congr. Logic, Method. and Philos. Sci. 1960*, pages 1–12, Stanford, 1962.

8. E. Clarke, O. Grumberg, K. McMillan, and X. Zhao. Efficient generation of counterexamples and witnesses in symbolic model checking. In *Proc. 32nd DAC*, pages 427–432, 1995.

9. E. Clarke, O. Grumberg, and D. Peled. *Model Checking.* MIT Press, 1999.

10. T. Eiter, G. Gottlob, and T. Schwentick. Second-order logic over strings: Regular and non-regular fragments. *Developments in Language Theory*, pages 37–56, 2001.

11. M. Fischer and R. Ladner. Propositional dynamic logic of regular programs. *JCSS*, 18:194–211, 1979.

12. P. Gastin and D. Oddoux. Fast LTL to büchi automata translation. In *Proc. 13th CAV*, LNCS 2102, pages 53–65, 2001.

13. R. Gerth, D. Peled, M. Vardi, and P. Wolper. Simple on-the-fly automatic verification of linear temporal logic. In *Protocol Specification, Testing, and Verification*, pages 3–18. Chapman & Hall, August 1995.

14. G. Gottlob, P. G. Kolaitis, and T. Schwentick. Existential second-order logic over graphs: Charting the tractability frontier. *JACM*, 51(2):312–362, 2000.

15. A. Gurfinkel and M. Chechik. Extending extended vacuity. In *5th FMCAD*, LNCS 2212, pages 306–321, 2004.

16. A. Gurfinkel and M. Chechik. How vacuous is vacuous. In *Proc. 10th TACAS*, LNCS 2988, pages 451–466, 2004.

17. J. Henriksen and P. Thiagarajan. Dynamic linear time temporal logic. *Annals of Pure and Applied Logic*, 96(1–3):187–207, 1999.

18. J. Hopcroft and J. Ullman. *Introduction to Automata Theory, Languages, and Computation.* Addison-Wesley, 1979.

19. O. Kupferman and M. Vardi. Vacuity detection in temporal model checking. *STTT*, 4(2):224–233, February 2003.

20. R. Kurshan. *FormalCheck User's Manual.* Cadence Design, Inc., 1998.

21. Z. Manna and A. Pnueli. *The Temporal Logic of Reactive and Concurrent Systems: Specification.* Springer-Verlag, Berlin, January 1992.

22. M. Purandare and F. Somenzi. Vacuum cleaning CTL formulae. In *Proc. 14th CAV*, LNCS 2404, pages 485–499, 2002.

23. M. Rabin. Decidability of second order theories and automata on infinite trees. *Transaction of the AMS*, 141:1–35, 1969.

24. M. Savelsberg and P. van emde Boas. Bounded tiling, an alternative to satisfiability. In *2nd Frege conference*, pages 354–363. Akademya Verlag, 1984.

25. A. Sistla and E. Clarke. The complexity of propositional linear temporal logic. *Journal ACM*, 32:733–749, 1985.

26. M. Vardi. Nontraditional applications of automata theory. In *Proc. STACS*, LNCS 789, pages 575–597, 1994.

27. M. Vardi and P. Wolper. Reasoning about infinite computations. *Information and Computation*, 115(1):1–37, November 1994.

Automatic Generation of Hints for Symbolic Traversal*

David Ward[1] and Fabio Somenzi[2]

[1] IBM Printing Systems Division
daveward@us.ibm.com
[2] University of Colorado at Boulder
Fabio@Colorado.EDU

Abstract. Recent work in avoiding the state explosion problem in hardware verification during breath-first symbolic traversal (BFST) based on Binary Decision Diagrams (BDDs) applies *hints* to constrain the transition relation of the circuit being verified [14]. Hints are expressed as constraints on the primary inputs and states of a circuit modeled as a finite transition system and can often be found with the help of simple heuristics by someone who understands the circuit well enough to devise simulation stimuli or verification properties for it. However, finding *good* hints requires one to constrain the transition system so that small intermediate BDDs arise during image computations that produce large numbers of reachable states. Thus, the ease of finding *good* hints is limited by the user's ability to predict their usefulness. In this paper we present a method to statically and automatically determine *good* hints. Working on the control flow graph(s) of a behavioral model of the circuit being analyzed, our algorithm extracts sets of related execution paths. Each set has a corresponding enabling predicate which is a candidate hint. Program slicing is employed to identify execution paths. Abstract interpretation and model checking are used to ascertain properties along these paths. Hints generated automatically using our technique result in orders-of-magnitude reductions in time and space requirements during state space exploration compared to BFST and are usually as good as those produced by someone who understands the circuit.

1 Introduction

Reachability analysis plays a central role in formal verification of sequential circuits. One of the state-of-the-art approaches for reachability analysis and formal verification of circuits modeled as finite transition systems exploits symbolic computations based on Binary Decision Diagrams (BDDs). However, the known state explosion problem may cause large intermediate BDDs during the exploration of the state space of a system. The conventional breadth-first search (BFS) strategy, used in most implicit model checking algorithms, is the main culprit. Researchers have approached this problem by devising techniques [5, 11, 1, 12, 14] that simplify the system model employed during BFS.

In [14] a method is proposed to use hints to guide the exploration of the state space. Hints are expressed as constraints on the primary inputs and states of a circuit modeled as a finite transition system. In [14], hints are classified into those that depend on

---

* This work was supported in part by SRC contract 2003-TJ-920.

D. Borrione and W. Paul (Eds.): CHARME 2005, LNCS 3725, pp. 207–221, 2005.

the invariants being checked and those that capture knowledge of the design. Hints are applied by constraining the transition relation of the system; the constrained traversal of the state space proceeds much faster than that of the unconstrained system (original transition relation). This method obtained orders-of-magnitude reductions in time and space requirements. Hints can often be found by someone who understands the design well enough to devise simulation stimuli or verification properties for it. However, identifying good hints can be a labor-intensive process requiring many attempts, and in many cases does not avoid the state space explosion problem. One reason it is hard to identify good hints immediately is due to the user's inability to predict, in most cases, the impact the hint will have on the intermediate BDDs during the image computations. Acceptance of this method by designers and verification engineers will certainly benefit from an efficient technique to devise good hints from a system being verified. Our purpose in this paper is to demonstrate how such hints can be automatically determined statically using program analysis techniques.

One effective way to attack the state explosion problem is to construct small transition systems to make automatic checking tractable, yet large enough to capture the information relevant to the property being checked—reachability in our case. Our method exploits these observations and can be summarized as follows: First, we translate the behavioral model into its control flow graph(s) and augment control and data dependency edges. We then partition the control flow graph(s) into subgraphs consisting of sets of valid execution paths. (Execution paths are paths that begins with the start node and end with the exit node whose enabling predicates are satisfiable.) The enabling predicates of these subgraphs are the candidates hints; pruning criteria are applied to discard inferior candidates. Finally, the surviving candidates are sorted to produce the final list of hints.

One feature of our approach is to borrow techniques from program analysis and apply them to hardware verification. The same ideas could be used to generate hints for software verification, but that is outside the scope of this paper. We regard the behavioral model in this paper as a program. The program analysis techniques employed to accomplish our objective are program slicing [15] to extract the subgraph(s) from the original control flow graph(s); abstract interpretation [5] to obtain relevant properties for each subgraph—e.g., checking whether program variables can be influenced by the primary inputs; and model checking of abstract models to identify false data dependencies, and estimate the impact of candidate hints on reachability analysis. The program dependence graph (PDG) [6, 13] is chosen for its efficient representation of control and data dependencies of program operations and its rich set of supporting algorithms.

Analysis of models using our technique is mostly achieved at a high level of abstraction (program dependency graph). Therefore, it remains feasible when the BDD-based analysis (BFS) of the original model is not. We validated our technique using a subset of the Verilog hardware description language (behavioral Verilog); however, we argue that it can be easily extended to any simple imperative language.

This paper is organized as follows: Section 2 reviews the background material. Section 3 discusses the procedure to extract valid execution paths (subgraphs) from the original control flow graph. Section 4 presents our experimental results, and Sect. 5 summarizes, outlines future work, and concludes.

2   Preliminaries

2.1   Guided Search for Least Fixpoints

Hints are used to speed up symbolic reachability analysis of transition systems with set of states Q and inputs W defined by a *transition relation* $T \subseteq Q \times W \times Q$ and *initial state set* $I \subseteq Q$. A triple (q_1, w, q_2) is in T if and only if the transition system can proceed from q_1 to q_2 when the input is w; in this case q_2 is a *successor* of q_1. State q is *reachable* from state q' if there exists a sequence of states $q_1, \ldots, q_n$ such that $q = q_1$, $q' = q_n$, and for $1 < i \leq n$, q_{i+1} is a successor of q_i. The reachability analysis problem consists of finding all states that are reachable from some state in I. For $S \subseteq Q$, let EY S denote all states that are successors of some state in S. Then reachability can be computed as a fixpoint: $\mu Z \,.\, I \cup \text{EY}\, Z$.

This fixpoint computation corresponds to *breadth-first search* (BFS) of the transition system starting from the initial states. In symbolic model checking, transition relations and sets of states are represented by their characteristic functions, which can be manipulated in various forms. In this paper we assume that (reduced, ordered) Binary Decision Diagrams (BDDs [3]) are used for this purpose. Success with symbolic computations depends on the algorithm's ability to keep the BDDs small. Several factors affect the size of BDDs, including the variable orders. Guided search, however, focuses on the facts that BFS may require the representation of sets of states that are intrinsically unsuitable for concise representation by BDDs, and that the BDDs that represent the full transition relation may be unwieldy while restrictions to subsets of transitions may dramatically shrink the BDDs.

Given a set of *hints*, $\tau_1, \tau_2, \ldots, \tau_k$ (where each τ_i is a transition relation obtained by constraining the inputs or state variables of the model) the computation of the reachable states can be decomposed into the computation of a sequence of fixpoints—one for each hint. If hints are chosen properly, the computation of least fixpoints can be substantially sped up [14]. If simple transition systems result for each τ_i, reachability analysis may proceed further compared to computing the model fixpoint directly, and in some cases go to completion by avoiding the memory explosion problem. There are several strategies to use hints. The one of [14] is based on the following result.

Theorem 1 ([14]). *Given a sequence of monotonic functionals $\tau_1, \tau_2, \ldots, \tau_k$ such that $\tau_i \leq \tau_k$ for $0 < i < k$, the sequence $\rho_0, \rho_1, \ldots, \rho_k$ of fixpoints defined by $\rho_0 = 0$ and*

$$\rho_i = \mu X \,.\, \rho_{i-1} \vee \tau_i(X), \quad 0 < i \leq k$$

monotonically converges to $\rho = \mu X.\tau_k(X)$; that is, $\rho_0 \leq \rho_1 \leq \cdots \leq \rho_k = \rho$.

The traditional BFS reachability analysis algorithm can be modified to take advantage of hints: first, each hint, in order, is used to constrain the original transition relation, the algorithm is allowed to run normally until all reachable states are reached. The starting point for each run is either the initial states, for the first hint, or the reached states from the previous run; finally, the original transition relation is restored and runs to completion or is terminated early due to time-space exhaustion. Its starting point is the set of reachable states produced by the last hint.

2.2   Control Flow Graph (CFG)

Many program analysis techniques work on graphs derived from the program text. Among these, the CFG is a directed graph that represents the flow of control of a program (hardware or behavioral model). Each node represents an assignment or branching statement S_i in a program P. Each directed arc represents flow of control from one node to another. A CFG can be extracted in a single pass traversal over P. (See the left part of Fig. 3.) In our implementation we create one CFG for each Verilog *always block*.

Definition 1 (Control Flow Graph (CFG)). *A control flow graph CFG is a directed graph $G = (V, E)$, where: (1) V is a finite set of nodes including two distinguished nodes of type* entry *and* exit. *All other nodes are of one of five types:* assignment, input, decision, no-op, *and* join. *(2) $E \subset V \times V$ is a control flow relation, whose elements are directed edges.*

We assume that the flow relation obeys restrictions. Specifically, we assume that the arcs can be partitioned into forward arcs and back arcs so that the forward arcs form a DAG in which all nodes are reachable from the entry node. We also assume that the exit node is reachable from all nodes in the CFG. Furthermore, each back edge goes from a node to another that dominates it. These assumptions imply *reducibility* of the CFG.

Intuitively, the different types of nodes map to the basic types of statements, and in fact we shall call the CFG nodes *statements*. The edges in E represent the transfer of control between statements. A path from the entry node to the exit node represent one clock cycle of a Verilog *always block*.

2.3   Control Dependence Analysis and Program Slicing

Control dependence represents the effect of conditional branches on the behavior of programs. Given two statements S_1 and S_2 in P, statement S_2 is control-dependent on S_1 if S_1 is a conditional branch statement and the control structure (enabling predicate) of P potentially allows S_1 to decide whether S_2 will be executed. Control dependence can be defined in terms of the CFG. Let S_1 and S_2 be two nodes of a CFG.

Definition 2 (Postdominance and Control Dependence). *S_1 is postdominated by S_2 in a CFG if all paths from S_1 to the exit node include S_2. S_2 is control dependent on S_1 if and only if:*

1. *There exists a path p from S_1 to S_2 such that S_2 postdominates every node of p;*
2. *S_1 is not postdominated by S_2.*

If S_2 is control dependent on S_1 in a CFG, then S_1 must have two outgoing edges. Following one of the edges always leads to S_2, while there is a path that uses the other edge and bypasses S_2. A control dependence edge can be added to the CFG to show the dependence relation. We refer to the set of control dependence edges as E_{cd}.

Control dependence is used to extract a static program slice. During the determination of hints, our goal is to retrieve pertinent information (valid paths, over-approximate reachable states, . . .) from the original model by analyzing the smallest subset of the original model that preserves the correct result. Program slicing allows us to efficiently and effectively achieve this goal. Program slicing statically identifies all statements that *might* affect the value of a given variable occurrence [15]. The statements selected constitute a *subprogram* with respect to the variable occurrence. For a statement S_i in a CFG, the static program slice with respect to S_i is the set of statements $S_1, S_2, S_3, \ldots$ in the CFG augmented with control dependence information that can reach S_i via a path of flow or control dependence edges [8]. The program slice for a set of statements S is simply the union of the program slice of each statement S_i.

2.4 Data Dependence Analysis and the Program Dependence Graph (PDG)

Given any two statements S_1 and S_2 (containing variable x) of a CFG, a data dependence relation may hold between them if one statement is an assignment to variable x and the other is a read access (use) of the same variable x. Let $OUT(S_i)$ be the left-hand side variable of S_i and $IN(S_i)$ be the set of right-hand side variables of S_i. For any two statements S_1 and S_2 in a CFG, data dependence is defined as follows:

Definition 3 (Data Dependence). *S_2 is data dependent on S_1 if and only if: (1) $\exists x \in IN(S_2) . x = OUT(S_1)$; and (2) there exists a path in the CFG from S_1 to S_2 such that no intervening statement is an assignment to x.*

We refer to the set of data dependence edges as E_{dd}. In practice, it is easy to check for the first condition of the definition, but not for the second. Hence, we add one data dependency arc to G_{dd} whenever the first condition is met, and then try to identify as many false dependencies as computationally feasible. False data dependencies do not affect the correctness of our procedure only the quality of the result. Hence, a small number of false dependencies is tolerable. We use data dependence information to cluster paths of the CFG into candidate hints and to determine the relative order of hints.

The PDG represent the control and data dependencies of a program. It can be defined in terms of the CFG; PDG $= (V, E \cup E_{cd} \cup E_{dd})$. The PDG derived from the model text is a lossless transformation of the original program. We can go back and forth from one to the other. We employ the program dependence graph (PDG) [6, 13] as our intermediate representation.

2.5 Abstract Interpretation

Our goal is to statically (and cheaply) determine pertinent information of a program that would otherwise be ascertained during run-time. More specifically, we would like to calculate the run-time behavior of a program without having to run it on all input data, and while guaranteeing termination of the analysis. Abstract interpretation [5] provides the necessary framework to accomplish our goal. In our hint generation procedure we use abstract interpretation to determine if a decision node depends on primary inputs or not. (See Sect. 3.2.) This use effectively corresponds to a reaching definition analysis [7]. Our abstraction will therefore need to capture information about whether input information can reach the definition of a variable. We replace the set of possible values for each variable with the set of values *NID* and *ID* ("not input dependent" and "may be input dependent" respectively). Initially, each variable is assigned the value NID, unless it is an input variable. Arguments and values of functions (e.g., integer operators, boolean operators) are now from the set $\{NID, ID\}$. The encoding of the semantics of the functions is simple—any argument with a value of ID causes the function to return ID, otherwise the function returns NID. At the completion of the analysis we can safely conclude that a variable with a value of NID is not influenced by the inputs. Such a variable is labeled an *internal decision variable*. Using this technique on our running example in Fig. 2 results in *state* being identified as an internal decision variable.

3   Hint Generation Algorithm

The hints generated to help symbolic traversal of a model graph should select subsets of transitions that allow reachability analysis to visit sets of states with many elements and compact representations. Since these representations are usually Binary Decision Diagrams [3], we shall simply say that the objective is to have many states with small BDDs. When a model has several major modes of operation—as when it can execute a set of instructions—enabling one mode at the time is often effective in keeping the BDD sizes under control. Our approach to producing hints automatically is based on identifying the different modes of operation from the Control-Flow Graph (CFG) of the model, and merging and prioritizing them according to their dependencies and their promise to reduce time and memory requirements. The process can be divided in three major phases corresponding to the dashed boxes in Fig. 1.

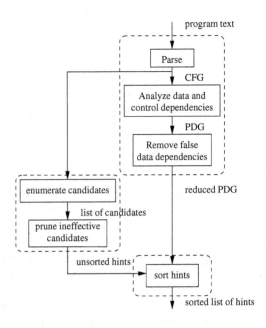

Fig. 1. Automatic hints generator methodology

- From the program text a CFG is extracted and from it a reduced program dependency graph (PDG) is created.
- From the CFG a list of candidate hints is compiled; ineffective hints are pruned.
- Using the reduced PDG, hints are sorted according to their dependencies and usefulness.

It is possible in principle for the list of hints produced by this process to be empty. This may result from exhaustion of computational resources, or because the procedure deems all candidates unworthy. However, we have not yet observed this outcome in practice, except for trivial models that contain no control flow statements. We now describe the three phases in more detail. Figures 2 and 3 show an example that is used throughout the rest of the paper to illustrate the algorithm.

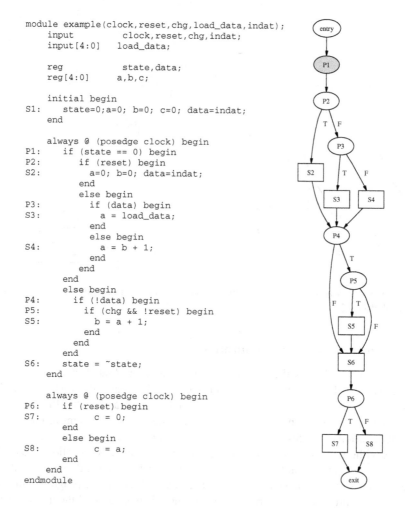

```
module example(clock,reset,chg,load_data,indat);
    input           clock,reset,chg,indat;
    input[4:0]      load_data;

    reg             state,data;
    reg[4:0]        a,b,c;

    initial begin
S1:     state=0;a=0; b=0; c=0; data=indat;
    end

    always @ (posedge clock) begin
P1:     if (state == 0) begin
P2:         if (reset) begin
S2:             a=0; b=0; data=indat;
            end
            else begin
P3:             if (data) begin
S3:                 a = load_data;
                end
                else begin
S4:                 a = b + 1;
                end
            end
        end
        else begin
P4:         if (!data) begin
P5:             if (chg && !reset) begin
S5:                 b = a + 1;
                end
            end
        end
S6:     state = ~state;
    end

    always @ (posedge clock) begin
P6:     if (reset) begin
S7:         c = 0;
        end
        else begin
S8:         c = a;
        end
    end
endmodule
```

Fig. 2. Example Verilog model (left) and serialized CFG (right)

On the left of Fig. 2 we show a Verilog model. The statements of the model are annotated with labels so that they can be traced through the transformations. The model contains a false data dependency (between S3 and S5) as well as cyclic data dependencies and therefore allows us to illustrate various aspects of the hint generation process. The PDG for this model with the control and data dependencies extracted is given in Fig. 3. To save space, the join nodes, where the two branches emanating from a decision node meet, have been merged into their successors. Moreover, to avoid clutter, the data dependency arcs are shown separately on the right, while control flow and control dependencies are jointly presented in one graph, by using thick lines for those arcs that represent both control flow and control dependency. Finally, the right part of Fig. 2 shows the serialized polar graph, which is introduced in Sect. 3.2.

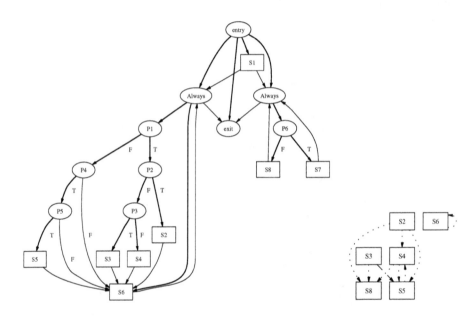

Fig. 3. Control flow and control dependency graph (left) and data dependency graph (right) for the model of Fig. 2

3.1   Removing False Data Dependencies

The program that defines the model to be analyzed is translated into a CFG, which is augmented with data dependency information to produce a PDG. (See Sect. 2.4.) Since the analysis is conservative, some data dependency arcs in the PDG are false. Since more data dependency arcs result in fewer degrees of freedom in the merging and prioritization of modes of operation, it is desirable to remove as many false arcs as possible, without incurring excessive costs. This is accomplished as follows. Each data dependency arc is tested in turn to determine whether the variable definition at the tail of the arc can actually reach the usage at its head by augmenting the program with *token variables*. The program slice corresponding to the token variable of the usage variable is extracted from the PDG. The check whether the definition can reach the usage is thus translated into the check for an invariant on the token variable of the usage variable.

Specifically, suppose that the dependency on the definition $S_1 : x := v_1$ of x by its use $S_2 : y := x$ is investigated. Two token variables, t_1 and t_2, are added to the program by making the following changes.

– Token variables t_1 and t_2 are added to the program defines.
– Assignments $t_1 := 0$ and $t_2 := 0$ are added to the beginning of the program.
– S_1 is changed to $x := v_1; t_1 := 1$.
– Every other assignment $S_i : x := v$ is changed to $S_i : x := v; t_1 := 0$.
– S_2 is changed to $y := x; t_2 := t_1$.

If in the program slice for t_2 no state is reachable in which $t_2 = 1$, then the data dependency arc from S_1 to S_2 is removed. We employ model checking to check the invariant $t_2 = 0$ in the augmented model. We are only interested in direct dependencies: Consider $S_1 : x := 2$, $S_2 : y := x$, and $S_3 : x := x + 1$. If S_3 is always executed between S_1 and S_2, the dependency arc between S_2 and S_1 is removed. However, the dependencies of S_3 on S_1, and of S_2 on S_3 imply, by transitivity, the one of S_2 on S_1.

Though program slicing may greatly reduce the cost of checking the $t_2 = 0$ invariant, this is not always the case; hence, each model checking run is allotted a short time to complete. If it does not finish, a less accurate, but less expensive test is applied. The augmented program slice is analyzed with abstract interpretation. If abstract interpretation fails to prove the invariant, the arc is (conservatively) retained.

Referring to Fig. 3, it is not hard to see that the data dependency between S3 and S5 is false. In fact, S3 requires `data` to be true for its execution, while S5 is only executed if `data` is false. The edge in the data dependency graph is correspondingly shown as a dashed line. The algorithm based on the token variables identifies the false data dependency. As a result the dashed arc is removed from the PDG.

3.2   Generating Candidate Hints

The modified PDG with (some) false data dependencies removed is one of the two inputs to the final step of our procedure that outputs a list of hints. The other input is a list of subgraphs of the CFG, each corresponding to a mode of operation. The subgraphs are identified by a procedure based on the enumeration of the paths from the entry node to the exit node of the CFG.

Depth-first search (DFS) of a graph classifies the arcs of a directed graph into forward, backward, and cross arcs [4]. The classification depends in general on the order in which nodes are visited. In a *reducible* CFG, however, the result is unique: The back arcs are precisely the return arcs of the looping constructs. Therefore, in the following we refer to the back arcs without reference to a specific DFS.

The graph obtained from the CFG by removing the back arcs is *polar*, that is, all nodes are reachable from the entry node and have a path to the exit node. Our procedure produces a list of candidate hints by partitioning the set of paths connecting the two poles of the graph obtained by removing the back arcs from the CFG. Each subset in the partition is a candidate for producing a hint (the enabling predicate obtained by conjoining the predicates along the path from the entry node to the exit node).

The partitioning algorithm is based on the notion of internal decision. A variable is an *internal decision variable* if it does not depend directly on the external inputs. Abstract interpretation is used to identify internal decision variables. A decision node of a CFG is an *internal decision node* if any variables appearing in the predicate attached to the node are internal decision variables. A hint should not constrain internal decision variables, lest it may contribute very few states to reachability analysis. Consider, for instance, an internal decision variable that is incremented modulo n at each iteration through the CFG. A hint that specifies the value for this variable will allow only one iteration of reachability analysis before reaching a fixpoint: As soon as the variable gets incremented, all transitions are disabled (remember that one clock cycle corresponds to executing one path from the entry node to the exit node). Internal decision variables are therefore treated specially in two ways:

1. Paths that diverge at an internal decision node are kept together in the partitioning.
2. Internal decision variables are existentially quantified from the predicates attached to decision nodes before they are used to form a hint.

To account for internal decision nodes in the partitioning of the paths, the polar graph is *serialized*. Let v be an internal decision node with children v_0 and v_1, and u be the corresponding join node with parents u_0 and u_1. Assume that u_0 is a descendant of v_0 and u_1 is a descendant of v_1. Then serialization of v replaces its predicate node with a no-op node; makes v_0 the only child of v; makes v_1 the successor of u_0, and u_1 the only parent of u. Which of the two children of v is regarded as v_0 is immaterial. The effect of serialization is to merge paths that should be kept in the same block of the partition into a single path. We call the result of serialization the *serialized polar graph*. DFS from the start node of this graph enumerates the paths connecting the two poles. The search procedure maintains the conjunction of the predicates of all the decision nodes currently on the stack. This conjunction is kept as a BDD; if it ever becomes false, then the search backtracks to skip the infeasible execution path. Serialization is applied to each always block individually. Finally, the resulting polar graphs are concatenated to form one polar graph for the whole model.

On the right in Fig. 2 one can see the serialized polar graph for our running example. There is one internal decision variable in this case: state, which causes P1 to be an internal decision node. The two children of P1, P2 and P4, are serialized. P1 becomes a no-op node (shown by the shaded background). In addition, the two serialized polar graphs from the two always blocks get concatenated.

Two additional techniques are used to reduce the number of blocks in which the paths of the serialized polar graphs are partitioned. When blocks are merged by these techniques, their predicates are disjoint. The two techniques are:

1. Distinct paths of the serialized polar graph may be merged if there are data dependencies among them. The merging takes place after the paths have been extracted from the graph. For each path, merging with another path is considered if there is some data dependency between the two. The merged path is evaluated by reachability analysis. If it does not require more time than the individual paths, and if it does not time out, it replaces the two candidates that were merged.
2. Array variables are treated specially. Addressing into an array can be regarded as conditional access to a set of scalar variables. For instance, $a[i] := 0$ corresponds to

$a[0] := 0$ if $i = 0$, $a[1] := 0$ if $i = 1$, and so on. This interpretation of array accesses is required in cases in which hints prescribe the order in which array elements should be enabled. (Such hints are sometimes effective in the presence of symmetry, since they help in reducing the sizes of BDDs that otherwise would encode all permutations of certain set of states.) However, in case of large arrays, expanding their accesses may greatly increase the number of paths. Therefore, the expansion is not initially performed. This leads to ignoring the address variable in the hints. If the resulting subgraphs time out during their evaluation by reachability analysis, the array assignments are gradually refined until a set threshold is reached.

The partitioning of the paths in the serialized polar graph is maintained as a list of predicates, each annotated with a list of CFG nodes, which carry the data dependency information.

The CFG of a complex model may have many candidates that would not contribute enough states to pay for themselves. Therefore, the set of candidates produced by the enumeration procedure is pared down. The selection of the best candidates is heuristic. We currently employ two criteria. The first favors subgraphs with more states reached during abstract interpretation or model checking. Very often, subgraphs in which variables can be controlled via primary inputs produce the best results. To see why, consider an assignment $x := y + z$, where y depends on other variables, whereas z is read from an external input. During reachability analysis, for any value of x and any value of y there is a value of z such that $x = y + z$. (Assuming signed integers.) Hence, the dependency on y, while present, is voided by the dependency on z.

The second selection criterion favors those subgraphs that result in smaller BDDs for the transition relations of the corresponding models. Ideally, we would have a criterion that accounts for both the number of states and the BDD sizes. However, it is difficult to accurately estimate both without going all the way to guided search. The pruning eliminates all candidates that prove inferior according to at least one heuristic.

The serialized polar graph of Fig. 2 has a total of 18 paths from entry to exit. Of these, only six are viable (their predicates are not false). For each of these paths we list the predicate and the list of assignment nodes appearing in them.

1. reset $\land$ ¬data $\land$ chg (S2, S6–7)
2. reset $\land$ ¬data $\land$ ¬chg (S2, S6–7)
3. reset $\land$ data (S2, S6–7)
4. ¬reset $\land$ data (S3, S6, S8)
5. ¬reset $\land$ ¬data $\land$ chg (S4–6, S8)
6. ¬reset $\land$ ¬data $\land$ ¬chg (S4, S6, S8).

The first three paths do not generate new states; therefore, they are pruned. The last two candidates have mutual data dependencies through S4 and S5; hence, they are merged into ¬reset $\land$ ¬data, (S4–6, S8). The result of the merger and the fourth path are forwarded to the final phase of the algorithm.

As another example consider the model CRC used in the experiments of Sect. 4. It is challenging for reachability analysis because of its complex transition relation. This model has four main modes of operation. One in which it resets its register; another in which it holds the current value; a third mode in which it loads data from the outside; and a fourth mode in which it computes the cyclic redundancy code. Four candidates are produced by the analysis of the CFG, one for each of these modes. The first two candidates are discarded because they yield no new states. The fourth candidate is discarded both because the corresponding transition relation is too large and because its reachability analysis times out. In fact, it is this mode of operation that makes BFS reachability analysis hard. The surviving candidate enables the load operation, which is exactly what a knowledgeable designer writing a hint would do. The load mode allows every state to be reached. Hence, guided search terminates using only the constrained transition system without having to restore the full transition relation.

3.3   Sorting the Hints

The final step of the procedure sorts the list of candidates using the information on data dependencies provided by the PDG. The order in which hints are applied may greatly influence their effectiveness. This is particularly the case when there are data dependencies between the variables occurring in different subgraphs. Suppose subgraphs P_1 and P_2 are such that variable x is assigned in P_1 by an input statement, while in P_2 it is assigned a constant value v. Suppose also that x is used in an assignment $y := x$ in P_2, and that that is the only assignment to y. Then, if the hint extracted from P_2 is applied before the hint derived from P_1, all the states reached after the two hints have been applied have $y = v$, whereas, if the order of application is reversed, there will be reachable states for each possible value of y.

In general, there will be cyclic dependencies among subgraphs. Hence, we proceed as follows. We form a Subgraph Dependency Graph (SDG) with one node for each subgraph. Each node of the SDG is the set of nodes in the PDG that make up the corresponding subgraph. An arc connects nodes u and v of the SDG iff there exists a data dependency arc (a, b) in the PDG such that $a \in u$, $b \in v$, and $a \neq b$. The ordering of the candidate subgraphs is obtained from the SDG. In particular the strongly connected components (SCCs) [4] of the SDG define a preorder on the subgraphs: We say that $u \preceq v$ if there is a path from u to v in the SDG. The final order $\leq$ is always a refinement of this preorder in the following sense: if $u \preceq v$ and $v \not\preceq u$, then $u \leq v$. However, an arbitrary total order that refines the preorder may not work well, if there are just a few large SCCs.

We decompose the problem of deriving a total order from the preorder defined by the SDG into two subproblems. The first is the one of linearizing the partial order defined by the SCC quotient graph of the SDG. The second is to find total orders for the nodes of each SCC. The total order of the subgraphs results from combining the solutions of these two subproblems in the obvious way.

Any topological sort of the nodes of the SCC quotient graph would satisfy the definition of order refinement. However, different orders result in BDDs of different sizes. It is normally advantageous to keep subgraphs adjacent in the order if they operate on common variables. Therefore, to sort the SCCs of the SDG we perform a depth-first search from the source nodes of the SCC quotient graph.

Sorting the nodes of an individual SCC is based on identifying a starting node, and then enumerating the elementary circuits of the SCC [10]. As we enumerate elementary circuits from the designated start node, we add nodes to the total order as they appear in some elementary circuit. We rely on the fact that the enumeration algorithm outputs short circuits first. We equate short circuits to tight interaction, and therefore put those nodes that have tighter interaction with the start node earlier in the order. The start node is the entry point to the SCC in the DFS that computed the quotient graph.

The SDG for the example of Fig .2 consists of two disconnected nodes. In this case the order of the two hints is chosen arbitrarily.

4 Experimental Results

We extended VIS 2.0 [2] as outlined in Sect. 3 to automatically produce hints. Experiments were conducted on a 1.8GHz Pentium IV machine with 512MB of RAM running Linux. We report the results of our experiments in Tables 1 and 2. We used ten circuits in our experiments. CRC computes a 32-bit cyclic redundancy code. BPB is a branch prediction buffer. S1269 is an 8-bit ALU. Rotator and Spinner are barrel shifters sandwiched between registers. B04 is a Verilog translation of the original b04 circuit from the ITC99 benchmark set [9]. It computes the minimum and maximum of a set of numbers. Vsa is a simple non-pipelined microprocessor that executes 12-bit instructions—ALU operations, loads, stores, conditional branches—in five stages: fetch, decode, execute, memory access, and write-back. Am2901 is a bit-sliced ALU and contains sixteen 4-bit registers organized into a register file, along with a 4-bit shift register. Am2910 is a microprogram sequencer.

Table 1. Experimental results for reachability analysis

Circuits	FFs	Reachable States	Times in seconds		
			BFS	Manual Hints	Auto Hints
CRC	32	4.295e+09	Mem. out	0.48	0.48
BPB	36	6.872e+10	124.22	0.55	0.22
s1269	37	1.31e+09	22.91	0.65	0.65
DAIO	56	2.95e+11	21.02	7.94	22.05
Rotator	64	1.845e+19	Mem. out	0.15	0.15
Spinner	65	3.689e+19	Mem. out	0.15	0.15
B04	66	5.650e+15	5883.28	1892.76	1892.76
Vsa	66	1.625e+14	4859.33	153.38	224.22
am2901	68	2.951e+20	Mem. out	1.79	1.87
am2910	99	1.610e+26	Mem. out	60.08	Mem. out

Table 1 compares reachability analysis with automatically generated hints against BFS runs and manual hints supplied by an expert user. Columns 1, 2, and 3 give the name of the circuit, number of flip-flops (state variables) and number of reachable states of the circuit. Columns 4, 5, and 6 compare run times for reachability analysis for BFS, manual hints, and automatic hints, respectively. The circuits in this table are mid-sized, but three of these circuits—CRC, Rotator, and Spinner—run out of memory for BFS. The automatic and manual hints were able to provide dramatic improvements to the traversal of these circuits, enabling completion times of a few seconds. Circuit

Table 2. Auto hint generation

Circuits	Total number of hint candidates	Final number of hints	time to produce hint(s)	Statistics	
				timeouts	Reachability completed
CRC	5	1	25	1	1
BPB	165	4	806	2	0
s1269	32	1	381	0	0
DAIO	576	1	422	0	0
Rotator	32	1	4	0	32
Spinner	32	1	4	0	32
B04	6	1	96	0	0
Vsa	23	7	61	3	0
am2901	82	3	123	0	0
am2910	48	1	76	0	0

B04 completes in about one third of the time taken by BFS when using hints. The automatically generated hint is in this case exactly the same as the manual hint. Three remaining circuits in Table 1, BPB, s1269, Vsa, and am2901, demonstrate 1–2 orders of magnitude improvements over BFS. Finally, circuit DAIO and am2910 does not show any improvement over BFS. It is remarkable that the quality of the automatically generated hints is, with one exception, quite comparable to that of the manual hints. (In a few cases, the hints are indeed the same.) The times to generate the hints are non-negligible for some examples, but quite acceptable especially considering that it is incurred only once. The hints, on the other hand, may be used many times.

Table 2 shows information collected during the experiments. Column 2 shows the total number of hints generated during the analysis of the example's CFG (the total number of acyclic paths in the serialized polar graph). The sizable number of hint candidates produced for BPB is attributed to the need to expand the array elements to compensate for the lack of robustness of our parser. However, this was not a limiting factor in that we were able to generate competitive hints after pruning and sorting. By contrast, the number of candidates for Vsa is small because expansion was not necessary.

The total number of hints after pruning and sorting is shown in Column 3. We were able to forego the pruning and sorting steps for CRC and Rotate after a completed reachability analysis of the candidate hint was realized (within a 15 CPU seconds). This reachability analysis showed that all states were reached with a hint, thereby eliminating the need to continue the generation process.

5   Conclusion

In this paper we have shown that state traversal guided by automatically generated hints can substantially speed up reachability analysis relative to BFS and produces hints comparable to manual hints. We have presented a procedure that analyzes the control flow graph derived from the program text (e.g., behavioral Verilog description) and partitions the execution paths into subgraphs corresponding to hint candidates. The candidates are ranked and ordered to produce a final list. Though our implementation is still a prototype, it has produced very encouraging results because the quality of the hints it generates rivals that of hints written by expert users. The times required to automatically generate hints sometimes exceed the guided search time, but remain acceptable, and should be reduced as our implementation matures.

Considerable work remains to be done in the area of automatic generation of hints. We need to strengthen our parser so that we can confirm the initial encouraging results on a larger selection of examples. We also need to address model checking of more general properties than just invariants and study the generation of property-specific hints.

References

[1] M. Abadi and L. Lamport. The existence of refinement mappings. *Theoretical Computer Science*, 82(2):253–284, 1991.

[2] R. K. Brayton et al. VIS. In *Formal Methods in Computer Aided Design*, pages 248–256. Springer-Verlag, Berlin, Nov. 1996. LNCS 1166.

[3] R. E. Bryant. Graph-based algorithms for Boolean function manipulation. *IEEE Transactions on Computers*, C-35(8):677–691, Aug. 1986.

[4] T. H. Cormen, C. E. Leiserson, and R. L. Rivest. *An Introduction to Algorithms*. McGraw-Hill, New York, 1990.

[5] P. Cousot and R. Cousot. Abstract interpretation: A unified lattice model for static analysis of programs by constructions or approximation of fixpoints. In *Proceedings of the ACM Symposium on the Principles of Programming Languages*, pages 238–250, 1977.

[6] J. Ferrante, K. J. Ottenstein, and J. D. Warren. The program dependence graph and its use in optimization. *ACM Transactions on Programming Languages and Systems (TOPLAS)*, 9(3):319–349, July 1987.

[7] J. Gustafsson, B. Lisper, R. Kirner, and P. Puschner. Input-dependency analysis for hard real-time software. In *International Workshop on Object-Oriented Real-Time Dependable System*, Oct. 2004.

[8] S. Horwitz and T. Reps. The use of program dependence graphs in software engineering. In *Fourteenth International Conference on Software Engineering*, 1992.

[9] ITC'99 benchmark home page. http://www.cerc.utexas.edu/itc99-benchmarks/bench.html.

[10] D. B. Johnson. Finding all the elementary circuits of a directed graph. *SIAM Journal on Computing*, 4:77–84, 1975.

[11] R. P. Kurshan. *Computer-Aided Verification of Coordinating Processes*. Princeton University Press, Princeton, NJ, 1994.

[12] K. L. McMillan. Verification of an implementation of Tomasulo's algorithm by compositional model checking. In A. J. Hu and M. Y. Vardi, editors, *Tenth Conference on Computer Aided Verification (CAV'98)*, pages 110–121. Springer-Verlag, Berlin, 1998. LNCS 1427.

[13] K. J. Ottenstein and L. M. Ottenstein. The program dependence graph in a software development environment. In *Symposium on Practical Software Development Environments*, pages 177–184, New York, NY, 1984.

[14] K. Ravi and F. Somenzi. Hints to accelerate symbolic traversal. In *Correct Hardware Design and Verification Methods (CHARME'99)*, pages 250–264, Berlin, Sept. 1999. Springer-Verlag. LNCS 1703.

[15] M. Weiser. Program slicing. *IEEE Transactions on Software Engineering*, 10(4):352–357, 1984.

Maximal Input Reduction of Sequential Netlists via Synergistic Reparameterization and Localization Strategies

Jason Baumgartner and Hari Mony

IBM Systems & Technology Group, Austin, TX 78758

Abstract. Automatic formal verification techniques generally require exponential resources with respect to the number of primary inputs of a netlist. In this paper, we present several fully-automated techniques to enable maximal input reductions of sequential netlists. First, we present a novel min-cut based localization refinement scheme for yielding a *safely* overapproximated netlist with minimal input count. Second, we present a novel form of reparameterization: as a trace-equivalence preserving structural abstraction, which provably renders a netlist with input count at most a constant factor of register count. In contrast to prior research in reparameterization to offset input growth during symbolic simulation, we are the first to explore this technique as a structural transformation for sequential netlists, enabling its benefits to general verification flows. In particular, we detail the synergy between these input-reducing abstractions, and with other transformations such as retiming which – as with traditional localization approaches – risks substantially increasing input count as a byproduct of its register reductions. Experiments confirm that the complementary reduction strategy enabled by our techniques is necessary for iteratively reducing large problems while keeping both proof-fatal design size metrics – register count and input count – within reasonable limits, ultimately enabling an efficient automated solution.

1 Introduction

Automatic formal verification techniques generally require exponential resources with respect to the number of primary inputs of a netlist. For example, the size of a transition relation may grow exponentially with respect to the number of inputs, in addition to state elements. The initial state encoding of a netlist may also grow exponentially complex with respect to the number of inputs used to encode that relation. Symbolic simulation – used for bounded model checking and induction – may require exponential resources with respect to the number of inputs multiplied by the unfolding depth. A large input count may thus render proof as well as falsification efforts inconclusive, and may arise through being inherent in the design under verification, or as the byproduct of a particular verification strategy – e.g., as the result of a register-reducing transformation such as localization or retiming, which are often critical to ensure that a large *register count* is not the fatal verification bottleneck on larger industrial designs.

Several techniques have been proposed to reduce the number of primary inputs of a netlist for specific verification algorithms. For example, the approach of enhancing

D. Borrione and W. Paul (Eds.): CHARME 2005, LNCS 3725, pp. 222–237, 2005.

symbolic simulation through altering the parametric representation of subsets of the input space via manual case splitting strategies was proposed in [1,2]. The approach of automatically reparameterizing unfolded variables during symbolic simulation to offset their increase over unfolding depth has also been explored, e.g., in [3,4,5]. Various approaches for reducing variable count in symbolic reachability analysis have been proposed, e.g., through early quantification of inputs from the transition relation [6], enhanced by partitioning [7] or overapproximation [8]. In this paper, we propose a novel set of fully-automated techniques to enable maximal input reductions of sequential netlists for *arbitrary* verification frameworks.

First, we present a novel form of reparameterization: as a sound and complete structural abstraction. Unlike prior research in reparameterization which focused upon its enhancement to symbolic simulation [3–5], we are the first to explore the use of this technique as a structural transformation for sequential netlists, enabling it to benefit general verification flows. We prove that this technique renders a netlist with input count at most a constant factor of register count, and discuss how it heuristically reduces register count and correlation. These reductions may thereby enhance the application of a variety of verification and falsification algorithms, including semi-formal search, reachability analysis, and emulation. Algorithm-specific reparameterization techniques may be complementarily applied to the resulting abstracted netlist, and are likely to benefit from its reduction. For example, in our experience, it is almost always worth performing aggressive reductions on the sequential netlist prior to unfolding to achieve a *simplify once, unfold many* optimization to bounded analysis, in this case reducing the amount of costly reparameterization needed over unfolding depth. More significantly, our structural reparameterization enables synergistic application with various other transformations such as retiming [9] and localization [10], which overall are capable of yielding dramatic iterative netlist reductions.

Second, we present a novel min-cut based localization refinement scheme tuned for yielding an overapproximated netlist with minimal input count. Unlike traditional localization approaches which refine entire next-state functions or individual gates, ours augments gate-based refinement by adding gates within a min-cut over the combinational logic driving the localized cone to minimize localized input count. A related approach was proposed in [10,11], where register-based localization is followed by the insertion of cut-points to a combinational min-cut between the localized inputs and sequentially-driven logic. Our approach improves upon this work as follows. **(1)** Whereas their approach *eliminates* gates from the logic deemed necessary by the refinement process, hence is prone to introducing spurious counterexamples to the already-overapproximated netlist, ours *adds* gates to the chosen refinement hence avoids this secondary overapproximation risk. **(2)** Their approach resolves spurious counterexamples caused by the secondary cut-point insertion by adding registers to the localized logic, whereas ours performs refinement at the level of individual gates, avoiding the addition of unnecessary registers while preserving minimal input count. **(3)** The ability of our technique to safely inject cut-points to sequentially-driven localized logic theoretically and practically improves upon the input reductions possible with their localization approach. Additionally, our approach is the first to address the use of localization to simplify initial value cones. Complex initial value cones arise in a variety of applications such as retiming, and may otherwise be fatal to proof analysis. Localization refinement algorithms may be used to reduce the input count of these cones, effectively attempting to overapproximate the *initial states* of the design in a property-preserving manner.

Third, we detail the synergy that these reparameterization and localization transformations have with each other, and also with other transformations such as retiming and redundancy removal [12–14]. For example, the former approaches break interconnections in the design and reduce correlation among its registers, enabling greater register reductions through subsequent retiming and localization. Retiming and localization eliminate registers which constitute bottlenecks to the reduction potential of reparameterization, enabling greater input reductions through subsequent reparameterization. Retiming and localization are powerful techniques for reducing register count, which is indeed a critical step in enabling automated proofs on larger netlists. However, these techniques often entail a dramatic proof-fatal increase in input count as a byproduct of their register reductions, which has been our primary motivation for the development of the techniques presented in this paper. We have often found in practice that the iterative application of such register-reducing and input-reducing transformations constitutes a necessary strategy to enable automated proofs on complex industrial designs.

The rest of this paper is organized as follows. In Section 2, we introduce various formalisms used throughout the paper; the reader well-versed in such notation may wish to skip this section. In Section 3, we discuss our structural parametric abstraction. In Section 4, we present our min-cut based localization refinement scheme. In Section 5, we detail synergies between these two transformations and various others. In Section 6, we present experimental results to illustrate the power and synergy of these techniques in reducing netlist size. In Section 7, we conclude this work.

2   Formalisms

Definition 1. A *netlist* is a tuple $N = \langle \langle V, E \rangle, G, T, Z \rangle$ comprising a finite directed graph with vertices V and edges $E \subseteq V \times V$, a semantic mapping from vertices to gate types $G : V \mapsto types$, and a set of *targets* $T \subseteq V$ correlating to a set of properties $AG(\neg t), \forall t \in T$. The function $Z : V \mapsto V$ is the initial value mapping.

Our verification problem is represented entirely as a netlist, comprising the *design under verification*, its *environment*, and its *property automata*. Our gate *types* define a set of primary inputs, registers (our only sequential gate type), and combinational gates with various functions, including constants. The type of a gate may place constraints upon its incoming edge count – e.g., each register has an indegree of one (whose source gate is referred to as its *next-state function*); primary inputs and constants have an indegree of zero. We denote the set of inputs as $I \subseteq V$, and the set of registers as $R \subset V$.

Definition 2. The *combinational fanin* of gate set U is defined as $\bigcup_{u \in U} cfi(u)$, where $cfi(u)$ is defined as u if $u \in R$, else $u \cup combinational fanin(\{v : (v, u) \in E\})$.

Definition 3. The *semantics of a netlist* N are defined in terms of semantic traces. We denote the set of all legal traces associated with a netlist by $P \subseteq [V \times \mathbb{N} \mapsto \{0, 1\}]$, defining P as the subset of functions from $V \times \mathbb{N}$ to $\{0, 1\}$ which are consistent with the following rule. Term u_j denotes the source vertex of the j-th incoming edge to v, implying that $(u_j, v) \in E$. The value of gate v at time i in trace p is denoted by $p(v, i)$.

$$p(v, i) = \begin{cases} s^i_{v_p} & : v \text{ is a primary input with sampled value } s^i_{v_p} \\ G_v\big(p(u_1, i), ..., p(u_n, i)\big) & : v \text{ is a combinational gate with function } G_v \\ p(u_1, i - 1) & : v \text{ is a register and } i > 0 \\ p\big(Z(v), 0\big) & : v \text{ is a register and } i = 0 \end{cases}$$

The initial values of a netlist represent the values that registers can take at time 0. We disallow registers from appearing in the combinational fanin of any initial value cones. We additionally disallow combinational cycles, which makes Definition 3 well-formed.

Definition 4. Gate sets $A \subseteq V$ and $A' \subseteq V'$ of netlists N and N', respectively, are said to be *trace equivalent* iff there exists a bijective mapping $\psi : A \mapsto A'$ such that:

- $\forall p \in P.\exists p' \in P'.\forall i \in \mathbb{N}.\forall a \in A.\ p(a, i) = p'\big(\psi(a), i\big)$
- $\forall p' \in P'.\exists p \in P.\forall i \in \mathbb{N}.\forall a \in A.\ p(a, i) = p'\big(\psi(a), i\big)$

Definition 5. A *cut of a netlist* is a partition of V into two sets: C and $\overline{C} = V \setminus C$. A cut induces two sets of *cut gates* $V_C = \{u \in C : \exists v \in \overline{C}.(((u, v) \in E) \vee (v \in R \wedge u = Z(v)))\}$, and $V_{\overline{C}} = \{u \in \overline{C} : \exists v \in C.(((u, v) \in E) \vee (v \in R \wedge u = Z(v)))\}$.

One may visualize a cut of netlist N as the composition [15] of netlists $N_C \parallel N_{\overline{C}}$, with V_C denoting inputs to $N_{\overline{C}}$ which are closed under the composition, and with $V_{\overline{C}}$ denoting inputs to N_C which are closed under the composition.

Definition 6. An *s-t cut* is a cut seeded with vertex sets $s \subseteq C$ and $t \subseteq \overline{C}$. An *s-t min-cut* refers to an *s-t cut* where V_C is of minimal cardinality.

Algorithmically, when computing an *s-t min-cut*, sets s and t will be selected according to some application-specific criteria, and provided as constraints to the min-cut solver. The structural reparameterization technique that we will introduce in Section 3 and the min-cut based localization technique that we will introduce in Section 4 both utilize an *s-t min-cut* algorithm for optimality. However, they use the result for different purposes, hence have different criteria for selecting s and t as will be discussed in the respective sections. Numerous algorithms have been proposed for the efficient computation of *s-t min-cuts*, for example, the *augmenting path* algorithm [16]. It is noteworthy that the optimality of our techniques is independent of the chosen algorithm, and of the chosen min-cut if multiple cuts of minimal cardinality exist.

3   Structural Parametric Abstraction

In this section we discuss our structural reparameterization technique. We prove the correctness and optimality of this fully-automated abstraction, and discuss the algorithms used for performing the abstraction as well as for lifting abstract traces to ones consistent with the original netlist.

Definition 7. Consider a cut $N_C \parallel N_{\overline{C}}$ of netlist N where N_C comprises inputs and combinational logic but no registers or target gates. A *structural reparameterization* of N is a netlist $N' = N'_C \parallel N_{\overline{C}}$ such that V_C of N is trace-equivalent to V'_C of N' under the bijective mapping implied by the composition onto $N_{\overline{C}}$.

1. Compute a cut $N_C \parallel N_{\overline{C}}$ of N using an *s-t min-cut* algorithm, specifying the inputs as s, and the initial value gates, next-state function gates, registers, and target gates as t.
2. Compute the range of the cut as the set of minterms producible at V_C as a function of the registers in its combinational fanin.
3. Synthesize the range via the algorithm of Figure 2. The resulting netlist N_C' is combinational, and includes V_C' which is trace-equivalent to V_C under composition with $N_{\overline{C}}$.
4. Replace each $v \in V_C$ by its correspondent in V_C', yielding abstract netlist $N' = N_C' \parallel N_{\overline{C}}$.

Fig. 1. Structural parametric abstraction algorithm

Theorem 1. Let $N_C \parallel N_{\overline{C}}$ be a cut of netlist N, and $N' = N_C' \parallel N_{\overline{C}}$ be a structural reparameterization of N. The gates of $N_{\overline{C}}$ in composition $N_C \parallel N_{\overline{C}}$ are trace-equivalent to those in $N_C' \parallel N_{\overline{C}}$ under the reflexive bijective mapping.

Proof. By Definition 5, any gate $u \in N_C$ which sources an edge whose sink is in $N_{\overline{C}}$, or is the initial value of a register in $N_{\overline{C}}$, is an element of V_C. Definition 3 thus implies that we may evaluate $N_{\overline{C}}$ of N from valuations to V_C independently of valuations to gates in $N_C \setminus V_C$; similarly for N' and V_C'. Since we compose each gate of V_C onto a trace-equivalent gate of V_C', this implies that $N_{\overline{C}}$ of N is trace-equivalent to $N_{\overline{C}}$ of N'. $\square$

Theorem 1 is related to the result that simulation precedence is preserved under Moore composition [15]. This theorem establishes the soundness and completeness of our structural parametric abstraction: we wish to replace N_C by a simpler netlist which preserves trace-equivalence, while ensuring that every target is in $\overline{C}$ and thereby preserving property checking. Numerous aggressive state-minimization techniques have been proposed for such purposes such as bisimulation minimization; however, such approaches tend to outweigh the cost of invariant checking [17]. Structural reparameterization is a more restrictive type of abstraction, though one which requires only lower-cost combinational analysis and is nonetheless capable of offering dramatic enhancements to the overall verification process.

We use the algorithm depicted in Figure 1 to perform the parametric abstraction. In Step 1, we compute an *s-t min-cut* of N. In Step 2, we compute the range of the cut using well-known algorithms as follows. For each $c_i \in V_C$, we introduce a distinct parametric variable p_{c_i}, and we denote the function of c_i – over registers and primary inputs in its combinational fanin – as $f(c_i)$. The range of the cut is $\exists I . \bigwedge_{i=1}^{|V_C|} (p_{c_i} \equiv f(c_i))$. In Step 3, we compute the replacement logic for N_C from the range. The replacement gate r_{c_i} for c_i may be computed using the algorithm of Figure 2, assuming that the range is represented as a BDD.[1] Note that the approach of [18] may also be used for this synthesis; the algorithm of Figure 2 is merely an alternative included herein for completeness, implemented using common algorithms and applicable to BDDs with inverted edges. When completed, each produced gate r_{c_i} is trace-equivalent to c_i.

Figure 3a illustrates an example netlist, where we wish to reparameterize a cut at gates g_1 and g_2. Gate g_1 has function $i_1 \not\equiv r_1$, and g_2 has function $i_2 \vee (i_3 \wedge r_2)$, where

---

[1] In [5], it is proposed to perform the range computation for symbolic simulation using SAT; their technique is also applicable in our framework for structural reparameterization.

```
for (i = 1, ..., |V_C|) {    // Process i in rank order of variables p_{c_i} in BDD range
    b_i       = ∃p_{c_{i+1}}, ..., p_{c_n}.range;
    forced_0_i = ¬b_i|_{p_{c_i}=1};    forced_1_i = ¬b_i|_{p_{c_i}=0};

    // SYNTH creates logic gates from BDDs. It creates a distinct primary input to synthesize
    // each p_{c_i}. It processes "forced" terms using a standard multiplexor-based synthesis,
    // using r_{c_1}, ..., r_{c_{i-1}} as selectors for nodes over p_{c_1}, ..., p_{c_{i-1}} variables,
    // and using registers as selectors for nodes over their corresponding variables.
    // OR, AND, NOT create the corresponding gate types.
    r_{c_i}   = OR(SYNTH(forced_1_i), AND(SYNTH(p_{c_i}), NOT(SYNTH(forced_0_i)))); }
```

Fig. 2. Range synthesis algorithm

$i_1, i_2, i_3 \in I$ and $r_1, r_2 \in R$. The range of this cut is $\exists i_1, i_2, i_3. ((p_{g_1} \equiv (i_1 \not\equiv r_1)) \wedge (p_{g_2} \equiv (i_2 \vee (i_3 \wedge r_2))))$ which simplifies to $\top$. Replacement gates r_{g_1} and r_{g_2} are thus parametric inputs p_{g_1} and p_{g_2}, respectively, and r_1 and r_2 are eliminated from the support of V_C' as illustrated in Figure 3b. While this abstraction is primarily intended for input elimination, this example illustrates its heuristic ability to reduce *correlation* between registers, here breaking any correlation through N_1 between the next-state functions of r_1 and r_2 and their respective present-state values. Additionally, note that if N_2 does not depend upon either of these registers (say r_2), that register will be eliminated from the abstracted netlist by reparameterization alone, illustrating the heuristic register elimination capability of this technique. This correlation reduction synergistically enables greater structural reductions through other transformation techniques such as retiming, as will be discussed in Section 5.

Theorem 2. The maximum number of primary inputs of the abstracted netlist N' generated by the algorithm of Figure 1 is $|T| + 2 \times |R|$.

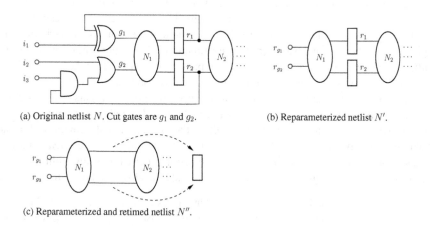

(a) Original netlist N. Cut gates are g_1 and g_2.

(b) Reparameterized netlist N'.

(c) Reparameterized and retimed netlist N''.

Fig. 3. Reparameterization example

Proof. An *s-t min-cut* algorithm may be guaranteed to return a netlist cut with $|V_C| \leq \min(|s|, |t|)$, as follows from the following analysis. The bound of $|s|$ follows from the existence of a cut where $C = s$. Noting that the min-cut is seeded with $s = I$, this guarantees that our algorithm cannot increase input count. The bound of $|t|$ follows by automatically preprocessing the netlist to ensure that each element of t has indegree of one,[2] and selecting $\overline{C} = t$. The seeded set t comprises the target gates, as well as the registers' initial value and next-state function gates – a set of cardinality $|T| + 2 \times |R|$. The resulting cut V_C may thus be upper-bounded in cardinality by $\min(|I|, |T| + 2 \times |R|)$. At most one input is required per element of V_C' in N', used in the synthesis of the parametric variable for that cut gate. The structural reparameterization thus replaces the $|I|$ inputs of N_C with the $|V_C'|$ inputs of N_C'.

Though we also add R to t, this does not alter the above bound because the only gates sourcing an edge into the registers – their next-state functions – are seeded into $\overline{C}$. This inclusion serves only to facilitate compositional reasoning, in that registers in the support of the synthesized range will appear in N' – whereas N_C and N_C' are disjoint.

Let U represent the set of gates which contain an input in their combinational fanin. Straight-forward analysis will demonstrate that N' will have at most $(|T \cap U| + |\{r \in R : Z(r) \in U\}| + |\{r \in R : \exists u_1 \in U.(u_1, r) \in E\}|)$ primary inputs, which often yields a significantly tighter bound in practice. □

There are several noteworthy points relating to Theorem 2. First, note that at most one parametric input may be required per register for abstract initial values. This illustrates the duality between structural initial values and reachable state data, which is often represented with one variable per register. Certain techniques have been proposed which lock reachability data into structural initial values. For example, retiming [9] uses symbolic simulation to compute retimed initial values. If an input is retimed by k time-steps, there may be k unfolded copies of that input in the retimed initial values. Our parametric abstraction offsets this input amplification within the initial value data, similarly to how reparameterizing symbolic simulators operate [4,5]. As another example, one may underapproximate the reachable states (e.g., via symbolic simulation), then form a new netlist by altering the initial values of the original netlist to reflect the resulting state set [19,5]. Second, aside from initial values, note that at most one parametric input per register is necessary for abstract next-state functions. This bound has significant potential for enhancing a variety of verification paradigms, especially when coupled with synergistic register-reduction techniques (e.g., localization and retiming).

Because our abstraction preserves trace-equivalence of all targets in $N_{\overline{C}}$, demonstrating that a target cannot be asserted within a bounded or unbounded time-frame on the abstracted netlist implies the same result on the original netlist. However, if a trace is obtained asserting a target in the abstracted netlist, that trace must be *lifted* to indicate an assertion of the corresponding target in the original netlist. Our algorithm for trace lifting is provided in Figure 4. In Step 1, we simulate the abstracted trace to ensure that

---

[2] This preprocessing entails "splitting" a gate v into gates v_1 and v_2. Gate v_1 has input connectivity and type identical to that of v, and fans out exclusively a new *buffer* gate v_2, which in turn inherits all fanout references of v (including fanout edges, as well as target and initial value references). A similar approach is used to ensure that $s \cap t = \emptyset$ in Step 1 of the algorithm of Figure 1, e.g., in case a next-state function is also an input.

---

1. Given partial trace p' of N', fully populate that trace up to the necessary length to assert the abstracted target, using binary simulation as per Definition 3 and injecting arbitrary values to any *don't cares* (unassigned values) of any primary inputs.
2. Cast a satisfiability check over V_C to obtain the same sequence of valuations as witnessed to V_C' in the populated trace p'. This check must be satisfiable since V_C' is trace-equivalent to V_C under composition with $N_{\overline{C}}$, and yields trace p''.
3. Return trace p produced by composing values to $N_{\overline{C}}$ from p' with values to N_C from p''.

Fig. 4. Parametric abstraction trace lifting algorithm

we have adequate deterministic valuations to V_C' and R' to enable the lifting. This is necessary because many verification algorithms produce *partial traces*, where certain valuations may be omitted for certain gates at certain time-steps. For example, in Figure 3b, parametric input r_{g_1} replaced gate g_1 of function $i_1 \not\equiv r_1$, eliminating r_1 from the support of V_C'. The abstracted trace p' is thus less likely to include valuations to r_1. In order to lift p', and thereby provide the proper sequence of valuations to i_1 to yield an identical sequence of valuations to V_C, the trace-lifting process must be aware of the valuations to r_1. After simulation populates the necessary valuations to p', a bounded satisfiability check in Step 2 will yield a trace p'' over N_C which provides the identical sequence of valuations to V_C. This check tends to require only modest resources regardless of netlist size, since register valuations in p' effectively break the k-step bounded analysis into k one-step satisfiability checks, each injecting the netlist into the state reflected in the corresponding time-step of the trace. Step 3 splices p' and p'' together, producing a consistent trace over the original netlist asserting the original target. This algorithm is similar to those for lifting traces over localized netlists (e.g., [20]); its primary difference is the binary simulation step, which reduces satisfiability resources and is enabled due to the soundness *and completeness* of our abstraction as per Theorem 1.

Related Work. The approach of automatically reparameterizing unfolded variables during symbolic simulation to offset their increase over unfolding depth has been explored in prior work, e.g., in [3,4,5]. Overall, our technique is complementary to this prior work: by transforming the sequential netlist prior to unfolding, we enable a *simplify once, unfold many* optimization to bounded analysis reducing the amount of costly reparameterization needed over unfolding depth. Nonetheless, input growth over unfolding depth is inevitable; while our technique reduces this growth, a reparameterizing symbolic simulator may nonetheless be beneficial for analysis of the abstracted netlist.

Our approach is most similar to that of [4], which computes a cut of a logic cone, then parametrically replaces that cut by a simpler representation which preserves trace-equivalence. Unlike [4], which seeks to improve the efficiency of BDD-based combinational analysis hence retains all computations as BDDs, ours converts the reparameterized representation to gates. We are the first to propose the use of reparameterization as a structural reduction for sequential netlists, enabling its benefits to arbitrary verification and falsification algorithms, in addition to enabling dramatic iterative reductions with synergistic transformations as will be discussed in Section 5. Our approach also enables an efficient trace lifting procedure, unlike the approach of [4].

1. Begin with an initial abstraction $\mathcal{A}$ of N such that $T \subseteq \overline{\mathcal{C}}$.
2. Attempt to prove or falsify each target in $\mathcal{A}$.
3. If the target is proven unreachable, this result is valid for N; return this result.
4. If a trace is obtained asserting the target in $\mathcal{A}$, search for a corresponding trace in N. If one is found, return this result.
5. Otherwise, the trace over $\mathcal{A}$ is spurious. Identify a refinement of $\mathcal{A}$ – i.e., a set of gates to move from $\mathcal{C}$ to $\overline{\mathcal{C}}$ – to eliminate the spurious trace. Repeat Step 2 with the refinement.

Fig. 5. Localization refinement algorithm

Optimality. Note that the algorithm of Figure 2 uses a single parametric input per cut gate. One may instead attempt a more aggressive synthesis of the range, using $\lceil \log_2 m \rceil$ variables to directly select among the m possible minterms on a per-state basis (for maximal m), similarly to the approach proposed in [1]. While this may yield heuristically lesser input count, we have found this approach to be inferior in practice since $\lceil \log_2 m \rceil$ is often nearly equivalent to the cut-width due to the density of the range, and since the resulting encoding tends to be of significantly greater combinational complexity resulting in an increase in the analysis resources needed by virtually all algorithms, including simulation, satisfiability, and BDD-based algorithms (the latter was also noted in [2]).

We may readily eliminate the $|T|$ contribution of the bound proven in Theorem 2 by using the structural target enlargement technique of [21]. In particular, we may replace each target $t_i \in T$ by the synthesis of the characteristics function of the set of states for which there exists an input valuation which asserts that target, i.e., by $\exists I.f(t_i)$.

We utilize an *s-t min-cut* algorithm to ensure maximal input reductions as per Theorem 2. However, the range computation of the resulting cut may in cases be prohibitively expensive. It therefore may be desired to choose a cut with larger cardinality, weakening reduction potential in favor of computational efficiency – though iterative abstractions may be performed to ultimately converge upon the min-cut with lesser resources. In [4] it is proposed to reparameterize a *group* U of a candidate cut $V_{\mathcal{C}}$ to eliminate inputs I_U which are in the combinational fanin of U but not $V_{\mathcal{C}} \setminus U$. This reduction may be accomplished in our framework by selecting a cut of $V_{\mathcal{C}} = U \cup (I \setminus I_U)$, noting that any inputs in $V_{\mathcal{C}}$ will merely be replaced by other inputs, hence may effectively be treated as non-quantifiable variables when computing the range (similarly to registers in $N_{\overline{\mathcal{C}}}$). We have found that an efficient way to select suboptimal cuts for incremental abstraction is to compute min-cuts over increasing subsets of the desired cut, enabling the earlier abstractions to simplify later abstractions by iteratively decreasing $|I|$.

4   Min-cut Based Localization

Definition 8. A *localization* $\mathcal{A}$ of N is a netlist obtained by computing a cut of N such that $T \subseteq \overline{\mathcal{C}}$, and by replacing $V_{\mathcal{C}}$ by a set of primary inputs $V'_{\mathcal{C}}$ of netlist $N'_{\mathcal{C}}$, resulting in $\mathcal{A} = N'_{\mathcal{C}} \| N_{\overline{\mathcal{C}}}$. This replacement is referred to as *injecting cut-points to $V_{\mathcal{C}}$*.

Localization differs from the parametric abstraction of Section 3 since it renders an *overapproximated* netlist which can simulate the original, though the converse may not be true. Because the overapproximation may result in a spurious assertion of a target, *refinement* is often used to tighten the overapproximation by increasing the size of $\overline{C}$, e.g., using the algorithm of Figure 5. For larger netlists, the localization may contain many thousands of inputs when using traditional approaches of selecting V_C to comprise only registers and inputs (e.g., [10,22]), or of refining individual gates. This large input count tends to render the BDD-based reachability analysis which is commonly used for the proof analysis in Step 2 infeasible. In [10,11], this problem is addressed by further overapproximating the localization by computing an *s-t min-cut* between its inputs and sequentially-driven gates (i.e., gates which have a register in their combinational fanin), and injecting cut-points to the resulting cut gates to significantly reduce localized input count. When a trace is obtained on the post-processed localization, an attempt is made to map that trace to the original localization. If the mapping fails, in [11] various heuristics are proposed to select registers to add for the next localization refinement phase, instead of directly addressing the causal post-process cut-point injection.

The min-cut based localization refinement scheme we have developed to minimize input growth is depicted in Figure 6. In Step 1, a new localization $\mathcal{A}'$ is created from $\mathcal{A}$ by adding a set of refinement gates, which may be selected using any of the numerous proposed refinement schemes (e.g., [11,20]). For optimality, however, we have found that the refinement should be at the granularity of individual gates vs. entire next-state functions to avoid locking unnecessary complex logic into the localization. In Step 2, an *s-t min-cut* $\langle \mathcal{C}_1, \overline{\mathcal{C}}_1 \rangle$ is computed over N. In Step 3, the gates of $\overline{\mathcal{C}}_1$ are added to $\mathcal{A}'$ to ensure that $\mathcal{A}'$ has as few inputs as possible while containing the original refinement of Step 1. Note that the newly-added gates are all combinational because all registers not already in $\mathcal{A}'$ are seeded into s, hence cannot be in $\overline{\mathcal{C}}_1$ which is the set added to $\mathcal{A}'$.

Unlike the approach of [10,11], which *eliminates* gates from the logic deemed necessary by the refinement process hence is prone to introducing spurious counterexamples, our min-cut based localization *adds* combinational logic to the refinement to avoid this risk while ensuring minimal input count. While the overapproximate nature of localization may nonetheless result in spurious counterexamples, our approach avoids the secondary overapproximation of theirs which is done without refinement analysis to heuristically justify its validity. Our more general approach also avoids adding unnecessary registers during refinement, since it has the flexibility to select which combinational logic to include. In our experience, many refinements may be addressed solely by altering the placement of the cut within the combinational logic. Additionally, our approach is often able to yield a localization with *lesser* input count due to its ability to safely inject cut-points at gates which are sequentially-driven by registers included in the localization, which their register-based localization does not support and their combinational cut-point insertion disallows to minimize its introduction of spurious counterexamples. Finally, our approach enables localization to simplify complex initial value cones, as the inclusion of register r does not imply the inclusion of its initial value cone. Only the subset of that cone deemed necessary to prevent spurious counterexamples will be added during refinement. This initial-value refinement capability has not been addressed by prior research, despite its utility – e.g., when coupled with techniques which lock reachability data into initial values such as retiming [9].

In a transformation-based verification framework [9,23], one could attempt to reduce the input count of an arbitrarily-localized netlist by using the parametric abstrac-

1. Select a set of gates to add to the refinement $\mathcal{A}'$ of $\mathcal{A}$ using an arbitrary algorithm. Let $\langle \mathcal{C}', \overline{\mathcal{C}}' \rangle$ be the cut of N corresponding to $\mathcal{A}'$.
2. Compute an *s-t min-cut* $\langle \mathcal{C}_1, \overline{\mathcal{C}}_1 \rangle$ over N, with all gates in $\overline{\mathcal{C}}'$ as t, and $I \cup (R \cap \mathcal{C}')$ as s.
3. Add $\overline{\mathcal{C}}_1$ to the refinement $\mathcal{A}'$.

Fig. 6. Min-cut based abstraction refinement algorithm

tion of Section 3 instead of using a min-cut based localization refinement scheme, or of overapproximately injecting cut-points to a combinational min-cut thereof as proposed in [10]. As per Theorem 2, this synergistic strategy is theoretically able to reduce input count to within a factor of two of register count. This bound is only possible due to the ability of reparameterization to abstract sequentially-driven logic. In contrast, the min-cut approach of [10] is taken with t being the set of all sequentially-driven gates, which is often much larger than the set of registers – hence input count may remain arbitrarily larger than register count with their approach. Reparameterization is thus a superior input-elimination strategy compared to the cut-point insertion of [10], and has the additional benefit of retaining soundness and completeness. Nevertheless, the dramatic input growth which may occur during traditional localization approaches often entails exorbitant resources for reparameterization to overcome on large netlists. We have therefore found that an input-minimizing localization scheme such as ours is necessary to safely minimize input growth *during* localization, to in turn enable the optimal input elimination of reparameterization with minimal resources.

5   Transformation Synergies

In a transformation-based verification (TBV) framework [9], various algorithms are encapsulated as *engines* which each receive a netlist, perform some processing on that netlist, then transmit a new, simpler netlist to a child engine. If a verification result (e.g., a proof or counterexample) is obtained by a given engine from a child engine, that engine must map that result to one consistent with the netlist it received before propagating that result to its parent – or suppress it if no such mapping is possible. Synergistic transformation sequences often yield dramatic iterative reductions – possibly several orders of magnitude compared to a single application of the individual techniques [23]. In this section we detail some of the synergies enabled and exploited by our techniques.

Theorem 2 illustrates that all register-reducing transformations (e.g., retiming [9], localization [10], redundancy removal [12,13,14], and structural target enlargement [21]) synergistically enable greater input reductions through structural reparameterization. For example, retiming finds a minimal-cardinality register placement to eliminate reparameterization bottlenecks caused by their arbitrary initial placement. Localization injects cut-points to the netlist, which when reparameterized enable reductions even at *deep* gates which previously had no inputs in their combinational fanin. Redundancy removal may enable *s-t min-cut* algorithms to identify smaller-cardinality netlist cuts.

In addition to its input reductions, structural reparameterization reduces register correlation as per Figure 3b. As with redundancy removal, this often enables subsequent localization to yield greater reductions, since the heuristic abstraction algorithms are less likely to identify unnecessary registers as being required to prevent spurious counterexamples. We have found iterative localization and reparameterization strategies to be critical to yield adequate simplifications to enable a proof *or* a counterexample result on many complex industrial verification problems. The concept of iterative localization strategies was also proposed in [22], leveraging the heuristics inherent in the SAT algorithms used for the abstraction to identify different subsets of the netlist as being necessary across the nested localizations, in turn enabling iterative reductions. Our TBV approach enables significantly greater reduction potential, since it not only allows the use of differing abstraction heuristics across nested localizations, but also allows arbitrary transformations to iteratively simplify the netlist between localizations to *algorithmically – not merely heuristically –* enable greater localization reductions. In cases, the result enabled through our iterative reductions was a *spurious* localization counterexample which could be effectively used by the causal prior localization engine for refinement. This illustrates the utility of our synergistic transformation framework for the generation of complex counterexamples for abstraction refinement, enabling a more general refinement paradigm than that of prior work, e.g., [10,11,22].

Retiming is limited in its reduction potential due to its inability to alter the register count of any directed cycle in the netlist graph, and its inability to remove all registers along *critical paths* of differing register count between pairs of gates [24]. Both reparameterization and localization are capable of eliminating such paths, enabling greater register reductions through retiming. This is illustrated in Figure 3b, where reparameterization eliminates the directed cycles comprising r_1 and r_2, enabling a subsequent retiming to eliminate those registers in Figure 3c. Retiming has the drawback of increasing input count due to the symbolic simulation used to calculate retimed initial values [9]. Both reparameterization and our min-cut based localization are capable of offsetting this input growth, enabling retiming to be more aggressively applied without risking a proof-fatal input growth, as we have otherwise witnessed in practice.

6   Experimental Results

In this section we provide experimental results illustrating the reduction potential of the techniques presented in this paper. All experiments were run on a 2GHz Pentium 4, using the IBM internal transformation-based verification tool *SixthSense*. The engines used in the experiments are as follows; each performs a cone-of-influence reduction.

- **COM**: a BDD- and SAT-based combinational redundancy removal engine [13].
- **RET**: a min-area retiming engine [9].
- **CUT**: a structural reparameterization engine as per Section 3.
- **LOC**: a min-cut based localization engine as per Section 4.

We present several sets of experiments in Table 1 to illustrate the power of and synergy between these engines. The first column indicates the name of the benchmark and the size metric being tracked in the corresponding row. The second reflects the size of

Table 1. Synergistic transformation experiments

S4863 [12]

	Initial	COM	RET	COM	CUT		Initial	COM	CUT	RET					Resources
Registers	101	101	37	37	21		101	101	34	0					1 sec
Inputs	49	49	190	190	37		49	49	21	21					34 MB

S6669 [12]

	Initial	COM	RET	COM	CUT		Initial	COM	CUT	RET					
Registers	303	186	49	49	0		303	186	138	0					1 sec
Inputs	80	61	106	81	40		80	61	40	40					35 MB

SMM

	Initial	COM	LOC	CUT	LOC	CUT	LOC	CUT						
Registers	36359	33044	760	758	464	167	130	129						229 sec
Inputs	261	71	2054	666	366	109	135	60						291 MB

MMU

	Initial	COM	LOC	CUT	LOC	CUT	RET	COM	CUT					
Registers	124297	67117	698	661	499	499	133	131	125					1038 sec
Inputs	1377	162	1883	809	472	337	1004	287	54					386 MB

RING

	Initial	COM	LOC	CUT	RET	COM	CUT	LOC	CUT	LOC	CUT	LOC	CUT	
Registers	20692	19557	266	262	106	106	106	65	65	49	48	47	35	745 sec
Inputs	2507	2507	568	280	726	587	480	452	376	330	263	259	64	240 MB

BYPASS

	Initial	COM	LOC	CUT	LOC	CUT	LOC	CUT	LOC	CUT	LOC	CUT	LOC	CUT	
Registers	11621	11587	311	306	265	265	216	212	164	154	127	124	101	95	240 sec
Inputs	432	410	501	350	333	254	248	216	203	156	154	123	110	79	175 MB

the original netlist; phase abstraction [25] was used to preprocess the industrial examples. The successive columns indicate the size of the problem *after* the corresponding transformation engine (indicated in the row labeled with the benchmark name) was run.

The first two examples in Table 1 are sequential equivalence checking proof obligations of SIS-optimized ISCAS89 benchmarks from [12]. The first presented flow demonstrates how **CUT** offsets the increase in input count caused by **RET**, and also the register reduction potential of **CUT** itself. The second flow additionally illustrates how reparameterization enhances the register-reduction ability of **RET**, enabling retiming to eliminate *all* registers from both benchmarks. **CUT** was able to eliminate significant register correlation – and thereby critical paths – in these benchmarks due to logic of the form $(i_1 \not\equiv r_1)$ and $i_2 \vee (i_3 \wedge r_2)$ as illustrated in Figure 3.

The remaining four examples are difficult industrial invariant checking problems. SMM and MMU are two different memory management units. RING validates the prioritization scheme of a network interface unit. BYPASS is an instruction decoding and dispatch unit. These results illustrate the synergistic power of iterative reparameterization and localization strategies, coupled with retiming, to yield dramatic incremental netlist reductions. The resulting abstracted netlists were easily discharged with reachability analysis, though otherwise were too complex to solve with reachability or induction. In SMM, the first **LOC** reduces register count by a factor of 43, though increases input count by a factor of 29 to 2054. Without our min-cut based localization, this input growth is even more pronounced. Refining entire next-state functions as per [10] yields 29221 inputs; their combinational cut-point injection may only eliminate 54 of these, as most of the logic is sequentially driven. **CUT** could eliminate 28514 of these, modulo resource limitations. If refining individual gates, we obtain 2755 inputs. In practice, we often witness an even more pronounced input growth through gate-based refinement (e.g., 3109 vs. 1883 inputs for MMU). In MMU, **LOC** and **CUT** enable a powerful **RET** reduction with input growth which is readily contained by a subsequent **CUT**. RING is a difficult example which **LOC** and **CUT** alone were unable to adequately reduce to enable reachability. **RET** brought register count down to an adequate level,

Table 2. Input counts with and without structural reparameterization prior to unfolding

Benchmark	$|R|$	$|I|$ Orig.	$|I'|$ Reparam.	$|R| \leq |I|$ Unfold Depth	$|R'| \leq |I'|$ Unfold Depth	$|I|$ Unfold Depth 25	$|I'|$ Unfold Depth 25	$|I|$ Unfold Depth 100	$|I'|$ Unfold Depth 100
LMQ	345	189	135 (29%)	6	8	3884	2735 (30%)	17309	12111 (30%)
DA_FPU	6348	534	240 (57%)	24	39	7038	3120 (56%)	47088	21120 (55%)
SQMW	13583	1271	421 (67%)	23	47	16356	4538 (72%)	111681	36113 (68%)

though increased input count substantially due to complex retimed initial values. A single **CUT** was unable to contain that input growth with reasonable resources, though the ability to safely overapproximate the initial value cones with **LOC** iteratively and synergistically enabled **CUT** to eliminate all but a single input per initial value cone.

Table 2 illustrates the utility of structural reparameterization prior to unfolding. Column 2 and 3 illustrate the register and input count of the corresponding redundancy-removed [13] netlists. Column 4 provides the input count of the reparameterized netlist; the numbers in parentheses illustrate percent reductions. Columns 5 and 6 illustrate the unfolding depth at which input count exceeds register count with and without reparameterization. This is the unfolding depth at which one may wish to use reparameterization within the symbolic simulator to *guarantee* a reduction in variable count [5]. Note that this depth is significantly greater for the abstracted than the original netlist. Practically, a bug may be exposed by the symbolic simulator *between* these depths, hence our approach may preclude the need for reparameterization on the unfolded instance. More generally, the *simplify once, unfold many* optimization enabled by our abstraction reduces the amount of costly reparameterization necessary over greater unfolding depths, and enables shallower depths to be reached more efficiently due to lesser variable count. Another noteworthy point is that register count is significantly greater than input count in these netlists (as is common with industrial designs). Reparameterization within symbolic simulators operates on parametric variables for the *registers*, and on the *unfolded* inputs which become comparable in cardinality to the registers. In contrast, our structural reparameterization operates solely upon parametric variables for the *cut gates* (bounded in cardinality by the abstracted input count, in turn bounded by the original input count as per the proof of Theorem 2), and on the *original* inputs: a set of significantly lesser cardinality, implying significantly lesser resource requirements.

Note also that we did not perform more aggressive transformations such as localization and retiming on the examples of Table 2. As illustrated by Table 1, doing such is clearly a beneficial strategy in our synergistic transformation framework. However, the purpose of this table is to demonstrate how our structural reparameterization alone benefits symbolic simulation. The final columns of this table indicate input count with and without reparameterization for unfolding depths of 25 and 100.

7   Conclusion

We have presented several fully-automated techniques for maximal input reduction of sequential netlists for arbitrary verification flows. **(1)** We introduced a structural reparameterization technique, which provably reduces input count to a constant factor of register count. This technique also heuristically reduces register count and correlation. **(2)** We introduced a min-cut based localization refinement scheme for *safely* overapproximating a netlist through minimal cut-point insertion. We also detailed the synergy between these two abstractions, along with other transformations such as retiming.

Overall, the transformation synergy enabled by our techniques comprise their greatest benefit, capable of yielding dramatic iterative reductions unachievable by any standalone approach. For example, a single reparameterization application is able to reduce our RING benchmark from 2507 to 2109 inputs. A single application of our min-cut-based localization is able to reduce RING to 568 inputs (and prior localization approaches substantially increase its input count). Our iterative transformations, however, bring RING down to 64 inputs, ultimately enabling efficient reachability analysis. Such a profound reduction is obviously capable of yielding dramatic improvements to virtually all search algorithms, including reparameterizing symbolic simulators. We have made extensive use of these reduction strategies in a variety of complex industrial verification tasks, both for proofs and falsification, in many cases obtaining a conclusive result that was otherwise unattainable. For example, with many larger netlists, we have found that traditional localization and retiming strategies alone may ultimately reduce register count to a reasonable level, though result in an abstracted netlist with far too many inputs for an automated proof. The techniques presented in this paper were largely motivated by such complications, and have to a large extent solved these problems.

Acknowledgments. The authors wish to thank Geert Janssen, Viresh Paruthi, Robert Kanzelman, Jessie Xu, and Mark Williams for their contributions to the TBV system used in our experiments, and Koen van Eijk for providing the benchmarks of [12].

References

1. P. Jain and G. Gopalakrishnan, "Efficient symbolic simulation-based verification using the parametric form of Boolean expressions," *IEEE Transactions on CAD*, April 1994.
2. M. D. Aagaard, R. B. Jones, and C.-J. H. Seger, "Formal verification using parametric representations of Boolean constraints," in *Design Automation Conference*, June 1999.
3. V. Bertacco and K. Olukotun, "Efficient state representation for symbolic simulation," in *Design Automation Conference*, June 2002.
4. I.-H. Moon, H. H. Kwak, J. Kukula, T. Shiple, and C. Pixley, "Simplifying circuits for formal verification using parametric representation," in *FMCAD*, Nov. 2002.
5. P. Chauhan, E. M. Clarke, and D. Kroening, "A SAT-based algorithm for reparameterization in symbolic simulation," in *Design Automation Conference*, June 2004.
6. S. Mador-Haim and L. Fix, "Input elimination and abstraction in model checking," in *FMCAD*, Nov. 1998.
7. H. Jin, A. Kuehlmann, and F. Somenzi, "Fine-grain conjunction scheduling for symbolic reachability analysis," in *Tools and Algos. Construction and Analysis of Systems*, April 2002.
8. P. Chauhan, E. Clarke, J. Kukula, S. Sapra, H. Veith, and D. Wang, "Automated abstraction refinement for model checking large state spaces using SAT based conflict analysis," in *FMCAD*, November 2002.
9. A. Kuehlmann and J. Baumgartner, "Transformation-based verification using generalized retiming," in *Computer-Aided Verification*, July 2001.
10. D. Wang, P.-H. Ho, J. Long, J. H. Kukula, Y. Zhu, H.-K. T. Ma, and R. F. Damiano, "Formal property verification by abstraction refinement with formal, simulation and hybrid engines," in *Design Automation Conference*, June 2001.

11. D. Wang, *SAT based Abstraction Refinement for Hardware Verification*. PhD thesis, Carnegie Mellon University, May 2003.
12. C. A. J. van Eijk, "Sequential equivalence checking without state space traversal," in *Design, Automation, and Test in Europe*, March 1998.
13. A. Kuehlmann, V. Paruthi, F. Krohm, and M. Ganai, "Robust Boolean reasoning for equivalence checking and functional property verification," *IEEE Transactions on CAD*, Dec. 2002.
14. H. Mony, J. Baumgartner, V. Paruthi, and R. Kanzelman, "Exploiting suspected redundancy without proving it," in *Design Automation Conference*, June 2005.
15. O. Grumberg and D. E. Long, "Model checking and modular verification," *ACM Transactions on Programming Languages and System*, vol. 16, no. 3, 1994.
16. L. R. Ford and D. R. Fulkerson, "Maximal flow through a network," *Canadian Journal of Mathematics*, vol. 8, 1956.
17. K. Fisler and M. Vardi, "Bisimulation and model checking," in *CHARME*, Sept. 1999.
18. J. H. Kukula and T. R. Shiple, "Building circuits from relations," in *CAV*, July 2000.
19. M. Awedh and F. Somenzi, "Increasing the robustness of bounded model checking by computing lower bounds on the reachable states," in *FMCAD*, Nov. 2004.
20. E. Clarke, A. Gupta, J. Kukula, and O. Strichman, "SAT based abstraction-refinement using ILP and machine learning techniques," in *Computer-Aided Verification*, July 2002.
21. J. Baumgartner, A. Kuehlmann, and J. Abraham, "Property checking via structural analysis," in *Computer-Aided Verification*, July 2002.
22. A. Gupta, M. Ganai, Z. Yang, and P. Ashar, "Iterative abstraction using SAT-based BMC with proof analysis," in *Int'l Conference on Computer-Aided Design*, Nov. 2003.
23. H. Mony, J. Baumgartner, V. Paruthi, R. Kanzelman, and A. Kuehlmann, "Scalable automated verification via expert-system guided transformations," in *FMCAD*, Nov. 2004.
24. C. Leiserson and J. Saxe, "Retiming synchronous circuitry," *Algorithmica*, vol. 6, 1991.
25. J. Baumgartner, T. Heyman, V. Singhal, and A. Aziz, "An abstraction algorithm for the verification of level-sensitive latch-based netlists," *Formal Methods in System Design*, (23) 2003.

A New SAT-Based Algorithm
for Symbolic Trajectory Evaluation

Jan-Willem Roorda and Koen Claessen

Chalmers University of Technology, Sweden
{jwr, koen}@cs.chalmers.se

Abstract. We present a new SAT-based algorithm for Symbolic Trajectory Evaluation (STE), and compare it to more established SAT-based techniques for STE.

1 Introduction

Symbolic Trajectory Evaluation (STE) [7] is a high-performance simulation-based model checking technique. It combines three-valued simulation (using the standard values 0 and 1 together with the extra value X, "don't know") with symbolic simulation (using symbolic expressions to drive inputs). STE has been extremely successful in verifying properties of circuits containing large data paths (such as memories, fifos, floating point units) that are beyond the reach of traditional symbolic model checking [1,6,5].

STE specifications are written in a restricted temporal language, where assertions are of the form $A \Longrightarrow C$; the *antecedent* A drives the simulation, and the *consequent* C expresses the conditions that should result. In the assertion variables are taken from a set of Boolean symbolic variables V.

In STE, two abstractions are used: (1) the value X can be used to abstract from a specific Boolean value of a circuit node, (2) information is only propagated forwards through the circuit and through time. A *trajectory* is a sequence of node assignments over time that meets the constraints of the circuit taking these abstractions into account. An STE-assertion $A \Longrightarrow C$ holds if each trajectory that satisfies A also satisfies C.

STE Model Checking. All current implementations of STE use symbolic simulation to compute a representation of the so-called *weakest* trajectory that satisfies the antecedent A. While computing this representation, it is checked if the trajectory also satisfies the consequent C. Such a weakest trajectory can be represented by means of BDDs and a dual-rail encoding. A pleasant property of STE is that the number of variables occurring in these BDDs only depends on the number of variables in the STE assertion, not on the size of the circuit.

An alternative way of implementing STE is to use SAT. Bjesse et al. [3] and Singerman et al. [9] independently implemented SAT-based STE by using a simulator that works on non-canonical Boolean expressions instead of BDDs. The STE symbolic simulator calculates a symbolic expression for the weakest trajectory satisfying the antecedent. After simulation, the propositional formula expressing that weakest trajectory satisfies the consequent is fed to a SAT-solver.

Bjesse et al. used SAT-based STE for bug finding for a design of an Alpha microprocessor. The authors report that SAT-based STE enabled them to find bugs as deep as

D. Borrione and W. Paul (Eds.): CHARME 2005, LNCS 3725, pp. 238–253, 2005.

with Bounded Model Checking, but with negligible run-times. Singerman et al. showed how SAT-based STE can be used for bug finding in *Generalized Symbolic Trajectory Evaluation* (GSTE). This bug finding method is called satGSTE. GSTE [10] is a generalization of STE that can verify properties over infinite time intervals. The core of the satGSTE algorithm is a SAT-based algorithm for (non-generalized) STE, as described above. At Intel, satGSTE is used for debugging and refining GSTE assertion graphs, thereby improving user productivity.

Contributions. We have developed an alternative, more efficient, method of verifying STE properties using SAT. The idea is that, instead of simulating the circuit and creating a symbolic expression for the *weakest* trajectory satisfying the antecedent but not the consequent, our algorithm generates a constraint problem that represents *all* trajectories satisfying the antecedent and not the consequent. We argue that this approach is much better suited for use with a SAT-solver.

A second contribution is an alternative STE semantics, that is closely related to our algorithm, and more faithfully describes the behaviour of existing STE algorithms.

In the following, we present our STE semantics, and show how to convert the semantic definitions directly into *primitive abstract constraints*. We then show how to implement these primitive abstract constraints using a SAT-solver, and compare running times on some benchmarks with other SAT-based approaches.

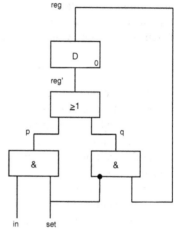

Fig. 1. Gate-level model of a memory cell circuit

p   = set AND in
q   = ¬set AND reg
reg' = p OR q

Fig. 2. Netlist of the circuit

2   Preliminaries

Circuits. A circuit is modeled by a set of node names $\mathcal{N}$ connected by logical gates and delay elements. $\mathcal{S} \subseteq \mathcal{N}$ is the set of state holding nodes, used to model delay elements. It is assumed that for every node n in $\mathcal{S}$, there is a node n' in $\mathcal{N}$ that models the value of that node in the next state.

It is common to describe a circuit in the form of a *netlist*. Here, a netlist is an acyclic list of definitions describing the relations between the values of the nodes. Consider for example the gate-level model of a memory cell circuit in Fig. 1. The netlist of this circuit is given in Fig. 1. Inverters are not modeled explicitly in our netlists, instead they occur implicitly for each mention of the negation operator ¬ on the inputs of the gates. Delay elements are not mentioned explicitly in the netlist either. Instead, for a register with output node n in the circuit, the input of the delay element is node n' which is mentioned in the netlist. So, from the netlist in Fig. 1 it can be derived that the node reg is the output of a delay element with input reg'. The netlists used here do not contain the initial values of delay elements. They are not needed as the STE abstraction assumes that the initial states of delay elements are unknown. For simplicity, we only allow AND-gates and OR-gates in netlists. It is, however, straightforward to extend this notion of netlists to include more operations.

Values. In STE, we can abstract away from specific Boolean values of a node taken from the set $\mathbb{B} = \{0, 1\}$, by using the value X, which stands for *unknown*. The set of signal values is denoted $\mathbb{V} = \{0, 1, X\}$. On this set an *information-ordering* $\leq$ is introduced. The unknown value X contains the least information, so $X \leq 0$ and $X \leq 1$, while 0 and 1 are incomparable. If $v \leq w$ it is said that v is *weaker* than w.

A *circuit state*, written $s : \mathbf{State}$, is a function from $\mathcal{N}$ to $\mathbb{V}$, assigning a value from $\mathbb{V}$ to each node in the circuit. A *sequence* $\sigma : \mathbb{N} \to \mathbf{State}$ is a function from a point in time to a circuit state, describing the behaviour of a circuit over time. The set of all sequences σ is written **Seq**.

Trajectory Evaluation Logic. STE assertions have the form $A \Longrightarrow C$. Here A and C are formulas in *Trajectory Evaluation Logic* (TEL). The only variables in the logic are time-independent Boolean variables taken from the set V of *symbolic variables*. The language is given by the following grammar:

$$f ::= n \text{ is } 0 \mid n \text{ is } 1 \mid f_1 \text{ and } f_2 \mid P \to f \mid \mathbf{N}f$$

where $n \in \mathcal{N}$ and P is a Boolean propositional formula over the set of symbolic variables V. The operator **is** is used to make a statement about the Boolean value of a particular node in the circuit, **and** is conjunction, $\to$ is used to make conditional statements, and **N** is the next time operator. Note that symbolic variables only occur in the Boolean propositional expressions on the left-hand side of an implication. The notation n **is** P, where P is a Boolean symbolic expression over the set of symbolic variables V, is used to abbreviate the formula: $(\neg P \to n \text{ is } 0)$ **and** $(P \to n \text{ is } 1)$.

The meaning of a TEL formula is defined by a satisfaction relation that relates valuations of the symbolic variables and sequences to TEL formulas. Here, the following notation is used: The time shifting operator σ^1 is defined by $\sigma^1(t)(n) = \sigma(t+1)(n)$. Standard propositional satisfiability is denoted by $\models_{\text{Prop}}$. Satisfaction of a trajectory evaluation logic formula f, by a sequence $\sigma \in \mathbf{Seq}$, and a valuation $\phi : V \to \mathbb{B}$ (written $\phi, \sigma \models f$) is defined by

$$
\begin{aligned}
\phi, \sigma \models n \text{ is } b &\equiv \sigma(0)(n) = b \ , \ b \in \{0, 1\} \\
\phi, \sigma \models f_1 \text{ and } f_2 &\equiv \phi, \sigma \models f_1 \text{ and } \phi, \sigma \models f_2 \\
\phi, \sigma \models P \to f &\equiv \phi \models_{\text{Prop}} P \text{ implies } \phi, \sigma \models f \\
\phi, \sigma \models \mathbf{N}f &\equiv \phi, \sigma^1 \models f
\end{aligned}
$$

n	$s_1(n)$
in	1
set	1
p	1
q	0
reg'	1
reg	X

n	$s_2(n)$
p	0
other	X

3   Stability Semantics

In STE model-checking two abstractions are used: (1) the value X can be used to abstract from a specific Boolean value of a circuit node, (2) information is only propagated forwards through the circuit (i.e. from inputs to outputs of gates) and through time (i.e. from time t to time $t + 1$). Given a circuit c, a *trajectory* is a sequence that meets the constraints of the circuit c, taking these abstractions

Fig. 3. Example states

into account. An STE-assertion $A \implies C$ holds if each trajectory that satisfies A also satisfies C.

For instance, for the memory cell given in Fig. 1, consider the assertion: p is 1 $\implies$ reg' is 1. The antecedent specifies the value 1 for node p, so each trajectory satisfying the antecedent should give node p value 1. As node reg' is the output of an OR-gate with input node p, the node reg' is, by forwards propagation, required to have value 1 in each such trajectory. Therefore the assertion is true in STE.

The assertion p is 1 $\implies$ set is 1 is, however, not true. Node set is the input to an AND-gate with output node p. But, as there is no *backwards* propagation of information in STE, a trajectory for the memory cell is allowed to give node p value 1 while giving node set value X at the same time point.

Also the assertion (in is 1) and (reg is 1) $\implies$ (reg' is 1) is not true in STE. Although for each *Boolean* value of node set, node reg' is, by forwards propagation, required to have value 1, the sequence giving both node set and reg' value X is a trajectory that satisfies the antecedent but not the consequent.

Semantics. Below we define a new semantics for STE. The reason we give a new semantics here is that the "classic" semantics of STE [7] cannot deal with combinatorial assertions. That is, it cannot deal with assertions that express a relation between circuit nodes at the same time-point. Because our algorithm (just as existing algorithms like the STE algorithm in Intel's in-house verification toolkit Forte [4]) can prove such properties, we needed a new semantics to prove our algorithm sound and complete.

Stable State Sets. To model this behaviour of STE, we propose to use *stable state sets*, written $F : \mathbb{P}(\mathbf{State})$ as circuit-models. The idea is that a (three-valued) state s is in the stable state set F_c of a circuit c if no more information about the circuit state at the *same* point in time can be derived by propagating the information in a *forwards* fashion. Later, we define trajectories in terms of stables state sets.

Example 1. In this example (and following examples), a state $s : \{p, q, r\} \to \mathbb{V}$ is written as a vector $s(p)s(q)s(r)$. Consider the circuit consisting of a single AND-gate with inputs p and q, and output r. The stable state set of this circuit is

$$F_c = \{ s \mid \text{if } s(\mathsf{p}) = s(\mathsf{q}) = 1 \text{ then } s(\mathsf{r}) = 1, \text{ if } s(\mathsf{p}) = 0 \text{ or } s(\mathsf{q}) = 0 \text{ then } s(\mathsf{r}) = 0 \}$$
$$= \{000, 010, 0\mathsf{X}0, 100, 111, 1\mathsf{X}0, 1\mathsf{X}1, 1\mathsf{X}\mathsf{X}, \mathsf{X}00, \mathsf{X}10, \mathsf{X}11, \mathsf{X}1\mathsf{X}, \mathsf{X}\mathsf{X}0, \mathsf{X}\mathsf{X}1, \mathsf{X}\mathsf{X}\mathsf{X}\}$$

The state 0X0 is in the stable state set, because if p $= 0$ then r $= 0$, but no new information about q can be derived. Also, XX1 is in the stable state set; the reason is that from r $= 1$, we cannot derive information about p or q by means of forwards propagation. The state 11X is not in the stable state set of the circuit; when p $= 1$ and q $= 1$, forwards propagation requires that also the output has value 1.   □

Given the netlist of a circuit, the circuit's stable state set is constructed by taking the intersection of all stable state sets belonging to each of the gates. The stable state sets of AND- and OR-gates with inputs p and q and output r are written $F_{\mathrm{AND}}(p, q, r)$ and $F_{\mathrm{OR}}(p, q, r)$, respectively. The definition of $F_{\mathrm{AND}}(p, q, r)$ is given in Example 1. The set $F_{\mathrm{OR}}(p, q, r)$ is defined similarly. Here, note that the stable state set of a gate is a set of states of the whole circuit and not a set of states of only the in- and outputs of the gate.

Example 2. The stable state set for the memory cell from Fig. 1 is given by:

$$F_c = F_{AND}(\text{set}, \text{in}, \text{p}) \cap F_{AND}(\neg\text{set}, \text{reg}, \text{q}) \cap F_{OR}(\text{p}, \text{q}, \text{reg}')$$

Consider the states s_1, s_2 given in Fig. 3. State s_1 is in the stable state set F_c as all node assignments are consistent and no new information can be derived. State s_2 given in Fig. 3 is also in the stable state set of the memory cell as from the node-assignment $p = 0$ no information can be derived by forwards propagation of information.   □

Trajectories. A trajectory is a sequence in which no more information can be derived by forwards propagation of information. Recall that for every delay element with output n the input to the delay element is called n'. Therefore, in a trajectory, the value of node n' at time t should be propagated to node n at time $t + 1$.

So, a sequence σ is a trajectory if for each time point $t \in \mathbb{N}$: (1) the state $\sigma(t)$ is a stable state, and (2) for each state holding node $n \in S$, the value of node n at time $t + 1$ contains at least the same information as the value of node n' at time t. More formally, the set of trajectories of a circuit c, written $F_c^{\rightarrow} : \mathbf{Seq}$, is defined by:

$$F_c^{\rightarrow} = \{ \sigma \mid \forall t \in \mathbb{N} . \sigma(t) \in F_c, \ \forall t \in \mathbb{N} . \forall n \in S . \sigma(t)(n') \leq \sigma(t+1)(n) \}$$

Stable Semantics of STE. Using the definition of trajectories of a circuit, we can now define the semantics of an STE assertion. A circuit c *satisfies* a trajectory assertion $A \Longrightarrow C$, written $c \models_{\rightarrow} A \Longrightarrow C$ iff for every valuation $\phi \in V \to \mathbb{B}$ of the symbolic variables, and for every trajectory τ of c, it holds that:

$$\phi, \tau \models A \ \Rightarrow \ \phi, \tau \models C.$$

Counter Examples. A valuation ϕ together with a trajectory τ that satisfies A but not C form a counter example of the STE assertion. Because any given STE assertion only refers to a finite number of points in time, only a finite part of the trajectory τ contains interesting information about the counter example. We call the *depth* d of an assertion the maximum number of nested occurrences of the next time operator $\mathbf{N}$. In order to construct a counter example for an assertion of depth d, it is enough to only consider the first d time points of the trajectory. We will use this fact in the next section.

4   A Constraint-Based Algorithm for STE

In this section, we describe how an STE assertion can be checked using a constraint solver that can solve sets of constraints built-up from a small set of *primitive abstract constraints* with a well-defined meaning. In the next section, we show how to concretely represent each of these primitive abstract constraints as a set of clauses in a SAT solver.

Constraints. A *constraint* $S \in \text{Constraint}(D)$ on a domain D is a syntactical object that restricts the elements of D to the set of *solutions* of the constraint. The semantics of constraints is given by the function sol : $\text{Constraint}(D) \to \mathbb{P}(D)$, yielding all solutions of a given constraint. Constraints can be combined by the conjunction operator &. The solutions of a conjunction of two constraints is the intersection of their sets of solutions, that is: $\text{sol}(S_1 \ \& \ S_2) = \text{sol}(S_1) \cap \text{sol}(S_2)$.

In the following, we present a constraint-based algorithm for STE. The idea is to translate a circuit c and an STE assertion $A \implies C$ into a constraint S, such that the STE assertion holds for the circuit if and only if the constraint S has no solutions. Each solution to S represents a counter example, a valuation ϕ and a trajectory τ that together satisfy A but not C.

Domain.   The solution domain D of our constraints consists of pairs (ϕ, σ) of valuations and sequences. For an STE assertion of depth d, we need only to consider the first d points in time. Therefore, the sequence part of a solution (ϕ, σ) is a function from time points $\{0, \ldots, d\}$ to states.

Given a circuit c and an assertion $A \implies C$, the final constraint for the STE problem, written $\mathsf{CEX}(c \models A \implies C)$, consists of 3 parts: (1) constraints that restrict the first d time points of the sequences considered to be the first d time points of trajectories of the circuit c, (2) constraints that restrict the sequences and valuations considered to satisfy the antecedent A, and (3) constraints that restrict the sequences and valuations considered to *not* satisfy the consequent C. Thus, if we find a solution that satisfies all three parts, we have found a counter example to the STE assertion. If we show that no such solution exists, we have shown that the STE assertion holds.

Trajectory Constraint.   Given a circuit c with stable state set F_c, we denote the constraint that restricts the first d time steps of the solutions to be trajectories of c by $\mathsf{TRAJ}(F_c, d)$. It consists of *stable state constraints*, denoted $\mathsf{STABLE}(F_c, t)$, that restrict each point in time t to be a stable state w.r.t. F_c, and of *transition constraints*, denoted $\mathsf{TRANS}(t, t+1)$, that connect the state holding nodes for each point in time t to the next point in time $t+1$:

$$\mathsf{TRAJ}(F_c, d) = \quad \mathsf{STABLE}(F_c, 0) \ \& \ \ldots \ \& \ \mathsf{STABLE}(F_c, d)$$
$$\& \ \mathsf{TRANS}(0, 1) \ \& \ \ldots \ \& \ \mathsf{TRANS}(d-1, d)$$

For a given STE assertion of depth d, only the first d points in time of a trajectory are interesting, and thus we only create constraints for the first d steps of the constraint.

The definition of the constraint $\mathsf{STABLE}(F_c, t)$ makes use of the primitive abstract constraints for the AND- and OR-gates, denoted $\mathsf{AND}(p_t, q_t, r_t)$ and $\mathsf{OR}(p_t, q_t, r_t)$. Here the notation n_t refers to the value of node n at time point t. We show how to concretely implement these constraints in the next section. For now, it is only important to know that the solutions to the constraints are exactly the ones allowed by their stable state sets. For example, for the AND-gate constraint it holds:

$$\mathsf{sol}(\mathsf{AND}(p_t, q_t, r_t)) \ = \ \{(\phi, \sigma) \mid \sigma(t) \in F_{\mathrm{AND}}(p, q, r)\}$$

To build the constraint $\mathsf{STABLE}(F_c, t)$ for the stable state of the circuit, we simply follow the structure of the netlist and conjoin the constraints for each gate together.

Example 3. The stable state constraint for the memory cell is given by:

$$\mathsf{AND}(\mathsf{set}_t, \mathsf{in}_t, \mathsf{p}_t) \ \& \ \mathsf{AND}(\neg\mathsf{set}_t, \mathsf{reg}_t, \mathsf{q}_t) \ \& \ \mathsf{OR}(\mathsf{p}_t, \mathsf{q}_t, \mathsf{reg}'_t) \qquad \qquad \square$$

For a given point in time t, and a circuit c, the transition constraint $\mathsf{TRANS}(t, t+1)$ is built up from primitive abstract constraints of the form $\mathsf{LT}(n_{t_1} \leq m_{t_2})$. The constraint

$\mathsf{LT}(n_{t_1} \leq m_{t_2})$ demands that the value of node n at time t_1 is weaker than the value of node m at time t_2. Here, we require:

$$\mathsf{sol}(\mathsf{LT}(n_{t_1} \leq m_{t_2})) = \{ (\phi, \sigma) \mid \sigma(t_1)(n) \leq \sigma(t_2)(m) \}$$

The definition of the constraint $\mathsf{TRANS}(t, t+1)$ then becomes:

$$\mathsf{TRANS}(t, t+1) = \&_{n \in S} \mathsf{LT}(n'_t \leq n_{t+1})$$

Example 4. For the memory cell, $\mathsf{TRAJ}(F_c, 2)$ is given by:

$$\mathsf{AND}(\mathsf{set}_0, \mathsf{in}_0, \mathsf{p}_0) \ \& \ \mathsf{AND}(\neg\mathsf{set}_0, \mathsf{reg}_0, \mathsf{q}_0) \ \& \ \mathsf{OR}(\mathsf{p}_0, \mathsf{q}_0, \mathsf{reg}'_0)$$
$$\& \ \mathsf{AND}(\mathsf{set}_1, \mathsf{in}_1, \mathsf{p}_1) \ \& \ \mathsf{AND}(\neg\mathsf{set}_1, \mathsf{reg}_1, \mathsf{q}_1) \ \& \ \mathsf{OR}(\mathsf{p}_1, \mathsf{q}_1, \mathsf{reg}'_1)$$
$$\& \ \mathsf{LT}(\mathsf{reg}'_0 \leq \mathsf{reg}_1) \qquad\qquad \square$$

Proposition 1. *For any circuit c, it holds that:*

$$\mathsf{sol}(\mathsf{TRAJ}(F_c, d)) = \{(\phi, \tau \restriction \{0, 1, .., d\}) \mid \tau \in F_c^{\rightarrow}\}.$$

Antecedent Constraint. In order to build the constraint for the antecedent, we need to define the concept of *defining formula*. Given an antecedent A, a node name n, a boolean value $b \in \mathbb{B}$, and a time point t, we can construct a propositional formula that is true exactly when A requires the node n to have value b at time point t. This formula is called the *defining formula*, and is denoted by $\langle A \rangle(t)(n = b)$.

Example 5. If the antecedent A is defined as $(a \wedge b) \rightarrow$ in is 0, then $\langle A \rangle(0)(\mathsf{in} = 0)$ is the formula $a \wedge b$, since only when $a \wedge b$ holds, does A require the node in to be 0. However, $\langle A \rangle(0)(\mathsf{in} = 1)$ is the false formula 0, since A never requires the node in to be 1. $\qquad \square$

The *defining formula* is defined recursively as follows:

$$\langle m \text{ is } b' \rangle(t)(n = b) = \begin{cases} 1, & \text{if } m = n, b' = b \text{ and } t = 0 \\ 0, & \text{otherwise} \end{cases}$$

$$\langle f_1 \text{ and } f_2 \rangle(t)(n = b) = \langle f_1 \rangle(t)(n = b) \vee \langle f_2 \rangle(t)(n = b)$$

$$\langle P \rightarrow f \rangle(t)(n = b) = P \wedge \langle f \rangle(t)(n = b)$$

$$\langle \mathbf{N}f \rangle(t)(n = b) = \begin{cases} \langle f \rangle(t-1)(n = b), & \text{if } t > 0 \\ 0, & \text{otherwise} \end{cases}$$

Note that for an antecedent of the form f_1 **and** f_2 to require that a node has a value, it is enough that one of the formulas f_1 or f_2 requires this.

The third primitive abstract constraint is called an *implication constraint*, and given a propositional formula P, a node n, time point t, and a boolean value b, is written $\mathsf{IMPLIES}(\ P \rightarrow (n_t = b)\ )$. The meaning of this constraint is required to be:

$$\mathsf{sol}(\mathsf{IMPLIES}(\ P \rightarrow (n_t = b)\ )) = \{(\phi, \sigma) \mid \text{if } \phi \models P \text{ then } \sigma(t)(n) = b \}$$

Lastly, the constraint for the antecedent, written $\mathsf{SAT}(A)$, is defined by:

$$\mathsf{SAT}(A) \;=\; \&_{0 \le t \le d}.\ \&_{n \in \mathcal{N}}.\ \&_{b \in \mathbb{B}}.\mathsf{IMPLIES}(\ \langle A \rangle(t)(n = b) \to (n_t = b)\ )$$

In other words, we take the conjunction of all requirements that the antecedent A might have on any node n at any time t with any value b.

Example 6. For the TEL formula $A = (\text{in is } a)$:

$$\mathsf{SAT}(A) = \mathsf{IMPLIES}(\ \neg a \to (\mathrm{in}_0 = 0)\ )\ \ \&\ \ \mathsf{IMPLIES}(\ a \to (\mathrm{in}_0 = 1)\ )$$

Proposition 2. *For every TEL-formula A of depth d:*

$$\mathsf{sol}(\mathsf{SAT}(A)) = \{(\phi, \sigma \restriction \{0, 1, .., d\}) \mid \phi, \sigma \models A\}.$$

Consequent Constraint. For the consequent, we should add a constraint that *negates* the requirements of the consequent on the values of the circuit nodes. In order to do so, we introduce a fresh symbolic variable k_t^n for each node[1] $n \in \mathcal{N}$ and time point $t \in \{0, \ldots, d\}$. We force the variable k_t^n to have value 0 if node n at time t satisfies the requirements of the consequent C. There are three cases when this happens: (1) C requires node n at time t to have value 1 and it has indeed value 1. (2) C requires node n at time t to have value 0 and it has indeed value 0. (3) C has no requirements on node n at time t. Finally, a constraint is introduced that requires that at least one of the k_t^n has value 1. This constrains the set of solutions to contain only solutions where at least one of the requirements of C is not fulfilled.

For the definition of negation of the consequent, two more primitive abstract implication constraints are introduced:

$$\mathsf{IMPLIES}(\ (P \text{ and } (n_t = b)) \to k_t^n = 0\ )$$
$$\mathsf{IMPLIES}(\ P \to k_t^n = 0\ )$$

The meaning of these constraints is given by:

$$\mathsf{sol}(\mathsf{IMPLIES}(\ (P \text{ and } (n_t = b)) \to k_t^n = 0\ ))$$
$$= \{(\phi, \sigma) \mid \text{if } \phi \models P \text{ and } \sigma(t)(n) = b \text{ then } \phi(k_t^n) = 0\}$$

$$\mathsf{sol}(\mathsf{IMPLIES}(\ P \to k_t^n = 0\ )) = \{(\phi, \sigma) \mid \text{if } \phi \models P \text{ then } \phi(k_t^n) = 0\}$$

Furthermore, a primitive abstract constraint that demands that at least one of the k_t^n has value 1, written $\mathsf{EXISTS}(k_t^n = 1)$ is needed. The meaning of this constraint is given by:

$$\mathsf{sol}(\mathsf{EXISTS}(k_t^n = 1)) =$$
$$\{(\phi, \sigma) \mid \text{ there exists an } n \in \mathcal{N} \text{ and a } 0 \le t \le d \text{ such that } \phi(k_t^n) = 1\}.$$

---

[1] As an optimization, in our implementation, variables are only introduced for those node and time point combinations that are actually referred to in the consequent.

Finally, the constraint for the negation of the consequent C, written $\mathsf{NSAT}(C)$, is defined below. Here, the first three constraints match the three cases given above.

$$
\begin{aligned}
\mathsf{NSAT}(C) = \\
\&_{n \in \mathcal{N}} \&_{0 \le t \le d} \; (\; &\mathsf{IMPLIES}(\; \langle C \rangle(t)(n = 0) \text{ and } n_t = 0 \to k_t^n = 0\;)\;\&\\
&\mathsf{IMPLIES}(\; \langle C \rangle(t)(n = 1) \text{ and } n_t = 1 \to k_t^n = 0\;)\;\&\\
&\mathsf{IMPLIES}(\; \neg\langle C \rangle(t)(n = 0) \wedge \neg\langle C \rangle(t)(n = 1) \to k_t^n = 0\;)\;)\\
\& \qquad &\mathsf{EXISTS}(k_t^n = 1)
\end{aligned}
$$

Example 7. For $C = (a \to (\text{reg is } 0))$ **and** $(b \to (\text{reg is } 1))$, $\mathsf{NSAT}(C)$ is given by:

$$
\begin{aligned}
&\mathsf{IMPLIES}(\; a \text{ and } \mathrm{reg}_0 = 0 \to k_0^{\mathrm{reg}} = 0\;)\\
\&\; &\mathsf{IMPLIES}(\; b \text{ and } \mathrm{reg}_0 = 1 \to k_0^{\mathrm{reg}} = 0\;)\\
\&\; &\mathsf{IMPLIES}(\; \neg a \wedge \neg b \to k_0^{\mathrm{reg}}\;)\;\&\;\mathsf{EXISTS}(k_t^n = 1)
\end{aligned}
$$
$\square$

Proposition 3. *For every TEL-formula C:*

$$
\mathsf{sol}(\mathsf{NSAT}(C)) = \{(\phi, \sigma \upharpoonright \{0, 1, .., d\}) \mid \phi, \sigma \not\models C\}
$$

The Constraint for an STE Assertion. is written $\mathsf{CEX}(c \models A \Longrightarrow C)$ and is defined by combining the trajectory constraint, the constraint for antecedent, and the constraint for the negation of the consequent.

$$
\mathsf{CEX}(c \models A \Longrightarrow C) = \mathsf{TRAJ}(F_c, d) \; \& \; \mathsf{SAT}(A) \; \& \; \mathsf{NSAT}(C)
$$

The correctness of the constraint formulation follows from Propositions 1,2 and 3.

Proposition 4. *For each circuit c and STE-assertion $A \Longrightarrow C$:*

$$
c \models_\to A \Longrightarrow C \quad \Leftrightarrow \quad \mathsf{sol}(\mathsf{CEX}(c \models A \Longrightarrow C)) = \emptyset
$$

5   Reducing Constraints to SAT-Problems

In this section, we show how we can instantiate the abstract constraints of the previous section to concrete SAT problems using a dual-rail encoding. First, we briefly restate the concept of a SAT-problem.

SAT Problems. A SAT-problem consists of set of *variables* W and a set of *clauses*. A *literal* is either a variable v or a negated variable $\bar{v}$. An *assignment* is a mapping $a : W \to \{0, 1\}$. For a negated variable $\bar{v}$, we define $a(\bar{v}) = \neg a(v)$. A clause, written $c = v_1 \vee v_2 \vee ... \vee v_n$, is said to be *satisfied* by an assignment a, if there exists an i such that $1 \le i \le n$ and $a(v_i) = 1$. A SAT-problem S is satisfied by an assignment a, written $a \models S$, if a satisfies every clause of S. The set of all satisfying assignments of a SAT-problem S is denoted $\mathsf{sa}(S)$.

SAT Problem for an STE Assertion. Given an STE assertion $A \Longrightarrow C$ for a circuit c the SAT problem for the assertion is denoted $\mathsf{CEX}_{\mathsf{SAT}}(c \models A \Longrightarrow C)$. This *concrete*

SAT-problem is build up from *concrete* primitive constraints in the same way as the *abstract* constraint $\mathsf{CEX}(c \models A \implies C)$ is built up from primitive *abstract* constraints in the previous section. So, in this section we only need to show how the primitive abstract constraints can be instantiated to concrete SAT problems.

The SAT-problem generated for an STE-assertion of depth d contains a SAT-variable v for each variable v in the set of symbolic variables V. Furthermore, for each node n in the set of nodes $\mathcal{N}$ of the circuit c, and for each time point $0 \le t \le d$ *two* SAT-variables are introduced, written n_t^0 and n_t^1.

The two variables n_t^0 and n_t^1 encode the ternary value of node n at time t using a dual-rail encoding. If both variables are false, the value of node n_t is X. If n_t^0 is true, and n_t^1 is false, the node has value 0, if n_t^0 is false, and n_t^1 is true, the node has value 1. We exclude the possibility that both n^0 and n^1 are true by adding a clause $\overline{n_t^0} \vee \overline{n_t^1}$ to the SAT-problem for each n and t. The function mapping a dual-rail encoded ternary value to the ternary value itself, written tern, is defined by: $\mathrm{tern}(0,0) = \mathsf{X}$, $\mathrm{tern}(1,0) = 0$, and $\mathrm{tern}(0,1) = 1$.

Solutions. A satisfying assignment a of such a SAT-problem is mapped to a solution (a tuple of an assignment of the symbolic variables and a sequence) by mapping the satisfying assignment a to the assignment of symbolic variables ϕ_a defined by $\phi_a(v) = a(v)$ and to a sequence σ_a defined by: $\sigma_a(t)(n) = \mathrm{tern}(a(n_t^0), a(n_t^1))$. So, the set of solutions for a SAT-problem is defined by: $\mathsf{sol}(S) = \{(\phi_a, \sigma_a) \mid a \in \mathsf{sa}(S)\}$

Concrete SAT-Problems for the Gates. The SAT-problem for the AND-gate with inputs p_t and q_t and output r_t should have as solutions the sequences in which all forwards propagation has taken place. That is: (1) if $p_t = q_t = 1$ then $r_t = 1$, (2) if $p_t = 0$ then $r_t = 0$, and (3) if $q_t = 0$ then $r_t = 0$.

Recall that for each node n and time point t the clause $\overline{n_t^0} \vee \overline{n_t^1}$ is in the SAT-problem. This clause excludes the possibility that both n_t^0 and n_t^1 are true at the same time. Because of this, there first requirement can be captured in clauses by:

$$\overline{p_t^1} \vee \overline{q_t^1} \vee r_t^1$$

Now, the SAT-problem for the AND-gate, written $\mathsf{AND}_{\mathsf{SAT}}(p_t, q_t, r_t)$ is defined below. The problem consists of three clauses, corresponding to the three requirements above.

$$\mathsf{AND}_{\mathsf{SAT}}(p_t, q_t, r_t) = \{\overline{p_t^1} \vee \overline{q_t^1} \vee r_t^1, \overline{p_t^0} \vee r_t^0, \overline{q_t^0} \vee r_t^0\}$$

Note that these clauses do not yield backwards propagation of information. The assignment $r_t^1 = 1, r_t^0 = 0$ and $p_t^0 = p_t^1 = q_t^0 = q_t^1 = 0$ is a satisfying assignment of the clause set. So, the sequence that gives value 1 to the output of an AND-gate, but value X to its two inputs is a solution of the SAT-problem.

The following property states that the concrete SAT-problem for the AND-gate has the same solutions as the corresponding abstract constraint.

Proposition 5. *For all nodes p, q, and r, and time-point t:*

$$\mathsf{sol}(\mathsf{AND}_{\mathsf{SAT}}(p_t, q_t, r_t)) = \{(\phi, \sigma) \mid \sigma(t) \in F_{\mathrm{AND}}(p, q, r)\} = \mathsf{sol}(\mathsf{AND}(p_t, q_t, r_t).)$$

Concrete SAT-Problems for Comparing Node Values. The SAT-problem for the constraint $LT(n_{t_1} \leq m_{t_2})$ is defined below. The first clause makes sure that if node n has value 0 at time t, node m at time t_2 has that value as well. The next clause states the same requirement for value 1.

$$LT_{SAT}(n_{t_1} \leq m_{t_2}) = \{ \overline{n_{t_1}^0} \vee m_{t_2}^0, \quad \overline{n_{t_1}^1} \vee m_{t_2}^1 \}$$

Proposition 6. *For all $t_1, t_2 \in \mathbb{N}$ and $n, m \in \mathcal{N}$:*

$$sol(LT_{SAT}(n_{t_1} \leq m_{t_2})) = \{ (\phi, \sigma) \mid \sigma(t_1)(n) \leq \sigma(t_2)(m) \} = sol(LT(n_{t_1} \leq m_{t_2})).$$

Concrete SAT-Problems for Implications. Methods to convert an arbitrary Boolean propositional formula to clauses are well-known. Typically, these methods introduce a fresh SAT-variable for each subexpression of the formula. Here, we abstract away from the details of such a method, and assume the existence of functions, cnf and lit that convert a Boolean propositional formula P on a set the set of variables V to a set of clauses $cnf(P)$ on the set of variables $V' \supseteq V$ and a corresponding literal $lit(p)$ such that (1) for all assignments $a : V \to \{0, 1\}$ there exists an assignment $a' : V' \to \{0, 1\}$ extending a such that $a' \models cnf(P)$, and (2) for all assignments $a : V' \to \{0, 1\}$ holds: $a \models cnf(P) \Leftrightarrow a(lit(P)) = a(P)$. Here $a(P)$ stands for the valuation of the expression P w.r.t. the assignment a.

Using these functions, the concrete SAT-problems for the implication constraints are defined. Given a Boolean propositional expression P, node $n \in \mathcal{N}$, time point $t \in \mathbb{N}$, the SAT problems for implications are defined as:

$$
\begin{aligned}
IMPLIES_{SAT}(P \to n_t = 0) &= cnf(P) \cup \{\overline{lit(P)} \vee n_t^0\} \\
IMPLIES_{SAT}(P \to n_t = 1) &= cnf(P) \cup \{\overline{lit(P)} \vee n_t^1\} \\
IMPLIES_{SAT}(P \to k_t^n = 0) &= cnf(P) \cup \{\overline{lit(P)} \vee \overline{k_t^n}\} \\
IMPLIES_{SAT}((P \text{ and } (n_t = 0)) \to k_t^n = 0) &= cnf(P) \cup \{\overline{lit(P)} \vee \overline{n_t^0} \vee \overline{k_t^n}\} \\
IMPLIES_{SAT}((P \text{ and } (n_t = 1)) \to k_t^n = 0) &= cnf(P) \cup \{\overline{lit(P)} \vee \overline{n_t^1} \vee \overline{k_t^n}\}
\end{aligned}
$$

Proposition 7. *For each Boolean propositional expression P, node $n \in \mathcal{N}$, time point $t \in \mathbb{N}$ and $b \in \{0, 1\}$, the following holds:*

$$
\begin{aligned}
sol(IMPLIES_{SAT}(P \to n_t = b)) &= sol(IMPLIES(P \to n_t = b)) \\
sol(IMPLIES_{SAT}(P \to k_t^n = 0)) &= sol(IMPLIES(P \to k_t^n = 0)) \\
sol(IMPLIES_{SAT}((P \text{ and } n_t = b) \to k_t^n = 0)) &= \\
sol(IMPLIES((P \text{ and } n_t = b) &\to k_t^n = 0))
\end{aligned}
$$

Finally, the concrete SAT-problem for the abstract constraint $EXISTS(k_t^n = 1)$ is needed. The constraint is constructed as a disjunction of all k_t^n where n ranges over the set of nodes of the circuit, and t over the time points 0 to d.

$$EXISTS_{SAT}(k_t^n = 1) = \vee_{n \in \mathcal{N}} \cdot \vee_{0 \leq t \leq d} k_t^n$$

Proposition 8. $sol(EXISTS_{SAT}(k_t^n = 1)) = sol(EXISTS(k_t^n = 1))$

6 Constraint vs. Simulation Based SAT-STE

The main difference between simulation-based SAT-STE and constraint-based SAT-STE is that the first generates a SAT problem representing the set of *weakest* trajectories satisfying the antecedent but not the consequent, while the latter generates a SAT-problem that represents *all* such trajectories. For this reason, simulation based SAT-STE generates much larger SAT-problems.

The difference in generated SAT-problems can be illustrated by considering a single AND-gate with input nodes p and q and output r. This AND-gate is assumed to be part of a larger circuit, but here we consider only the clauses generated for the AND-gate. In constraint based SAT-STE, clauses are generated that make sure that the solutions represent *all* trajectories. In simulation-based SAT-STE however, the set of solutions to the SAT-problem represents only the set of *weakest* trajectories. Therefore, the clauses for the AND-gate do not only contain the clauses mentioned in Sect. 5, but also require the following: if forward propagation cannot derive a Boolean value for the output, then the output has value X. The following extra requirements are thus generated: if $p = q = $ X then $r = $ X, if $p = $ X and $q = 1$ then $r = $ X, and if $p = 1$ and $q = $ X then $r = $ X. So, for an AND-gate, simulation-based SAT-STE requires twice as many clauses as constraint-based STE. A similar result holds for other gates. Therefore, simulation-based SAT-STE generates much larger SAT-problems than constraint-based STE.

Optimization. An advantage of STE is that when model checking a small part of a large circuit (for instance an adder within a complete microprocessor) we can set the inputs to the irrelevant parts of the circuit to X. Then, during simulation, all node values of the irrelevant parts receive value X, and only the values of the nodes in the part of interest are represented in the resulting symbolic expressions for the weakest trajectory.

In our algorithm, we represent all trajectories. Therefore, in the pure form of the algorithm, constraints are generated for all gates, even for the gates for which the output node would directly receive value X in a simulation based algorithm. Therefore, we apply a simple and light-weight optimization to our algorithm: if symbolic simulation yields a scalar value $(0, 1$ or X$)$ for a node, the node receives this value in our algorithm and no constraints are generated for the gates driving the node. For all other gates constraints are generated as described in Sect. 5.

7 Results

We have implemented two algorithms: CON-SAT STE, performing constraint-based SAT-STE, and SIM-SAT STE, performing simulation-based SAT-STE. We compare the CON-SAT algorithm and SIM-SAT algorithms with each other.

As a reference point, we also compare with Bounded Model Checking (BMC) [2]. BMC can be used to verify STE assertions by interpreting the assertion as an LTL formula; the completeness threshold [2] is simply the depth of the assertion. Note that BMC solves a different problem, as it does not use STE's three-valued abstraction.

To make the comparison between the algorithms fair, the same SAT-solver (the latest version of MiniSAT [8]) is used for all methods. The benchmarks were run on a cluster of PCs with AMD Barton XP2800+ processors and each with one gigabyte of memory.

	#nodes ($\times 10^3$)	Verification Time(s)			Bug Finding Time(s)			#variables ($\times 10^3$)			#clauses ($\times 10^3$)		
		BMC	CON	SIM	BMC	CON	SIM	BMC	CON	SIM	BMC	CON	SIM
shifter-64	5	8.4	2.4	17	0.0	0.0	0.0	5	9	9	19	24	41
shifter-128	19	175	36	364	0.0	0.0	0.1	18	35	35	72	89	158
shifter-256	71	3443	500	8127	1.6	0.3	1.1	69	137	137	275	343	613
shifter-512	275	time out	5621	time out	3.8	0.7	1.6	271	537	537	1101	1344	2451
mem-10-4	27	13	12	21	9.4	8.1	17	18	27	27	47	51	84
mem-11-4	55	78	47	83	24	44	82	37	53	53	94	102	168
mem-12-4	115	367	222	435	371	157	197	74	107	107	188	205	336
mem-13-4	238	2215	876	1449	1947	564	1087	147	213	213	377	410	672
mem-14-4	492	8066	3612	5524	9626	1970	3194	295	426	426	754	819	1343
treemem-10-4	14	2.6	0.6	3.7	0.0	0.4	3.7	14	18	18	39	39	63
treemem-11-4	29	5.0	3.9	15	0.1	4.4	7.3	29	37	37	78	78	127
treemem-12-4	57	22	21	62	22	21	17	57	74	74	156	156	254
treemem-13-4	115	106	107	281	98	102	160	115	147	147	311	311	508
treemem-14-4	229	476	452	1153	434	427	1059	229	295	295	623	623	1016
con-6-10-4	15	0.9	0.9	4.3	0.7	0.6	1.1	15	20	20	41	41	67
con-6-11-4	30	3.9	5.1	16	1.7	2.0	13	30	39	39	82	82	135
con-6-12-4	61	22	25	70	12	17	40	60	78	78	164	165	270
con-7-13-4	118	116	123	298	97	49	70	118	153	153	320	321	525
con-7-14-4	237	431	512	1170	204	257	665	236	305	305	641	643	1051

Fig. 4. Benchmarks on instances of generically-sized circuits

First, we performed benchmarks on instances of generically-sized circuits, designed by ourselves. The properties we consider for these circuits are: (1) shifter-w; for a variable shifter of width w, full correctness using *symbolic indexing* [5], (2) (tree-)mem-a-d; for a (tree shaped) memory with address width a and data width w, the property that reading an address after writing a value to it yields the same value, and (3) con-c-a-d; for a memory controller with a cache of address width c, a memory of address width a and data width d, the property that reading an address after writing yields the same value, both for the cache and the memory. The times needed to solve the problems and the numbers of variables and clauses in each SAT-problem are given in Fig. 4.

The results show, as expected, that the number of SAT variables for CON-SAT-STE and SIM-SAT-STE are about equal — two variables are introduced for each relevant node and time point. Also as expected, the number of clauses is much larger for SIM-SAT-STE, as explained in Sect. 6. Furthermore, CON-SAT-STE solves the the STE problems much faster than SIM-SAT-STE, something we believe is caused by the reduction in problem size.

For the shifter-n and mem-a-d benchmarks, CON-SAT STE performs better than BMC. For the tree-mem-a-d and con-c-a-d benchmarks the two methods perform comparably. So, in some cases the abstractions used in STE can be beneficial when using SAT-based methods. The reader should, however, realize that the point of this paper is not to advocate the usage of SAT-based STE over BMC or BDD-based STE. Bjesse et al. and Singerman et al. have already shown that SAT-based STE is a useful complement to BDD-based STE and BMC in industrial settings [3,9]. The point of this paper is to present an algorithm that improves upon the algorithms used by Bjesse and Singerman.

The second set of circuits have been supplied to us by Intel Strategic CAD Labs. The circuits are part of a tutorial for GSTE. In Fig. 5 we compare the performance of BMC, BDD-based STE, SIM-SAT-STE and CON-SAT-STE for the verification of

	#nodes $(\times 10^3)$	Verification Time(s)				#variables $(\times 10^3)$			#clauses $(\times 10^3)$		
		BDD	BMC	CON	SIM	BMC	CON	SIM	BMC	CON	SIM
cam (full enc.)	5	time out	1.6	1.6	1.6	4	4	4	8	8	8
cam (plain enc.)	5	time out	1.8	0.9	11	4	5	6	10	11	16
cam (cam enc.)	5	0.1	2.6	2.4	4.2	4	5	6	8	10	16
mem	25	0.3	11	13	23	41	43	60	109	101	175

Fig. 5. Benchmarks on circuits from Intel's GSTE tutorial

several properties of the Content Addressable Memory (CAM) and the memory circuit from this tutorial. Forte [4] was used to perform BDD-based STE. For the CAM, we verify the associative read property using three symbolic indexing schemes from Pandey et al [5]. The CAM contains 16 entries, has a data-width of 64 bits and a tag-width of 8 bits. For the memory, the property that reading address D after writing value V to address D yields value V is verified. Standard symbolic indexing is used. The memory has an address-width of 6 bits, and a data-width of 128 bits.

Pandey et al. show in [5] that verifying the associative read property of CAMs using BDD-based STE is highly non-trivial. The problem is that the straight-forward specification (which they call the *full encoding*) of the property leads to a BDD blowup. They present an improved specification, called the *plain encoding*, that results in smaller BDDs, but that still causes a BDD blow up. Only the most efficient (and complex) specification they introduce, called the *cam encoding*, yields small enough BDDs to make verification of the property go through.

Also for these benchmarks, CON-SAT-STE produces smaller and easier to solve SAT-problems then SIM-SAT-STE. Moreover, the experiments confirm the results of Pandey et al: BDD-based STE cannot be used to verify CAMs using the full or plain encoding. In these experiments, the performance of SAT-based STE is more robust. No matter which encoding is used for verifying the associative read property of the CAM, the SAT-based methods manage to verify the property. This can be explained as follows. The efficiency of a BDD-based STE verification run is highly dependent on the number of variables in the BDDs involved. BDD-based verification methods are usually not able to handle problems with more than several hundred variables. Therefore, symbolic indexing methods minimizing the number of symbolic variables in an STE-assertion are crucial to the efficiency of BDD-based STE. SAT-solvers, on the other hand, have proved to be much less dependent on the number of variables. Therefore, symbolic indexing techniques, minimizing the number of variables, are much less relevant for SAT-based STE.

Reflection. Constraint-based SAT-STE generates smaller problems that are easier to solve than simulation-based SAT-STE, on all our benchmarks. We realize that the problem set we used is quite limited, but we believe it nevertheless indicates the usefulness of our approach.

Plain BMC sometimes outperforms SAT-based STE. Although this is an interesting observation, BMC cannot replace SAT-based STE because it implements a different semantics. For instance, at Intel, the satGSTE tool is used to help develop specifications in GSTE model checking [9]. Here, SAT-based STE is used to get quick feedback when debugging or refining a GSTE assertion graph. In this setting, it is *essential* to have a model checking method that implements the *same semantics* as BDD-based STE, but is not as sensitive to BDD-blow up . This is where SAT-based STE comes in.

8   Conclusions and Future Work

Bjesse et al. and Singerman et al. have shown that SAT-based STE is a useful complement to BDD-based STE and BMC in industrial settings [3,9]. Their algorithms are based on simulation, and generate a SAT-problem that represents the set of weakest trajectories satisfying the antecedent but not the consequent of an STE assertion.

We have presented a new constraint-based SAT-algorithm for STE. Instead of generating a SAT-problem that represents the set of weakest trajectories satisfying the antecedent but not the consequent, our algorithm generates a SAT problem whose solutions represent *all* trajectories satisfying the antecedent but not the consequent. The advantage of representing the set of all such trajectories in the SAT problem (instead of just the weakest trajectories) is that smaller SAT-problems are generated.

Benchmarks, both on circuits designed by ourselves and on circuits taken from Intel's GSTE tutorial, show that our constraint based SAT algorithm for STE performs significantly better than current simulation based algorithms.

Future Work. Intel's satGSTE tool [9] is a bug finding method for GSTE, it implements a *bounded* version of GSTE: only a finite subset of all finite paths in a GSTE assertion graph is considered. Currently the core of the satGSTE tool is a simulation-based SAT-STE algorithm. We conjecture that replacing the tool with a constraint-based SAT-STE algorithm might significantly improve the performance of the tool.

Furthermore, we would like to investigate whether we can use SAT for doing full (unbounded) GSTE model checking. Finally, in (G)STE finding the right specification can be very time consuming. Therefore, we would like to investigate whether SAT can be used to implement a form of *automatic specification refinement* for (G)STE.

Acknowledgment. We are grateful for an equipment grant from Intel Corporation.

References

1. Mark Aagaard, Robert B. Jones, Thomas F. Melham, John W. O'Leary, and Carl-Johan H. Seger. A methodology for large-scale hardware verification. In *Proceedings of the Third International Conference on Formal Methods in Computer-Aided Design*, 2000.
2. Armin Biere, Alessandro Cimatti, Edmund Clarke, and Yunshan Zhu. Symbolic model checking without BDDs. *Lecture Notes in Computer Science*, 1579:193–207, 1999.
3. P. Bjesse, T. Leonard, and A. Mokkedem. Finding bugs in an Alpha microprocessor using satisfiability solvers. In *Proceedings of the 13th International Conference of Computer-Aided Verification*, 2001.
4. http://www.intel.com/software/products/opensource/tools1/verification.
5. Manish Pandey, Richard Raimi, Randal E. Bryant, and Magdy S. Abadir. Formal verification of content addressable memories using symbolic trajectory evaluation. In *34th Design Automation Conference (DAC'97)*, pages 167–172. Association for Computing Machinery.

6. Tom Schubert. High level formal verification of next-generation microprocessors. In *Proceedings of the 40th conference on Design automation*, pages 1–6. ACM Press, 2003.
7. Carl-Johan H. Seger and Randal E. Bryant. Formal verification by symbolic evaluation of partially-ordered trajectories. *Formal Methods in System Design: An International Journal*, 6(2):147–189, March 1995.
8. Niklas Eén & Niklas Sörensson. An extensible SAT-solver. In *Proceedings of the 6th International Conference on Theory and Applications of Satisfiability Testing (SAT2003)*, 2003.
9. Jin Yang, Rami Gil, and Eli Singerman. satGSTE: Combining the abstraction of GSTE with the capacity of a SAT solver. In *Designing Correct Circuits (DCC'04)*, 2004.
10. Jin Yang and C.-J. H. Seger. Introduction to generalized symbolic trajectory evaluation. In *IEEE International Conference on Computer Design: VLSI in Computers & Processors (ICCD '01)*, pages 360–367, Washington - Brussels - Tokyo, September 2001. IEEE.

An Analysis of SAT-Based Model Checking Techniques in an Industrial Environment

Nina Amla, Xiaoqun Du, Andreas Kuehlmann, Robert P. Kurshan, and Kenneth L. McMillan

Cadence Design Systems

Abstract. *Model checking* is a formal technique for automatically verifying that a finite-state model satisfies a temporal property. In model checking, generally Binary Decision Diagrams (BDDs) are used to efficiently encode the transition relation of the finite-state model. Recently model checking algorithms based on Boolean satisfiability (SAT) procedures have been developed to complement the traditional BDD-based model checking. These algorithms can be broadly classified into three categories: (1) *bounded model checking* which is useful for finding failures (2) hybrid algorithms that combine SAT and BDD based methods for unbounded model checking, and (3) purely SAT-based unbounded model checking algorithms. The goal of this paper is to provide a uniform and comprehensive basis for evaluating these algorithms. The paper describes eight bounded and unbounded techniques, and analyzes the performance of these algorithms on a large and diverse set of hardware benchmarks.

1 Introduction

A common method used in formal verification is *model checking* [7,26]. Generally, Binary Decision Diagrams (BDDs) [4] are used to symbolically represent the set of states. This approach, known as *symbolic model checking* [5], has been successfully applied in practice. Unfortunately, BDDs are very sensitive to the type and size of the system. For instance common designs like multipliers can not be represented efficiently with BDDs. Due to recent advances in tools [19,23,11] that solve the Boolean satisfiability problem (SAT), formal reasoning based on SAT is proving to be an viable alternative to BDDs.

Bounded Model Checking (BMC) [3] is a SAT-based technique where a system is unfolded k times and encoded as a SAT problem to be solved by a CNF-based SAT solver. A satisfying assignment returned by the SAT solver corresponds to a counterexample of length k. If the problem is determined to be unsatisfiable, the SAT solver produces a proof of the fact that there are no counterexamples of length k. A different approach, called *circuit-based* BMC [15], uses the circuit structure to make BMC more efficient. The circuit is unfolded incrementally and at each step equivalent nodes are identified and merged to simplify the circuit. BMC, while successful in finding errors, is incomplete: there is no efficient way to decide that the property is *true*. Recently several complete model checking algorithms have been developed that use SAT-based quantifier

D. Borrione and W. Paul (Eds.): CHARME 2005, LNCS 3725, pp. 254–268, 2005.
© IFIP International Federation for Information Processing 2005

elimination [20,10], ATPG methods [12], and combinations of SAT-based BMC with techniques like BDD-based model checking [6,22], induction [27] and interpolation [21].

Since users have limited resources for the verification of systems, it is important to know which of these new SAT-based algorithms is most effective. This paper presents an experimental analysis of these bounded and unbounded algorithms in an attempt to address this issue. Unlike previous efforts that compared SAT-based BMC to BDD-based and explicit state methods (cf. [8,1]), this paper focuses only on SAT-based techniques. In Section 2 we give an overview of the eight algorithms we evaluated. A more comprehensive survey of SAT-based techniques can be found in [25]. We describe our experimental framework in Section 3. We compare the various algorithms on a set of over 1000 examples drawn from actual hardware designs. Section 4 presents our results and analysis. We conclude and discuss future work in Section 5.

2   Overview of the Algorithms

2.1   Preliminaries

A model $M = (S, I, T, L)$ has a set of states S, a set of initial states $I \subseteq S$, a transition relation $T \subseteq S \times S$, and a labeling function $L : S \rightarrow 2^A$ where A is a set of atomic propositions. For the purposes of this paper, we shall consider only invariant properties specified in the logic LTL. The construction given in [16] can be used to reduce model checking of safety properties to checking invariant properties. The syntax and semantics of LTL and other temporal logics is not given here but can be found in [9].

Given a finite state model M and a safety property p, the model checking algorithm checks that M satisfies p, written $M \models p$. The forward reachability algorithm starts at the initial states and computes the *image*, which is the set of states reachable in one step. This procedure is continued until either the property is falsified in some state or no new states are encountered (a fixed point). The backward reachability algorithm works similarly but starts from the states where the property is *false* and computes the *preimage*, which is the set of states that can reach the current states in one step. The representation and manipulation of the sets of states can be done explicitly or with Binary Decision Diagrams (BDDs). In the sequel, we shall refer to BDD-based model checking as MC.

2.2   DPLL-Style SAT Solvers

The Boolean satisfiability problem (SAT) is to determine if a given Boolean formula has a satisfying assignment. This is generally done by converting the formula into Conjunctive Normal Form (CNF), which can be efficiently solved by a SAT solver. A key operation used in SAT solvers is *resolution*, where two clauses $(a \vee b)$ and $(\neg a \vee c)$ can be resolved to give a new clause $(b \vee c)$. Modern

DPLL-style SAT solvers [19,23,11] make assignments to variables, called *decisions*, and generate an implication graph which records the decisions and the effects of Boolean constraint propagation. When all the variables are assigned, the SAT solver terminates with the satisfying assignment. But if there is a *conflict*, which is a clause where the negation of every literal already appears in the implication graph, a conflict clause is generated through resolution. This conflict clause is added to the formula to avoid making those assignments again. The SAT solver then backtracks to undo some of the conflicting assignments. The SAT solver terminates with an *unsatisfiable* answer when it rules out all possible assignments. The resolution steps used in generating the conflict clauses can now be used to produce a *proof of unsatisfiability*.

2.3   SAT-Based Bounded Model Checking

Bounded Model Checking (BMC) [3] is a restricted form of model checking, where one searches for a counterexample (CEX) in executions bounded by some length k. In this approach the model is unfolded k times, conjuncted with the negation of the property, and then encoded as a propositional satisfiability formula. Given a model M and an invariant property p, the BMC problem is encoded as follows:

$$BMC(M, p, k) = I(s_0) \wedge \bigwedge_{i=0}^{k-1} T(s_i, s_{i+1}) \wedge \bigvee_{i=0}^{k} \neg p(s_i)$$

The formula can be converted into CNF and solved by a SAT solver. If the formula is satisfiable, then the property is *false*, and the SAT solver has found a satisfying assignment that corresponds to a counterexample of length k. In the unsatisfiable case, there is no counterexample of length k and a proof of unsatisfiability can be obtained from the SAT solver.

2.4   Circuit-Based Bounded Model Checking

In circuit-based BMC the circuit structure is exploited to enhance efficiency. Rather than translating the problem into a CNF formula directly, circuit-based BMC uses an intermediate representation, called And-Inverter Graphs (AIGs) [15], that keeps the circuit structure. The use of AIGs allows the application of the *SAT-sweeping* technique [14], where one identifies equivalent nodes using a SAT solver and merges these equivalent nodes to simplify the circuit represented by the AIG. Random simulation is used to pick candidate pairs of nodes that have identical simulation results, and a SAT solver is used to check whether the XOR of the two candidate nodes can ever be satisfied. If not, the nodes are equivalent and can be merged to simplify the AIG. If the XOR of the nodes is satisfiable, the SAT solver will give a witness that shows how the nodes can obtain different values. This witness can be used to show the in-equivalence of other nodes to reduce the number of candidate pairs for equivalence-finding. After the completion of SAT-sweeping, the simplified AIG is translated into a CNF formula for BMC.

2.5   CEX-Based Abstraction Refinement

Counterexample-based abstraction-refinement [17] is an iterative technique that starts with BDD-based MC on an initial conservative abstraction of the model. If MC proves the property on the abstraction then the property is *true* on the full model. However, if a counterexample A is found, it could either be an actual error or it may be spurious, in which case one needs to refine the abstraction to rule out this counterexample. The process is then repeated until the property is found to be *true*, or until a real counterexample is produced.

The counterexample-based method in [6] used BMC to concretize the counterexample by solving the following:

$$BMC(M, p, k, A) = I(s_0) \land \bigwedge_{i=0}^{k-1} T(s_i, s_{i+1}) \land \bigvee_{i=0}^{k} \neg p(s_i) \land \bigwedge_{i=0}^{k} A_i$$

where A_i is a constraint that represents the assignments in the abstract counterexample A in time frame i. If this formula is determined to be satisfiable then the satisfying assignment represents a counterexample on the concrete model. In the unsatisfiable case, the method [6] analyzes the proof of unsatisfiability generated by the SAT solver to find a set of constraints whose addition to the abstraction will rule out this spurious counterexample. Since the BMC problem includes the constraints in the abstract counterexample A, one can guarantee that A is eliminated by adding all variables that occur in the proof to the existing abstraction. The pseudocode is shown in Figure 1.

procedure cex-based (M,p)
1. generate initial abstraction M'
2. while *true* do
3.   if $MC(M', p)$ holds then return *verified*
4.   let $k = $ length of abstract *counterexample* A
5.   if $BMC(M,p,k,A)$ is SAT then return *counterexample*
6.   else use proof of UNSAT P to refine M'
7. end while
end

Fig. 1. SAT-based counterexample procedure

2.6   Proof-Based Abstraction Refinement

The proof-based algorithm in [22] also iterates through SAT-based BMC and BDD-based MC. It starts with a short BMC run, and if the problem is satisfiable, an error has been found. If the problem is unsatisfiable, the proof of unsatisfiability is used to guide the formation of a new conservative abstraction on which BDD-based MC is run. In the case that the BDD-based model checker proves the property then the algorithm terminates; otherwise the length k' of the counterexample generated by the model checker is used as the next

procedure proof-based (M,p)
1. initialize k
2. while *true* do
3.   if *BMC(M,p,k)* is SAT then return *counterexample*
4.   else
5.   derive new abstraction M' from proof P
6.   if $MC(M',p)$ holds then return *verified*
7.   else set k to length of counterexample k'
8. end while
end

Fig. 2. Proof-based procedure

BMC length. Notice that only the length of the counterexample generated by the BDD-based MC is used. This method creates a new abstraction in each iteration, in contrast to the counterexample method which refines the existing abstraction. Since this abstraction includes all the variables in the proof of unsatisfiability for a BMC run up to depth k, we know that any counterexample obtained from model checking this abstract model will be of length greater than k. Therefore, unlike the counterexample method, this algorithm eliminates *all* counterexamples of length k in a single unsatisfiable BMC run. This procedure, shown in Figure 2, is continued until either a failure is found in the BMC phase or the property is proved in the BDD-based MC phase. The termination of the algorithm hinges on the fact that the value of k' increases in every iteration.

2.7   Induction-Based Model Checking

The induction-based method in [27] uses a SAT solver as the decision procedure for a special kind of induction called k-induction. In this type of induction, one attempts to prove that a property holds in the current state, assuming that it holds in the previous k consecutive states. In addition, for completeness, one has to add an additional constraint that specifies that the states along a path must be unique. This is formalized as follows:

$$Base(M, p, k) = I(s_0) \wedge \bigwedge_{i=0}^{k-1} T(s_i, s_{i+1}) \wedge \bigvee_{i=0}^{k} \neg p(s_i)$$

$$Step(M, p, k) = \bigwedge_{0 \leq i < j \leq k} s_i \neq s_j \wedge \bigwedge_{i=0}^{k} T(s_i, s_{i+1}) \wedge \bigwedge_{i=0}^{k} p(s_i) \wedge \neg p(s_{k+1})$$

A counterexample has been found if the base condition is satisfiable; otherwise the value of k is increased until both conditions are unsatisfiable, which means the property holds. The pseudocode is shown in Figure 3.

procedure k-induction (M,p)
1. initialize $k = 0$
2. while *true* do
3.   if $Base(M, p, k)$ is SAT then return *counterexample*
4.   else if $Step(M, p, k)$ is UNSAT then return *verified*
5. $k = k + 1$
6. end while
end

Fig. 3. The k-induction procedure

2.8   Interpolation-Based Model Checking

An *interpolant* $\mathcal{I}$ for an unsatisfiable formula $A \wedge B$ is a formula such that: (1) $A \Rightarrow \mathcal{I}$ (2) $\mathcal{I} \wedge B$ is unsatisfiable and (3) $\mathcal{I}$ refers only to the common variables of A and B. Intuitively, $\mathcal{I}$ is the set of facts that the SAT solver considers relevant in proving the unsatisfiability of $A \wedge B$.

The interpolation-based algorithm [21] uses interpolants to derive an over-approximation of the reachable states with respect to the property. This is done as follows (Figure 4). The BMC problem $BMC(M, p, k)$ is solved for an initial depth k. If the problem is satisfiable, a counterexample is returned, and the algorithm terminates. If $BMC(M, p, k)$ is unsatisfiable, the formula representing the problem is partitioned into $Pref(M, p, k) \wedge Suff(M, p, k)$, where $Pref(M, p, k)$ is the conjunction of the initial condition and the first transition, and $Suff(M, p, k)$ is the conjunction of the rest of the transitions and the final condition. The interpolant $\mathcal{I}$ of $Pref(M, p, k)$ and $Suff(M, p, k)$ is computed. Since $Pref(M, p, k) \Rightarrow \mathcal{I}$, it follows that $\mathcal{I}$ is *true* in all states reachable from $I(s_0)$ in one step. This means that $\mathcal{I}$ is an over-approximation of the set of states reachable from $I(s_0)$ in one step. Also, since $\mathcal{I} \wedge Suff(M, p, k)$ is unsatisfiable, it also follows that no state satisfying $\mathcal{I}$ can reach an error in $k - 1$ steps. If $\mathcal{I}$ contains no new states, that is, $\mathcal{I} \Rightarrow I(s_0)$, then a fixed point of the reachable set of states has been reached, thus the property holds. If $\mathcal{I}$ has new states then R' represents an over-approximation of the states reached so far. The algorithm then uses R' to replace the initial set I, and iterates the process of solving the BMC problem at depth k and generating the interpolant as the over-approximation of the set of states reachable in the next step. The property is determined to be *true* when the BMC problem with R' as the initial condition is unsatisfiable, and its interpolant leads to a fixed point of reachable states. However, if the BMC problem is satisfiable, the counterexample may be spurious since R' is an over-approximation of the reachable set of states. In this case, the value of k is increased, and the procedure is continued. The algorithm will eventually terminate when k becomes larger than the diameter of the model.

2.9   Quantification-Based Model Checking

There are many approaches [25] to doing quantifier elimination which is a key step in reachability analysis. The purely SAT-based quantifier elimination procedure introduced in [20] works by enumeration of all the satisfying assignments.

procedure interpolation (M, p)
1. initialize k
2. while *true* do
3.   if $BMC(M, p, k)$ is SAT then return *counterexample*
4. $R = I$
5.   while true do
6. $M' = (S, R, T, L)$
7.   let $C = Pref(M', p, k) \wedge Suff(M', p, k)$
8.   if C is SAT then break (goto line 15)
9.   /* C is UNSAT */
10.   compute interpolant $\mathcal{I}$ of $Pref(M', p, k) \wedge Suff(M', p, k)$
11. $R' = \mathcal{I}$ is an over-approximation of states reachable from R in one step.
12.   if $R \Rightarrow R'$ then return *verified*
13. $R = R \vee R'$
14.   end while
15.   increase k
16. end while
end

Fig. 4. Interpolation procedure

The SAT solver is modified to generate all the satisfying assignments by adding blocking clauses to the problem each time an assignment is found. The SAT solving process is continued until no new solutions are found. A blocking clause, which refers only to the state variables, represents the negation of a state cube. This quantification procedure yields a purely SAT-based method for computing the preimage in backward symbolic model checking.

A recent quantification-based method [10] uses a circuit representation of the blocking constraints and use a hybrid solver that works directly on this representation. This enables circuit cofactoring with respect to the input assignments to simplify the circuit graph in each enumeration step. This results in more solutions in each enumeration step and thus far fewer enumerations steps. It is reported in [10] that this method outperforms the technique described in [20]. We implemented the basic cofactoring-based quantification approach in our framework. Our implementation did not include the heuristics provided in [10] to select values for unassigned inputs in the satisfying cube; we just use the complete input assignment provided by the SAT solver in that enumeration step. We also did not use functional hashing in the simplification process but we did use structural hashing.

2.10 ATPG-Based Model Checking

Automatic Test Pattern Generation (ATPG) is an approach that adapts DPLL-style SAT techniques to a structural representation of a circuit. The ATPG-based algorithm in [12] combines the structure guided search strategy of ATPG with the faster implication procedures and conflict-based learning in SAT solvers. They use a circuit representation, a CNF clause database and a mapping between both representations. The method conducts a backward search, using an ATPG-based back-tracing traversal method, from the states where the property is *false*. The search strategy, which is a mixture of DFS and BFS, is based on a cost function that measures the number of states traversed. A counterexample is generated if an initial state is reached during the search; otherwise the property is proved to be *true* if the entire backward reachable set of states does not intersect with the initial state set. This procedure is complete because the search is efficiently bounded by using additional Boolean constraints to mark visited states as already reached and hence never to be visited again.

3   Experimental Framework

In order to measure the relative performance of the algorithms described in the previous section, we implemented all the methods except the ATPG-based method SATORI, which was developed at University of Santa Barbara [12]. We developed a flexible experimental framework that allows external tools, like SATORI, to be integrated with little effort. We use a simple intermediate representation that can be translated easily and efficiently into the input language of various tools. This interface also enables us to plug and play with different SAT solvers and BDD packages.

3.1   Benchmarks

In the context of commercial software development, a good benchmark suite must be large, diverse, and representative of real customer designs. The data collection must be fully automated, and must complete within a reasonable amount of time so that the benchmark suite can be used as a regression suite for tracking the performance of the software over time.

Our benchmark suite included approximately 85 hardware designs, accumulated through many years of customer interaction. The sizes of these designs ranged from a few hundred to more than 100,000 lines of HDL code. Each design in our benchmark suite contained from one up to a few hundred properties to check. Some of the properties were duplicates because they were instantiated from the same property declaration in similar parts of a design. To make our benchmark suite as diverse as possible, we removed all duplicate properties, where two properties were considered duplicates if the model had the same number of state and combinational variables, and that the running times were within 10% of each other.

There were properties that none of the algorithms could finish within a reasonable amount of time. We removed most of these properties from our benchmark suite because they were not useful for comparing the relative performance of the algorithms. We did keep some of these properties to track performance improvements of the algorithms over time. This resulted in a total of 1182 properties for the 85 designs in our benchmark suite. Out of these 1182 properties, 803 of them are passes, 364 of them are failures, and the remaining 15 properties have unknown results.

3.2   Data Collection

Each ⟨property, algorithm⟩ pair corresponds to one run for data collection. This meant we needed 1182 runs for each technique, hence it was important that we set up our test environment so that the experiments finished within a reasonable amount of time. To do this, we set a time limit of 3600 seconds for each property. We found in our experiments that a majority of the runs finished within this time limit.

We used a computer server farm for data collection. In our experiments, we use 10 identical Redhat Enterprise Linux machines, each with an AMD Opteron CPU at 2GHZ and 4GB of available memory. We partitioned our entire set of runs into multiple jobs, each job consisting of a small set of runs. These jobs are submitted to the server farm and launched whenever a CPU is free. To ensure the accurate collection of data, no other jobs are permitted on a CPU when it is running one of our data collection jobs; also, a data collection job cannot be started unless a machine has at least 4GB of free memory.

4   Results and Analysis

In our experiments, except for SATORI, we used the same SAT solver and BDD-based model checker for all the techniques. The SAT solver is incremental [29], in the sense that it is possible to add/delete clauses and restart the solver, while maintaining all previously inferred conflict clauses that were not derived from deleted clauses. An important point to note is that all methods were run with default settings and there was no tuning done with respect to specific examples.

Table 1. Summary Table for the Bounded Technique

Depth	# Props	SAT-BMC		CIR-BMC	
		# Fin	Avg Time	# Fin	Avg Time
10	1182	1179	10.9	1178	15.0
25	1182	1175	28.8	1177	23.8
50	1182	1168	73.3	1170	53.3
100	1182	1153	174.0	1158	117.0

For the bounded model checking techniques, we set a time limit of 3600 seconds and did four runs with depth limits of 10, 25, 50 and 100. We measured the number of problems that were resolved within the time limit and the average time taken per property (over all the properties regardless of whether an algorithm finished or not) by both methods. Table 1 presents these results. We can see that, after depth 25, the circuit-based approach takes less time on average. We plot the run time at depth 100 for both algorithms in Figure 5, a point below the diagonal line indicates that circuit BMC was faster on that example. In all the tables and plots, the time for any unresolved property is taken to be

3600 seconds even if the method ran out of memory in far less time. The data shows that the savings due to SAT sweeping in circuit-based BMC outweighs the overhead at the larger depths.

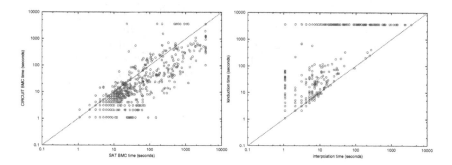

Fig. 5. Plot of time in seconds. Left: X-axis is SAT BMC and Y-axis is Circuit BMC at depth 100. Right: X-axis is Interpolation and Y-axis is K-induction.

For the unbounded techniques, we set a time limit of 3600 seconds for verification, and measure the number of problems that were resolved within this time limit. Table 2 reports the number of resolved problems and average time taken per property. As a baseline, we include the results for a forward traversal BDD-based MC method in Table 2. It is interesting to note that all the SAT-based algorithms, except the k-induction method, do better than BDD-based model checking with respect to the number of problems resolved and average time taken. However, we shall not include BDD-based MC in any further discussions since it is not in the scope of this paper. We also see that the interpolation method resolved more problems and had a lower average running time than the other techniques. Since the interpolation method is the most robust, in the sense that it resolves the largest number of problems, we plotted the run time of the other five unbounded algorithms versus the interpolation algorithm. These are shown in Figures 5 to 7. The plots indicate that in general the interpolation method is faster and more robust than the other methods, however there are still many cases where the other techniques do better.

Tables 3 and 4 present the number of problems resolved, average time, average final depth and average number of state variables (size), for only the resolved failing and passing problems respectively. The depth information was not available for the ATPG-based method and is therefore excluded from both tables. We also report the number of "wins" with respect to time, where a win is attributed to a particular algorithm if it does better than all others with respect to running time. In the case of a tie, which we defined to be two runs where the difference was less than 5% of the run time, we award a win for both methods.

The failing properties in our benchmark suite can be roughly characterized with respect to depth as follows: 91% failed at a depth of 25 or less with 24% of the failures at a depth of 2, 7% failed between a depth of 26 till 100 and 2% failed

Table 2. Summary Table for the Unbounded Techniques

Algorithm	# Props	# Resolved	Total time	Avg. Time
BDD	1182	876	1171716	991.3
proof-based	1182	1121	269377	227.9
cex-based	1182	1054	520570	439.3
cofactor	1182	874	1154459	976.7
atpg-based	1182	992	756480	640.0
kinduction	1182	513	2417662	2045.4
interpolation	1182	1157	118791	100.5

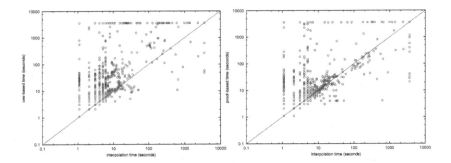

Fig. 6. Plot of time in seconds. Left: X-axis is Interpolation and Y-axis is CEX-based. Right: X-axis is Interpolation and Y-axis is Proof-based.

at a depth greater than 100. The data in Table 3 for the bounded techniques is cumulative, in the sense that we report the total running time at depths 10, 25 and 50 for an error found at depth 45. Since the maximum depth checked was 100, the bounded techniques were not able to find failures that occurred at depths greater than 100 and this is reflected in the number of failures. Table 3 shows some interesting trends for the failing properties. Not surprisingly we see that, with respect to average run time, both bounded techniques do better than all others on the failing properties. However, since the bounded techniques were employed at fixed depths, this made finding the shallow errors, like the failures at depth 2, more expensive than necessary. The interpolation and proof-based techniques are competitive with the bounded techniques in number of wins but the proof-based technique is clearly the faster of the two. The k-induction method is effective in finding the shallow failures, as is evident in the low run time when it does resolve a problem. The correspondingly low depth numbers in Table 3 are due to the fact that the k-induction method ran out of memory fairly early in 662 cases. The mixed DFS/BFS search strategy of the ATPG-based method could cause the technique to miss errors if it chooses to do DFS early and may explain why it does poorly on failures. This is consistent with the results reported in [24] which show that a purely BFS search is more robust than a purely DFS search on failing properties. Another possibility is that, on

Table 3. Summary Table for the Failing Properties

Algorithm	Failures				
	# Props	# Wins	Avg Time	Avg Size	Avg Depth
sat-bmc	351	230	9.6	106	15
circuit-bmc	350	219	14.1	106	15
proof-based	359	216	22.1	111	19
cex-based	341	119	58.6	88	17
cofactor	268	157	71.8	60	18
atpg-based	295	144	119.6	54	-
kinduction	340	171	17.6	97	7
interpolation	362	224	31.6	112	16

Table 4. Summary Table for the Passing Properties

Algorithm	Passes				
	# Props	# Wins	Avg Time	Avg Size	Avg Depth
proof-based	762	380	54.9	115	30
cex-based	713	237	51.7	101	23
cofactor	606	457	48.0	109	7
atpg-based	697	427	53.4	111	-
kinduction	173	107	19.1	14	14
interpolation	795	701	21.9	130	22

these examples, the set of states grows faster with backward exploration than with forward exploration. This could in part explain why the cofactoring method does poorly as well. Both the ATPG and cofactoring methods have a much lower average size which suggests that these methods are unable to resolve the larger examples.

For the passing properties, the interpolation technique is the fastest and solves more properties than the other methods. The proof-based technique is the closest in terms of the number of properties resolved but is significantly slower on average. We see that the proof-based method does better than the counterexample-based method, despite the fact that the counterexample-based method proves properties at lower depths on average. This is largely due to the number of iterations done by the counterexample-based method, most of them done refuting counterexamples at the same depth (see [2] for a detailed analysis). The data in Table 4 indicates that the interpolation method is able to prove the properties at a lower depth than the proof-based method. This suggests that the approximate image computation is more effective on these examples than the corresponding BDD-based MC phase in the proof-based method. The k-induction method does rather poorly since checking the k-induction step is expensive as the value of k gets larger. As mentioned earlier, the size of the BMC problem for the step case is often too large causing the SAT-solver to run out of memory. As reported in [18], removing the simple path constraints and trading completeness for efficiency may improve the performance of this method. The ATPG-based and cofactoring methods have a high number of wins and are comparable to the proof-based method in running time. Both methods do backward reachability and cube enlargement but, while their performance signatures are similar, the ATPG method appears to be more robust. The cofactoring method has a low average depth which seems to suggest that a large and rapidly growing backward reachable state space could be contributing to the difference. The search strategy of ATPG-based method permits on-the-fly pruning of the search space, which could be beneficial in such situations. However, we do not have enough data on the ATPG method to validate this conjecture. Furthermore, as observed in [10], using the heuristics to enlarge the satisfying state set in the cofactoring technique has a significant impact on performance.

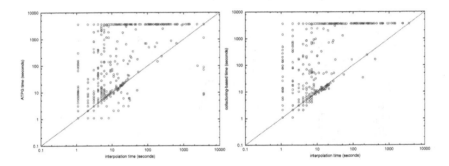

Fig. 7. Plot of time in seconds. Left: X-axis is Interpolation and Y-axis is ATPG-based. Right: X-axis is Interpolation and Y-axis is Cofactoring-based.

5   Conclusions and Future Work

This paper compares eight bounded and unbounded SAT-based algorithms on a large set of industrial benchmarks. Our experiments show that although the interpolation technique is the most efficient and robust overall, there were still many examples where the other techniques did better. This is evident in the number of wins in Tables 3 and 4. Therefore, it would be useful to find ways to apply the best algorithm for each task. One way to do this is to run the algorithms in parallel and terminate the slower ones as soon as the first finishes. Another approach would be to combine the various algorithms in a way that exploits their strengths, like the hybrid method in [2] that combines the proof-based and counterexample-based methods.

   For future work, we plan to integrate the VIS model checker into our experimental framework. We believe that methods implemented in VIS would provide some interesting comparisons. The conjecture that the simple path restriction in k-induction hinders performance could be evaluated by using the more sophisticated technique described in [18]. Furthermore, we could compare the counterexample-based technique in [28] that uses a generalized counterexample that is derived from the sequence of reachable states approximations computed by the model checker. Finally it would be useful to evaluate the circuit-based BMC solver described in [13] which uses BDDs to help in the solution of SAT instances given in CNF.

Acknowledgments. The authors thank Kwang-Ting Cheng, Feng Lu, Ganapathy Parthasarthy and Madhu Iyer for help in integrating SATORI.

References

1. N. Amla, R. Kurshan, K. McMillan, and R. Medel. Experimental analysis of different techniques for bounded model checking. In *TACAS*, 2003.
2. N. Amla and K. McMillan. A hybrid of counterexample-based and proof-based abstraction. In *FMCAD*, 2004.
3. A. Biere, A. Cimatti, E. Clarke, and Y. Zhu. Symbolic model checking without BDDs. In *TACAS*, 1999.
4. R. E. Bryant. Graph-based algorithms for boolean function manipulations. *IEEE Transactions on Computers*, 1986.
5. J. R. Burch, E. M. Clarke, K. L. McMillan, D.L. Dill, and J. Hwang. Symbolic model checking: 10^{20} states and beyond. In *LICS*, 1990.
6. P. Chauhan, E. Clarke, J. Kukula, S. Sapra, H. Veith, and D. Wang. Automated abstraction refinement for model checking large state spaces using sat based conflict analysis. In *FMCAD*, 2002.
7. E.M. Clarke and E. A. Emerson. Design and synthesis of synchronization skeletons using branching time temporal logic. In *Workshop on Logics of Programs*, 1981.
8. F. Copty, L. Fix, R. Fraer, E. Giunchiglia, G. Kamhi, A. Tacchella, and M. Vardi. Benefits of bounded model checking at an industrial setting. In *CAV*, 2001.
9. E. A. Emerson. Temporal and modal logic. In *Handbook of Theoretical Computer Science, Volume B: Formal Models and Sematics*, 1990.
10. M. Ganai, A. Gupta, and P. Ashar. Efficient SAT-based unbounded symbolic model checking using circuit cofactoring. In *ICCAD*, 2004.
11. E. Goldberg and Y. Novikov. Berkmin: A fast and robust sat-solver. In *DATE*, 2002.
12. M. Iyer, G. Parthasarathy, and K.T. Cheng. SATORI- an efficient sequential SAT solver for circuits. In *ICCAD*, 2003.
13. H. Jin and F. Somenzi. CirCUs: Hybrid satisfiability solver. In *SAT*, 2004.
14. A. Kuehlmann. Dynamic transition relation simplification for bounded property checking. In *ICCAD*, 2004.
15. A. Kuehlmann, V. Paruthi, F. Krohm, and M. Ganai. Robust Boolean reasoning for equivalence checking and functional property verification. In *TCAD*, 2003.
16. O. Kupferman and M. Vardi. Model checking of safety properties. In *Formal Methods in System Design*, 2001.
17. R. Kurshan. *Computer-aided Verification of Coordinating Processes: The Automata-Theoretic Approach*. Princeton University Press, 1994.
18. B. Li, C. Wang, and F. Somenzi. A satisfiability-based approach to abstraction refinement in model checking. In *Workshop on BMC*, 2003.
19. J. Marques-Silva and K. Sakallah. GRASP: A search algorithm for propositional satisfiability. *IEEETC: IEEE Transactions on Computers*, 48, 1999.

20. K. McMillan. Applying SAT methods in unbounded symbolic model checking. In *CAV*, 2003.
21. K. McMillan. Interpolation and SAT-based model checking. In *CAV*, 2003.
22. K. McMillan and N. Amla. Automatic abstraction without counterexamples. In *TACAS*, 2003.
23. M. W. Moskewicz, C. F. Madigan, Y. Zhao, L. Zhang, and S. Malik. Chaff: Engineering an Efficient SAT Solver. In *DAC*, 2001.
24. G. Parthasarathy, M. Iyer, K.T. Cheng, and L.C. Wang. A comparison of BDDs, BMC, and sequential SAT for model checking. In *High-Level Design Validation and Test Workshop*, 2003.
25. M. Prasad, A. Biere, and A. Gupta. A survey of recent advances in sat-based formal verification. In *STTT*, 2005.
26. J.P. Queille and J. Sifakis. Specification and verification of concurrent systems in CESAR. In *Proc. of the 5th International Symposium on Programming*, 1982.
27. M. Sheeran, S. Singh, and G. Stalmarck. Checking safety properties using induction and a SAT-solver. In *FMCAD*, 2000.
28. C. Wang, B. Li, H. Jin, G. Hachtel, and F. Somenzi. Improving ariadne's bundle by following multiple threads in abstraction refinement. In *ICCAD*, 2003.
29. J. Whittemore, J. Kim, and K. Sakallah. Satire: A new incremental satisfiability engine. In *DAC*, 2001.

Exploiting Constraints in Transformation-Based Verification

Hari Mony[1,2], Jason Baumgartner[1], and Adnan Aziz[2]

[1] IBM Systems & Technology Group
[2] The University of Texas at Austin

Abstract. The modeling of design environments using constraints has gained widespread industrial application, and most verification languages include constructs for specifying constraints. It is therefore critical for verification tools to intelligently leverage constraints to enhance the overall verification process. However, little prior research has addressed the applicability of transformation algorithms to designs with constraints. Even when addressed, prior work lacks optimality and in cases violates constraint semantics. In this paper, we introduce the theory and practice of *transformation-based verification* in the presence of constraints. We discuss how various existing transformations, such as redundancy removal and retiming, may be optimally applied while preserving constraint semantics, including *dead-end states*. We additionally introduce novel constraint elimination, introduction, and simplification techniques that preserve property checking. We have implemented all of the techniques proposed in this paper, and have found their synergistic application to be critical to the automated solution of many complex verification problems with constraints.

1 Introduction

Constraints are pervasively used across a variety of verification frameworks. For example, the compositional verification framework advocates verifying a system by checking properties of its components using *assume-guarantee* reasoning. The assumptions that a component's environment needs to satisfy are often modeled using constraints. The modeling of verification environments using constraints has gained widespread industrial acceptance [1], and most industrial verification languages include constructs to specify constraints – for example, PSL [2], CBV [3], and *e* [4]. Constraints are also used to implement case-splitting strategies to enhance complex verification tasks, for example, arithmetic and datapath correctness [5,6].

Given their pervasiveness, it is important for verification algorithms to leverage constraints to enhance the overall verification process. However, it is even more critical to preserve constraint semantics during this process. The concept of *transformation-based verification* (TBV) has been proposed to synergistically apply various automated transformation algorithms to simplify and decompose complex problems into simpler problems which may be solved with exponentially lesser resources [7,8]. However, little prior research has addressed the applicability of various transformation algorithms in the presence of constraints. Additionally, in some cases prior research lacks optimality, and does not even guarantee the preservation of constraint semantics. For example, an

D. Borrione and W. Paul (Eds.): CHARME 2005, LNCS 3725, pp. 269–284, 2005.

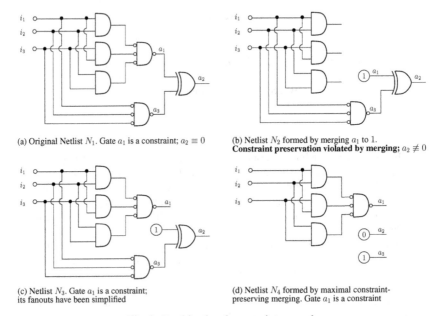

(a) Original Netlist N_1. Gate a_1 is a constraint; $a_2 \equiv 0$

(b) Netlist N_2 formed by merging a_1 to 1.
Constraint preservation violated by merging; $a_2 \not\equiv 0$

(c) Netlist N_3. Gate a_1 is a constraint;
its fanouts have been simplified

(d) Netlist N_4 formed by maximal constraint-
preserving merging. Gate a_1 is a constraint

Fig. 1. Combinational constraint example

approach for simplifying a combinational netlist in the presence of constraints is proposed in [9] as part of a Boolean-reasoning framework, which suffers these weaknesses.

Constraint-preserving testcase generation for simulation has been widely resear-
ched, e.g., in [10,11]. These solutions, however, do not address preservation of *dead-
end constraints* which entail states for which there is no legal input stimulus. Dead-end
constraints tend to reduce the efficiency of explicit-state analysis, as well as semi-formal
search; when a dead-end state is reached, the only recourse is to backtrack to an earlier state. Though dead-end constraints are considered *user errors* in certain method-
ologies [10], they are specifiable in a variety of languages, and in cases are powerful
constructs for modeling verification tasks and case-splitting strategies [5].

Constraint Challenges to TBV. Constraints specify conditions that must hold in any
state explored by a verification algorithm. To illustrate the impact of constraints, consider the combinational netlist illustrated in Figure 1. In the original netlist N_1, gate
a_2 could evaluate to 1 (e.g., if $i_1 = 1$ and $i_2 = i_3 = 0$) or 0 (e.g., if $i_1 = i_2 = i_3 = 0$).
However, labeling gate a_1 as a constraint would force at least two of i_1, i_2, i_3 to evaluate to 1, in turn forcing gate a_3 to evaluate to 1 and a_2 to evaluate to 0. For optimality,
it is desirable to leverage the constraint to simplify the netlist accordingly. In [9], a
structural conjunctive decomposition of the constraint is proposed, traversing each constraint gate fanin-wise through AND gates and stopping at inversion points and other
gate types, merging each of these terminal gates to constant ONE. Applying this algorithm to netlist N_1, gate a_1 will be merged to constant ONE. However, this merging
fails to preserve constraint semantics as gate a_2 in the resulting netlist N_2 could evaluate to 1 (if $i_1 = i_2 = i_3 = 0$). This demonstrates that redundancy removal applications
must take precautions when leveraging constraints to increase their reduction potential.

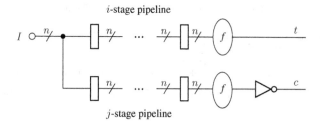

i-stage pipeline

j-stage pipeline

Fig. 2. Sequential constraint example

In a sequential netlist, constraints pose additional challenges as illustrated by the example depicted in Figure 2. Constraint c disallows precisely the input sequences that can evaluate t to 1. If $j > i$, then t can evaluate to 1 as the constraint precludes such paths only at a later time-step. If on the other hand $j \leq i$, constraint c prevents t from ever evaluating to 1. This demonstrates that temporal abstractions like retiming [7], which may effectively alter the values of i and j, must take precautions to ensure that constraint semantics are preserved through their transformations.

Contributions. In this paper we make several fundamental contributions to improving the efficiency of constraint-based verification frameworks [1].

1. We are the first to discuss how various existing automated transformation algorithms may be optimally applied in a property-preserving manner to designs with constraints. Table 1 enumerates these transformations, along with an overview of the corresponding challenges and solutions. *Overapproximation* refers to the risk of the transformation yielding spurious counterexamples. *Underapproximation* refers to the risk of the transformation yielding an incorrect proof of correctness.
2. We introduce fully-automated techniques for eliminating, introducing, and simplifying constraints in a property-preserving manner, enumerated in Table 2.

We have implemented all of these techniques in a verification toolset. We have found each of these techniques to be useful in the verification of designs with constraints. Fur-

Table 1. Contributions to enable transformations in the presence of constraints

Section	Technique	Challenge	Solution
3	Redundancy Removal	Merging within constraint cones may lead to overapproximation.	Disallow merging within a constraint cone, if redundancy proof *requires* that constraint.
4	Retiming	Varying lags of targets and constraints may lead to overapproximation as well as underapproximation.	Force identical lags across all target and constraint gates in retiming graph. Re-apply unfolded constraints to recurrence structure.
5	Target Enlargement	Transition-function based methods may lose correlation between constraint and target cones, leading to overapproximation.	Force application of constraints to each functional preimage prior to input quantification.
6	Reparameter-ization	Dead-end states may be lost through the transformation, leading to overapproximation.	Re-apply dead-end states as a simplified constraint.
7	Phase Abstraction	State folding may cause underapproximation if targets and constraints are of different *phase*.	Methodologically require all targets and constraints to be of the same phase.
8	C-Slow Abstraction	State folding may cause underapproximation if targets and constraints are of different *colors*.	Methodologically require all targets and constraints to be of the same color.
8	C-Slow Abstraction	Abstraction loses correlation across differing mod-c time-frames, causing overapproximation.	Methodologically disallow constraints that are not amenable to mod-c reasoning.

Table 2. Constraint transformation contributions

Section	Technique	Description
10	Constraint Elimination	Replace the constraint with an *accumulator circuit* to *remember* whether the constraint signal has been previously violated; conjunct to the target.
11	Constraint Introduction	Attempt to derive conditions after which targets are never hittable; add as constraints.
12	Constraint Simplification	Attempt to replace a constraint with its preimage, to reduce the size of its cone and enable its elimination through reparameterization.

thermore, we have found that the *synergistic* application of these techniques is capable of yielding dramatic improvements to the verification of such designs, enabling conclusive results to problems that we have otherwise found unsolvable. Though we focus on the application of these techniques to formal verification, their structural nature enables their benefits to arbitrary frameworks, including testcase generation and synthesis.

2   Formalisms

In this section, we provide formalisms used throughout the paper. A reader well-versed in hardware verification may wish to skip this section, using it as a reference.

Definition 1. A *netlist* is a tuple $N = \langle \langle V, E \rangle, G, T, C, Z \rangle$ comprising a finite directed graph with vertices V and edges $E \subseteq V \times V$, a semantic mapping from vertices to gate types $G : V \mapsto types$, a set of *targets* $T \subseteq V$ correlating to a set of properties $AG(\neg t), \forall t \in T$, and a set of *constraints* $C \subseteq V$. The function $Z : V \mapsto V$ is the symbolic initial value mapping.

Our verification problem is represented entirely as a netlist, comprising the *design under verification*, its *environment*, and its *property automata*. Our gate *types* define a set of primary inputs, registers (our only sequential gate type), and combinational gates with various functions, including constants. The type of a gate may place constraints upon its incoming edge count – e.g., each register has an indegree of one (whose source gate is referred to as its *next-state function*); primary inputs and constants have an indegree of zero. We denote the set of inputs as $I \subseteq V$, and the set of registers as $R \subset V$. The initial values of a netlist represent the values that registers can take at time 0. We disallow registers from appearing in any initial value functions. Furthermore, we do not allow combinational cycles in a legal netlist.

Definition 2. The *semantics of a netlist* N are defined in terms of semantic traces. We denote the set of all legal traces associated with a netlist by $P \subseteq [V \times \mathbb{N} \mapsto \{0, 1\}]$, defining P as the subset of functions from $V \times \mathbb{N}$ to $\{0, 1\}$ which are consistent with the following rule. The value of gate v at time i in trace p is denoted by $p(v, i)$. Term u_j denotes the source vertex of the j-th incoming edge to v, implying that $(u_j, v) \in E$.

$$p(v, i) = \begin{cases} s_{v_p}^i & : v \text{ is a primary input with sampled value } s_{v_p}^i \\ G_v\big(p(u_1, i), ..., p(u_n, i)\big) & : v \text{ is a combinational gate with function } G_v \\ p(u_1, i - 1) & : v \text{ is a register and } i > 0 \\ p\big(Z(v), 0\big) & : v \text{ is a register and } i = 0 \end{cases}$$

1. Guess the *redundancy candidates* – i.e., suspected-equivalent gate sets.
2. Attempt to prove that each pair of candidates is truly equivalent.
3. If any of the candidate pairs cannot be proven equivalent, refine them and goto Step 2.
4. The redundancy candidates are accurate; the corresponding gates may be merged.

Fig. 3. Generic redundancy removal algorithm

The length of a trace p is defined as $length(p) = \min\{i : \exists c \in C. \, p(c, i) = 0\}$. A target t is said to be hit in a trace t at time i iff $(p(t, i) = 1) \wedge (i < length(p))$. We define $hit(p, t)$ as the minimum i at which t is hit in trace p, or -1 if no such i exists.

Definition 3. Netlists N and N' are said to be *property-preserving trace equivalent* with respect to target sets T and T' respectively, iff there exists a bijective mapping $\psi : T \mapsto T'$ such that:

- $\forall p \in P. \exists p' \in P'. \forall t \in T. \big(hit(p, t) = hit(p', \psi(t))\big)$
- $\forall p' \in P'. \exists p \in P. \forall t \in T. \big(hit(p, t) = hit(p', \psi(t))\big)$

3   Redundancy Removal

Redundancy removal (e.g., [9,12]) is the process of demonstrating that two gates in a netlist always evaluate to the same value. Once a pair of redundant gates are identified, the netlist may be simplified by *merging* one of the gates onto the other; i.e., by replacing each fanout reference to one gate by a reference to the other. For property checking, it is sufficient to reason about the prefix *length* of a trace as per Definition 2. Constraints therefore generally cause more gates to appear redundant (within this prefix) than otherwise. For optimality, redundancy removal algorithms should thus leverage the constraints to increase their reduction potential. For example, when using the framework of Figure 3, the algorithms which identify redundancy candidates in Step 1 and the algorithms which prove each of the candidates redundant in Step 2 must leverage the constraints to avoid a loss of reduction potential. However, as per Figure 1b, once redundant gates have been identified, proper care must be taken while merging them to avoid violating constraint semantics.

Theorem 1. Consider gate u which is not in the cone of constraint set $U \subseteq C$. Gate u may be merged onto any other gate v while preserving property checking provided that the proof of $u \equiv v$ does not require the trace-prefixing effect of constraints $C \backslash U$.

Proof. (Sketch) Since $u \equiv v$ within all valid trace prefixes, the only risk of violating property checking due to this merge is that the constraining power of a constraint gate is diminished as per Figures 1a-1b. By Definition 2, the merge of u onto v only alters the evaluation of gates in the fanout of u. However, since the trace-prefixing effect of no constraint in the fanout of u was leveraged to enable the merge, this merge cannot diminish the constraining power of the resulting netlist.   □

Theorem 1 illustrates that gates outside of the cone of the constraints may be merged without violating constraint semantics, though care must be taken when merging gates within the cones of the constraints to ensure that their constraining power is not diminished. Netlist N_4 of Figure 1d illustrates the result of optimal property-preserving redundancy removal of netlist N_1. In Section 6, we will address the property-preserving elimination of gates within the cones of constraints whose trace-prefixing may be used to enable that elimination via the technique of structural reparameterization.

4   Retiming

Retiming is a synthesis optimization technique capable of reducing the number of registers of a netlist by relocating them across combinational gates [13].

Definition 4. A *retiming* of netlist N is a gate labeling $r : V \mapsto \mathbb{Z}$, where $r(v)$ is the *lag* of gate v, denoting the number of registers that are moved backward through v. A *normalized retiming* r' may be obtained from an arbitrary retiming r, and is defined as $r' = r - \max_{v \in V} r(v)$.

In [7], normalized retiming is proposed for enhanced invariant checking. The retimed netlist $\tilde{N}$ has two components: **(1)** a sequential *recurrence structure* $\tilde{N}'$ which has a unique representative for each combinational gate in the original netlist N, and whose registers are placed according to Definition 4, and **(2)** a combinational *retiming stump* $\tilde{N}''$ obtained through unfolding, representing retimed initial values as well as the functions of combinational gates for prefix time-steps that were effectively discarded from the recurrence structure. It is demonstrated in [7] that each gate $\tilde{u}'$ within $\tilde{N}'$ is trace-equivalent to the corresponding u within N, modulo a temporal skew of $-r(u)$ time-steps. Furthermore, there will be $-r(u)$ correspondents to this u within $\tilde{N}''$, each being trace-equivalent to u for one time-step during this temporal skew. Property checking of target t is thus performed in two stages: a bounded check of the time-frames of t occurring within the unfolded retiming stump, and a fixed-point check of $\tilde{t}'$ in the recurrence structure. If a trace is obtained over $\tilde{N}'$, it may be mapped to a corresponding trace in N by reversing the $\langle gate,\ time \rangle$ relation inherent in the retiming.

Theorem 2. Consider a normalized retiming where every target and constraint gate is lagged by the same value $-i$. Property checking will be preserved provided that:

1. the i-step bounded analysis of the retiming stump enforces all constraints across all time-frames, and
2. every retimed constraint gate, as well as every unfolded time-frame of a constraint referenced in a retimed initial value in $\tilde{N}'$, is treated as a constraint when verifying the recurrence structure.

Proof. (Sketch) Correctness of (1) follows by construction of the bounded analysis. Correctness of (2) follows from the observation that: **(a)** every gate lagged by $-i$ time-steps (including all targets and constraints) is trace-equivalent to the corresponding original gate modulo a skew of i time-steps, and **(b)** the trace pruning caused by constraint violations within the retiming stump is propagated into the recurrence structure by reapplication of the unfolded constraint gates referenced in the retimed initial values.   □

Compute $f(t)$ as the function of the target t to be enlarged;
Compute $f(c_i)$ as the function of each constraint c_i;
$B_0 = \exists I.(f(t) \wedge \bigwedge_{c_i \in C} f(c_i));$
for $(k = 1; \neg done; k{+}{+})$ {   // Enlarge up to arbitrary termination criteria $done$
   If t may be hit at time $k-1$ while adhering to constraints, return the corresponding trace;
   $B_k = \exists I.(preimage(B_{k-1}) \wedge \bigwedge_{c_i \in C} f(c_i));$
   Simplify B_k by applying $B_0, \ldots, B_{k-1}$ as $don't\ cares;$
}
Synthesize B_k using a standard multiplexor-based synthesis as the enlarged target $t';$
If t' is proven unreachable, report t as unreachable;
If trace p' is obtained hitting t' at time j {
   Cast a k-step constraint-satisfying unfolding from the state in p' at time j to hit $t;$
   Concatenate the resulting trace p'' onto p' to form trace p hitting t at time $k + j;$ return $p;$ }

Fig. 4. Target enlargement algorithm

The min-area retiming problem may be cast as a minimum-cost flow problem [13]. One may efficiently model the restriction of Theorem 2 by *renaming* the target and constraint gates to a single vertex in the retiming graph, which inherits all fanin and fanout edges of the original gates. This modeling forces the retiming algorithm to yield an optimal solution under the equivalent-lag restriction. While this restriction may clearly impact the optimality of the solution, it is generally necessary for property preservation.

5   Structural Target Enlargement

Target enlargement [14] is a technique to render a target t' which may be hit at a shallower depth from the initial states of a netlist, and with a higher probability, than the original target t. Target enlargement uses preimage computation to calculate the set of states which may hit target t within k time-steps. A transition-function vs. a transition-relation based preimage approach may be used for greater scalability. Inductive simplification may be performed upon the k-th preimage to eliminate states which hit t in fewer than k time-steps. The resulting set of states may be synthesized as the enlarged target t'. If t' is unreachable, then t must also be unreachable. If t' is hit in trace p', a corresponding trace p hitting t may be obtained by casting a k-step bounded search from the state hitting t' in p' which is satisfiable by construction, and concatenating the result onto p' to form p. The modification of traditional target enlargement necessary in the presence of constraints is depicted in Figure 4.

Theorem 3. The target enlargement algorithm of Figure 4 preserves property checking.

Proof. (Sketch) The constraint-preserving bounded analysis used during the target enlargement process will generate a valid trace, or guarantee that the target cannot be hit at times $0, \ldots, k - 1$, by construction. To ensure that the set of enlarged target states may reach the original target along a trace which does not violate constraints, the constraint functions are conjuncted onto each preimage prior to input quantification. The correctness of *target unreachable* results, as well as the trace lifting process, relies upon the fact that there exists an k-step extension of any trace hitting t' which hits t as established in [14], here extended to support constraints.   □

There is a noteworthy relation between retiming a target t by $-k$ and performing a k-step target enlargement of t; namely, both approaches yield an abstracted target which may be hit k time-steps shallower than the corresponding original target. Recall that with retiming, we retimed the constraints in lock-step with the targets. With target enlargement, however, we retain the constraints intact. There is one fundamental reason for this distinction: target enlargement yields sets of states which only preserve the *hittability* of targets, whereas retiming more tightly preserves trace equivalence modulo a time skew. This relative weakness of property preservation with target enlargement is due to its input quantification and preimage accumulation via the don't cares. If preimages were performed to *enlarge* the constraints, there is a general risk that a trace hitting the enlarged target while preserving the enlarged constraints may not be extendable to a trace hitting the original target, due to possible conflicts among the input valuations between the constraint and target cones in the original netlist. For example, a constraint could evaluate to 0 whenever an input i_1 evaluates to 1, and a target could be hittable only several time-steps after i_1 evaluates to 1. If we enlarged the constraint and target by one time-step, we would lose the unreachability of the target under the constraint because we would quantify away the effect of i_1 upon the constraint.

6   Structural Reparameterization

Definition 5. A *cut of a netlist* is a partition of V into two sets: C and $\overline{C} = V \setminus C$. A cut induces a set of *cut gates* $V_C = \{u \subseteq C : \exists v \in \overline{C}.(((u,v) \in E) \vee (v \in R \wedge u = Z(v)))\}$.

Reparameterization techniques, e.g., [15], operate by identifying a cut of a netlist graph V_C, enumerating the valuations sensitizable to that cut (its *range*), then synthesizing the range relation and replacing the fanin-side of the cut by this new logic. In order to guarantee soundness and completeness for property checking, one must generally guarantee that target and constraint gates lie on the cut or its fanout. Given parametric variables p^i for each cut gate V_C^i, the range is computable as $\exists I. \bigwedge_{i=1}^{|V_C|} (p^i \equiv f(V_C^i))$. If any cut gate is a constraint, its parametric variable may be forced to evaluate to 1 in the range to ensure that the synthesized replacement logic inherently reflects the constrained input behavior. This cut gate will then become a constant ONE in the abstracted netlist, effectively being discarded.

While adequate for combinationally-driven constraints and a subset of sequentially-driven constraints, this straight-forward approach does not address the preservation of dead-end states. A postprocessing approach is thus necessary to identify those abstracted constraints which have dead-end states, and to re-apply the dead-end states as constraints in the abstracted netlist. This check consists of computing $\exists I.f(c_i)$ for every constraint gate c_i used to constrain the range. If not a tautology, the result represents dead-end states for which no input valuations are possible, hence a straight-forward multiplexor-based synthesis of the result may be used to create a logic cone to be tagged as a constraint in the abstracted netlist.

Theorem 4. Structural reparameterization preserves property checking, provided that any constraints used to restrict the computed range are re-applied as simplified dead-end constraints in the abstracted netlist.

Proof. (Sketch) The correctness of reparameterization without dead-end constraints follows from prior work, e.g., [15]. Note that reparameterization may replace any constraints by constant ONE in the abstracted netlist. Without the re-application of the dead-end states as a constraint, the abstracted netlist will thus be prone to allowing target hits beyond the dead-end states. The re-application of the dead-end states as a constraint closes this semantic gap, preserving falsification as well as proofs.   □

To illustrate the importance of re-applying dead-end constraints during reparameterization, consider a constraint of the form $i_1 \wedge r_1$ for input i_1 and register r_1. If this constraint is used to restrict the range of a cut, its replacement gate will become a constant ONE hence the constraint will be effectively discarded in the abstracted netlist. The desired byproduct of this restriction is that i_1 will be forced to evaluate to 1 in the function of all cut gates. However, the undesired byproduct is that the abstracted netlist will no longer disallow r_1 from evaluating to 0 without the reapplication of the dead-end constraint $\exists i_1.(i_1 \wedge r_1)$ or simply r_1. Because this re-application will ensure accurate trace-prefixing in the abstracted netlist, the range may be simplified by applying the dead-end state set as *don't cares* prior to its synthesis as noted in [11].

7   Phase Abstraction

Phase abstraction [16] is a technique for transforming a *latch-based* netlist to a register-based one. A latch is a gate with two inputs (*data* and *clock*), which acts as a buffer when its *clock* is active and holds its last-sampled *data* value (or initial value) otherwise. Topologically, a k-phase netlist may be k-colored such that latches of color i may only combinationally fan out to latches of color $((i + 1) \mod k)$; a combinational gate acquires the color of the latches in its combinational fanin. A modulo-k counter is used to clock the latches of color $(j \mod k)$ at time j. As such, the initial values of only the $(k-1)$ colored latches propagate into other latches. Phase abstraction converts one color of latches into registers, and the others into buffers, thereby reducing state element count and temporally *folding* traces modulo-k, which otherwise stutter.

Phase abstraction may not preserve property checking for netlists with constraints as illustrated by the following example. Assume that we have a 2-phase netlist with a target gate of color 1, and a constraint gate of color 0 which is unconditionally violated one time-step after the target evaluates to 1. Without phase abstraction, the target may be hittable since the constraint prefixes the trace only on the time-step after the target evaluates to 1. However, if we eliminate the color-0 latches via phase abstraction, the constraint becomes violated concurrently with the target's evaluation to 1, hence the target becomes unhittable. Nonetheless, there are certain conditions under which phase abstraction preserves property checking as per the following theorem.

Theorem 5. If each constraint and target gate is of the same color, phase abstraction preserves property checking.

Proof. *(Sketch)* The correctness of phase abstraction without constraints has been established in prior work, e.g., [16]. Because every constraint and target gate are of the same color i, they update concurrently at times j for which $((j \bmod k) = i)$. Phase abstraction will merely eliminate the stuttering at intermediate time-steps, but not temporally skew the updating of the constraints relative to the targets. Therefore, the trace prefixing of the constraints remains property-preserving under phase abstraction. $\Box$

Automatic approaches of attempting to establish the criteria of Theorem 5, e.g., via *padding* pipelined latch stages to the constraints to align them with the color of the targets, are not guaranteed to preserve property checking. The problem is that such approaches unconditionally delay the trace prefixing of the constraints, hence even a contradictory constraint which can never be satisfied at time zero – which thus renders all targets unhittable – may become contradictory only at some future time-step in the range $1, \ldots, (k-2)$. After phase abstraction, this delay will be either zero or one time-step; in the latter case, we have opened a hole during which phase abstracted targets may be hit, even if they are truly unhittable in the original netlist. Nonetheless, in most practical cases, one may methodologically specify their desired verification problem in a way that adheres to the criteria of Theorem 5.

8 C-Slow Abstraction

C-slow abstraction [17] is a state folding technique which is related to phase abstraction, though is directly applicable to register-based netlists. A c-slow netlist [13] has registers which may be c-colored such that registers of color i may only combinationally fan out to registers of color $((i + 1) \bmod c)$; a combinational gate acquires the color of the registers in its combinational fanin. Unlike k-phase netlists, the registers in a c-slow netlist update every time-step hence generally never stutter. Additionally, the initial value of every register may propagate to other registers. C-slow abstraction operates by transforming all but a single color of registers into buffers, thereby reducing register count and temporally *folding* traces modulo-c. To account for the initial values which would otherwise be lost by this transformation, an unfolding approach is used to inject the retained registers into all states reachable in time-frames $0, \ldots, (c-1)$.

As with phase abstraction, if the target and constraint gates are of differing colors, this abstraction risks converting some hittable targets to unhittable due to its temporal collapsing of register stages. Additionally, even the criteria of requiring all target and constraint gates to be of the same color as with Theorem 5 is not guaranteed to preserve property checking with c-slow abstraction. The problem is due to the fact that c-slow netlists do not stutter mod c. Instead, each time-step of the abstracted netlist correlates to c time-steps of the original netlist, with time-steps $i, c + i, 2 \cdot c + i, \ldots$ being evaluated for each $i < c$ *in parallel* due to the initial value accumulation. Reasoning across mod c time-frames is intrinsically impossible with c-slow abstraction; thus, in the abstracted netlist, there is generally no way to detect if a constraint was effectively violated at time $a \cdot c + i$ in the original netlist when evaluating a target at time $(a + 1) \cdot c + j$ for $i \neq j$. Even with an equivalent-color restriction, c-slow abstraction thus risks becoming *overapproximate* in the presence of constraints. Nonetheless, methodologically, constraints which are not amenable to this state-folding process are of little practical utility in c-slow netlists. Therefore, in most cases one may readily map an abstracted counterexample trace to one consistent with the original netlist, e.g., using satisfiability analysis to ensure constraint preservation during intermediate timesteps.

9   Approximating Transformations

Overapproximating Transformations. Various techniques have been developed for attempting to reduce the size of a netlist by overapproximating its behavior. Any target proven unreachable after overapproximation is guaranteed to be unreachable before overapproximation. However, if a target is hit in the overapproximated netlist, this may not imply that the corresponding target is hittable in the original netlist. Localization [18,19] is a common overapproximation technique which replaces a set of cut gates of the netlist by primary inputs. The abstracted cut can obviously simulate the behavior of the original cut, though the converse may not be possible.

Overapproximating transformations are directly applicable in the presence of constraints. Overapproximating a constraint cone only weakens its constraining power. For example, while the cone of target t and constraint c may overlap, after localizing the constraint cone it may only comprise localized inputs which do not appear within the target cone, thereby losing all of its constraining power on the target. Such constraint weakening is merely a form of overapproximation, which must already be addressed by the overall overapproximate framework. Both counterexample-based [18] and proof-based [19] localization schemes are applicable to netlists with constraints, as they will both attempt to yield a minimally-sized localized netlist such that the retained portion of the constraint and target cones will guarantee unreachability of the targets.

Underapproximating Transformations. Various techniques have been developed to reduce the size of a netlist while underapproximating its behavior. For example, unfolding only preserves a time-bounded slice of the netlist's behavior; case splitting (e.g., by merging inputs to constants) may restrict the set of traces of a netlist. Underapproximating transformations may safely be applied to a netlist with constraints, as underapproximating a constraint cone only strengthens its power. For example, if a constraint is of the form $i_1 \vee i_2$, underapproximating by merging i_1 to constant **ZERO** will force i_2 to constant **ONE** in the underapproximated netlist even though a target may be hit in the original netlist only while assigning i_2 to a 0. However, this restriction – which may cause unreachable results for targets which were hittable without the underapproximation – must already be addressed by the overall underapproximate framework. Target hits on the underapproximated netlist still imply valid hits on the original netlist even in the presence of constraints. Extensions to underapproximate frameworks to enable completeness – e.g., diameter bounding approaches for *complete* unfolding, and complete case splitting strategies – are directly applicable in the presence of constraints.

10   Constraint Elimination

Given the challenges that they pose to various algorithms, one may wish to eliminate constraints in a property-preserving manner. In Figure 5c, we introduce a general constraint elimination algorithm.

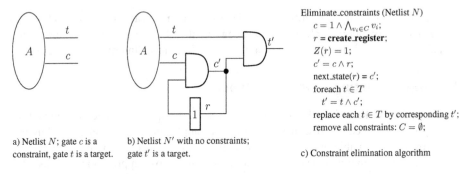

Eliminate_constraints (Netlist N)
$$c = 1 \land \bigwedge_{v_i \in C} v_i;$$
$r = \mathbf{create\_register};$
$Z(r) = 1;$
$c' = c \land r;$
$\mathrm{next\_state}(r) = c';$
foreach $t \in T$
$\quad t' = t \land c';$
replace each $t \in T$ by corresponding t';
remove all constraints: $C = \emptyset;$

a) Netlist N; gate c is a constraint, gate t is a target.

b) Netlist N' with no constraints; gate t' is a target.

c) Constraint elimination algorithm

Fig. 5. Property-preserving constraint elimination

Theorem 6. The constraint elimination algorithm of Figure 5c is a *property-preserving* transformation.

Proof. Consider any trace p that hits target t in netlist N at time i. Note that netlist N' has the same set of gates as N in addition to gates c', r, and t'. Consider the trace p' of N' where all common gates have the same valuations over time as in p, and gates c', r and t' are evaluated as per Definition 2. Because t is hit at time i, $\forall j \leq i.\big(p(c, j) = 1\big)$, and thus by construction of c', $\forall j \leq i.\big(p'(c', j) = 1\big)$. Because $t' = t \land c'$, we also have $\forall j \leq i.\big(p(t, j) = p'(t', j)\big)$. It may similarly be proven that for any trace p' that hits target t' at time i, there exists an equivalent trace p that hits target t at time i. □

Performing the constraint elimination transformation in Figure 5 enables arbitrary verification and transformation algorithms to be applied to the resulting netlist without risking the violation of constraint semantics. However, this approach could result in significant performance degradation for both types of algorithms:

- Transformation algorithms (particularly redundancy removal) lose their ability to leverage the constraints for optimal simplification of the netlist.
- Falsification algorithms may waste resources analyzing uninteresting states, i.e., from which no target may subsequently be hit due to c' evaluating to 0.
- The tactical utility of the constraints for case-splitting strategies is lost.

11   Constraint Introduction

It follows from the discussion of redundancy removal in Section 3 that reduction potential may be increased by constraints. It may therefore be desirable to derive constraints that may be introduced into the netlist while preserving property checking, at least temporarily to enhance a particular algorithm.

Theorem 7. Consider netlist N with gate g. If no target in T may be hit along any trace after gate g evaluates to 0, then g may be labeled as a constraint while preserving property checking.

Proof. If gate g is labeled as a constraint, by Definition 2, we will only reason about the prefix *length* of traces wherein gate g always evaluates to 1. Since no target in T may be hit along any trace after gate g evaluates to 0, by Definition 3, netlist N' formed from N by labeling gate g as a constraint is property-preserving trace equivalent to N.   □

Taking the example netlist of Figure 5b, any of the gates c, c', and r may be labeled as a constraint provided that we may establish the corresponding condition of Theorem 7, effectively reversing the transformation of Figure 5c. While this proof may in cases be as difficult as property checking itself, we propose an efficient heuristic algorithm for deriving such constraint candidate gates as follows. Similar to the approach of [20], we may localize each of the targets, and use a preimage fixed-point computation to underapproximate the number of time-steps needed to hit that target from a given set of states. Any state not reached during this fixed-point may never reach that target. The intersection of such state sets across all targets represents the conditions from which no target may subsequently be hit. While the approach of [20] proposes only to use this set to steer semi-formal analysis away from useless states, we propose to synthesize the resulting conditions as a constraint in the netlist to enhance reduction potential.

Note that these constraints are in a sense *redundant* because no target hits may occur after they evaluate to 0 anyway. Therefore, instead of forcing all algorithms to adhere to these constraints which may have an associated overhead, we may treat these as *verification don't cares* so that algorithms may choose to either use these constraints to restrict evaluation of the netlist, or to ignore them. Note that certain verification algorithms, e.g., SAT-based search, may inherently *learn* such conditions and direct their resources accordingly. Ours is a more general paradigm which enables leveraging this information for arbitrary algorithms, particularly to enhance reduction potential.

12   Constraint Simplification

In this section, we discuss a general approach to simplify constraints. We also discuss an efficient implementation of this paradigm which attempts to replace a constraint with its preimage, heuristically trying to reduce the size of the constraint cone and enable the elimination of that constraint through reparameterization.

We define $prop\_p(t, c)$ as the target gate resulting from applying the constraint elimination algorithm of Figure 5c specifically to target t and gate c.

Theorem 8. Consider a netlist N with constraint c_1 and gate c_2. If $\forall t \in T.\big(prop\_p(t, c_1) \equiv prop\_p(t, c_2)\big)$ without the trace-prefixing of constraint c_1, then converting N into N' by labeling c_2 as a constraint instead of c_1 is a property-preserving transformation.

Proof. Since $\forall t \in T.\big(prop\_p(t, c_1) \equiv prop\_p(t, c_2)\big)$ without the trace-prefixing entailed by constraint c_1, this proof follows directly from Definition 3 and Theorem 6.   □

Theorem 8 illustrates that in certain cases, we may modify the constraint gates in a netlist while preserving property checking. Practically, we wish to exploit this theorem to shrink the size of the constraint cones and thereby effectively strengthen their reduction potential. Note that the structural reparameterization algorithm in Section 6 is able to eliminate constraints which have no dead-end states. This is in a sense an optimal

```
while (¬done)   // Iterate until arbitrary termination criteria done
    Apply structural reparameterization to simplify constraint c;
    If constraint c has been eliminated by reparameterization, break;
    // Else, note that c has been simplified to its dead-end states
    If (prop_p(t, c) ≡ prop_p(t, struct_pre(c)))
        c = struct_pre(c);
    else break; // constraint c cannot be safely replaced by its preimage
```

Fig. 6. Heuristic constraint simplification algorithm

transformation, as the constraining power of the constraints are thereafter reflected in the netlist structure itself and effectively filters the input stimulus applied to the netlist. Given these motivations, we present a heuristic constraint simplification algorithm.

Definition 6. The *structural preimage* of a gate u which has no inputs in its combinational fanin, $struct\_pre(u)$, is a logic cone obtained by replacing each register gate $v \in R$ in the combinational fanin of gate u with its corresponding next-state function.

The algorithm of Figure 6 attempts to iteratively simplify, and ultimately eliminate, the constraints in a property-preserving manner. At each iteration, reparameterization is used to replace the current constraint by its dead-end states. Note that this step will eliminate the constraint if it entails no dead-end states. Otherwise, we attempt to simplify the resulting sequential constraint by replacing it with its structural preimage, using Theorem 8 to validate that this replacement preserves property checking. If this check fails (either through refutation or excessive resource requirements), then the algorithm terminates. Otherwise, the algorithm iterates with the resulting simplified constraint.

To illustrate how this algorithm works in practice, consider its application on constraint c in the netlist of Figure 2. If $j \leq i$, constraint c can be iteratively replaced by its preimage until it becomes combinational, at which point reparameterization will outright eliminate it. If $j > i$, constraint c can be simplified by shrinking j to $i + 1$, at which point the check based upon Theorem 8 fails causing the iterations to terminate.

Practically, the equality check of Figure 6 tends to be computationally expensive. However, this check can be simplified as per the following theorem.

Definition 7. The *structural initialization* of a gate u which has no inputs in its combinational fanin, $struct\_init(u)$, is a logic cone obtained by replacing each register gate $v \in R$ in the combinational fanin of gate u with its corresponding initial value function. The initial value constraint of u is defined as $init\_cons(u) = init\_r \vee struct\_init(u)$, where $init\_r$ is a register whose initial value is **ZERO** and next-state function is **ONE**.

Theorem 9. Consider a netlist N with constraint c_1. If $\forall t \in T.(prop\_p(t, c_1) \implies prop\_p(t, struct\_pre(c_1)))$ in N with the trace-prefixing entailed by constraint c_1, then converting N into N' by labeling $struct\_pre(c_1)$ and $init\_cons(c_1)$ as constraints instead of c_1 is a property-preserving transformation.

Proof. **(1)** The implication proof in N means that within the prefix of any trace, either the two gates evaluate to the same value, or $prop\_p(t, c_1)$ evaluates to 0 and $prop\_p(t, struct\_pre(c_1))$ to 1. The latter condition cannot happen since within any prefix, constraint c_1 must evaluate to 1, which implies that t cannot evaluate to 1 and $prop\_p(t, c_1)$ to 0 concurrently. The implication proof thus ensures that if t is asserted within any prefix at time i, then $struct\_pre(c_1)$ must evaluate to 1 at times 0 to i.

(2) Since N and N' have the same set of gates, they also have the same set of traces; only the constraint sets differ. The trace prefixing of N' is stricter than that of N as follows. (a) All traces prefixed at time 0 because of constraint c_1 in netlist N are also prefixed at time 0 because of constraint $init\_cons(c_1)$ in N'. (b) All traces prefixed at time $i + 1$ because of constraint c_1 in netlist N are prefixed at time i because of constraint $struct\_pre(c_1)$ in N'.

(3) For property-preservation, we must only ensure that target t cannot be asserted during time-steps that were prefixed in N' but not N. During such time-steps, c_1 evaluates to 1, and $struct\_pre(c_1)$ to 0, hence $prop\_p\big(t, struct\_pre(c_1)\big)$ must evaluate to 0. The proof of this implication check thus requires $prop\_p(t, c_1)$ to evaluate to 0 at such time-steps, ensuring that t evaluates to 0.   □

Practically, we have found that the trace-prefixing of c_1 substantially reduces the complexity of the proof obligation of Theorem 9 vs. Theorem 8, e.g., by enabling low cost inductive proofs. This check tends to be significantly easier than the property check itself, as it merely attempts to validate that the modified constraint does not *alter* the hittability of the target along any trace, independently of whether the target is hittable or not. Additionally note that $init\_r$ can readily be eliminated using retiming.

13 Conclusion

We have discussed how various automated netlist transformations may be optimally applied while preserving constraint semantics, including *dead-end states*. We have additionally introduced fully-automated techniques for constraint elimination, introduction, and simplification. We have implemented each of these techniques in the IBM internal transformation-based verification tool *SixthSense*. The synergistic application of these techniques has been critical to the automated solution of many complex industrial verification problems with constraints, which we otherwise were unable to solve.

Due to the relative lack of availability of complex sequential netlists with constraints, we do not provide detailed experimental results. The only relevant benchmarks we are aware of are a subset of the IBM FV Benchmarks [21]. These constraints are purely sequential, thus preventing their optimal elimination through reparameterization alone. However, we were able to leverage transformations such as retiming and constraint simplification to enable reparameterization to optimally eliminate 2 of 2 constraints from IBM_03 and IBM_06; 3 of 4 from IBM_10; 5 of 8 from IBM_11; and 11 of 14 from IBM_24.

References

1. C. Pixley, "Integrating model checking into the semiconductor design flow," in *Electronic Systems Technology & Design*, 1999.
2. Accelera. PSL LRM, http://www.eda.org/vfv.
3. M. Kaufmann, A. Martin, and C. Pixley, "Design constraints in symbolic model checking," in *Computer-Aided Verification*, 1998.

4. Y. Hollander, M. Morley, and A. Noy, "The *e* language: A fresh separation of concerns," in *Technology of Object-Oriented Languages and Systems*, 2001.
5. P. Jain and G. Gopalakrishnan, "Efficient symbolic simulation-based verification using the parametric form of Boolean expressions," *IEEE Transactions on CAD*, April 1994.
6. M. D. Aagaard, R. B. Jones, and C.-J. H. Seger, "Formal verification using parametric representations of Boolean constraints," in *Design Automation Conference*, June 1999.
7. A. Kuehlmann and J. Baumgartner, "Transformation-based verification using generalized retiming," in *Computer-Aided Verification*, July 2001.
8. H. Mony, J. Baumgartner, V. Paruthi, R. Kanzelman, and A. Kuehlmann, "Scalable automated verification via expert-system guided transformations," in *FMCAD*, Nov. 2004.
9. A. Kuehlmann, V. Paruthi, F. Krohm, and M. Ganai, "Robust Boolean reasoning for equivalence checking and functional property verification," *IEEE Transactions on CAD*, Dec. 2002.
10. J. Yuan, K. Shultz, C. Pixley, H. Miller, and A. Aziz, "Modeling design constraints and biasing in simulation using BDDs," in *ICCAD*, 1999.
11. J. Yuan, K. Albin, A. Aziz, and C. Pixley, "Constraint synthesis for environment modeling in functional verification," in *Design Automation Conference*, 2003.
12. H. Mony, J. Baumgartner, V. Paruthi, and R. Kanzelman, "Exploiting suspected redundancy without proving it," in *Design Automation Conference*, 2005.
13. C. Leiserson and J. Saxe, "Retiming synchronous circuitry," *Algorithmica*, vol. 6, 1991.
14. J. Baumgartner, A. Kuehlmann, and J. Abraham, "Property checking via structural analysis," in *Computer-Aided Verification*, July 2002.
15. J. Baumgartner and H. Mony, "Maximal input reduction of sequential netlists via synergistic reparameterization and localization strategies," in *CHARME*, Oct. 2005.
16. J. Baumgartner, T. Heyman, V. Singhal, and A. Aziz, "An abstraction algorithm for the verification of level-sensitive latch-based netlists," *Formal Methods in System Design*, (23) 2003.
17. J. Baumgartner, A. Tripp, A. Aziz, V. Singhal, and F. Andersen, "An abstraction algorithm for the verification of generalized C-slow designs," in *Computer-Aided Verification*, July 2000.
18. E. Clarke, A. Gupta, J. Kukula, and O. Strichman, "SAT based abstraction-refinement using ILP and machine learning techniques," in *Computer-Aided Verification*, July 2002.
19. K. L. McMillan and N. Amla, "Automatic abstraction without counterexamples," in *Tools and Algorithms for Construction and Analysis of Systems*, April 2004.
20. P. Bjesse and J. Kukula, "Using counter example guided abstraction refinement to find complex bugs," in *Design Automation and Test in Europe*, 2004.
21. IBM Formal Verification Benchmark Library. http://www.haifa.il.ibm.com/projects/verification/RB_Homepage/fvbenchmarks.html.

Identification and Counter Abstraction for Full Virtual Symmetry

Ou Wei, Arie Gurfinkel, and Marsha Chechik

Department of Computer Science, University of Toronto
{owei, arie, chechik}@cs.toronto.edu

Abstract. Symmetry reduction is an effective approach for dealing with the state explosion problem: when applicable, it enables exponential statespace reduction. Thus, it is appealing to extend the power of symmetry reduction to systems which are "not quite symmetric". Emerson et al. identified a class of these, called *virtually* symmetric [9]. In this paper, we study symmetry from the point of view of abstraction, which allows us to present an efficient procedure for identifying full virtual symmetry. We also explore techniques for combining virtual symmetry with symbolic model-checking and report on experiments that illustrate the feasibility of our approach.

1 Introduction

Symmetry reduction (e.g., [7,10]) is a technique for combating the state explosion problem in model-checking. Symmetry is naturally exhibited in systems or protocols that consist of synchronization and coordination of several identical processes. Such symmetry can be seen as a form of redundancy, and model checking can then be performed on the symmetry-reduced quotient structure which is bisimilar to, and often substantially smaller than, the original system structure. Unfortunately, many protocols are not symmetric: even in cases where process descriptions exhibit a high degree of similarity, a slight difference among them results in an asymmetric global behavior. To extend symmetry reduction to such systems, Emerson et al. [9] defined *virtual symmetry* as the most general condition under which the structure of a system is bisimilar to its symmetry-reduced quotient structure, and thus symmetry reduction can be applied.

Although virtual symmetry increases a potential domain of problems that can be symmetry reduced, its practical application depends on successful solutions to the following questions: (1) How does one identify virtual symmetry without building the entire system (which is typically infeasible)? (2) How does one apply the knowledge that a system is virtually symmetric to effectively solve the resulting *symbolic* model-checking problem?

In this paper, we answer these questions for *fully* virtually symmetric systems, i.e., systems which are virtually symmetric up to exchanging the roles of processes. This form of symmetry typically arises in systems composed of processes which are similar but not identical due to different priorities for accessing a shared resource. An example of such a system is Readers-and-Writers (R&W): a variant of a well-known mutual exclusion protocol (MUTEX), where writer processes are given a higher priority than

D. Borrione and W. Paul (Eds.): CHARME 2005, LNCS 3725, pp. 285–300, 2005.

reader processes for entering the critical section [9]. Like full symmetry, full virtual symmetry may lead to an exponential reduction on the statespace of the system.

We start by formalizing the connection between symmetry reduction and abstraction in Section 3, and use it to derive an alternative (and simpler) characterization of virtual symmetry. The remainder of the work reported here is based on this characterization.

We then address the problem of effectively identifying full virtual symmetry. In practice, full symmetry of a system is ensured by restricting its description using a special syntax [11,12]. In Section 4, we show that lack of regularity in asymmetric systems makes it difficult to capture the restrictions that ensure full virtual symmetry syntactically. However, based on our characterization of virtual symmetry, we show that identification of full virtual symmetry can be reduced to satisfiability of a quantifier-free Presburger (QFP) formula built directly from the syntactic description of the system.

Afterwards, we turn to the problem of combining symbolic model-checking with symmetry reduction. The naive construction of a symmetry-reduced quotient structure requires building an orbit relation, which defines the orbit equivalence between states. Clarke et al. [7] proved that BDD-based symbolic representation of the orbit relation is often exponential. Thus, it was assumed that symmetry and symbolic model-checking do not mix well. However, Emerson et al. [11,12] have shown that the quotient of a fully symmetric system can be constructed without the orbit relation via a *generic representatives* (or counter abstraction) technique. In Section 5, we extend this technique to handle fully virtually symmetric systems.

In Section 6, we report on experiments of identifying full virtual symmetry and applying counter abstraction-based symbolic model-checking on two families of systems. Section 7 concludes the paper and compares our result with related work.

2   Background

We assume that the reader is familiar with symmetry reduction. Below, we recall some specific concepts and fix the notation.

Structures and Simulations. A structure M is a pair (S, R) where S is a finite set of states and $R \subseteq S \times S$ is the transition relation. The domain of R is denoted by $Dom(R) \triangleq \{s \in S \mid \exists t \in S \cdot (s,t) \in R\}$. We use $s \to t$ and (s,t) interchangeably to denote a transition in R.

Let $M_1 = (S_1, R_1)$ and $M_2 = (S_2, R_2)$ be two structures. Then, M_2 *simulates* M_1 with respect to a relation $\rho \subseteq S_1 \times S_2$, denoted by $M_1 \preceq_\rho M_2$, if and only if for $(s_1, s_2) \in \rho$, the following condition holds:

$\forall t_1 \in S_1 \cdot (s_1, t_1) \in R_1 \Rightarrow \exists t_2 \in S_2 \cdot (s_2, t_2) \in R_2 \wedge (t_1, t_2) \in \rho$

Furthermore, M_2 is *bisimilar* to M_1 with respect to ρ, denoted by $M_1 \equiv_\rho M_2$, if both $M_1 \preceq_\rho M_2$ and $M_2 \preceq_{\rho^{-1}} M_1$.

Symmetry Reduction. Let $M = (S, R)$ be a structure and G be a permutation group on S. The group G induces an equivalence partition on S. The equivalence class of a state s is called the *orbit* of s under G, defined by $\theta_G(s) \triangleq \{s' \in S \mid \exists \sigma \in G \cdot \sigma(s) = s'\}$. We use $\theta(s)$ to denote the orbit of s when G is clear from the context. The extension of θ to a set of states $Q \subseteq S$ is defined by $\theta(Q) \triangleq \bigcup_{s \in Q} \theta(s)$.

The *quotient structure* of M induced by G is $M^G = (S^G, R^G)$ where $S^G \triangleq \{\theta(s) \mid s \in S\}$, and $\forall s, t \in S \cdot (\theta(s), \theta(t)) \in R^G \Leftrightarrow \exists s' \in \theta(s) \cdot \exists t' \in \theta(t) \cdot (s', t') \in R$. A permutation group G is an *automorphism group* for M if it preserves the transition relation R, i.e., $\forall s, t \in S \cdot (s, t) \in R \Rightarrow \forall \sigma \in G \cdot (\sigma(s), \sigma(t)) \in R$. A structure M is called *symmetric* with respect to a permutation group G, if G is an automorphism group for it. In this case, M is bisimilar to its symmetry-reduced quotient structure.

Theorem 1. [7,10] *Let $M = (S, R)$ be a structure, G be a permutation group acting on S, and $\rho_G \triangleq \{(s, \theta(s)) \mid s \in S\}$. Then, $M \equiv_{\rho_G} M^G$ if G is an automorphism group for M.*

Note that temporal logics such as CTL* and modal μ-calculus are invariant under bisimulation [5]. Therefore, model checking a temporal logic formula φ on M can be reduced to model checking φ on M^G, provided that the atomic propositions of φ are preserved by ρ_G.

Compositional Structures. Symmetry reduction is often applied to a parallel composition of similar processes. Such a composition is modeled by a structure whose statespace is assignments of local states to each process.

Let $I = [1..n]$ be the index set of n processes which have the same set of local states $\mathcal{L}$. The composition of the processes is modeled by a *compositional structure* $M = (S, R)$, where $S = \mathcal{L}^n$. Then a global state s in S is an n-tuple $(l_1, \ldots, l_n) \in \mathcal{L}^n$. For each $i \in I$, we use $s(i)$ to denote the value of l_i, i.e., the current local state of the ith process, P_i, at s. Let $K \subseteq I$ be a set of processes. The *group counter* of a local state L with respect to K is a function $\#L[K] : \mathcal{L}^n \to [0..n]$ such that for any global state s, $\#L[K](s) = |\{i \in K \mid s(i) = L\}|$. That is, $\#L[K](s)$ is the number of processes in K whose current state at s is L. In particular, if $K = I$, we use $\#L$ to denote $\#L[I]$, and call $\#L$ the *total counter* of L.

The *full symmetry group* of I, i.e., the group of all permutations acting on I, is denoted by $Sym(I)$. A permutation $\sigma \in Sym(I)$ is extended to act on a state s of a compositional structure M as follows: $\forall i, j \in I \cdot \sigma(s)(i) = s(j) \Leftrightarrow \sigma(i) = j$. In the rest of the paper, we do not distinguish between a permutation group on S or I. A structure M is called *fully* symmetric if M is symmetric with respect to $Sym(I)$.

3 Abstraction and Virtual Symmetry

In this section, we formalize the connection between symmetry reduction and abstraction. We then show how this connection can be used to establish a necessary and sufficient condition for the application of symmetry reduction. This condition, referred to by Emerson et al. as *virtual symmetry* [9], generalizes the notion of automorphism-based symmetry [7,10] (see Theorem 1) and increases the applicability of symmetry reduction.

Given a structure $M = (S, R)$ and a set of *abstract* states S_α, an *abstraction* $\alpha : S \to S_\alpha$ is a total function that maps each state $s \in S$ to a state $a \in S_\alpha$. S and S_α are the *concrete* and the *abstract* statespaces, respectively. We define $\gamma : S_\alpha \to 2^S$ to be a *concretization function* that maps each abstract state s_α to a set of concrete states corresponding to it, i.e., $\gamma(a) \triangleq \{s \in S \mid \alpha(s) = a\}$. Following [8], we extend α to the

Table 1. A mapping between abstraction and symmetry reduction

Abstraction	Symmetry Reduction
abstract statespace : S_α	orbits induced by G: S^G
abstraction function : α	orbit function θ_G: $\alpha_G(s) \triangleq \theta_G(s)$
concretization function : γ	identity function: $\gamma_G(\theta_G(s)) \triangleq \theta_G(s)$
existential abstraction of R : $R_\alpha^{\exists\exists}$	quotient of R with respect to G: R^G
abstract equivalence: $\alpha(s) = \alpha(t)$	orbit equivalence: $\theta(s) = \theta(t) \Leftrightarrow \exists \sigma \in G \cdot s = \sigma(t)$

transition relation as follows. A relation $R_\alpha^{\exists\exists} \subseteq S_\alpha \times S_\alpha$ is an *existential abstraction* of R where $(a, b) \in R_\alpha^{\exists\exists}$ if and only if R has a transition between *some* concretizations of a and b; $R_\alpha^{\forall\exists}$ is a *universal abstraction* where $(a, b) \in R_\alpha^{\forall\exists}$ if and only if R has a transition from *every* concretization of a to *some* concretization of b:

$$R_\alpha^{\exists\exists} \triangleq \{(a,b) \mid \exists s \in \gamma(a) \cdot \exists t \in \gamma(b) \cdot R(s,t)\} \qquad \text{(existential abstraction)}$$
$$R_\alpha^{\forall\exists} \triangleq \{(a,b) \mid \forall s \in \gamma(a) \cdot \exists t \in \gamma(b) \cdot R(s,t)\} \qquad \text{(universal abstraction)}$$

Accordingly, we define $M_\alpha^{\exists\exists} = (S_\alpha, R_\alpha^{\exists\exists})$ and $M_\alpha^{\forall\exists} = (S_\alpha, R_\alpha^{\forall\exists})$ to be the existential and the universal abstractions of M, respectively.

Theorem 2. *Let* $\rho \subseteq S \times S_\alpha$ *be a relation defined as* $\rho \triangleq \{(s,a) \mid \alpha(s) = a\}$. *Then* M *is* ρ-*bisimilar to* $M_\alpha^{\exists\exists}$ *if and only if* $M_\alpha^{\exists\exists}$ *is isomorphic to* $M_\alpha^{\forall\exists}$: $M_\alpha^{\exists\exists} \equiv_\rho M \Leftrightarrow M_\alpha^{\exists\exists} = M_\alpha^{\forall\exists}$.

Symmetry reduction of a structure $M = (S, R)$ with respect to a permutation group G can be seen as a form of abstraction. Formally, let S^G, the set of orbits of S, be the abstract statespace, and let an abstraction $\alpha_G : S \to S^G$ map each state to its orbit, i.e., $\alpha_G(s) \triangleq \theta(s)$. Under this interpretation, the quotient M^G of M is equivalent to the existential abstraction of M. A mapping between key concepts in abstraction and symmetry reduction is summarized in Table 1.

Using this connection between symmetry and abstraction, we reinterpret Theorem 2 as a necessary and sufficient condition for bisimilarity between M and its quotient M^G. Note that

$$R_\alpha^{\exists\exists} = R_\alpha^{\forall\exists} \text{ if and only if } (s,t) \in R \Rightarrow \forall s' \in \gamma(\alpha(s)) \cdot \exists t' \in \gamma(\alpha(t)) \cdot (s',t') \in R$$

In the context of symmetry reduction, $\gamma(\alpha(s))$, the abstract equivalence class of s, is simply its orbit $\theta(s)$. Furthermore, s and s' share an orbit, i.e., $s' \in \theta(s)$ if and only if there exists a permutation $\sigma \in G$ such that $s' = \sigma(s)$. Combining the above, we obtain the following theorem.

Theorem 3. *Let* $M = (S, R)$ *be a structure,* G *be a permutation group acting on* S, *and* $\rho_G \triangleq \{(s, \theta(s)) \mid s \in S\}$. *Then,* $M \equiv_{\rho_G} M^G$ *if and only if*

$$\forall s, t \in S \cdot (s,t) \in R \Rightarrow \forall \sigma \in G \cdot \exists \sigma' \in G \cdot (\sigma(s), \sigma'(t)) \in R \qquad (1)$$

Note that Theorem 3 is a generalization of Theorem 1 since G is no longer required to be an automorphism group for M, and thus M is not necessarily symmetric with respect to G.

Definition 1. *A structure M is* virtually *symmetric with respect to a permutation group G if and only if $M \equiv_{\rho_G} M^G$.*

The problem of establishing a necessary and sufficient condition for a quotient M^G to be bisimilar to M has also been addressed by Emerson et al. [9]. Unlike us, they do not use abstraction, but proceed directly to show that M is virtually symmetric with respect to G if and only if it can be "completed" to a structure M' such that M' is both symmetric with respect to G and bisimilar to M. Thus, Theorem 3 provides an alternative (and, in our opinion, much simpler) characterization of virtual symmetry. In the rest of the paper, we show how this new characterization leads to an efficient symbolic model-checking algorithm for a large class of asymmetric systems.

4   Full Virtual Symmetry Identification using Constraints

In this section, we address the problem of identifying full virtual symmetry. Notice that we cannot simply use Condition (1) of Theorem 3 since it requires building the transition relation of the structure, which may not be feasible. We begin by reviewing existing modeling languages for specifying fully symmetric systems in Section 4.1 and then extend them to asymmetric systems in Section 4.2. In Section 4.3, we discuss conditions that ensure that the specified system is fully virtually symmetric, and show how to decide these conditions using constraints derived directly from the system description in Section 4.4.

4.1   Modeling Symmetric Systems

Consider an asynchronous composition of n processes $\{P_1, \ldots, P_n\}$ executing a common concurrent program. Each process is specified using a finite directed graph, called a *synchronization skeleton* [6]. Nodes in the graph represent states of the process, and edges, labeled with boolean expressions called *guards*, represent guarded transitions. For example, a synchronization skeleton of a process participating in MUTEX is shown in Figure 1(a). A MUTEX process has 3 states: Non-critical (N), Trying (T), and Critical (C); it can enter states N and T freely, but can only enter the state C if no other process is currently in state C.

When all processes have identical synchronization skeletons, their asynchronous composition can be specified using a single skeleton P. This skeleton can be seen as a template from which skeletons of each individual process are instantiated. Thus, Figure 1(a) is also a synchronization skeleton *template* for MUTEX.

A synchronization skeleton template P defines a compositional structure $M(P)$ in which a (global) transition results from a local transition of some process. For example, in the three-process MUTEX, $M(P)$ has a transition from (N, N, T) to (N, N, C) because the third process, P_3, can move from T to C.

Note that when each transition guard in P is invariant under any permutation of process indices, the structure $M(P)$ is unchanged by any permutation of process indices; that is, it is fully symmetric [11]. For example, the three-process MUTEX is fully symmetric since if the guard $(\#C = 0)$ is true in a state s, it is also true in a state $\sigma(s)$ for any permutation $\sigma \in Sym([1, 2, 3])$. Symmetry reduction of a fully symmetric

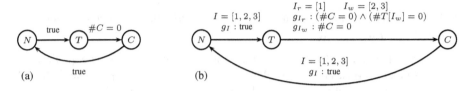

Fig. 1. (a) Synchronization Skeleton for MUTEX. (b) GSST for three-process R&W.

Table 2. Basic guard elements for ensuring full symmetry

Basic Elements	Predicates on Total Counters
$\forall i \cdot l_i = L, \forall i \cdot l_i \neq L$	$\#L = n, \#L = 0$
$\exists i \cdot l_i = L, \exists i \cdot l_i \neq L$	$\#L \geq 1, \#L \leq n - 1$
$\exists i \neq j \cdot l_i = L \wedge l_j = L$	$\#L \geq 2$

system can often yield an exponential reduction in the number of states. In practice, full symmetry of a synchronization skeleton is ensured by restricting basic elements of the guards to the ones shown in the left column of Table 2, where $l_i = L$ is true in a state s if the ith process is in a state L, i.e., $s(i) = L$. The basic elements can be equivalently expressed using total counters, as shown in the right column of Table 2 [11].

4.2 Modeling Asymmetric Systems

In this paper, we are interested in applying symmetry reduction to asymmetric systems composed of many similar, but not identical processes, such as R&W mentioned in Section 1. In this case, since the condition for entering the critical section is different between the two groups of processes (writers have a higher priority than readers), the system cannot be modeled by a single synchronization skeleton. Thus, for such asymmetric systems, we need both a more general modeling formalism, and an approach to identify whether the system is fully virtually symmetric. To address the first problem, we define a *generalized synchronization skeleton template*.

Definition 2. *A* generalized synchronization skeleton template *(GSST) for an asynchronous system with n processes is a tuple $P = (\mathcal{L}, \mathcal{R}, I, \tau)$, where $\mathcal{L}$ is a finite set of (local) states, $\mathcal{R} \subseteq \mathcal{L} \times \mathcal{L}$ is a (local) transition relation, $I = [1..n]$ is the index set, and $\tau : \mathcal{R} \rightarrow [I \rightarrow G]$ is a labeling function that labels each transition with a guard for each process. Here, $G : \mathcal{L}^n \rightarrow \{true, false\}$ is a set of transition guards.*

We assume that for any local transition $u \rightarrow v \in \mathcal{R}$, $u \neq v$, i.e., no self-loops are allowed in a GSST.

Definition 3. *A GSST $P = (\mathcal{L}, \mathcal{R}, I, \tau)$ defines an asynchronous structure $M(P) = (S, R)$, where $S = \mathcal{L}^{|I|}$ is the global statespace, and $R \subseteq S \times S$ is the global transition relation defined as follows:*

(a) *for any local transition $u \rightarrow v \in \mathcal{R}$,*
$$R_{u \rightarrow v}(s, t) \triangleq \exists i \in I \cdot (s(i) = u \wedge t(i) = v \wedge s \models \tau(u \rightarrow v)(i) \wedge \forall j \neq i \cdot s(j) = t(j))$$
(b) $R \triangleq \bigcup_{r \in \mathcal{R}} R_r.$

Intuitively, $R_{u \to v}$ is the set of all global transitions resulting from some process changing its state from u to v. We say that $s \to t \in R$ is a result of firing a local transition $u \to v$ if $s \to t$ is in $R_{u \to v}$.

For a local transition $r \in \mathcal{R}$, the labeling function $\tau : \mathcal{R} \to [I \to G]$ can be seen as: (a) a partition $\Pi_r = \{I_1, \ldots, I_d\}$ of processes into process groups, (b) an index mapping function $\pi : I \to \Pi_r$, and (c) a function $\eta : \Pi_r \to G$ assigning a guard to each process group, i.e., for any $i \in I$, $\tau(r)(i) = \eta(\pi(i))$. For example, in the GSST for the three-process R&W shown in Figure 1(b), the guards for the local transition $T \to C$ are described by partitioning the processes into two groups: $I_r = \{P_1\}$ (readers) and $I_w = \{P_2, P_3\}$ (writers). Readers have the guard $g_{I_r} : (\#C = 0) \land (\#T[I_w] = 0)$, and writers $g_{I_w} : \#C = 0$. Note that this allows us to model not only the static process partitioning, i.e., $\forall r, r' \in \mathcal{R} \cdot \Pi_r = \Pi_{r'}$, but a dynamic one as well, that is, processes can be divided into different groups at different local transitions.

Motivated by R&W, we restrict our attention to a counter-based syntax of guards. Formally, a guard for a transition $u \to v$ is a boolean combination of *group counter constraints* on the local state u, i.e., $\#u[I_k] \bowtie b$, or *total counter constraints* on any local states, i.e., $(\sum_i \#L_i) \bowtie b$, where b is a positive integer, and $\bowtie$ is one of $\{\leq, \geq, = \}$. For example, in Figure 1(b), $\#C = 0$ means no process is currently in the local state C, whereas $\#T[I_w] = 0$ means that no *writer* process is currently in T.

4.3   Full Virtual Symmetry in Asynchronous Structures

In this section, we show how to identify whether a system specified by a GSST is fully virtually symmetric.

Let P be a GSST and r be a transition in P. If all processes at r belong to the same group, i.e., $|\Pi_r| = 1$, then the transition guard is defined on total counters and is independent of any permutation of process indices. Furthermore, if this is the case for all transitions in P, then P is just a synchronization skeleton, and the underlying structure $M(P)$ is fully symmetric (see Section 4.1). In general, when P contains a transition r with $|\Pi_r| > 1$, even restricting guards to just total counter constraints is not sufficient to ensure that $M(P)$ is fully virtually symmetric. For example, consider the GSST shown in Figure 1(b) and assume that we change the guard g_{I_r} of the transition $T \to C$ to $(\#C = 0) \land (\#T = 2)$. In this case, $M(P)$ contains a global transition from $s = (N, N, T)$ to $t = (N, N, C)$ corresponding to the process P_3 entering state C. Let $\sigma \in Sym(I)$ be a permutation that switches process indices 1 and 3. Then, the only two states reachable from $\sigma(s) = (T, N, N)$ are $t_1 = (T, T, N)$ and $t_2 = (T, N, T)$. Since neither t_1 nor t_2 can be obtained by applying a permutation $\sigma' \in Sym(I)$ to t, transitions in the form $\sigma(s) \to \sigma'(t)$ are *not* in $M(P)$ for any permutation σ'; hence, $M(P)$ is not fully virtually symmetric.

As illustrated by the example above, it is difficult to capture the restrictions that ensure full virtual symmetry syntactically. The difficulty comes from lack of regularity in asymmetric systems. Therefore, we seek an algorithmic way to identify symmetry. As mentioned before, we cannot simply use Condition (1) of Theorem 3 since it requires building the transition relation of $M(P)$.

Notice that in our example, full virtual symmetry is broken at a global transition resulting from firing a local transition where the processes are partitioned into several groups. We generalize from this example and show that virtual symmetry of a structure is equivalent to virtual symmetry of each transition relation subset defined by a local transition. This allows us to decompose the problem of identifying virtual symmetry of a system along *local* transitions. Formally, we establish the following theorem.

Theorem 4. *Given a GSST $P = (\mathcal{L}, \mathcal{R}, I, \tau)$ and a permutation group $G \subseteq Sym(I)$, the structure $M(P) = (S, R)$ is virtually symmetric with respect to G if and only if each transition relation subset R_r is virtually symmetric with respect to G, where $R \triangleq \bigcup_{r \in \mathcal{R}} R_r$.*

The "if" direction of Theorem 4 is trivial: a union of virtually symmetric transition relations is virtually symmetric. For the "only if" direction, by Theorem 2, we know that R is virtually symmetric with respect to G if and only if $R_{\alpha_G}^{\exists\exists} = R_{\alpha_G}^{\forall\exists}$. With the aid of Theorem 5 given below and obtained from the perspective of abstraction, we show that $(R_r)_{\alpha_G}^{\exists\exists} = (R_r)_{\alpha_G}^{\forall\exists}$ for each R_r, i.e., R_r is virtually symmetric with respect to G.

Let $M' = (S', R')$ be a structure, and $\alpha : S' \to S_\alpha$ be an abstraction function. We define a restriction of R' to a pair of abstract states (a, b) as

$$R'_{|(a,b)} \triangleq \{(s, t) \in R' \mid s \in \gamma(a) \wedge t \in \gamma(b)\}$$

Note that $R' = \bigcup_{a,b \in S_\alpha} R'_{|(a,b)}$, and the universal and the existential abstractions of R' coincide if and only if they coincide for each $R'_{|(a,b)}$. The following theorem generalizes this observation.

Theorem 5. *Let $M' = (S', R')$ be a structure, $\alpha : S' \to S_\alpha$ be an abstraction function, and $R' = \bigcup_{i \in [1..k]} R'_i$ such that $\forall i \in [1..k] \cdot \exists D \subseteq S' \times S' \cdot R'_i = \bigcup_{(s,t) \in D} R'_{|(\alpha(s), \alpha(t))}.$ Then, $(R')_\alpha^{\forall\exists} = (R')_\alpha^{\exists\exists} \Leftrightarrow \forall i \in [1..k] \cdot (R'_i)_\alpha^{\forall\exists} = (R'_i)_\alpha^{\exists\exists}.$*

Recall that in the context of symmetry reduction, $\alpha_G(s)$ is equivalent to $\theta(s)$ (see Table 1). We claim that each R_r satisfies the precondition of Theorem 5 by showing that $R_r = \bigcup_{(s,t) \in R_r} R_{|(\theta(s), \theta(t))}$. That is, we need to show that if a transition $s \to t$ is a result of firing a local transition r, then for any permutations $\sigma, \sigma' \in G$, a transition $\sigma(s) \to \sigma'(t)$ is a result of firing r as well. This holds from the following observations: (a) two states s_1 and s_2 share an orbit only if they agree on total counters, and (b) a global transition $s \to t$ is a result of firing a local transition $u \to v$ if and only if $\#u$ at s is one more than that at t, $\#v$ at s is one less than that at t, and the total counters of other local states at s and t are the same. For example, consider two global transitions $s \to t$ and $s' \to t'$ such that $s' \in \theta(s)$, and $t' \in \theta(t)$. Since s and t agree with s' and t', respectively, on total counters, then if $s \to t$ is in R_r, $s' \to t'$ must be in R_r as well. Therefore, virtual symmetry of R implies virtual symmetry of each R_r. This concludes the proof of Theorem 4.

When G is the full symmetry group $Sym(I)$, Theorem 4 can be simplified further since here two states share an orbit *if and only if* they agree on total counters. Note that if R_r is fully virtually symmetric, i.e., $(R_r)_{\alpha_G}^{\forall\exists} = (R_r)_{\alpha_G}^{\exists\exists}$, then $Dom(R_r)$ contains its orbit $\theta(Dom(R_r))$, which follows from the definitions of existential and universal abstractions. On the other hand, if $Dom(R_r)$ contains $\theta(Dom(R_r))$, then for any pair of states s and s' in the same orbit, if $s \to t$ is in R_r for some state t, then there exists a state t' such that $s' \rightarrow t'$ is in R_r. Furthermore, t and t' agree on total counters, and thus belong to the same orbit. Hence, by Theorem 3, R_r is fully virtually symmetric. Since $\theta(Dom(R_r))$ always contains $Dom(R_r)$, we obtain the following theorem.

Theorem 6. *Given a GSST $P = (\mathcal{L}, \mathcal{R}, I, \tau)$, the structure $M(P) = (S, R)$ is fully virtually symmetric if and only if $\forall r \in \mathcal{R} \cdot \theta(Dom(R_r)) = Dom(R_r)$.*

Thus, we have reduced the problem of checking virtual symmetry of R, a global property of the entire system, to a local property of each transition subset R_r.

4.4   Constraint-Based Identification of Full Virtual Symmetry

In this section, we present a technique for identifying full virtual symmetry based on Theorem 6. Specifically, we construct Presburger formulas representing sets of states directly from the description of the GSST.

By Theorem 4, checking whether a structure $M(P)$ is fully virtually symmetric is equivalent to checking whether R_r is fully virtually symmetric for each local transition r of the GSST P. Note that if all processes belong to the same group at a local transition r, i.e., $|\Pi_r| = 1$, then R_r is fully symmetric and no check is required. Otherwise, when $|\Pi_r| > 1$, by Theorem 6, we need to check whether the domain of R_r, $Dom(R_r)$, is equal to its orbit, $\theta(Dom(R_r))$. In this section, we show that both $Dom(R_r)$ and $\theta(Dom(R_r))$ can be represented by Presburger formulas and their equivalence can be reduced to checking satisfiability of a Quantifier Free Presburger (QFP) formula.

We illustrate the procedure on the $T \rightarrow C$ transition of the R&W whose GSST is shown in Figure 1(b). The counter-based syntax of the guards provides a compact representation of a set of states in the structure $M(P)$ using Presburger formulas on group counters. The formula $\varphi_{T \rightarrow C}$ representing $Dom(R_{T \rightarrow C})$ is constructed based on the transition guards in the GSST as follows. According to the interleaving semantics, a state s is in $Dom(R_{T \rightarrow C})$ if and only if either a reader or a writer process can move from T to C at s. In the first case, s must satisfy the guard g_{I_r}, and since the current local state of the reader process is T, s satisfies $g_{I_r} \wedge \#T[I_r] \geq 1$; similarly, in the second case, s satisfies $g_{I_w} \wedge \#T[I_w] \geq 1$. Therefore, $Dom(R_{T \rightarrow C})$ can be represented by the formula $\varphi_{T \rightarrow C} = \varphi_{T \rightarrow C, I_r} \vee \varphi_{T \rightarrow C, I_w}$, where

$$\varphi_{T \rightarrow C, I_r} \triangleq g_{I_r} \wedge \#T[I_r] \geq 1 \wedge inv_{T \rightarrow C} \qquad \varphi_{T \rightarrow C, I_w} \triangleq g_{I_w} \wedge \#T[I_w] \geq 1 \wedge inv_{T \rightarrow C}$$

and the invariant $inv_{T \rightarrow C}$, defined as the conjunction of the constraints in the left column of Table 3, represents the statespace of the system. Note that $\varphi_{T \rightarrow C}$ is still defined only on group counters since $\#C$ is equivalent to $\#C[I_r] + \#C[I_w]$. In general, for a local transition r, the formula φ_r representing $Dom(R_r)$ is a disjunction of formulas representing subsets of $Dom(R_r)$ with respect to each process group.

We now show how to derive a formula $\tilde{\varphi}_r$ representing $\theta(Dom(R_r))$ from φ_r. For simplicity, assume that P contains only two local states, X and Y, and the processes are partitioned into two groups. Let $Dom(R_r)$ and the invariant of the statespace be represented by $\varphi_r(X_1, X_2, Y_1, Y_2)$ and $inv_r(X_1, X_2, Y_1, Y_2)$, respectively. Then $\tilde{\varphi}_r$ representing $\theta(Dom(R_{T \rightarrow C}))$ is defined as

$$\tilde{\varphi}_r(X_1, X_2, Y_1, Y_2) \triangleq \exists X_1', X_2', Y_1', Y_2'. \ (inv_r(X_1, X_2, Y_1, Y_2) \wedge \varphi_r(X_1', X_2', Y_1', Y_2') \\ \wedge X_1 + X_2 = X_1' + X_2' \wedge Y_1 + Y_2 = Y_1' + Y_2')$$

Table 3. Invariant for the three-process R&W

Constraints	Meaning
$0 \leq \#N[I_r]$ $0 \leq \#T[I_r]$ $0 \leq \#C[I_r]$ $0 \leq \#N[I_w]$ $0 \leq \#T[I_w]$ $0 \leq \#C[I_w]$	each group counter is a positive integer
$\#N[I_r] + \#T[I_r] + \#C[I_r] = 1$ $\#N[I_w] + \#T[I_w] + \#C[I_w] = 2$	there is one reader process and two writer processes

That is, a state s satisfies $\tilde{\varphi}_r$ if and only if there exists a state s' satisfying φ_r ($s' \in Dom(R_r)$) and s and s' agree on total counters, i.e., they are in the same orbit. Since $Dom(R_r)$ is a subset of $\theta(Dom(R_r))$, $Dom(R_r) = \theta(Dom(R_r))$ if and only if the sentence $\psi = \exists X_1, X_2, Y_1, Y_2 \cdot (\tilde{\varphi}_r \wedge \neg\varphi_r)$ is unsatisfiable. Since ψ contains only existential quantifiers, this is equivalent to unsatisfiability of a QFP formula obtained from ψ by removing all quantifiers, which can be checked using any existing decision procedure for QFP [3,16,17].

Note that while the satisfiability problem of a Presburger formula has a worst-case super-exponential complexity, satisfiability of a QFP formula is NP-complete [14]. Furthermore, the number of local transitions in a GSST that need to be checked is expected to be small, since we are interested in asynchronous systems in which processes are relatively similar to one another. Indeed, if the processes differ significantly, it does not seem appropriate to consider full virtual symmetry at all. In practice, the structure of the guards often leads to further optimizations of the decision procedure. As illustrated by experiments in Section 6, full virtual symmetry can be identified efficiently when the guards are defined on a small number of local states.

5   Counter Abstraction for Full Virtual Symmetry

The naive way of constructing a symmetry-reduced quotient structure requires a representative function for choosing a state as the unique representative from each orbit [7,5]. The abstract transition relation is then defined on the set of representatives. For symbolic model-checking, computation of the representative function requires building an orbit relation which, for many groups, including the full symmetry group, has a BDD representation that is exponential in the minimum of the number of processes and the number of local states in each process [7], decreasing the effectiveness of symbolic model-checking.

An alternative is to use *generic representatives* (or a counter abstraction) technique proposed by Emerson at el. [11,12], which avoids building the orbit relation. As we have seen before, under the full symmetry group, states in the same orbit agree on all total counters. Thus, each orbit can be uniquely represented by values of these counters. For example, in the three-process MUTEX, the orbit $\{(N, T, T), (T, N, T), (T, T, N)\}$ is represented by a tuple $(1, 2, 0)$ which corresponds to the counters of states N, T and C. In this section, we extend the counter-based abstraction technique to handle fully virtually symmetric structure specified by a GSST. The key idea is that instead of using the orbit relation, a structure isomorphic to the quotient structure is constructed on the statespace of total counters directly from the GSST.

For the rest of this section, let $P = (\mathcal{L}, \mathcal{R}, I, \tau)$ be a GSST of a fully virtually symmetric system with local states $\mathcal{L} = \{L_1, \ldots, L_m\}$ and process indices $I = [1..n]$. A *counter abstraction* $\alpha : S \rightarrow S_\alpha$ on the structure $M(P) = (S, R)$ is constructed using a set of assignments to a vector $\mathbf{x} = (x_1, \ldots, x_m)$ of m counter variables ranging over $[0..n]$. Each variable x_i corresponds to a total counter $\#L_i$ of a local state L_i. Since there are n processes, the sum of the values of $\mathbf{x}$ must always equal n. Therefore,

$$S_\alpha \triangleq \{(c_1, \ldots, c_m) \in [0..n]^m \mid \sum_{i=1}^{m} c_i = n\}$$

The abstraction function $\alpha : S \rightarrow S_\alpha$ maps a state $s \in S$ to an abstract state $a \in S_\alpha$ if and only if for each $i \in I$, $a(i)$ equals $\#L_i(s)$. The concretization function $\gamma : S_\alpha \rightarrow 2^S$ maps an abstract state a to an orbit θ where states in θ agree with a on total counters. In what follows, let R_α denote the existential abstraction of R with respect to α.

Theorem 7. *Given a GSST P and a counter abstraction α, the abstract structure $M(P)_\alpha = (S_\alpha, R_\alpha)$ is isomorphic to the quotient structure $M(P)^{Sym(I)} = (S^{Sym(I)}, R^{Sym(I)})$ via a bijection $h : S_\alpha \rightarrow S^{Sym(I)}$, where $\forall s \in S \cdot h(\alpha(s)) \triangleq \theta(s)$.*

The above definition of $M(P)_\alpha$ guarantees that the abstract transition relation R_α can be constructed directly from P for a fully virtually symmetric system. Since existential abstraction distributes over union, and $R = \bigcup_{r \in \mathcal{R}} R_r$ by Definition 3, it follows that $R_\alpha = \bigcup_{r \in \mathcal{R}} (R_r)_\alpha$. Therefore, we only need to show how to construct $(R_r)_\alpha$ for a local transition r.

We start by illustrating the construction in the case of an unguarded local transition r. If r is of the form $L_i \rightarrow L_j$, then r can be fired from a global state s if and only if s contains a process whose current state is L_i; in other words, $Dom(R_r)$ is $\#L_i \geq 1$. Furthermore, if $s \rightarrow t$ is in R_r, then the counters $\#L_i$ and $\#L_j$ at t are one less and one more than those at s, respectively. From the definition of existential abstraction, for any abstract states a and b, a transition $a \rightarrow b$ is in $(R_r)_\alpha$ if and only if $s \rightarrow t \in R_r$ for some $s \in \gamma(a)$ and $t \in \gamma(b)$. Therefore,

$$(R_r)_\alpha \equiv x_i \geq 1 \wedge (x_i := x_i - 1; \ x_j := x_j + 1)$$

which is a formula over counter variables. Generalizing from this example, we obtain that for every local transition r of the form $L_i \rightarrow L_j$,

$$(R_r)_\alpha \equiv g_r \wedge (x_i := x_i - 1; \ x_j := x_j + 1)$$

where g_r is a formula defined over counter variables $\mathbf{x}$ representing the "existential" abstraction of $Dom(R_r)$. Specifically,

$$a \models g_r \Leftrightarrow \exists s \in \gamma(a) \cdot s \in Dom(R_r)$$

Since $M(P)_\alpha$ is isomorphic to the quotient structure, the above construction allows us to combine symmetry reduction and symbolic model-checking without building the orbit relation. The only remaining problem is the construction of the formula g_r for an arbitrary local transition r, and in the rest of this section, we show how to do this for cases where r is guarded by (a) a single guard on total counters, (b) multiple guards on total counters, and (c) multiple guards on group counters of the source state of r and arbitrary total counters.

Case (a). Let r be a local transition $L_i \rightarrow L_j$. Suppose r is guarded by a single guard g, i.e., $|\Pi_r| = 1$. Then $Dom(R_r)$ can be represented by $\psi_r = (\#L_i \geq 1 \wedge g)$, i.e., $s \in Dom(R_r)$ if there is at least one process at s in local state L_i and s satisfies g. Let $sub(\psi_r)$ denote a formula obtained from ψ_r by replacing each occurrence of a total counter with its corresponding counter variable. For example, $sub(\#L_i \geq 0) = (x_i \geq 0)$ and $sub(\#L_i \geq 1 \wedge \#L_j \leq 3) = (x_i \geq 1 \wedge x_j \leq 3)$. Since g contains only total counter constraints, we define $g_r \triangleq sub(\#L_i \geq 1 \wedge g)$. Note that this procedure constructs a counter abstraction for a fully symmetric synchronization skeleton, and is effectively equivalent to the *generic representatives* approach of Emerson and Trefler [11].

Case (b). Suppose that r is guarded by multiple guards, i.e., $|\Pi_r| = d > 1$, but each guard is expressed using only total counters. In this case, $Dom(R_r)$ is represented by $\psi_r = \bigvee_{k \in [1..d]}(\#L_i[I_k] \geq 1 \wedge g_{I_k})$, where g_{I_k} is the guard for the process group I_k. Since ψ_r depends on group counters, we cannot simply define g_r to be $sub(\psi_r)$. However, R_r is fully virtually symmetric, so $Dom(R_r) = \theta(Dom(R_r))$ by Theorem 6, and $\theta(Dom(R_r))$ is representable by $\tilde{\psi}_r = (\#L_i \geq 1 \wedge (\bigvee_{k \in [1..d]} g_{I_k}))$. Thus, we define $g_r \triangleq sub(\tilde{\psi}_r)$.

Case (c). Finally, we look at the case where the guards of r depend on group counters. In this case, $\tilde{\psi}_r$ defined above still contains group counters. However, this problem can be solved for cases where group counters in guards for a transition $r : L_i \rightarrow L_j$ are defined only over L_i.

First, let $Q \subseteq S$ be some non-empty set of states given by some formula ψ defined only on group counters of L_i. That is,

$$\psi = \bigwedge_{k \in [1..d]}(min_k \leq \#L_i[I_k] \leq max_k)$$

where $\{min_k\}$ and $\{max_k\}$ are positive integers. Then the orbit $\theta(Q)$ under $Sym(I)$ is given by the formula

$$\tilde{\psi} = (min \leq \#L_i \leq max)$$

where

$$min \triangleq \sum_{k \in [1..d]} min_k \qquad max \triangleq \sum_{k \in [1..d]} max_k$$

For example, suppose there are only two local states, L_1 and L_2, $d = 2$, and Q is given by $\psi = (1 \leq \#L_1[I_1] \leq 4) \wedge (1 \leq \#L_1[I_2] \leq 4)$. Then $\theta(Q)$ is $\tilde{\psi} = (2 \leq \#L_1 \leq 8)$ since for any state s in S satisfying $\tilde{\psi}$ there exists a state s' in S satisfying ψ such that s and s' agree on total counters of L_1 and L_2, i.e., they are in the same orbit. Furthermore, if Q is encoded by a conjunction $\psi^t \wedge \psi^g$, where ψ^t and ψ^g are defined only on total and group counters, respectively, then the orbit of Q is given by $\psi^t \wedge \tilde{\psi}^g$.

Second, suppose a guard g_{I_k} contains group counter constraints. Let $Dom(R_r)_{I_k}$ denote the subset of $Dom(R_r)$ containing states in which the local transition r of some process in the group I_k can be fired. If the formula ψ_{r,I_k} representing $Dom(R_r)_{I_k}$ can be decomposed as $\psi_{r,I_k} = \psi^t_{r,I_k} \wedge \psi^g_{r,I_k}$, then a total counter formula representing $\theta(Dom(R_r)_{I_k})$ is computed as described above. Otherwise, ψ_{r,I_k} can be converted to a DNF, and formulas corresponding to the orbit of each clause are computed as above. Since $Dom(R_r) = \bigcup_{k \in [1..d]} Dom(R_r)_{I_k}$, and θ distributes over union, i.e., $\theta(Q_1 \cup Q_2) = \theta(Q_1) \cup \theta(Q_2)$, we can define $\tilde{\psi}_r$ representing $\theta(Dom(R_r))$ as a disjunction of the clause formulas. Finally, $\tilde{\psi}_r$ depends only on total counters; thus, we define g_r to be $sub(\tilde{\psi}_r)$.

For example, the domain of the transition $T \to C$ of the R&W shown in Figure 1(b), is the union of the domain for the readers and that of the writers. For readers,

$$Dom(R_{T \to C})_{I_r} \equiv \#T[I_r] >= 1 \wedge \#T[I_w] = 0 \wedge \#C = 0$$
$$\equiv \#T[I_r] = 1 \wedge \#T[I_w] = 0 \wedge \#C = 0$$

since there is only one reader. Using only total counters, the orbit $\theta(Dom(R_{T \to C})_{I_r})$ is represented by $\tilde{\psi}_r = (\#T = 1 \wedge \#C = 0)$. Similarly, for the writers,

$$Dom(R_{T \to C})_{I_w} \equiv \#T[I_w] \geq 1 \wedge \#C = 0$$

and the orbit $\theta(Dom(R_{T \to C})_{I_w})$ is represented by $\tilde{\psi}_w = (\#T \geq 1 \wedge \#C = 0)$. Finally, $g_{T \to C}$ is defined by $sub(\tilde{\psi}_r \vee \tilde{\psi}_w) = (\#T \geq 1 \wedge \#C = 0)$.

6   Experiments

In this section, we report on experiments of identifying full virtual symmetry and performing counter abstraction-based symbolic model-checking on two examples: generalized R&W (GR&W) and asymmetric sharing of resources (ASR) [9]. We used the Omega library [16] to check for full virtual symmetry as described in Section 4, and used NuSMV [4] as the model-checker for both the direct and the counter abstraction-based analysis : for each example, we constructed NuSMV programs to represent the original and the counter abstracted systems and then run NuSMV to check properties.

In GR&W, we assumed that each process has m local states $\{L_1, \ldots, L_m\}$, where L_m represents the critical section. Each process can move from L_i to L_{i+1} ($i \in [1..m-2]$) and return from L_m to L_1 freely. The processes are partitioned into d groups, each of size q, based on their priorities: a process cannot access the critical section if another process with higher priority is waiting for it. The property we verified was $AG(\#L_m \leq 1)$. The second example, ASR, is motivated by the drinking philosophers problem [9]. It exhibits full virtual symmetry induced by the asymmetric sharing of resources, where n processes have different permissions to access r critical resources, and the number of processes that can be waiting for each resource and using it is bounded. We checked whether it is possible for all critical resources to be used at the same time, i.e., $EF(\bigwedge_{i \in [1..r]}(\#C_i > 0))$. The experiments were performed on a Sun Fire V440 server (4@1.3GHz, USPARC3i, 16384M). The results of the direct (*NuSMV*) and the counter abstraction-based (*Symmetry Reduction with Counter Abstraction*) analysis are summarized in Table 4, where dashes indicate that verification did not complete due to either memory or time limits. Where appropriate, we separate the checking time into identifying symmetry (*CkSym*) and checking the resulting reduced model (*ModelCk*). For ASR, we also reported the results of computing the set of reachable states first, before evaluating the property (the -f option of NuSMV).

The experiments show that counter abstraction provides a significant reduction in both memory and CPU usage. Memory usage grows slowly with the number of processes, which indicates that the method is applicable for systems comprised of a large number of processes.

In these examples, the time it took to identify full virtual symmetry was relatively small. One reason is that the guards depend only on a small number of process groups and local states. Otherwise, more specialized solvers may be useful. For example, iden-

Table 4. Experimental results for generalized R&W and asymmetric sharing of resources

	Parameter	NuSMV			Symmetry Reduction with Counter Abstraction				
		BDD Nodes Allocated	Mem. (MB)	Time (sec.)	BDD Nodes Allocated	Mem. (MB)	CkSym	ModelCk	Total
Generalized R&W	**d (q=20, m=10)**								
	5	51,778,281	931	241	25,146	7	0.07	0.27	0.34
	10	-	-	-	31,772	8	0.83	0.53	1.36
	15	-	-	-	38,927	8	5.09	1.26	6.35
	m (d=5, q=20)								
	10	51,778,281	931	241	25,146	7	0.07	0.27	0.34
	20	121,392,365	2,041	837	130,891	10	0.07	0.59	0.66
	30	-	-	-	379,336	14	0.07	1.35	1.42
	q (d=10, m=20)								
	10	121,408,515	2,040	742	131,010	10	0.80	0.58	1.38
	30	-	-	-	187,469	12	0.81	24.14	24.95
	50	-	-	-	195,653	13	0.75	67.21	67.96
Asymmetric Sharing of Resources	**n (r=2)**								
	20	597,911	18	2.11	77,885	8	0.10	0.78	0.88
	30	2,443,114	51	8.19	179,389	10	0.10	1.74	1.84
	40	8,151,508	151	30.74	427,075	14	0.10	4.35	4.45
	80	57,163,279	1,001	2928.81	289,566	18	0.10	36.83	36.93
	n (r=3)								
	20	1,896,771	43	10.39	182,799	10	0.15	1.55	1.70
	30	11,503,014	216	78.46	403,628	14	0.15	3.64	3.79
	40	44,877,253	782	43108.92	390,715	17	0.15	9.68	9.83
	80	-	-	-	420,347	20	0.15	80.61	80.76
	n (r=5)								
	40	-	-	-	67,060	19	0.30	28.31	28.61
	80	-	-	-	342,060	39	0.30	279.89	280.19
	n (r=10)								
	40	-	-	-	484,260	48	3.00	251.87	254.87
	80	-	-	-	671,318	153	3.00	1409.53	1412.53
Asym. Sharing of Resources (reachable states)	**n (r=2)**								
	20	635,791	19	2.24	5,575	6.9	0.10	0.13	0.23
	30	2,557,272	53	8.91	6,589	6.9	0.10	0.14	0.24
	40	8,543,329	159	34.47	10,165	7	0.10	0.15	0.25
	80	57,375,594	1,006	528.25	18,611	7.2	0.10	0.25	0.35
	n (r=3)								
	20	1,927,302	43	8.07	11,634	7	0.15	0.15	0.30
	30	11,591,335	220	61.14	14,616	7.1	0.15	0.18	0.33
	40	42,633,638	805	1614.32	21,647	7.3	0.15	0.21	0.36
	80	-	-	-	38,913	7.7	0.15	0.39	0.54
	n (r=5)								
	40	-	-	-	71,925	8.2	0.30	0.49	0.79
	80	-	-	-	133,034	9.5	0.30	1.03	1.33
	n (r=10)								
	40	-	-	-	394,722	14	3.00	2.55	5.55
	80	-	-	-	404,477	18	3.00	6.13	9.13

tifying symmetry of GR&W with $d = 100$ and $q = 20$ took us many hours with the Omega library and only 17 seconds with the pseudo-Boolean solver (PBS) [1].

7 Conclusion and Related Work

The problem of exploiting symmetry reduction in model checking has been studied by many researchers, e.g., [2,7,10,13]. To extend symmetry reduction to asymmetric systems, Emerson and his colleagues first proposed "looser" notions of *near* symmetry and *rough* symmetry [11], and finally virtual symmetry [9] which subsumes the previous two. In this paper, we give an alternative (and simpler) characterization of virtual symmetry from the perspective of abstraction.

The problem of identifying full symmetry has been avoided by imposing restrictions on the specification language [11,12,13]. However, lack of regularity in asymmetric systems makes it difficult to capture the restrictions that ensure full virtual symmetry syntactically. Emerson et al. proposed a combinatorial condition for checking virtual symmetry based on counting the missing transitions [9], which seems to require the construction of the transition relation. With our characterization of virtual symmetry, we avoid this problem by checking satisfiability of a QFP formula built from the system description.

To combine full symmetry reduction and symbolic model-checking, Emerson et al. [11] proposed a *generic representatives* technique, also known as a counter abstraction [15]. In this paper, we have extended this technique to fully virtually symmetric systems. The generic representatives technique was later applied to fully symmetric systems on processes communicating via shared variables [12], and the experiments show that it is superior to other methods, such as multiple representatives [7]. We plan to do the same for fully virtually symmetric systems in the future.

We believe that our techniques have a potential to significantly increase the scope of systems to which symmetry reduction can be effectively applied. Note that our work assumed that group counters occurring in a guard are defined only on the source state (see Section 5). While this did not pose a problem for examples we have tried, we do not know what the consequences of this restriction are, and would like to explore these further.

Acknowledgments. We would like to thank Thomas Wahl and anonymous referees for their useful comments on the paper. This work has been financially supported by the Ontario Graduate Scholarship, IBM Fellowship and NSERC.

References

1. F. Aloul, A. Ramani, I. Markov, and K. Sakallah. "PBS: A Backtrack Search Pseudo-Boolean Solver". In *SAT'02*, pp. 346–353, 2002.
2. S. Barner and O. Grumberg. "Combining Symmetry Reduction and Under-Approximation for Symbolic Model Checking". In *CAV'02*, vol. 2404 of *LNCS*, pp. 93–106, 2002.
3. C. Barrett and S. Berezin. "CVC Lite: A New Implementation of the Cooperating Validity Checker". In *CAV'04*, vol. 3114 of *LNCS*, pp. 515–518, 2004.

4. A. Cimatti, E. Clarke, F. Giunchiglia, and M. Roveri. "NUSMV: a new Symbolic Model Verifier". In *CAV'99*, vol. 1633 of *LNCS*, pp. 495–499, 1999.
5. E. Clarke, O. Grumberg, and D. Peled. *Model Checking*. MIT Press, 1999.
6. E.M. Clarke and E.A. Emerson. "Design and Synthesis of Synchronization Skeletons for Branching Time Temporal Logic". In *Logic of Programs*, vol. 131 of *LNCS*, 1981.
7. E. Clarke, R. Enders, T. Filkorn, and S. Jha. "Exploiting Symmetry in Temporal Logic Model Checking". *FMSD*, 9(1-2):77–104, 1996.
8. D. Dams, R. Gerth, and O. Grumberg. "Abstract Interpretation of Reactive Systems". *ACM TOPLAS*, 2(19):253–291, 1997.
9. E. Emerson, J. Havlicek, and R. Trefler. "Virtual Symmetry Reduction". In *LICS'00*, pp. 121–131, 2000.
10. E. Emerson and A. Sistla. "Symmetry and Model Checking". *FMSD*, 9(1-2):105–131, 1996.
11. E. Emerson and R. Trefler. "From Asymmetry to Full Symmetry: New Techniques for Symmetry Reduction in Model Checking". In *CHARME'99*, LNCS 1703, pp. 142–157, 1999.
12. E. Emerson and T. Wahl. "On Combining Symmetry Reduction and Symbolic Representation for Efficient Model Checking". In *CHARME'03*, LNCS 2860, pp. 216–230, 2003.
13. C. Ip and D. Dill. "Better Verification Through Symmetry". *FMSD*, 9(1-2):41–75, 1996.
14. C. Papadimitriou. "On the Complexity of Integer Programming". *J. ACM*, 28(4):765–768, 1981.
15. A. Pnueli, J. Xu, and L. Zuck. "Liveness with $(0, 1, \infty)$-Counter Abstraction". In *CAV'02*, vol. 2404 of *LNCS*, pp. 107–122, 2002.
16. W. Pugh. "The Omega Test: A Fast and Practical Integer Programming Algorithm for Dependence Analysis". *Comm. of the ACM*, August 1992.
17. P. Wolper and B. Boigelot. "An Automata-Theoretic Approach to Presburger Arithmetic Constraints". In *SAS'95*, vol. 1785 of *LNCS*, pp. 21–32, 1995.

On the Verification of
Memory Management Mechanisms

Iakov Dalinger*, Mark Hillebrand*, and Wolfgang Paul

Saarland University, Computer Science Dept., 66123 Saarbrücken, Germany
{dalinger, mah, wjp}@wjpserver.cs.uni-sb.de

Abstract. We report on the design and formal verification of a complex processor supporting address translation by means of a memory management unit (MMU). We give a paper and pencil proof that such a processor together with an appropriate page fault handler simulates virtual machines modeling user computation. These results are crucial steps towards the seamless verification of entire computer systems.

1 Introduction

1.1 The Challenge of Verifying Entire Systems

In the spirit of the famous CLI stack [1] the research of this paper aims at the formal verification of entire computer systems consisting of hardware, compiler, operating system, communication system, and applications. Working with the Boyer-Moore theorem prover [2] the researchers of the CLI stack project succeeded as early as 1989 to prove formally the correctness of a system which provided the following components: a non pipelined processor [3], an assembler [4], a compiler for a simple imperative language [5], a rudimentary operating system kernel [6] written in machine language. This kernel provided scheduling for a fixed number of processes; each process had the right to access a fixed interval of addresses in the processor's physical memory. An attempt to access memory outside these bounds lead to an interrupt. Interprocess communication and system calls apparently were not provided.

From 1989 to 2002 to the best of our knowledge no project aiming at the formal verification of entire computer systems was started anywhere. In [7] J S. Moore, principal researcher of the CLI stack project, declares the formal verification of a system 'from transistor to software level' a grand challenge problem. A main goal of the Verisoft project [8] funded by the German Federal Government is to solve this challenge.

This paper makes two necessary steps towards the verification of entire complex systems. (i) We report about the formal verification of a processor with memory management units (MMUs). MMUs provide hardware support for address translation; address translation is needed to implement address spaces provided by modern operating

---

* Work partially funded by the German Federal Ministry of Education and Research (BMBF) in the framework of the Verisoft project under grant 01 IS C38. Work of the second author was also partially funded by IBM Entwicklung GmbH Böblingen.

D. Borrione and W. Paul (Eds.): CHARME 2005, LNCS 3725, pp. 301–316, 2005.

systems. (ii) We present a paper and pencil correctness proof for a virtual memory emulation based on a very simple page fault handler. As the formal treatment of I/O devices is an open problem [7] we state the correctness of a swap memory driver as an axiom.

In companion papers we address the verification of I/O devices, of a compiler for a C-like language with in-line assembler code, and of an operating system kernel [9–11].

1.2   Overview of This Paper

In Sect. 2 we briefly review the standard formal definition of the DLX instruction set architecture (ISA) for virtual machines. We emphasize interrupt handling. In Sect. 3 on physical machines we enrich the ISA by the standard mechanisms for operating system support: (i) user and system mode; (ii) address translation in user mode. In Sect. 4 we present a construction of a simple MMU and prove its correctness under nontrivial operating conditions. In pipelined processors separate MMUs are used for instruction fetch and load / store. In Sect. 5 we show how the operating conditions for both MMUs can be guaranteed by hardware *and* software implementation. Sect. 6 gives the main new arguments of the processor correctness proof under these software conventions. In Sect. 7 we present a simple page fault handler. We show that a physical machine with this handler emulates a virtual machine. In Sect. 8 we conclude and sketch further work.

1.3   Related Work

The processor verification presented here extends work on the VAMP presented in [12,13]. The treatment of external interrupts is in the spirit of [14,15]. Formal proofs are in PVS [16] and—except for limited use of its model checker—interactive. All formal specifications and proofs are on our website.[1] We stress that some central lemmas in [12,14] (e.g. on Tomasulo schedulers) have similar counterparts that can be proven using the rich set of automatic methods for hardware verification. How to profit from these methods in correctness proofs of entire processors continues to be an amazingly difficult topic of research. Some recent progress is reported in [17].

As for the new results of this paper: we are not aware of previous work on the verification of MMUs. We are also not aware of previous theoretical work on the correctness of virtual machine simulations.

2   Virtual Machines

2.1   Notation

We denote the concatenation of bit strings $a \in \{0, 1\}^n$ and $b \in \{0, 1\}^m$ by $a \circ b$. For bits $x \in \{0, 1\}$ and positive natural numbers $n \in \mathbb{N}^+$ we define inductively $x^1 = x$ and $x^n = x^{n-1} \circ x$. Thus, for instance $0^5 = 00000$ and $1^2 = 11$.

Overloading symbols like $+$, $\cdot$, and $<$ we will allow arithmetic on bit strings $a \in \{0, 1\}^n$. In these cases arithmetic is binary modulo 2^n (with nonnegative representatives). We will consider $n = 32$ for addresses or registers and $n = 20$ for page indices.

---

[1] http://www-wjp.cs.uni-sb.de/forschung/projekte/VAMP/

Table 1. Special purpose registers. Indices 01100 to 01111 are not assigned.

Address	Name	Meaning	Address	Name	Meaning
00000	SR	Status register	00111	IEEEf	IEEE flags
00001	ESR	Exception status reg.	01000	FCC	Floating point (FP)
00010	ECA	Exception cause reg.			condition code
00011	EPC	Exception PC	01001	pto	Page table origin
00100	EDPC	Exception DPC	01010	ptl	Page table length
00101	Edata	Exception data	01011	Emode	Exception mode
00110	RM	Rounding mode	10000	mode	Mode

We model memories m as mappings from addresses a to byte values $m(a)$. For natural numbers d we denote by $m_d(a)$ the content of d consecutive memory cells starting at address a, so $m_d(a) = m(a+d-1) \circ \cdots \circ m(a)$. For $d = 4\mathrm{K} = 2^{12}$ and a a multiple of 4K, we call $m_d(a)$ a *page* and 4K the *page size*. We split virtual addresses $va = va[31:0]$ into page index $va.px = va[31:12]$ and byte index $va.bx = va[11:0]$. Thus, $va = va.px \circ va.bx$. For page indices px and memories m we abbreviate $page(m, px) = m_{4\mathrm{K}}(px \circ 0^{12})$.

2.2 Specifying the Instruction Set Architecture

Virtual machines are the hardware model visible for user processes. Its parameters are:

- The number V of pages of accessible virtual memory. This defines the set of accessible virtual addresses $VA = \{a \mid 0 \le a < V \cdot 4\mathrm{K}\}$.
- The number $e \in \mathbb{N}$ of external interrupt signals.
- The set $VSA \subseteq \{0,1\}^5$ of addresses of user visible special purpose registers. Table 1 shows the entire set of special purpose registers that will be visible for a *physical* machine. For the virtual machine only the registers RM, $IEEEf$, and FCC will be visible. Hence $VSA = \{00110, 00111, 01000\}$.
- The status register $SR \in \{0,1\}^{32}$. This is the vector of mask bits for the interrupts.

Formally, the configuration of a virtual machine is a 7-tuple $c_V = (c_V.PC, c_V.DPC, c_V.GPR, c_V.FPR, c_V.SPR, c_V.vm, c_V.p)$ with the following components:

- The normal program counter $c_V.PC \in \{0,1\}^{32}$ and the delayed program counter $c_V.DPC \in \{0,1\}^{32}$, used to implement the delayed branch mechanism (cf. [15]).
- The general purpose register file $c_V.GPR : \{0,1\}^5 \to \{0,1\}^{32}$, the floating point register file $c_V.FPR : \{0,1\}^5 \to \{0,1\}^{32}$, and the special purpose register file $c_V.SPR : VSA \to \{0,1\}^{32}$.
- The byte addressable virtual memory $c_V.vm : VA \to \{0,1\}^8$.
- The write protection function $c_V.p : \{va.px \mid va \in VA\} \to \{0,1\}$. Virtual addresses in the same page have the same protection bit.

Let C_V be the set of virtual machine configurations. An instruction set architecture (ISA) is formally specified as a transition function $\delta_V : C_V \times \{0,1\}^e \to C_V$ mapping configurations $c_V \in C_V$ and a vector of external event signals $eev \in \{0,1\}^e$ to the next configuration $c'_V = \delta_V(c_V, eev)$. For the DLX instruction set we outline the formal definition of this function emphasizing interrupt handling.

The instruction $I(c_V) = c_V.vm_4(c_V.DPC)$ to be executed in configuration c_V is found in the four bytes in virtual memory starting at the address of the delayed PC. The opcode $opc(c_V) = I(c_V)[31:26]$ consists of the leading six bits of the instruction. Many instructions can be decoded just from the opcode, e.g. a load word instruction is recognized by $lw(c_V) = (opc(c_V) = 100011)$. The type of an instruction determines how the bits outside the opcode are interpreted. For instance, if the opcode consists of all zeros we have an R-type instruction, $R\text{-}type(c_V) = (opc(c_V) = 0^6)$. Other instruction types are defined in a similar way. Depending on the instruction type the register destination address $RD(c_V)$ is found at different positions in the instruction, namely $RD(c_V) = I(c_V)[15:11]$ if $R\text{-}type(c_V)$ and $RD(c_V) = I(c_V)[20:16]$ otherwise. Similarly, one can define register source addresses $RS1(c_V)$ and $RS2(c_V)$, the sign extended immediate constant $simm(c_V)$, etc. The effective address of a load / store instruction is computed as the sum of the general purpose register addressed by $RS1(c_V)$ and the sign extended immediate constant, $ea(c_V) = c_V.GPR(RS1(c_V)) + simm(c_V)$. A load word instruction reads four bytes of virtual memory starting at address $ea(c_V)$ into the general purpose register addressed by $RD(c_V)$. This can be expressed by equations like $lw(c_V) \implies (c'_V.GPR(RD(c_V)) = c_V.vm_4(ea(c_V)))$.

Components of the configuration that are not listed on the right-hand side of the implication are meant to be unchanged. This definition, however, ignores both internal and external interrupts; therefore even for virtual machines it is an oversimplification.

2.3 Interrupts

We define a predicate $JISR(c_V, eev)$ (jump to interrupt service routine) depending on both the current configuration c_V and the current values $eev \in \{0,1\}^e$ of the external interrupt event signals. Only if this signal stays inactive does the above equation hold, so $(\neg JISR(c_V, eev) \wedge lw(c_V)) \implies (c'_V.GPR(RS1(c_V)) = c_V.vm_4(ea(c_V)))$.

For physical machines an activation of the $JISR$ signal has a well defined effect on the program counters and the special purpose registers. The effect on virtual machine computations however is that control is handed over to the operating system kernel. This effect can only be defined in a model that includes the operating system kernel.[2]

For the definition of signal $JISR(c_V, eev)$ for physical machines, we consider the 32 interrupts from Table 2 with indices $j \in IP = \{0, \ldots, 31\}$. For virtual machines we ignore page fault interrupts, thus we only consider $j \in IV = IP \setminus \{3, 4\}$. The activation of signal $JISR(c_V, eev)$ can be caused by the activation of external interrupt lines $eev[j]$ or internal interrupt event signals $iev(c_V)[j]$. We define the cause vector by $ca(c_V, eev)[j] = eev[0]$ for $j = 0$, by $ca(c_V, eev)[j] = eev[j-12]$ for $j > 0$ external, and by $ca(c_V, eev)[j] = iev(c_V)[j]$ otherwise.

Formally, external interrupts are input signals for the next state computation while internal interrupts are functions of the current configuration. E.g. a definition of the misalignment signal is

$$mal(c_V) = iev(c_V)[2] = \neg(4 \mid c_V.DPC) \vee (ls(c_V) \wedge \neg(d(c_V) \mid ea(c_V)))$$

---

[2] We do not treat this further; see the (german) lecture notes [18] or [9] for details.

Table 2. Interrupts

j	Name	Meaning	Mask.	Ext.	j	Name	Meaning	Mask.	Ext.
0	reset	Reset	No	Yes	7	fovf	FP overflow	Yes	No
1	ill	Illegal instruction	No	No	8	funf	FP underflow	Yes	No
2	mal	Misaligned access	No	No	9	finx	FP inexact result	Yes	No
3	pff	Page fault on fetch	No	No	10	fdbz	FP division by zero	Yes	No
4	pfls	Page fault on load / store	No	No	11	finv	FP invalid operation	Yes	No
5	trap	Trap	No	No	12	ufop	Unimpl. FP operation	No	No
6	xovf	Fixed point overflow	Yes	No	>12	$io[j]$	Device interrupt j–12	Yes	Yes

with $u \mid v$ indicating divisibility, $ls(c_V)$ indicating the presence of a load / store instruction, and $d(c_V) \in \{1, 2, 4, 8\}$ indicating its memory access width in bytes.

For virtual machines, but not for physical machines, reading or writing special purpose registers other than RM, $IEEEf$, and FCC is illegal. Reading or writing these registers is achieved with commands `movi2s` or `movs2i`; the register address is given by the instruction field $SA(c_V) = I(c_V)[10 : 6]$. Thus the illegal instruction signal $ill(c_V) = iev(c_V)[1]$ has an implicant $(movi2s(c_V) \lor movs2i(c_V)) \land (SA(c_V) \notin VSA)$.

The interrupt cause for a maskable interrupt j is ignored if the associated status register bit $SR[j]$ is zero. So, we define the masked vector mca by $mca(c_V, eev)[j] = ca(c_V, eev) \land c_V.SR[j]$ for j maskable and $mca(c_V, eev)[j] = ca(c_V, eev)$ otherwise. An interrupt occurs if at least one masked cause bit is on; so, $JISR(c_V, eev) = 1$ iff there exists $j \in IV$ with $mca(c_V, eev)[j] = 1$.

3 Physical Machines

Physical machines are the sequential programming model of the hardware as seen by the programmer of an operating system kernel. Compared with virtual machines, more details are visible in configurations $c_P \in C_P$ of physical machines.

- All special purpose registers are visible. Formally $c_P.SPR : PSA \rightarrow \{0, 1\}^{32}$ with $PSA \subseteq \{0, 1\}^5$ consisting of the addresses in Table 1. We abbreviate $c_P.x = c_P.SPR(x)$ where x is the name of a special purpose register.
  The mode register $c_P.mode$ distinguishes between system mode ($c_P.mode = 0$) and user mode. In system mode accessing special purpose registers is legal.
- Page faults are visible; in the definition of $JISR$ the full set of indices IP is used.
- For physical machines the next state $\delta_P(c_P, eev)$ is defined also for an active signal $JISR(c_P, eev)$, starting execution of the interrupt service routine (ISR) in system mode. See [15] for details. In system mode physical machines can legally execute an `rfe` (return from exception) instruction.
- Instead of a uniform virtual memory the (system) programmer now sees two memories: physical memory $c_P.pm$ and swap memory $c_P.sm$.
- In user mode accesses to physical memory are translated.

In the remainder of this section we specify a single-level translation mechanism and model I/O operations with the swap memory.

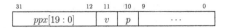

Fig. 1. Page Table Entry

3.1   Address Translation

In user mode, i.e. if $c_P.mode = 1$, memory accesses to virtual addresses $va = c_P.DPC$ and $va = ea(c_P)$ are subject to address translation: they either cause a page fault or are redirected to the translated physical memory address $pma(c_P, va)$.

Let us define $pma(c_P, va)$ first. The page table entry address for virtual address va is defined as $ptea(c_P, va) = c_P.pto \cdot 4K + 4 \cdot va.px$ and its page table entry is defined as $pte(c_P, va) = c_P.pm_4(ptea(c_P, va))$. As shown in Fig. 1, the page table entry is composed of three components, the physical page index $ppx(c_P, va) = pte(c_P, va)[31 : 12]$, the valid bit $v(c_P, va) = pte(c_P, va)[11]$, and the protection bit $p(c_P, va) = pte(c_P, va)[10]$. We define the physical memory address by concatenating the physical page index and the va's byte index $pma(c_P, va) = ppx(c_P, va) \circ va.bx$.

For the definition of page faults, let the flag $w \in \{0, 1\}$ be active for write operations. The page fault flag $pf(c_P, va, w)$ is set if (i) the virtual page index $va.px$ is greater or equal the number of accessible pages $V = c_P.ptl + 1$, (ii) the valid bit $v(c_P, va)$ is false, or (iii) the write flag w and the protection bit $p(c_P, va)$ are active, indicating a write attempt to a protected page. So, overall $pf(c_P, va, w) = (va.px \geq V) \vee \neg v(c_P, va) \vee w \wedge p(c_P, va)$. Thus, all entries $pte(c_P, va)$ with $pf(c_P, va, w) = 0$ are located in the *page table* $PT(c_P) = c_P.pm_{4 \cdot V}(c_P.pto \circ 0^{12})$.

A page fault on fetch occurs if $pff(c_P) = c_P.mode \wedge pf(c_P, c_P.DPC, 0)$. In the absence of such a fault, we define the instruction word by $I(c_P) = c_P.pm_4(iaddr(c_P))$ where $iaddr(c_P) = pma(c_P, c_P.DPC)$ in user mode and $iaddr(c_P) = c_P.DPC$ otherwise. Let $ls(c_P)$ and $s(c_P)$ indicate the presence of a load / store resp. a store instruction. In the absence of a page fault on fetch, a page fault on load / store occurs if $pfls(c_P) = c_P.mode \wedge ls(c_P) \wedge pf(c_P, ea(c_P), s(c_P))$.

Multi-level address translation can be formally specified similarly, see e.g. [19].

3.2   Modeling an I/O Device

In order to handle page faults, one has to be able to transfer pages between the physical memory $c_P.pm$ and the swap memory $c_P.sm$, implemented with an I/O device. For a detailed (minimal) treatment of this process four things are necessary:

1. Define I/O ports as a portion of memory shared between the CPU and the device.
2. Specify the detailed protocol of the I/O devices.
3. Construct a driver program, say, with three parameters passed on (distinct) fixed addresses in physical memory: a physical page index $ppxp(c_P)$, a swap memory page index $spxp(c_P)$, and a physical-to-swap flag $p2s(c_P)$ indicating whether the page transfer is from physical to swap memory ($p2s(c_P) = 1$) or vice versa.
4. Show: if the driver is started in configuration c_P and never interrupted, it eventually reaches a configuration c'_P with

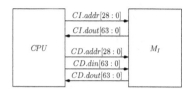

Fig. 2. Memory Interface

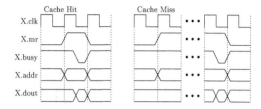

Fig. 3. Timing Diagrams for Read Accesses

$$page(c_P'.sm, spxp(c_P)) = page(c_P.pm, ppxp(c_P)) \quad \text{if} \quad p2s(c_P) = 1 \; ;$$
$$page(c_P'.pm, ppxp(c_P)) = page(c_P.sm, spxp(c_P)) \quad \text{if} \quad p2s(c_P) = 0 \; .$$

5. Furthermore show: (i) program control returns to the location of the call of the driver, (ii) except for certain book keeping information no other parts of the configuration change, and (iii) the driver never leaves its own code region.

Here, we assume the existence of a correct driver as an axiom; in [11] we deal with this problem on a fundamental level.

4   Construction and Local Correctness of MMUs

We refer to the hardware configuration by h. Its components are registers $h.R$, often shortly written as R. For cycles t and hardware signals or registers x we denote by x^t the value of x during cycle t.

4.1   Memory Interface

We construct MMUs for processors with two first level caches, an instruction cache CI for fetches and a data cache CD for load / store instructions. Thus the CPU communicates with the memory system via two sets of busses: one connecting the CPU with the instruction cache and the other one with the data cache (data bus width is 64 bits, cf. Fig. 2). We use the same protocol for both busses. Examples of the protocol are shown in Fig. 3 for a read access with and without a cache hit. The properties of the bus protocol are:

1. Accesses last from the activation of a request signal (in the example mr) until the busy signal is turned off. Optimally, this happens in the same cycle.
2. Read and write requests may not be given simultaneously: $\neg(mr \wedge mw)$
3. During an access, CPU inputs to the memory system must be kept stable.
4. Liveness: if Conditions 2 and 3 are fulfilled, every access eventually ends.

The memory system satisfies shared memory semantics: for cycles t, for $0 \le b < 8$, and addresses a we define $last_b(a, t)$ as the last cycle t' before t, when a write access to byte b of address a ended (necessarily via the data cache). Now assume a read access to cache X with address a ends in cycle t. Then the result on bus $X.dout$ is $X.dout^t[8 \cdot$

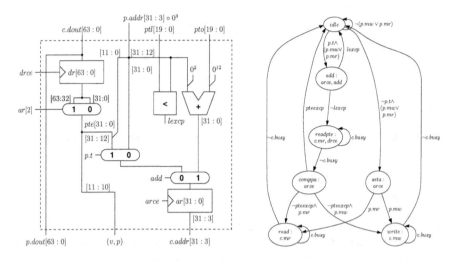

Fig. 4. MMU Datapaths and Control Automaton.

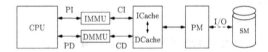

Fig. 5. Processor and MMUs

$b + 7 : 8 \cdot b] = CD.din^{last_b(a,t)}[8 \cdot b + 7 : 8 \cdot b]$. This definition permits to define the state of the two port memory system $m(h)$ at time t by $m(h^t)(a \cdot 8 + b) = CD.din^u$ where $u = last_b(a, t)$. For a formal and complete version of this definition (including initialization), the construction of a split cache system, and a transcript of a formal correctness proof, see [13–Pages 1–110]. Guaranteeing that the CPU keeps inputs stable (Condition 3) during *all* accesses (even when an interrupt is detected deeper down in the pipeline) requires the construction of *stabilizer circuits* for both ports of the memory system. For details see [13–Section 4.4].

4.2   MMU Construction and Operating Conditions

Figure 4 shows datapaths and control automaton of a simple non-optimized MMU implementation. Two copies of this MMU are placed between the CPU and the caches as shown in Fig. 5. In user mode this MMU will only perform address translation under non trivial operating conditions. Consider an access of the CPU to the MMU lasting from a start cycle *ts* to an end cycle $te \geq ts$. We have to require that no signal or register x from the groups below changes during the access, so $x^t = x^{ts}$ holds for $ts \leq t \leq te$.

G1. Inputs from the CPU to the MMU; these are $p.dout$, $p.addr$, $p.mr$, and $p.mw$.
G2. The CPU registers $h.mode$, $h.pto$, and $h.ptl$ relevant for translation.

G3. In case of a translated access the page table entry used for translation, the shared memory content $m(h)_4(ptea)$ with $ptea = h.pto \cdot 4K + 4 \cdot p.addr.px$.

G4. For reads with physical address pa, the shared memory content $m(h)_8(pa)$.

Analogous to Sect. 3.1 one can define for hardware configurations h and virtual addresses va a page table entry address $ptea(h, va)$, a page table entry $pte(h, va)$, and a physical memory address $pma(h, va)$. Note that under the operating conditions the virtual address va, the translation $pma(h, va)$, and, for reads, the data read from the memory stay the same during the whole access.

Assuming these operating conditions, the MMU's correctness proof is relatively straightforward. Guaranteeing them will be a considerably tougher issue.

4.3   Local MMU Correctness

There is an obvious case split on the kind and result of the access: (i) read / write, (ii) translated / untranslated, (iii) with / without exception. For each of the cases two lemmas about the control and the datapath of the MMU have to be proven. The proofs of these lemmas are easy and not given here. For example, the next two lemmas state the correctness for a translated read without exception. In this case, the page table entry and the memory operand are read in states *readpte* and *read* resp. By s^+ we denote the fact that the control stays in state s until the busy signal is taken away by the cache.

Lemma 1. *For a translated read without exception the path through the control automaton is* $idle \rightarrow add \rightarrow readpte^+ \rightarrow comppa \rightarrow read^+ \rightarrow idle$.

Lemma 2. *The result* $p.din^{te}$ *of a translated read without exception from a virtual address* $va = p.addr^{ts} \circ 0^3$ *is* $p.dout^{te} = m(h^{ts})_8(pma(h^{ts}, va))$.

5   Guaranteeing the Operating Conditions

Stable inputs from the CPU to the MMUs (Condition $G1$) can be guaranteed by using stabilizer circuits similar to those mentioned in Sect. 4.1. Condition $G4$ for loads can be guaranteed if stores are performed in-order by the memory unit. Guaranteeing the remaining operating conditions (Conditions $G2$, $G3$, and $G4$ for fetch) requires a software convention *and* a hardware construction.

5.1   Software Synchronization Convention

Consider sequential computations of the physical machine $(c_P^0, c_P^1, \dots)$. Formally, for all steps i we have $c_P^{i+1} = \delta_P(c_P^i, eev^i)$. Recall that for such machines the instruction address $iaddr(c_P)$ depends on $c_P.mode$ (cf. Sect. 3.1) and the instruction $I(c_P)$ fetched in configuration c_P is defined as $I(c_P) = c_P.pm_4(iaddr(c_P))$.

We define an instruction as *synchronizing* if the pipeline of the processor is drained before the (translation of the) fetch of the next instruction starts. The VAMP processor already has such an instruction, namely a movs2i instruction with *IEEEf* as source.[3]

---

[3] This instruction reads the floating point interrupts accumulated *so far*.

We now also define the $\mathtt{rfe}$ instruction as synchronizing and let the predicate $sync(c_P)$ indicate that instruction $I(c_P)$ is synchronizing.

Synchronizing instructions must be used to resolve RAW hazards for instruction fetch to prevent modification of an instruction in a pipelined machine after it has already been (pre-) fetched. Formally, let $u < w$ be two instruction indices. We require the existence of an index v with $u < v < w$ and $sync(c_P^v)$ under the following two conditions: 1. If $I(c_P^u)$ writes to $iaddr(c_P^u)$. 2. If $I(c_P^u)$ writes to the page table entry at address $ptea(c_P^w.DPC)$ that is read for *user mode* instruction fetch. The first condition is already needed in pipelined machines without address translation [12,14].

Clearly, Condition 1 addresses operating condition $G4$ in case of a fetch, whereas Condition 2 addresses $G3$. In hardware one has to address operating condition $G2$ and to implement pipeline drain once a synchronizing instruction is decoded.

5.2 Hardware Mechanisms for Synchronization

The VAMP processor has a two stage pipeline for instruction fetch and instruction decode, followed by a Tomasulo scheduler. For details see [12,13,20]. Thus, there are many register stages S, e.g. IF for instruction fetch and ID for instruction decode.

The clocking and stalling of individual stages is achieved by a *stall engine*. For an introduction to stall engines see [15]; for improvements see [13,20]. Three crucial data structures / signals are associated with each stage S in the stall engine:

1. The full bit $full_S$ is on if stage S has meaningful data. Clearing it flushes the stage.
2. The local busy signal $busy_S$ is on if the circuits with inputs from register stage S do not produce meaningful data at the end of a cycle.
3. The update enable signals ue_S is like a clock enable signal. If ue_S is active in a cycle, the stage S receives new data in the next cycle.

Let $busy'_{IF}$ be the busy signal of the instruction fetch stage of the VAMP without MMUs. We define a new busy signal by $busy_{IF}(h) = busy'_{IF}(h) \vee \neg fetch(h)$ where the signal $fetch(h)$ is almost the read signal for the instruction MMU (as noted before, the read signal of the instruction MMU is stabilized to satisfy $G1$).

Signal $fetch$ is turned on if (i) no instruction changing registers pto, ptl and $mode$ is in progress and (ii) no synchronizing instruction is in decode. Instructions in progress can be in the instruction decode stage, i.e. in its instruction register I, or they are issued but not completed, thus they are in the Tomasulo scheduler and its data structures. In a Tomasulo scheduler an instruction in progress which changes a register r from a register file is easily recognized by an inactive valid bit $r.v$. Thus we define $fetch(h) = h.pto.v \wedge h.ptl.v \wedge h.mode.v \wedge fetch'(h)$ where function $fetch'(h)$ has to take care of instructions in the decode stage. Using predicates like $rfe()$ which are already defined for configurations also for the contents of the instruction register, we define

$$fetch'(h) = \neg(h.full_{ID} \wedge (sync(I) \vee movi2s(I) \vee rfe(I))) .$$

In the VAMP processor synchronizing instructions stay in the instruction decode stage until they can immediately proceed to the write-back stage.

6   Processor Correctness

6.1   Correctness Criteria

We are using correctness criteria based on scheduling functions from [13,14,15,20]. Register stages S of the hardware configuration h come in three flavours:

- Visible stages (with respect to the physical machine from Section 3): these stages are (i) PCs with the program counters $h.PC$, $h.DPC$, (ii) RF with the register files $h.GPR$, $h.SPR$, and $h.FPR$, (iii) stage mem' with the specified memory. This memory is not represented directly by hardware registers; instead it is simulated by the memory system with caches with the function $m(h)$ (cf. Sect. 4.1).
- Invisible stages: the registers of these stages store intermediate results used in the definition of the sequential physical machine. Stage ID with the instruction register $h.IR$ stores values $I(c_P)$, stage mem with the address input register $h.PD.addr$ for the data MMU stores $ea(c_P)$, etc.
- Stages from the data structures of the Tomasulo scheduler.

We map hardware stages S and hardware cycles t to instruction numbers i via the scheduling function sI. Assume $sI(S,t) = i$. The intention is to relate the contents of the registers in stage S in hardware configuration h^t to the physical machine configuration c_P^i (and its derived components). We distinguish the following cases.

For visible registers R from stages $S \neq mem'$ we require $h^t.R = c_P^i.R$. Thus the specified value of visible hardware register R in cycle t is the same as the value of R in the specification machine before execution of the i-th instruction. Similarly, we require for the stage $S = mem'$ that $m(h^t) = c_P^i.pm$ and for invisible registers R in stage S that $h^t.R = R(c_P^i)$. Specific correctness criteria are used for the data structures of the Tomasulo scheduler. For details see [20].

The three main definitions for scheduling functions that make this work are: (i) In-order fetch: The fetch scheduling function is incremented if the instruction decode stage receives a new instruction, $sI(fetch, t+1) = sI(fetch, t) + 1$ for $ue_{ID}^t = 1$, and stays unchanged otherwise. (ii) The scheduling of a stage S' that is not updated does not change. Hence, $ue_{S'}^t = 0$ implies $sI(S', t+1) = sI(S', t)$. (iii) If data is clocked in cycle t from stage S to S' we set $sI(S', t+1) = sI(S, t) + 1$ if S' is visible and otherwise $sI(S', t+1) = sI(S, t)$.

Thus intuitively an instruction number $i = sI(S, t)$ accompanies the data through the pipeline; upon reaching a register in a visible stage S' however, the register receives the value *after* the i-th instruction, i.e. before instruction $(i+1)$.

6.2   Correctness Proof with External Interrupt Signals

In general pipelined processors do not finish execution of one instruction per cycle. As there are more cycles t than instructions i there are necessarily more external interrupt events signals eev_h^t at the hardware level than event signals eev^i seen by the sequential physical machine. For the computation of the latter, given as $c_P^{i+1} = \delta_P(c_P^i, eev^i)$, one has to define the interrupt signals eev^i seen by the physical machine from the signals eev_h^t seen by the hardware machine. This has already been observed in [14,15].

The VAMP processor, as most processors with Tomasulo schedulers, *samples* external interrupt signals in the write-back stage. Each instruction i is in this stage only for a single cycle. Call this cycle $t = WB(i)$. The correctness proof then works with $eev^i = eev_h^t$. It is a matter of protocol between processor and devices that no harm comes from that, i.e. no interrupts are lost [11].

6.3 Correctness Proof

We give the new part of the VAMP correctness proof for a translated instruction fetch without exceptions. The other new cases are handled similarly. Thus consider a translated read access on the instruction port of the CPU lasting from cycle ts to cycle te. Let $i = sI(\textit{fetch}, ts)$ and let $t \in \{ts, \ldots, te\}$ be any cycle of the access. Let us abbreviate the address of the double word containing instruction $I(c_P^i)$ by $va := c_P^i.DPC$ $[31:3] \circ 0^3$. From program counter correctness we conclude that in cycle t the address bus of the instruction MMU holds the (upper 29 bits) of va, so $PI.addr(h^t) = va$ $[31:3]$.

Let $i_1 = sI(RF, t) \leq i$ be the instruction in the register file stage in cycle t. By the construction of the fetch signal all instructions $x < i$ that update a special purpose register $R \in \{pto, ptl, mode\}$ have already left the pipe at cycle ts (also no instruction $x > i$ can enter the pipe while instruction $I(c_P^i)$ is being fetched). By additionally using the correctness criterion for R, we may conclude for t as above that $c_P^i.R = c_P^{i_1}.R = h^t.R$ and hence $pa_1 := ptea(c_P^i, va) = ptea(h^t, va)$.

Let $i_2 = sI(\textit{mem}', t)$. By Condition 2 of the software sync-convention all instructions $x < i$ that write to the address pa_1 have left the pipe already at cycle ts. Using correctness of the memory stage we get $c_P^i.pm_4(pa_1) = c_P^{i_2}.pm_4(pa_1) = m(h^t)_4(pa_1)$ and therefore $pa_2 := pma(c_P^i, va) = pma(h^t, va)$. By Condition 1 of the software sync-convention all instructions that write to the physical memory address pa_2 have left the pipe at cycle ts. As above we get $c_P^i.pm_8(pa_2) = c_P^{i_2}.pm_8(pa_2) = m(h^t)_8$ (pa_2).

Hence the operating conditions for the MMU are fulfilled and at time te it returns the double word $PI.dout(h^{te}) = m(h^{ts})_8(pa_2) = c_P^i.pm_8(pa_2)$. By selecting the appropriate half of this double word via bit 2 of the delayed program counter, at the end of cycle te we clock $I(c_P^i)$ into the instruction register I. Since $sI(ID, te + 1) = i$, we have shown hardware correctness for the considered case:

Lemma 3. $h^{te+1}.I = I(c_P^i) = I(c_P^{sI(ID, te+1)})$

7 Virtual Machine Simulation

In this section we outline an *informal* proof that a physical machine with a page fault handler can simulate virtual machines (here: only a single one). Making these arguments precise is not trivial; we give some details in Sect. 8.

We extend the definitions of physical page index $ppx(c_P, va)$ and valid bit $v(c_P, va)$ to page indices by $ppx(c_P, px) = ppx(c_P, px \circ 0^{12})$ and $v(c_P, px) = v(c_P, px \circ 0^{12})$.

Fig. 6. Memory Map. Addresses are given as page indices.

7.1 Memory Map of the Physical Machine

We partition the physical memory $c_P.pm$ into user memory and system memory, cf. Fig. 6. Addresses below $abase \cdot 4K$ are used by the page fault handler and the swap memory driver. Starting at address $abase \cdot 4K$ we allocate $a > 1$ pages of user memory with indices $UP = \{a' \in \{0,1\}^{20} \mid abase \leq a' < abase + a\}$. Likewise, we have a swap page index $sbase$ and use $sma(va) = sbase \cdot 4K + va$ to store va on swap.

We list below the data structures used by the handler and some invariants:

- A process control block PCB to save the registers of the virtual processor.
- The page table PT as defined by the address translation mechanism (Sect. 3.1).
- The physical page index MRL of the most recently loaded page.
- A variable $b \in \{-1, \ldots, a-1\}$ and an array D of size a holding virtual page indices. User page indices $0 \leq u \leq b$ we call *full*; we require for them $v(c_P, D[u]) \wedge ppx(c_P, D[u]) = abase + u$ and $D[u] < V$ where $V = c_P.ptl + 1$ denotes the number of accessible virtual pages. Otherwise, for $b < u < a$ we require $\neg v(c_P, D[u])$. Hence, valid translations map to the user memory, which is of crucial importance.
- Parameters $ppxp$, $spxp$, and $p2s$ of the swap memory driver (cf. Sect. 3.2).

7.2 Simulation Relation

For virtual machine configurations c_V and physical machine configurations c_P we define a simulation relation $B(c_V, c_P)$ stating that c_P encodes c_V. We require that the invariants of the previous subsection hold for the physical machine and that the physical machine is in user mode ($c_P.mode = 1$). Furthermore: (i) The write protection function is encoded in the protection bits of the page tables. Formally, for all virtual addresses va we require $c_V.p(va) = p(c_P, va)$. (ii) The user memory acts as a (write-back) cache for the swap memory. For virtual page indices px we require $page(c_V.vm, px) = page(c_P.pm, ppx(c_P, px))$ if $v(c_P, px)$ and $page(c_V.vm, px) = page(c_P.sm, sbase + px)$ otherwise.

Lemma 4 (Step lemma). *Let c_V and c_P be as above, assume no page fault in configuration c_P. Then, without external interrupts $B(c_V, c_P) \implies B(\delta_V(c_V, 0^e), \delta_P(c_P, 0^e))$.*

7.3 Page Fault Handler and Software Conditions

We describe a very simple handler that is never interrupted itself. Thus the handler needs only to save the general purpose registers of the physical processor into the PCB. Via the exception cause ECA we determine, if a page fault occurred. For page fault on fetch, $ECA[3:0] = 10^3$; for page fault on load / store, $ECA[4:0] = 10^4$. The virtual address xva causing the page fault is $xva = EDPC$ in the former case, $xva = EDATA$ else. It is easy to deal with page table length or protection exceptions: we stop the simulation. Thus assume a page fault occurred in a configuration c_P because the exception virtual page was invalid. Moreover assume $B(c_V, c_P)$ for a virtual machine configuration c_V. From this we get $page(c_P.sm, sbase + xv) = page(c_V.vm, xv)$ where $xv = xva.px$.

If $b < a$, not all user pages are full. We increment b and let $e = abase + b$ denote the physical page index where we later swap in the exception virtual page.

Otherwise, a victim physical page index vp must be selected from the user pages. The most recently loaded page is never chosen to avoid deadlock, so $vp \in UP \setminus \{MRL\}$. Let $vp = abase + u$. Using the table D we determine the matching victim virtual page index $vv = D[u]$ of the virtual page stored at physical page vp. Because $B(c_V, c_P)$ holds and $ppx(c_P, vv) = abase + u = vp$ we have

$$page(c_V.vm, vv) = page(c_P.pm, ppx(c_P, vv)) = page(c_P.pm, vp) .$$

We copy the victim page to swap memory by running the driver with parameters $(ppxp, spxp, p2s) = (vp, sbase + vv, 1)$. Then we clear the valid bit of page vv, reaching a configuration c_P' with $v(c_P', vv) = 0$ and $page(c_P'.sm, sbase + vv) = page(c_P.pm, vp) = page(c_V.vm, vv)$. Thus, the simulation relation $B(c_V, c_P')$ still holds. We set $e = vp$.

Now we swap in the exception virtual page to the physical page with index e by running the driver with parameters $(ppxp, spxp, p2s) = (e, sbase + xv, 0)$. We end up in a configuration c_P'' with $page(c_P''.pm, e) = page(c_P.sm, sbase + xv) = page(c_V.vm, xv)$. Then we update the page table entry of xv and the data structures by $v(c_P''', xv) = 1$, by $ppx(c_P''', xv) = e$, by $D[e - abase] = xv$, and by $MRL = e$ in a later configuration c_P'''. Thus, $B(c_V, c_P''')$ and the invariants hold for c_P'''. Finally, the handler restores the user registers from the PCB and executes an rfe instruction. By inspection of the handler we see that the software sync-convention holds.

7.4   Simulation Theorem

Theorem 1. *For all computations $(c_V^0, c_V^1, \ldots)$ of the virtual machine there is a computation $(c_P^0, c_P^1, \ldots)$ of the physical machine and there are step numbers $(s(0), s(1), \ldots)$ such that for all i and $S = s(i)$ we have $B(c_V^i, c_P^S)$.*

Proof. We prove the claim by induction on i. We assume that the initialization code establishes after a certain number of steps $S = s(0)$ that $b = -1$, all virtual pages are invalid and stored in swap memory, and the simulation relation $B(c_V^0, c_P^S)$ holds.

Concluding from i to $i + 1$, we examine the configuration after the next non-page-faulting user step. We set $s(i + 1) = \min\{s' \geq s(i) \mid c_P^{s'}.mode \land \neg pfls(c_P^{s'}) \land \neg pff(c_P^{s'})\} + 1$. The minimum always exists since the victim page of a page fault is not the page swapped in for the previous page fault. Thus, there are zero to two page faults from steps $s(i)$ to $s(i + 1) - 1$; for $s(i + 1) = s(i) + 1$ one step of the virtual machine is simulated in one step of the physical machine. The theorem's claim is implied by page fault handler correctness and the step lemma (Sects. 7.2 and 7.3).

8   Summary and Further Work

We have presented two main results. First, we have reported on the formal verification of the VAMP with (simple) MMUs (Sects. 4 to 6). The correctness proof for an MMU alone is simple, but depends on nontrivial operating conditions. Guaranteeing these requires a variety of arguments, from intricate arguments about the hardware (e.g. Sect. 5.2) to the format of page fault handlers (Sect. 7.3). Second, arguing on low level software we have shown that physical machines with suitable page fault handlers simulate virtual machines. Since operating systems support multitasking and virtual memory, these results are crucial steps towards verifying entire computer systems.

Presently we see three directions for further work. (i) The formal verification of processors with memory-mapped I/O devices, pipelined MMUs, multi level translation and translation look aside buffers. A mathematical model of a hard disk can be found in [11]. (ii) The formal proof of our virtual memory simulation theorem. This is part of an ongoing effort to verify an entire operating system kernel in the Verisoft project [8]. Mathematical proofs can be found in [18]. (iii) The verification of memory management mechanisms for shared memory multiprocessors. The thesis [19] contains such results.

References

1. Boyer, R.S., ed.: Special issue on system verification. (JAR) **5** (1989)
2. Boyer, R.S., Moore, J S.: A Computational Logic Handbook. Academic Press (1988)
3. Hunt, W.A.: Microprocessor design verification. In *JAR* [1] 429–460
4. Moore, J S.: A mechanically verified language implementation. In *JAR* [1] 461–492
5. Young, W.D.: A mechanically verified code generator. In *JAR* [1] 493–518
6. Bevier, W.R.: Kit and the short stack. In *JAR* [1] 519–530
7. Moore, J S.: A grand challenge proposal for formal methods: A verified stack. In Aichernig, B.K., Maibaum, T.S.E., eds.: 10th Colloquium of UNU/IIST '02, Springer (2003) 161–172
8. The Verisoft Consortium: The Verisoft Project. http://www.verisoft.de/ (2003)
9. Gargano, M., Hillebrand, M., Leinenbach, D., Paul, W.: On the correctness of operating system kernels. In Hurd, J., Melham, T., eds.: TPHOLs '05. LNCS, Springer (2005)
10. Leinenbach, D., Paul, W., Petrova, E.: Towards the formal verification of a C0 compiler: Code generation and implementation correctness. In Aichernig, B., Beckert, B., eds.: SEFM '05, IEEE Computer Society (2005)
11. Hillebrand, M., In der Rieden, T., Paul, W.: Dealing with I/O devices in the context of pervasive system verification. In: ICCD '05, IEEE Computer Society (2005) To appear.
12. Beyer, S., Jacobi, C., Kröning, D., Leinenbach, D., Paul, W.: Instantiating uninterpreted functional units and memory system: Functional verification of the VAMP. In Geist, D., Tronci, E., eds.: CHARME '03, Springer (2003) 51–65
13. Beyer, S.: Putting It All Together: Formal Verification of the VAMP. PhD thesis, Saarland University, Saarbrücken, Germany (2005)
14. Sawada, J., Hunt, W.A.: Processor verification with precise exceptions and speculative execution. In Hu, A.J., Vardi, M.Y., eds.: CAV '98, Springer (1998) 135–146
15. Müller, S.M., Paul, W.J.: Computer Architecture: Complexity and Correctness. Springer (2000)

16. Owre, S., Shankar, N., Rushby, J.M.: PVS: A prototype verification system. In Kapur, D., ed.: CADE '92, Springer (1992) 748–752
17. Aagaard, M., Ciubotariu, V., Higgins, J., Khalvati, F.: Combining equivalence verification and completion functions. In Hu, A., Martin, A., eds.: FMCAD '04, Springer (2004) 98–112
18. Paul, W., Dimova, D., Mancino, M.:   Skript zur Vorlesung Systemarchitektur. `http://www-wjp.cs.uni-sb.de/publikationen/Skript.pdf` (2004)
19. Hillebrand, M.: Address Spaces and Virtual Memory: Specification, Implementation, and Correctnesss. PhD thesis, Saarland University, Saarbrücken, Germany (2005)
20. Kröning, D.: Formal Verification of Pipelined Microprocessors. PhD thesis, Saarland University, Saarbrücken, Germany (2001)

Counterexample Guided Invariant Discovery for Parameterized Cache Coherence Verification*

Sudhindra Pandav, Konrad Slind, and Ganesh Gopalakrishnan

School of Computing, University of Utah
{sudhindr, slind, ganesh}@cs.utah.edu

Abstract. We propose a heuristic-based method for discovering inductive invariants in the parameterized verification of safety properties. The promise of the method stems from powerful heuristics we have identified for verifying the cache coherence of directory based protocols. The heuristics are based on syntactic analysis of counterexamples generated during verification, combined with simple static analysis of the predicates involved in the counterexamples to construct and refine inductive invariants. The heuristics were effective in filtering irrelevant predicates as well as keeping the sizes of the generated inductive invariants small. Contributions are: (i) the method is an efficient strategy for discovering inductive invariants for practical verification; (ii) the heuristics scaled smoothly from two small to one large cache coherence protocol (of complexity similar to commercial cache coherence protocols); (iii) the heuristics generate relevant auxiliary invariants which are easily verifiable in few seconds; and (iv) the method does not depend on special verification frameworks and so can be adapted for other verification tools. The case studies include German, FLASH, and a new protocol called German-Ring. The properties verified include mutual exclusion and data consistency.

1 Introduction

Parameterized verification methods—which verify systems comprised of multiple identical components for an arbitrary number of these components—are of growing importance in formal verification. Most parameterized verification techniques for safety properties (such as cache coherence) are based on discovering inductive invariants. Despite the large amount of research conducted in this area, there is no general-purpose inductive invariant discovery method that has been shown to be uniformly good across a spectrum of examples. High-level descriptions of large systems contain enough state variables that even after applying common reduction strategies, such as symmetry reduction, abstraction, and efficient fixpoint computation algorithms, the system is far too large for automated verification methods—let alone parameterized methods. Practical verification therefore demands some kind of symbiotic interaction between the user and the automated verification machinery to construct invariants that imply the safety

---

* Supported by NSF Grant CCR-0219805 and SRC Contract 1031.001.

D. Borrione and W. Paul (Eds.): CHARME 2005, LNCS 3725, pp. 317–331, 2005.

property. Such a verification method should not only help solve the verification problem but also help open a dialog between verification engineers and system designers who may exchange their knowledge about important system invariants.

In this paper, we discuss heuristics that have allowed us to generate invariants that are just strong enough to verify safety properties of cache coherence protocols. We build our heuristics in the context of a decision procedure for the equality fragment of first order logic with uninterpreted functions (**EUF**) [1]. The goal of these heuristics is to (i) cut down the number of invariants that are needed for verifying the proof goal, and (ii) filter out irrelevant facts (predicates) in the formation of inductive invariants. Our starting point is a concrete model of the system and a safety property to be verified. We start the system from an unconstrained state and symbolically simulate it for a single step. We then use an **EUF** decision procedure to check that the next state obtained from symbolic simulation satisfies the safety property, assuming the hypothesis that the start state satisfies it. Naturally, we are bound to get a failure case as we started from an unconstrained start state. We then construct invariants based on syntactic analysis of such failure cases obtained during the verification process. The syntactic analysis of the counterexamples is conceptually simple and can be easily automated. We deploy efficient filtering heuristics to minimize the predicates that make up the invariants. These heuristics, although context-dependent, are a kind of static analysis and may be done (only once) before the verification process starts. The heuristics are intuitive from a designer's point of view and can be automated for any cache coherence protocol. The idea behind the generated invariants is to constrain the start state to be within the set of reachable states such that the safety property holds. The process stops when the safety property and all the invariants are proved. Note that *our method is primarily intended* for verifying the safety property with respect to a model that has been thoroughly debugged through simulation as well as perhaps even formally verified for small non-parametric instances of, say, 3-4 nodes. This fact justifies why a user would react to a counterexample by strengthening the invariant—and not suspecting that the model is incoherent. This mindset as well as division of labor in achieving parametric verification is nothing new.

On simple but realistic examples, our heuristics worked without *any* adaptations; in other cases, the method still offered a structured approach to invariant discovery that had to be adapted only to a mild degree in an example-specific manner. In all three of our case studies[1]—namely the original German protocol [2], the FLASH protocol, and the high-level version of a completely new industrial protocol (which we call *German-Ring*) used in the IBM z990 multibook microprocessor complex [3]—our approach resulted in modestly sized inductive invariants.

We used the UCLID tool [4] for our experiments. UCLID provides a reasonably efficient collection of decision procedures for the logic of *Equality with Uninter-*

---

[1] The proof scripts, UCLID reference models, and the first author's MS thesis are available at http://www.cs.utah.edu/formal_verification/charme05_pandav. Please contact the first author for details.

preted Functions (**EUF**). On our examples, UCLID's runtime was under a few seconds. Our method relies on UCLID's ability to generate concrete counterexamples. These counterexamples are analyzed in order to come up with invariant strengthenings. *Our key contributions are in terms of the manner in which we analyze counterexamples and discover invariant strengthenings.* We believe our methods can be based on other counterexample-generating decision procedures for sufficiently expressive fragments of first-order logic.

1.1 Related Work

Since the work of German [5], if not before, there has been a significant amount of research on automating the discovery of invariants, see [6,7,8,9] for a (non-exhaustive) list of efforts. In spite of the sophistication of these techniques, the process of finding invariants is still mostly manual. Also these methods tend to discover far too many invariants (equivalent to one large invariant with many conjuncts), and there is currently no good way of deciding which ones are useful.

Predicate abstraction based methods [10,11] to construct inductive invariants automatically require complex quantified predicates. Das used predicate abstraction for verifying mutual exclusion for FLASH [12], albeit on a simpler model. Automated predicate discovery [10] tends to discover large predicates, and so cannot be applied for verifying large protocols like FLASH. Lahiri [13] developed a theory of automatically discovering indexed predicates to be used to construct inductive invariants; predicates are iteratively discovered by computing weakest preconditions, which can generate many superfluous predicates at each stage. It requires manual filtering to get rid of useless predicates (which needs human expertise); also, for large protocols like FLASH, the iteration may fail to converge to a fixpoint. The method of invisible invariants [14] is a collection of automated heuristics to construct auxiliary invariants. The heuristics compute the reachable set of states for a finite instance of the system and then generalize to construct an assertion, which is checked for inductiveness. However, the method is only known to work on a restricted class of systems, to which protocols like FLASH do not belong.

For the FLASH protocol, there have been few previous attempts at discovering inductive invariants for the *data consistency property*; namely, Park [15] in the setting of the PVS theorem prover and Chou et.al. [16] in the setting of Murphi. Park also proved *sequential consistency property* for FLASH (delayed mode). Efficient abstraction-based techniques for parameterized verification have been proposed in [16]. These techniques are suggested by a theory based on simulation proofs, by which one can justifiably use "non-interference lemmas", generated from counter examples, to refine the abstract model and prove the safety property. The lemmas are generated from counter example analysis, but the analysis is not syntax-driven, as in our approach. McMillan used compositional model checking for the safety and liveness property verification of the FLASH protocol [17]. The Cadence SMV tool has various built-in abstractions and symmetry reductions to reduce an infinite state system to finite state, which is then model checked. The user has to provide auxiliary lemmas, though few, and has to decompose the proof to be discharged by symbolic model checking. This requires significant human skill and knowledge for proving conjectures and driving the tool. In our method, we do not need such human intervention in using the tool. Rather, expertise is needed in picking relevant predicates for our filtering heuristics. Fortunately, such intervention occurs at the higher level of protocol design, which can help designers in not only understanding their protocols better, but also in communicating insights at that level to designers. In contrast to proofs done in the context of specialized tools such as Cadence SMV, our method can be employed in the context of more general-purpose tools such as UCLID or CVC-Lite that have **EUF** decision procedures which generate concrete counterexamples. Emerson and Kahlon [18] verified the German protocol by reducing it to a snoopy protocol and then invoking their proposition to automatically verify the reduced snoopy protocol. The reduction is manually performed and requires expertise. It is not clear whether such a method can be applied to FLASH. Recently, Bingham and Hu [19] proposed a new finite-state symbolic model checking algorithm for safety property verification on a broad class of infinite-state transition systems. They presented a method to reduce a conjunctively guarded protocol to a broadcast protocol on which their algorithm can be applied. They automatically verified German's protocol for data consistency within a minute. It is not clear, however, whether such a method can be scaled to work on large protocols like FLASH.

2   Overview of the Invariant Discovery Process

We model a protocol with a set of *state variables* $\mathcal{V}$. The values assigned to state variables characterize the state of the system. We also use a set of *input variables* $\mathcal{I}$, which can be set to arbitrary values on each step of operation. The value assigned to each input variable is nondeterministically chosen from the domain, thus modeling the concurrent nature of the protocol.

A protocol is formalized by $\mathcal{M} = \langle \mathcal{V}, \theta, \Delta \rangle$, a rule-based state machine, where

- $\mathcal{V}$ is a set of *state variables*. A *state* of the system M provides a type-consistent interpretation of the system variables $\mathcal{V}$. Let Σ denote the set of states over $\mathcal{V}$.
- θ is an boolean **EUF** formula describing the set of initial states $I \subseteq \Sigma$.
- Δ is a set of nondeterministic *rules* describing the transition relation $R \subseteq \Sigma^2$. Syntactically, each rule $\delta \in \Delta$ can be expressed as: $g \rightarrow a$, where g is a predicate on state variables and input variables and a is a *next state function (action)* expression. If g holds, a is executed: this assigns next state values to a subset $\mathcal{W}$ of state variables; any other state variables are unchanged when the transition is taken. If the guards of multiple rules hold at the same time, just one of the rules is picked up nondeterministically for execution.

2.1   Syntax Based Heuristics

For all cache coherence protocols that we are aware of—at least a dozen, including industrial ones—cache coherence can be stated as the safety property

$$\forall i, j. \, ((i \neq j) \wedge cache(i) = exclusive) \Rightarrow cache(j) \neq exclusive$$

The data consistency property of coherence protocols and the invariants we generate also enjoy a syntactically similar shape. Thus our method focuses on properties of the form

$$P : \forall \mathcal{X}. \, \mathcal{A}(\mathcal{X}) \Rightarrow \mathcal{C}(\mathcal{X}) \tag{2.1}$$

where $\mathcal{X}$ is the set of *index variables* and $\mathcal{A}$ and $\mathcal{C}$ are the antecedent and consequent of the formula, expressed using boolean connectives.

Let $\mathcal{P} = SP \wedge \bigwedge_i Q_i$ be the conjunction of the safety property SP and the invariants Q_i we generate. We can also treat $\mathcal{P}$ as a set of candidate invariants. Initially $\mathcal{P} = SP$, as we start with empty set of auxiliary invariants. Let D be the decision procedure for the logic of **EUF**. Our method of inductive invariant checking works as follows:

1. Pick a property P from the set $\mathcal{P}$ for verification [2]. Use the decision procedure D to verify that P holds for the initial state of the system.
2. Perform a one-step symbolic simulation of the system, moving from a general symbolic state s to a successor state t according to the transition relation. Use the decision procedure D to verify that the property P holds in the successor state t, assuming the conjunction of invariants $\mathcal{P}$ holds in start state s. We verify a formula of the form $\mathcal{P}(s) \Rightarrow P(t)$. If the result is **true**, we are done with the verification of property P. Otherwise, there are three possible failure cases, determined by the way in which the property can hold in the first state s and not hold in the second state t. The failure case is selected arbitrarily by the decision procedure.
3. Synthesize new formula Q from *syntactic analysis* and heuristics for the corresponding failure case. Add it to the system i.e., $\mathcal{P}' = \mathcal{P} \wedge Q$; go to (2). The intuition behind the new formula is to introduce a constraint that would not only get rid of the absurd failure (typically a scenario from an unreachable state space), but also trim the search space just enough to prove the property.

We iterate till all the properties in $\mathcal{P}$ are proved to be inductive.

A failure (or a counterexample) is a tuple $\langle \sigma^s, \delta', \sigma^t \rangle$ where σ^s, σ^t gives the start and next state interpretation for the system variables in the start and the next states respectively, and δ' is the (instantiated) transition rule. We say an interpretation σ satisfies a boolean formula F (denoted as $\sigma \models F$) if F is *true* under the interpretation σ. The syntactic evaluation of a formula F under an interpretation σ is denoted by $\langle F \rangle_\sigma$. Before we discuss the analysis of each failure case, a few definitions that we will need in the discussion:

Given an interpretation σ and a boolean formula F, the *satisfying core* of F under interpretation σ ($SC(F, \sigma)$) returns a maximal subformula, F', of F such that $\langle F' \rangle_\sigma \wedge (F' \Rightarrow F)$. The maximal subformula can be easily computed by traversing the syntax tree of F in a top-down manner. For example, if $F =$

---

[2] We start with the safety property SP. Then select the property in the order in which it is generated to be a potential invariant.

$a_1 \vee a_2 \ldots \vee a_n$ then $SC(F, \sigma) = \bigvee_i \{a_i | \langle a_i \rangle_\sigma = \textbf{true}\}$. The intuition is to capture as much information from the formula F provided by the interpretation σ that satisfies F.

Similarly, we define the *violating core* of a formula F under interpretation σ to be a maximal subformula, F' such that $\neg \langle F' \rangle_\sigma \wedge (\neg F' \Rightarrow \neg F)$.

The *action core* of a variable v for the transition rule $\delta : g \rightarrow a$ under the interpretation σ is the conjunction of the cores of the guard and the conditions in the nested ITE expression that assigns the next state value in the action a. Before we formally define the action core, we first define the set of boolean conditions in the nested ITE expression that leads to the next state assignment of v. Let

$$C(a(v)) = \begin{cases} \{c\} \cup C(t) \cup C(e) & \text{if } a(v) = ITE(c, t, e) \\ \{\} & \text{otherwise} \end{cases}$$

We divide the above set into two, one set contains conditions that are satisfied in the ITE expression ("then conditions") and other that are not ("else conditions"). Let

$$I(a(v)) = \{c \in C(a(v)) | \langle c \rangle_\sigma = \textbf{true}\}$$
$$J(a(v)) = \{c \in C(a(v)) | \langle c \rangle_\sigma = \textbf{false}\}$$

Finally, the action core of a variable v for the rule $\delta : g \rightarrow a$ under the interpretation σ is given by:

$$AC(v, \delta, \sigma) = \begin{aligned} & SC(g, \sigma) \\ & \wedge \bigwedge_{c \in I(a(v))} SC(c, \sigma) \\ & \wedge \bigwedge_{c \in J(a(v))} \neg VC(c, \sigma) \end{aligned}$$

The action core helps determine the predicates that were responsible for the next state assignment to state variable v by executing the transition rule δ under the interpretation σ. Since the guard g of the rule δ executed has to be satisfied, the satisfying core $SC(g, \sigma)$ is always included in the action core computation. Then, if the assignment expression for state variable v is a nested ITE we also conjunct the satisfying or the violating core of the boolean conditions in the nested ITE that were satisfied or violated respectively for reaching the assignment.

Now we discuss each failure case analysis:

Failure case I $(\sigma^s \models \mathcal{A} \wedge \sigma^s \models \mathcal{C}), (\sigma^t \models \mathcal{A} \wedge \sigma^t \not\models \mathcal{C})$

For this case, it is clear that the state transition rule δ' in question has assigned some of the variables in the consequent $\mathcal{C}$ leading to the failure. Let $S_\mathcal{C}$ be the set of such state variables. For each state variable $v \in S_\mathcal{C}$, we compute the *action core*, $AC(v, \delta', \sigma^s)$. Conjoin these action cores to obtain a formula $\mathcal{G}' = \bigwedge_{v \in S_\mathcal{C}} AC(v, \delta', \sigma^s)$. Let $\mathcal{A}' = SC(\mathcal{A}, \sigma^s)$ be the satisfying core of the antecedent. The idea behind the various *cores* is to minimize the predicates that make up our assertions. At the end of this process, we generate the following assertion

$$\mathcal{A}' \Rightarrow \neg \mathcal{G}' \tag{2.2}$$

The idea behind this formula is to disallow the conditions that lead to the violation of the consequent, if an over-approximation of the antecedent holds.

Failure case II $(\sigma^s \not\models \mathcal{A} \wedge \sigma^s \not\models \mathcal{C}), (\sigma^t \models \mathcal{A} \wedge \sigma^t \not\models \mathcal{C})$

In this case, the transition rule has assigned some variable in $\mathcal{A}$, since the truth value of $\mathcal{A}$ went from false to true when going from σ^s to σ^t. However, the failed consequent is just propagated from one state to other. Thus, we seek to suppress those conditions in the guard and action expressions of the rule δ' that led to the next state assignment satisfying the antecedent. We first determine the violating subformula of $\mathcal{C}$, $\mathcal{C}' = VC(\mathcal{C}, \sigma^s)$ (note that $\sigma^s \not\models \mathcal{C}'$, means $\sigma^s \models \neg \mathcal{C}'$). Let $S_{\mathcal{A}}$ be the set of variables in the antecedent that got assigned. Again as in failure-case **I**, for each variable $v \in S_{\mathcal{A}}$ we compute the action core $AC(v, \delta', \sigma^s)$. We then compute the *precondition* $\mathcal{G}' = \bigwedge_{v \in S_{\mathcal{A}}} AC(v, \delta', \sigma^s)$. This was the condition that fired the counterexample rule δ' and led to the next state assignment violating the property of interest. We therefore generate the following assertion to deal with failure case **II**:

$$\neg \mathcal{C}' \Rightarrow \neg \mathcal{G}' \tag{2.3}$$

The basic idea is to not allow a rule propagate the failed consequent to the next state.

Failure case III $(\sigma^s \not\models \mathcal{A} \wedge \sigma^s \models \mathcal{C}), (\sigma^t \models \mathcal{A} \wedge \sigma^t \not\models \mathcal{C})$

This case is the rarest, the main reason being that it arises for protocols that are buggy.[3] The transition rule δ' has assigned values to state variables present in both the antecedent and consequent, leading to violation. Under no circumstances, should any transition rule assign values conflicting with the invariance property. This failure case helped us identify modeling errors in our experimental studies.

2.2   Filtering Heuristics

In contrast to the failure analysis above, the heuristics we now discuss are context-dependent and can be applied only on cache coherence protocols. The motivation for them is that the major component of $\mathcal{G}'$ in the assertions 2.2, 2.3, consists of predicates from the guard g'. Large cache coherence protocols like FLASH have guards with many predicates: retaining all predicates from the guard g' in the assertion would be impractical. To remedy this, we filter irrelevant predicates from a guard. We came up with the filtering heuristics based on the empirical observations we made from our case studies.

Rules in cache coherence protocols can be categorized into two classes: *P-rules*, which are initiated by the requesting processor (*home* or *remote*); and *N-rules*, which are initiated by a message from the network. Messages in the network can be classified, as either **requests** or **grants**. A request message typically is from a caching node to the home node (such as *Get* and *GetX* in FLASH

---

[3] Parameterized verification is an expensive process and typically should be attempted only after finite-state model-checking has extensively ferreted out bugs.

Table 1. Filtering Heuristics: The numbers in the last column refers to the order in which the predicates must be picked. For example, if the counterexample has a N-rule of request msg type being processed by the home, then we construct assertion by picking predicates on directory variables first. If we are not able to prove this assertion inductive, then we *add* the predicates on environment variables to the assertion and check for inductiveness.

Rule (R)	Msg Type (m)	Client Type (c)	**Filter:** pick predicates on
P-rule	request	home	*local variables*
		remote	*directory variables*
N-rule	request	home	(1) *directory variables,* (2) *environment variables*
		remote	*channel variables describing the* (1) *type* (2) *sender of the msg*
	grant	—	*channel variables describing the msg type*

or *req_shared* and *req_exclusive* in German). A grant message is a message typically sent by *home* node to a *remote* node (such as *Put* and *PutX* in FLASH or *grant_shared* and *grant_exclusive* in German). All non-request messages, which are part of a pending transaction, such as invalidations, invalidation acknowledgments, *etc.* can be regarded as grants.

We also classify the state variables of cache coherence protocols in four types: *local* variables — describing the state of a caching agent such as `cache_state`, `cache_data`, ...; *directory* variables — such as `dir_dirty`, `excl_granted`, ...; *channel* variables — describing the shared communication channels, such as `ch2`, `unet_src`, ...; and *environment* variables — explaining the state of the transaction or global state. For example, the variable `current_command` in the German protocol explains the command that is currently being processed, and the variable `some_others_left` in FLASH which determines whether there are any *shared* copies.

Our filtering heuristics are based on the above classifications, and are summarized in Table 1. The predicates filtered by the heuristics are characterized by the *type* of the state variables on which they are expressed. We tabulate these context-dependent filtering heuristics based on our empirical observations. We found them to be very efficient in constructing invariants. Let us look at an instance how we apply the filtering heuristics. In German, `rule5` treats what happens when the home nodes receives a `inv_ack` message from a remote node. The guard of the rule is:

$$(\texttt{home\_current\_command} \neq \texttt{empty}) \wedge (\texttt{ch2(i)} = \texttt{invalidate\_ack})$$

This rule is a N-rule with message type **grant**. According to Table 1 one must pick predicates on channel variables describing the message type. Thus the relevant predicate from this guard is $(\texttt{ch2}(i) = \texttt{invalidate\_ack})$ and we need not consider the predicate $(\texttt{home\_current\_command} \neq \texttt{empty})$.

As can be seen, the filtering heuristics are a kind of static analysis. The tabular form of filtering heuristics (see Table 1) has resemblance to the tables that designers use for design cache coherence protocols. Those tables explain the action taken by a processing node for different protocol scenarios. We just order the state variables involved and choose predicates on them from the guard of the counterexample rule. So, these heuristics can be easily developed upon even by the designer which can not only aid the verification process but also encourage co-ordination between a verification expert and a designer in industrial setting.

Other Heuristics. Apart from the above heuristics for filtering predicates from the guard, other simple techniques can be useful:

Specialization: In cache coherence protocols, the home node has a distinguished status; therefore, if the counterexample deals with the home node, then the new invariant should not be generalized for all nodes and is applicable only for the home node.

Consistency Requirement: Sometimes, the right hand side of an assignment to a state variable is another variable. Imagine the property to be verified has a predicate $p = r$ in the consequent, where p, r are term variables. This is common in data consistency properties. Suppose also that $a(p) = q$ where a is the action function for the counterexample rule δ and q is a variable. In such cases, we cannot rely solely on boolean conditions in the guard and ITEs of the action to construct invariants, as the problem lies in the requirement that the state variable q has to be consistent too. The invariant should include a predicate on the consistency of this value. For example, if p and q are term variables and the consequent of the property has the predicate $p = i$, then we construct the invariant of the form $g' \Rightarrow (q = i)$.

3   A Detailed Illustration on the German Protocol

The 'German' directory based protocol was proposed as a verification benchmark by Steven German [2], and it provides a good illustration of our method. Our UCLID model of the protocol extends that developed by Lahiri [20] with a data-path description obtained from the Murphi model in [16]; the model is available from our website. For lack of space, and since the German protocol has been a popular example [16,14,13,18,11], we do not seek to explain the protocol here.

Coherence Property Verification. To start, let the coherence property

$$P : \forall i, j. \left((i \neq j) \land cache(i) = exclusive \right) \Rightarrow cache(j) = invalid$$

be symbolically simulated for one step as described in the previous section.

Counterexample 1: The decision procedure returns a counterexample in which the start state satisfies coherence (node i is *invalid* while j is *exclusive*). The client id `cid` chosen for execution is the node i, which receives a `grant_exclusive` message from the **home** node ("home" hereafter). The rule chosen for execution is `rule8`, which changes the cache state of `cid` to exclusive upon receiving this message. This violates coherence after `rule8` is executed.

Analysis: The start state doesn't satisfy both the antecedent of P (since $cache(i) = invalid$) and the consequent (since $cache(j) = exclusive$): thus P is vacuously satisfied. The rule assigns next state value to `cache(cid)` such that the antecedent holds in the next state and the violated consequent just propagates itself from start state to next state. Thus this is a class **II** counterexample as defined in Section 2.1. The boolean guard of the rule (obtained after beta-reduction) is `ch2(cid) = grant_ex`. We now let the syntax guide us in constructing a new assertion. First, we compute the violated core of the consequent, which in this case is the consequent itself. So $\mathcal{C}' = (cache(j) = exclusive)$. Then we compute the action core for the state variable, `cache`, which is the only state variable in the antecedent updated in the action of the counterexample rule. Thus $\mathcal{G}' = (ch2(cid) = grant\_ex)$. We now need to eliminate the input variable `cid` from $\mathcal{G}'$. Since the counterexample gives the same interpretation to both i and `cid`, `cid` may be replaced by i. Thus the constructed auxiliary assertion is, according to Formula 2.3:

$$I_1 : \forall i, j.\ cache(j) \neq invalid \Rightarrow ch2(i) \neq grant\_ex$$

Filtering heuristics do not apply since $\mathcal{G}'$ has just a single predicate. With I_1 in the system to prune the search space, we again check P for correctness.

Counterexample 2: We now obtain a new counterexample: node i is in exclusive state in the start state (thus satisfying the antecedent of P), while node j is in invalid state (thus satisfying the consequent of P). Thus P holds in the start state. We also have node j receiving a $grant\_sh$ message from `home`. The client id `cid` chosen for execution is the node j, and the rule is `rule7`. This rule changes the cache state of the client to *shared*, if the client has received a shared grant from home. Thus we have node j in shared state while node i has exclusive rights in the next state, which violates P.

Analysis: This counterexample is of type **I**. The state variable `cache` appears in the consequent and gets updated by the action. We compute the action core for `cache`, which is the guard $ch2(cid) = grant\_sh$. The assertion is built according to the formula 2.2; replacing the input variable `cid` by its corresponding index variable i. The constructed auxiliary assertion is

$$I_2 : \forall i, j.\ cache(i) = exclusive \Rightarrow ch2(j) \neq grant\_sh$$

With the auxiliary assertions I_1 and I_2 in the system, the property P is successfully proved. Note that both invariants I_1 and I_2 were constructed by following the recipe suggested in the analysis. We did not need any protocol dependent heuristics or filterings, as the involved guards were of small sizes. Of course, the auxiliary assertions remain to be proved.

Filtering Heuristics. Now we discuss an application of the filtering heuristics. While following our approach in verifying assertion I_2, we obtained a counterexample in an application of `rule9`. The start state has node i in exclusive state and node j is the `current_client`, satisfying the guard of the transition rule. In the next state the client j has been granted `grant_shared` message by the home node, as mandated by `rule9`, but node i is still in exclusive state, thus violating assertion I_2. This counterexample is of type **I**. The rule describes home granting shared access to a client, if the client has requested shared access, home has not granted exclusive access to any other node, and the response message channel is empty. The calculated precondition $\mathcal{G}'$

`current_command = req_sh` $\wedge$ `¬exclusive_granted` $\wedge$ `ch2(current_client) = empty`

has three boolean predicates. Having all of them in the refined assertion would perhaps be more than needed to construct an inductive version of I_2. Therefore, we use our filtering heuristics to prune $\mathcal{G}'$. The counterexample rule, `rule9`, is an **N-rule** of **request** type being processed by the *home* node. According to the heuristics suggested for **N-rule request** (see Table 1), therefore, the predicate on the directory variable, `exclusive_granted` is chosen, as it is the most crucial one in decision making. The predicate `current_command=req_sh`, which explains the request message, is irrelevant since the concurrent nature of a cache coherence protocol should allow request messages any time while the system is running. Also, the predicate checking the emptiness of the shared channel, `ch2(current_client)=empty`, doesn't yield a global constraint. Therefore, the strengthened assertion I_2 is:

$$I_{2.1} : \forall i, j.\, cache(i) = exclusive \Rightarrow ch2(j) \neq grant\_sh \wedge exclusive\_granted$$

After a few further steps, we arrive at the final version of $I_{2.1}$ (call it $I_{2.n}$):

$$I_{2.n} : \forall i, j.\, ((i \neq j) \wedge cache(i) = exclusive) \Rightarrow$$
$$(ch2(j) \neq grant\_sh \wedge exclusive\_granted \wedge$$
$$ch3(j) \neq inv\_ack \wedge ch2(j) \neq inv \wedge \neg inv\_list(j) \wedge \neg sh\_list(j))$$

The structure of the formula to be synthesized into an inductive invariant can be easily mechanized based on the case analysis of counterexamples. We blindly followed the above counterexample based analysis and the filtering heuristics to construct all the auxiliary invariants for verifying the coherence property.

Data Consistency Verification. The datapath property is

$$\forall i.\, ((\neg exclusive\_granted \Rightarrow (memdata = auxdata)) \wedge \qquad (3.1)$$
$$((cache(i) \neq invalid) \Rightarrow (cache\_data(i) = auxdata)))$$

To verify data consistency, we needed just two additional invariants beyond those discovered to verify the coherence property. Both the invariants were generated from the counterexamples that violated the consistency requirement. We will examine one such invariant. When we ran UCLID to check 3.1, we obtained a counterexample where the start state has node i receiving *grant_ex* message from *home*, but the data variable of the channel `ch2` carrying the message had a value different from `auxdata`. The transition rule was `rule8`. The action of the rule assigns `cache_data` for node i the value possessed by `ch2_data`, which is not `auxdata`, thus violating data consistency. So, following the consistency requirement heuristic (see Section 2.2), we invent the following auxiliary invariant:

$$D_1 := \forall i.\, (ch2(i) = grant\_ex) \Rightarrow (cache2\_data(i) = auxdata)\,.$$

4   Summary of Verifications

Besides the German protocol, we have also applied our method to the data-path and controlpath verification of FLASH and the controlpath verification of German-Ring. We now briefly summarize how our method performed on all the verifications.

German. We needed a total of 9 invariants to completely verify the coherence property of German. It took us a day to come up with the invariants. The total time taken by UCLID to prove the properties was 2.16s.

The earlier manual proof by Lahiri needed 29 invariants and took 8 hours for UCLID to finish the verification. Lahiri also applied an indexed predicate discovery method [13] to construct inductive invariants for the German proto-col. He derived a single indexed invariant, which required a manually provided predicate on the auxiliary variable `last_granted`. Note that auxiliary variables do not participate in decision making and so such predicates cannot be discov-ered, unless they are part of the property to be proven. For that reason, our invariants do not depend on auxiliary variables. Lahiri also generated a dual indexed inductive invariant automatically. However, this invariant had 28 predi-cates, against just 13 needed for constructing our invariants (most of them dual indexed), and took 2813 seconds of UCLID time, as against 2.16 seconds needed for ours.

We also verified data consistency for German; it required two additional invariants. It took couple of hours to modify the model to include datapath variables and finish the verification.

FLASH. The FLASH model was translated from the SMV model of McMil-lan [17]. We first verified coherence: no two nodes can be in the exclusive state. Surprisingly, no predicates on the directory were needed to prove the safety property except `dir_dirty`; this contrasts with the German coherence property verification which pulled out almost the entire logic of the protocol. This clearly points out that it is a waste of time and effort to generate invariants irrelevant to the proof of the safety property. We also verified data consistency for FLASH. New data variables for the cache, history variables, and auxiliary variables were introduced. These variables do not appear in the guards of rules; however, the data consistency property had predicates on these variables, so our method was effective. Certain counterexamples showed scenarios that seem hard to humanly imagine. For example, FLASH allows parallel operations like *replacement* to occur while another critical transaction is pending. These operations affect im-portant directory variables, and so invariants involving these directory variables had to be strengthened. The filtering heuristics were very highly used in con-structing the invariants. Many of the counterexamples had rules of N-rule grant type processed by a *remote* node, especially involving the scenario where inval-idation acknowledgements are pending. Invariants involving directory variables such as `shlist` (keeps track of the nodes having a shared copy of cacheline) and `real` (keeps track of number of invalidations sent in the system) were difficult to construct as they needed to be precisely strengthened.

It took just 7 invariants [21] to prove the mutex property for FLASH, containing just 9 predicates and UCLID took 4.71s to complete the verification. Surprisingly, none of these invariants needed predicates on directory variables other than `dir_dirty`, thus explaining the fact that we use only the information that would be just enough to imply the safety property. An additional 15 invariants were required to prove the consistency property and UCLID took 18.68s to automatically verify them. This shows the difference in efforts and time needed to verify different safety properties, and how our method efficiently adapts to such verifications by saving tool processing time and human effort. These invariants had predicates on almost all directory variables. Overall, it took us 3 days to discover all the invariants needed to imply the data consistency property from the counterexample guided discovery process.

German-Ring. We applied our method to verify a high-level description of the protocol used in the IBM z990 superscalar multiprocessor [3], provided to us by Steven German. This is an unconventional protocol, where caches communicate by sending messages on a bidirectional ring. The destination node for a message in the ring is computed by arithmetic calculations using $\mod, \times$ and $\div$.

The invariants were constructed using just the counterexample analysis explained in subsection 2.1, without the need of filtering heuristics. Since the UCLID language doesn't support arithmetic operators like $\mod, \times, \div$ where the arguments are variables, we could not model the ring topology of the protocol. Instead, we modeled an approximation in which nodes can send messages arbitrarily to any node in the system. However, the rules behind message passing/processing and all state changes were completely modeled as in the high-level specification of the German-Ring protocol. We were able to prove the coherency property, no matter how the caches are arranged.

In the verification, our heuristics generated two invariants sufficient to verify the safety property. It took us two days to complete the entire verification process including modeling of the protocol and generating the invariants.

5   Automation

We now briefly explain how the syntactic analysis of counterexample and the heuristics can be automated.

Automation. Given an interpretation, the computation of satisfiability, violating and action cores can be easily automated. When a property fails, the counterexample returned by a decision procedure is an assignment to variables that are used in the system and property description. This assignment is the interpretation that is used to decide to which failure case the counterexample belongs. The corresponding transition rule is determined and the satisfiability core of the guard is computed for the interpretation. Then we use our *filtering heuristics* (this can be a manual process too) to filter the predicates from the satisfying core formula of the guard. We would use this filtered formula to construct the invariant. Depending on the failure case, the corresponding core for the antecedent and consequent of the property is also computed. The action core computation for the variables in the property that are assigned in the action of the rule is also computed. Finally, the appropriate invariant is generated by applying the formulas 2.2,2.3. All the steps in the computation, except perhaps filtering heuristics, can be easily automated as they perform basic extraction and manipulation of boolean formulas. Providing a system that automates these steps and also provides a good interface for applying heuristics and backtracking is useful future work.

How to Detect Over-strengthening? A crucial issue is how do we detect whether we are over-strengthening the invariant or not. At present, we do not have a concrete solution to this problem. We detect this in a very crude way when we learn that we are picking the same predicates from the guard of the transition rule involved in the counterexample that has already been used in the invariant constructed so far. This signals that we are moving in circles and should backtrack to the point where we can pick some other predicate suggested by the priority ordering in filtering heuristics.

6   Conclusions

We have discussed new invariant generation techniques for the safety property verification of cache coherence protocols, using a simple counterexample based analysis. Our heuristics have been successfully applied to verify the mutual exclusion and data consistency properties of the German and FLASH cache coherence protocols. We were also pleasantly surprised at how effective they were on the new German-Ring protocol. The invariants that our method generates are sufficient but *lean*: just sufficient to prove the desired properties. Such invariants typically offer sharper insights into the behavior of a system compared to "flooding" the scene with too many invariants.

Industry level cache coherence protocols are too complicated for any current formal verification system to handle automatically. Our heuristics can help tackle this important problem by guiding manual deductive verification of such protocols, and by being able to generate simple auxiliary invariants easily from the counter example analysis. Our method is more general than previous approaches that were often pursued in the context of special verification frameworks. In contrast, our method can be applied in the context of any decision procedure for **EUF** logics that generate concrete counterexamples.

We have focused on constructing auxiliary invariants for safety property verification. We do not know whether such counterexample based analysis can be adapted for liveness property verification. Some of the issues that could be explored in future work are: (1) almost all the steps in the counterexample analysis and the heuristics can be automated; (2) it would be interesting to adapt our methods to *k-step* inductive invariant checking of safety properties for cache coherence protocols.

References

1. J. R. Burch and D. L. Dill. Automatic verification of pipelined microprocessor control. In *CAV'94*, volume 818 of *LNCS*, pages 68–80. Springer, 1994.
2. S. German. Personal Communication.
3. T. J. Siegel, E. Pfeffer, and J. A. Magee. The IBM eServer z990 microprocessor. *IBM J. Res. Dev.*, 48(3-4):295–309, 2004.
4. R. E. Bryant, S. K. Lahiri, and S. A. Seshia. Modeling and verifying systems using a logic of counter arithmetic with lambda expressions and uninterpreted functions. In *CAV'02*, volume 2404 of *LNCS*, pages 78–92. Springer, 2002.
5. S. German and B. Wegbreit. A synthesizer of inductive assertions. *IEEE Trans. Software Eng.*, 1(1):68–75, 1975.
6. Z. Manna and A. Pnueli. *Temporal verification of reactive systems: Safety.* Springer-Verlag, 1995.
7. A. Tiwari, H. Rueß, H. Saïdi, and N. Shankar. A technique for invariant generation. In Tiziana Margaria and Wang Yi, editors, *TACAS'01*, volume 2031 of *LNCS*, pages 113–127. Springer-Verlag, 2001.
8. N.Bjorner, A. Browne, and Z. Manna. Automatic generation of invariants and intermediate assertions. *Theor. Comput. Sci.*, 173(1):49–87, 1997.
9. S. Bensalem, Y. Lakhnech, and H. Saïdi. Powerful techniques for the automatic generation of invariants. In *CAV'96*, volume 1102 of *LNCS*, pages 323–335. Springer, 1996.
10. S. Das and D. L. Dill. Counter-example based predicate discovery in predicate abstraction. In *FMCAD'02*, volume 2517 of *LNCS*, pages 19–32. Springer, 2002.
11. K. Baukus, Y. Lakhnech, and K. Stahl. Parameterized verification of a cache coherence protocol: Safety and liveness. In *VMCAI'02*, volume 2294 of *LNCS*, pages 317–330. Springer, 2002.
12. S. Das, D. Dill, and S. Park. Experience with predicate abstraction. In *CAV'99*, volume 1633 of *LNCS*, pages 160–171. Springer, 1999.
13. S.K. Lahiri and R. Bryant. Indexed predicate discovery for unbounded system verification. In *CAV'04*, volume 3114 of *LNCS*, pages 135–147. Springer, 2004.
14. A. Pnueli, S. Ruah, and L. Zuck. Automatic deductive verification with invisible invariants. In *TACAS'01*, volume 2031 of *LNCS*, pages 82–97. Springer, 2001.
15. S. Park and D. L. Dill. Verification of flash cache coherence protocol by aggregation of distributed transactions. In *SPAA'96*, pages 288–296. ACM Press, 1996.
16. P.K. Mannava C.T. Chou and S. Park. A simple method for parameterized verification of cache coherence protocols. In *FMCAD'04*, volume 3312 of *LNCS*, pages 382–398. Springer, 2004.
17. K. McMillan. Parameterized verification of the FLASH cache coherence protocol by compositional model checking. In *CHARME'01*, volume 2144 of *LNCS*, pages 179–195. Springer, 2001.
18. E.A. Emerson and V. Kahlon. Exact and efficient verification of parameterized cache coherence protocols. In *CHARME'03*, volume 2860 of *LNCS*, pages 247–262. Springer, 2003.
19. J. D. Bingham and A. J. Hu. Empirically efficient verification for a class of infinite-state systems. In *TACAS'05*, volume 3440 of *LNCS*, pages 77–92. Springer, 2005.
20. S. Lahiri. Personal Communication.
21. S. Pandav, K. Slind, and G. Gopalakrishnan. Mutual exclusion property verification of FLASH cache coherence protocol. Technical Report UUCS-04-010, School of Computing, University of Utah, 2004.

Symbolic Partial Order Reduction for Rule Based Transition Systems

Ritwik Bhattacharya[1], Steven German[2], and Ganesh Gopalakrishnan[1,*]

[1] School of Computing, University of Utah
{ritwik, ganesh}@cs.utah.edu
[2] IBM T.J. Watson Research Center
german@watson.ibm.com

Abstract. *Partial order (PO) reduction methods* are widely employed to combat state explosion during model-checking. We develop a partial order reduction algorithm for rule-based languages such as Murphi [4] based on the observation that for finite-state systems, independence conditions used for PO reduction can be encoded as boolean propositions and checked using SAT methods. Comparisons against static-analysis based PO reduction algorithms have yielded encouraging results.

1 Introduction

Partial order (PO) reduction helps combat state explosion by avoiding redundant interleavings [3] among *independent* transitions [12,6,10], generating a representative subset of all interleavings. Traditional PO reduction algorithms rely on syntactic methods (e.g. based on occurences of shared variables) to compute the independence relation. Unfortunately, in the presence of complex data structures like records and arrays, such as is common with cache coherence protocols encoded in languages such as Murphi [4] and TLC [9], these algorithms do not work well — even if concurrent accesses to these aggregate structures occur at disjoint sites. By conducting a deeper semantic analysis based on Boolean SAT methods, one can overlook such 'false sharings' and achieve PO reduction. This short paper sketches our explicit enumeration model checking algorithms for PO reduction that benefit from a SAT-based analysis for independence.

There has been extensive research on partial order reduction methods [3]. Few previous works address reduction for formalisms without processes. Partial order reduction algorithms have also been proposed for symbolic state exploration methods [1]. The algorithm there is based on a modified breadth first search, since symbolic state exploration is essentially breadth first. The *in-stack check* of the traditional partial order algorithm is replaced by a check against the set of visited states. An alternative to the traditional runtime ample set computation algorithm is discussed in [8].

* Supported in part by NSF Award ITR-0219805 and SRC Contract 1031.001.

D. Borrione and W. Paul (Eds.): CHARME 2005, LNCS 3725, pp. 332–335, 2005.

2   Partial Order Reduction

Two transitions are *independent* if, whenever they are enabled together at a state, (i) firing either one does not disable the other (*enabledness*), and (ii) firing them in either order leads to the same state (*commutativity*). A transition is *invisible* with respect to a property if it does not change the truth values of any of the atomic propositions occurring in the property. The ample-set method proceeds by performing a modified depth-first search where, at each state, a subset of all the enabled transitions is chosen, called the *ample set*. Transitions from the ample set are then the only ones pursued from that state. This leads to a subset of the entire state space being explored. It is important to ensure that for each path in the full graph, there is a *representative* path in the reduced graph. The following conditions, adapted from [3], guarantee the existence of such representative paths: **C0** : An ample set is empty if and only if there are no enabled transitions. **C1:** Along every path in the full state graph that starts at a state s, the following must hold - if there is an enabled transition that depends on a transition in the ample set, it is not taken before some transition from the ample set is taken. **C2** : If a state is not fully expanded, then every transition in the ample set is invisible. **C3**[1]**:** There is at least one transition in every ample set that leads to a state not on the current dfs stack, which ensures that at least one transition in the ample set does not create a cycle.

3   Implementing PO Reductions for Murphi

We compute the independence relation by encoding the *enabledness* and *commutativity* relations as boolean propositions, and using a SAT solver to conservatively check them. First, we take the code fragments defining the guards and actions, and transform them into equivalent Lisp S-expressions. These are then combined to form S-expressions representing the *enabledness* and *commutes* relations for each pair of transitions, which are symbolically evaluated to produce formulas over finite data types. We do this over the entire syntax of Murphi, handling loops (by unrolling), procedures, and functions in the process. To check commutativity, for example, the SAT solver is given a formula of the form $g_1(S) \wedge g_2(S) \Rightarrow t_1(t_2(S)) \neq t_2(t_1(S))$ for an arbitrary S (perhaps unreachable — this being the source of conservativeness). If satisfiable, t_1 and t_2 are potentially non-commuting; otherwise, they are commuting. The invisibility checks can similarly be encoded as boolean formulas and symbolically evaluated.

Constructing the Ample Set: Our algorithm for constructing the ample set is shown in Figure 1. Line 2 picks an enabled, invisible transition (called the *seed transition*) at each state, and tries to form an ample set using this transition. Once a seed transition has been chosen, lines 5–7 compute the transitive closure of the ample set with respect to the dependence relation. Lines 11–15 check for a violation of the **C1** condition. If there is no violation, lines 16–19 check whether at least one of the transitions in the ample set leads to a state not on the current

---

[1] For a proof of the sufficiency of this form of the condition see [7].

```
1  proc ample(s) {
2    ample := { pick_new_invisible(enabled(s)) };
3    if (empty(ample))
4      return enabled(s);
5    while (exists_dependent(enabled(s),ample)) {
6      ample := ample + all_dependent(enabled(s),ample);
7    }
8    non_ample := all_transitions \ ample;
9    if ((ample = enabled(s)) or exists_visible(ample))
10     return enabled(s);
11   for (t_d in disabled(s))
12     if (dependent(t_d, ample))
13       for (t_o in non_ample)
14         if (t_o != t_d and !leavesdisabled(t_o,t_d))
15           return enabled(s);
16   for (t_a in ample) {
17     if (!(t_a(s) in onstack(s)))
18       return ample;
19   }
20   return enabled(s);
21 }
```

Fig. 1. Ample set construction algorithm for Murphi

stack. If this is the case, we return this ample set. Otherwise, we return the set of all enabled transitions.

4 Results and Conclusions

Our algorithms have been implemented in the **POeM** tool [2], which extends Murphi. We have run **POeM** on examples of varying sizes, and the results are shown in Table 1. Significant reduction is achieved in a number of the examples, the most dramatic being the dining philosophers benchmark labeled DP in the table, where, for 10 philosophers, there is over 99% reduction. The symbolic PO algorithm always does better than the static algorithm in our examples, in terms of the number of states generated. GermanN refers to German's cache protocol for N nodes. It currently yields insignificant reductions because of the existence of transitions dependent only in unreachable states. We are working on strengthening the guards with local invariants, to restrict the independence checks to reachable states.

Instead of SAT, better results might be obtained through higher level decision procedures for quantifier free formulas with equality, finite arithmetic and arrays [11,5], especially given the possibility of initially representing Murphi procedures and functions using uninterpreted functions.

Table 1. Performance of partial order reduction algorithm

Example	Unreduced		Static PO		Symbolic PO	
	States	Time	States	Time	States	Time
Bakery	33	0.14	33	0.14	21	0.14
Burns	82010	2.65	82010	5.02	81542	8.76
Dekker	100	0.17	100	0.17	90	0.17
Dijkstra4	864	0.29	864	0.29	628	0.31
Dijkstra6	11664	0.62	11664	0.88	6369	0.98
Dijkstra8	139968	6.65	139968	13.15	57939	35.32
DP4	112	0.22	112	0.22	26	0.22
DP6	1152	0.27	1152	0.27	83	0.25
DP10	125952	13.85	125952	17.27	812	0.34
DP14	>20000	>60	>20000	>60	7380	1.4
Peterson2	26	0.15	26	0.15	24	0.15
Peterson4	22281	0.3	22281	0.53	14721	0.58
German3	28593	0.43	28593	0.78	28332	1.31
German4	566649	31.15	566649	39.9	562542	72.43

References

1. Rajeev Alur, Robert K. Brayton, Thomas A. Henzinger, Shaz Qadeer, and Sriram K. Rajamani. Partial-order reduction in symbolic state space exploration. In *Computer Aided Verification*, pages 340–351, 1997.
2. R. Bhattacharya. http://www.cs.utah.edu/formal_verification/poem-0.4.tar.gz.
3. Edmund M. Clarke, Orna Grumberg, and Doron Peled. *Model Checking*. MIT Press, December 1999.
4. David L. Dill, Andreas J. Drexler, Alan J. Hu, and C. Han Yang. Protocol verification as a hardware design aid. In *International Conference on Computer Design*, pages 522–525, 1992.
5. C. Flanagan, R. Joshi, X. Ou, and J.B. Saxe. Theorem Proving Using Lazy Proof Explication. In *Computer Aided Verification*, pages 355–367, 2003.
6. Patrice Godefroid. Using partial orders to improve automatic verification methods. In *Computer Aided Verification*, pages 176–185, 1990.
7. G.J. Holzmann, P. Godefroid, and D. Pirottin. Coverage preserving reduction strategies for reachability analysis. In *Proc. 12th Int. Conf on Protocol Specification, Testing, and Verification, INWG/IFIP*, Orlando, Fl., June 1992.
8. R. Kurshan, V.Levin, M.Minea, D.Peled, and H. Yenigün. Static partial order reduction. In *Tools and Algorithms for the Construction and Analysis of Systems (TACAS '98)*, pages 345–357, 1998.
9. Leslie Lamport. *Specifying Systems: The TLA+ Language and Tools for Hardware and Software Engineers*. Pearson Education, Inc., 2002.
10. Doron Peled. All from one, one for all: On model checking using representatives. In *Computer Aided Verification*, pages 409–423, 1993.
11. Aaron Stump, Clark W. Barrett, and David L. Dill. CVC: A Cooperating Validity Checker. In *Computer Aided Verification*, pages 500–504, 2002.
12. Antti Valmari. A stubborn attack on state explosion. In *Computer Aided Verification*, pages 156–165, 1990.

Verifying Timing Behavior by Abstract Interpretation of Executable Code

Christian Ferdinand and Reinhold Heckmann

AbsInt Angewandte Informatik GmbH
Stuhlsatzenhausweg 69, D-66123 Saarbrücken, Germany
info@absint.com
http://www.absint.com

Abstract. Many tasks in safety-critical embedded systems have hard real-time characteristics. **AbsInt**'s worst-case execution time analyzer **aiT** can estimate precise and safe upper bounds for the WCETs of program tasks, thus providing the basic input for verifying the real-time behavior of embedded applications.

1 Introduction

Failure of a safety-critical embedded system may result in the loss of life or in large damages. Utmost carefulness and state-of-the-art machinery have to be applied to make sure that such a system is working properly. To do so lies in the responsibility of the designer(s). The proper working of an embedded system includes faultless working of the underlying hardware and software ensuring the production of correct output at appropriate times. Failure to meet deadlines may be as unacceptable as producing wrong output. A tool such as **AbsInt**'s **aiT** can efficiently determine upper bounds for the Worst-Case Execution Time (WCET) of code snippets given as routines in executables. The predicted WCETs can be used to determine an appropriate scheduling scheme for the tasks and to perform an overall schedulability analysis in order to guarantee that all timing constraints will be met [1].

The determination of the WCET of a task is a difficult problem because of the characteristics of modern software and hardware. Caches, branch target buffers, and pipelines are used in virtually all performance-oriented processors. Consequently the timing of the instructions depends on the execution history. Hence, the widely used classical methods of predicting execution times are not generally applicable. Software monitoring and dual-loop benchmark change the code, what in turn changes the cache behavior. Hardware simulation, emulation, or direct measurement with logic analyzers can only determine the execution time for some fixed inputs.

In contrast, abstract interpretation can be used to efficiently compute a safe approximation for all possible cache and pipeline states that can occur at a program point in any program run with any input. These results can be combined with ILP (Integer Linear Programming) techniques to safely predict the worst-case execution time and a corresponding worst-case execution path.

D. Borrione and W. Paul (Eds.): CHARME 2005, LNCS 3725, pp. 336–339, 2005.

2   Worst-Case Execution Time Prediction by aiT

AbsInt's **aiT** WCET analyzer tools get as input an executable, user annotations, a description of the (external) memories and buses (i.e. a list of memory areas with minimal and maximal access times), and a task (identified by a start address). A task denotes a sequentially executed piece of code (no threads, no parallelism, and no waiting for external events). This should not be confused with a task in an operating system that might include code for synchronization or communication. Effects of interrupts, IO and timer (co-)processors are not reflected in the predicted runtime and have to be considered separately (e.g., by a quantitative analysis).

aiT operates in several phases. First a *decoder* reads the executable, identifies the instructions and their operands, and reconstructs the control flow [2]. The reconstructed control flow is annotated with the information needed by subsequent analyses and then translated into CRL (Control-Flow Representation Language). The annotated control-flow graph serves as the input for all further analyses.

The decoder can find the target addresses of absolute and pc-relative calls and branches, but may have difficulties with target addresses computed from register contents. Thus, **aiT** uses specialized decoders that are adapted to certain code generators and/or compilers. They usually can recognize branches to a previously stored return address, and know the typical compiler-generated patterns of branches via switch tables. Yet non-trivial applications may still contain some computed calls and branches (in handwritten assembly code) that cannot be resolved by the decoder and require user annotations. Such annotations may list the possible targets of computed calls and branches, or tell the decoder about the address and format of an array of function pointers or a switch table used in the computed call or branch.

Value analysis tries to determine the values in the processor registers for every program point and execution context. Often it cannot determine these values exactly, but only finds safe lower and upper bounds, i.e. intervals that are guaranteed to contain the exact values. The results of value analysis are used to determine possible addresses of indirect memory accesses—important for cache analysis—and in loop bound analysis.

WCET analysis requires that upper bounds for the iteration numbers of all loops be known. **aiT** tries to determine the number of loop iterations by *loop bound analysis*, but succeeds in doing so for simple loops only. Bounds for the iteration numbers of the remaining loops must be provided as user annotations. Loop bound analysis relies on a combination of value analysis and pattern matching, which looks for typical loop patterns. In general, these loop patterns depend on the code generator and/or compiler used to generate the code that is being analyzed. There are special **aiT** versions adapted to various generators and compilers.

Cache analysis classifies the accesses to main memory. The analysis in our tool is based upon [3], which handles analysis of caches with LRU (Least Recently Used) replacement strategy. However, it had to be modified to reflect the non-

LRU replacement strategies of common microprocessors: the pseudo-round-robin replacement policy of the ColdFire MCF 5307, and the PLRU (Pseudo-LRU) strategy of the PowerPC MPC 750 and 755. The modified algorithms distinguish between sure cache hits and unclassified accesses. The deviation from perfect LRU is the reason for the reduced predictability of the cache contents in case of ColdFire 5307 and PowerPC 750/755 compared to processors with perfect LRU caches [4].

Pipeline analysis models the pipeline behavior to determine execution times for a sequential flow (basic block) of instructions. It takes into account the current pipeline state(s), in particular resource occupancies, contents of prefetch queues, grouping of instructions, and classification of memory references as cache hits or misses. The result is an execution time for each instruction in each distinguished execution context.

Using the results of the micro-architecture analyses, *path analysis* determines a safe estimate of the WCET. While the analyses described so far are based on abstract interpretation, integer linear programming is used for path analysis. The program's control flow is modeled by an integer linear program [5] so that the solution to the objective function is the predicted worst-case execution time for the input program.

Detailed information about the WCET, the WCET path, and the possible cache and pipeline states at any program point are visualized in the aiSee tool [6].

3   Dependence on Target Architectures

There are **aiT** versions for PowerPC MPC 555, 565, and 755, ColdFire 5307, ARM7 TDMI, HCS12/STAR12, TMS320C33, C166/ST10, Renesas M32C/85 (prototype), and Tricore 1.3 (under construction).

Decoders are automatically generated from processor specifications defining instruction formats and operand meaning. The CRL format used for describing control-flow graphs is machine-independent. *Value Analysis* must interpret the operations of the target processor. Hence, there is a separate value analyzer for each target, but features shared by many processors (e.g., branches based on condition bits) allowed for considerable code sharing among the various value analyzers.

There is only one cache analyzer with a fixed interface to pipeline analysis. It is parameterized on cache size, line size, associativity, and replacement strategy. Each replacement strategy supported by **aiT** is implemented by a table for line age updates that is interpreted by the cache analyzer.

The pipeline analyzers are the most diverse part of **aiT**. The supported target architectures are grouped according to the complexity of the processor pipeline. For each group a common conceptual and coding framework for pipeline analysis has been established, in which the actual target-dependent analysis must be filled in by manual coding.

4   Precision of aiT

Since the real WCET is not known for typical real-life applications, statements about the precision of **aiT** are hard to obtain. For an automotive application running on MPC 555, one of **AbsInt**'s customers has observed an overestimation of 5–10% when comparing **aiT**'s results and the highest execution times observed in a series of measurements (which may have missed the real WCET). For an avionics application running on MPC 755, Airbus has noted that **aiT**'s WCET for a task typically is about 25% higher than some measured execution times for the same task, the real but non-calculable WCET being in between. Measurements at **AbsInt** have indicated overestimations ranging from 0% (cycle-exact prediction) till 10% for a set of small programs running on M32C, TMS320C33, and C166/ST10.

5   Conclusion

aiT is a WCET tool for industrial usage. Information required for WCET estimation such as computed branch targets and loop bounds is determined by static analysis. For situations where **aiT**'s analysis methods do not succeed, a convenient specification and annotation language was developed in close cooperation with **AbsInt**'s customers. Annotations for library functions (RT, communication) and RTOS functions can be provided in separate files by the respective developers (on source level or separately).

   aiT enables development of complex hard real-time systems on state-of-the-art hardware, increases safety, and saves development time. Precise timing predictions enable the most cost-efficient hardware to be chosen. As recent trends, e.g., in automotive industries (X-by-wire, time-triggered protocols) require knowledge on the WCETs of tasks, a tool like **aiT** is of high importance.

References

1. Stankovic, J.A.:   Real-Time and Embedded Systems.   ACM 50th Anniversary Report on Real-Time Computing Research. (1996) http://www-ccs.cs.umass.edu/sdcr/rt.ps.
2. Theiling, H.: Extracting safe and precise control flow from binaries. In: Proceedings of the 7th Conference on Real-Time Computing Systems and Applications, Cheju Island, South Korea (2000)
3. Ferdinand, C.: Cache Behavior Prediction for Real-Time Systems. PhD thesis, Saarland University (1997)
4. Heckmann, R., Langenbach, M., Thesing, S., Wilhelm, R.: The influence of processor architecture on the design and the results of WCET tools. Proceedings of the IEEE **91** (2003) 1038–1054 Special Issue on Real-Time Systems.
5. Theiling, H., Ferdinand, C.: Combining abstract interpretation and ILP for microarchitecture modelling and program path analysis. In: Proceedings of the 19th IEEE Real-Time Systems Symposium, Madrid, Spain (1998) 144–153
6. AbsInt Angewandte Informatik GmbH: aiSee Home Page. (http://www.aisee.com)

Behavior-RTL Equivalence Checking Based on Data Transfer Analysis with Virtual Controllers and Datapaths

Masahiro Fujita

VLSI Design and Education Center, The University of Tokyo,
2-11-16 Yayoi, Bunkyo-ku, Tokyo, 113-0032, Japan
fujita@ee.t.u-tokyo.ac.jp

Abstract. A behavior-RTL equivalence checking method based on bottom-up reasoning is presented. Behavior and RTL descriptions are converted into dependence graphs from which virtual controllers/datapaths are generated. Actual equivalence checking is based on isomorphism analysis on dependence graphs and also virtual controllers/datapaths. First equivalence classes on partial computations are extracted by using Boolean reasoning on virtual controllers/datapaths. Then these equivalence classes are used to prove the equivalence of the entire descriptions in a bottom-up way.

1 The Proposed Verification Method

In this paper, we propose a way to verify equivalence by establishing mappings between behavior and RTL descriptions. We first extract "classes of equivalent partial computations". Using these accumulated correspondences, the equivalence checking problem can be solved by establishing mappings on the entire design descriptions followed by reasoning about them in a bottom-up fashion. This is a similar technique to combinational equivalence checking methods based on internal equivalent points, such as the one in [1]. We map given behavior and RTL descriptions into virtual controllers and datapaths [2] and then reason about those design descriptions. The virtual controllers and datapths can make it possible to separately reason about "timing" and "data computations" and can establish correspondence among partial computations in a bottom-up way. Our verification methods have four steps as follows:

(Step 1) Generate system dependence graph (SDG), which represents dependencies among statements in design descriptions, and virtual controllers/datapaths from both behavior and RTL descriptions

(Step 2) Gather information on equivalence classes on partial computations on SDG. In this step, if necessary equivalence classes are computed by analyzing virtual controllers/datapaths as well as SDG. When analyzing virtual controllers/datapaths, apply reachability computation on virtual controllers to decide equivalence of partial computations.

(Step 3) Perform graph matching between the SDGs for behavior and RTL descriptions by using equivalence classes computed in (Step 2).

(Step 4) If the result of (Step 3) gives matching on SDGs, we conclude that the behavior and RTL descriptions are equivalent. Otherwise go back to (Step 2), and try to get more equivalence classes. If no more equivalence classes are available,

D. Borrione and W. Paul (Eds.): CHARME 2005, LNCS 3725, pp. 340–344, 2005.
© Springer-Verlag Berlin Heidelberg 2005

we generate a computation path which differentiates computations in the two SDGs as a counter example.

Please note that the counter example generated in (Step 4) may not be a real computer example, since in (Step 2) we may not be able to gather all equivalence classes. That is, there are cases where our results are false-negative.

The system dependence graph that we are using in the proposed equivalence checking method is generated by program slicers. Program slicing [3] is a technique by which related portions of the programs are extracted based on user-specified criteria. In the program slicing tools, internally control flow graphs and also so called system dependence graphs (SDG) are generated. SDG represents all static dependencies among statements in terms of control, data, and interference. In our method, we are using control flow graphs and SDGs generated by program slicers when generating virtual controllers and virtual datapaths. Our program slicer [4] is targeting SpecC language [5] and also C/C++ descriptions, and so combined descriptions in those languages can also be processed. The slicing program generates the corresponding control flow graphs (CFGs) and system dependence graphs (SDGs) as a unified graph.Then they are further processed to generate virtual controllers/datapaths.

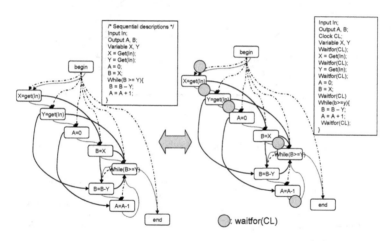

Fig. 1. Behavior and RTL descriptions and their System Dependence Graph (SDG)

Now we illustrate the above verification method with examples. An example behavior description and a corresponding RTL one that is supposed to implement the behavior description are shown in the boxes of Figure 1. They are computing divisions, and the first input from the input port, In, is divided by the second input form the input port, and the output, A, is the quotient and the output B is the remainder at the end of the computation. The division is very straightforwardly computed by counting up how many times the value of the divider can be extracted. The semantics of the descriptions are obvious from the descriptions, and we do not explain them here except for "waitfor(CL)" statement. It is the statement that determines the clock boundary in RTL descriptions to fix the scheduling of the RTL descriptions. All statements surrounded by neighboring two waitfor(CL) statements must be executed within the same clock cycle. Since waitfor(CL) statements are the only difference, these two descriptions should be recognized to be equivalent. However, the values of output signals, A and B, may not be equal for every clock cycle, since behavior description has no fixed scheduling in the terms of clock timing. So in this case we assume that with an appropriate use of attribute statements [2] what should be compared is defined as to check the values of the outputs at the end of computation only. The SDGs for the two descriptions are also shown in Figure 1. The difference is just the existence of several "waitfor(CL)" statements in RTL, and so the two SDGs are easily recognized as "matching", that is, they are isomorphic other than nodes for "waitfor(CL)". We basically use graph isomorphism check for identifying equivalence of computations, and equivalence classes are used to make matching on sub-graphs..

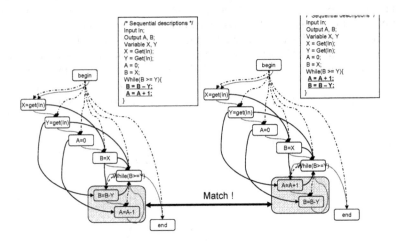

Fig. 2. Identification of equivalences of subgraphs in SDG I a bottom-up way

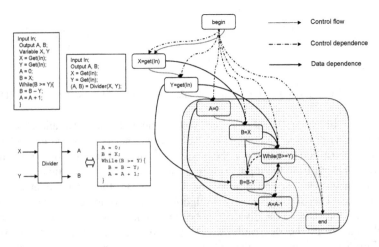

Fig. 3. Bottom-up reasoning by identifying sub-graphs for "division" circuit/computation

For more complicated cases, first of all equivalence class are first computed as explained in (Step 2) in the previous section. For example, the equivalence checking on the two descriptions shown in Figure 2 is processed as follows. Here we are comparing the two descriptions inside the boxes. The only difference between the two is the order of executions of the two underlined statements. Since they are independent with each other, these statements compute exactly the same. This can be easily checked by traversing the SDGs and make sure they are independent. Then we can have an equivalence class for these statements and use it for the comparison of the two SDGs generated from the descriptions as shown in Figure 2. After identifying the equivalence class, the two SDGs are isomorphic and so the descriptions are equivalent. Figure 3 shows a more complicated case. In this example, the portion of the original description for division computation is replaced by a divider circuit as shown in the left-top part of the figure. First of all, we try to prove with loop-invariants that the while-loop part in the original description is computing division. With appropriate loop invariants, we can decompose the verification problem for the while-loop into the ones for non-loops. The decomposed verification can be processed as Boolean reasoning problems with virtual controllers/datapaths. Once that is finished, the equivalence for the entire SDGs can be again by checking their isomorphism.

Figure 4 shows another example between sequential and parallel descriptions. In such cases, we first extract sequential behaviors from parallel ones by identifying synchronization statements, such as "notify" and "wait" and using them to generate sequential orders of executions. The extracted behaviors are then compared with the original sequential ones in terms of graph isomorphism utilizing equivalence classes.

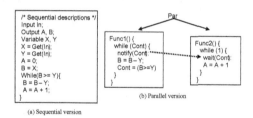

Fig. 4. Sequential and parallel description comparison by first extracting sequential behaviors from parallel ones

2   Experimental Results

We have tried several SpecC descriptions, such as the SpecC examples shown in SpecC manuals, e.g., elevator system, parity checker, and so on. Also, we have verified two versions of internet PPP protocol descriptions. These examples are ranging from one hundred to a couple of thousands lines of SpecC codes. Also, in the case of designs generated by SoC Environment, a system level design/synthesis tool developed by UC Irvine [5], the difference between two successive synthesis steps in the tool is very limited, and the analysis on partial computation equivalence classes becomes very simple but very useful. Several tens of thousands lines of SpecC descriptions can be verified with the proposed methods for such cases, including description on MPEG4 encoders.

References

[1] A. Kuehlmann and F. Krohm, "Equivalence Checking Using Cuts and Heaps", in Proceedings of the 34th ACM/IEEE Design Automation Conference 1997.

[2] M. Fujita, "On equivalence checking between behavioral and RTL descriptions", HLDVT 2004, Nov. 2004. Also see http://www.cad.t.u-tokyo.ac.jp for more reference.

[3] M. Weiser, "Program slices: Formal, psychological, and practical investigations of an automatic program abstraction", PhD thesis, University of Michigan, 1979.

[4] K. Tanabe, S. Sasaki, M. Fujita, "Program slicing for system level designs in SpecC", IASTED Conference on Advances in Computer Science and Technology, Nov. 2004.

[5] SoC Environment, University of California, Irvine. http://www.cecs.uci.edu/~cad/sce.html.

Deadlock Prevention in the ÆTHEREAL Protocol*

Biniam Gebremichael[1], Frits Vaandrager[1], Miaomiao Zhang[1,**], Kees Goossens[2],
Edwin Rijpkema[2], and Andrei Rădulescu[2]

[1] ICIS, Radboud University Nijmegen, The Netherlands
[2] Philips Research Laboratories, Eindhoven, The Netherlands

Abstract. The ÆTHEREAL protocol enables both guaranteed and best effort communication in an on-chip packet switching network. We discuss a formal specification of ÆTHEREAL and its underlying network in terms of the PVS specification language. Using PVS we prove absence of deadlock for an abstract version of our model.

1 Introduction

The ÆTHEREAL protocol [2,4] has been proposed by Philips to enable both guaranteed and best-effort communication in an on-chip packet switching network. The design of such a protocol, which has to meet all the functional and correctness requirements for best-effort and guaranteed traffic, is a difficult task. Typically, the designers play around with thousands of design alternatives before they commit to one. It is difficult to keep track of all design alternatives in a systematic way, and to make sure that the choices that have been made are consistent. Our contribution is that: (1) for one of the numerous design alternatives we produced a detailed, precise and highly modular formal model in PVS [1], and (2) within this model we were able to establish a key correctness criterion for the absence of deadlock. We believe that our work illustrates that formal specification languages, such as the typed higher-order logic supported by PVS, can be most useful to document complex designs, to help designers to clarify design choices and to resolve problematic inconsistencies in an early stage of the design process.

An extended version of our paper is available as technical report [3]. We refer to [3] for a much more detailed explanation of the ÆTHEREAL protocol, in particular of the routing algorithm that prevents deadlock. The report also describes in great detail how we formally modeled[1] the protocol in PVS and how we proved absence of deadlock for an abstracted version of the model. Finally, it evaluates our experiences in modeling the ÆTHEREAL protocol, discusses related work and points at interesting topics for future work.

---

* Supported by PROGRESS project TES4199, Verification of Hard and Softly Timed Systems (HaaST).
** Currently affiliated with Tongji University, China.

[1] The PVS sources are available at
http://www.cs.ru.nl/ita/publications/papers/biniam/noc/.

D. Borrione and W. Paul (Eds.): CHARME 2005, LNCS 3725, pp. 345–348, 2005.
© IFIP International Federation for Information Processing 2005

2   The ÆTHEREAL **Protocol**

A network on chip, like any other network, is composed of nodes and edges between them. The nodes are classified into two groups depending on their position in the network, namely network interfaces and routers. Network interfaces are the service access points of the network. An interface that initiates a communication request is called an *active network interface port* (ANIP), and an interface that responds to a communication request is called a *passive network interface port* (PNIP). Routers provide the connectivity of the network. They do not initiate or respond to communication but just route packets from one interface to another. Each node in the network has a number of (bounded) buffers to store packets that have arrived and are waiting to leave.

Within a packet switching network it is relatively easy to offer a best-effort (BE) communication service, in which packets can be delayed to an arbitrary amount of time, and it is not possible to give a worst-case estimation. The main goal of the ÆTHEREAL protocol [4] is to also provide a guaranteed-throughput (GT) service within a network on chip. This is done by first reserving the resources (links) needed for the GT service for the entire duration of the service. The challenging part is to set up a new GT service using the BE services, which do not give any timing guarantee. Due to the limited buffer size (which are also shared by already running GT services) a deadlock scenario can easily occur, and the ÆTHEREAL protocol has to avoid such circumstance at all times. Once a GT connection is established, data may flow through this connection without difficulty. An important instrument for the establishment of a GT connection is the *slot tables*. Each routers is equipped with such a table, in order to book-keep which outgoing link is reserved for a given incoming link at a given slot time.

Establishing a GT connection starts when a source ANIP sends a BE SETUP packet to a destination PNIP. This SETUP packet will try to reserve all the links in the path that lead to the destination. The intention is that the GT service will follow the same path for its entire duration. The destination PNIP may not be connected to the ANIP directly, therefore the SETUP packet may have to pass through a number of routers, or the buffers of the routers as shown in Fig. 1. Each router has a separate unit (or buffer) called *reconfiguration unit (rcu)*, where the management of the slot table take place. During reservation request, an outgoing link is reserved if the link is free during the requested slot time, otherwise the request is denied. If the reservation is accepted, the SETUP packet is passed over to the next router, and the process goes on. If every reservation request is successful in all the nodes in the path (including the destination), then the destination PNIP sends a BE positive acknowledgment packet (ACK) to the source (the arrow with ∗∗ in Fig. 1). We say that the GT-connection has been established when the source receives the ACK packet. Subsequently, the GT service can start as scheduled. However if at some point in the path a node rejects the reservation request, the node will send a BE negative acknowledgment packet (NACK) to the source (the arrow with ∗ in Fig. 1). When the source ANIP receives NACK, it means (1) the GT-connection can not start, and (2) it has to unreserve the reservations it made. Note that the nodes between the source up to the node where the SETUP packet was rejected, do not know that the setup process has failed. For this purpose the ANIP sends a BE tear-down (TDOWN) packet to unreserve what has been reserved earlier. This TDOWN packet follows the

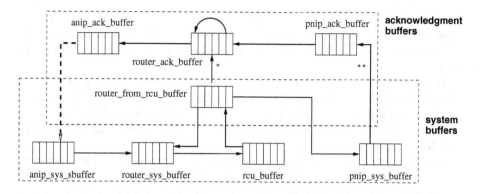

Fig. 1. Dependency graph between buffers

same path as the preceding SETUP packet. Like SETUP packets, TDOWN packets visit every router on the path and update the slot tables accordingly.

One thing that may possibly go wrong during GT connection set-up is buffer overflow. This is handled by controlling the flow of packets locally (between adjacent nodes) and globally. As shown in Fig 1 local flow control is between adjacent nodes (or more specifically, adjacent buffers), and the global (or end to end) flow control is handled within ANIPs. For local control, the sender node maintains a local credit counter for every adjacent buffer. This counter records how much space is left in the receiver's buffer, and a packet is sent to this buffer only if it is not full. End-to-end flow control is introduced to prevent ANIPs from flooding the network. An end to end flow control counter is maintained locally by every ANIP in the network. Each time an ANIP sends a SETUP packet, its credit is decremented by one, and each time the ANIP receives an ACK or NACK its credit is incremented by one. Initially an ANIP has a credit which is equivalent to the size of the buffer in which acknowledgment packets are received in the ANIP (anip_ack_buffer). Thus, ANIPs may only send SETUP packets if they can accommodate the resulting acknowledgment packets.

A key idea to prevent deadlock in ÆTHEREAL is to have separate classes of buffers for system (SETUP, TDOWN) and acknowledgment (ACK, NACK) packets, and to ensure that there are no routing cycles within a buffer class. This separation is illustrated in Fig. 1 as a buffer dependency graph. The buffer dependency graph of a network on chip is defined to be a directed graph whose vertices are buffers and whose edges correspond to possible routings from one buffer to another. A key property that we proved for our PVS model of ÆTHEREAL is that there is no routing from an acknowledgment buffer to a system buffer, with the exception that in an ANIP a NACK packet may be routed to a system buffer as a TDOWN packet. Thus, if a path involves ANIP buffers then it may contain a cycle. But, as we will argue in the following section, even in this case no deadlock will occur.

3   Deadlock Involving an ANIP

Communication in a network on chip takes place via synchronous transmission of packets from one buffer to another buffer. Each transmission is signaled by the advancement of a time slot [4]. The behavior of a complete network can be modeled conveniently by a state machine in which the states are the configurations of the network at a given time slot and the transitions correspond to the synchronous transmission of packets from one buffer to another.

A state is identified by the values of the following variables: (a) the content of the buffers, (b) local and end to end credits, (c) the slot tables, and (d) the time slot. Initially, all buffers and slot tables are empty. The local credit is equal to the buffer capacity it refers to, and the end to end credit is equal to capacity of the acknowledgment buffer of the ANIP. The time slot is zero.

The control transitions of the network can be structured as three sequential steps called *read*, *execute* and *write*. These three phases together constitute a single control transition in the state machine. We say that there is a transition (or `step(s1,s2)`), from a state `s1` to another state `s2`, if `s2` can be reached from `s1` by executing the three sequential steps. The set of reachable states is the set of all states that can be computed by recursive application of `step(s1,s2)`, starting from the initial state. We say that a reachable state `s` has a *deadlock* if there are a list of buffers `lb`, which are full in `s` and which form a cycle in the dependency graph.

In order to prove that there is no reachable state with a deadlock, we proceed by assuming the converse. Suppose that there is a state with a deadlock. This means that there is a list of full buffers containing ANIP buffers and this list forms a cycle. Moreover, this means that the system and acknowledgment buffers of the ANIP are full and yet there is an incoming packet from the network to this ANIP. But as explained above, the end-to-end flow control forbids such scenarios, because the ANIP could not have sent more packets than the capacity of its acknowledgment buffer. Formally, using PVS, we established (for an abstract version of our model) a number of system invariants which in combination imply that such a scenario will never arise.

References

1. J. Crow, S. Owre, J. Rushby, N. Shankar, and M. Srivas. A tutorial introduction to PVS. In *Workshop on Industrial-Strength Formal Specification Techniques*, Boca Raton, Florida, April 1995.
2. Om Prakash Gangwal, Andrei Rădulescu, Kees Goossens, Santiago González Pestana, and Edwin Rijpkema. Building predictable systems on chip: An analysis of guaranteed communication in the æthereal network on chip. In P. van der Stok, editor, Philips Research Book Series, chapter 1. Kluwer, 2005.
3. B. Gebremichael, F. Vaandrager, and M. Zhang. Formal models of guaranteed and best-effort services for network on chip. Technical Report ICIS-R05016, Radboud University Nijmegen, 2005.
4. Kees Goossens, John Dielissen, and Andrei Rădulescu. The Æthereal network on chip: Concepts, architectures, and implementations. *IEEE Design and Test of Computers*, 22(5), Sept-Oct 2005. Special issue on Networks on Chip.

Acceleration of SAT-Based Iterative Property Checking

Daniel Große and Rolf Drechsler

Institute of Computer Science, University of Bremen, 28359 Bremen, Germany
{grosse, drechsle}@informatik.uni-bremen.de

Abstract. Formal property checking is used to check whether a circuit satisfies a temporal property or not. An important goal during the development of properties is the formulation of general proofs. Since assumptions of properties define the situations under which the commitments are checked, in order to obtain general proofs assumptions should be made as general as possible. In practice this is accomplished iteratively by generalizing the assumptions step by step. Thus, the verification engineer may start with strong assumptions and weakens them gradually.

In this paper we propose a new approach to speed up SAT-based iterative property checking. This process can be exploited by reusing conflict clauses in the corresponding SAT instances of consecutive property checking problems. By this the search space is pruned, since recomputations of identical conflicts are avoided.

1 Introduction

Nowadays, for successful circuit designs *Property Checking* (PC) is very important. Typically such a property consists of two parts: an *assume part* which should imply the *proof part*. In the last years tools based on *Satisfiability* (SAT) performed better than classical BDD-based approaches since SAT procedures do not suffer from the potential "size explosion" of BDDs. In SAT-based PC the initial SAT instance is generated from the circuit description together with the property to be proven. Usually, the largest part will result from the unrolled circuit description. In comparison, the parts for the commitments, assumptions, and the extra logic are much smaller. From a practical perspective, during PC as long as no design bug is found the circuit design remains unchanged, but the verification engineer modifies and adds new properties. Thus, the PC tool is used interactively. For the verification engineer on the one hand, proving becomes more easy if the assumptions of a property are very strong, i.e. the property is very restrictive and argues only over a small part of the design space. On the other hand, such proofs are not very general. Hence in practice, the formulation of a property is an iterative process. E.g., the engineer starts writing a property with strong assumptions. Then, the engineer stepwise weakens some of the assumptions to obtain a more general proof.

The basic idea is to exploit the iterative process of PC. As can be seen only a very small part of the verification problem changes in consecutive PC runs

D. Borrione and W. Paul (Eds.): CHARME 2005, LNCS 3725, pp. 349–353, 2005.

if the assumptions are weakened. Re-computations can be avoided if learned information is reused for consecutive SAT problems. *Bounded Model Checking* (BMC) as introduced in [1] reduces the verification problem to a SAT problem and then searches for counter-examples in executions whose length is bounded by k time steps. For BMC, it has been suggested to reuse constraints on the search space deduced in instance k for solving the consecutive instance $k + 1$ faster [4]. However, in [4] this concept is only used during the proof of a single or more fixed properties.

In this paper we use BMC as described in [5], thus, a property only argues over a finite time interval and during the proof there is no restriction to reachable states. In contrast to [4], here two SAT instances for slightly different PC problems are considered and information from the two properties with respect to the underlying circuit is utilized. This enables to reuse learned conflict clauses in the SAT instance of the consecutive PC problem.

2   Acceleration of Iterative Property Checking

In this section the approach for reusing conflict clauses during iterative PC is presented. Before the details are given, the work flow is illustrated in Figure 1.

At first the design and the property are compiled into an internal representation. In this step information to allow for a syntactic comparison between properties is stored in the data base (A). Then the internal representation is converted into a BMC problem expressed as a CNF formula. While solving this SAT instance the references to the clauses that lead to a new conflict clause are stored in a data structure. After termination of the SAT solver this conflict clause information can be related to the single assumptions and commitments of the checked property. Finally this information is minimized and added to the data base (B). Now assume that PC is repeated but the property has been weakened. Then, this is detected (X) and before the BMC problem is given to the SAT solver conflict clauses are read from the data base, analyzed and reused (Y), if possible.

Let M be the set of clauses resulting from the translation of the design D, let P be the set of clauses resulting from the property p. Then P can be partitioned into $P = A \cup C \cup R$, where A are the clauses from the assumptions,

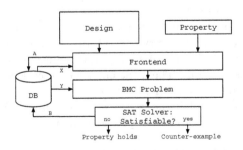

Fig. 1. Property Checking Flow

C from the commitments and R the clauses to "glue" the assumptions and the commitments of the property together. Now consider two consecutive runs of the property checker for the unchanged design D and for two properties p^F (first) and p^S (second). Assume that the property p^S has been derived from the property p^F by weakening some of the assumptions. Let $P^F = A^F \cup C^F \cup R^F$ be the resulting clauses of the property of the first run and $P^S = A^S \cup C^S \cup R^S$ the clauses for the second run, respectively. Further assume that the variables in P^S are renamed with a variable mapping function which maps a variable from the second set of variables V_S to the according variables of the variable set V_F from the first run. Then the following holds:

1. $C^S = C^F$, since the commitments of properties p^S and p^F are equal.
2. $R^S = R^F$ since the variables to combine the assumptions and commitments can be identified.
3. $A^S \subset A^F$ because the assumptions of p^S are weaker than the assumptions of p^F.

Since the clauses M of the design do not change only the clauses resulting from the two properties p^F and p^S have to be compared. Under the assumptions and conclusions from above the following holds:

$$P^F - P^S = (A^F \cup C^F \cup R^F) - (A^S \cup C^S \cup R^S) = A^F - A^S$$

With this result it can be concluded that all conflict clauses can be reused which are *not* a result of an implication caused by a clause of $A^F - A^S$. In other words we have to identify the conflict clauses which have been deduced exclusively from the intersection of the two consecutive PC problems. This intersection is given by $(M \cup P^F) \cap (M \cup P^S) = M \cup A^S \cup C^F \cup R^F$. Thus, for each conflict clause of the first run the sequence of clauses which produced that conflict clause have to be determined, since with this information we can exactly identify the source of the conflict in terms of the two properties p^F and p^S. This becomes possible, if we further know which clauses have been produced by the design, the individual expressions in the assume part and the individual expressions of the proof part of both properties. Finally for a conflict clause cl the minimal source information is stored which allows to check if cl was produced by a clause of the design or by an assume expression or a proof expression. Altogether it can be decided which conflict clauses of the first run can be reused to speed up the current proof.

3   Experimental Results

To allow for access of necessary information during PC we have implemented a SAT-based property checker on top of zChaff [3]. All experiments have been carried out in the same system environment on an Athlon XP 2800 with 1 GByte main memory. The following experiments always consist of two steps. First, for a circuit a property with "overly" strong assumptions is proved. This is done with and without our approach to measure the time overhead. Next, we prove

Table 1. Overhead for arbiter

Cells	Property	Clauses	Literals	Result	Time (sec) std	reuse
100	mutualexclusion	240,776	541,742	holds	9.15	9.57
100	lowestWins_50	161,399	363,193	holds	14.15	14.49
200	mutualexclusion	961,576	2,163,542	holds	176.65	177.78
200	lowestWins_50	642,799	1,446,393	holds	588.30	590.45

Table 2. Acceleration for arbiter

Cells	Property	Clauses	Literals	Result	Time (sec) std	reuse	Reused Cl. (%)	Speed-up
100	mutualexclusion	161,076	362,442	holds	13.26	13.01	20.23	1.0
100	lowestWins_50	161,247	362,839	holds	8.71	4.54	100.00	1.9
200	mutualexclusion	642,176	1,444,942	holds	1078.80	343.77	6.23	3.1
200	lowestWins_50	642,347	1,445,339	holds	656.35	22.70	100.00	28.9

the same property but in a more general version, i.e. some of the assumptions of the property have been weakened. In this case we measure the speed-up that can be achieved by reusing conflict clauses.

In a first series of experiments we considered a scalable bus arbiter that has been studied frequently in formal hardware verification (see e.g. [2]). The considered properties for the arbiter circuit are mutual exclusion of the outputs of the arbiter and lowestWins. The second property states that if exactly one token is set and no cell is waiting and exactly the request i is high then the corresponding acknowledgement i will be set in the same clock cycle. In Table 1 the overhead for our approach is given for different arbiter instances (column *Cells*). In the second column the name of the considered property is shown. The next two columns provide information on the corresponding SAT instance. In column *Result* it is shown whether the property holds or not. Next, the run time needed without and with our approach is given in column *std* and column *reuse*, respectively. The difference between the two given run times is the time needed to store learned information into the data base. As can be seen the overhead is negligible, i.e. less than 1% of the run time for the larger examples.

The achieved improvement of the proposed approach for the arbiter is shown in Table 2. E.g. in the weakened variant of the property mutualexclusion the assumption that no arbiter cell is waiting is no longer assumed. The first seven columns give similar information as in Table 1. Because the considered properties have been weakened the resulting number of clauses and literals decreases. However, since for each property learned information can be found in the data base, conflict clauses can be reused. Thus, column *Reused Cl.* gives the percentage of reused clauses. In the last column the achieved speed-up is shown. As can be seen for the 100 cell arbiter in case of the property mutualexclusion no speed-up results. But for the three remaining examples a significant speed-up was obtained, i.e. up to nearly a factor of 30.

Table 3. Overhead for FIFO

Size	Property	Clauses	Literals	Result	Time (sec)	
					std	reuse
64	nochange	68,077	156,723	holds	14.82	14.92
128	nochange	156,595	361,173	holds	101.83	102.03

Table 4. Acceleration for FIFO

Size	Property	Clauses	Literals	Result	Time (sec)		Reused Cl. (%)	Speed-up
					std	reuse		
64	nochange	68,072	156,712	holds	14.80	2.16	100.00	6.9
128	nochange	156,590	361,162	holds	101.72	6.42	100.00	15.8

In a second series of experiments we studied FIFOs of different depth. As a property we prove that the content of a FIFO does not change under the assumption that no write operation is performed. In the initial version of this property it has also been assumed that no read operation is performed. Similar information as for the arbiter examples is provided in Tables 3 and 4, respectively. Also in this case for larger examples a speed-up of more than a factor of 10 can be observed.

References

1. A. Biere, A. Cimatti, E. Clarke, and Y. Zhu. Symbolic model checking without BDDs. In *Tools and Algorithms for the Construction and Analysis of Systems*, volume 1579 of *LNCS*, pages 193–207. Springer Verlag, 1999.
2. D. Große and R. Drechsler. *CheckSyC*: An efficient property checker for RTL SystemC designs. pages 4167–4170, 2005.
3. M.W. Moskewicz, C.F. Madigan, Y. Zhao, L. Zhang, and S. Malik. Chaff: Engineering an efficient SAT solver. In *Design Automation Conf.*, pages 530–535, 2001.
4. Ofer Shtrichman. Pruning techniques for the SAT-based bounded model checking problem. pages 58–70, 2001.
5. K. Winkelmann, H.-J. Trylus, D. Stoffel, and G. Fey. A cost-efficient block verification for a UMTS up-link chip-rate coprocessor. In *Design, Automation and Test in Europe*, volume 1, pages 162–167, 2004.

Error Detection Using BMC in a Parallel Environment

Subramanian K. Iyer[1], Jawahar Jain[2], Mukul R. Prasad[2], Debashis Sahoo[3], and Thomas Sidle[2]

[1] University of Texas at Austin, Austin, TX 78712, USA
[2] Fujitsu Labs of America, Sunnyvale, CA 94085, USA
[3] Stanford University, Stanford CA 94305, USA

Abstract. In this paper, we explore a parallelization of BMC based on state space partitioning. The parallelization is accomplished by executing multiple instances of BMC independently from different seed states. These seed states are *deep* states, selected from the reachable states in different partitions. In this scheme, all processors work independently of each other, thus it is suitable for scaling verification to a grid-like network. Our experimental results demonstrate improvement over existing approaches, and show that the method can scale to a large network.

1 Introduction

Satisfiability based Bounded Model Checking (SAT-BMC) [2] approaches are the preferred method for detecting error states that are not very deep. However, these techniques can become quite expensive when many time-frames are required to be analyzed. BDD based approaches are better choices for those "deep cases" where the image BDDs remain moderately small as constructing large BDDs for many image steps can be very expensive. Thus the class of problems which may require many steps of image analysis to detect the error, *but* where BDD sizes grow large, remain an attractive research target.

Our approach is to create a method that can find various candidate deep states which can be *seeds* from which SAT-BMC can be run in *parallel* to explore the adjacent state space. Starting from such potential deep seed states, multiple BMC runs may be able to reach further deep states, and locate errors, which may be out of reach for existing methods.

Generating Seed States: For a few initial steps of reachability, rapid progress can be made using BDDs. To control the size of BDDs using state space analysis we use state-space partitioning [5]. Deep states provided from such local BFS traversals can be used to provide initial seed states to subsequent BMC runs. Since the BDD runtime is directly proportional to the size of the graphs, we further limit the size of partitions using an under-approximation based method on top of partitioned BDDs.

Using Seed States: We augment our ideas of combining Partitioning and BMC by generating multiple instances of BMC and run each such case in parallel on

D. Borrione and W. Paul (Eds.): CHARME 2005, LNCS 3725, pp. 354–358, 2005.

a grid of computers. This idea looks even more attractive when we consider that large computing grids are slowly becoming available in many computing environments [1].

For a detailed description of background, survey of related work, and explanation of terminology, the reader may refer to the full version of this paper. [4]

2   Algorithm

We believe there are two key ideas for deep exploration. The first is to go deep using BDDs at the expense of completeness, by ensuring that BDD sizes remain tractable. This is accomplished by the use of partitioning and underapproximation. The second idea is starting multiple BMC runs, one from each seed. To keep the runtime practical we make these runs in parallel by using the computing power of a grid. This is a non-conventional way of parallelizing BMC. For the circuits where the BDD based exploration is able to build the transition relation cheaply our method appears to overcome the main shortcoming of classical SAT-BMC which is its inability to perform deep state exploration.

To summarize, our algorithm has following two stages:

1. Generate deep seed-states using partitioning and approximation techniques
2. Distribute seeds on the grid focussing on minimizing unnecessary runs.

Generate Deep Seeds: We perform a full traversal of the state space by partitioning the transition relation, as well as the computed sets of states so that both the graphs and associated calculations remain tractable. When the BDD calculations are no longer manageable, we perform successive under-approximations. At each step of image computation, we use a subset of the actual set of states. Such massive under-approximation may result in successive traversal not always leading to a deeper state. However, probabilistically speaking, if the number of states in any computed image set is more than the sum in the previous steps, as is often the case, then there is a high probability that with successive application of "smaller" image function obtained from a partition of the transition relations, most nodes in our path of deep-traversal will indeed be deep.

Parallel Seed SAT: In order to determine the initial seed states for SAT, we use the following two approaches: Firstly, a small number of BDD based partitions are explored fully and CNF clauses are written out at regular intervals, say every 5 steps. Alternatively, a large number of partitions are explored very rapidly with under-approximation, and the resulting deep states are used to seed SAT. By making multiple BMC runs, starting from various points along the state traversal, we can ensure that at least a subset of the BMC executions start from a deep state. Since all BMC runs can be made in parallel so this leads to a non-traditional method of parallelizing BMC.

The Proposed Algorithm:

1. *Partition_reach*: Use state partitioning in reachability to get different and divergent paths exploring state space.

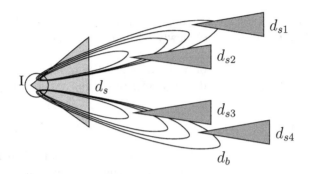

Fig. 1. Seeding multiple SAT-BMC runs from POBDD reachability

2. *Approx_Partition_reach*: Do reachability analysis with under-approximation – during each image computation, pick a subset of the newly found reachable states and add it to reachable set in order to avoid BDD blowup problems.
3. *Generate_seed*: At regular intervals, whenever a threshold is crossed, store the seeds and pass it to a new instance of the SAT solver.
4. *Start_Seeded_SAT*: From each of these seeds, run an instance of SAT-based BMC up to a small enough depth.
5. *Run_in_Parallel*: Run one SAT instance on each machine of the grid.
6. *Termination_condition*: Allow BDD exploration and all SAT explorations to continue in parallel until bug is seen or timeout is reached.

3   Results

In this section, we present our experimental results on some industrial circuits. Several of these properties are deep and pose some difficulty for SAT-BMC as well as simulation based methods. The experiments are run on a grid of computers that include up to 100 independent Xeon CPUs (1.5 to 2.3 GHz) running linux. We use an in-house grid middle-ware, CyberGrip [1], developed at Fujitsu Labs Limited, Japan, for managing jobs executed on the grid. Our program is implemented on top of VIS-2.0 and uses CUDD BDD package and zchaff SAT-solver. The POBDD algorithm is run on a single processor but the CNF files generated are transfered to different nodes on the grid where a BMC run is fired in parallel.

Details of Experiments: Random simulation, using VIS-2.0 upto 100,000 steps is unable to find a bug in any of the circuits in the benchmark. We perform simulation to find deep states and seed BMC from there. This is similar to the approach of [3], except that we use a different random seed for each simulation depth. For each circuit, we run simulation, in steps of 1,000 from 2,000 to 10,000. When the depth is reached, we pick the state reached at the end of the simulation and seed SAT from there.

Table 1. Comparison of the time taken in seconds by various approaches

	Num.	Error	Existing					Proposed			Num.
			Total Time (sec)					Time (sec)			
Ckt	latches	Depth	BDD	POBDD	BMC	Sim	Sim/BMC	Seed	BMC	Total	CPU
b1	125	59	7	**3.2**	T/O	NB	167	3.2	N/A	**3.2**	1
b2	70	85	3.4	**2**	T/O	NB	115	2	N/A	**2**	1
b3	66	23	1.9	**1.3**	T/O	NB	268	1.3	N/A	**1.3**	1
b4	66	59	1.9	**1.3**	T/O	NB	3097	1.3	N/A	**1.3**	1
b5	170	36	T/O	T/O	T/O	NB	2758	27	36	**63**	9
b6	201	29	3148	2857	T/O	NB	1407	156	20	**176**	3
b7	123	60	**258**	976	T/O	NB	T/O	35	429	464	14
b8	169	23	T/O	T/O	T/O	NB	T/O	198	55	**253**	28
b9	148	27	T/O	T/O	T/O	NB	T/O	280	1580	**1860**	70

"T/O" is a timeout of 2 hrs, "NB" means no bug found.

Table 1 shows the time taken by different methods: Existing approaches are invariant checking using BDDs and POBDDs; SAT-BMC; simulation to 5,000 steps and an application of SAT solver after 5,000 steps. The last four columns of Table 1 shows the details of time spent by the proposed method: the time taken for (a) POBDD based reachability to discover the seed state, (b) the SAT-solver to find the bug from there, (c) the total time and (d) the number of CPUs of the grid that are actually used. We allow each method to run for 2 hours. The results for all the methods are shown in table 1. Note that the proposed method is the only one that is able to find the error in benchmarks b8 and b9.

4   Conclusions

Based upon our analysis of the experimental results, we believe that the proposed hybrid method has various benefits. It is computationally inexpensive in terms of overhead and an alternate way of parallelizing SAT-based BMC – each of many processors can execute a BMC from a different set of initial states. The only data that is passed over the network is at the very beginning, after that no synchronization is required, until termination. Such parallelization has no interdependence at all, and can therefore very effectively utilize a number of processors in a large grid, without creating communication overhead between the processors. This method also effectively exploits the advantage of symbolic BDD based search as well as SAT. If there are a large number of partitions or if certain partitions are difficult, performing cross-over images between them can be difficult, and this may be the bottleneck in getting to the error. This can be overcome by SAT based BMC, which is "locally complete" from its originating point and does not compute sets of states.

Although a very large grid was available, in typical experiments only a small number of CPUs were used. This suggests significant scope to improve the quality of results and possibility to tackle larger problems with further research.

References

[1] Akira Asato and Yoshimasa Kadooka. Grid Middleware for Effectively Utilizing Computing Resources: CyberGRIP. In *Fujitsu Scientific and Technical Journal*, volume 40, pages 261–268, 2004.

[2] Edmund Clarke, Armin Biere, Richard Raimi, and Yunshan Zhu. Bounded Model Checking Using Satisfiability Solving. *Formal Methods in System Design*, 19(1):7–34, July 2001. Kluwer Academic Publishers.

[3] Pei-Hsin Ho, Thomas Shiple, Kevin Harer, James Kukula, Robert Damiano, Valeria Bertacco, Jerry Taylor, and Jiang Long. Smart Simulation Using Collaborative Formal and Simulation Engines. In *Proc. of the IEEE/ACM International Conference on Computer-Aided Design*, pages 120–126, November 2000.

[4] Subramanian Iyer, Jawahar Jain, Mukul Prasad, Debashis Sahoo, and Thomas Sidle. Error Detection using BMC in a Parallel Environment. In *Technical Report, Department of Computer Sciences, University of Texas at Austin*, 2005.

[5] Debashis Sahoo, Subramanian Iyer, Jawahar Jain, Christian Stangier, Amit Narayan, David L. Dill, and E. Allen Emerson. A Partitioning Methodology for BDD-based Verification. In *Formal Methods in Computer-Aided Design*, volume 3312 of *Lecture Notes in Computer Science*, pages 399–413. Springer-Verlag, January 2004.

Formal Verification of Synchronizers

Tsachy Kapschitz and Ran Ginosar

VLSI Systems Research Center, Electrical Engineering Department
Technion–Israel Institute of Technology, Haifa 32000, Israel
ran@ee.Technian.ac.il

Abstract. Large Systems on Chips (SoC) comprise multiple clock domains, and inter-domain data transfers require synchronization. Synchronizers may fail due to metastability, but when using proper synchronization circuits the probability of such failures can be made negligible. Failures due to unexpected order of events (caused by interfacing multiple unrelated clocks) are more common. Correct synchronization is independent of event order, and can be verified by model checking. Given a synchronizer, a correct protocol is guessed, verification rules are generated out of the protocol specification, and the model checker applies these rules to the given synchronizer. An alternative method verifies correct data transfer and seeks potential data missing or duplication. Both approaches require specific modeling of multiple clocks, allowing for non-determinism in their relative ordering. These methods have been applied successfully to several synchronizers.

1 Introduction

Large systems of chip are typically partitioned into multiple clock domains. Clock frequencies of the various domains and their relative phases may be unknown a-priori, and may also change dynamically [1]. Data transfers between different clock domains require synchronization [2]. When data enters a domain and happens to change exactly when the receiving register is sampling its input may cause that register to become metastable and fail [3]. This problem is mitigated by properly employing synchronizers. This paper describes methods for formal verification of synchronizers using model-checking [4].

Synchronizers are designed to allow certain time for metastability resolution. The amount of resolution time is determined according to the desired level of probability of failures. In this paper we assume that sufficient time has been allowed and no failures are expected. However, following metastability the synchronizer may resolve non-deterministically to either 0 or 1, and consequently proper synchronization is still not guaranteed. To mitigate that non-determinism, synchronizers are encapsulated in a bidirectional handshake protocol. The goal of formal verification is to guarantee correct execution of that protocol.

There are too many known synchronizer types and synchronization protocols, and it may be infeasible to define a single specification that could be used to verify all of them. Instead, we employ structural analysis to recognize synchronizers and to sort them into several a-priori known types. For each type, a set of properties has been defined, which, when proven to hold, guarantee correctness.

D. Borrione and W. Paul (Eds.): CHARME 2005, LNCS 3725, pp. 359–362, 2005.
© Springer-Verlag Berlin Heidelberg 2005

The paper describes how to generate formal verification executions of RuleBase (a model checker [5] using PSL [6]) for given synchronizers. We start with modeling of multiple clocks in Section 0. Next, in Section 0, we describe control verification method, based on converting the specification into PSL assertions. Data verification, which is not specification-dependent, is presented in Section 0. A more detailed description is given in [7].

2 Modeling Multiple Clocks

The model checker (MC) [5] performs its algorithms in a sequence of atomic *ticks*. Each synchronous component of the system being verified (the *design system*) is assumed to operate in atomic *clock cycles*. Common model checking assumes a single clock, but synchronizers must be verified while observing multiple clocks. Thus, we need to add special modeling of multiple clocks to our specification.

Clock modeling depends on how the clocks of the two domains are inter-related. If the two clocks are unrelated, they are modeled as two free variables. When the frequencies of the two clocks are assumed related by a rational number m/n (WLOG $m>n$) [8], then we specify to the MC that between any two edges of CLK2 there should be N active edges of CLK1, where $\lfloor m/n \rfloor \leq N \leq \lceil m/n \rceil$ (see [7]). A wide range of m/n ratios may be covered in a single execution of the MC if m/n is specified as a non-deterministic variable.

3 Control Verification

As stated above, data transferred between two mutually asynchronous clock domains are wrapped by a handshake protocol, implemented with control signals between the domains. We consider verification of the protocol by examining the control signals. The desired synchronizer handshake protocols are specified by means of STG (Signal Transition Graphs) that define the order of events (logic level transitions) in the synchronizer [9]. In this section we discuss how to convert the synchronizer STG directly into PSL assertions.

We first generate assertions to prove that if a signal transition event is enabled, it eventually happens. Each event has its own condition that enables its execution. In STG, the condition is fulfilled by a marking (a mapping of tokens to arcs) where all arcs incoming into the event carry tokens, enabling firing of the event. The condition is converted into a rule that verifies that the enabled transition actually takes place before the enabling state is changed [7]:

```
AG ( EnablingState(E) -> Transition(E) before !EnablingState(E) )
```

Next, we generate assertions that verify that events take place only when enabled:

```
AG (Transition(E) -> SetOfEnablingStates)
```

To verify that the given synchronizer complies with the specification STG, we prove the correctness of the constituent events with the above rules. The correct ordering of events is then implied by the ordering allowed by the STG.

4 Data Verification

Verifying the synchronizer control, presented in the previous section, is subject to two limitations: First, it is protocol specific--the rules depend on the specific STG and cannot in general be applied to other synchronizers. Second, the STG may need to be modified (e.g. to satisfy complete state coding [10]), in order to enable rule derivation [7]. In this section we present *data verification* of the actual data transfer, irrespective of the control handshake protocol. If the controller has an error, it will be discovered through data verification. The goal of data transfer verification is to prove that any data item sent by the sender is eventually sampled exactly once by the receiver.

The data transfer part of a synchronizer is shown in Fig. 1. The verifier interprets the loading of data DIN into the leftmost register as an attempt by the sender to send it. A sampling into the rightmost register is interpreted as an attempt by the receiver to receive data. The verifier must prove that no data item is either missed or sampled more than once by the receiver.

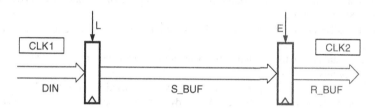

Fig. 1. Cross-domain data transfer structure

The first verification rule checks data integrity:

```
AG ( CLK1 & L & DIN(0)=1 ->
     next_event( CLK2 & E )( S_BUF(0)=1 ))
```

A similar rule can be written for the value 0. Integrity is checked only for a single data bit because all the other bits will behave in the same way, as guaranteed by structural verification. In addition to data integrity, we should verify that:

- Data is not duplicated—the receiver does not sample the data if the sender did not send any:

```
AG ( CLK2 & E -> AX ( (CLK1 & L) before (CLK2 & E) ))
```

- Data is not missed—the receiver eventually receives data that was sent by the sender:

```
AG ( CLK1 & L -> AX ( (CLK2 & E) before! (CLK1 & L) ))
```

In words, between any two send events there must be one reception, and vice versa. The second assertion uses the strong *before!* operator (with !) to verify that the event (CLK2 & E) eventually takes place even if the subsequent event (CLK1 & L) does not happen at all.

5 Conclusions

We have demonstrated two methods for synchronizer verification using model checking. For *control verification*, a specification (in terms of STG) is employed to derive PSL assertions that are subsequently applied to the design. For *data verification* we seek correct data transfers (each sent data item is received exactly once) while ignoring the control operation. Both methods require specific modeling of multiple clocks, allowing for non-determinism in their relative ordering.

These methods have been applied successfully to a number of synchronizers, such as the two-flip-flop synchronizer, a dual clock FIFO, and an Adaptive Predictive Synchronizer [8].

References

[1] A. Iyer and D. Marculescu, "Power Efficiency of Voltage Scaling in Multiple Clock, Multiple Voltage Cores", *IEEE/ACM Int. Conf. on Computer Aided Design (ICCAD)*, pp. 379-386, Nov. 2002.

[2] W. J. Dally and J. W. Poulton, "Digital System Engineering", Cambridge University Press, 1998.

[3] L. Kleeman, A. Cantoni, "Metastable behavior in digital systems", *IEEE Design and Test of Computers*, pp. 4-19, Dec. 1987.

[4] E.M. Clarke, O. Grumberg and D.A. Peled, "Model Checking", The MIT Press, 2000.

[5] I. Beer, S. Ben-David, C. Eisner, A. Landver, "RuleBase: an industry-oriented formal verification tool", *Design Automation Conference*, pp. 665-660 June 1996.

[6] M. Gordon, J. Hurd and K. Slind, "Executing the formal semantics of the Accellera Property Specification Language by mechanised theorem proving," *CHARME*, LNCS 2860, pp. 200–215, 2003.

[7] T. Kapschitz and R.Ginosar, "Formal Verification of Synchronizers," CCIT Tech. Rep. 536, EE Dept., Technion, 2005.

[8] U. Frank and R. Ginosar, "A Predictive Synchronizer for Periodic Clock Domains," *PATMOS*, LNCS 3254, pp. 402–412, 2004.

[9] T. A. Chu, C. K. C. Leung, T. S. Wanuga, "A Design Methodology for Concurrent VLSI Systems", in Proc. of ICCD, 407-410, 1985.

[10] J. Cortadella, M. Kishinevsky, A. Kondratyev, L. Lavagno, A. Yakovlev, "Complete state encoding based on the theory of regions", *2nd Int. Symp. Asynchronous Circuits and Systems*, pp. 36-47, March 1996.

A Parameterized Benchmark Suite of Hard Pipelined-Machine-Verification Problems[*]

Panagiotis Manolios[1] and Sudarshan K. Srinivasan[2]

[1] College of Computing
[2] School of Electrical & Computer Engineering,
Georgia Institute of Technology, Atlanta GA-30318
manolios@cc.gatech.edu
darshan@ece.gatech.edu

Abstract. We present a parameterized suite of benchmark problems arising from our work on pipelined machine verification, in the hopes that they can be used to speed up decision procedures. While the existence of a large number of CNF benchmarks has spurred the development of efficient SAT solvers, the benchmarks available for more expressive logics are quite limited. Our work on pipelined machine verification has yielded many problems that not only have complex models, but also have complex correctness statements, involving invariants and symbolic simulations of the models for dozens of steps. Many of these proofs take hundreds of thousands of seconds to check using the UCLID decision procedure and SAT solvers such as Zchaff and Siege. More complex problems can be generated by using PiMaG, a Web application that we developed. PiMaG generates problems in UCLID, SVC, and CNF formats based on user-provided parameters specifying features of the pipelined machines and their correctness statements.

1 Introduction

Fueled in part by advances in SAT solving, there is currently wide interest in obtaining efficient decision procedures for richer logics [1, 4]. As is the case with SAT solving technology [10, 11], efficiency does not mean better worst-case behavior; rather, it means better behavior on problems "arising in practice." In contrast to the situation for SAT, where hard CNF problems arising in practice are readily available, the supply of hard benchmark problems for more expressive logics is quite limited. We believe that by providing such problems we can help spur the growth of efficient decision procedures; to this end, we provide a parameterized suite of benchmarks in UCLID [2], SVC, and CNF formats that can be used to evaluate decision procedures and SAT solvers.

The core benchmark suite comprises of 210 benchmarks generated from our work on refinement based pipelined machine verification [7, 8]. We also developed PiMaG (Pipelined Machine Generator), a Web application that can be used to automatically generate complex benchmarks based on user provided parameters [9]. The benchmarks include not only the models, but also the properties to be proved, which include invariants, symbolic simulation steps, and arithmetic.

---

[*] This research was funded in part by NSF grants CCF-0429924 and IIS-0417413.

D. Borrione and W. Paul (Eds.): CHARME 2005, LNCS 3725, pp. 363–366, 2005.
© IFIP International Federation for Information Processing 2005

The paper is organized as follows. In Section 2, we briefly describe the refinement-based correctness theorems. In Section 3, we describe the pipelined machine models being verified, and in Section 4, we describe the benchmark suite, the tool, and give an overview of the running times we obtained in checking these benchmarks using the UCLID decision procedure [2] and the Siege SAT solver [11]. We conclude in Section 5.

2 Correctness Theorems

The benchmarks arise from our work on refinement-based pipelined machine verification. We use the notion of Well-Founded Equivalence Bisimulation (WEB) refinement to show pipelined machines and their instruction set architecture (ISA) have the same safety and liveness properties up to stuttering [5, 6]. Refinement proofs are relative to *refinement maps*, functions from pipelined machine states to ISA states, that show us how to view a pipelined machine state as an ISA state. For example, refinement maps have to hide the pipeline components that do not appear in the ISA. In [7], it is shown how to automate the proof of WEB-refinement in the context of pipelined machine verification. Our benchmark problems use three different refinement maps; two of them are based on commitment [5, 6] and one is based on flushing [3].

The idea with commitment is that partially completed instructions are invalidated and the programmer visible components are rolled back to correspond with the last committed instruction. Flushing is a kind of dual of commitment, where partially completed instructions are made to complete without fetching any new instructions. Using refinement maps based on commitment requires the use of invariants, but they can be automatically generated [7]. We use two different types of invariants that lead to two types of commitment proofs, one of which tends to lead to significantly faster verification times [8].

3 Pipelined Machine Models

The pipelined machine models are obtained by starting from a base model and extending it with various features to obtain more complex models. The most complex model in the core benchmark suite is shown in Figure 1. The base processor model is a 6 stage pipelined machine with fetch, decode, execute, memory1, memory2, and write back stages. The pipeline stages memory1 and memory2 provide for a two-cycle memory access. Instruction types such as ALU instructions with register-register and register-immediate addressing modes, branch, loads, and stores are implemented. The base processor model is extended with features such as a pipelined fetch stage, branch prediction, an instruction queue, an instruction cache, a data cache, and a write buffer.

The pipelined machine models are described using the UCLID specification language at the term-level. The data path is abstracted away using terms (integers) and much of the combinational circuit blocks that are common between the pipelined machine and its instruction set architecture (ISA) are abstracted using uninterpreted functions. The register file and the memory are modeled using lambda expressions.

We use the following naming convention for the pipelined machine models. The model name starts with a number followed optionally by the characters "i", "d", "w",

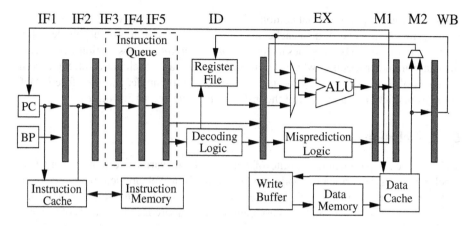

Fig. 1. High-level organization of the most complex processor model with 10 pipeline stages, instruction queue of length 3, instruction and data cache, and write buffer

"b", and "n", which indicate the presence of an instruction cache, a data cache, a write buffer, branch prediction abstraction scheme 1, and branch prediction abstraction scheme 2, respectively. The number indicates the number of pipeline stages. If no branch prediction is used, the model predicts not taken.

4   Benchmarks

We have generated a core suite of 210 benchmarks that are available in UCLID, SVC, and CNF formats. The benchmarks are obtained from the pipelined machine models described in Section 3 using flushing and the two commitment refinement maps. Even more complex benchmarks can be generated by our tool PiMaG. The benchmarks and tool are available on the Web [9].

The benchmark naming conventions are as follows: the first letter is either "f", "c", or "g" and indicates the use of flushing, commitment approach 1, or commitment approach 2, respectively. Then the name of the pipelined machine model, as described in Section 3, follows. For machines based on commitment approach 1 only, there is an optional suffix which can either be "-i" or "-r", indicating that only the invariant proof, or only the refinement proof should be generated, respectively.

We checked many of the benchmarks using the UCLID decision procedure (Version 1.0), and the Siege SAT solver (variant 4). The UCLID decision procedure compiles UCLID specifications to SAT problems or to SVC formulas. All the benchmarks are unsatisfiable and the verification times vary from a few seconds for the simpler models to hundreds of thousands of seconds to being too complex for Siege to handle (*e.g.*, f9idw and f10id, f10idw, f9bidw, f10bid, f10bidw, f9nidw, f10nid, and f10nidw).

To obtain even more complex problems, PiMaG can be used to automatically generate pipelined machine models, their ISA specifications, and their refinement theorems. PiMaG takes seven parameters, the first specifies if the base model has 6 or 7 stages, the second selects the refinement map used, the third provides the length of the instruction queue, the fourth specifies what combination of the following three optional features to include: instruction cache, data cache, and write buffer, the fifth provides the length of the write buffer, the sixth specifies the type of branch prediction abstraction scheme, and the final parameter specifies what set of formats to generate benchmarks for. Some combinations of parameters can be too large for the tools to handle, and therefore PiMaG enforces restrictions on the size of the instruction queue and write buffer.

5   Conclusions

We presented a parameterized suite of benchmarks in various formats arising from pipelined machine verification and developed PiMaG, a Web application that can generate arbitrarily complex models and their correctness statements. Some of the benchmarks are quite complex and their verification takes hundreds of thousands of seconds; other benchmarks cannot be handled using state-of-the art tools such as UCLID and the Siege SAT solver. Our goal in making these benchmarks readily available is to help evaluate and stimulate further research in efficient decision procedures and SAT solvers.

References

[1] C. Barret, L. M. de Moura, and A. Stump. The satisfiability modulo theories competition (SMT-COMP'05), 2005. See URL http://www.csl.sri.com/users/-demoura/smt-comp.

[2] R. E. Bryant, S. K. Lahiri, and S. Seshia. Modeling and verifying systems using a logic of counter arithmetic with lambda expressions and uninterpreted functions. In E. Brinksma and K. Larsen, editors, *Computer-Aided Verification–CAV 2002*, volume 2404 of *LNCS*, pages 78–92. Springer-Verlag, 2002.

[3] J. R. Burch and D. L. Dill. Automatic verification of pipelined microprocessor control. In *Computer-Aided Verification (CAV '94)*, volume 818 of *LNCS*, pages 68–80. Springer-Verlag, 1994.

[4] L. M. de Moura and H. Rueß. An experimental evaluation of ground decision procedures. In *Computer aided verification (CAV'04)*, pages 162–174, 2004.

[5] P. Manolios. Correctness of pipelined machines. pages 161–178.

[6] P. Manolios. *Mechanical Verification of Reactive Systems*. PhD thesis, University of Texas at Austin, August 2001. See URL http://www.cc.gatech.edu/~manolios/-publications.html.

[7] P. Manolios and S. Srinivasan. Automatic verification of safety and liveness for xscale-like processor models using web refinement. In *Design, Automation, and Test in Europe (DATE'04)*, 2004.

[8] P. Manolios and S. K. Srinivasan. A computationally efficient method based on commitment refinement maps for verifying pipelined machines. In *Formal Methods and Models for Codesign (MEMOCODE)*, July 2005. Accepted to appear.

[9] P. Manolios and S. K. Srinivasan. A parameterized benchmark suite of hard pipelined-machine-verification problems, 2005. See URL http://www.cc.gatech.edu/-manolios/benchmarks/charme.html.

[10] M. W. Moskewicz, C. F. Madigan, Y. Zhao, L. Zhang, and S. Malik. Chaff: Engineering an efficient SAT solver. *Design Automation Conference (DAC'01)*, pages 530–535, 2001.

[11] L. Ryan. Siege homepage. See URL http://www.cs.sfu.ca/~loryan/-personal.

Improvements to the Implementation of Interpolant-Based Model Checking

João Marques-Silva

Technical University of Lisbon,
IST/INESC-ID, Portugal
jpms@sat.inesc-id.pt

Abstract. The evolution of SAT technology over the last decade has motivated its application in model checking, initially through the utilization of SAT in bounded model checking (BMC) and, more recently, in unbounded model checking (UMC). This paper addresses the utilization of interpolants in UMC and proposes two techniques for improving the original interpolant-based UMC algorithm. These techniques include improvements to the computation of interpolants, and redefining the organization of the unbounded model checking algorithm given the information extracted from interpolant computation.

1 Introduction

The utilization of Boolean Satisfiability (SAT) in Model Checking has been the subject of intensive research in recent years. The main result of this effort has been a number of very competitive incomplete and complete algorithms for checking safety properties (see [3] for a comprehensive list of references and an extended version of this paper). Moreover, SAT-based model checking has also been rapidly adopted by industry, and a number of vendors have included SAT-based Model Checking in their tools. This paper describes preliminary work on optimizing the utilization of interpolants in SAT-based model checking [4]. Two techniques are proposed and evaluated. First, we propose the computation of interpolants directly from the proof trace and skip the generation of the resolution proof, and study the implementation of techniques for eliminating redundancy from the computed interpolants. Second, we propose to utilize information from the fixed-point checks of the UMC algorithm for redefining the organization of the UMC algorithm.

2 Interpolant-Based Unbounded Model Checking

The generic propositional formula associated with SAT-based bounded model checking is the following [2]:

$$\psi_{\text{BMC}}^{j,k} = \psi_I(Y/Y_0) \wedge \bigwedge_{i=0}^{k-1} \psi_T(Y/Y_i, Y'/Y_{i+1}) \wedge (\bigvee_{i=j}^{k} \neg\psi_S^i) \tag{1}$$

D. Borrione and W. Paul (Eds.): CHARME 2005, LNCS 3725, pp. 367–370, 2005.

This formula represents the unfolding of the state machine for k computation steps, where $\psi_I(Y/Y_0)$ represents the initial state, $\psi_T(Y/Y_i, Y'/Y_{i+1})$ represents the transition relation between states X_i and X_{i+1}, and ψ_S^i represents the target property in computation step i. Given the BMC propositional formula $\psi_{\text{BMC}}^{j,k}$, it is straightforward to generate a CNF formula $\varphi_{\text{BMC}}^{j,k}$. The resulting formula can then be evaluated by a SAT solver. Recent work on SAT-based UMC has addressed the utilization of interpolants [4], with quite promising experimental results. McMillan's [4] interpolant-based UMC algorithm can be organized into two main phases: a BMC step, where the circuit is unfolded, and the existence of a counterexample is checked, and a UMC step, where the existence of a fixed-point is tested. Whereas the first phase corresponds essentially to the standard BMC algorithm, the second phase requires the iterative computation of interpolants until a fixed-point is reached or a (possibly) false counterexample is identified. See [3] for a detailed description of McMillan's UMC algorithm.

3   Optimizations to the Basic UMC Algorithm

This section addresses two optimizations to the basic interpolant-based UMC algorithm proposed by McMillan [4]. First, we address the construction and simplification of interpolants. Afterwards, we show how to exploit the information from the interpolant iteration phase for rescheduling either the UMC or the BMC loops. As noted by McMillan [4], interpolants obtained from unsatisfiability proofs are highly redundant Boolean expressions. In [4] the author proposes the utilization of BDDs, but no details are provided. For complex problem instances, that yield hard instances of SAT, with large unsatisfiability proofs, the interpolants before simplification can reach extremely large sizes. Our experience has been that interpolants before simplification can be more than two orders of magnitude larger than the resulting interpolants after simplification. Moreover, although modern SAT solvers can easily be instructed to generate proof traces, the generation of the actual unsatisfiability proof must be performed after the SAT solver terminates and the proof trace is concluded. A key observation is that one can avoid generating the unsatisfiability proof, and construct the interpolant directly from the proof trace.

Next we outline two algorithms for creating interpolants directly from proof traces. We should note that the organization of the two algorithms allows fairly different results in terms of the worst-case memory requirements, as illustrated in Section 4 for real-world model checking problem instances. Moreover, both algorithms utilize Reduced Boolean Circuits [1] for representing Boolean expressions, thus ensuring that constants and duplicate nodes are eliminated.

The first algorithm consists of a breadth-first traversal of the proof trace, that at each node creates a Boolean expression as indicated by the definition of interpolant (see [4]). We refer to this approach as the BFS algorithm. A key drawback of the BFS algorithm is that a large number of Boolean expressions need to be created, most of which are eventually deleted by applying the simplification techniques described above. Hence, the BFS algorithm often spends a large amount of time creating Boolean expressions that are eventually eliminated. The second algorithm consists of a depth-first traversal of the proof trace, applying the simplification techniques described above wherever possible, and eliminating depth-first visits whenever the (constant) value of a Boolean expression is known. We refer to this second approach as the DFS algorithm.

Next, we address techniques for exploiting the information provided by the UMC step of the UMC algorithm. Suppose the current unfolding size consists of K time frames. Moreover, assume the interpolant iteration procedure is executed I times, until a (possibly) false counterexample is identified. According to the definition of computed interpolants, this means that the target property cannot be satisfied within $K + I - 1$ time frames. As a result, the property cannot be satisfied for any unfolding with size no greater than $K + I - 1$ time frames. Hence, instead of a fixed policy of incrementing the size of the unfolding by INC time frames, we can safely consider the size of the next unfolding to be $K + I$ time frames. Observe that the information from interpolant computation can be used for other purposes. For example, instead of rescheduling the BMC loop to $K + I$ time steps, we can simply utilize a SAT solver more effective at *proving unsatisfiability*, and check the fixed-point earlier than $K + I$ time steps. Moreover, and since the information from the interpolant iteration procedure allows rescheduling the BMC loop, we can also reschedule the next unfolding for which to iterate interpolants and check the existence of a fixed-point, i.e. the UMC step. In general, this can be done for every unfolding at which the BMC step is evaluated.

The potential gains introduced with rescheduling can be significant. Assume a state machine and safety property such that a counterexample can be identified with an unfolding of T time frames. Moreover, assume that the BMC loop increases the unfolding by 1 time frame each time, that the initial unfolding size is 1, and that the interpolant iteration procedure runs for $T - K$ iterations for an unfolding size of K time frames (observe that if a counterexample exists, then we cannot iterate the computation of interpolants more than $T - K$ times). In this case, rescheduling guarantees that the UMC step is invoked only once, and so the number of times the SAT solver is invoked is $2 + 2 \times (T - 1) = O(T)$. In contrast, without rescheduling, the number of times the SAT solver is invoked is $T + 2 \times \sum_{i=1}^{T-1}(T - i) = O(T^2)$.

4   Results

In order to evaluate the effectiveness of the proposed techniques we implemented the algorithm described in [4], and integrated the optimizations described in the previous section. Moreover, a state of the art SAT solver was used. The experiments have been run under Linux RH 9, on a Pentium 2.8 GHz machine, with 1 GByte of RAM. Two classes of instances are considered. First, we consider a set of standard counters, for which a counterexample exists. For these instances the property requires not all state bits to be simultaneously assigned value 1. Second, we consider a set of instances (I11, I12, I21, I31, I32 and I33) obtained

Table 1. Experimental results

Instance	BFS & No-reschedule	DFS & Reschedule BMC
4bit-counter	0.31	0.09
5bit-counter	3.86	0.84
6bit-counter	21.36	10.41
7bit-counter	1780.68	175.69
I12	255.77	272.47
I11	75.28	81.89
I31	83.51	90.08
I32	19.66	14.89
I33	17.44	13.09
I21	24.93	26.48
Total Time	2282.8	685.9

from real-world examples. For these instances, I11, I12, I21 and I31 do not have a counterexample, whereas I32 and I33 have counterexamples.

Some preliminary results are shown in Table 1. Two configurations are considered: the BFS algorithm with no rescheduling, and the DFS algorithm with rescheduling. In both cases interpolants are computed directly from the proof trace. The results indicate that the proposed techniques are promising, allowing an average speedup of 3.3 over our base implementation of the UMC algorithm.

5   Conclusions

This paper proposes techniques for improving the utilization of interpolants in SAT-based unbounded model checking. As the results illustrate, improvements can be obtained from a careful implementation of the interpolant computation algorithm, and from exploiting the information provided by the procedure for iterating the computation of interpolants. For specific classes of instances, both artificially generated and obtained from industrial designs, the improvements can exceed several orders of magnitude. The utilization of interpolants in SAT-based model checking shows promise for future improvements, mostly related with exploiting the information represented by computed interpolants. Moreover, additional effective techniques for reducing the final or intermediate size of interpolants may play a crucial role in the utilization of interpolants in SAT-based model checking.

References

1. P. A. Abdulla, P. Bjesse, and N. Eén. Symbolic reachability analysis based on SAT solvers. In *Proc. TACAS*, 2000.
2. A. Biere, A. Cimatti, E. Clarke, and Y. Zhu. Symbolic model checking without BDDs. In *Proc. TACAS*, March 1999.
3. J. Marques-Silva. Optimizing the utilization of interpolants in SAT-based model checking. Technical Report RT-01-05, INESC-ID, January 2005.
4. K. L. McMillan. Interpolation and SAT-based model checking. In *Proc. CAV*, 2003.

High-Level Modelling, Analysis, and Verification on FPGA-Based Hardware Design

Petr Matoušek, Aleš Smrčka, and Tomáš Vojnar

FIT, Brno University of Technology, Božetěchova 2, CZ-612 66 Brno, Czech Republic
{matousp, smrcka, vojnar}@fit.vutbr.cz

Abstract. The paper presents high-level modelling and formal analysis and verification on an FPGA-based multigigabit network monitoring system called Scampi. UPPAAL was applied in this work to establish some correctness and throughput results on a model intentionally built using patterns reusable in other similar projects. Some initial experiments with parametric analysis using TREX were performed too.

1 Introduction

Implementation of network components in hardware is a trend in advanced high-speed network technologies which applies also for the network monitor and analyser Scampi developed within the Liberouter project [4] that we consider here. The Scampi analyser is implemented in FPGA on a special add-on card. FPGA-based hardware provides a similar functionality of a system as software implemented on general microprocessors. However, in comparison to a software solution, programmable hardware is very fast—it allows Scampi to communicate in multiples of gigabits per second.

In the paper (and its full version [3]), we discuss our experience from high-level modelling and formal analysis and verification of certain important correctness and throughput properties of Scampi. Our analysis of the system started with a preliminary manual analysis, which we do not discuss here, and then continued by an application of automated formal analysis and verification methods. We divide the model of Scampi we used for automated formal analysis and verification into three kinds of components: a model of the environment (generators), a model of buffers (queues, channels), and a model of executive units. We show how the different model components may be constructed and especially in the case of generators and buffers, we obtain general templates that may be reused in different models of systems of the considered kind. Next, we discuss the properties we handled by automated formal analysis and verification using UPPAAL [5] and—in some initial attempts for a parametric analysis—TREX [1].

2 The Design of Scampi

Scampi is a network adapter working at the speed of 10 Gbps. The system consists of several components—input buffers, preprocessing units (a header field extractor—HFE), and searching units (a lookup processor—LUP and processing units—PU). The Scampi adapter reads data from one input port and distributes them into four independent paths working in parallel. An IP packet is processed

D. Borrione and W. Paul (Eds.): CHARME 2005, LNCS 3725, pp. 371–375, 2005.

by an HFE unit at first where the IP header is translated into a unified header containing adjusted data like the source/destination IP address, MAC address, port number, VLAN tag, etc. Then, the unified header is processed by a lookup

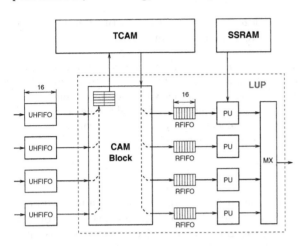

processor, see Fig. 1, where it is classified according to some pre-defined rules. Searching of the LUP consists of packet matching (parallel searching) encoded into a TCAM memory (Content Address Memory) and of additional sequential searching in an SSRAM memory performed by PU.

Fig. 1. The structure of the Lookup Processor

The results give us information what to do with the packet—e.g., to increment the number of dangerous packets found, to forward the packet to the software layer over Scampi, to broadcast the packet, or to simply release the packet from the Scampi system.

3   Modelling Scampi

We now sketch models of several components of Scampi important for its correctness and throughput analysis—their detailed description can be found in [3].

In our approach, we recognise three basic types of components that occur in some form in many complex systems: (i) *waiting FIFO queues* (buffers, channels)—deterministic, stochastic, or non-deterministic; lossy queues, delayed queues, etc., (ii) *executive components*—multiplexers, processing units (lookup processors, preprocessing units), etc., and (iii) *environment*—generators of incoming requests (packets) or output units consuming the results.

Modelling Waiting Queues. A FIFO queue is a typical abstract data structure that contains a sequence of stored data. Here, we abstract away the content of the queue items and we concentrate only on the number of items in the queue. FIFO queues are

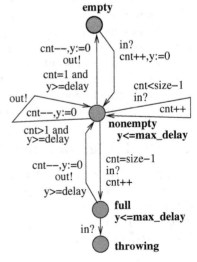

Fig. 2. A model of a delayed queue

used to represent transmitting channels, intermediate buffers between a process-ing unit and a memory, etc. We can have lossy queues where some data may be lost. There are delayed queues where data are delayed. We can model bounded or unbounded queues, or we can also deal with queues where a symbolic con-stant value—a parameter—defines the maximum length of the queue. We try to model all these queues without expecting any highly specialised features of the modelling language.

In Figure 2 there is a model of a delayed FIFO queue where every request is guaranteed to be delayed at least *delay* time units before it is released, but at maximum *max_delay* time units. The delayed queue is modelled using timed automata. Transitions that release an element of the queue are augmented with time constraints allowing to release an item only if the $y \geq delay$ guard is satisfied ensuring the lower bound on the delay. The upper bound is ensured by the $y \leq max\_delay$ invariants of the appropriate states. This pattern of a waiting queue was applied to model four UHFIFO queues and four RFIFO queues of the Scampi system working in parallel.

Modelling Executive Components. While creating a model, one often has to reflect the goal of the verification. In our case, we are interested in timing of the components. If executive components have an accurate timing plan, we distinguish two kinds of states in the model. The first is an urgent state that we use for observers. The second type is a state that models delays of the system. The latter kind of a state has an incoming transition resetting a clock ($t :=$ 0), an invariant that defines a time constraint over the clock ($t \leq delay$), and an outgoing transition constrained by a condition on the clock ($t = delay$). Using these principles, we modelled the TCAM memory, PU, and multiplexer components of the LUP.

We are interested in the minimum guaranteed throughput of the system which can be calculated from the size S of an incoming packet in bits—we take

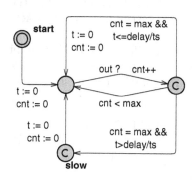

Fig. 3. A timed automaton MX for throughput checking

the minimum possible size which is the worst case in the given setting, the average delay D of the rule matching process in time slots for the worst possible scenario, and the size T of a time slot in seconds: $throughput = S/(D*T)$. We approximate the average delay for the worst case from the worst delay possible for transmitting x results (a user chosen, reason-ably large value). To compute the worst delay for x results, we can use a counter of outgoing results and a clock. When the counter reaches x, the system fires a transition to an observer state (the slow state in Fig. 3) provided the clock value is greater than the allowed delay.

The analysis of the throughput is then based on manually finding the minimum value of the delay (by running model checking several times) such that the system does not reach slow.

4   Verified Properties

Verification by UPPAAL. Let us now mention a few examples of properties (written in CTL) that we verified over the above presented models—more can be found in [3]: (i) $A \square \neg deadlock$—no deadlock is possible in the system. (ii) $A \square \neg (RFIFO0.full \lor RFIFO1.full \lor RFIFO2.full \lor RFIFO3.full)$—this property holds even if the RFIFO size is 2. It means that RFIFO can be replaced by a one-place buffer. We can use a similar property on other queues and see whether some data is thrown away. (iii) $A \square \neg MX.slow$—this property expresses the throughput checking mentioned above. The property is satisfied when the delay for 1000 counted results is set at least to 16000 time slots (the average delay for the worst case is 16 time slots). Now, we can calculate the minimum system throughput (from the smallest supported packets—64 bytes) caused by the Lookup Processor: $(64 * 8 \ bits)/(16 * 20 * 10^{-9} \ seconds) = 1.6 \ Gbps$.

Parametric Verification by TREX. Parametric verification is a technique that can help one to discover values of the parameters of the system that satisfy certain pre-defined constraints and cause the system to behave in a certain way. Here, we are interested in the length of buffers preventing a buffer overflow and in an optimal timing of the system maximizing the throughput of the system. At first, we used a similar model as for UPPAAL for which the analysis did not finish. So, we started to go from the simple building blocks of the system.

We created a simple parametric model of the FIFO queue with three parameters: the maximal length of the queue $FIFOsize$, the rate of incoming request uh_time, and the rate of reading data from the queue $read\_time$. At first, we asked what values the buffer $UHFIFO$ overflows for. We get the following results: If $uh\_time \geq read\_time$, the queue never overflows, and the length of the buffer is not important. If $uh\_time < read\_time$, the analysis does not finish. After setting the initial size of the queue $FIFOsize = 3$, we found that the buffer overflows if $4 * read\_time = uh\_time$. Then, we asked how many packets are accepted until the first one is dropped.

In the future, we plan to apply TREX to more specific parts of the Scampi system abstracted in a suitable way and we also intend to experiment with alternative (perhaps newly developed or improved) symbolic representations in TREX (e.g., based on parameterized intervals).

Acknowledgements. The work was supported by the FP5 projects No. IST-2001-32603 and IST-2001-32404, the CESNET activity "Programmable hardware", and the Czech Grant Agency project No. 102/04/0780.

References

1. A. Bouajjani, A. Collomb-Annichini, and M. Sighireanu. TReX: A tool for Reachability Analysis of Complex Systems. In *Proc. of CAV'01, LNCS* 2102, 2001. Springer-Verlag.

2. J. Holeček, T. Kratochvíla, V. Rehák, D. Šafránek, and P. Simeček. How to Formalize FPGA Hardware Design. Technical Report 4/2004, CESNET, October 2004.
3. P. Matoušek, A. Smrčka, and T. Vojnar. High-Level Modeling, Analysis, and Verification of Scampi2. Technical report, CESNET, 2005. To appear.
4. J. Novotný, O. Fučík, and D. Antoš. Project of IPv6 Router with FPGA Hardware Accelerator. In *Proc. of FPL'03*, *LNCS* 2778, 2003. Springer-Verlag.
5. P. Pettersson and K.G. Larsen. UPPAAL2k. *Bulletin of the European Association for Theoretical Computer Science*, 70:40–44, February 2000.

Proving Parameterized Systems: The Use of Pseudo-Pipelines in Polyhedral Logic

Katell Morin-Allory[1] and David Cachera[2]

[1] TIMA, 46 avenue Félix Viallet, 38031 Grenoble, France
[2] IRISA - ENS Cachan (Bretagne),
Campus de Beaulieu F-35042 Rennes, France

1 Introduction

The polyhedral model mixes recurrence equations over polyhedral domains and affine dependency functions. This model provides a unified framework for reasoning about regular systems composed of both hardware and software parts. Systems are described in a generic manner through the use of symbolic parameters, and structuring mechanisms allow for hierarchical specifications. The ALPHA language [3] and the MMAL-PHA environment [4] provide a syntax and a programming environment to define and manipulate polyhedral equation systems. High-level system specifications are refined through a user-guided series of automatic transformations, down to an implementable description, from which may be derived C code or a VHDL architecture. For hardware components and interfaces, control signals are generated to validate computations or data transfers. The use of systematic and semi-automatic rewritings together with the clean semantic basis provided by the polyhedral model should ensure the correctness of the final implementation. However, interface and control signal generators are not certified, and hand-made optimisations are still performed to tune the final result. As a consequence, the correctness of control signals has to be checked at the lower level of description, in the presence of *symbolic parameters*. A formal verification tool that benefits from the intrinsic regularity of the model has been developed to (partially) certify low-level system descriptions [2], based on polyhedra manipulation. The present work develops new strategies to prove a wider class of formulae. The basic idea is to detect particular patterns in the definition of signals, that characterise the propagation of known values along spatial or temporal dependencies, and to define a widening operator that allows for the automatic determination of how this propagation can be useful in the proof process.

2 The Polyhedral Model

An Example of a Modelled System. We introduce the model on the example of a system designed to compute a sequence of matrix-vector products. It consists of a linear array of N cells, N being a symbolic parameter carrying any integer value. The vector coefficients and the N column of the matrix are input sequentially, and each cell computes one coefficient of the output vector. Input vector coefficients and output values are propagated from left to right in the array, through register A. The behaviour of each

D. Borrione and W. Paul (Eds.): CHARME 2005, LNCS 3725, pp. 376–379, 2005.
© IFIP International Federation for Information Processing 2005

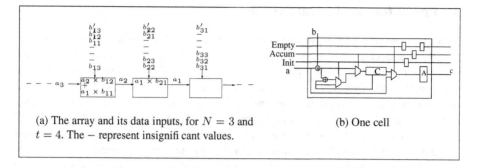

(a) The array and its data inputs, for $N = 3$ and $t = 4$. The $-$ represent insignificant values.

(b) One cell

Fig. 1. Structure of an array computing a matrix-vector product

cell depends on its position in the array and on the time elapsed since the beginning of the computation. Three boolean *control signals* are thus added to precisely control the behaviour of operators and registers: when *Init* is set to true, it initialises register C, *Accum* accumulates the product $a \times b$ in C and *Empty* outputs the value of register C in register A.

Describing This System in the Polyhedral Model. Each signal is represented by a function called a *polyhedral variable*. The vector of all cells registers A is a mapping from $\mathbb{N} \times [0, N]$ to the boolean set. This mapping is defined by an *affine recurrence equation* composed of three *branches*:

$$
A = \begin{cases}
\{t, i \mid t = 0; 0 \le i \le N\} : & 0 & (1) \\
\{t, i \mid i = 0\} : & a.(t, i \to t) & (2) \\
\{t, i \mid t > 0; 0 < i \le N\} : & \text{if Empty}.(t, i \to t, i) \text{ then } C.(t, i \to t - 1, i) & \\
& \text{else } A.(t, i \to t - 1, i - 1) & (3)
\end{cases}
$$

Let us focus on the third branch: $\{t, i \mid t > 0; 0 < i \le N\}$ denotes a *polyhedral domain*, i.e., a subset of $\mathbb{Z}^n$ bounded by a finite number of hyperplanes. The dimension of this domain (2 in this example) is also the dimension of variable A. Terms like $(t, i \to t - 1, i - 1)$ denote *dependency functions*, i.e., affine mappings between polyhedral domains. We concentrate on *uniform* dependencies, *i.e.* translations by a vector: dependency $(t, i \to t - 1, i - 1)$ is the translation by vector $(-1, -1)$. The "." notation denotes the composition of functions: $C.(t, i \to t - 1, i)$ thus represents the mapping $(t, i) \mapsto C(t - 1, i)$. Note that we have a *self-dependency* on A in (3). A *polyhedral system* is a set of such affine recurrence equations. Polyhedral systems are *parameterised* with symbolic parameters that are in turn defined on polyhedral domains, and can be seen as additional dimensions on all variables. We only consider systems for which an order in which computations should take place, has been determined, and assume that a particular index (say, the first one, denoted t) is considered as the *temporal index*. Such a system is called a *scheduled system*.

The combination of recurrence equations with polyhedral domains provide a rich mathematical and computational basis for program transformations. RTL descriptions can thus be obtained by derivation from a high-level algorithmic description.

3   Proofs for Polyhedral Systems

To formally establish properties of systems described in the polyhedral model, such as validity of a given control signal on a given set of time and space indices, we have developed a proof method and a proof tool[1]. Properties of the system are described in a so-called *polyhedral logic*: a formula is of the form $\mathcal{D} : e \downarrow v$, where $\mathcal{D}$ is a polyhedral domain, e a polyhedral multidimensional expression, and v a boolean scalar value. Proofs for such formulae are constructed by means of a set of inference rules, that are of two kinds: (i) "classical" propositional rules, and (ii) rules specific to the model, based on heuristics using rewritings and polyhedral computations (*e.g.* intersection of polyhedra). The proof tool uses these rules to automatically construct a proof tree, whose root is the initial formula we want to prove. This tool is able to establish simple inductive properties in connection with propagation of boolean values in multidimensional arrays. If formula $\mathcal{D} : e \downarrow v$ is proved, the soundness of the set of rules ensures that the value of e on $\mathcal{D}$ is v. If the proof construction fails on a given node, this node is called a *pending leaf*.

4   Pseudo-Pipelines and Widenings

Since the proof rules described in Section 3 are not complete, we have developed new heuristics to increase the effectiveness of our tool, based on the notion of *pseudo-pipelines*. In a hardware system, pipelined variables are used to transmit values from cell to cell without modifying them. We extend this notion to a less specific one by allowing a more general form of dependencies.

Definition 1 (Pseudo-Pipeline). *A* pseudo-pipeline *is a polyhedral variable X such that one of its branch is defined by an expression e such that:(a) e is in disjunctive (resp. conjunctive) normal form, (b) e contains at least one occurrence of X, (c) each conjunct (resp. disjunct) of e is either a single occurrence of X composed with a dependency d, or a polyhedral expression without any occurrence of X.*

A general form for a pseudo-pipeline is $X = \begin{cases} \mathcal{D}_1 : X.d \wedge e \\ \mathcal{D}_2 : f \end{cases}$ where e and f are polyhedral expressions. Like pipelines, pseudo-pipelines frequently appear in low-level description of systems, since they are used to compute reduction of boolean operators over a given set of signals, either in a temporal or spatial dimension.

The notion of pseudo-pipeline is a syntactic one. A pseudo-pipeline is characterised by a *propagation direction d*, which corresponds to the self-dependency occurring in its defining expression. The fundamental property of pseudo-pipelines is informally stated as follows: *If a pseudo-pipeline X of propagation direction d is true (resp. false) on a given point z_0, then there exists a domain $\mathcal{D}_{d,z_0}$ on which X is true (resp. false). $\mathcal{D}_{d,z_0}$ is an extension (potentially infinite) of $\{z_0\}$, either in the direction of d, or in the opposite one, depending on the boolean operators and truth values involved.*

This property illustrates the propagation of a value for one instance in a domain. It can be generalised to a whole domain by iteratively computing the image (or preimage) of the domain by the dependency: we widen the domain in the dependency direction. Since the domain $\mathcal{D}_{d,z_0}$ is not strictly a polyhedral domain, we have to extend it by taking its convex hull. The formal definition of our widening operator is:

Definition 2 (Widening Along a Dependency). *Let $\mathcal{D}$ be a domain of dimension n and d a dependency from $\mathbb{Z}^n$ to $\mathbb{Z}^n$. The widening of domain $\mathcal{D}$ by dependency d is the set:*

$$\mathcal{D} \mathbin{\widetilde{\nabla}} d = convex.hull(\{z \mid \exists z_0 \in \mathcal{D}, \exists i \in \mathbb{N}, \; z = d^i(z_0)\})$$

The alternative representation of polyhedra, as linear combinations of lines, rays and vertices, allow for a simple computation of convex hulls.

Use of Widenings in the Proof Construction. We now show how widenings are used to generate new lemmas. Let $f = \mathcal{D} : e \downarrow v$ be a formula labelling a pending leaf in the proof tree. For all variables occurring in e, a procedure is used to detect if it is a pseudo-pipeline. Let X be such a variable, and d the dependency associated to X in e. In the definition of X, we look for a subdomain $\mathcal{D}_0$ where X is defined by a boolean constant v', and we determine the direction d' of propagation. This direction is given by either d or d^{-1}, depending on the value of v'. The domain $\mathcal{D}_0 \mathbin{\widetilde{\nabla}} d'$ is then computed and intersected with $d(\mathcal{D})$, the domain on which the dependency d is valid. Let $\mathcal{D}'$ be the resulting domain. All occurrences of $X.d$ defined on $\mathcal{D}'$ may now be substituted by v'. Formula f is thus simplified by this substitution and we get formula $f' = \mathcal{D} : e' \downarrow v'$. Formulae f and f' are semantically equivalent. The proof construction then resumes with formula f' with these new domains and equations.

5 Conclusion

In this paper, we have presented heuristic strategies to generate new lemmas in order to improve the efficiency of proofs for systems described in the polyhedral model. Specifications of the system are described in a polyhedral logic close to the model, and the general proof mechanism relies on proof rules that exploit the expressivity and the computational power of the model. The proposed strategies consist in detecting particular value propagation schemes in the equations defining the variables, and to widen the index domains on which the proof has to be made. The proof rules are implemented within MMALPHAusing the PolyLib [5] . The heuristics greatly improve the effectivity of our verification tool. The proof tool is intended to work at a relatively low description level in the synthesis flow. At this level of detail, there are many signals defined by means of pipelines or pseudo-pipelines. As an example, our heuristics were able to establish the correctness of a hardware arbiter for mutual exclusion.

References

1. D. Cachera and K. Morin-Allory. Proving parameterized systems: the use of a widening operator and pseudo-pipelines in polyhedral logic. Technical report, TIMA, April 2005.
2. D. Cachera and K. Morin-Allory. Verification of safety properties for parameterized regular systems. *Trans. on Embedded Computing Sys.*, 4(2):228–266, 2005.
3. C. Mauras. *Alpha : un langage équationnel pour la conception et la programmation d'architectures systoliques.* PhD thesis, Univ. Rennes I, France, December 1989.
4. D.K. Wilde. A library for doing polyhedral operations. Technical Report 785, IRISA, Rennes, France, jan 1993.
5. D.K. Wilde. The Alpha language. Technical Report 999, IRISA, Rennes, France, jan 1994.

Resolving Quartz Overloading

Oliver Pell and Wayne Luk

Department of Computing, Imperial College,
180 Queen's Gate London SW7 2AZ, UK
{op, wl}@doc.ic.ac.uk

Abstract. Quartz is a new declarative hardware description language with polymorphism, overloading, higher-order combinators and a relational approach to data flow, supporting formal reasoning for design verification in the same style as the Ruby language. The combination of parametric polymorphism and overloading within the language involves the implementation of a system of constrained types. This paper describes how Quartz overloading is resolved using satisfiability matrix predicates. Our algorithm is a new approach to overloading designed specifically for the requirements of describing hardware in Quartz.

1 Introduction

The term overloading, or ad-hoc polymorphism, describes the use of a single identifier to produce different implementations depending on context, the standard example being the use of "+" to represent addition of both integers and floating point numbers in most programming languages. Parametric polymorphism covers the case when a function is defined over a range of types but acts in the same way for each type, a typical example is the length function for lists. The functional language Haskell uses type classes [1] to combine overloading with parametric polymorphism using the Hindley/Milner type system [2].

Quartz is a new declarative hardware description language, intended to combine features found in the Pebble [3] and Ruby [4] languages. The language includes polymorphism with type inference and support for overloading, however previous approaches to combining type inference and overloading in software languages are not ideal for Quartz. This paper describes how Quartz overloading is resolved using a system of *satisfiability matrix predicates* which extend the Hindley/Milner type system to support overloading without using type classes.

Matrix predicates provide a generalisation of the basic type system that maintains full inference of types without any explicit definitions, in contrast to type classes which require explicit class and instance declarations.

2 Motivation

A Quartz description is composed of a series of blocks which are defined by their name, interface type, local definitions and body statements. A block's interface

D. Borrione and W. Paul (Eds.): CHARME 2005, LNCS 3725, pp. 380–383, 2005.

is divided, in a relational style, into a domain and a range. *Primitive blocks* represent hardware or simulation primitives and control the function of the circuit, while *composite blocks* contain statements which control the structure and inter-connections of the primitives.

Quartz has a simple but strong type system with three basic signal types for wires, integers and booleans. Quartz also supports both tuples and vectors of signals. The signal assignment operation "=" is overloaded to allow the assignment of static values to wires. Quartz blocks can be overloaded by defining multiple blocks with the same name, a mechanism that has a number of uses:

– Primitive blocks can be overloaded when multiple hardware primitives are available which essentially carry out the same operation e.g. a two-input adder and a constant-coefficient adder.
– Higher-order combinators can be overloaded when multiple blocks have the same basic function but slightly different parameterisations. It is sometimes useful to supply "hint" parameters to combinators to aid in the generation of parameterised output.
– Composite blocks can be overloaded with primitive ones as "wrappers" around the primitives e.g. if only a two-input adder primitive is available it may still be desirable to define an overloaded (composite block) constant-coefficient adder which instantiates the adder primitive appropriately.

In order to achieve this our general requirements, which differ substantially from typical software languages, are:

1. We have no interest in run-time polymorphism. We wish to eliminate polymorphism and overloading during elaboration.
2. We wish to minimise extensions to the syntax. Where possible overloading should be inferred, reducing designers' concerns so that they can work at a higher level of abstraction.
3. It is necessary to be able to express complex constraints between types in order to allow the overloading of blocks without a common type pattern.
4. It is necessary to support overloading of blocks with different numbers of parameters.
5. We can assume a *closed world* environment and have no need to support separate compilation since all libraries are expected to be available as source.

Evaluated against these requirements, type classes do not seem an appropriate mechanism for providing overloading in Quartz: although they support run-time polymorphism, this is not useful; the language must be extended with extensive class and instance declarations; single-parameter type classes (as in the Haskell specification) can not express complex constraints between types and while multi-parameter type classes can type inference is then undecidable; they do not easily support overloading blocks with different numbers of parameters; and inferred types are sometimes ambiguous due to the *open world* assumption.

To meet these requirements, we use a system based around a language of satisfiability matrix predicates – matrices that represent possible values of a type and relationships between type variables. This system minimises ambiguity and can express n-ary constraints between type variables clearly and easily.

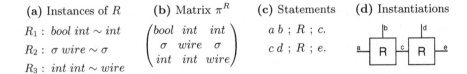

(a) Instances of R (b) Matrix π^R (c) Statements   (d) Instantiations

R_1 : bool int $\sim$ int

R_2 : σ wire $\sim$ σ

R_3 : int int $\sim$ wire

$\begin{pmatrix} bool & int & int \\ \sigma & wire & \sigma \\ int & int & wire \end{pmatrix}$

$a\,b\,;\,R\,;\,c.$

$c\,d\,;\,R\,;\,e.$

Fig. 1. Multiple instance types can be represented as a satisfiability matrix

(a)

$\begin{pmatrix} - & - & - \\ int & wire & int \\ int & int & wire \end{pmatrix}$

(b)

$\begin{pmatrix} int & wire & int & wire & int \\ int & wire & int & int & wire \\ int & int & wire & wire & wire \end{pmatrix}$

(c)

$\begin{pmatrix} int & wire & int & wire & int \\ - & - & - & - & - \\ int & int & wire & wire & wire \end{pmatrix}$

Fig. 2. Evolution of a predicate matrix during type checking

3   Satisfiability Matrix Predicates

Our system is implemented as a conservative extension to Robinson's unification algorithm [5] to support satisfiability matrices. We will introduce our system with an example. Suppose there are multiple, overloaded instances of a block R with types as in Fig. 1(a) (where σ is a polymorphic type variable). The types of these three instances can be represented as a predicate matrix π^R as shown in Fig. 1(b) where each row of the matrix contains the type for an instance and there is a column for each argument position.

Suppose then it is desired to type check the two Quartz statements in Fig. 1(c), which instantiate two R blocks as shown in Fig. 1(d), where a is known to have type *int*, b has unknown type β, c has unknown type γ and d and e have type *wire*.

Because there are two instantiations of the R block which could have different types, two matrices π^R and $\pi^{R'}$ will be used during type checking. The inference process attempts to unify each argument type with the appropriate column in the matrix. Type checking the first statement involves three unification operations: $unify(int, \pi_0^R)$, $unify(\beta, \pi_1^R)$ and $unify(\gamma, \pi_2^R)$ (where subscripts indicate the column number).

Unifying a type with a matrix column involves unifying that type with every element in the column. If this operation generates a substitution within the matrix, this substitution is applied along that row of the matrix. If a column element does not unify then that row is removed from the matrix. The result of the three unification operations above is shown in Fig. 2(a), note that the first row did not match and has been removed while *int* has been substituted for the unknown type σ. The operations have bound the type variables β and γ into the matrix: $\{\beta \mapsto \pi_1^R, \gamma \mapsto \pi_2^R\}$.

When type checking the second statement the type of c (γ) must be unified with $\pi_0^{R'}$ however it is already bound into the first matrix so matrices π^R and $\pi^{R'}$ must be merged. This produces a single matrix, shown in Fig. 2(b), with one row for each valid possible combination of types from the two source matrices where the two columns bound to type γ could be unified. Type checking continues by unifying the type of d (int) across the appropriate matrix column, which was $\pi_1^{R'}$ but is now π_3^R in the new matrix. The type int does not match with all elements in the column and so one row is eliminated as shown in Fig. 2(c).

Finally the type of signal e ($wire$) is unified with π_4^R which matches a single matrix row. The overloading is resolved with the type mapping $\{\beta \mapsto int, \gamma \mapsto wire\}$. The first R block is selected as R_3 with type $int\ int \sim wire$ and the second R block is selected as R_2 with type $wire\ wire \sim wire$.

The case when a type constructor with unknown type variables within it, such as the tuple (ϕ, ψ), is unified with a matrix column needs to be handled separately. The full type is unified across the original column while new columns are generated in the matrix for the unknown type variables to be bound to. The operation $unify\big((\phi, \psi), \pi_0^R\big)$ applied to the original π^R would return the substitution $\{\phi \mapsto \pi_3^R, \psi \mapsto \pi_4^R\}$ and the matrix would be left with a single row of $\big((\phi', \psi')\ wire\ (\phi', \psi')\ \phi'\ \psi'\big)$ where the tuple has been substituted for σ.

Satisfiability matrices can also support blocks with different numbers of parameters by extending the Quartz type system with an empty/void type Ω, which can be used to "pad" matrices and block types so that they are all the same length. Ω only unifies with itself so blocks with the wrong number of parameters are eliminated from the matrix when unification fails.

During type checking predicate matrices grow (due to mergers) and shrink (due to non-matching rows being eliminated) before reaching a point where overloading can be resolved. It is often possible to substantially optimise matrices to reduce their size, for example by merging identical columns.

4   Conclusion

Satisfiability matrices permit the expression of complex n-ary constraints between types and the overloading of Quartz blocks without extending the language syntax. We believe our system is superior to type classes for overloading in Quartz and other similar hardware description languages. Future work includes investigating the theoretical properties of satisfiability matrices and developing optimisation strategies to minimise the amount of matrix data stored.

References

1. Wadler, P., Blott, S.: How to make ad-hoc polymorphism less ad hoc. In: Proc. POPL '89, ACM Press (1989) 60–76
2. Milner, R.: A theory of type polymorphism in programming. J. Comput. Syst. Sci. **17** (1978) 348–375
3. Luk, W., McKeever, S.: Pebble: a language for parameterised and reconfigurable hardware design. In Proc. FPL'98. LNCS 1482, Springer-Verlag (1998) 9–18
4. Jones, G., Sheeran, M.: Circuit design in Ruby. In Staunstrup, J., ed.: Formal Methods for VLSI Design, North-Holland/Elsevier (1990) 13–70
5. Robinson, J.A.: A machine-oriented logic based on the resolution principle. J. ACM **12** (1965) 23–41

FPGA Based Accelerator for 3-SAT Conflict Analysis in SAT Solvers

Mona Safar[1], M. Watheq El-Kharashi[2], and Ashraf Salem[3]

[1] Computer and Systems Department, Ain Shams University, Cairo, Egypt
[2] University of Victoria, Victoria, Canada
[3] Mentor Graphics Egypt, Cairo, Egypt

Abstract. We present an FPGA-based accelerator for 3-SAT clause evaluation and conflict diagnosis and propose an approach to incorporate it in solving the Combinational Equivalence Checking problem. SAT binary clauses are mapped onto an implication graph and the ternary clauses are kept in an indexed clause database and mapped into the clause evaluator and conflict analyzer on FPGA.

1 Introduction

Algorithms to solve SAT involve many compute-intensive, logic bit-level, and highly parallelizable operations that make reconfigurable computing appealing [1]. Various approaches have been proposed to accelerate SAT solving using reconfigurable computing [2]. An important module of any SAT solver is a clause evaluator that checks the consistency of variables assignment. Conflict diagnosis [3] helps pruning search space. We present an FPGA-based 3-SAT clause evaluator and conflict analyzer.

Combinational Equivalence Checking (CEC) is a widely used formal verification methodology for digital systems. Due to its hardness, current checkers mostly combine multiple checking engines, like BDD [4], SAT [5], and SAT/BDD [6]. We propose an approach to incorporate our clause evaluator to accelerate SAT-based CEC.

2 FPGA Based 3-SAT Clause Evaluator and Conflict Analyzer

The architecture of our clause evaluator (Fig. 1) consists of a 3-input LUT acting as 3-input OR gate for each ternary clause, and an active low priority encoder that detects conflict when a clause is unsatisfiable and returns to the host the clause index. The value of each variable is encoded in two bits corresponding to its positive and negative literals. If the value of the variable is "0" or "1", the encoding is "01" or "10", respectively. The encoding "11" indicates that the variable is free.

Since same architecture is used for different SAT instances, except for the literal configurations, direct modification can be done on the bitstream reducing the synthesis and place-and-route overhead. Run-time reconfiguration can be used for dynamic clause addition. It also allows configurations larger than the available FPGA capability [1]. For large number of variables, virtual wires time multiplexing can be used [7].

D. Borrione and W. Paul (Eds.): CHARME 2005, LNCS 3725, pp. 384–387, 2005.

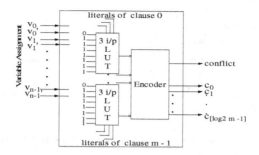

Fig. 1. The clause evaluator, n is the number of variables, m is the number of ternary clauses, and (C_0 C_1 ..... $C_{[log2m-1]}$) represents the binary equivalent of the first clause that evaluates to 0

Table 1. Number of 4-input LUTs occupied by the encoder component for DIMACS instances

Instance	# Clauses	# 4-input LUTs
aim-50-1_6-z-j[1]	80	178
aim-50-6_0-z-j	300	692
aim-100-2_0-z-j	200	453
aim-100-3_4-z-j	340	811
dubois21	168	390
dubois30	240	545
pret60-xx[2]	160	370
pret150-xx	400	1007

Table 1 shows the number of 4-input LUTs needed for the encoder part of the architecture for some cases from DIMACS benchmark suite. AIM, DUBOIS, and PRET families consist of ternary clauses, so they map directly into our architecture.

3 SAT-Based CEC Accelerator

Since SAT is an NP complete problem, using it in CEC transforms a problem that in worst case takes exponential time in the number of the circuit inputs into another problem that takes exponential time in the number of variables. Interestingly, most of the clauses of CNF formula produced by combinational circuits are binary that can be easily mapped onto an implication graph [8]. Ternary or more clause information can guide the search. A conflict arises when one of these clauses is unsatisfiable. Conflict diagnosis determines the backtracking level which helps pruning the search space [3].

Fig. 2 illustrates our proposed software/reconfigurable hardware accelerator for SAT-based CEC. The software running on the host computer first converts the

---

[1] zzzz is "no" or "yes1", the former denoting a no-instance and the latter a single-solution yes-instance. j means simply the jth instance at that parameter.
[2] xx is the horn percentage, it can take values 25,40,60 or 75.

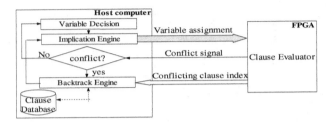

Fig. 2. The general view of our software/ reconfigurable hardware SAT based CEC accelerator

Table 2. ISCAS'85 benchmark circuits clauses specification

Miter Circuit	Unrestricted SAT formula		3-SAT formula	
	# Binary clauses	# Ternary or more clauses	# Binary clauses	# Ternary clauses
C432	678	373	850	487
C499	504	1077	614	1187
C1908	3234	978	3728	1352
C6288	9662	4862	9692	4892
C7552	12716	4299	13882	5409

The accelerator software algorithm

```
While(True){
  if(dir==forward){
    if(!Decide()) { Formula=SAT;  break; }
    process_implication();
    clause_evaluator(var);
    if(conflict=read_conflict()){
      conflict_clause_index=read-index();
      dir=backward;  //backtrack
    }
    else λ = λ +1;
  }
  if(dir==backward){
    B=Backtrack_level();
    if(B==NULL) { Formula=unSAT;  break; }
    undo(λ ,B);
    λ=B;
    if(!Tried_both_ways()){
      complement_value();
      clause_evaluator(var);
      if(conflict=read_conflict())
        conflict_clause_index=read-index();
      else{ λ = λ +1;  dir=forward; }
    }
  }
}
```

structural description of the miter circuit into 3-SAT formula. The binary clauses are mapped into an implication graph. The ternary clauses are kept in an indexed clause database on the host computer and mapped into the clause evaluator on the FPGA.

Initially all variables are free except for the miter output which is restricted to the value "1". Selecting a free variable and assigning a value to it is done by the software running on the host computer. A decision level is associated with each selected assignment. The implication engine derives the direct and transitive implications of this assignment by operating on the implication graph generated from the binary clauses. The consistency of the variables binding with the ternary clauses is checked at each decision level via the clause evaluator. In case of conflict, the backtracking engine, aided by the conflicting clause index, determines the predecessor set of variables that are responsible for the conflict and hence performs nonchronological backtracking, which helps pruning the search space. The algorithm is shown on the next page. *clause_evaluator( )* sends variables assignment to the FPGA. The FPGA sends back a conflict indication and the index of the unsatisfied clause, if any.

Our architecture 3-SAT restriction is imposed on the structural description of the circuit by having gates of a maximum fan-in of 2, which adds new variables and increases the number of binary and ternary clauses (see Table 2).

4 Conclusions

We presented FPGA-based clause evaluator and conflict detector and proposed a new approach for the combinational equivalence-checking problem. In our approach, the SAT binary clauses are treated on the software side where they are mapped onto an implication graph. The ternary clauses are kept in an indexed clause database and mapped onto the clause evaluator and conflict detector on FPGA. The need for accelerating the ternary clause evaluation is proved using the ISCAS'85 benchmark.

References

1. K. Compton and S. Hauck: Reconfigurable Computing: A Survey of Systems and Software. ACM computing Surveys, Vol. 34, no. 2 (June 2002) 171-210
2. I Skliarova and A. B. Ferrari: Reconfigurable Hardware SAT Solvers: A Survey of Systems IEEE Transactions on Computers, Vol. 53, no. 11 (November 2004) 1449-1461
3. L. M. Silva and K. A. Sakallah: GRASP: A Search Algorithm for Propositional Satisfiability. IEEE Trans. Computers, Vol. 48, no. 5 (May 1999) 506-521
4. R. E. Bryant: Graph-Based Algorithms for Boolean Function Manipulation. IEEE Trans. on Computers, Vol. C-35, No. 8 (August 1986)
5. J. P. Marques-Silva and L. Guerra e Silva: Solving Satisfiability in Combinational Circuits. IEEE Design and Test of Computers (July-August 2003) 16-21
6. S. Reda and A. Salem: Combinational Equivalence Checking using Boolean Satisfiability and Binary Decision Diagrams. IEEE/ACM Design, Automation and Test in Europe (March 2001) 122-126
7. P. Zhong, M. Martonosi, P. Ashar, and S. Malik: Using Configurable Computing to Accelerate Boolean Satisfiability. IEEE Trans. Computer Aided Design of Integrated Circuits and Systems, Vol. 18, no. 6 (June 1999) 861-868
8. T. Larrabee: Test Pattern generation using Boolean Satisfiability. IEEE Transactions on 2Computer Aided Design, Vol. 11, no. 1 (January 1992) 4-15

Predictive Reachability Using a Sample-Based Approach

Debashis Sahoo[1], Jawahar Jain[3], Subramanian K. Iyer[2],
David Dill[1], and E. Allen Emerson[2]

[1] Stanford University, Stanford CA 94305, USA
[2] University of Texas at Austin, Austin, TX 78712, USA
[3] Fujitsu Lab. of America

Abstract. BDD based reachability methods suffer from lack of robustness in performance, whereby it is difficult to estimate which one should be adopted for a given problem. We present a novel approach that examines a few short *samples* of the computation leading to an automatic, robust and modular way of reconciling the various methods for reachability. Our approach is able to intelligently integrate diverse reachability techniques such that each method can possibly get enhanced in efficiency. The method is in many cases orders of magnitude more efficient and it finishes all the invariant checking properties in VIS-Verilog benchmarks.

1 Introduction

BDD based reachability methods suffer from wild inconsistency in performance, whereby it is difficult to estimate which method should be adopted for a given problem. We analyze four different ways of doing reachability analysis, forward or backward reachability using partitioned [4] or unpartitioned BDDs [1, 2] for state set representation. It is often the case that though one method can compute reachability easily, the others find it very difficult. In this paper, we present a completely automatic strategy to determine the more effective method by running a few short *samples* of the above methods. These samples provide a short initial sampling of the performance of the various methods by observing the initial computations until a predefined cutoff in BDD size is reached. This approach determines the best direction for reachability analysis as well as the effectiveness of performing state space partitioning. Note that each method has its own domain of applicability. We have designed our approach so that it can benefit from the strengths of each method.

Importantly, at the end of the independently run samples, we allow all their computation to be shared. This can significantly enhance the performance of each technique. In many cases the reduction in reachability time for standard OBDD methods can be dramatic when its reached state set is augmented using information from POBDD samples.

2 Prediction Using Short Samples

We use a sample-based algorithm to predict the effective method. A *sample* for an algorithm is a short initial computation using that algorithm.

D. Borrione and W. Paul (Eds.): CHARME 2005, LNCS 3725, pp. 388–392, 2005.

The algorithm runs one sample each of the backward and forward partitioned reachability followed by forward and backward symbolic monolithic (non-partitioned) reachability. This order is chosen because we find backward reachability and partitioned reachability more suitable for finding bugs. Therefore, if there is a "easy" bug, then it can be found during the sampling process. The samples are run until a predefined size *cutoff* is exceeded. This cutoff is small enough to allow efficient performance of symbolic operations and is set at a fixed multiple of the representation size of the state transition relation.

If the samples themselves do not finish the computation, they are used to predict the most effective approach for the rest of the computation. Firstly, the appropriate direction is determined from the samples of symbolic forward and backward reachability. We use the number of images completed as measure for deciding the most effective method.

After selecting the direction, the algorithm tries to predict whether partitioned reachability is more effective than the monolithic approach, where state sets are represented as single BDDs. This is done by considering the number of states reached by samples run using both approaches in the selected direction. If the total number of reachable states explored by either method is significantly better than that of the other method, then we have a winner. If this number is comparable for both approaches, then a meaningful metric to break the tie seems to be the *rate of coverage* defined as number of states covered vs. corresponding time.

In this manner, the samples are used to pick a method that is likely to be the most effective method.

2.1 Augmenting the State Sets

To avoid the repeated overlapping computations, after deciding the effective method the algorithm augments the initial states and the invariant by adding the states reached by all samples. In the forward direction, the reachability analysis starts from the union of the reached states using both forward samples. Likewise, the error set, which is set of states that satisfy the negation of the invariant, is replaced by the union of the sets states reached by the two backward samples. If the direction of computation is backward, then the error states are the start set and the augmented initial states are the target. This allows the computations performed by the samples to be reused.

In the next section, we describe our experiments and analyze the results.

3 Experiments

We compare the methodology proposed in this paper with the forward and backward reachability approaches of VIS and static partitioned reachability analysis. We compute one sample each in forward and backward directions, using partitioned as well as non-partitioned data structures for the state set in reachability. Our current package is not optimized with respect to partitioned exploration of state space. For example, it doesn't implement all the efficient heuristics presented in [3, 5].

Table 1. Invariant Checking on ALL Vis-Verilog benchmarks that take more than 10 minutes in at least one of the methods

ckt_inv	Inv Res : Pass / Fail	Time in sec.				
		Static Pobdd Fwd	Static Pobdd Bwd	Vis Fwd	Vis Bwd	Trace Based
(a) Advantage due to intersection of Forward and Backward						
vsa16a_7	F	2610	808	2146	458	77
vsaR_1	F	M	124	24558	56	54
(b) Advantage due to POBDD State Space Representation						
am2901_1	F	T	67	T	431	68
ball_6	F	175	T	T	T	103
ball_7	F	22	T	3530	T	45
palu_1	F	1.0	684	714	4630	1.8
sp_product_1	P	50	T	740	507	52
(c) Addition of Partitioned Traces Makes Subsequent Unpartitioned Reachability Easier						
FIFOs_1	P	M	M	2986	T	1973
blackjack_1	P	5750	T	2273	T	1234
blackjack_2	P	6268	T	20565	T	979
blackjack_4	P	5795	T	2259	T	1307
ns3_1	P	43569	T	16840	19166	5269
ns3_5	P	T	T	14696	T	6456
ns3_6	P	48721	M	28063	T	4938
ns3_7	P	M	T	22612	T	7220
(d) Robust Predictive Capability: Timeouts Avoided						
am2910_1	F	660	5.3	T	2.0	5.8
b12_1	F	48	9528	48	2561	77
b12_2	F	T	T	T	8019	25535
b12abs_2	F	2977	449	163	536	446
blackjack_3	F	1054	T	3371	T	1337
blackjack_5	P	62752	T	2614	T	13259
crc_1	F	20459	1.5	T	0.9	1.5
eight_1	P	4.5	1194	1.1	173	5.8
eight_2	P	4.6	2466	1.1	344	6.2
mm_product_1	P	600	T	49	352	154
ns3_2	P	M	8895	21602	16454	24903
ns3_3	P	T	85851	T	2050	4751
ns3_4	P	M	24477	24539	3770	6263
ns3_8	P	71494	T	6268	29196	50938
ns3_9	P	81048	3174	18247	479	9373
ns3_10	P	75011	2834	9518	604	12946
ns3_11	P	60490	10.9	51166	8.2	10.9
ns3_12	P	65219	27.3	49968	8.2	25.7
rotate32_1	F	53033	1.5	51078	0.7	1.5
s1269b_1	P	3351	1.3	12994	0.7	1.3
s1269b_5	P	3379	3.5	13677	0.6	3.5
soapLTL4_1	P	254	T	80.1	T	408
soap_1	P	176	T	45.6	T	181
soap_2	P	77.3	T	30.1	T	81.9
soap_3	P	47.8	T	46.4	T	80.9
spinner32_1	F	33356	8.3	43264	1.9	9.5
vsa16a_1	P	M	43.0	T	18.4	42.6
vsa16a_2	P	T	27.6	T	16.8	27.4
vsa16a_4	P	T	41.5	T	19.2	41.3
vsa16a_5	P	M	42.1	T	18.8	41.6
vsa16a_6	F	2499	60.5	1387	25.5	61.0
vsa16a_8	F	2498	61.7	1387	27.4	59.8

"T" is Timeout of 86,400 s; "M" is Memory out of 500 MB.

All experiments were run on identical dual processor Xeon machines. They were allowed to run for a maximum time of one day, and the memory available to each run was bounded by 500MB.

Benchmarks

For experiments on reachability and invariant checking, we chose the public domain circuits from the VIS-Verilog [7] benchmark suite. In the following, we indicate property number i of circuit named ckt as ckt_i. Table 1 shows the runtime for checking the invariants of the VIS-verilog benchmark circuits for five methods. The entry "T" and "M" in the table represents a timeout limit of 1 day and memory out limit of 500MB.

4   Conclusion

In this paper, we presented an automatic self-tuning sample-based approach to address the inconsistency in performance of the BDD based reachability techniques. Many of the circuits time-out on one or other direction of reachability and some abort even when using partitioning. However, we find that the circuits aborted by backward are finished by forward and vice-versa in many cases. Note, the samples enable one to automatically select the appropriate method and the performance of the sample-centric approach is very robust and always significantly better than the worst. Such cases are shown in Table 1 (d). The table shows that the completely automatic sample-based approach is able to pick the right method from a set of different methods by using short samples of their initial reachability computation.

In a few cases, the wrong method may be picked, but even so, the sample-based approach is able to complete, due to the information available from the other samples. A more detailed version of this paper can be obtained from *http://verify.stanford.edu/PAPERS/dsahoo-charme05-e.pdf* [6].

Acknowledgments

The authors thank Fujitsu Laboratories of America, Inc for their gifts to support the research. Prof. Emerson thanks the NSF for support via grants CCR-009-8141 and CCR-020-5483. Prof. Dill thanks the NSF for support via grants CCR-012-1403. Any opinions, findings, and conclusions or recommendations expressed in this publication are those of the author(s) and do not necessarily reflect the views of the National Science Foundation.

References

[1] R. Bryant. Graph-based Algorithms for Boolean Function Manipulation. *IEEE Transactions on Computers*, C-35:677–691, 1986.

[2] O. Coudert, C. Berthet, and J. C. Madre. Verification of sequential machines based on symbolic execution. In *Proc. of the Workshop on Automatic Verification Methods for Finite State Systems*, 1989.

[3] S. Iyer, D. Sahoo, C. Stangier, A. Narayan, and J. Jain. Improved symbolic Verification Using Partitioning Techniques. In *Proc. of CHARME 2003*, volume 2860 of *Lecture Notes in Computer Science*, 2003.

[4] A. Narayan. et. al., Reachability Analysis Using Partitioned-ROBDDs. In *ICCAD*, pages 388–393, 1997.

[5] D. Sahoo, S. Iyer, J. Jain, C. Stangier, A. Narayan, David L. Dill, and E. Allen Emerson. A partitioning methodology for bdd-based verification. In Alan J. Hu and Andrew K. Martin, editors, *FMCAD*, volume 3312 of *Lecture Notes in Computer Science*, pages 399–413. Springer, 2004.

[6] D. Sahoo, J. Jain, S. Iyer, David L. Dill, and E. Allen Emerson. Predictive reachability using a sample-based approach. In *http://verify.stanford.edu/PAPERS/dsahoo-charme05-e.pdf*, 2005.

[7] VIS. Verilog Benchmarks http://vlsi.colorado.edu/~ vis/.

Minimizing Counterexample of ACTL Property

ShengYu Shen, Ying Qin, and SiKun Li

School of Computer Science,
National University of Defense Technology of China
{syshen, qy123, skli}@nudt.edu.cn

Abstract. Counterexample minimization tries to remove irrelevant variables from counterexamples, such that they are easier to be understood. For the first time, we proposes a novel approach to minimize loop-like and path-like counterexamples of ACTL properties. For a counterexample $s_0 \ldots s_k$, our algorithm tries to extract a succinct cube sequence $c_0 \ldots c_k$, such that paths run through $c_0 \ldots c_k$ are all valid counterexamples. Experimental result shows that our algorithm can significantly minimize ACTL counterexamples. [1]

1   Preliminaries

BDD contain two terminal nodes and a set of variable nodes. Attribute **value(u)** is associated with terminal nodes u. Every variable node has two outgoing edges: **llow(u)** and **high(u)**. A variable **var(u)** is associated with every node u.

Symbolic model checking with BDD is first proposed by K.McMillan [1], which is implemented by procedure **Check** that takes a CTL formula and returns BDD of those states that satisfy the formula.

Assume the state variable set of Kripke structure $M = \langle S, I, T, L \rangle$ is $V = \{v_0, \ldots, v_n\}$. A state $s \in S$ can be seen as assignments to V, which is denoted by $s = \{v_0 \leftarrow b_0, \ldots, v_n \leftarrow b_n\}$, with $b_i \in \{0,1\}$ are boolean constant. Assume $V' = \{v_{i_0}, \ldots, v_{i_m}\}$ is a subset of V, then projection of s to V' is defined as

$$s|_{V'} = \{v_{i_0} \leftarrow b_{i_0}, \ldots, v_{i_m} \leftarrow b_{i_m}\} \tag{1}$$

A state set $S' \subseteq S$ is a **cube** iff there exists $V' = \{v_{i_0}, \ldots, v_{i_m}\} \subseteq V$ and $\{b_{i_0}, \ldots, b_{i_m}\}$, such that $S' == \{s| \; s|_{V'} == \{v_{i_0} \leftarrow b_{i_0}, \ldots, v_{i_m} \leftarrow b_{i_m}\}\}$

Assume state s is in state set S', then c is a cube guided by s in S' iff $s \in c \subseteq S'$. We denote c by **GuidedCube(S', s)**, it can be computed as below.

Algorithm 1: Computing $GuidedCube(S', s)$

1. Assume $s = \{v_0 \leftarrow b_0, \ldots, v_n \leftarrow b_n\}$.
2. $c = \phi$ $V' = \phi$ are all empty set
3. $cn=$root node of BDD of S'

---

[1] Supported by Chinese NSF under Grant No.90207019 and No.60403048; the Chinese 863 Program under Grant No. 2002AA1Z1480.

D. Borrione and W. Paul (Eds.): CHARME 2005, LNCS 3725, pp. 393–397, 2005.

4. while(cn isn't a terminal node)
   (a) assume $var(cn)$ is v_i
   (b) if($b_i == 0$) then $cn = low(cn)$ else $cn = high(cn)$
   (c) $c = c \cup \{v_i \leftarrow b_i\}$ $V' = V' \cup \{v_i\}$
5. $GuidedCube(S', s) = \{s' | \ s'|_{V'} == c\}$

2   Minimizing Counterexample of ACTL Property

Existing approaches[2] can only deal with path-like counterexamples of invariant $AG \ f$. For the first time, this paper proposes a novel approach to minimize loop-like and path-like counterexamples of ACTL properties. Due to duality of ACTL and ECTL, we will focus on minimizing witness of ECTL formula.

To make a witness $s_0 \ldots s_k$ more easy to be understood, some state variables must be removed. So a minimized witness must be a cube sequence $c_0 \ldots c_k$. We define the criteria that it must satisfied.

Definition 1 (Criteria of Minimized Witness of ECTL Property). *Assume $s_0 \ldots s_k$ is a witness of an ECTL property f. Cube sequence $c_0 \ldots c_k$ is the minimized witness of $s_0 \ldots s_k$ iff*

1. $s_i \in c_i (0 \le i \le k)$
2. *Every path $s'_0 \ldots s'_k$ that satisfy $\bigwedge_{0 \le i \le k} s'_i \in c_i$ must be witness of f*

We will discuss minimizing witness of EX, EU and EG below.

2.1   Minimizing Witness of EX and EU

Assume $PreImage(S')$ is a procedure that computes pre-image of S'. We can minimize $EX f$ witness $s_0 s_1$ and $E[fUg]$ witness $s_0 \ldots s_{k-1}$ in the following way:

Algorithm 2: Minimizing Witness of $EX \ f$

1. $c_1 = GuidedCube(Check(f), s_1)$
2. $c_0 = GuidedCube(PreImage(c_1), s_0)$

Algorithm 3: Minimizing Witness of $E[f \ U \ g]$

1. $c_{k-1} = GuidedCube(Check(g), s_{k-1})$
2. for $i = k - 2$ to 0
3. $c_i = GuidedCube(PreImage(c_{i+1}) \cap Check(f), s_i)$

Correctness proof is omited due to space limitation.

2.2   Minimizing Witness of EG

A loop-like witness of EGf contains two segments: a stem $s_0 \ldots s_m$ and a loop $s_m \ldots s_n$. We will first prove the following theorem below.

Theorem 1. *Assume a loop-like witness of EGf contains two segments: a stem $s_0 \ldots s_m$ and a loop $s_m \ldots s_n$. Then a cube sequence $c_0 \ldots c_n$ is its minimized witness if the following 4 equations hold true*

$$\bigwedge_{0 \leq i \leq n} s_i \in c_i \tag{2}$$

$$c_n \subseteq PreImage(c_m) \wedge \bigwedge_{m \leq i \leq n-1} c_i \subseteq PreImage(c_{i+1}) \tag{3}$$

$$\bigwedge_{0 \leq i \leq m-1} c_i \subseteq PreImage(c_{i+1}) \tag{4}$$

$$\bigwedge_{0 \leq i \leq n} c_i \subseteq Check(f) \tag{5}$$

Proof. By equation (2), the 1st criteria of Definition 1 is satisfied.

Assume a path $s_0' \ldots s_n'$ satisfy $T(s_n', s_m') \wedge \bigwedge_{0 \leq i \leq n} s_i' \in c_i$. By equation (5), $\bigwedge_{0 \leq i \leq n} M, s_i' \models f$.

Thus this theorem is proven.

We compute an approximation of $c_m \ldots c_n$ with following algorithm.

Algorithm 4: $Min(x)$

1. $c_m = x$
2. $c_n = GuidedCube(PreImage(c_m) \cap Check(f), s_n)$
3. For $i = n - 1$ to m
4. $c_i = GuidedCube(PreImage(c_{i+1}) \cap Check(f), s_i)$
5. return c_m

To compute $c_m \ldots c_n$ that satisfies equation (3), we first let

$$C = Check(EGf) \tag{6}$$

And then run $Min(C)$. Cube sequence $c_m \ldots c_n$ obtained in this way satisfies almost all $\subseteq$ relation in equation (3), except $c_n \subseteq PreImage(c_m)$.

So we need to run Algorithm 4 iteratively, and obtain the following sequence:

$$Min(C), Min^2(C), \ldots Min^t(C), \ldots \tag{7}$$

We terminate above iteration only when $Min^{t-1}(C) \subseteq Min^t(C)$, at which $c_n \subseteq PreImage(c_m)$ and equation (3) can be satisfied. So we must prove that iteration in equation (7) is terminable with following theorems.

Theorem 2. *$Min(x)$ is monotonic. (Proof is omited due to space limitation)*

Theorem 3. *$C \supseteq Min(C)$*

Table 1. Experimental Result

Cex name	Cex length	Original cex		Minimized cex	
		Number of. Variables.	Run time	Number of Variables	Run time
P1	13	1027	0.12	244	0.12
P2	7	308	0.01	172	0.02
L1	64	975	0.991	791	1.45
L2	76	1140	1.26	942	1.96
L3	75	1125	2.83	929	4.09
L4	22	858	0.19	510	0.24
L5	22	858	0.28	467	0.33
L6	22	858	0.16	455	0.17
L7	22	858	0.12	408	0.17

Proof. By Algorithm 4, for every state $s'_m \in Min(C)$, there is a path $s'_m s'_{m+1} \cdots s'_n s_m"$, such that $s_m" \in C$. That is to say, there is an infinite path p starting from $s_m"$, and f holds true at all states along p.

By Algorithm 4, f holds true on all states of $s'_m s'_{m+1} \cdots s'_n s_m"$.

Thus, we can concatenate $s'_m s'_{m+1} \cdots s'_n s_m"$ and p, to form a new path p'. f hold true at all states along p'. Thus, p' is witness of M, $s'_m \models EGf$.

By equation (6), we can conclude that $s'_m \in C$.

Thus, $C \supseteq Min(C)$ is proven.

Theorem 4. *The iteration in equation (7) is terminable.*

Proof. By Theorem 2 and 3, it is obvious that : $C \supseteq Min(C) \ldots \supseteq Min^t(C) \ldots$. So $\exists t . Min^{t-1}(C) == Min^t(C)$ hold true. Thus, this theorem is proven.

Thus, we can construct minimized witness $c_m \ldots c_n$ in the following way:

Algorithm 5: Minimizing Witness of $EG\ f$

1. $c_m = Min^t(C)$
2. $c_n = GuidedCube(PreImage(c_m) \cap Check(f), s_n)$
3. for $i = n - 1$ to 0
4. $c_i = GuidedCube(PreImage(c_{i+1}) \cap Check(f), s_i)$

3   Experimental Result

We implement our algorithm in NuSMV, and perform experiments on NuSMV's benchmarks. All experiments run on a PC with 1GHz Pentium 3.

Table 1 presents experimental result. The 1st column lists the name of counterexamples. P1 and P2 are path-like counterexamples. All others are loop-like counterexamples. The 2nd column lists their length. The 3rd column lists the number of variables in original counterexamples. The 4th column lists the time taken by NuSMV to generate these counterexamples. The 5th column lists the number of variables in minimized counterexamples. The last column lists the run time of our approach.

From the experimental result, it is obvious that our algorithm can significantly minimize counterexamples.

References

1. K.L.McMillan. Symbolic model checking. Kluwer Academic Publishers, 1993.
2. K. Ravi and F. Somenzi. Minimal assignments for bounded model checking. In TACAS'04,LNCS 2988, pages 31-45, 2004.

Data Refinement for Synchronous System Specification and Construction*

Alex Tsow and Steven D. Johnson

System Design Methods Laboratory,
Computer Science Department,
Indiana University

Abstract. *Design derivation*, a correct-by-construction system design method, specifies behavior with abstract datatypes. Refining these abstract datatypes is necessary for architectural decomposition. A new transformation primitive enables data refinement by generalizing term level injective homomorphisms to system equivalence.

Data refinement enables high levels of behavioral specification without sacrificing meaningful architectural decompositions. When behavior is specified over abstract datatypes the boundaries of a target architecture often cut across the borders of its datatypes. Consider SECD *(stack, environment, code, dump)*, an abstract machine for LISP's operational semantics, where each "register" holds nested pairs of atoms. Typical implementations represent this recursive datatype as reference(s) to a heap. The memory that holds the reference value (a register) and the memory that holds the heap cells (a RAM) are architecturally distinct. A target architecture which separates the register file from the RAM is exposed only upon refinement of the specification data types.

The standard underlying model is that of mutually corecursive equations defined over first-order terms with stream semantics. Below is a simple corecursive system of equations and its solution set (streams over integers).

$$
\begin{array}{ll}
\texttt{X = 1 ! (+* X 1*)} & \texttt{X = (1, 2, 3, ...)} \\
\texttt{Y = \quad (-* X)} & \texttt{Y = (-1, -2, -3, ...)}
\end{array}
\tag{1}
$$

Definition of *sequential signals* is by destruction (expressed as arguments to the constructor !), i.e. X is a stream of integers whose head is the integer 1, and whose tail is (+* X 1*). The suffix * indicates the "lifting" of a term level function or constant to the stream level: e.g. 1* is a stream of 1s and +* is componentwise addition. The remaining signals are *combinational*, defined by lifted versions of term combinators; e.g. Y is the componentwise negation of X.

For simple lifting as just described, term level identities generalize to stream level identities, so local term *replacement* is one of the core transformations in the derivation algebra [1]. First order algebraic terms, unlike streams and other corecursive datatypes [3], are easily manipulated by standard theorem provers.

---

* This research is supported, in part, by the National Aeronautics and Space Association under the Graduate Student Researchers Program, NGT-1-010009.

D. Borrione and W. Paul (Eds.): CHARME 2005, LNCS 3725, pp. 398–401, 2005.

Thus, local term replacement provides a hook for integration with other toolsets. By commutativity of addition, the equations

$$X = 1 \ ! \ (+* \ X \ 1*) \quad \text{and} \quad X = 1 \ ! \ (+* \ 1* \ X) \tag{2}$$

have the same solutions. Given this orthogonality, we usually eliminate the * annotation unless the context demands its use.

The refinement approach uses term level algebraic identities to express injective homomorphisms between types. The following diagram expresses the homomorphism r between abstract stacks of integers S and their implementation using references I to heaps expressed as a memory M of cells $I \times \mathbb{Z}$ addressed by I and a "next-unallocated-cell" pointer of type I.

() denotes function application, [] denotes tuple construction, integer ordinals are tuple accessors. The reference value, memory, and horizon pointer bindings are defined by v=(0th (r s)), m=(1st (r s)), and i=(2nd (r s)), respectively.

Even with a complete term-level characterization, term replacement is insufficient for local *representation translation*. Local translation allows different representations of the same abstract type in the same system, enables multi-level modeling, and promotes interaction. We can not change a sequential signal's type in the present system algebra. To this end, we introduce a new transformation which adds a new sequential signal of the implementation type, and replaces the target signal with an abstraction coercion from the implementation signal.

Theorem 1. *Let A and R be two sorts with functions $r : A \to R$ and $a : R \to A$ such that for all $x \in R$, $(a \ (r \ x)) = x$. Let $X = x0 \ ! \ (T \ X)$ be an equation in a system description. Replacing X's equation with*

$$\begin{aligned} X &= (a \ X') \\ X' &= (r \ x0) \ ! \ (r \ (T \ X)) \end{aligned} \tag{4}$$

preserves the solution for X and

$$(r \ X) = X' \tag{5}$$

is a valid stream-level identity.

This transformation combined with subsequent applications of the coercion identities over r (e.g. (3) and (5)), eliminates references to X's in X''s equation, thereby completing the refinement.

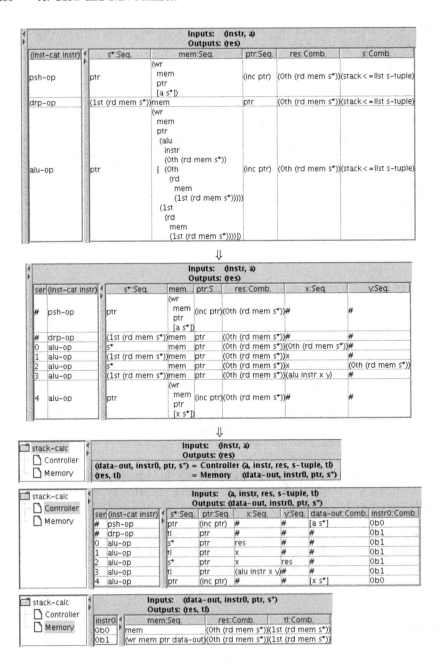

Fig. 1. The top table fully expand the refinement coercions, and splits the tupled signal into its three components as in (7). The next step *serializes* the deeply nested term guarded by `alu-op`. A column of integers in the decision table represent linear control flow that is invisible to external observers. The last step is a factorization that separates the memory from its referencing registers.

The following expressions are behavioral descriptions of a simple stack calculator. There are two input streams: an instruction token `instr` and an integer `a`. The function `inst-cat` classifies instructions as `psh-op`, `drp-op`, and `alu-op`.

The *behavior table* [2,4] explicitly enumerates the `case` key and branches in its decision table (left hand column), while indicating the signal updates in the action table (right-hand columns). Column headings indicate whether the signal is combinational or sequential. Current implementations omit display of initial values for sequential signals.

```
(stack-calc instr a) = res
where
  s  = (push mt 0) !
       (case (inst-cat instr)
         (push s a)
         (pop s)
         (push
           (pop
             (pop s))
           (alu instr
             (top s)
             (top (pop s)))))
  res = (top s)
```

Inputs: (instr, a) Outputs: (res)		
(inst-cat instr)	s:Seq.	res:Comb.
psh-op	(push s a)	(top s)
drp-op	(pop s)	(top s)
alu-op	(push (pop (pop s)) (alu instr (top s) (top (pop s))))	(top s)

$$(6)$$

The application of Theorem 1 to sequential signal `s` in (6) generates a new signal `s'` of the implementation type, where `r` coerces the `case` statement. Functions commute with `case` branches; the first branch (the upper left cell of the action table) is rewritten using the identities from (3), (5), and explicit binding of components in `s'=[s* mem ptr]`:

```
(r (push s a))
  = [(2nd (r s)) (wr (1st (r s)) (2nd (r s)) [a (0th (r s))]) (inc (2nd (r s)))]
  = [(2nd s') (wr (1st s') (2nd s') [a (0th s')]) (inc (2nd s'))]
  = [ptr (wr mem ptr [a s*]) (inc ptr)]
```
$$(7)$$

This reduction continues in each `case` branch, corresponding to the behavior table rows for signal `s`. When complete, the tuple `s'=[s* mem ptr]` is split into its three component signals. Remaining references to the abstract type `s` are satisfied by the combinational application of the homomorphism's inverse: `s = (stack<=llst s')` (Starfish's coercion naming conventions are more verbose than `r` and `a`). Figure 1 shows the full expansion of refinement identities in (6), serialization of actions guarded by `alu-op`, and a factorization separating memory from its reference registers.

References

1. S. D. Johnson. Manipulating logical organization with system factorizations. In *Hardware Specification, Verification and Synthesis: Mathematical Aspects*, July 1989.
2. S. D. Johnson and A. Tsow. Algebra of behavior tables. In *Lfm2000: Fifth NASA Langley Formal Methods Workshop, Proceedings*, 2000.
3. P. S. Miner. *Hardware Verification using Coinductive Assertions*. PhD thesis, Computer Science Department, Indiana University, USA, June 1998. T.R. No. 510.
4. A. Tsow and S. D. Johnson. Visualizing system factorizations with behavior tables. In *FMCAD 2000, Proceedings*, 2000.

Introducing Abstractions via Rewriting[*]

William D. Young

Department of Computer Sciences,
The University of Texas at Austin
byoung@cs.utexas.edu

Abstract. Mechanically assisted proofs of properties of a complex system require an accurate formal model of the system. If the model is too detailed the proof becomes intractible. We outline techniques for automatically "retrofitting" a detailed low-level model with abstractions that facilitate reasoning about the properties of a model. The abstractions are introduced through semantics-preserving rewrite rules. We have applied this technique to the Rockwell-Collins AAMP7 processor model and been able to improve significantly the analyzability of the model.

Mechanically assisted proofs of properties of a complex system require a formal model of the system. However, if the model is too detailed the proof may become intractible because of the overwhelming morass of low-level detail that must be managed. This is especially true if portions of the model are machine generated. This was the case with the Rockwell Collins AAMP7 processor model.[1,3] This is a very low-level specification of the AAMP7 instruction-level semantics and was partly generated by macro expansion from an imperative notation embedded in the ACL2 formal logic. Because of the lack of abstraction, the model is hard to understand and difficult to reason formally about.

Our goal was to prove properties of machine language programs for the AAMP7 using the existing formal model as an operational semantics. However, the model proved too low-level for our purposes. Rather than reconstruct it, we developed techniques for automatically "retrofitting" the detailed low-level model with abstractions to facilitate reasoning about properties of the system. The abstractions are introduced through semantics-preserving rewriting. We have applied this technique to the AAMP7 model and been able to improve significantly the analyzability of the model. We used the ACL2 system[2] to manage the process, the ACL2 rewriter to replace complex terms by more abstract versions, and the theorem prover to assure that the process preserves semantic equivalence.

In addition to providing a more intelligible and accessible formal characterization of the AAMP7 instruction-level semantics, there was a rather surprising

---

[*] This work was supported at the University of Texas at Austin by a contract from Rockwell Collins, Project #450117702, *Instruction-level Model of the AAMP7 in ACL2*.

D. Borrione and W. Paul (Eds.): CHARME 2005, LNCS 3725, pp. 402–405, 2005.

additional benefit. The addition of abstractions illuminated numerous inefficien-cies; the abstracted model could actually be faster than the low-level model.

1   The AAMP7 Model

The AAMP7 model is a detailed instruction-level model of the Rockwell-Collins AAMP7 microprocessor. Executable specifications for the AAMP7 processor were written in the logic of ACL2[2] and formally analyzed to satisfy a vari-ety of properties, including well-formedness of definitions, type restrictions on the arguments to functions, and formal relationships among various functions in the specification. All of these proofs were mechanically checked using the ACL2 theorem prover. The model comprises many megabytes of formal specification, executable code, and supporting theory.

To make the specification more perspicuous, a macro was defined that allows specifying the semantics of individual AAMP7 instructions in an imperative style. For example, the op-addu function below describes the semantics of the AAMP7 addu operation, which takes two 16-bit unsigned values from the top of the stack, adds them using modular unsigned integer arithmetic, and pushes the result back onto the stack.

```
(defun op-addu (st)
  (aamp *state->state*
        (pop ux) (pop uy) (push (uword16 (+ ux uy)))
        st))
```

Here, aamp is a macro defined within ACL2 that interprets its arguments as follows: The first argument specifies that this function is a state to state (as op-posed to a value-returning) transformation. The effect on the state is equivalent to executing the listed pseudo-instructions in sequence. Local variables such as ux and uy are introduced where needed.

The aamp macro essentially embeds within ACL2 a readable and intuitive, imperative language for specifying operation semantics. But because ACL2 is an applicative language, expansion of the macro must emulate this imperative nota-tion by translating it into an applicative form. The required translation is quite complex. The list of instructions in the body of the aamp form is transformed into a nested series of accesses and updates on a record of some 60 fields that represents the processor state. The expansion contains conditional branches for reset, trap and interrupt behaviors, user versus supervisor modes, and all of the possible exceptions that could arise. Details of the modular arithmetic and bit string manipulations involved in AAMP7 address computation and instruction execution are revealed. When macro-expanded, the call (op-addu st) takes over 1200 lines (as formatted on my screen).

Because the semantics is defined using macros that are eliminated by ACL2 during preprocessing, there are essentially *no intermediate abstractions* between the easily comprehensible definition of op-addu above and the "real story" that confronts the user of ACL2 attempting to reason about a program involving the addu operation.

2   Introducing Abstractions

Our solution was to develop automated techniques to introduce conceptual abstractions into the existing specification. The approach we took was to identify recurring low-level forms within the AAMP7 specification, and mechanically rewrite them into a more abstract and perspicuous form. This in turn may reveal a second level of abstract notions, which can then be introduced mechanically, and so on.

For example: in the expansion of (op-addu st), the following form appears numerous times: (wfixn 8 16 k). This is a standard locution generated by the aamp macro for coercing an arbitrary value k into an unsigned 16-bit integer. This suggest introducing an abstraction for this concept, say (fix16 k). Using the ACL2 macro facility, we defined a new syntax to add such abstractions.

```
(defabstractor fix16 (x) (wfixn 8 16 x))
```

This form defines a new function symbol fix16 of one argument and introduces a rewrite rule to unconditionally replace occurrences of expressions of the form (wfixn 8 16 x) with the corresponding expression (fix16 x). To prevent looping the non-recursive function fix16 is also "disabled" to prevent it from being automatically expanded by the prover. Whenever ACL2 subsequently encounters an expression of the form (wfixn 8 16 x), it will replace it with the corresponding expression (fix16 x).

This simple idea is surprisingly powerful. Using these abstractor functions, we can construct a hierarchy of abstractions, and begin to build an "algebra" of rewrites for our specification domain. For example, updates to different state components can be commuted and multiple, redundant and offsetting updates to the same state component can be collapsed into a single update.

As an example, within the macro-expansion of (op-addu st), the following expression appears:

```
(ash (makeaddr (aamp.denvr st)
        (gacc::wfixn 8 16 (logext 32 (+ -1 (gacc::wfixn 8 16
        (+ 1 (gacc::wfixn 8 16 (+ 1 (aamp.tos st)))))))))) 1)
```

Under the assumption that certain intermediate results are representable, this entire expression reduces to: (stack-address 1 st). Because the same basic forms are used throughout the AAMP7 specification, a relatively small collection of well-chosen abstraction functions provide enormous conceptual clarity.

Using our abstraction approach, we generate for each AAMP7 instruction a theorem that characterizes its operational semantics, assuming that we are executing in the "expected" case. For example, for the addu instruction we assume:

1. the reset, trap, and interrupt flags are not asserted;
2. the top-of-stack and program counter computations are within bounds;
3. the PMU is configured to allow the accesses required.

Under these conditions, our semantic theorem says that the state resulting from stepping the machine over an addu instruction is like the input state except that:

1. the sum of the top two stack elements replaces the second stack element;
2. the top-of-stack pointer is incremented;
3. the next instruction byte has been pre-fetched;
4. the pc is incremented;
5. two temporary locations contain specific values.

Subsequently, symbolically stepping the AAMP7 model on an `addu` instruction can be accomplished by applying this rewrite rule, which provides an alternative semantics for the `addu` operation. This semantics is significantly easier to deal with in a proof context than the definition, and allows conceptualizing execution at the level of the abstraction functions, rather than having to deal with the low-level details.

The introduction of abstractions had a rather surprising side benefit: the abstracted versions are more computationally efficient. The macro-expansion in the original emulates an imperative program in an applicative context. The result is a set of nested updates to the state, many of which are redundant, cumulative, or offsetting. The fog of detail in the macro-expanded version tends to hide these inefficiencies. The abstracted version, on the other hand, reveals obvious simplifications that can be implemented as rewrites. Our abstract semantic function for `addu`, for example, replaced several dozen distinct state updates with six. Moreover, since the abstracted, optimized version is proven semantically equivalent to the original, we could replace the original simulator with one that runs our more efficient versions.

We have demonstrated an approach to "retrofitting" an existing low-level specification with abstractions. This is a potentially valuable tool for rendering a complex low-level specification more intelligible and more amenable to formal analysis. Moreover, even a specification that was designed for efficient execution may have inefficiencies that are hidden by complexity. The abstraction process may make such inefficiencies more readily apparent. This effort re-emphasizes the value of abstraction to manage complexity and to facilitate proof. But it also suggests that it is possible in some cases to introduce abstraction into an existing specification.

References

1. David Greve, Matthew Wilding, and David Hardin. High-speed, analyzable simulators. In M. Kaufmann, P. Manolios and J Moore, editors, *Computer-Aided Reasoning: ACL2 Case Studies*, Kluwer Academic Press: Boston, 2000.
2. M. Kaufmann, P. Manolios, and J Moore. *Computer-Aided Reasoning: An Approach.* Kluwer Academic Press, Boston, 2000.
3. Matthew Wilding, David Greve, and David Hardin. Efficient simulation of formal processor models. *Formal Methods in System Design*, 18(3):233–248, May 2001.

A Case Study: Formal Verification of Processor Critical Properties

Emmanuel Zarpas

IBM Haifa Research Laboratory
zarpas@il.ibm.com

1 Introduction

Over the past ten years, the Formal Methods group at the IBM Haifa Research Lab has made steady progress developing tools and techniques that bring the power of model checking to the community of hardware designers and verification engineers, making it an integral part of the design cycle for many projects. Several IBM and non-IBM design teams have successfully integrated RuleBase [2], the IBM formal methods tool, into their design cycles. In this paper we present a case study describing the formal verification of critical properties in a recent processor. Because the details of the design and the specifications are highly proprietary, this paper focuses on the process, techniques and experience involved in the formal verification of the critical properties. We report here experiences on two units, named here for confidentiality reasons unit A and B.

2 Design Under Formal Verification

Unit A. The original implementation of this unit had about 15,000 flip-flops and 220,000 gates, which is a challenge for *complete* formal methods. We checked about 200 properties in order to verify the critical properties of the unit as thoroughly as possible. We found 35 bugs. Three of these bugs were found after the first tape out of the SoC. We were also able to highlight the remaining weaknesses to the design team and the SoC architect (so they could fix them).

The design cannot reach one of the critical states in less than 600 cycles. This was proved to be far too deep for Bounded Model Checking [3]. The Discovery engine, the main BDD symbolic model checking engine used by RuleBase, proved to be the only engine able to cope with the problem. Even so, as the design grew larger and significantly more complex, we had to restrict the model. By the end of the project, it became impossible to check properties without the use of severe environment restrictions, see the first line of Table 1 for average data about models and Discovery runs. SAT-based bounded model checking could still be used for the design, but only for bounds lower than 200. We made a decision to override internal design variables in order to allow the design to reach all critical states within about twenty cycles and therefore achieve a reasonable level of coverage.

D. Borrione and W. Paul (Eds.): CHARME 2005, LNCS 3725, pp. 406–409, 2005.

At the very end of the project, progress made in model checking technologies allowed us to check properties without overriding any internal variables or any restrictions of the behavior of control input variables. Using interpolation-based techniques as in [4] allowed us to prove two thirds of our properties, including some of the most sensitive properties. Our interpolation-based engine was able to prove these properties in a surprisingly short amount of time. Indeed when this engine was able to prove a property it was usually with an interpolant computed with a low bound (e.g. 10 or 15). In general, the engine was either able to prove a property quickly or unable to do it. For the remaining properties, we used incremental bounded model checking [5]. Second line of table 1 summarizes average data about models and runs. Of course, using bounded model checking, we could prove properties only with a bound. Reachability depths computed for the intermediate models made us think that the bounds (in the k=1000-1500 range) we used were probably high enough to prove most of the properties checked. However, this approach implied solving extremely big CNFs, indeed our SAT solver had to fight with CNFs of more than 20 million variables and 60 million clauses. With such CNFs memory becomes an issue, we had to work on a 8 GB 64-bit machine. Even though, each property often took more than 24 hours to be checked up to the relevant bound.

Unit B. The B unit we checked had two main phases. Phase 1 lasts for several hundred thousand cycles. This makes model checking for these properties nearly impossible as is. To circumvent this problem, we used a checkpoint generated by simulation to give our model an initial state at the beginning of Phase 2 (main unit B concerns are mainly for Phase 2). As initial states, we took a subset of the reachable states in the first cycle of Phase 2. Consequently, we did not get full coverage. A bug could be missed, for example, if the only path to this bug is through a Phase 1 state that was outside the subset used. Nevertheless, using this method, we obtained a level of verification far better than any that could be obtained using simulation or semi-formal methods.

The original implementation of B unit had about 1200 flip-flops and 12500 gates. Because this not very large, we were able to check each rule in reasonable amount of time (anywhere from a few minutes to less than an hour). The design encompassed a 2^{19} counter making reachability analysis, and therefore on-the-fly model checking, impracticable. The Discovery engine allowed us to perform to perform an over-approximation of the reachable states by disregarding the counter variables. At this point we were able to use a classical backward fix-point computation search. In general, this proved to be a good solution for this design (see third line of Table 1). As a results a dozen bugs were found very quickly in an already mature design.

3   Lessons

According to users survey [2], the three most difficult activities related to Rule-Base use are writing environments to cope with size, understanding design details and modifying design for size. As we saw in previous section, technology progresses do make a difference in tackling big size designs, however in many cases brute strength is not enough. The [2] discussion about dealing with the size problem is still up to date, so we will focus here on processes considerations usually disregarded in the literature, though critical for projects successes.

Designer Support is Critical. For verification engineers, their relationship with designers is one of the main challenges in verification projects, especially when the verification engineers act *de facto* as consultants. It is not surprising that we found it far easier to collaborate with skilled designers. Even if designers do not carry out any formal verification on their own, they need the time and availability to support the verification efforts being done on their design. First, the specifications are generally not detailed enough for formal verification work. The designer therefore has to give further explanations to the formal verification engineers and help them define properties and models. In addition, the designer plays an essential role in reviewing traces (either false negatives or real bugs) and giving feedback in a timely manner.

Have the "Classical" Verification Team Involved. The more formal verification is embedded into the "classical" verification process, the better. Ultimately, the use of formal verification should be a part of the entire verification strategy. Even the system architecture should accommodate formal verification, for example by taking into account that formal works better on small blocks than on big ones (a very light case of design for verifiability). However, if the formal verification engineers do not belong to the "classical" verification team, as it is often the case, coordination should be established. The verification lead should closely review the bugs found by formal methods on a regular basis, including properties checked or not and model restrictions made. This is very important in order to get a good cooperation with simulation teams and the maximum benefit and return on investment for formal verification.

Write General Environments (Top Down Approach). In order to create a model, the behavior of input signals of the designs need to be defined. We model input signals behavior using the PSL [1] modeling layer. A safe approach involves starting with an environment as general as possible. A non-existential property proved with an abstract environment will still hold for the "real life" environment. If false negatives appear, the environment can be refined during the verification process. In addition, abstract environments tend to be simpler and easier to write. As a result, it is usually better to start with a general environment and refine it when needed. Indeed, starting with a very precise, very detailed environment will take a long time to write, debug and tune and therefore waste designer time, a most precious resource. By refining a general environment, you very well could never have to reach such a level of detail, and even so, it is likely to be at a late stage of the verification project and after achieving some results. Bottom up approach is more risky: it is very easy to lose considerable time in tuning in a precise way complex behaviors for some inputs signals with no significant gains. Very often some abstracted behavior would have done as well.

Write Simple Properties. The RuleBase property language is PSL. PSL is simple to learn, yet the way it is used to write properties can have a significant impact on a formal verification project. The simpler the property the better. Simpler properties are easier to write, easier to understand, and easier to maintain. Even more important, the more complex a property is, the more difficult it will be to tune it and the more designer time, a rare and precious resource, will be required. It makes sense to start writing the simplest properties you can imagine for your model. This will allow you to assess your model and determine if it represents the design, its complexity, whether it is suitable for formal methods, or whether it should be made smaller by some restrictions. Many very important properties can be expressed in a relatively simple manner. We found that checking even trivial properties uncovered bugs. For example we found two bugs in A unit by checking that a signal was actually a pulse. When you want to write a complex rule, there is often a simpler version, or a simpler rule (either stronger or weaker) that will find the same bugs. It makes sense to first seek out the simpler rule. You may not be able to avoid writing and checking complex properties, however it is a safe policy to write them during a second iteration.

4   Conclusions

In this paper, we showed how skilled use of a state-of-art formal methods tool can allow checking critical properties in very important designs, in spite of technical difficulties. The author wishes to thank I. Holmes, J. Liberty and Kanna Shimizu for their support on design verification.

Table 1. Average values for Unit A and B models and engines runs. Depth is the number of cycles needed to complete reachability analysis.

	Depth	#State vars	#gates	BDD nodes allocated	Memory Usage (MB)	Discovery runtimes	BMC runtimes	Interpolant runtimes
Unit A (int.)	1420	520	4670	$1.3 * 10^7$	260	10 h		
Unit A (final)		1760	24000				48 h +	1 h
Unit B	979	305	7640	$6.7 * 10^6$	63	0.25 h		

References

1. Accelera. PSL LRM. http://www.eda.org/vfv/
2. S. Ben-David *et al.* Model Checking in IBM. In Formal Methods in System Design, 22, 2003.
3. A. Biere *et al.* Symbolic Model Checking Without BDDs. TACAS'99.
4. K. L. McMillan. Interpolation and SAT-based Model Checking. CAV'03.
5. O. Shtrichman. Pruning techniques for the SAT-based bounded model checking problem. CHARME'01, 2001.

Author Index

Amla, Nina   254
Axelsson, Emil   5
Aziz, Adnan   269

Baumgartner, Jason   222, 269
Bhattacharya, Ritwik   332
Bloem, Roderick   35
Bustan, Doron   191
Büttner, Wolfram   1

Cachera, David   376
Chakrabarti, Arindam   50
Chatterjee, Krishnendu   50
Chechik, Marsha   65, 285
Chockler, Hana   176
Ciardo, Gianfranco   146
Claessen, Koen   5, 238

Dalinger, Iakov   301
Dill, David   388
Drechsler, Rolf   349
Du, Xiaoqun   254

El-Kharashi, M. Watheq   384
Emerson, E. Allen   388

Ferdinand, Christian   336
Fisler, Kathi   176
Flaisher, Alon   191
Fujita, Masahiro   340

Gebremichael, Biniam   345
German, Steven   332
Ginosar, Ran   359
Goossens, Kees   345
Gopalakrishnan, Ganesh   317, 332
Große, Daniel   349
Grumberg, Orna   129, 191
Gurfinkel, Arie   65, 285

Heckmann, Reinhold   336
Henzinger, Thomas A.   50
Heyman, Tamir   129
Hillebrand, Mark   301

Hsiao, Michael S.   81
Hunt Jr., Warren A.   20

Ifergan, Nili   129
Imai, Masaharu   2
In der Rieden, Thomas   3
Iyer, Subramanian K.   354, 388

Jacobi, Christian   114
Jain, Jawahar   354, 388
Jobstmann, Barbara   35
Johnson, Steven D.   398

Kapschitz, Tsachy   359
Kitajima, Akira   2
Kuehlmann, Andreas   254
Kupferman, Orna   50, 191
Kurshan, Robert P.   254

Lamport, Leslie   162
Leinenbach, Dirk   3
Li, SiKun   393
Luk, Wayne   380

Majumdar, Rupak   50
Manolios, Panagiotis   363
Marques-Silva, João   367
Matoušek, Petr   371
McMillan, Kenneth L.   254
Mony, Hari   222, 269
Morin-Allory, Katell   376

Pandav, Sudhindra   317
Paruthi, Viresh   114
Paul, Wolfgang   3, 301
Pell, Oliver   380
Prasad, Mukul R.   81, 354

Qin, Ying   393

Reeber, Erik   20
Rijpkema, Edwin   345
Roorda, Jan-Willem   238
Rădulescu, Andrei   345

Safar, Mona   384
Sahoo, Debashis   354, 388
Salem, Ashraf   384
Schuster, Assaf   129
Sheeran, Mary   5
Shen, ShengYu   393
Sidle, Thomas   354
Slind, Konrad   317
Smrčka, Aleš   371
Somenzi, Fabio   207
Srinivasan, Sudarshan K.   363
Staber, Stefan   35

Tsow, Alex   398

Vaandrager, Frits   345
Vardi, Moshe Y.   191
Velev, Miroslav N.   97
Vojnar, Tomáš   371

Ward, David   207
Weber, Kai   114
Wei, Ou   285

Young, William D.   402
Yu, Andy Jinqing   146

Zarpas, Emmanuel   406
Zhang, Liang   81
Zhang, Miaomiao   345

Lecture Notes in Computer Science

For information about Vols. 1–3625

please contact your bookseller or Springer

Vol. 3728: V. Paliouras, J. Vounckx, D. Verkest (Eds.), Integrated Circuit and System Design. XV, 753 pages. 2005.

Vol. 3726: L.T. Yang, O.F. Rana, B. Di Martino, J. Dongarra (Eds.), High Performance Computing and Communcations. XXVI, 1116 pages. 2005.

Vol. 3725: D. Borrione, W. Paul (Eds.), Correct Hardware Design and Verification Methods. XII, 412 pages. 2005.

Vol. 3718: V.G. Ganzha, E.W. Mayr, E.V. Vorozhtsov (Eds.), Computer Algebra in Scientific Computing. XII, 502 pages. 2005.

Vol. 3717: B. Gramlich (Ed.), Frontiers of Combining Systems. X, 321 pages. 2005. (Subseries LNAI).

Vol. 3715: E. Dawson, S. Vaudenay (Eds.), Progress in Cryptology – Mycrypt 2005. XI, 329 pages. 2005.

Vol. 3714: H. Obbink, K. Pohl (Eds.), Software Product Lines. XIII, 235 pages. 2005.

Vol. 3713: L. Briand, C. Williams (Eds.), Model Driven Engineering Languages and Systems. XV, 722 pages. 2005.

Vol. 3712: R. Reussner, J. Mayer, J.A. Stafford, S. Overhage, S. Becker, P.J. Schroeder (Eds.), Quality of Software Architectures and Software Quality. XIII, 289 pages. 2005.

Vol. 3711: F. Kishino, Y. Kitamura, H. Kato, N. Nagata (Eds.), Entertainment Computing - ICEC 2005. XXIV, 540 pages. 2005.

Vol. 3710: M. Barni, I. Cox, T. Kalker, H.J. Kim (Eds.), Digital Watermarking. XII, 485 pages. 2005.

Vol. 3708: J. Blanc-Talon, W. Philips, D. Popescu, P. Scheunders (Eds.), Advanced Concepts for Intelligent Vision Systems. XXII, 725 pages. 2005.

Vol. 3706: H. Fuks, S. Lukosch, A.C. Salgado (Eds.), Groupware: Design, Implementation, and Use. XII, 378 pages. 2005.

Vol. 3703: F. Fages, S. Soliman (Eds.), Principles and Practice of Semantic Web Reasoning. VIII, 163 pages. 2005.

Vol. 3702: B. Beckert (Ed.), Automated Reasoning with Analytic Tableaux and Related Methods. XIII, 343 pages. 2005. (Subseries LNAI).

Vol. 3699: C.S. Calude, M.J. Dinneen, G. Păun, M. J. Pérez-Jiménez, G. Rozenberg (Eds.), Unconventional Computation. XI, 267 pages. 2005.

Vol. 3698: U. Furbach (Ed.), KI 2005: Advances in Artificial Intelligence. XIII, 409 pages. 2005. (Subseries LNAI).

Vol. 3697: W. Duch, J. Kacprzyk, E. Oja, S. Zadrożny (Eds.), Artificial Neural Networks: Formal Models and Their Applications – ICANN 2005, Part II. XXXII, 1045 pages. 2005.

Vol. 3696: W. Duch, J. Kacprzyk, E. Oja, S. Zadrożny (Eds.), Artificial Neural Networks: Biological Inspirations – ICANN 2005, Part I. XXXI, 703 pages. 2005.

Vol. 3695: M.R. Berthold, R. Glen, K. Diederichs, O. Kohlbacher, I. Fischer (Eds.), Computational Life Sciences. XI, 277 pages. 2005. (Subseries LNBI).

Vol. 3694: M. Malek, E. Nett, N. Suri (Eds.), Service Availability. VIII, 213 pages. 2005.

Vol. 3693: A.G. Cohn, D.M. Mark (Eds.), Spatial Information Theory. XII, 493 pages. 2005.

Vol. 3692: R. Casadio, G. Myers (Eds.), Algorithms in Bioinformatic. X, 436 pages. 2005. (Subseries LNBI).

Vol. 3691: A. Gagalowicz, W. Philips (Eds.), Computer Analysis of Images and Patterns. XIX, 865 pages. 2005.

Vol. 3690: M. Pěchouček, P. Petta, L.Z. Varga (Eds.), Multi-Agent Systems and Applications IV. XVII, 667 pages. 2005. (Subseries LNAI).

Vol. 3687: S. Singh, M. Singh, C. Apte, P. Perner (Eds.), Pattern Recognition and Image Analysis, Part II. XXV, 809 pages. 2005.

Vol. 3686: S. Singh, M. Singh, C. Apte, P. Perner (Eds.), Pattern Recognition and Data Mining, Part I. XXVI, 689 pages. 2005.

Vol. 3685: V. Gorodetsky, I. Kotenko, V. Skormin (Eds.), Computer Network Security. XIV, 480 pages. 2005.

Vol. 3684: R. Khosla, R.J. Howlett, L.C. Jain (Eds.), Knowledge-Based Intelligent Information and Engineering Systems, Part IV. LXXIX, 933 pages. 2005. (Subseries LNAI).

Vol. 3683: R. Khosla, R.J. Howlett, L.C. Jain (Eds.), Knowledge-Based Intelligent Information and Engineering Systems, Part III. LXXX, 1397 pages. 2005. (Subseries LNAI).

Vol. 3682: R. Khosla, R.J. Howlett, L.C. Jain (Eds.), Knowledge-Based Intelligent Information and Engineering Systems, Part II. LXXIX, 1371 pages. 2005. (Subseries LNAI).

Vol. 3681: R. Khosla, R.J. Howlett, L.C. Jain (Eds.), Knowledge-Based Intelligent Information and Engineering Systems, Part I. LXXX, 1319 pages. 2005. (Subseries LNAI).

Vol. 3679: S.d.C. di Vimercati, P. Syverson, D. Gollmann (Eds.), Computer Security – ESORICS 2005. XI, 509 pages. 2005.

Vol. 3678: A. McLysaght, D.H. Huson (Eds.), Comparative Genomics. VIII, 167 pages. 2005. (Subseries LNBI).

Vol. 3677: J. Dittmann, S. Katzenbeisser, A. Uhl (Eds.), Communications and Multimedia Security. XIII, 360 pages. 2005.

Vol. 3676: R. Glück, M. Lowry (Eds.), Generative Programming and Component Engineering. XI, 448 pages. 2005.

Vol. 3675: Y. Luo (Ed.), Cooperative Design, Visualization, and Engineering. XI, 264 pages. 2005.

Vol. 3674: W. Jonker, M. Petković (Eds.), Secure Data Management. X, 241 pages. 2005.

Vol. 3673: S. Bandini, S. Manzoni (Eds.), AI*IA 2005: Advances in Artificial Intelligence. XIV, 614 pages. 2005. (Subseries LNAI).

Vol. 3672: C. Hankin, I. Siveroni (Eds.), Static Analysis. X, 369 pages. 2005.

Vol. 3671: S. Bressan, S. Ceri, E. Hunt, Z.G. Ives, Z. Bellahsène, M. Rys, R. Unland (Eds.), Database and XML Technologies. X, 239 pages. 2005.

Vol. 3670: M. Bravetti, L. Kloul, G. Zavattaro (Eds.), Formal Techniques for Computer Systems and Business Processes. XIII, 349 pages. 2005.

Vol. 3666: B.D. Martino, D. Kranzlmüller, J. Dongarra (Eds.), Recent Advances in Parallel Virtual Machine and Message Passing Interface. XVII, 546 pages. 2005.

Vol. 3665: K. S. Candan, A. Celentano (Eds.), Advances in Multimedia Information Systems. X, 221 pages. 2005.

Vol. 3664: C. Türker, M. Agosti, H.-J. Schek (Eds.), Peer-to-Peer, Grid, and Service-Orientation in Digital Library Architectures. X, 261 pages. 2005.

Vol. 3663: W.G. Kropatsch, R. Sablatnig, A. Hanbury (Eds.), Pattern Recognition. XIV, 512 pages. 2005.

Vol. 3662: C. Baral, G. Greco, N. Leone, G. Terracina (Eds.), Logic Programming and Nonmonotonic Reasoning. XIII, 454 pages. 2005. (Subseries LNAI).

Vol. 3661: T. Panayiotopoulos, J. Gratch, R. Aylett, D. Ballin, P. Olivier, T. Rist (Eds.), Intelligent Virtual Agents. XIII, 506 pages. 2005. (Subseries LNAI).

Vol. 3660: M. Beigl, S. Intille, J. Rekimoto, H. Tokuda (Eds.), UbiComp 2005: Ubiquitous Computing. XVII, 394 pages. 2005.

Vol. 3659: J.R. Rao, B. Sunar (Eds.), Cryptographic Hardware and Embedded Systems – CHES 2005. XIV, 458 pages. 2005.

Vol. 3658: V. Matoušek, P. Mautner, T. Pavelka (Eds.), Text, Speech and Dialogue. XV, 460 pages. 2005. (Subseries LNAI).

Vol. 3657: F.S. de Boer, M.M. Bonsangue, S. Graf, W.-P. de Roever (Eds.), Formal Methods for Components and Objects. VIII, 325 pages. 2005.

Vol. 3656: M. Kamel, A. Campilho (Eds.), Image Analysis and Recognition. XXIV, 1279 pages. 2005.

Vol. 3655: A. Aldini, R. Gorrieri, F. Martinelli (Eds.), Foundations of Security Analysis and Design III. VII, 273 pages. 2005.

Vol. 3654: S. Jajodia, D. Wijesekera (Eds.), Data and Applications Security XIX. X, 353 pages. 2005.

Vol. 3653: M. Abadi, L. de Alfaro (Eds.), CONCUR 2005 – Concurrency Theory. XIV, 578 pages. 2005.

Vol. 3652: A. Rauber, S. Christodoulakis, A M. Tjoa (Eds.), Research and Advanced Technology for Digital Libraries. XVIII, 545 pages. 2005.

Vol. 3650: J. Zhou, J. Lopez, R.H. Deng, F. Bao (Eds.), Information Security. XII, 516 pages. 2005.

Vol. 3649: W.M. P. van der Aalst, B. Benatallah, F. Casati, F. Curbera (Eds.), Business Process Management. XII, 472 pages. 2005.

Vol. 3648: J.C. Cunha, P.D. Medeiros (Eds.), Euro-Par 2005 Parallel Processing. XXXVI, 1299 pages. 2005.

Vol. 3646: A. F. Famili, J.N. Kok, J.M. Peña, A. Siebes, A. Feelders (Eds.), Advances in Intelligent Data Analysis VI. XIV, 522 pages. 2005.

Vol. 3645: D.-S. Huang, X.-P. Zhang, G.-B. Huang (Eds.), Advances in Intelligent Computing, Part II. XIII, 1010 pages. 2005.

Vol. 3644: D.-S. Huang, X.-P. Zhang, G.-B. Huang (Eds.), Advances in Intelligent Computing, Part I. XXVII, 1101 pages. 2005.

Vol. 3643: R. Moreno Díaz, F. Pichler, A. Quesada Arencibia (Eds.), Computer Aided Systems Theory – EUROCAST 2005. XIV, 629 pages. 2005.

Vol. 3642: D. Ślezak, J. Yao, J.F. Peters, W. Ziarko, X. Hu (Eds.), Rough Sets, Fuzzy Sets, Data Mining, and Granular Computing, Part II. XXIII, 738 pages. 2005. (Subseries LNAI).

Vol. 3641: D. Ślezak, G. Wang, M. Szczuka, I. Düntsch, Y. Yao (Eds.), Rough Sets, Fuzzy Sets, Data Mining, and Granular Computing, Part I. XXIV, 742 pages. 2005. (Subseries LNAI).

Vol. 3639: P. Godefroid (Ed.), Model Checking Software. XI, 289 pages. 2005.

Vol. 3638: A. Butz, B. Fisher, A. Krüger, P. Olivier (Eds.), Smart Graphics. XI, 269 pages. 2005.

Vol. 3637: J. M. Moreno, J. Madrenas, J. Cosp (Eds.), Evolvable Systems: From Biology to Hardware. XI, 227 pages. 2005.

Vol. 3636: M.J. Blesa, C. Blum, A. Roli, M. Sampels (Eds.), Hybrid Metaheuristics. XII, 155 pages. 2005.

Vol. 3634: L. Ong (Ed.), Computer Science Logic. XI, 567 pages. 2005.

Vol. 3633: C. Bauzer Medeiros, M. Egenhofer, E. Bertino (Eds.), Advances in Spatial and Temporal Databases. XIII, 433 pages. 2005.

Vol. 3632: R. Nieuwenhuis (Ed.), Automated Deduction – CADE-20. XIII, 459 pages. 2005. (Subseries LNAI).

Vol. 3631: J. Eder, H.-M. Haav, A. Kalja, J. Penjam (Eds.), Advances in Databases and Information Systems. XIII, 393 pages. 2005.

Vol. 3630: M.S. Capcarrere, A.A. Freitas, P.J. Bentley, C.G. Johnson, J. Timmis (Eds.), Advances in Artificial Life. XIX, 949 pages. 2005. (Subseries LNAI).

Vol. 3629: J.L. Fiadeiro, N. Harman, M. Roggenbach, J. Rutten (Eds.), Algebra and Coalgebra in Computer Science. XI, 457 pages. 2005.

Vol. 3628: T. Gschwind, U. Aßmann, O. Nierstrasz (Eds.), Software Composition. X, 199 pages. 2005.

Vol. 3627: C. Jacob, M.L. Pilat, P.J. Bentley, J. Timmis (Eds.), Artificial Immune Systems. XII, 500 pages. 2005.

Vol. 3626: B. Ganter, G. Stumme, R. Wille (Eds.), Formal Concept Analysis. X, 349 pages. 2005. (Subseries LNAI).